The Moral Psychology H<!-- -->

The Moral Psychology Handbook

John M. Doris and the Moral Psychology Research Group

Fiery Cushman, John M. Doris, Joshua D. Greene, Gilbert Harman, Daniel Kelly, Joshua Knobe, Edouard Machery, Ron Mallon, Kelby Mason, Victoria McGeer, Maria W. Merritt, Shaun Nichols, Joseph M. Paxton, Alexandra Plakias, Jesse J. Prinz, Erica Roedder, Adina L. Roskies, Timothy Schroeder, Walter Sinnott-Armstrong, Chandra Sekhar Sripada, Stephen Stich, Valerie Tiberius, Liane Young

OXFORD
UNIVERSITY PRESS

OXFORD

UNIVERSITY PRESS

Great Clarendon Street, Oxford OX2 6DP
United Kingdom

Oxford University Press is a department of the University of Oxford.
It furthers the University's objective of excellence in research, scholarship,
and education by publishing worldwide. Oxford is a registered trade mark of
Oxford University Press in the UK and in certain other countries

First published 2010
First published in paperback 2012
Reprinted 2013

British Library Cataloguing in Publication Data
Data available

Library of Congress Cataloging in Publication Data
Data available

ISBN 978-0-19-965548-9

Contents

List of Abbreviations

ACC	anterior cingulate cortex
ASL	American Sign Language
CAD	contempt and community; anger and autonomy; disgust and divinity
DDE	Doctrine of Double Effect
DLPFC	dorsolateral prefrontal cortex
EMG	electromyography
fMRI	functional magnetic resonance imaging
FTD	frontotemporal dementia
IAT	Implicit Association Test
JOLS	judgments of overall life satisfaction
LST	life-satisfaction theory
MRS	Modern Racism Scale
NBA	National Basketball Association
OFC	orbitofrontal cortex
PFC	prefrontal cortex
SES	socioeconomic status
SWB	subjective well-being
VBLS	values-based life-satisfaction (account)
VIM	Violence Inhibition Mechanism
VM	ventromedial
VMPC	ventromedial prefrontal cortex

Contributors

Fiery Cushman is Assistant Professor in the Cognitive, Linguistic, and Psychological Sciences Department at Brown University. His research focuses on the psychological mechanisms of moral judgment, their developmental origins, and their evolutionary history. His research combines methods in adult and developmental psychology, neuropsychology, neuroscience, experimental economics, and formal modeling.

John M. Doris is Professor in the Philosophy–Neuroscience–Psychology Program and Philosophy Department, Washington University in St. Louis. Doris works at the intersection of psychology, cognitive science, and philosophical ethics, and has authored or co-authored papers in this region for such publications as *Noûs, Bioethics, Cognition, Philosophy and Phenomenological Research, Midwest Studies in Philosophy, The Australasian Journal of Philosophy*, and the *Oxford Handbook of Contemporary Philosophy*. Doris authored *Lack of Character* (Cambridge, 2002) and is currently working on *Talking to Our Selves*, to appear with Oxford University Press. Doris has been awarded fellowships from Michigan's Institute for the Humanities, Princeton's University Center for Human Values, the National Humanities Center, the American Council of Learned Societies, and (three times) the National Endowment for the Humanities. In 2007, he was awarded the Society for Philosophy and Psychology's Stanton Prize for interdisciplinary research in philosophy and psychology.

Joshua D. Greene is the John Ruth and Hazel Associate Professor of the Social Sciences at Harvard University and the director of the Moral Cognition Lab. He studies moral judgment and decision-making using behavioral experiments, functional magnetic resonance imaging (fMRI), and other empirical methods. Greene has a Ph.D. in philosophy, and much of his scientific research is motivated by traditionally philosophical questions. He is recipient of the 2012 Stanton Prize, awarded by the Society for Philosophy and Psychology.

Gilbert Harman is James S. McDonnell Distinguished University Professor of Philosophy at Princeton University. He is the author or co-author of nine books, including *Explaining Values* (Oxford, 2000) and (with Sanjeev Kulkarni) *Reliable Reasoning* (MIT, 2007), and *An Elementary Introduction to Statistical Learning Theory* (Wiley, 2011). He has edited or co-edited four others, including *Conceptions of the Human Mind* (Erlbaum, 1993).

Daniel Kelly is an assistant professor in the Philosophy Department at Purdue University. His research interests are at the intersection of the philosophy of mind, cognitive science, and moral theory. He is the author of *Yuck! The Nature and Moral Significance of Disgust*, and has published papers on moral judgment, social norms, racial cognition, and cross-cultural diversity.

Joshua Knobe is an associate professor of cognitive science and philosophy at Yale University. Most of his research is in the new field of experimental philosophy. In his work in this field, he has conducted experimental studies about people's intuitions concerning intentional action, causation, consciousness, group agency, racial prejudice, reason, explanation, freedom, and moral responsibility. Above all, he is interested in the ways in which moral considerations can affect people's judgments about what seem to be purely, scientific, questions.

Edouard Machery is currently an associate professor of philosophy in the Department of History and Philosophy of Science at the University of Pittsburgh. His research focuses on the philosophical issues raised by psychology and neuropsychology, with a special interest in concepts, moral psychology, the relevance of evolutionary biology for understanding cognition, modularity, and the nature, origins, and ethical significance of prejudiced cognition. He has published more than 60 articles and chapters on these topics in journals such as *Analysis, Behavioral and Brain Sciences, The British Journal for the Philosophy of Science, Cognition, Mind & Language, Philosophy and Phenomenological Research*, and *Philosophy of Science*. In his first book, *Doing without Concepts* (Oxford, 2009), he argues that drastic conceptual changes are required to make sense of the research on concepts in psychology and neuropsychology. He is currently working on a new book examining critically the methodology of psychology and cognitive neuroscience. He is also involved in the development of experimental philosophy, having published several noted articles in this field.

Ron Mallon is an associate professor and Director of the Philosophy–Neuroscience–Psychology Program at Washington University in St. Louis. He has authored or co-authored papers in *Cognition, Ethics, Journal of Political Philosophy, Midwest Studies in Philosophy, Mind and Language, Noûs, Philosophy and Phenomenological Research, Philosophy of Science, Social Neuroscience, Social Philosophy*, and *Social Theory and Practice*. His research is in social philosophy, philosophy of cognitive psychology, and moral psychology.

Kelby Mason is a graduate student in the Department of Philosophy at Rutgers University. His work is in the philosophy of psychology.

Maria W. Merritt is a Core Faculty member of the Johns Hopkins Berman Institute of Bioethics and Assistant Professor in the Department of International Health at the Johns Hopkins Bloomberg School of Public Health in Baltimore, Maryland, USA, with a secondary appointment in the Department of Philosophy at the Johns Hopkins Krieger School of Arts and Sciences. She earned her B.S. in Biology from Wake Forest University, her B.A. in Philosophy and Modern Languages from the University of Oxford, and her Ph.D. in philosophy from the University of California, Berkeley. Merritt completed post-doctoral training in the Department of Bioethics at the National Institutes of Health. Prior to joining the faculty at Johns Hopkins, she taught philosophy at the College of William and Mary and held a Faculty Fellowship at the Edmond J. Safra Foundation Center for Ethics at Harvard University. At Johns Hopkins, Merritt is a faculty affiliate and advisory board member of the Johns Hopkins-Fogarty African Bioethics Training Program. Her current research interests include global health ethics, international research ethics, moral philosophy, and moral psychology. Merritt's work as an author or co-author includes articles published in *AIDS, American Journal of Public Health, Bulletin of the WHO, Ethical Theory and Moral Practice, Ethics, JAMA, Journal of Empirical Research on Human Research Ethics, Journal of Moral Philosophy, Kennedy Institute of Ethics Journal, PLoS Medicine*, and *Yale Journal of Health Policy, Law, and Ethics*.

Shaun Nichols holds a joint appointment in philosophy and cognitive science at the University of Arizona. He is author of *Sentimental Rules: On the Natural Foundations of Moral Judgment* (Oxford, 2004), co-author (with Stephen Stich) of *Mindreading: An Integrated Account of Pretense, Self-awareness and Understanding Other Minds* (Oxford, 2003), and co-editor (with Joshua Knobe) of *Experimental Philosophy* (Oxford, 2008).

Alexandra Plakias is a postdoctoral research fellow at the Northern Institute of Philosophy at the University of Aberdeen. Her research concerns moral psychology, metaethics, and the intersection of the two. She has published papers on moral disagreement and moral relativism, and on the role of disgust in moral judgment.

Jesse J. Prinz is Distinguished Professor of Philosophy at the City University of New York, Graduate Center. His research focuses on the perceptual, emotional, and cultural foundations of human psychology. His books include *Furnishing the Mind: Concepts and Their Perception Basis* (MIT, 2002), *Gut Reactions: A Perceptual Theory of Emotion* (Oxford, 2004), and *The Emotional Construction of Morals* (Oxford, 2007). All of his research in the cognitive sciences bears on traditional philosophical questions. Prinz's work is a contemporary extension of the classical empiricist tradition in philosophy, which emphasizes experience, rather than innate knowledge, and disembodied, amodal representations in thought.

Erica Roedder graduated cum laude from Stanford University and will receive her Ph.D. in philosophy from New York University. She has co-authored several papers in philosophy of psychology and is particularly interested in cognitive biases.

Adina L. Roskies, Associate Professor of Philosophy at Dartmouth College, has pursued a career in both philosophy and neuroscience. Her research and writing has focused on philosophy of mind, philosophy of science, and ethics, including neuroethics. She received a Ph.D. in neuroscience and cognitive science in 1995 from the University of California, San Diego, and did a post-doctoral fellowship in cognitive neuroimaging at Washington University in St. Louis, using positron emission tomography and functional magnetic resonance imaging (fMRI). After serving two years as senior editor of *Neuron*, she went on to complete a Ph.D. in philosophy at the Massachusetts Institute of Technology in 2004. Dr. Roskies joined the Dartmouth faculty in the fall of 2004. She has been a visiting fellow in philosophy at the Australian National University and the University of Sydney. She was a project fellow on the MacArthur Law and Neuroscience Project. Her work has been supported by grants and fellowships from National Institutes of Health, the McDonnell–Pew Foundation, and the Mellon Foundation. Dr. Roskies is the author of numerous articles published in academic journals. She was awarded both the William James Prize and the Stanton Prize by the Society of Philosophy and Psychology.

Timothy Schroeder received his B.A. from the University of Lethbridge and his Ph.D. from Stanford University. After starting his career at the University of Manitoba, he is now Associate Professor of Philosophy at Ohio State University. He works on the philosophy of mind and moral psychology, and these interests intersect in his book, *Three Faces of Desire* (Oxford, 2004).

Walter Sinnott-Armstrong is Chauncey Stillman Professor in Practical Ethics in the Department of Philosophy at Duke University. He taught at Dartmouth College 1981-2009 after receiving his B.A. from Amherst College and his Ph.D. from Yale University. He is currently Vice-Chair of the Board of Officers of the American Philosophical Association and was Co-director of the MacArthur Law and Neuroscience Program. He has published extensively on ethics (theoretical and applied), philosophy of law, epistemology, philosophy of religion, and informal logic. His current research focuses on empirical moral psychology as well as law and neuroscience.

Stephen Stich is Board of Governors Professor of Philosophy and Cognitive Science at Rutgers University and Honorary Professor of Philosophy at the University of Sheffield. He has written extensively on issues in cognitive science, philosophy of language, philosophy of mind, epistemology, moral theory, and philosophical methodology. Stich is a Fellow of the American Academy of Arts and Sciences and was the first recipient of the American Philosophical Association's Gittler Award for outstanding scholarly contribution to the philosophy of the social sciences. In 2007, he received the Jean Nicod Prize sponsored by the French Centre National de la Recherche Scientifique.

Valerie Tiberius is Professor of Philosophy at the University of Minnesota. Her research interests include moral psychology, prudential virtues, and well-being. Her recent book, *The Reflective Life: Living Wisely With Our Limits* (Oxford, 2008), explores how we ought to think about practical wisdom and living a good life given what we now know about ourselves from empirical psychology. She is currently working on a textbook on moral psychology, *Moral Psychology: A Contemporary Introduction*, that will be published by Routledge.

Liane Young is Assistant Professor of Psychology at Boston College. She studies the cognitive and neural basis of human moral judgment, focusing especially on the roles of emotion and mental state reasoning. Her work employs the methods of cognitive neuroscience: functional neuroimaging, studying patient populations with specific cognitive and neural deficits, and modulating activity in specific brain areas using transcranial magnetic stimulation. Young received her Ph.D. in psychology from Harvard University in 2008, and her B.A. in Philosophy from Harvard University in 2004. In 2006 Young was awarded the William James Prize by the Society of Philosophy and Psychology for a paper on moral judgment in patients with brain damage.

Introduction

JOHN M. DORIS

It is not always good, as the proverbial curse reminds us, to live in interesting times.[1] But for moral psychology, times have lately been both interesting and good: research at the intersection of human mentation and human morality is flourishing as never before. A central reason for this encouraging circumstance is an unprecedented *interdisciplinarity*: investigators in both philosophy and the human sciences are now freely drawing on resources from well beyond the confines of their fields.

Things weren't always so. In the academy, the study of morality has historically been a special province of philosophy, while the study of mental processes has, for the past century or so, largely been the province of psychology and allied sciences. At the same time, recent philosophy has been largely speculative or theoretical (despite the robust empirical interests of many canonical philosophers), while the methods of contemporary psychology have characteristically been empirical or experimental (despite the robust theoretical interests of many canonical psychologists). The results have been uneven: philosophy has often been light on fact, and psychology has often been light on theory.

Yet the discipline of moral psychology is, as the name intimates, a hybrid inquiry, informed by both ethical theory and psychological fact. Different practitioners will, quite reasonably, favor different admixtures of fact and theory, but central questions in the field— *What is the nature of moral judgment? Why do people behave well or badly?*—want empirically informed answers, while developing these answers in theoretically sophisticated ways requires delicate inquiry in philosophical ethics.

Starting in the late 1960s, the increasing influence of philosophical naturalism and cognitive science, particularly in epistemology and philosophy of mind,

---

[1] "May you live in interesting times" is often said to be Chinese in origin, although its provenance is uncertain (see Shapiro, 2006: 669).

set the stage for an interdisciplinary study of morality in philosophy, while in psychology, the demise of behaviorism enabled empirical investigation of an increasing variety of topics, including those that had previously been under the ambit of philosophical ethics. Since the early 1990s, such inquiry has increased exponentially, and by the twenty-first century's inception, not only were philosophers and psychologists liberally sampling the empirical and theoretical riches available in their sister disciplines, they had begun to collaboratively produce research aimed at illuminating problems that had previously been treated within the borders of individual fields. The result is not a new discipline, since research appropriately termed moral psychology has long been produced in a variety of subfields, but a *resituated* discipline, one straddling disciplinary boundaries or—better yet—regarding such demarcations as of little more than administrative interest.

In 2003, a small group of philosophers, excited by these crumbling prohibitions, met to discuss how the conversation might best be continued, and at that meeting the Moral Psychology Research Group was formed. At length, we decided to write a book, and at considerably greater length, a book was written. That book is this *Handbook*. Along the way, a number of talented philosophers and scientists have joined our numbers, and while we've been hard at our labors, so have many others, and there's now far more good work in moral psychology than we can do justice to here.

For this reason, we have not here embarked on the fool's errand of attempting a comprehensive survey. Not every important topic has been treated with a chapter, and the chapters themselves, as a rule, favor focus over comprehensiveness. We've also declined to pursue another fool's errand: the pretense of impartiality. Happily, our field is marked by lively disagreement, and progress sometimes required taking sides, even where the authors of different chapters—and sometimes the *same* chapter—have disagreed about what side should be taken. While we've aspired to balanced reporting on the controversial issues, we've more than occasionally adopted editorial positions. The result is not survey, but argumentative survey. Nevertheless, we hope that collectively, the chapters achieve what a *Handbook* should achieve: a wide-ranging statement of what moral psychology is about, and why it matters.

References

Shapiro, F. 2006. *Yale Book of Quotations*. New Haven, CT: Yale University Press.

1

Evolution of Morality[1]

EDOUARD MACHERY AND RON MALLON

> Biology provides a broad source of information about humans that has no substitute. It clarifies long-standing paradoxes. It shows that some things have indeed been missing from the debates about morality, and that they have been missing because the process of organic evolution that gave rise to all forms of life has been left out of the discussions.
>
> (Alexander, 1987: xvii)

Walking in Darwin's footsteps, numerous philosophers, psychologists, anthropologists, and biologists have turned toward evolutionary theory to provide a scientific understanding of morality.[2] In spite of their differences, these thinkers concur on the provocative claim that morality is an evolved part of human nature, much like a tendency to weave nets is an evolved part of spiders' nature.

This claim is supposed to have far-reaching implications in moral philosophy (e.g. Gibbard, 1990; D'Arms, ms). Proponents of evolutionary ethics have often attempted to justify specific moral norms by appealing to the evolution of morality (e.g. Spencer, 1892; Richards, 1986, 1989; Rottschaefer & Martinsen, 1990; Rottschaefer, 1991, 1998; Casebeer, 2003a).[3] The claim that morality evolved has also been used as a premise for various skeptical arguments about

---

[1] We would like to thank Steve Downes, Richard Joyce, Stefan Linquist, and particularly John Doris and Stephen Stich for their comments on previous versions of this chapter.

[2] Darwin (1871); Kropotkin (1902); Huxley (1894/1989); Waddington (1942); Trivers (1971); Singer (1981, 2000); Boehm (1982, 1999); Alexander (1987); Ruse & Wilson (1985); Frank (1988); Gibbard (1990); Irons (1991); Fiske (1991); Wright (1994); Cronk (1994); Dennett (1995); Kitcher (1998, 2006a, b); Wilson (2002); Levy (2004); Allen & Bekoff (2005); Krebs (2005); Joyce (2006); Hauser (2006). Lahti (2003) and Prinz (2008: ch. 7) are more skeptical.

[3] Evolutionary ethics is a specific philosophical tradition. In spite of their diversity, evolutionary ethicists concur that evolutionary theory leads to specific conclusions in normative ethics (i.e. that some particular moral norms are justified or unjustified). For a historical overview of this philosophical tradition, see Farber (1994).

morality (Ruse, 1986; Woolcock, 2000; Joyce, 2000, 2006; Street, 2006, 2008; for critical discussion, see, e.g., Sober, 1994; Copp, 2008).

While it matters philosophically whether or not morality is a product of evolution, we find ourselves agreeing with Darwall, Gibbard, and Railton's complaint that "more careful and empirically informed work on the nature or history or function of morality is needed (. . .) [p]erhaps unsurprisingly, very little such work has been done even by some of those who have recommended it most firmly" (1992: 34). Fifteen years after they expressed this complaint in their well-known article "Toward fin de siècle ethics: Some trends," it remains unclear whether, and in which sense, morality evolved. Our goal in this chapter is to answer these questions. Specifically, we propose to clarify the claim that morality evolved by distinguishing three possible versions of this claim and to review the evidence in support of each. We conclude that two versions of the claim that morality evolved are relatively well supported, but that they are unlikely to yield significant philosophical payoffs, while the stronger version, which is of real interest to philosophers, is in fact empirically unsupported.

Here is how we proceed. In Section 1, we examine a First interpretation of the claim that morality evolved—one on which *some components of moral psychology* have evolved. We argue that this claim is uncontroversial although it can be very difficult to show that some particular components of moral psychology really evolved. In Section 2, we turn to a second interpretation of the claim that morality evolved, the claim that *normative cognition*—that is, the capacity to grasp norms and to make normative judgments—is a product of evolution. We argue that normative cognition might well have evolved, and that it may even be an adaptation. Finally, we turn to the philosophically most interesting interpretation of the claim that morality evolved. In Section 3, we set out the view that *moral cognition*, understood as a special sort of normative cognition, is the product of evolution, and we argue that the evidence adduced in support of the view is unpersuasive.[4] We conclude by expressing our skepticism about the philosophical implications that can be drawn from the literature on the evolution of morality.

---

[4] We do not tackle here a whole range of issues that are often associated with the topic "evolution and morality." In particular, we do not discuss the philosophical tradition of evolutionary ethics, and we only indirectly examine the meta-ethical implications of the evolution of morality.

1. The Evolution of Components of Moral Psychology

1.1. *The Project*

As noted in the introduction, the claim that morality evolved can be interpreted in at least three different ways. The first interpretation asserts that specific components (e.g. emotions, dispositions, rule-based reasoning systems, or concepts) of moral psychology or specific behaviors typically associated with morality evolved. Some evolutionary theorists ask whether some of these components or behaviors evolved, whether they are adaptations, how they could have contributed to fitness, and whether they evolved exclusively in the hominid taxon or in other taxa.

Frans de Waal's work is a good illustration of this approach (e.g. de Waal, 1996; Preston & de Waal, 2002; see also Darwin, 1871; Bekoff, 2004). He is interested in whether some of the emotions, dispositions, and cognitive competences that underlie moral behaviors—e.g. empathy and the recognition of norms—are present in our closest extant relatives, the apes, as well as in more distant relatives, such as old-world and new-world monkeys. Thus, when he defines his project at the beginning of *Good Natured*, he asks, "Do animals show behavior that parallels the benevolence as well as the rules and regulations of human moral conduct? If so, what motivates them to act this way? And do they realize how their behaviors affect others?" (1996: 3).

This interpretation of the claim that morality evolved strikes us as not at all contentious although specific hypotheses about the evolution of particular components of moral psychology may be controversial. It is highly plausible that some moral emotions have an evolutionary history because many emotions have a long evolutionary history (e.g. Fessler & Haley, 2003). And the cognitive architecture of morality also relies on various components of social cognition, many of which also have a long evolutionary history (e.g. Fessler, 1999; Stone, 2006).

Although the idea is fairly uncontroversial, showing that a specific component of moral psychology evolved is difficult. In the remainder of this section, we focus on what is perhaps the main difficulty: before looking for the homologues[5] of human moral traits[6] in other species, such as chimpanzees, researchers should establish that these traits are good candidates for being evolved traits.

1.2. *Fairness in Non-Human Primates?*

De Waal has long argued that many important components of moral psychology, such as the sense of fairness and numerous fairness-related emotions, e.g. gratitude (Brosnan & de Waal, 2002) and inequity aversion (Brosnan & de Waal, 2003; Brosnan, 2006), are homologous to psychological systems in other primates.[7] Here, we focus critically on de Waal's claim that there is evidence for a precursor of the human sense of fairness among female brown capuchins (Brosnan & de Waal, 2003; for related results with chimpanzees, see Brosnan, Schiff, & de Waal, 2005; and for dogs, see Rangea, Horna, Viranyi, & Hubera, 2009). Our goal is not to challenge the idea that many components of our moral psychology (psychological systems, emotions, etc.) evolved: as noted above, this claim strikes us as non-controversial. Rather, focusing on the example of the sense of fairness, our goal is to illustrate how difficult it is to show that some particular component evolved because some traits that might seem to be good candidates for being evolved traits might, on further examination, turn out to be poor ones.

Brosnan and de Waal's experimental design is clever. Capuchins, which have been trained to exchange coins for foods, are put in two adjacent cages. They are given a coin and have to give it back in order to receive a piece of food, which is visible in a transparent bowl in front of them. In one condition, the two capuchins are given a similar recompense, a piece of cucumber. In a second condition, one monkey receives a piece of cucumber, while the second monkey receives a piece of grape (a highly valued food). In a third condition, one monkey receives a piece of cucumber, while the second monkey is given a piece of grape without having to exchange it for a coin. Brosnan and de Waal measure the rate of rejection by monkeys, i.e. the number of cases where the monkeys do not exchange the coin or throw it. The results are surprising:

---

[5] As a first approximation, two traits are homologues if they are modifications of a single ancestor trait (see, e.g., the human eye and the chimpanzee eye) or if one is the modification of the other (see, e.g., the human eye and the eye of humans' and chimpanzees' last common ancestor) (for discussion, see Brigandt, 2003; Griffiths, 2006). Homologues are not necessarily very similar: for instance, mammals' arms and bats' wings are homologous, although they look quite different (at least superficially).

[6] "Trait" is a term of art in evolutionary biology. It refers to the physiological, behavioral, psychological, etc. properties of organisms (e.g. bipedality or a specific skull structure). This use is obviously different from the use of "trait" in the controversy about character in psychology and in ethics.

[7] De Waal (1996); Flack & de Waal (2000). See also Trivers (1971); Bekoff (2001, 2004).

female capuchins reject at a much higher rate the piece of cucumber when the other capuchin is given a grape for a coin and at an even higher rate when the other capuchin is given a grape for free.[8]

Brosnan and de Waal argue that this is tentative evidence for expectations about fair distributions of food, that is, for norms of fair distribution, as well as evidence for social emotions similar and homologous to human moral outrage. They write (2003: 299):

People judge fairness based both on the distribution of gains and on the possible alternatives to a given outcome. Capuchin monkeys, too, seem to measure reward in relative terms, comparing their own rewards with those available, and their own efforts with those of others. They respond negatively to previously acceptable rewards if a partner gets a better deal. Although our data cannot elucidate the precise motivations underlying these responses, one possibility is that monkeys, similarly to humans, are guided by social emotions. These emotions, known as 'passions' by economists, guide human reactions to the efforts, gains, losses and attitudes of others.

And, in a related paper (2004: 140), they add:

[C]apuchin monkeys react negatively when another individual gets a better reward for the same or less effort on a specific task. This finding suggests that precursors to inequity aversion are present in animals from which our lineage split millions of years ago.

We are skeptical, and we now argue that it is unlikely that capuchins obey a norm of fair distribution of windfall gains that is homologous with any human fairness norm. Let us emphasize that we are not denying that the sense of fairness—the tendency to find some actions fair and others unfair—has plausibly evolved. Our claim is more specific: we question whether Brosnan and de Waal's work provides evidence that a specific norm of fairness—the equal distribution of windfall profits—is a homologue present among capuchins and humans. We then use the example of Brosnan and de Waal's research to draw some cautionary conclusions about the search for homologues of the components of human morality.

First, Brosnan and de Waal (2003) found no effect for male capuchins (but see van Wolkenten et al., 2007). This is curious if Brosnan and de Waal have really identified a homologue of a human norm of fair distribution of windfall gains. Among humans, there is some variation in how males and females

---

[8] A control condition ensures that this result is not a mere effect of the presence of highly valued food. Note however that Brosnan, Freeman, & de Waal (2006) failed to replicate capuchin monkeys' aversion to inequity in a different experimental design, and that Bräuer, Call, & Tomasello (2006) failed to replicate chimpanzees' aversion to inequity. Brosnan and de Waal's design has also been severely criticized (Dubreuil, Gentile, & Visalberghi, 2006; but see van Wolkenten, Brosnan, & de Waal, 2007). We will bracket these issues here.

behave in similar situations (e.g. Andreoni & Vesterlund, 2001; Solnick, 2001). However, in an economic game called "the dictator game," both males and females are disposed to reject low offers (Solnick, 2001), suggesting that both get upset when windfall gains are shared unequally.[9]

In addition, Henrich (2004) has noted two problems with Brosnan and de Waal's proposal (but see Brosnan & de Waal's [2004] reply). First, in similar conditions, humans tend to react very differently from female capuchins. When they are offered a deal that they judge to be unfair, humans in many cultures reject this deal, when such a rejection hurts the person who offered the deal (Henrich et al., 2004). However, when rejecting the deal does not hurt the person who offered it, which is a situation analogous to the second and third conditions in Brosnan and de Waal's experiment, people tend to accept the deal, in sharp contrast with capuchins (Bolton & Zwick, 1995).

One could argue on behalf of Brosnan and de Waal that Henrich's first objection is unconvincing. Henrich is certainly correct that humans do not behave similarly to capuchin monkeys. However, it is plausible that in situations that are analogous to Brosnan and de Waal's experiments, humans in many cultures feel annoyed and angry. But because they are able to control their anger and to act in their best interest, humans accept the offer, when rejecting the offer would not hurt its author. By contrast, capuchins are not able to control their anger and are thus unable to act in their best interest. It would be easy to test the hypothesis that in situations that are similar to Brosnan and de Waal's conditions 2 and 3, humans and capuchins react similarly in that they both feel anger. In particular, focusing on humans, one could examine whether there is any facial micro-expression of anger (micro-expressions are facial expressions of emotions that last only a fraction of second because the agent tries to suppress or control her emotion). One could also examine whether the brain areas involved in negative emotions (particularly the insula) and in executive control (the dorsolateral prefrontal cortex and the anterior cingulate cortex) are activated in these situations.

More troubling is Henrich's second criticism. Henrich and colleagues have documented that there is much cross-cultural normative diversity in the norms bearing on the distribution of windfall gains (Henrich et al., 2004, 2005). For instance, Americans believe that a fair distribution of such gains consists in splitting them equally. By contrast, in a few small-scale societies, such

---

[9] A "dictator game" is one in which a windfall is divided by one person ("the dictator"), and the resulting distribution can be accepted or rejected by the other. If it is rejected, the two persons get nothing. Because even a small share of a windfall is better than nothing, economic rationality suggests that parties should accept even small shares rather than reject an unfair distribution.

as the Machiguengas of the Peruvian Amazon, people seem to expect the beneficiaries of windfall gains to keep the gain for themselves.

Of course, by itself, variation, including cultural variation, does not show that a trait (i.e., in the present case, the norm of splitting windfall gains equally) has not evolved. To begin with, different adaptations can be selected for in different human populations. Moreover, a trait can also be designed so as to take different forms in different environments, including different social environments (see, e.g., Draper & Belsky, 1990). Finally, a given adaptation often varies across environments because the environment in which organisms develop influences its development.

However, in this specific case, cultural variation suggests that the norm about the fair allocation of windfall gains was not selected for. If this norm is really present in capuchins (as de Waal and colleagues would have it), then it is very ancient: it had already evolved 30 million years ago, before the platyrrhines (the phylum to which capuchins belong) and the catarrhines (the phylum to which humans belong) split. If it is that ancient, then it should plausibly be species-typical, exactly like vision is. However, the cross-cultural research suggests that it varies across cultures, undermining the hypothesis that the norm of splitting windfall gains equally is an evolved trait that is homologous in capuchins and humans. Rather than being a trait homologous to old-world monkeys and humans, what is fair in the kind of situations considered by Brosnan and de Waal or by Henrich and colleagues is determined by the culture-specific norms governing economic interactions.

Henrich's second comment illustrates what is maybe the most important difficulty that accompanies attempts to discover homologues of human moral traits. Suppose that one is interested, as de Waal or Bekoff are, in finding homologues of some of the traits (emotions, norms, concepts, etc.) that constitute human moral cognition (and not in establishing that these traits are themselves evolved). Because two traits are homologues only if they evolved from a common ancestor trait, such a research project assumes that the relevant components of human moral cognition have evolved or, at least, that they are good candidates for being evolved traits. Thus, before looking for homologues of a given component of human moral cognition, it would seem important to ensure that there are no strong reasons to doubt that this component really evolved.[10] The existence of a trait in only a few cultures, its emergence in

---

[10] If one's interest does not lie in finding homologues of the components of human moral cognition, but in showing that these components themselves evolved, then it is appropriate to look for plausible homologues even if there are some reasons to doubt that the relevant components really evolved. For finding plausible homologues of some components of human moral cognition would provide very strong evidence that these components evolved.

some recent, historical times, or its acquisition by means of a domain-general learning mechanism are strong reasons to doubt that this trait evolved. Thus the cross-cultural variation of how windfall gains should be shared suggests that the norm of splitting windfall gains equally is unlikely to be an evolved trait. It is then pointless to look for homologues of this norm.

1.3. *Summary: The Evolution of Psychological Components of Moral Psychology*

Researchers often focus on some components of moral psychology, such as the norm of fairness. Then they attempt to determine the evolutionary history of these components, by studying whether other species, particularly other primates, also possess the relevant traits. We have argued that this first interpretation is uncontroversial: some, and perhaps many, components of moral psychology evolved. At the same time, hypotheses about the evolution of specific components are difficult to establish, in part because some traits that might seem to be good candidates for having evolved may, on further examination, turn out to be poor candidates. Looking for homologues of the components of moral psychology requires careful attention to a range of data from multiple fields of scientific inquiry to ensure that there are no strong reasons to doubt that these components evolved. Cultural psychology and anthropology are needed to establish that this trait is not culturally local while developmental psychology is needed to show that it is not acquired by means of a domain-general learning mechanism. In this section, we illustrated this difficulty by discussing Brosnan and de Waal's claim to have found a homologue of the human fairness norm about windfall gains.

As noted in the introduction, the claim that morality evolved is often supposed to have far-reaching implications in moral philosophy, but little attention has been dedicated to examining whether and in which sense morality evolved. Now, we have just argued that, under at least one interpretation, it is uncontroversial that it did: some components of moral cognition evolved. So, one might ask, what follows from the evolution of morality in this sense? As we shall now see, very little.

It is important to distinguish three strategies for answering this question. First, one might ask whether anything of interest in moral philosophy follows from the claim that some components of moral cognition evolved. We believe that the answer is probably negative since we do not see how the argument would go, and indeed we know of no philosopher who argued to significant philosophical conclusion from this premise. Second, one might attempt to derive moral conclusions from the evolution of *specific* components of moral cognition. For instance, D'Arms (ms) argues that research on the evolution of "self-righteous anger"—the anger directed at people who are not angered by others' moral violations—has moral consequences. Arguments of this kind can take one of the following two forms. First, one could propose to derive moral norms about dispositions to act, character traits, etc. from facts about the functions of these dispositions and character traits.[11] For instance, Casebeer contends that "moral facts are reducible to functional facts" (2003b: 67). Although we do not have the space to discuss this first kind of argument at length, we are not sanguine about it. Although some normative propositions might be reducible to functional propositions—e.g. the claim that an organ is working as it should might be reducible to the claim that it fulfilled its function—we doubt that this can be done from moral propositions without falling prey to some version of the open question argument (see Joyce, 2006 for further criticism of Casebeer). The second type of argument is illustrated by D'Arms's discussion of the normative consequences of the evolution of self-righteous anger. D'Arms correctly notes that research on the evolution of a morally relevant trait can improve our knowledge about what this trait is or what it does. For instance, research on the evolution of self-righteous anger improves our understanding of the effect of self-righteous anger on the social stability of norms. And what a trait is or does is surely relevant to whether one should morally have this trait. Although this kind of argument is the most promising way of deriving moral consequences from some evolutionary findings about a specific component of morality, it is noteworthy that these consequences are not derived from the fact that this component evolved, but rather from what it is or what it does. So, just like the two strategies discussed above, this argumentative strategy does not establish that moral consequences follow from the evolution of the components of moral cognition.

2. The Evolution of Normative Cognition

We now turn to the second interpretation of the claim that morality evolved. Researchers interested in this second interpretation focus on normative cognition in general: they contend that normative cognition evolved (and often, that it is an adaptation). In this section, we explain this claim in more detail, and we argue that there is a small, but suggestive, body of evidence that normative cognition is an adaptation.

---

[11] In this context, functions are understood etiologically: roughly, y is the function of x if and only if the fact that x does y explains why x exists. For instance, the function of shame is to motivate people to apologize for having broken some norms if shame was selected for during evolution (and as a result, exists nowadays) because of this effect.

2.1. *Normative Cognition*

Although the nature of norms is a controversial topic in the social sciences (e.g. McAdams, 1997), we offer an informal account that should be acceptable to many social scientists. As we shall understand them, norms are attitudes toward types of actions, emotions, thoughts, or other traits. These norms are typically shared by many members of a given group and regulate people's behaviors, thoughts, emotions, characters, and so on. Their content essentially involves deontic concepts, such as SHOULD or OUGHT. Such norms can prescribe or forbid a thought, behavior, or any other characteristic, and may be associated with a disposition to punish those individuals who do not comply with the norms.

Normative cognition is underwritten by a complex cognitive architecture. People learn and assimilate, explicitly and implicitly, numerous norms; they are motivated to comply with them; and they typically expect others to comply with them. Emotions are also a key component of this cognitive architecture. Several negative emotions are triggered by norm violations (Haidt, 2003; Fessler & Haley, 2003). Norm violators are likely to feel shame or guilt (depending on which emotion is emphasized in their culture).[12] Victims of norm violations and third parties are likely to feel anger or disgust toward norm violators. These emotions motivate behavior: the anticipation of feeling ashamed and guilty motivates avoiding the violation of norms, shame and guilt motivate reparative behavior, and anger motivates punishment (e.g. Fehr & Gächter, 2002; Haidt & Sabini, 2000). Disgust causes third parties to distance themselves from norm violators, which results in the loss of cooperative opportunities for the norm violators. Anticipatory fear of shame or guilt often motivates norm compliance (Fessler, 2007).[13] In addition to these negative emotions, positive emotions are caused by norm compliance. People feel elevation when others endure some cost to comply with certain norms (Haidt, 2003).

It is remarkable, however, there has been little systematic work on human normative cognition. One exception is Chandra Sripada and Stephen Stich's (2006) article. Sripada and Stich argue for the existence of two cognitive systems subserving the psychology of norms: an acquisition mechanism and an implementation mechanism. The function of the acquisition mechanism is to learn the norms that are prevalent in one's culture, while the function

---

[12] Research shows that in some cultures (e.g. Indonesia), people are more prone to feel shame than guilt when they violate a norm, while in other cultures (e.g. the USA), they are more prone to feel guilt than shame (Benedict, 1946; Fessler, 2004).

[13] For instance, according to J. Heinrich (personal communication, 10/21/2007), Fijians are constantly weighing the prospects of feeling shame when they make decisions.

of the implementation mechanism is to store representations of these norms, to produce some intrinsic desires to comply with them, and to motivate people to punish norm violators. While their hypothesis is consistent with the existence of innate representations of norms, Sripada and Stich speculate that the implementation mechanism does not store any innate representation of norms. Rather, children, and sometimes adults, need to learn the prevalent norms of their social community.

2.2. *How to Study the Evolution of Normative Cognition?*

Many researchers' work on the evolution of morality is best understood as being about the evolution of normative cognition in general, since they do not single out a specific kind of norms (i.e. moral norms).[14]

Before going any further, it is worth noting that there are many ways to investigate the evolution of a trait. It is particularly useful to distinguish two related claims. To claim that a trait *evolved* is simply to claim that the trait has a phylogenetic history, and one project would be to inquire into this history.[15] That is, one can study what changes took place in the psychology of our primate ancestors during the evolution of normative cognition (just as one can study the evolution of the human eye by identifying the changes that took place during the evolution of the mammalian eye). A stronger claim is that normative cognition constitutes an *adaptation*. An adaptation is a specific sort of evolved trait—i.e. a trait whose evolution is the result of natural selection. Since not all products of evolution are adaptations, someone who conjectures that normative cognition is an evolved trait can also examine whether it is an adaptation, the by-product of another adaptation, or an evolutionary accident. In addition, if one proposes that normative cognition is an adaptation, one should consider what its evolutionary function might be—that is, what selective forces might have driven its evolution.

2.3. *Evidence that Normative Cognition is an Adaptation*

Sociological and psychological evidence suggests that normative cognition is an adaptation. We consider these two types of evidence in turn (for further evidence, see Cummins, 1996b).

Norms, either informal or formal, are ancient: the historical record has no trace of a society without norms. Furthermore, norms are universal (although

---

[14] See, particularly, Fiske (1991); Bowles & Gintis (1998); Richerson, Boyd, & Henrich (2003); Gintis, Bowles, Boyd, & Fehr (2003); Nowak & Sigmund (2005).

[15] Phylogeny is the change of lineages through time. One looks at an evolved trait in a given species from a phylogenetic perspective when one considers how this trait results from changes to the traits possessed by the ancestor species of the species under consideration.

the content of norms varies tremendously across cultures). Small-scale societies are typically regulated by informal norms, while large-scale societies are typically regulated by informal and formal norms. All known societies also have policing mechanisms that ensure people's compliance with the prevalent norms (Brown, 1991). These policing mechanisms naturally vary across cultures. In some societies, but not in all, policing is the socially sanctioned role of a dedicated group of individuals (e.g. policemen, Iran's "moral" police [a branch of the Islamic Revolutionary Guard], etc.). In addition, in all societies, informal social practices contribute to ensure people's compliance with the prevalent norms (Boehm, 1999). These include gossip (Dunbar, 1996) and various forms of ostracism (Brown, 1991). Finally, as noted by Sripada and Stich (2006), norms permeate people's life: few behaviors and decisions are immune to the influence of some norm or other.

The antiquity and universality of norms is evidence that normative cognition evolved. When a trait is ancient and universal, it is either because it can be easily acquired by individual learning or by social learning, or because a developmental system is designed to ensure its regular development. In the latter case, but not in the former case, the universality and antiquity of a trait is evidence that it evolved. Ancient and universal traits that are *not* evolved, such as the belief that the sun rises every morning, are easy to acquire from one's physical and social environment (Dennett, 1995). Since it is difficult to see how one could acquire the capacity for normative attitudes toward thoughts, behaviors, and other traits—i.e. a capacity for norms—from one's environment (in contrast to acquiring specific norms, which can obviously be learned), it is plausible that normative cognition evolved.

Turning from sociological to psychological considerations, evidence suggests that people are endowed with a reasoning capacity that is specific to the domain of norms. While people reason poorly about non normative matters, they are adept at reasoning about normative matters (for review, see Cosmides & Tooby, 2005). Both Western and non-literate Shuar Amazonian subjects easily determine in which situations deontic conditionals, such as "If you eat mongongo nut (described as an aphrodisiac in the cover story), then you must have a tattoo on your chest" (described as a mark denoting married status), are violated, while they are surprisingly poor at determining in which situations indicative conditionals, such as ("If there is a red bird in the drawing on top, then there is an orange on the drawing below"), are false (Cosmides, 1989; Sugiyama, Tooby, & Cosmides, 2002). Although the interpretation of these findings remains somewhat controversial (e.g. Sperber, Cara, & Girotto, 1995), they suggest to us that people are distinctively adept at detecting norm violation.

Furthermore, just like adults, young children are much better at reasoning about the violations of deontic conditionals than about the falsity of indicative conditionals (Cummins, 1996a; Harris & Núñez, 1996). For instance, Cummins (1996a) showed 3-year-old children some toy mice and told them that some, but not all, could squeak. She also told them that some squeaky mice were inside the house, while others were outside. Finally, she told children that a cat was hunting mice outside the house, but only when they squeaked. Half of the children were told that Queen Minnie Mouse had told the mice, "It's not safe outside for the squeaky mouse, so all squeaky mice *are* in the house." Those children were then asked to say which mice must be examined to see whether Minnie Mouse was right. The other half was told that Queen Minnie Mouse had told the mice, "It's not safe outside for the squeaky mouse, so all squeaky mice *must stay* in the house." Those children were then asked to say which mice must be examined to see whether Minnie Mouse's rule has been broken. While almost 65% of 3-year-olds answered correctly the second question, only 30% of them answered correctly the first question. These findings suggest that the capacity to reason about norms develops early (as early as children's fourth year) and in a distinctive manner (since it seems independent from children's capacity to reason about conditionals in general).

The existence of a cognitive system that seems dedicated specifically to produce good reasoning about norms from an early age on provides some suggestive evidence that normative cognition is an adaptation.[16] Generally, the functional specificity of a trait is (defeasible) evidence that it is an adaptation. Furthermore, the fact that a trait develops early and that its development is distinctive—it is independent from the development of other traits—suggests that natural selection acted on its developmental pathway. The early development of a psychological trait suggests that it is not acquired as a result of our domain-general learning capacity; the distinctive development of a psychological trait suggests that it is not acquired as a by-product of the acquisition of another psychological capacity (for further discussion, see Machery, forthcoming). Thus, evidence tentatively suggests not only that normative cognition is an evolved trait, but also that it is an adaptation.

The findings just considered provide suggestive (though inconclusive) evidence that normative cognition is an adaptation. It is instructive to anticipate

---

[16] Note that this claim is independent of Cosmides and Tooby's more specific claims about the form the adaptation takes (e.g. Cosmides & Tooby, 2005). It might even be compatible with critiques of Cosmides and Tooby (Fodor, 2000) according to which differential reasoning about norm violations is due to the use of deontic concepts in the norms themselves (see Cosmides & Tooby, 2008a, 2008b, 2008c; Fodor, 2008; Mallon, 2008).

Section 3 and to compare these findings with the body of evidence typically adduced to support the claim that moral cognition, conceived as a specific kind of normative cognition, evolved. While researchers often claim that moral cognition, conceived as a specific kind of normative cognition, is universal, we shall argue in the next section that the evidence for this claim is lacking. By contrast, the evidence for the antiquity and universality of norms is extremely solid. We shall also challenge the claim that a key component of moral cognition—i.e. grasping the distinction between properly moral norms and conventional norms—develops early and reliably. By contrast, although the research on adults' and children's capacity to reason with deontic conditionals is not entirely uncontroversial, it is on safer ground. In this case, psychologists have indeed typically not challenged the claim that people reason better with deontic conditionals than with indicative conditions; rather, they have focused on how this difference is to be explained.

2.4. *"How-Possible" Models of the Selection of Normative Cognition*

In addition to this small, but suggestive, body of evidence that normative cognition in general is an adaptation, several models show how normative cognition *could* have been selected for during the evolution of hominids.[17] These "how-possible" models (Brandon, 1990) do not establish how normative cognition actually evolved: evidence is lacking to answer this question. But these models show, first, that the hypothesis that normative cognition was selected for is consistent with our knowledge of evolution; second, the selection of normative cognition in evolutionary models is robust: in several possible evolutionary situations—those represented by the how-possible models—normative cognition would have been selected for.[18]

Since the 1980s, Robert Boyd, Peter Richerson, and their colleagues have developed a series of models explaining how norms can be stable in a community. Here, we present two of their models informally. In a well-known model, Boyd and Richerson (1992) have shown that punishment (actions inflicting a cost on norm violators) can stabilize any norm, including norms that prescribe costly behaviors such as cooperation. Suppose for an instant that punishment is cost-free—the punisher does not endure any cost when she punishes. By violating a norm, norm violators might get some

---

[17] By contrast, the models that account for the evolution of morality, understood as a specific form of normative cognition, are not particularly plausible (see Section 3).

[18] Boyd & Richerson (1992); Henrich & Boyd (2001); Boyd et al. (2003); Gintis et al. (2003); Richerson et al. (2003); Richerson & Boyd (2005); Boyd & Mathew (2007); Hauert et al. (2007).

benefit or might avoid some cost, when norm compliance is costly. However, because they are punished, violators suffer a cost and do less well than those who comply with norms, but avoid punishing ("lazy norm compliers") and those who comply with norms and enforce them ("punishers"). If successful behaviors tend to become common in a population (maybe because they are imitated by others), then compliance with norms will prevail. Thus punishment can stabilize norms. Importantly, in this model, norm compliance does not depend on the content of the norms, only on the punishment of norm violators. Thus different norms might be stabilized in different societies, consistent with the diversity of norms across cultures.

But, of course, punishment is not cost-free, although, in humans, it might be low-cost because of the development of weapons and of language (which allows people to hurt others by gossiping negatively about them). Because punishment is not cost-free, lazy norm compliers do better than punishers. Thus compliance without punishment might become more common in a population at the expense of compliance with punishment (Boyd & Richerson, 1992). However, if lazy norm compliers become more common, norm violators will in turn increase in frequency, because they will be less often punished. This will prevent the stabilization of norms. How, then, is norm compliance obtained?

This problem has been addressed in various ways. One could first suggest that punishment itself is a norm, and that lazy norm compliers get punished when they fail to punish norm violators, a type of punishment called "metapunishment" or "second-order punishment" (Boyd & Richerson, 1992). However, this suggestion only pushes the problem one step further, because metapunishment is itself costly.

Henrich and Boyd (2001) have proposed an alternative solution (for a different model, see Boyd et al., 2003). In their model, behaviors are transmitted culturally, but biased by *conformism* and *prestige*. Conformist bias means that common behaviors are more likely to be transmitted than rare behaviors, while prestige bias means that high-payoff behaviors are more likely to be transmitted than low-payoff behaviors. Conformism favors the cultural transmission of the prevalent behaviors, whatever these are, while prestige-biased transmission can undermine norm compliance, punishment, and metapunishment, because these can be costly. Suppose now that, in a population, everybody complies with the norms, but fails to punish norm violators (everybody is *a lazy norm complier*). An intruder who fails to comply with the norms (*a norm violator*) would be better off than these lazy norm compliers, and prestige bias would tend to lead others to become norm violators, providing that this bias was stronger than the countervailing bias to conform with the more common compliant behavior. So, where conformism is weak, norm violation will become common.

Consider now a second case. Everybody complies with the norms and punishes violators (everybody is *a punisher*). An intruder norm violator would not be better off than the common punishers, because she would be punished. But an intruder *lazy norm complier* would be better off than the common punishers, since she would not get punished (since she complies with the norms) and would avoid the cost of punishing others. By contrast, punishers would pay the cost of punishing the other punishers who would fail by mistake to comply with the prevalent norms. The extent of a lazy norm complier's advantage over the punishers depends on how costly it is to punish and on how often punishers fail to comply by accident with the prevalent norms.[19] If this advantage is large enough to offset the advantage conformism gives to punishers' common behavior (that is, to offset the fact that due to people's conformism, common behaviors are more likely to be imitated by others than rare behavior), compliance with the norms without punishing would become common. If lazy norm compliers replace the punishers in a population, the norm violators will ultimately invade this population.

Now, consider a third case. Everybody complies with norms, punishes violators, and punishes non-punishers (everybody is *a metapunisher*). An intruder lazy norm complier would not be better off than the common metapunishers, because she would be punished for non-punishing the metapunishers' accidental norm violations. But an intruder who would comply with the prevalent norms, punish violators, but fail to punish those who fail to punish (*a lazy punisher*) would be better off than the common metapunishers because she would not be punished (she complies with the norms) and because she would avoid the cost of punishing the failure to punish. By contrast, metapunishers would pay the cost of punishing those metapunishers who would fail by mistake to punish the metapunishers who by mistake violate a norm. However, the advantage of a lazy punisher over the metapunishers is smaller than the advantage of a lazy norm complier over the punishers, for the former advantage depends on *two* mistakes, i.e. a metapunisher failing by accident to comply with a prevalent norm and another metapunisher failing by accident to punish the accidental non-compliance. The lazy punisher's advantage is thus less likely to offset the advantage conformism gives to the common metapunishing behavior. Of course, the same argument applies at further orders of punishment. Thus, even if conformism is weak, it can stabilize punishment at some order

---

[19] This punisher is a cooperator who fails to cooperate by accident. Think for instance of someone who was unable to fulfill her promise to pick up a friend at the airport because her car failed to start.

of punishment. If punishment is stable, then norm compliance is itself stable. Thus Henrich and Boyd show that with a small amount of conformism that stabilizes metapunishment (or some higher-order punishment), costly norm compliance is stable: compliance with the prevalent norms, even at one's own cost, is more likely to be culturally transmitted than non-compliance with these norms.

Now, suppose that, as this and other models suggest is possible, cultural transmission stabilized norms during human evolution. Because norm violators were punished for violating the prevalent norms and because lazy norm compliers were punished for not punishing norm violators, both norm violators and lazy norm compliers incurred costs that punishers (who comply with the norms and punish) did not incur. Our ancestors who were good at learning the prevalent norms and who were motivated to comply with them and to punish norm violators might thus have had a fitness advantage over people who learned badly the prevalent norms or had a weak (if any) motivation to comply with them. Thus natural selection might have favored some important elements of the architecture of normative cognition—a disposition to learn prevalent norms, a disposition to comply with norms, and a disposition to punish norm violators.

2.5. *Summary: The Evolution of Normativity*

In this section, we have focused on a second interpretation of the claim that morality evolved: normative cognition—the capacity to grasp and apply norms—evolved. A small body of evidence suggests that normative cognition evolved by natural selection. Furthermore, several how-possible models show how normative cognition could have been selected for during the evolution of the human species.

Importantly, this conclusion is cold comfort to those philosophers who want to get some philosophical mileage out of evolutionary findings. This is particularly clear when one focuses on the argument that the evolution of morality would undermine the authority of moral norms (e.g. Ruse, 1986; Joyce, 2006). Suppose that this argument from the evolution of morality is meant to hang on the reading of the claim that morality evolved considered in this section: normative cognition in general evolved. While this argument would then rest on a premise that is supported by a small, but convincing body of evidence, it would have very troubling consequences. If the evolution of normative cognition really undermines the authority of moral norms, then it should also undermine the authority of *any* kind of norms (including epistemic norms), for there is no reason why *only* the authority of moral norms would be undermined by the evolution of the capacity to grasp norms *tout court*.

The unpalatable nature of this conclusion would plausibly give grounds for concluding that the argument from the evolution of morality is flawed. The upshot should be clear: if the claim that the evolution of morality undermines the authority of morality is to be plausible at all, it has to be based on an interpretation of the claim that morality evolved different from the one considered in this section. In our view, it is no accident that when philosophers have attempted to derive philosophical implications from the hypothesis that morality evolved, they have typically focused on a third reading of this hypothesis. We now turn to this reading.

3. The Evolution of Moral Normativity

3.1. *The Project*

Researchers who endorse the third version of the claim that morality evolved start by drawing a distinction among different types of normative cognition and by singling out one specific type of normative cognition, which they call "morality." They then proceed to argue for the evolution of this type of normative cognition. Consider each step of this project.

3.1.1. *Morality as a Type of Normativity*   As we saw in Section 2, normative cognition includes the capacity to grasp norms, to make normative judgments, and to be motivated to act according to the norms that one endorses.[20] Norms have to do with the regulation of people's actions, emotions, thoughts, or other traits. They specify what kinds of behaviors, emotions, thoughts, or other characteristics are mandatory, permissible, or recommended.[21] In turn, normative judgments consist in judging that behaviors, emotions, and thoughts (one's own or others') are unconditionally mandatory, permissible, or recommended.[22]

Turn now to the claim that moral cognition is a distinctive type of normative cognition. The basic idea is that moral norms are a distinct type of

[20] We distinguish grasping a norm from making a normative judgment because research on psychopathy suggests that it is possible to grasp a norm without endorsing it (Roskies, 2003; but see Levy, 2007; Prinz, 2008, ch. 1).

[21] For a discussion of normativity, see, e.g., Gibbard (1990: 61–80) and Railton (1999).

[22] Note that saying that a behavior (emotion, etc.) is unconditionally mandatory (permissible, etc.) is not the same as saying that it is universally mandatory (permissible, etc.)—that is, that it is mandatory for everybody. One can make unconditional normative judgments that apply only to some groups of people. For instance, one could judge that some actions are permissible for adults, but not for children, that some actions are forbidden for some particular social groups, such as a caste, etc.

norm and that related entities like moral judgments, moral motivations, and moral behaviors and thoughts are similarly distinct. For the sake of simplicity, we focus our discussion here especially on norms and normative judgments. There are many kinds of normative judgments, and moral judgments are only one of them. Other kinds of normative judgments might include judgments about what is rational (e.g. "you shouldn't believe that, given what else you believe"), aesthetically appropriate ("one should never wear green pants with a yellow shirt"), prudent ("if you want to live a long life, you should wear your seatbelt"), and conventionally expected ("if you are satisfied with the service, the tip should be at least 20%"). The first interpretation of the claim that morality is the product of evolution rests on the idea that moral judgments provide a *distinctive* means of regulating or evaluating actions, emotions, intentions, or character.

Richard Joyce's (2006) book *The Evolution of Morality* provides a particularly clear illustration of the kind of research considered here (see also Ruse, 1986; D'Arms, 2000; Joyce, 2008a, b). Focusing on moral judgments, he proposes that seven properties distinguish moral judgments and moral behaviors from other kinds of normative judgments:

- Moral judgments (as public utterances) are often ways of expressing conative attitudes, such as approval, contempt, or, more generally, subscription to standards; moral judgments nevertheless also express beliefs; i.e., they are assertions.
- Moral judgments pertaining to action purport to be deliberative considerations irrespective of the interests/ends of those to whom they are directed; thus they are not pieces of prudential advice.
- Moral judgments purport to be inescapable; there is no "opting out."
- Moral judgments purport to transcend human conventions.
- Moral judgments centrally govern interpersonal relations; they seem designed to combat rampant individualism in particular.
- Moral judgments imply notions of desert and justice (a system of "punishments and rewards").
- For creatures like us, the emotion of guilt (or "a moral conscience") is an important mechanism for regulating one's moral conduct. (2006: 70–71)

He adds that "so long as a kind of value system satisfies *enough* of the above, then it counts as a moral system" (71).

While Joyce clearly intends his list to function not as a checklist of necessary and sufficient conditions, but rather as something like a cluster concept, it is worth emphasizing that his claim is substantive and provocative precisely because of the rich characterization of moral judgments that he offers. That is, according to his account, moral judgments have many distinctive properties that differentiate them from other sorts of normative judgments. In expressing skepticism about whether the capacity to make moral judgments is a product of evolution, we mean specifically to doubt Joyce's view and others like it. We do not doubt that there exists some thin description of the class of moral judgments that could be offered such that, under this description, the capacity to make moral judgments would be the product of evolution.[23] We deny the claim that when moral judgments are richly described, the capacity to make them is a product of evolution.

3.1.2. *Morality as an Evolved Trait* After characterizing distinctively moral cognition—for example, after characterizing moral norms as a distinct kind of norm or moral judgments as a distinct kind of normative judgment—researchers conjecture that such distinctively moral cognition is an evolved trait. Remember that in Section 2 we distinguished two related ways of studying the evolution of a trait. One could simply claim that morality, as a specific kind of normative cognition, *evolved*. One would then study what changes took place in the psychology of our primate ancestors during the evolution of the grasp of distinctively moral norms and of the capacity to make moral judgments. Since, as noted in Section 2.2, not all products of evolution are adaptations, someone who conjectures that the capacity to grasp moral norms and the capacity to make moral judgments are evolved traits can also examine whether they constitute an adaptation (as Dennett, 1995, Kitcher, 1998, and Joyce, 2006 have claimed), whether it is a by-product of another adaptation, or whether it is an evolutionary accident (Williams, 1988). In addition, if one proposes that the grasp of moral norms and the capacity to make moral judgments constitute an adaptation, one should consider what its evolutionary function might be—that is, what selective forces might have driven its evolution.

Joyce, for example, suggests that the capacity to make moral judgments is a specifically human adaptation for motivating us to act in a prosocial way. In essence, moral judgments provided our ancestors with compelling reasons to act in ways that typically favor others and that can be detrimental to themselves (see also Dennett, 1995). As a result, moral judgments reliably caused prosocial behavior. Moreover, loosely following Robert Frank (1988), Joyce contends that because moral judgments can be linguistically expressed, they signal to

---

[23] Indeed, as we have seen in Section 2, we allow that normative cognition *tout court*—as opposed to distinctively moral normative cognition—may well be a product of evolution.

others that we are committed to act in a prosocial way. The capacity to make moral judgments was favored by natural selection because reliable prosocial behavior and the signaling of one's dispositions to act in a prosocial way were favored during the evolution of the human species, possibly because prosocial behaviors were reciprocated.

Joyce is not the only researcher to claim that the capacity to make moral judgments, understood as a distinct type of normative judgment, is an adaptation. In *Moral Minds*, Marc Hauser (2006) contends that, like the language faculty, the moral faculty is a distinct psychological adaptation, although he has little to say about its evolutionary function (2006: xvii):

> The central idea of this book is simple: we evolved a moral instinct, a capacity that naturally grows within each child, designed to generate rapid judgments about what is morally right or wrong based on an unconscious grammar of action.[24]

In contrast to these projects, we see little reason to believe that the grasp of distinctively moral norms and the capacity to make moral judgments, understood as a specific kind of normative judgments, evolved at all, and so we doubt that they constitute an adaptation, a by-product, or an evolutionary accident. We conjecture that in this respect, the capacity to grasp moral norms and the capacity to make moral judgments might be similar to chess or handwriting. The capacities to play chess and to write involve various evolved cognitive traits (e.g. visual recognition and memorization of rules for the former), but they did not evolve. Similarly, we conjecture that the capacity to grasp moral norms and the capacity to make moral judgments involve various evolved cognitive traits (including, as we proposed in Section 2, a disposition to grasp norms in general), but they themselves did not evolve. In any case, as we shall argue now, none of the available evidence suggests that they did.

In the remainder of Section 3, we look critically at two different forms of argument for the claim that moral cognition evolved:

(1) There are plausible adaptationist models that predict its selection. Thus the grasp of moral norms and the capacity to make moral judgments are likely to be an adaptation and, *a fortiori*, to have evolved.

(2) The universality and innateness of the capacity to grasp moral norms and to make moral judgments is evidence that it is an evolved trait.

---

[24] For other approaches to the evolution of moral cognition, understood as a distinct type of normative cognition, see Darwin (1871), Ruse & Wilson (1985), Ruse (1986), Dennett (1995: chs. 16–17), Kitcher (1998), Singer (2000), and Levy (2004).

3.2. Adaptationist Models of the Evolution of Morality

It is common to argue that a trait is an adaptation by showing that there are plausible adaptationist models that predict the selection of this trait. For instance, some sociobiologists have provided this kind of argument in support of the hypothesis that female orgasm is an adaptation: they have argued this because it is plausible that, among our ancestors, those females who were able to have orgasms were more motivated to have sex and, as a result, were more likely to have descendants than those females who had no orgasm (for review and criticism, see Lloyd, 2005). This kind of argument has been severely criticized in the philosophy of biology because it involves telling just-so stories that cannot be supported by any available evidence (Gould & Lewontin, 1979; Kitcher, 1985).[25] Here, we do not discuss the value of this kind of argument in general. Rather, we criticize specific adaptationist models of the evolution of morality. We argue that these models do not support the claim that moral cognition, conceived as a distinct kind of normative cognition, was selected for. We first consider models that appeal to *reciprocal altruism*, then we consider models that are based on *indirect reciprocity*, before finally raising a general problem for all current adaptationist models of the evolution of morality.

Many adaptationist models of the evolution of morality appeal to a specific evolutionary mechanism, reciprocal altruism (Figure 1.1). The notion of reciprocal altruism was developed by evolutionary biologist Robert Trivers as a possible explanation of altruistic behavior among non-related organisms (Trivers, 1971).[26] The idea goes roughly as follows: a gene G for an altruistic trait T is favored by natural selection if T benefits discriminatively recipients who are likely to reciprocate in the future. Reciprocation is delayed and may be of a different kind (as happens, e.g., when chimps exchange grooming for political support, a phenomenon reported in Foster et al., 2009). To use a toy example, a gene G for sharing food is favored by natural selection if the bearer of G shares food with individuals that are likely, at some point in the future, to reciprocate by acting in a way that increases the fitness of the bearer

[25] Gould and Lewontin illustrated just-so stories with sociobiologist David Barash's work on bluebirds (but see Alcock, 2001: 65–68). Having observed that male bluebirds attack significantly more stuffed males near their nets before than after the eggs were laid, Barash speculated that males' aggressiveness toward other males was an evolved disposition for avoiding cuckoldry. Although this hypothesis seems to make sense of the trait under consideration, Gould and Lewontin argued that it was simply an untestable speculation. Research on the evolution of human brain size or human language offers numerous other examples.

[26] In evolutionary biology, a trait is said to be altruistic if it reduces the individual relative fitness of the bearer of the trait (the cost of the trait for the bearer) while increasing the individual relative fitness of another individual (see Chapter 5 of this volume on altruism).

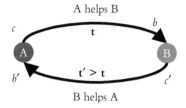

Figure 1.1. Reciprocal altruism

Note: c and c' stand for the costs of the altruistic actions for the agents A and B, b and b' for the benefits bestowed upon the beneficiaries of the actions, A and B ($c < b'$, $b > c'$), and t and t' for the times of the actions.

of G. According to Triver's model, three conditions have to be met for reciprocal altruism to explain the evolution of altruism. First, for the two individuals involved in a reciprocal interaction, the cost of being altruistic (in units of fitness) must be lower than the benefit received from the reciprocator's altruism. The cost of sharing food for the bearer of G must be lower than the benefit taken from the reciprocation at a later time. Second, the benefit of altruism must be withheld from those individuals who did not reciprocate in the past—usually called "cheaters." The bearer of G should refrain from sharing food with those individuals who did not reciprocate in the past. Third, individuals must interact repeatedly, so that the cost to cheaters of foregone protracted reciprocal interactions (in units of fitness) is greater than the benefit cheaters take from non-reciprocating. The bearer of G must share food with individuals with whom she is likely to interact often, so that not benefiting from food sharing over a long period of time is more costly than avoiding the cost of reciprocating a past benefit.

It is likely that reciprocal altruism fails to explain a range of human altruistic behaviors. As we saw, Trivers's idea is that if interactions between two individuals last for long enough, traits that benefit discriminatively those individuals that are likely to reciprocate will be favored by natural selection. This hypothesis fails to explain why people are disposed to benefit individuals with whom they will probably have no further interaction. For instance, people regularly tip waiters while on vacations, even though they will have no further interactions with them.

To explain away this difficulty, one might suggest that our ancestors lived in close-knit societies, where interactions were typically repeated. As a result, we evolved cooperative dispositions that do not distinguish between interactions that are likely and interactions that are unlikely to be repeated. In substance, we evolved to treat every interaction as if it was likely to be repeated (e.g. Johnson, Stopka, & Knights, 2003). This reply won't do, however (Fehr &

Henrich, 2003). Anecdotal reports and experimental evidence in behavioral economics show that people effortlessly distinguish between interactions that are unlikely to be repeated and long-term cooperative situations, and that they behave differently in these two types of situations. For instance, in experimental contexts, people tend to be less generous and helpful in the first type of situations than in the later type of situations (e.g. Gächter & Falk, 2002). Thus it does not seem to be the case that we behave cooperatively in some non-repeated interactions (e.g. when we tip strangers) because we evolved to treat every interaction as if it is likely to be repeated.[27]

Moreover, it is unclear whether our ancestors really lived in small and close-knit communities. Reciprocal altruism can explain the selection of altruistic behaviors only if our ancestors were able to discriminate between those individuals who failed to reciprocate altruistic acts ("cheaters") and those who did reciprocate, that is, only if they were able to remember who did what. The larger the group in which our ancestors belonged and the more fluid membership in residential units was,[28] the less likely it is that this condition was met. Paleoanthropological evidence suggests that at least for the last 50,000 years, our ancestors have lived in large groups of several thousands of members—too large for them to have been able to remember who did what (see Richerson & Boyd, 1998, 1999 for a detailed review of the evidence). Furthermore, as Richerson and Boyd write (1999: 254), "Foraging societies are simple by comparison with modern societies, but even the simplest contemporary hunting and gathering peoples, like !Kung San and the peoples of Central Australia, link residential units of a few tens of people to create societies of a few hundred to a few thousand people." Migrations and long-distance economic exchanges have also characterized the life of our ancestors for maybe several hundreds of thousands of years (McBrearty & Brooks, 2000). Finally, in many modern hunter-gatherer societies, membership in residential units is fluid (see, e.g., Hill, 2003 on the Ache; Smith, 2004 on the Hadza).

Clearly, these findings do not establish beyond doubt that reciprocal altruism could not explain the evolution of altruism. Morality could have evolved before our ancestors lived in large and fluid groups. Furthermore, even if our ancestors lived in large and fluid groups, they might have interacted altruistically only with a small number of group members. Nonetheless, the body of evidence about the size and fluidity of the social groups that have been common during

[27] One could object that people might have learned to override their tendency to behave altruistically, a tendency that could have been selected for by reciprocal altruism. We concede that this is a possibility, but we believe that some evidence would be required to substantiate this hypothesis.

[28] Membership is fluid when people can easily join and leave residential groups. When membership is fluid, people are more likely to interact with strangers.

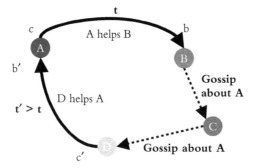

Figure 1.2.   Indirect reciprocity
Note: c and c′ stand for the costs of the altruistic actions for the agents A and D, b and b′ for the benefits bestowed upon the beneficiaries of the actions, B and A (c < b′), and t and t′ for the times of the actions.

part of the evolution of our species casts at least some doubt on the importance of reciprocal altruism for understanding the evolution of altruism.

A better reply to the charge that reciprocal altruism fails to explain a range of human altruistic behaviors consists in extending the notion of reciprocal altruism. Evolutionary biologist Richard Alexander (1987) has done precisely this with the notion of indirect reciprocity.[29] Roughly, the idea is that a trait that benefits another individual will be favored by natural selection if the possession of this trait increases the probability of benefiting from the altruism of a third party. One way to characterize indirect reciprocity is in terms of reputation. The possessor of the altruistic trait increases her reputation and people with a good reputation are the target of others' altruism (see Figure 1.2).

Prominent researchers, including Trivers himself, have proposed that while originally developed to explain altruism in a large range of species (including some species of fish), reciprocal altruism and indirect reciprocity also explain the evolution of morality in humans. Alexander puts it succinctly (1987: 77): "Moral systems are systems of indirect reciprocity."[30,31]

---

[29] The theory of indirect reciprocity has been developed by, among others, the mathematician Karl Sigmund and the theoretical biologist Martin Nowak, but a detailed discussion of their work is beyond the scope of this chapter (see, e.g., Nowak & Sigmund, 1998, 2005; Panchanathan & Boyd, 2004; for critical discussion, see Leimar & Hammerstein, 2001; Panchanathan & Boyd, 2003).

[30] Alexander's view is in fact more complex. For him, group selection is another cause of the evolution of morality.

[31] Joyce concurs, writing: "My own judgment is that . . . the process that most probably lies behind [the emergence of an innate faculty for making moral judgments] is indirect reciprocity, but it is not an objective of this book to advocate this hypothesis with any conviction" (2006: 44). Nowak & Sigmund (2005) make a similar claim, but their work is perhaps better interpreted as an instance of the second explanatory project that goes under the heading "the evolution of morality" (Section 2).

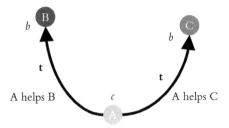

Figure 1.3. Public goods
Note: *c* stands for the cost of the altruistic action for the agent A, *b* for the benefit bestowed upon the beneficiaries of the actions, B and C, and *t* for the time of the action.

In spite of its impressive pedigree, the hypothesis that reciprocal altruism or indirect reciprocity selected for moral cognition, as a distinct kind of normative cognition, faces serious challenges. Following Sripada (2005), we highlight three shortcomings of this hypothesis. First, reciprocal altruism and indirect reciprocity are supposed to explain the evolution of behaviors in pairwise interactions, while moral behavior does not always take place in the context of pairwise interactions. For instance, morally sanctioned altruistic behaviors often benefit a large number of people, as is illustrated by the sacrifice of soldiers for their country.

One could propose to extend Trivers's reciprocal altruism to interactions that do not take place in pairs. This kind of situation is typically modeled by means of a public-goods game (aka, *n*-person prisoner's dilemma) (Figure 1.3).

Thus one could examine whether a trait that benefits the other members of the group conditional on the altruism of all the other members (or of a specific proportion of these group members) could be favored by natural selection, if interactions between the members of this group lasted long enough.[32] However, Boyd and Richerson (1988) have shown that natural selection is unlikely to favor this kind of trait (for critical discussion, see Johnson, Price, & Takezawa, 2008). Their model presents a dilemma. On the one hand, if altruists were to benefit others only when *every* other member of the group they belong to behaves altruistically, they would be unlikely to ever behave altruistically when this group is large and they would not reap the benefits of long-term cooperation. Their fitness would then not be higher than the fitness of non-altruists. On the other hand, if altruists were to behave altruistically when *most* (in contrast to all) members of their group behave altruistically,

---

[32] Altruistic behavior is often called "cooperation," and altruists are often called "cooperators" in the literature about the evolution of altruism.

they would then behave altruistically even when their group included some non-altruists. The fitness of altruists would then be lower than the fitness of non-altruists. Thus, on both horns of this dilemma, altruists have a lower fitness than non-altruists. Consequently, reciprocal altruism cannot explain the evolution of altruism in large groups.

Second, reciprocal altruism and indirect reciprocity are designed to explain the evolution of altruism (in a biological sense: acting in a way that increases others' fitness) while many moral norms have little to do with altruism because they do not regulate social interactions. For example, there are various apparently moral prohibitions against eating particular types of food. But it is very unclear how one can extend these two evolutionary mechanisms to account for the evolution of moral norms—like food taboos—that are not related to altruism.[33]

Third, neither reciprocal altruism nor indirect reciprocity can account for the link between morality and punishment. If reciprocal altruism or indirect reciprocity really explained the evolution of morality, people would be disposed to exclude from cooperation agents who violate moral norms. However, when an agent commits morally reprehensible actions, rather than merely terminating cooperation with this agent, people are disposed to punish her.[34] A large body of evidence in psychology and in behavioral economics highlights the link between punishment and morality. For instance, Haidt and Sabini (2000) showed subjects several videos of unjust actions. When asked to decide between various endings, subjects were more satisfied when the agent suffered for her action than when the victim pardoned the agent (see Fehr & Fischbacher, 2004 for consistent behavioral evidence).

To summarize, because the main adaptationist models of the evolution of morality appeal to direct or indirect reciprocity, they seem badly tailored to account for three key properties of moral cognition: moral norms do not exclusively (nor even primarily) bear on pairwise interactions; many moral norms have nothing to do with altruism; and violations of norms are punished.

---

[33] One might object that morality evolved for governing reciprocal interactions and, once present, came to govern other behaviors, such as incest avoidance. It is indeed common that a trait that was selected for a given function is put to other uses. Although we do not know any decisive reason to reject this hypothesis, it strikes us as an ad hoc extension of the hypothesis that reciprocal altruism or indirect reciprocity explains the evolution of morality.

[34] One could perhaps reject the distinction between punishing a norm violator and terminating cooperative interactions with a norm violator by arguing that the latter is a form of punishment. In reply, we highlight the importance of the distinction between punishing and terminating a cooperative relation. The former consists in imposing a cost on the norm violator, the latter in preventing the norm violator from gaining future benefits. Given that imposing a cost on the norm violator is typically costly (see Section 2), it is puzzling that people would go out of their way to punish others, while there is no mystery why people would stop cooperating when cooperating is not in their best interest.

For these three reasons, we view these models with skepticism. Their existence provides little support to the claim that moral cognition evolved.

3.3. *Distinctive Properties of Evolved Traits*

In addition to providing adaptationist models, it is also common to argue for the evolution of a trait by showing that this trait possesses some properties that are distinctive either of evolved traits or of adaptations. Here we focus successively on three alleged properties: moral norms are a cultural universal; complex moral norms are acquired in spite of impoverished stimuli; and very young children reason about norms and have harm-related emotions.

3.3.1. *Universality of Moral Norms*   It is often said that there is no culture without a system of moral norms. Joyce writes (2006: 134): "[m]orality (by which I mean the tendency to make moral judgments) exists in all human societies we have ever heard of." Similarly, Hauser contends that "[t]he principles [of the moral faculty] constitute the universal moral grammar, a signature of the species" (2006: 53). And the universality of moral norms is taken to be evidence that it evolved.[35]

To evaluate this argument properly, it is important to keep in mind that the claim that morality is present in every culture is not just the assertion that one finds norms in every culture. Rather, it asserts that in every culture, one finds norms that possess the properties that distinguish moral norms from other kinds of norms according to the characterization used by a given evolutionary researcher. Thus, when Joyce asserts that morality is present in every culture, he is claiming that in every known culture, one finds norms that have most of the seven properties he uses to single out moral norms from other kinds of norms (see above).

But why should we believe that moral norms are present in all known cultures? Researchers often bluntly assert this claim (e.g. Dwyer, 2006: 237) or illustrate it with ancient or exotic codes of norms. Thus Joyce refers to the norms in the Egyptian Book of the Dead and in the Mesopotamian epic of Gilgamesh (2006: 134–135). We find this casual use of the anthropological and historical literature problematic. The problem is not so much that these researchers have not examined a large number of cultures and historical periods to substantiate the claim that moral norms are ancient and pancultural. Rather, the problem is that because they fail to clearly distinguish *norms* from *moral*

---

[35] For a brief discussion of the evidential connection between universality and evolution, see Section 2.3.

norms, the evidence they allude to merely supports the claim that norms are universal, but not the much more controversial claim that moral norms are universal (see Stich, 2008 for a similar point).

What anthropology and history show beyond reasonable doubt is that all known cultures have norms. In all cultures, some actions are prohibited while others are mandatory and some character traits are disvalued while others valued. Sanctions and rewards for behaviors and personal attributes are good candidates for being cultural universals. But because moral norms are conceived as a distinct type of norm and moral judgments as a distinct kind of normative judgment, the universality of norms should not be confused with the universality of *moral* norms. For a given researcher (e.g. Hauser, Dwyer or Joyce) to support the hypothesis that moral norms are universal thus requires far more than citing exotic and ancient codes. It requires him or her to show that such codes amount to an expression of morality, that is, to show that the norms in these codes possess the properties that distinguish moral norms from other kinds of norms according to the researcher's rich characterization of moral norms and judgments. However, to our knowledge, the relevant research has not been done. Furthermore, the richer the characterization of moral norms and judgments is, the less likely it is that norms in other cultures will count as moral norms and thus that moral norms will be a universal.

Let's illustrate this point with an example. In the sixth century, the Catholic Church prohibited Christians from being buried with their wealth and it recommended (but did not require) that part of one's wealth be given to the Church (Duby, 1996: 56–58). This is a clear example of a norm. But the existence of this norm in Europe fifteen centuries ago provides no support whatsoever for the hypothesis that moral norms are universal since it is unclear whether it is a moral norm—that is, since it is unclear whether it possesses the properties that distinguish moral norms. Instead of merely noting that this norm exists, Joyce and other researchers would have to show that it possesses the properties that (for them) distinguish moral cognition from other kinds of normative cognition. This is a very difficult task, and it is far from obvious whether the norms found in other cultures possess the properties that characterize moral norms according to their rich characterization.[36]

---

[36] Joyce has recently defended the claim that morality is universal (Joyce, 2008b). He asserts that there is probably no society where all the norms are prudential or hypothetical, noting that whenever norm violations are viewed as transgressions and as punishable, the norms violated are not merely hypothetical or prudential. He views this as evidence that moral norms are universal. We are not convinced by this argument, for one cannot infer that *moral* norms are universal from the fact that *categorical* norms are universal.

What might explain philosophers', psychologists', and anthropologists' confusion between the universality of norms and the universality of moral norms is the fact that they find in various cultures and times some norms that are somewhat similar to the norms they themselves view as moral. For instance, many cultures have norms against harming others, such as prohibition against in-group harm. But this fact does not show that all cultures have a system of moral norms, for, again, it is unclear whether these norms are moral norms in all the cultures in which they hold.

3.3.2. *The Moral/Conventional Distinction*   The second piece of evidence adduced to support the hypothesis that morality evolved relies on the research on the moral/conventional distinction by developmental psychologist Elliot Turiel (Dwyer, 2006: 239–242; Joyce, 2006: 134–137; Hauser, 2006: 291).[37] In substance, Turiel and colleagues argue that very early on, and panculturally, children distinguish two types of norms, called "moral norms" and "conventional norms." Moral norms are those norms that are judged to hold independently from the authority of any individual or institution, that are judged to be universally applicable, that are justified by appeal to the harm done to others, to their rights, or to justice, and whose violations are judged to be serious. Conventional norms are those norms whose force depends on authority, that are judged to be only locally applicable, that are justified by reference to convention, and whose violations are judged to be less serious than the violations of moral norms.

Joyce concludes that "[t]hese results from developmental psychology strongly suggest that the tendency to make moral judgments is innate" (2006: 137). The argument from the universality and early development of the so-called moral/conventional distinction to the evolution of morality is best viewed as a poverty of the stimulus argument (Dwyer, 1999, 2006; Mikhail, 2000). According to this type of argument, developed most famously by Chomsky (1975), the fact that a trait, such as the capacity to speak a language, develops reliably, while the environmental stimuli are variable and impoverished, is evidence that this trait is innate (for discussion, see Cowie, 1999; Laurence & Margolis, 2001; Pullum & Scholz, 2002). Innateness is then often taken to be evidence that the trait under consideration is the product of evolution or sometimes that it is an adaptation.[38] It is tempting to apply this form of argument

---

[37] See, e.g., Turiel (1983); Nucci (2001); Smetana (1981); Blair (1995); Smetana et al. (1999).

[38] The evidential connection between being innate and having evolved (or being an adaptation) is not straightforward. The acquisition of some evolved traits involves learning, while some innate traits (such as some genetic diseases) are not evolved. For the sake of the argument, we take for granted here

to the distinction between moral norms and conventional norms. Turiel and others have argued that even very young children grasp the distinction between moral norms and other kinds of norms. It is dubious whether young children could have learned this distinction because the evidence needed to learn is often missing and because, when it is not missing, it is unreliable. For instance, Dwyer notes that caregivers' reactions to norms violations are unlikely to distinguish the two types of norms because, as she puts it (2006: 240), "(s)ome parents get just as hot under the collar about conventional transgressions as they do about moral transgressions." Furthermore, explicit moral instruction would not distinguish between different kinds of norms because moral norms are not linguistically distinguished from other norms: consider, e.g., "You ought to put your fork on the left of your plate" and "You ought to keep your promises." One might then conclude that the distinction between moral norms and conventional norms is innate.

The poverty of the stimulus argument about the so-called moral/conventional distinction is unsound. The research on this distinction has a long and respectable history, and it is received wisdom in much of contemporary psychology. Recently, however, a growing body of evidence has emerged that challenges the research tradition on the distinction between moral and conventional norms in psychology (Gabennesch, 1990; Haidt et al., 1993; Kelly et al., 2007).[39]

First, as Gabennesch (1990) has convincingly argued, the common wisdom—endorsed by Dwyer and others—that very early on, children view some norms as social conventions is poorly supported by the evidence. Carter and Patterson (1982) found that half of their second- and fourth-grader subjects judged that table manners (e.g. eating with one's fingers) were not variable across cultures and that they were authority-independent. Similarly, Shweder and colleagues (1987: 35) concluded that among American children under 10, "there [was] not a single practice in [their] study that is viewed predominantly in conventional terms" (see Gabennesch, 1990 for many other references). Because many children do not understand early on that some norms are conventional, the poverty of the stimulus argument about the moral/conventional distinction mischaracterizes the nature of the moral knowledge of young children. Furthermore, because people come to understand slowly and rather late

that this connection can be drawn. In addition, we bracket the debate about what innateness is and about whether the notion of innateness is confused (for discussion, see, e.g., Samuels, 2002; Mallon & Weinberg, 2006; Griffiths, Machery, & Linquist, 2009).

[39] For further critical discussion of the poverty of the stimulus argument under consideration, see Nichols (2005) and Prinz (2008). We also note that we do not reject poverty of the stimulus arguments in general.

in their adolescence that some norms are mere social conventions, the amount of evidence children and adolescents might rely on to come to understand this distinction (whatever it amounts to—see below) is much less impoverished than is assumed by the poverty of the stimulus argument.

More important, the research on the so-called moral/conventional distinction assumes that being authority-independent, being universal, being associated with serious violations, and being justified by appeal to harm, justice, or rights form a cluster of co-occurring properties (Kelly et al., 2007). That is, it is assumed that when a norm is judged to be authority-independent, it is also judged to be universal, it is justified by appeal to harm, justice, or rights, and the violations of this norm are judged to be serious. By contrast, when a norm is judged to be authority-dependent, it is not judged to be generalizable to other cultures, it is justified by appeal to conventions, and the violations of this norm are judged to be less serious. However, research shows that this assumption is unsubstantiated. People judge some actions (e.g. having sex with a dead chicken before eating it or cleaning the bathroom with the national flag) to be serious and authority-independent, but do not justify the relevant norms by appeal to harm, justice, or rights (Haidt et al., 1993). People are also sometimes reluctant to generalize to other cultures norms that are justified by appeal to harms, and they sometimes view these norms as authority-dependent (Kelly et al., 2007; but see Sousa, 2009; Sousa, Holbrook, & Piazza, 2009 for discussion). It thus appears that the four properties assumed to set apart moral norms may not form a cluster of co-occurring properties at all.[40] If this is the case, it is unclear what the claim that early on children distinguish moral norms from conventional norms amounts to, putting into jeopardy the poverty of the stimulus argument about the moral/conventional distinction.

3.3.3. *Developmental Evidence*   In addition to the two alleged pieces of evidence discussed above (the presence of moral norms in every culture and the early development of the moral/conventional distinction), other aspects of human psychological development have been mentioned as evidence for the evolution of morality. However, as we now argue, they do not constitute evidence that moral cognition, understood again as a specific kind of normative cognition, evolved, rather than evidence that normative cognition evolved.

We have seen in Section 2 that children understand deontic conditionals, such as "It's not safe outside for the squeaky mouse, so all squeaky mice *must*

---

[40] One could object that although the four properties assumed to set apart moral norms do not necessarily occur together, they still *tend* to co-occur, forming something like a homeostatic cluster (Boyd, 1991). However, Kelly and colleagues' work tentatively suggests that these properties do not tend to co-occur, since most possible combinations seem to occur.

stay in the house" much earlier and much better than indicative conditionals, such as "It's not safe outside for the squeaky mouse, so all squeaky mice *are* in the house" (Cummins, 1996a; Harris & Núñez, 1996). One might be tempted to argue that the capacity to identify the violation of deontic conditionals early on provides evidence for the evolution of morality (Joyce, 2006; Dwyer, 2006).

This is certainly a very interesting finding, one that suggests that normative cognition might be the product of evolution by natural selection (as noted in Section 2). However, it is unclear how this finding is supposed to support the idea that moral cognition proper, understood as a specific kind of normative cognition, rather than normative cognition in general, evolved, since the norms in the stories presented to children by Cummins and by Harris and Núñez were not moral. More generally, deontic conditionals are not exclusively used in specifically moral reasoning.

One could perhaps argue that infants' empathic reaction to others' suffering and the early development of helping behaviors in children provide evidence for the evolution of morality. For instance, Dwyer concludes that "this work strongly suggests that some basic moral capacities are in place quite early in development" (2006: 237). However, again, it is unclear how the early development of empathy and of helping behaviors is supposed to support the hypothesis that morality is a product of evolution. Certainly, empathy is morally sanctioned in modern, Western cultures and helping is often morally prescribed. But all this shows is that empathy and some behavioral tendencies that are morally sanctioned in modern, Western cultures are present at an early stage of children's psychological and behavioral development. This is perfectly consistent with moral norms being a culture-specific kind of norms and with moral cognition being a culture-specific kind of normative cognition that recruits early developing, maybe evolved psychological traits, such as empathy and some behavioral tendencies.

To summarize, while many philosophers, psychologists, and anthropologists have claimed that morality is a product of the evolution of the human species, the evidence for this claim is weak at best. First, we do not know whether moral norms are present in every culture: because researchers endorse rich characterizations of what moral norms are, it is not obvious that norms that have the distinctive properties of moral norms will be found in every culture, and, in any case, researchers have simply not shown that, in numerous cultures, there are norms that fit some rich characterization of moral norms. Second, the claim that early on children display some complex moral knowledge in spite of variable and impoverished environmental stimuli is based on the research on the moral/conventional distinction. Although this research remains widely accepted in much of psychology, a growing body of evidence has highlighted its shortcomings. Third, the other pieces of evidence often cited in the literature on the evolution of morality do not constitute evidence that moral norms and moral judgments, understood as a specific type of norms and normative judgments, evolved, rather than evidence that normative cognition evolved.

3.4. *Summary: The Evolution of a Specifically Moral Normativity*

In this section, we have focused on the idea that moral cognition, conceived as a distinct kind of normative cognition, evolved. We have argued that the scenarios typically advanced to explain the selection of this specific form of normative cognition are unconvincing, and that the arguments and evidence commonly adduced to support the hypothesis that morality evolved are at best inconclusive.

This conclusion is philosophically significant. As noted already, it is commonly argued that the evolution of morality undermines the authority of moral norms. At the end of Section 2, we noted that this argument cannot plausibly hang on the hypothesis that normative cognition in general evolved (the second interpretation of the claim that morality evolved) although this hypothesis is supported by a small, but suggestive, body of evidence. Rather, it should hang on the third interpretation that morality evolved—i.e. moral cognition, conceived as a distinct kind of normative cognition, is the product of evolution—and this is indeed the way it has typically been presented.

Most philosophers have focused on evaluating the truth of the conditional, "If morality (understood as a particular type of normative cognition) evolved, the authority of moral norms is undermined" (e.g. Joyce, 2006; Street, 2006, 2008; Copp, 2008). However, no agreement has been reached on whether this conditional should be accepted. Our discussion shows that this lack of agreement might not matter since it turns out that there is little reason to believe that moral cognition, understood as a particular type of normative cognition, evolved. The claim that the authority of moral norms is undermined by the evolution of morality therefore depends on an unsupported premise, and so it does not threaten the authority of moral norms.

4. Conclusion

So, did morality evolve? We have shown that this question has no single answer, because it is understood in various ways. Some researchers focus on the evolutionary history of specific components of moral psychology. So understood, it is uncontroversial that morality evolved: although establishing that some particular morally relevant trait has evolved can be especially difficult, there is little doubt that numerous traits have a long evolutionary history. However, philosophers are unlikely to be moved by this conclusion, since it is unclear whether it has any philosophically significant implication.

By arguing that morality evolved, other researchers contend that normative cognition is an adaptation. We have argued that, although somewhat speculative, this claim is supported by a small, but suggestive, body of sociological and psychological evidence as well as by a robust set of how-possible evolutionary models. We view the fact that norms are ancient and universal and that from a very early age on, people are distinctively adept at reasoning about normative matters, as evidence that normative cognition evolved by natural selection. But again, we argued that this conclusion is cold comfort to philosophers hoping to draw conclusions undermining the authority of moral norms from the evolution of morality.

Finally, other researchers characterize moral cognition as a distinct kind of normative cognition, which includes the grasp of a specific kind of norms (i.e. moral norms) and a capacity to make a specific kind of normative judgments (i.e. moral judgments). They then endorse the provocative claim that we evolved to grasp this specific kind of norms and to make this specific kind of normative judgments. By contrast, we have argued that the evidence usually adduced to support the hypothesis that morality (so characterized) evolved is far from conclusive. While some adaptationist models, inspired by evolutionary biologists' research on altruism, are touted as suggesting that morality is an adaptation, we have argued that they are not well tailored to explain how morality evolved. Researchers also assert that the universality and innateness of morality show that it evolved. But a critical look at the evidence reveals that it is unclear whether morality is universal and innate.

As we noted in the introduction, the hypothesis that morality evolved is often assumed to have significant philosophical implications. The evolution of morality features in arguments attempting to justify specific norms and in various skeptical arguments about morality. Although our discussion has not directly focused on evaluating these arguments, it has led us to skepticism about a crucial premise. While the first reading of the claim that morality evolved is uncontroversial, and while its second reading is supported by a small, but suggestive, body of evidence, these two readings do not seem to yield significant philosophical payoffs. While the third reading—morality, understood as a distinct type of normative cognition, evolved—is more likely to yield such payoffs, on close consideration, it turns out to be empirically unsupported.

References

Alcock, J. (2001). *The Triumph of Sociobiology*. New York: Oxford University Press.

Alexander R. D. (1987). *The Biology of Moral Systems*. Hawthorne, NY: Aldine de Gruyter.

Allen, C., & Bekoff, M. (2005). Animal play and the evolution of morality: An ethological approach. *Topoi, 24,* 125–135.

Andreoni, J., & Vesterlund, L. (2001). Which is the fair sex? Gender differences in altruism. *Quarterly Journal of Economics, 116,* 293–312.

Bekoff, M. (2001). Social play behavior: Cooperation, fairness, trust, and the evolution of morality. *Journal of Consciousness Studies, 8,* 81–90.

——(2004). Wild justice and fair play: Cooperation, forgiveness, and morality in animals. *Biology and Philosophy, 19,* 489–520.

Benedict, R. (1946). *The Chrysanthemum and the Sword: Patterns of Japanese Culture.* Boston, MA: Houghton Mifflin.

Blair, R. J. R. (1995). A cognitive developmental approach to morality: Investigating the psychopath. *Cognition, 57,* 1–29.

Boehm, C. (1982). The evolutionary development of morality as an effect of dominance behavior and conflict interference. *Journal of Social and Biological Structures, 5,* 413–421.

——(1999). *Hierarchy in the Forest: The Evolution of Egalitarian Behavior.* Cambridge, MA: Harvard University Press.

Bolton, G. E., & Zwick, R. (1995). Anonymity versus punishment in ultimatum bargaining. *Games and Economic Behavior, 10,* 95–121.

Boyd, R. (1991). Realism, anti-foundationalism and the enthusiasm for natural kinds. *Philosophical Studies, 61,* 127–148.

Boyd, R., & Mathew, S. (2007). A narrow road to cooperation. *Science, 316,* 1858–1859.

Boyd, R., & Richerson, P. J. (1988). The evolution of reciprocity in sizable groups. *Journal of Theoretical Biology, 132,* 337–356.

——(1992). Punishment allows the evolution of cooperation (or anything else) in sizable groups. *Ethology and Sociobiology, 13,* 171–195.

Boyd, R., Gintis, H., Bowles, S., & Richerson, P. J. (2003). The evolution of altruistic punishment. *Proceedings of the National Academy of Sciences, 100,* 3531–3535.

Bowles, S., & Gintis, H. (1998). The moral economy of community: Structured populations and the evolution of prosocial norms. *Evolution and Human Behavior, 19,* 3–25.

Brandon, R. (1990). *Organism and Environment.* Princeton, NJ: Princeton University Press.

Bräuer, J., Call, J., & Tomasello, M. (2006). Are apes really inequity averse? *Proceedings of the Royal Society of London B, 273,* 3123–3128.

Brigandt, I. (2003). Homology in comparative, molecular, and evolutionary developmental biology: The radiation of a concept. *Journal of Experimental Zoology (Molecular and Developmental Evolution), 299,* 9–17.

Brosnan, S. F. (2006). Nonhuman species' reactions to inequity and their implications for fairness. *Social Justice Research, 19,* 153–185.

Brosnan, S. F., & de Waal, F. B. M. (2002). A proximate perspective on reciprocal altruism. *Human Nature, 13,* 129–152.

—— (2003). Monkeys reject unequal pay. *Nature, 425,* 297–299.

—— (2004). Reply to Henrich and Wynne. *Nature, 428,* 140.

Brosnan, S. F., Freeman, C., & de Waal, F. B. M. (2006). Partner's behavior, not reward distribution, determines success in an unequal cooperative task in capuchin monkeys. *American Journal of Primatology, 68,* 713–724.

Brosnan, S. F., Schiff, H. C., & de Waal, F. B. M. (2005). Tolerance for inequity may increase with closeness in chimpanzees. *Proceedings of the Royal Society of London, Series B, 1560,* 253–258.

Brown, D. E. (1991). *Human Universals.* New York: McGraw-Hill.

Carter, D. B., & Patterson, C. J. (1982). Sex roles as social conventions: The development of children's conceptions of sex-role stereotypes. *Child Development, 18,* 812–824.

Casebeer, W. D. (2003a). *Natural Ethical Facts: Evolution, Connectionism, and Moral Cognition.* Cambridge, MA: MIT Press.

—— (2003b). An argument for "new wave" Aristotelianism. *Politics and the Life Sciences, 22,* 67–69.

Chomsky, N. (1975). *Reflections on Language.* New York: Pantheon.

Copp, D. (2008). Darwinian skepticism about moral realism. *Philosophical Issues, Interdisciplinary Core Philosophy, 18,* 186–206.

Cosmides, L. (1989). The logic of social exchange: has natural selection shaped how humans reason? Studies with the Wason selection task. *Cognition, 31,* 187–276.

Cosmides, L., & Tooby, J. (2005). Neurocognitive adaptations designed for social exchange. In D. M. Buss (ed.), *The Handbook of Evolutionary Psychology.* Hoboken, NJ: Wiley, 584–627.

—— (2008a). Can a general deontic logic capture the facts of human moral reasoning? How the mind interprets social exchange rules and detects cheaters. In W. S. A. Armstrong (ed.), *Moral Psychology, volume 1: The Evolution of Morality.* Cambridge, MA: MIT Press, 53–120.

—— (2008b). Can evolutionary psychology assist logicians? A reply to Mallon. In W. S. A. Armstrong (ed.), *Moral Psychology, volume 1: The Evolution of Morality.* Cambridge, MA: MIT Press, 131–136.

—— (2008c). When falsification strikes: A reply to Fodor. In W. S. A. Armstrong (ed.), *Moral Psychology, volume 1: The Evolution of Morality.* Cambridge, MA: MIT Press, 143–164.

Cowie, F. (1999). *What's Within? Nativism Reconsidered.* Oxford: Oxford University Press.

Cronk, L. (1994). Evolutionary theories of morality and the manipulative use of signals. *Zygon: Journal of Religion and Science, 29,* 81–101.

Cummins, D. D. (1996a). Evidence of deontic reasoning in 3- and 4-year-olds. *Memory and Cognition, 24,* 823–829.

Cummins, D. D. (1996b). Evidence for the innateness of deontic reasoning. *Mind & Language, 11*, 160–190.

D'Arms, J. (2000). When evolutionary game theory explains morality, what does it explain? *The Journal of Consciousness Studies, 7*, 296–300.

—— (ms). Self-righteous anger: A case study in evolutionary ethics.

Darwall, S., Gibbard, A., & Railton, P. (1992) Toward fin de siècle ethics: Some trends. *Philosophical Review, 101*, 115–189.

Darwin C. (1871). *The Descent of Man and Selection in Relation to Race.* 1874 edn. London: John Murray.

Dennett, D. C. (1995). *Darwin's Dangerous Idea: Evolution and the Meanings of Life.* New York: Simon & Schuster.

Draper, P., & Belsky, J. (1990). Personality development in evolutionary perspective. *Journal of Personality, 58*, 141–162.

Dubreuil, D., Gentile, M. S., & Visalberghi, E. (2006). Are capuchin monkeys (Cebus apella) inequity averse? *Proceedings of the Royal Society of London B, 273*, 1223–1228.

Duby, G. (1996). *Féodalité.* Paris: Gallimard.

Dunbar, R. I. M. (1996). *Grooming, Gossip, and the Evolution of Language.* Cambridge, MA: Harvard University Press.

Dwyer, S. (1999). Moral competence. In K. Murasugi & R. Stainton (eds.), *Philosophy and Linguistics.* Boulder, CO: Westview Press, 169–190.

—— (2006). How good is the linguistic analogy? In P. Carruthers, S. Laurence, & S. Stich. *The Innate Mind: Culture and Cognition.* Oxford: Oxford University Press, 237–256.

Farber, P. (1994). *The Temptation of Evolutionary Ethics.* Berkeley, CA: University of California Press.

Fehr, E., & Fischbacher, U. (2004). Third-party punishment and social norms. *Evolution and Human Behavior, 25*, 63–87.

Fehr, E., & Gächter, S. (2002). Altruistic punishment in humans. *Nature, 415*, 137–140.

Fehr, E., & Henrich, J. (2003). Is strong reciprocity a maladaptation? In P. Hammerstein (ed.), *Genetic and Cultural Evolution of Cooperation.* Cambridge, MA: MIT Press, 55–82.

Fessler, D. M. T. (1999). Toward an understanding of the universality of second order emotions. In A. Hinton (ed.), *Beyond Nature or Culture: Biocultural Approaches to the Emotions.* New York: Cambridge University Press, 75–116.

—— (2004) Shame in two cultures: Implications for evolutionary approaches. *Journal of Cognition and Culture, 4*, 207–262.

—— (2007) From appeasement to conformity: Evolutionary and cultural perspectives on shame, competition, and cooperation. In J. L. Tracy, R. W. Robins, & J. P. Tangney (eds.), *The Self-conscious Emotions: Theory and Research.* New York: Guilford Press, 174–193.

Fessler, D. M. T., & Haley, K. J. (2003) The strategy of affect: Emotions in human cooperation. In P. Hammerstein (ed.), *The Genetic and Cultural Evolution of Cooperation.* Cambridge, MA: MIT Press, 7–36.

Fiske, A. P. (1991). *Structures of Social Life: The Four Elementary Forms of Human Relations*. New York: Free Press.

Flack, J. C., & de Waal, F. B. M. (2000). "Any animal whatever": Darwinian building blocks of morality in monkeys and apes. *Journal of Consciousness Studies, 7*, 1–29.

Fodor, J. A. (2000). Why we are so good at catching cheaters. *Cognition, 75*, 29–32.

——(2008). Comment on Cosmides and Tooby. In W. S. A. Armstrong (ed.), *Moral Psychology, volume 1: The Evolution of Morality*. Cambridge, MA: MIT Press, 137–142.

Foster, M. W., Gilby, I. C., Murray, C. M., Johnson, A., Wroblewski, E. E., & Pusey, A. E. (2009). Alpha male chimpanzee grooming patterns: Implications for dominance "style". *American Journal of Primatology, 71*, 136–144.

Frank, R. H. (1988). *Passions within Reason: The Strategic Role of the Emotions*. New York: W. W. Norton & Company.

Gabennesch, H. (1990). The perception of social conventionality by children and adults. *Child Development, 61*, 2047–2059.

Gächter, S., & Falk, A. (2002). Reputation or reciprocity? Consequences for labour relations. *Scandinavian Journal of Economics, 104*, 1–25.

Gibbard, A. (1990). *Wise Choices, Apt Feelings*. Cambridge, MA: Harvard University Press.

Gintis, H., Bowles, S., Boyd, R., & Fehr, E. (2003). Explaining altruistic behavior in humans, *Evolution and Human Behavior, 24*, 153–172.

Gould, S. J., & Lewontin, R. (1979). The spandrels of San Marco and the Panglossian paradigm: a critique of the adaptationist programme. *Proceedings of the Royal Society B, 205*, 581–598.

Griffiths, P. E. (2006). Function, homology, and character individuation. *Philosophy of Science, 73*, 1–25.

Griffiths, P. E., Machery, E., & Linquist, S. (2009). The vernacular concept of innateness. *Mind & Language, 24*, 605–630.

Haidt, J. (2003). The moral emotions. In R. J. Davidson, K. R. Scherer, & H. H. Goldsmith (eds.), *Handbook of Affective Sciences*. Oxford: Oxford University Press, 852–870.

Haidt, J., & Sabini, J. (2000). What exactly makes revenge sweet? Unpublished manuscript.

Haidt, J., Koller, S., & Dias, M. (1993). Affect, culture, and morality, or is it wrong to eat your dog? *Journal of Personality and Social Psychology, 65*, 613–628.

Hamilton, W. (1964). The evolution of social behavior. *Journal Theoretical Biology, 7*, 1–52.

Harris, P. L., & Núñez. M. (1996). Understanding of permission rules by preschool children. *Child Development, 67*, 1572–1591.

Hauert, C., Traulsen, A., Brandt, H., Nowak, M. A., & Sigmund, K. (2007). Via freedom to coercion: The emergence of costly punishment. *Science, 316*, 1905–1907.

Hauser, M. D. (2006). *Moral Minds: How Nature Designed Our Universal Sense of Right and Wrong*. New York: Ecco.

Hauser, M. D., Cushman, F., Young, L., Jin, K.-X. R., & Mikhail, J. (2007). A dissociation between moral judgments and justifications. *Mind & Language, 22*, 1–21.

Henrich, J. (2004). Inequity aversion in capuchins. *Nature, 428*, 139.

Henrich, J., & Boyd, R. (2001). Why people punish defectors: Weak conformist transmission can stabilize costly enforcement of norms in cooperative dilemmas. *Journal of Theoretical Biology, 208*, 79–89.

Henrich, H., Boyd, R., Bowles, S., Camerer, C., Fehr, E., & Gintis, H. (2004). *Foundations of Human Sociality.* New York: Oxford University Press

Henrich, J., Boyd, R., Bowles, S., Camerer, C., Fehr, E., Gintis, H., McElreath, R., Alvard, M., Barr, A., Ensminger, J., Hill, K., Gil-White, F., Gurven, M., Marlowe, F., Patton, J. Q., Smith, N., & Tracer, D. (2005). "Economic man" in cross-cultural perspective: Behavioral experiments in 15 small-scale societies. *Behavioral and Brain Sciences, 28*, 795–855.

Hill, K. (2003). Altruistic cooperation during foraging by the Ache, and the evolved human predisposition to cooperate. *Human Nature, 13*, 105–128.

Huxley, T. H. (1894/1989). *Evolution and Ethics.* J. Paradis and G. C. Williams (eds.). Princeton, NJ: Princeton University Press.

Irons, W. (1991). How did morality evolve? *Zygon, 26*, 49–89.

Johnson, D. D. P., Price, M. E., & Takezawa, M. (2008). Renaissance of the individual: Reciprocity, positive assortment, and the puzzle of human cooperation. In C. Crawford & D. Krebs (eds.), *Foundations of evolutionary psychology.* New York: Lawrence Erlbaum, 331–352.

Johnson, D. D. P., Stopka, P., & Knights, S. (2003). The puzzle of human cooperation. *Nature, 421*, 911–912.

Joyce, R. (2000). Darwinian ethics and error. *Biology and Philosophy, 15*, 713–732.

—— (2006). *The Evolution of Morality.* Cambridge, MA: MIT Press.

—— (2008a). Précis of *The Evolution of Morality. Philosophy and Phenomenological Research, 77*, 213–218.

—— (2008b). Replies. *Philosophy and Phenomenological Research, 77*, 245–267.

Kelly, D., Stich, S. P., Haley, K. J., Eng, S., J., & Fessler, D. M. T. (2007). Harm, affect, and the moral/conventional distinction. *Mind & Language, 22*, 117–131.

Kitcher, P. (1985). *Vaulting Ambition: Sociobiology and the Quest for Human Nature.* Cambridge, MA: MIT Press.

—— (1998). Psychological altruism, evolutionary origins, and moral rules. *Philosophical Studies, 98*, 283–216.

—— (2006a). Biology and ethics. In D. Copp (ed.), *The Oxford Handbook of Ethical Theory.* New York: Oxford University Press, 163–185.

—— (2006b). Between fragile altruism and morality: Evolution and the emergence of normative guidance. In G. Boniolo & G. de Anna (eds.), *Evolutionary Ethics and Contemporary Biology.* New York: Cambridge University Press, 159–177.

Krebs, D. L. (2005). The evolution of morality. In D. Buss (ed.), *The Handbook of Evolutionary Psychology.* Hoboken, NJ: John Wiley & Sons, 747–771.

Kropotkin, P. (1902). *Mutual Aid: A Factor in Evolution*. London: McClure Phillips and Co.

Lahti, D. C. (2003). Parting with illusions in evolutionary ethics. *Biology and Philosophy, 18*, 639–651.

Laurence, S., & Margolis, E. (2001). The poverty of the stimulus argument. *British Journal for Philosophy of Science, 52*, 217–276.

Leimar, O., & Hammerstein, P. (2001). Evolution of cooperation through indirect reciprocity. *Proceedings of the Royal Society of London (B), 268*, 745–753.

Levy, N. (2004). *What Makes us Moral? Crossing the Boundaries of Biology*. Oxford: Oneworld Publications.

—— (2007). The responsibility of the psychopath revisited. *Philosophy, Psychiatry, & Psychology, 14*, 129–138.

Lloyd, E. A. (2005). *The Case of the Female Orgasm: Bias in the Science of Evolution*. Cambridge, MA: Harvard University Press.

Machery, E. (Forthcoming). Discovery and confirmation in evolutionary psychology. In J. J. Prinz (ed.), *Oxford Handbook of Philosophy of Psychology*. Oxford: Oxford University Press.

Mallon, R. (2008). Ought we to abandon a domain-general treatment of "ought"? In W. S. A. Armstrong (ed.), *Moral Psychology, volume 1: The Evolution of Morality*. Cambridge, MA: MIT Press, 121–130.

Mallon, R., & Weinberg, J. (2006). Innateness as closed-process invariantism. *Philosophy of Science, 73*, 323–344.

McAdams, R. H. (1997). The origin, development, and regulation of social norms. *Michigan Law Review, 96*, 338–443.

McBrearty, S., & Brooks, A. S. (2000). The revolution that wasn't: A new interpretation of the origin of modern human behavior. *Journal of Human Evolution, 39*, 453–563.

Mikhail, J. (2000). Rawls' linguistic analogy: A study of the "generative grammar" model of moral theory described by John Rawls in *A theory of justice*. PhD thesis, Cornell University, p. 375.

Nichols, S. (2004). *Sentimental Rules: On the Natural Foundations of Moral Judgment*. New York: Oxford University Press.

—— (2005). Innateness and moral psychology. In P. Carruthers, S. Laurence, & S. Stich (eds.), *The Innate Mind: Structure and Content*. New York: Oxford University Press, 353–370.

Nowak, M. A., & Sigmund, K. (1998). Evolution of indirect reciprocity by image scoring. *Nature, 393*, 573–577.

—— (2005). Evolution of indirect reciprocity. *Nature, 437*, 1291–1298.

Nucci, L. (2001). *Education in the Moral Domain*. Cambridge: Cambridge University Press.

Panchanathan, K., & Boyd, R. (2003). A tale of two defectors: The importance of standing for the evolution of indirect reciprocity. *Journal of Theoretical Biology, 224*, 115–126.

Panchanathan, K., & Boyd, R. (2004). Indirect reciprocity can stabilize cooperation without the second-order free rider problem. *Nature, 432,* 499–502.

Preston, S. D., & de Waal, F. B. M. (2002). The communication of emotions and the possibility of empathy in animals. In S. Post, L. G. Underwood, J. P. Schloss & W. B. Hurlburt (eds.), *Altruistic Love: Science, Philosophy, and Religion in Dialogue.* New York: Oxford University Press, 284–308.

Prinz, J. J. (2007). *The Emotional Construction of Morals.* Oxford: Oxford University Press.

——(2008). Acquired moral truths. *Philosophy and Phenomenological Research, 77,* 219–227.

Pullum, G. K., and Scholz, B. C. (2002). Empirical assessment of stimulus poverty arguments. *The Linguistic Review, 19,* 9–50.

Railton, P. (1999). Normative force and normative freedom: Hume and Kant, but no Hume *versus* Kant. *Ratio, 12,* 320–353.

Rangea, F., Horna, L., Viranyi, Z., & Hubera, L. (2009). The absence of reward induces inequity aversion in dogs. *Proceedings of the National Academy of Sciences, 106,* 340–345.

Richards, R. J. (1986). A defence of evolutionary ethics. *Biology and Philosophy, 1,* 265–293.

——(1989). Dutch objections to evolutionary ethics. *Biology and Philosophy, 4,* 331–343.

Richerson, P. J., & Boyd, R. (1998). The evolution of human ultra-sociality. In I. Eibl-Eibisfeldt & F. Salter (eds.), *Ideology, Warfare, and Indoctrinability.* Oxford: Berghan Books, 71–95.

——(1999). The evolutionary dynamics of a crude super organism. *Human Nature, 10,* 253–289.

——(2005). *Not by Genes Alone: How Culture Transformed Human Evolution.* Chicago: University of Chicago Press.

Richerson, P. J., Boyd, R., & Henrich, J. (2003). The cultural evolution of human cooperation. In P. Hammerstein (ed.), *The Genetic and Cultural Evolution of Coopera-tion.* Cambridge MA: MIT Press, 357–388.

Roskies, A. (2003). Are ethical judgments intrinsically motivational? Lessons from "acquired sociopathy." *Philosophical Psychology, 16,* 51–66.

Rottschaefer, W. A. (1991). The insufficiency of supervenient explanations of moral actions: Really taking Darwin and the naturalistic fallacy seriously. *Biology and Philosophy, 6,* 439–445.

——(1998). *The Biology and Psychology of Moral Agency.* Cambridge: Cambridge University Press.

Rottschaefer, W. A., & Martinsen, D. (1990). Really taking Darwin seriously: An alternative to Michael Ruse's Darwinian metaethics. *Biology and Philosophy, 5,* 149–173.

Ruse, M. (1986). *Taking Darwin Seriously.* Oxford: Basil Blackwell.

Ruse, M., & Wilson, E. O. (1985). Moral philosophy as applied science. In E. Sober (ed.), *Conceptual Issues in Evolutionary Biology.* Cambridge, MA: MIT Press, 421–438.

Samuels, R. (2002). Nativism in cognitive science. *Mind & Language, 17*, 233–265.

Shweder, R. A., Mahapatra, M., & Miller, J. (1987). Culture and moral development. In J. Kagan and S. Lamb (eds.), *The Emergence of Morality in Young Children.* Chicago, IL: University of Chicago Press, 1–82.

Singer, P. (1981). *The Expanding Circle: Ethics and Sociobiology.* Oxford: Oxford University Press.

——(2000). *A Darwinian Left: Politics, Evolution, and Cooperation.* New Haven, CT: Yale University Press.

Smetana, J. (1981). Preschool children's conceptions of moral and social rules. *Child Development, 52*, 1333–1336.

Smetana, J., Toth, S., Cicchetti, D., Bruce, J., Kane P., & Daddis, C. (1999). Maltreated and nonmaltreated preschoolers' conceptions of hypothetical and actual moral transgressions. *Developmental Psychology, 35*, 269–281.

Smith, E. A. (2004). Why do good hunters have higher reproductive success? *Human Nature, 15*, 343–364.

Sober, E. (1994). Prospects for an evolutionary ethics. In E. Sober, *From a Biological Point of View.* Cambridge: Cambridge University Press, 93–113.

Solnick, S. J.(2001). Gender differences in the ultimatum game. *Economic Inquiry, 39*, 189–200.

Sousa, P. (Forthcoming). On testing the "moral law." *Mind & Language.*

Sousa, P., Holbrook, C., & Piazza, J. (Forthcoming). The morality of harm. *Cognition.*

Spencer, H. (1892). *The Principles of Ethics.* London: Williams and Northgate.

Sperber, D., Cara, F., & Girotto, V. (1995). Relevance theory explains the selection task. *Cognition, 52*, 3–39.

Sripada, C. (2005). Punishment and the strategic structure of moral systems. *Biology and Philosophy, 20*, 707–789.

Sripada, C., & Stich, S. (2006). A Framework for the Psychology of Norms. In P. Carruthers, S. Laurence, & S. Stich (eds.), *The Innate Mind: Culture and Cognition.* Oxford: Oxford University Press, 280–301.

Stich, S. P. (2008). Some questions about the evolution of morality. *Philosophy and Phenomenological Research, 77*: 228–236.

Stone, V. E. (2006). Theory of mind and evolution of social intelligence. In J. T. Cacioppo, P. S. Visser, & C. L. Pickett (eds.), *Social Neuroscience: People Thinking about Thinking People.* Cambridge, MA: MIT Press, 103–130.

Street, S. (2006). A Darwinian dilemma for realist theories of value. *Philosophical Studies, 127*, 109–166.

——(2008). Reply to Copp: Naturalism, normativity, and the varieties of realism worth worrying about. *Philosophical Studies, Interdisciplinary Core Philosophy, 18*, 207–228.

Sugiyama, L. S., Tooby, J., & Cosmides, L. (2002). Cross-cultural evidence of cognitive adaptations for social exchange among the Shiwiar of Ecuadorian Amazonia. *Proceedings of the National Academy of Sciences, 99*, 11537–11542.

Trivers, R. (1971). The evolution of reciprocal altruism. *Quarterly Review of Biology, 46*, 35–57.

Turiel, E. (1983). *The Development of Social Knowledge*. Cambridge: Cambridge University Press.

de Waal, F. B. M. (1996). *Good Natured: The Origins of Right and Wrong in Humans and Other Animals*. Cambridge, MA: Harvard University Press.

Waddington, C. H. (1942) *Science and ethics*. London: Allen & Unwin.

Williams, G. C. (1988). Huxley's evolution and ethics in sociobiological perspective. *Zygon, 23*, 383–407.

Wilson, D. S. (2002). *Darwin's Cathedral: Evolution, Religion and the Nature of Society*. Chicago, IL: University of Chicago Press.

van Wolkenten, M., Brosnan, S. F., & de Waal, F. B. M. (2007). Inequity responses of monkeys modified by effort. *Proceedings of the National Academy of Science, 104*(47): 18854–18859.

Woolcock, P. G. (2000). Objectivity and illusion in evolutionary ethics: Comments on Waller. *Biology and Philosophy, 15*, 39–60.

Wright, R. (1994). *The Moral Animal*. New York: Pantheon Books.

2

Multi-system Moral Psychology

FIERY CUSHMAN, LIANE YOUNG, AND JOSHUA D. GREENE

In the field of moral psychology, a number of theoretical proposals that were at one time regarded as unconnected at best—and, at worst, contradictory—are showing signs of reconciliation. At the core of this emerging consensus is a recognition that moral judgment is the product of interaction and competition between distinct psychological systems. Our goal is to describe these systems and to highlight directions for further inquiry.

Recent research in moral psychology has focused on two challenges to the long-dominant cognitive development paradigm conceived by Piaget and nurtured by Kohlberg (Kohlberg, 1969; Piaget, 1965/1932; Turiel, 1983, 2005). The first challenge claims that moral judgment takes the form of intuition, accomplished by rapid, automatic, and unconscious psychological processes (Haidt, 2001; Hauser, 2006: 1; Mikhail, 2000; Schweder & Haidt, 1993; see also Damasio, 1994: 165–201), *contra* the cognitive developmentalists' assumption that moral judgment is the product of conscious, effortful reasoning. A central motivation for this challenge comes from studies demonstrating people's inability to articulate a rational basis for many strongly held moral convictions (Haidt, 2001; Cushman, Young, & Hauser, 2006; Hauser, Cushman, Young, Jin, & Mikhail, 2007; Mikhail, 2000). The second and related challenge claims that moral judgment is driven primarily by affective responses (Blair, 1995; Damasio, 1994; Greene & Haidt, 2002; Schweder & Haidt, 1993), *contra* the cognitive developmentalists' focus on the deliberate application of explicit moral theories and principles to particular cases. Evidence for the role of affect is largely neuroscientific (Shaich Borg, Hynes, Van Horn, Grafton, & Sinnott-Armstrong, 2006; Ciaramelli, Muccioli, Ladavas, & di Pellegrino, 2007; Damasio, 1994; Greene, Nystrom, Engell, Darley, & Cohen, 2004; Greene, Sommerville, Nystrom, Darley, & Cohen, 2001; Koenigs et al., 2007; Mendez, Anderson, & Shapria, 2005), but also includes behavioral studies of moral judgment using affective manipulations (Valdesolo

& DeSteno, 2006; Schnall, Haidt, Clore, & Jordan, 2008; Wheatley & Haidt, 2005).

The evidence that moral judgment is driven largely by intuitive emotional responses is strong, but it does not follow from this that emotional intuition is the whole story. Concerning the role of intuition, the research of Kohlberg and others indicates a truly astonishing regularity in the development of explicit moral theories and their application to particular dilemmas (Kohlberg, 1969). Recent studies show that while people cannot offer principled justifications for some of their moral judgments, they are quite able to do so for others (Cushman et al., 2006), and that people alter some moral judgments when asked to engage in conscious reasoning (Pizarro, Uhlmann, & Bloom, 2003) or presented with appropriate opportunities (Lombrozo, 2008). Others studies implicate reasoning processes in moral judgment using brain imaging (Greene et al., 2004) and reaction time data (Greene et al., 2008). Together, these studies seem to capture an important and relatively common experience: deliberation about right and wrong, informed by an awareness of one's explicit moral commitments.

In fact, the claim that moral judgment depends on affective responses at all has been met with skepticism, for instance by champions of "universal moral grammar" (Huebner, Dwyer, & Hauser, 2008; Hauser, 2006; Mikhail, 2000). They observe that moral judgment requires computations performed over representations of agents, intentions, and causal relationships in order to output judgments of "right" and "wrong." Information processing of this sort necessarily precedes an affective response, the argument goes, and thus it must be that moral judgment leads to affect, not the other way around.

Reconciling these apparent alternatives—intuitive versus rational,[1] affective versus cognitive[2]—is therefore a focal point of research. In our view, the most successful attempts share a common insight: moral judgment is accomplished by multiple systems. Here, we pursue a dual-process approach in which moral judgment is the product of both intuitive and rational psychological processes, and it is the product of what are conventionally thought of as "affective" and "cognitive" mechanisms. As we shall see, a dual-process model of moral judgment can explain features of the data that

---

[1] By contrasting intuitive versus "rational" processes of moral judgment we aim to capture the common social psychological distinction between automatic (rapid, effortless, involuntary) and controlled (slow, effortful, voluntary) processes. Our purpose in choosing the term "rational" is not to imply the normative optimality of a particular decision, but rather to imply the use of deliberative reasoning in reaching that decision.

[2] For more on the somewhat artificial, but undeniably useful distinction between affect and cognition, see Greene (2007).

unitary models cannot: dissociations in clinical populations, cognitive conflict in healthy individuals, and so on.

The new challenge we face is to understand the specific features of distinct systems and the processes of integration and competition among them. In this chapter, we begin by reviewing the evidence in favor of a division between a cognitive system and an affective system for moral judgment. Next, we argue that the cognitive system operates by "controlled" psychological processes whereby explicit principles are consciously applied, while affective responses are generated by "automatic" psychological processes that are not available to conscious reflection. Thus, we suggest, the cognitive/affective and conscious/intuitive divisions that have been made in the literature in fact pick out the same underlying structure within the moral mind. Finally, we consider a set of Humean hypotheses according to which moral principles deployed in conscious cognition have affective origins.

The present chapter focuses exclusively on two psychological systems that shape moral judgments concerning physically harmful behavior. Psychological researchers have often noted, however, that the moral domain encompasses much more than reactions to and prohibitions against causing bodily harm (Darley & Shultz, 1990; Gilligan, 1982/1993: 19; Haidt, 2007; Schweder & Haidt, 1993). Other sub-domains of morality might include the fair allocation of resources, sexual deviance, altruism and care, respect for social hierarchy, and religious devotion, for instance. Several authors have suggested that independent psychological systems are responsible for judgments in several of these domains, and we regard such conjectures as plausible. Our focus on two systems that are important for judgments concerning harm is not presented as a complete account of moral psychology. On the contrary, we hope that the dual-process model explored here will eventually be understood as part of a larger constellation of psychological systems that enable the human capacity for moral judgment.

1. A Dual-Process Model of Moral Judgment

Moral dilemmas come in many flavors, and a perennial favorite in moral philosophy forces a choice between harming one person and letting many people die, as in the classic trolley dilemmas (Foot, 1967; Thomson, 1985). In a case that we shall call the switch dilemma, a runaway trolley threatens to run over and kill five people. Is it morally permissible to flip a switch that will redirect the trolley away from five people and onto one person instead, thus saving five lives at the cost of one? In a large web survey, most people said that it is (Hauser et al., 2007.) This case contrasts with the footbridge dilemma. Here, one person is standing next to a larger person on a footbridge spanning the tracks, in between the oncoming trolley and the five. In this case, the only way to save the five is to push the large person off of the footbridge and into the trolley's path, killing him, but preventing the trolley from killing the five. (You can't stop the trolley yourself because you're not big enough to do the job.) Most people surveyed said that in this case trading one life for five is not morally permissible. It appears that most ordinary people, like many philosophers, endorse a characteristically consequentialist judgment ("maximize the number of lives saved") in first case and a characteristically deontological judgment ("harm is wrong, no matter what the consequences are") in the second. (For a discussion of why we consider it legitimate to refer to these judgments as "characteristically deontological" and "characteristically consequentialist," see Greene, 2007.) This pair of dilemmas gives rise to the "trolley problem," which, for decades, philosophers have attempted to solve (Fischer & Ravizza, 1992; Kamm, 1998, 2006). What makes people judge these cases differently?

Greene and colleagues' dual-process theory of moral judgment (Greene et al., 2001, 2004; Greene, 2007) attempted to characterize the respective roles of affect and controlled cognition in people's responses to these dilemmas (Greene et al., 2001). Specifically, Greene and colleagues proposed that the thought of harming someone in a "personal" way, as in the footbridge dilemma, triggers a negative emotional responses that says, in effect, "That's wrong, don't do it!" According to their theory, this emotional alarm bell overrides any consequentialist inclination to approve of the five-for-one trade off. In contrast, people tend to say that redirecting the trolley in the switch case is morally permissible because the "impersonal" nature of this action fails to trigger a comparable emotional response. In the absence of such a response, consequentialist moral reasoning ("Five lives are worth more than one") dominates the decision. The core insight of this proposal is that our discrepant judgments in the switch and push cases may not come from the operation of a single psychological system, but rather from competition between two distinct psychological systems.

Putting this proposal to the empirical test, Greene and colleagues examined the neural activity of people responding to various "personal" and "impersonal" moral dilemmas. As predicted, they found that brain regions associated with emotion (and social cognition more broadly) exhibited increased activity in response to "personal" moral dilemmas such as the footbridge case. These brain regions included a region of the medial prefrontal cortex (Brodmann's area 9/10) that was damaged in the famous case of Phineas Gage, the nineteenth-century railroad foreman whose moral behavior became severely disordered after a tragic accident sent a metal tamping iron through his eye socket and out of the top of his head (Damasio, 1994: 3; Macmillan, 2000). In contrast, and also as predicted, Greene and colleagues found that brain regions associated with controlled cognitive processes such as working memory and abstract reasoning exhibited increased activity when people were responded to "impersonal" moral dilemmas such as the switch case.

Building on this finding, Greene and colleagues conducted a second study (Greene et al., 2004). Whereas their first study identified patterns of neural activity associated with the kind of dilemma in question ("personal" vs. "impersonal"), the second study identified patterns of neural activity associated with the particular judgments people made ("acceptable" vs. "unacceptable"). They focused their analysis on difficult dilemmas in which harming someone in a "personal" manner would lead to a greater good. Here is an example of a particularly difficult case, known as the crying baby dilemma:

Enemy soldiers have taken over your village. They have orders to kill all remaining civilians. You and some of your townspeople have sought refuge in the cellar of a large house. Outside, you hear the voices of soldiers who have come to search the house for valuables. Your baby begins to cry loudly. You cover his mouth to block the sound. If you remove your hand from his mouth, his crying will summon the attention of the soldiers who will kill you, your child, and the others hiding out in the cellar. To save yourself and the others, you must smother your child to death. Is it appropriate for you to smother your child in order to save yourself and the other townspeople?

Subjects tend to take a long time to respond to this dilemma, and their judgments tend to split fairly evenly between the characteristically consequentialist judgment ("Smother the baby to save the group") and the characteristically deontological judgment ("Don't smother the baby"). According to Greene and colleagues' dual-process theory, the characteristically deontological responses to such cases are driven by prepotent emotional responses that nearly everyone has. If that's correct, then people who deliver characteristically consequentialist judgments in response to such cases must override their emotional responses.

This theory makes two predictions about what we should see in people's brains as they respond to such dilemmas. First, we would expect to see increased activity in a part of the brain called the anterior cingulate cortex (ACC), which, in more dorsal subregions, reliably responds when two or more incompatible behavioral responses are simultaneously activated, i.e. under conditions of "response conflict" (Botvinick, Braver, Barch, Carter, & Cohen, 2001). For example, if one is presented with the word "red" written in green ink, and one's task is to name the color of the ink, then one is likely to experience response conflict because the more automatic word-reading response ("red") conflicts with the task-appropriate color-naming response ("green") (Stroop, 1935). According to this dual-process theory, the afore-mentioned difficult dilemmas elicit an internal conflict between a prepotent emotional response that says "No!" and a consequentialist cost–benefit analysis that says "Yes." Consistent with this theory, Greene and colleagues found that difficult "personal" dilemmas like the crying-baby case elicit increased ACC activity, relative to easier "personal" dilemmas, such as whether to kill your boss because you and others don't like him, in which reaction times are shorter and judgments are more overwhelmingly negative. Second, we would expect to see increased activity in a part of the brain known as the dorsolateral prefrontal cortex (DLPFC). This part of the brain is the seat of "cognitive control" (Miller & Cohen, 2001) and is necessary for overriding impulses and for "executive function" more broadly. Once again, if the characteristically deontological judgment is based on an intuitive emotional response, then giving a characteristically consequentialist response requires overriding that response, a job for the DLPFC. As predicted, Greene and colleagues found that consequentialist judgments in response to difficult "personal" dilemmas ("Smother the baby in the name of the greater good") are associated with increased activity in the DLPFC relative to the activity associated with trials on which deontological judgments were made.

These neuroimaging results support a dual-process theory of moral judgment in which distinct "cognitive" and emotional processes sometimes compete. But a consistent association between neural activity and behavior cannot provide conclusive evidence that the neural activity is a cause of the behavior. To provide stronger evidence for such causal relationships, one must intervene on the neural process. In a recent study, Greene and colleagues (2008) did this by imposing a "cognitive load" on people responding to difficult "personal" moral dilemmas like the crying-baby dilemma. People responded to the moral dilemmas while simultaneously monitoring a string of digits scrolling across the screen. The purpose of this manipulation is to disrupt the kind of controlled cognitive processes that are hypothesized to support consequentialist moral judgments. They found, as predicted, that imposing a cognitive load slowed down characteristically consequentialist judgments, but had no effect on characteristically deontological judgments. (Deontological judgments were in fact slightly faster under cognitive load, but this effect was not statistically significant.)

A complementary tactic is to manipulate the relevant emotional responses, rather than the capacity for cognitive control. Valdesolo and DeSteno (2006) did this by presenting either comedic video clips or affectively neutral video clips to two groups of subjects who then responded to versions of the switch and footbridge dilemmas. They reasoned as follows: if people judge against pushing the man in front of the trolley because of a negative emotional response, then a dose of positive emotion induced by watching a short comedic sketch from *Saturday Night Live* might counteract that negative response and make their judgments more consequentialist. As predicted, the researchers found that people who watched the funny video were more willing to endorse pushing the man in front of the trolley.

Yet another method for establishing a causal relationship between emotion and moral judgment is to test individuals with selective deficits in emotional processing. This approach was first taken by Mendez and colleagues (2005) in a study of patients with frontotemporal dementia (FTD), a disease characterized by deterioration of prefrontal and anterior temporal brain areas. FTD patients exhibit blunted emotion and diminished regard for others early in the disease course. Behavioral changes include moral transgressions such as stealing, physical assault, and unsolicited or inappropriate sexual advances. Mendez and colleagues presented FTD patients with versions of the switch and footbridge dilemmas and found, as predicted, that most FTD patients endorsed not only flipping the switch but also pushing the person in front of the trolley in order to save the five others. Mendez and colleagues suggest that this result is driven by the deterioration of emotional processing mediated by the ventromedial prefrontal cortex (VMPC). Since neurodegeneration in FTD affects multiple prefrontal and temporal areas, however, firm structure—function relationships cannot be ascertained from this study.

To fill this gap, moral judgment has since been investigated in patients with more focal VMPC lesions—that is, lesions involving less damage to other structures. Like FTD patients, VMPC lesion patients exhibit reduced affect and diminished empathy, but unlike FTD patients, VMPC lesion patients retain broader intellectual function. Thus VMPC patients are especially well suited to studying the role of emotion in moral judgment. Koenigs, Young, and colleagues (2007) tested a group of six patients with focal, adult-onset, bilateral lesions of VMPC to determine whether emotional processing subserved by VMPC is in fact necessary for deontological moral judgment. In this study patients evaluated a series of impersonal and personal moral scenarios, used by Greene and colleagues in the neuroimaging work discussed above. VMPC patients responded normally to the impersonal moral scenarios, but for the personal scenarios the VMPC patients were significantly more likely to endorse committing an emotionally aversive harm (e.g. smothering the baby) if a greater number of people would benefit. That is, they were more consequentialist. A second lesion study conducted by Ciaramelli and colleagues (2007) produced consistent results. Thus these lesion studies lend strong support to the theory that characteristically deontological judgments are—in many people, at least—driven by intuitive emotional responses that depend on the VMPC, while characteristically consequentialist judgments are supported by controlled cognitive processes based in the DLPFC.

It is worth noting that this dual-process theory, and the body of evidence that supports it, run counter to the traditional philosophical stereotypes concerning which normative positions are most closely allied with emotion vis-à-vis controlled cognition. Historically, consequentialism is more closely allied with the "sentimentalist" tradition (Hume, 1739/1978), while deontology is more closely associated with Kantian (1785/1959) rationalism. According to the dual-process theory, this historical stereotype gets things mostly backwards. The evidence suggests that characteristically deontological judgments are driven primarily by automatic emotional responses, while characteristically consequentialist judgments depend more on controlled cognition (Greene, 2007). Of course, this association between emotion and deontology, on the one hand, and consequentialism and controlled cognition, on the other, is bound to be overly simple. In what follows, we present a more nuanced picture of the interactions between cognition and affect that support both characteristically consequentialist and characteristically deontological moral judgments.

2. Intuition and Affect: A Common System?

The division between affective and cognitive systems of moral judgment proposed by Greene and colleagues is by now well supported. Several critics have noted, however, that early formulations of the theory left many details of the affective system unspecified (Cushman et al., 2006; Hauser, 2006: 8; Mikahil, 2007). Taking the specific example of the trolley problem, what is it about the footbridge dilemma that makes it elicit a stronger emotional responses than the switch dilemma? As Mikhail (2000) observed, this question can be answered in at least two complementary ways. On a first pass, one can provide a descriptive account of the features of a given moral dilemma that reliably produce judgments of "right" or "wrong." Then, at a deeper level, one can provide an explanatory account of these judgments with reference to the specific cognitive processes at work.

A natural starting point for the development of a descriptive account of our moral judgments is the philosophical literature, which in the last half-century has burgeoned with principled accounts of moral intuitions arising from hypothetical scenarios (e.g. Fischer & Ravizza, 1992). The most prominent philosophical account of the trolley problem is a moral principle called the "Doctrine of Double Effect," or DDE. According to proponents of the DDE, the critical difference between the switch and footbridge cases is that the large man in the footbridge case is *used* to stop the train from hitting the five, whereas the death of the victim in the switch dilemma is merely a *side-effect* of diverting the trolley away from the five. In its general form, the DDE states that it is impermissible to use a harm as the means to achieving a greater good, but permissible to cause a harm as a side-effect of achieving a greater good. Setting aside its validity as a moral principle, we may ask whether the DDE is an accurate descriptive account of the moral judgments of ordinary people.

The characteristic pattern of responses elicited by the trolley problem provides some evidence for this view, but the DDE is certainly not the only account for subjects' judgments of these cases. Another obvious distinction between the footbridge and switch cases is that the former involves physical contact with the victim, while the latter occurs through mechanical action at a distance (Cushman et al., 2006). At a more abstract level, the footbridge case requires an intervention on the victim (pushing the large man), while the bystander case merely requires an intervention on the threat (turning the trolley) (Waldman & Dieterich, 2007).

In order to isolate the DDE from these sorts of alternative accounts, Mikhail (2000) tested subjects on a modified version of the switch dilemma. Both cases involve a "looped" side track that splits away from, and then rejoins, the main track (Figure 2.1). Five people are threatened on the main track, and they are positioned beyond the point where the side track rejoins. Thus, if the train were to proceed unimpeded down either the main track or the side track, the five would be killed. In the analog to the footbridge case, there is a man standing on the side track who, if hit, would be sufficiently large to stop the train before it hit the five. In the analog to the switch case, there is a weighted object on the side track that, if hit, would be sufficiently large to stop the train before it hit the five. However, standing in front of the weighted object is a man who would first be hit and killed. These cases preserve the distinction between harming as a *means* to saving five (when the man stops the train) and harming as a *side-effect* of saving five (when an object stops the train and a man dies incidentally). However, neither involves physical contact, and both require a direct intervention on the trolley rather than the victim.

Mikhail found that subjects reliably judged the looped means case to be morally worse than the looped side-effect case, although the size of the effect was markedly smaller than the original switch/footbridge contrast. These results suggest that the DDE is an adequate descriptive account for at least

Means case

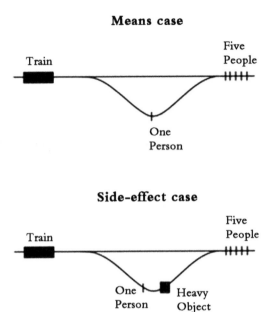

Side-effect case

Figure 2.1.

some part of the moral distinction between the fat man and bystander cases. A follow-up study involving several thousand subjects tested online replicated this effect, and found it to be remarkably consistent across variations in age, gender, educational level, exposure to moral philosophy, and religion (Hauser et al., 2007). While the specific wording of Mikhail's "loop" cases has been criticized (Greene et al., 2009; Waldman & Dieterich, 2007), subsequent research has demonstrated use of the DDE across multiple controlled pairs of moral dilemmas (Cushman et al., 2006).

These initial studies establish that DDE is at least part of an accurate description of subjects' moral judgments, but leave open the explanatory question: how is the means/side-effect distinction manifested in the psychological systems that give rise to moral judgment? Several related proposals have been offered (Cushman, Young, & Hauser, in preparation; Greene et al., 2009; Mikahil, 2007), but we will not discuss these in detail. In short, all three share the claim that when harm is used as the means to an end it is represented as being intentionally inflicted to a greater degree than when harm is produced as a side-effect. Cushman and colleagues (in preparation) provide evidence that that this relationship holds even in non-moral cases. That is, when somebody brings about a consequence as a means to accomplishing a goal, participants are more likely to judge that the effect was brought about intentionally than when somebody brings about a consequence as a foreseen side-effect of their goal. Many details remain to be worked out in providing a mechanistic account of the DDE in producing moral judgments, but it is likely to involve representations of others' mental states.

Several studies have explored another dimension of the cognitive processes underlying the DDE: specifically, whether they operate at the level of conscious awareness. Hauser et al. (2007) selected a subset of participants who judged killing the one to be impermissible in the loop means case but permissible in the loop side-effect case and asked them to provide a justification for their pattern of judgments. Of twenty-three justifications analyzed, only three contained a principled distinction between the two cases (e.g. "the man's death is a by-product rather than direct goal of trying to save the five men"). Subsequent research has replicated this result with a much larger group of participants, demonstrating the general inability of a majority of individuals to provide a sufficient justification for a variety of double effect cases (Cushman et al., 2006).

These results illustrate a phenomenon that Haidt has termed "moral dumbfounding" (Bjorklund et al., 2000). Moral dumbfounding occurs when individuals make moral judgments that they confidently regard as correct, but then cannot provide a general moral principle that accounts for their specific judgment. One example is the moral prohibition against incest among con-senting adults. Haidt and Hersh (2001) told subjects about a brother and sister who make love, but who use highly reliable contraception to avoid pregnancy, are rightly confident that they will suffer no negative emotional consequences, are able to keep their activities private, and so on. Presented with such cases, subjects often insist that the siblings' actions are morally wrong, despite the fact that they cannot provide more general justification for this judgment.

Haidt and colleagues argue that these difficult-to-justify moral judgments are generated by rapid, automatic, unconscious mental processes—in short, intuitions. Moreover, research indicates that these intuitions are supported by affective processing. For instance, subjects' moral judgments are harsher when made in a physically dirty space (Schnall, Haidt, Clore, & Jordan, 2008). It appears that subjects' feelings of disgust brought about by the dirty space were misattributed to the moral vignettes they judged, implicating disgust as an affective contributor to intuitive moral judgments. In another study, Wheatley and Haidt (2005) hypnotized subjects to experience disgust when they heard a key target word, such as "often." When subjects were told apparently innocent stories that contained this word—for example, a story about cousins who often visit the zoo, or a student council officer who often picks discussion topics—some made moralistic allegations against the protagonists, saying for instance, "It just seems like he is up to something," or that the he is a "popularity-seeking snob."

In summary, there is research suggesting that the DDE characterizes patterns of moral intuition, and research suggesting that affective responses underlie certain moral intuitions. This raises a clear question: does contemplating harm used as the means to an end trigger an affective response that in turn generates moral judgments consistent with the DDE? We suggest that the answer is yes: although the DDE alone cannot be fashioned into a complete descriptive account of the conditions under which affective processes are engaged in moral judgments of harmful acts, there are good reasons to suppose that it captures part of the story. The DDE is among the features that distinguish "personal" from "impersonal" dilemmas used to validate the dual-process model (Greene et al., 2001; Koenigs et al., 2007; Mendez et al., 2005; Valdesolo & DeSteno, 2006). A subsequent study by Shaich Borg and colleagues (2006) also revealed increased neural activity in brain regions associated with emotion, such as the VMPC, during the judgment of cases involving the use of harm as a means to a greater good. These data suggest that the use of harm as a means may play a specific role in engaging affective processes of moral judgment. However, the stimuli used have often not been sufficiently well controlled, leaving room for multiple interpretations.

We draw several conclusions from this collective body of data. First, the processes that shape moral judgment often operate below the level of conscious awareness, in the sense that individuals are often unable to articulate the basis for moral judgments derived from them. Second, these unconscious mechanisms operate over representations of agents and actions, causes and intentions, and so on, in ways that can be captured by fairly general principles such as the DDE. Third, although aspects of these unconscious mechanisms may involve the processing of information without emotional valence, evidence suggests that emotion plays some causal role in generating the ultimate moral judgment. Finally, the very sorts of features that seem to guide intuitive moral judgments also seem to guide affective moral judgments. A parsimonious account of these data clearly stands out: the research programs into the affective basis of moral judgment and research programs into the intuitive basis of moral judgment have been investigating the same kind of psychological process.

3. Reasoning from Deontological Principles

While the research described above associates conscious, principled reasoning with characteristically consequentialist moral judgment and emotional intuition with characteristically deontological moral judgment, other evidence suggests that this pattern need not hold in all cases. Consider, first, deontological philosophy. It seems that philosophical reasoning can lead to judgments that are not consequentialist and that are even strikingly counterintuitive. (See, e.g., Kant's [1785/1983] infamous claim that it would be wrong to lie to a would-be murderer in order to save someone's life.) Even when intuitions inspire putative deontological distinctions, reasoning can then determine their actual role in a normative theory, determining whether and the extent to which we should take them seriously. To adapt a dictum from evolutionary biology: intuition proposes, reason disposes.

But philosophers aren't the only ones providing evidence of non-consequentialist reasoning that appears to be conscious, principled, and deliberate. Let's return briefly to the patients with emotional deficits due to VMPC damage (Koenigs et al., 2007). The sketch we provided of their performance on personal scenarios was just that—a sketch. The full picture is both richer and messier. The personal moral scenarios on which VMPC patients produced abnormally consequentialist judgments could in fact be subdivided into two categories: "low-conflict" or easy scenarios and "high-conflict" or difficult scenarios. Low-conflict scenarios elicited 100% agreement and fast reaction times from healthy control subjects; high-conflict scenarios elicited disagreement and slow responses. All high-conflict scenarios featured a "consequentialist" option in which harm to one person could serve to promote the welfare of a greater number of people. Low-conflict scenarios, by contrast, typically described situations in which harm to one person served another person's purely selfish ends, for example, throwing one's baby in a dumpster to avoid the financial burden of caring for it. In these cases, the VMPC patients judged the actions to be wrong, just as normal individuals do.

How do VMPC patients arrive at the "appropriate" answer on low-conflict or easy personal moral scenarios? One proposal is that low-conflict scenarios pit a strong emotional response to the harmful action against a weak case for the alternative. According to this proposal, VMPC subjects could have generated the normal pattern of judgments on low-conflict scenarios because they retained sufficiently intact emotional processing to experience an aversion to the harm. This proposal isn't entirely plausible, however, in light of the fact that the VMPC subjects tested show abnormal processing of even highly charged emotional stimuli.

According to an alternative proposal, VMPC patients reasoned their way to conclusions against causing harm. The difference between low-conflict and high-conflict scenarios is driven by the absence of conflicting moral norms in the low-conflict scenarios and the presence of conflicting moral norms in the high-conflict scenarios. As described above, high-conflict scenarios described situations that required harm to one person to help other people. The decision of whether to endorse such harm presents participants with a moral dilemma, in the sense that they have distinct moral commitments demanding opposite behaviors. Regardless of the decision, either a norm against harming or a norm against not helping is violated. Low-conflict scenarios, on the other hand, typically described situations that required harm to one person in order to help only oneself. Thus it is possible that an uncontested moral norm against harming someone purely for self-benefit guides judgment. Alternatively, the VMPC patients could be applying the same utilitarian principles that they applied to the high-conflict cases, judging, for example, that the financial benefits to the young mother are outweighed by the harm done to her infant.

There were some low-conflict dilemmas featuring situations in which harm to one person was required to save other people. These scenarios, however, feature actions that violate widely understood moral norms, for instance norms against child prostitution, cannibalism, and the violation of a patient's rights by his doctor. The pattern of data thus suggests that patients with compromised emotional processing are able to use their intact capacity for reasoning to apply clear moral norms to specific situations.

Finally, ordinary people appear capable of bringing explicit moral principles to bear on particular cases in service of moral judgment. In contrast to the distinction between intended and foreseen harm, which appears to be intuitively generated and then justified *post hoc*, the distinction between killing and letting die (or, more generally, between action and omission) may commonly be consciously deployed in the first place. Cushman and colleagues (2006) asked people to justify patterns of their own judgments that were consistent with these two distinctions. They found that many people were able to explicitly produce a version of the action/omission distinction, while very few were able to explicitly produce a version of the distinction between intended and foreseen harm. Thus it is at least possible that ordinary people engage in moral reasoning from some version of the action/omission distinction, just as some philosophers do. Even more revealing is a reanalysis of that data showing that participants who were able to *articulate* the action/omission distinction showed significantly greater *use* of the distinction in their prior judgments. This link between having a principle and using that principle provides stronger evidence that explicit moral reasoning can play a role in the process of moral judgment.

Further evidence for the role of moral reasoning—albeit a limited role—comes from a study by Lombrozo (2008). Participants were asked several questions designed to reveal whether they adhered to a more consequentialist or more deontological moral theory. For instance, they were asked whether it is "never permissible" to murder (Lombrozo designated this a deontological response), "permissible" if it would bring about a greater good (consequentialist), or "obligatory" if it would bring about a greater good (strong consequentialist). They were also asked to make a moral judgment of two specific cases: the "switch" and "push" variants of the trolley problem. Subjects' general commitments with their judgment of particular cases, but this effect was limited in a revealing way. As predicted, subjects whose general commitments were consequentialist exhibited greater consistency in their moral judgments of the "push" and "switch" cases. This effect only emerged, however, when the "push" and "switch" cases were judged side by side. When specific judgments were made sequentially, there was no effect of subjects' general moral commitments. This suggests that moral reasoning can be triggered in some specific contexts, but not in others.

We expect that further research will uncover further evidence for conscious, principled reasoning in moral judgments. The examples offered here serve to support its potential role in non consequentialist moral judgments—adding important detail to the dual-process model.

4. The Pervasive Role of Affect

So far we have considered the general properties of two different processes that shape moral judgment: a deliberate, effortful process that reasons about specific cases from explicit abstract principles, and a rapid, automatic process of moral judgment that generates affective responses to specific cases on the basis of mental processes inaccessible to conscious reflection. We have also begun to characterize these systems at a more computational level, specifying the content of their moral rules: a general principle favoring welfare-maximizing behaviors appears to be supported by controlled cognitive processes, while a principle prohibiting the use of harm as a means to a greater good appears to be part of the process that generates intuitive emotional responses. We conclude by turning to a crucial, unanswered question: how do these principles get into our heads?

Elsewhere Greene has suggested that some of our emotionally driven moral judgments have an innate and evolutionarily adaptive basis (Greene & Haidt, 2002; Greene, 2003, 2007). Recent research demonstrating sophisticated social evaluation in preverbal infants has begun to lend credence to this view (Hamlin, Wynn, & Bloom, 2007). At the very least, it points the way towards research paradigms that could support a nativist hypothesis. While we look forward eagerly to progress on this front, here we will not pursue the question of the developmental or adaptive origins of the principles at work on the intuitive emotional side of the dual-process divide.

Our aim in this section is instead to consider the origins of the cognitive commitment to a utilitarian principle favoring welfare-maximizing choices (hereafter, the "welfare principle"). We explore the Humean (1739/1978) hypothesis that utilitarian judgment, despite its association with controlled cognition (Greene et al., 2004) and its prominence in the presence of emotional deficits (Mendez et al., 2005; Koenigs et al., 2007; Ciaramelli et al., 2007), itself has an affective basis. Put simply, we suggest that affect supplies the primary motivation to regard harm as a bad thing, while "cognition" uses this core statement of value to construct the utilitarian maximum that we ought to act so as to minimize harm. The result is the welfare principle. Below, we sketch out two versions of this hypothesis in greater detail.

They begin with a proposal by Greene (2007) distinguishing two kinds of emotional responses: those that that function like alarm bells and those that function like currencies. This distinction is meant to capture the difference between deontological intuitions and utilitarian reasoning, but it is also offered as a broader distinction that operates beyond the moral domain. The core idea is that alarm-bell emotions are designed to circumvent reasoning, providing absolute demands and constraints on behavior, while currency emotions are designed to participate in the process of practical reasoning, providing negotiable motivations for and against different behaviors. For example, the amygdala, which has been implicated in responses to personal moral dilemmas, reliably responds to threatening visual stimuli such as snakes and faces of out-group members (LeDoux, 1996: 166; Phelps et al., 2000). Thus the amygdala is a good candidate for a region that is critical for supporting at least some alarm-bell emotions. In contrast, Knutson and colleagues (2005) have identified a set of meso-limbic brain regions that appear to represent expected monetary value in a more graded fashion, with distinct regions tracking a stimulus's reward magnitude, reward probability, and expected value. These regions, in a rather transparent way, support currency-like representations.

Above, we argued that strongly affective deontological intuitions are triggered when types of harms occur, perhaps those that involve physical contact and use harm as a means to accomplishing a goal. The emotional response is like an alarm bell because it is designed to make a clear demand that is extremely difficult to ignore. This response can be overridden with substantial effort (cognitive control), but it is not designed to be negotiable. The prohibition of certain physical harms seems to be just an example of a broader class of alarm-bell emotions. For instance, research on "protected values" (Baron & Spranca, 1997) and "sacred values" (Tetlock, Kristel, Elson, Green, & Lerner 2000) in moral judgment suggests that people sometimes treat harm to the environment as non-negotiable as well. Outside the moral domain, the strong disgust response to eating contaminated food also seems to have an alarm-like character: most people are not willing to negotiate eating feces.

Whereas alarm-bell emotions treat certain types of physical harms as non-negotiable, it is precisely the defining feature of the "welfare principle" that harms are negotiable. One person's life counts for one-fifth as much as five people's lives, and the relative costs and benefits of lives, among other outcomes, are weighed against each other to determine the best course of action. Here, again, the case of moral decision-making is presumed to be one case of a much broader phenomenon. The desire for ice cream on a hot summer day is an example of a currency emotion: it supplies a reason to pursue the Good Humor truck, but this reason can be traded off against others, such as maintaining a slim poolside profile. Currency-like emotions function by adding a limited measure of motivational weight to a behavioral alternative, where this weighting is designed to be integrated with other weightings in order to produce a response. Such emotional weightings say, "Add a few points to option A" or "Subtract a few points from Option B,", rather than issuing resolute commands.

Above, we suggested that affect supplies the primary motivation to regard harm as bad. Once this primary motivation is supplied, reasoning proceeds in a currency-like manner. But we still must explain the origin of the primary motivation to regard harm as bad. Is it located in the alarm-bell response to personal harms, or in an independent currency response? Each hypothesis has pros and cons.

According to the "alarm-bell" hypothesis, the primary motivation not to harm is ultimately derived from the alarm-bell emotional system that objects to things like pushing a man in front of a train. When people attempt to construct general principles that account for their particular "alarm-bell" moral intuitions, one of the first things they notice is that their intuitions respond negatively to harm. This gives rise to a simple moral principle: "harm is bad." Combined with a general cognitive strategy of minimizing bad things (i.e. practical reasoning), the result is the welfare principle. Represented as such, the welfare principle can become a basis for controlled, conscious processes of reasoning. Critically, reasoning on the basis of an explicit welfare principle can occur in a currency-like manner. The alarm-bell hypothesis locates the *origins* of the welfare principle in a process of theory-construction over alarm-bell responses, but maintains the view that the *operation* of the welfare principle occurs in a currency-like manner that engages controlled reasoning processes.

According to this hypothesis, the welfare principle takes hold not because it offers a fully adequate descriptive account of our intuitive moral judgments (which it does not), but because it is simple, salient, and accounts for a large proportion of our intuitive judgments (which it does). Ultimately, the same mechanism can also give rise to more complex moral principles. For instance, Cushman and colleagues (in preparation) have explored this hypothesis in the particular cases of the doctrine of double effect and doctrine of doing and allowing.

The principle virtue of the alarm-bell hypothesis is its parsimony: by explaining the origins of the welfare principle in terms of an independently hypothesized alarm-bell aversion to harm, it can provide a motivational basis for controlled cognitive moral reasoning without invoking any additional primary affective valuation. It can also explain why utilitarian moral judgment is preserved in individuals who experience damage to frontal affective mechanisms: the welfare principle has already been constructed on the basis of past affective responses. But one shortcoming of the alarm-bell hypothesis is that it leaves unexplained how a theory of one's own moral intuitions gives rise to practical reasoning. When an individual regards her own pattern of moral intuitions and notes, "I *seem to think* harm is bad," will this lead automatically to the conclusion "Harm *is a reason* not to perform a behavior"? At present, we lack a sufficient understanding of the interface between cognition and affect to answer this difficult question. It seems plausible that a descriptive theory of one's motivations could become a motivational basis for practical reasoning, but it also seems plausible that it might not.

Philosophers will note that the alarm-bell hypothesis paints an unflattering portrait of philosophical utilitarianism because it characterizes the welfare principles as a sort of crude first pass, while characterizing deontological principles as more subtle and sophisticated. People's intuitive judgments are often consistent with the welfare principle, but it is clear that in many cases they are not—for instance, in the footbridge version of the trolley problem. If the welfare principle is designed to capture our intuitive moral judgments as a whole, then it would receive about a B+, getting things descriptively right much of the time, but getting things descriptively wrong much of the time, too.

The currency hypothesis is more friendly toward utilitarianism/consequentialism as a normative approach. According to the currency hypothesis, we are furnished with certain currency-like affective responses *independently* of our alarm-bell responses. For instance: harm is bad, regardless of who experiences it. Benefits are good, regardless of who experiences them. More harm is worse than less harm. More benefits are better than fewer benefits. Small harms can be outweighed by large benefits. Small benefits can be outweighed by large harms. And so on.

Notice that these premises assign a valence to outcomes (harm is bad), and even ordinal relationships among outcomes (more harm is worse), but they do not assign cardinal values to particular outcomes. Thus they specify the general structure of utilitarian thinking, but do not specify how, exactly, various harms and benefits trade off against one another. According to the currency process, utilitarian thinking is the product of a rational attempt to construct a set of practical principles that is consistent with the constraints imposed by the aforementioned premises. It is an idealization based on the principles that govern the flow of emotional currency. One might say that it is a union between basic sympathy and basic math.

Note that the operational mechanisms upon which the currency hypothesis depends—the math, so to speak—overlap substantially with the mechanisms upon which the alarm-bell hypothesis depends. Both accounts posit that explicit utilitarian principles arise from a combination of abstract reasoning and affect. The key difference is the source of the affect: generalization from alarm-bell responses prohibiting harm versus an independent set of currency-like valuations of harms and benefits.

The principal virtue of the currency hypothesis is that utilitarian cost–benefit reasoning looks very much like cost–benefit reasoning over other currency-like responses. The welfare principle functions very much as if there were a negotiable negative value placed on harm—and, for that matter, a negotiable positive value placed on benefits. Also, in contrast to the alarm-bell hypothesis, it is apparent how the currency-like weighting of costs and benefits directly and necessarily enters into practical reasoning. This tight fit comes with a slight expense in parsimony, however. The currency hypothesis demands two separate types of affective response to harm of independent origin: an alarm-bell response to a select set of harms, and a currency-like response to a larger set of harms. It also implies that currency-like responses are preserved in individuals with frontal-lobe damage, since they continue to reason from the welfare principle.

As noted earlier, the currency hypothesis is more friendly toward philosophical utilitarianism. According to this view, utilitarians are not simply doing a poor job of generalizing over the body of their alarm-bell moral intuitions. Instead, their judgments are based indirectly on a distinct set of currency-like emotional responses. Is it better to rely on currency-like emotions to the exclusion of alarm-like emotions? Perhaps. The alarm-like emotions that drive people's non-utilitarian judgments in response to trolley dilemmas appear to be sensitive to factors that are hard to regard as morally relevant, such as whether the action in question involves body-contact between agent and victim (Cushman et al., 2006). Taking the charge of bias one step further, Greene et al. (2009) hypothesizes that the DDE is a by-product of the computational limitations of the processes that govern our intuitive emotional responses. Borrowing some computational machinery from Mikhail (2000), he argues that the controlled cognitive system based in the DLPFC has the computational resources necessary to represent the side-effects of actions, while the appraisal system that governs our emotional responses to actions like the one in the footbridge dilemma lacks such resources. As a result, our emotional responses have a blind spot for harmful side-effects, leading us to draw a moral distinction between intended and foreseen harms, i.e. the DDE.

Although the alarm-bell and currency hypotheses vary in detail, they both reject philosophical moral rationalism in that they (a) require a specification of primitive goods before practical reasoning (including utilitarian reasoning) can proceed and (b) locate these primitives in our affective responses. Moreover, these hypotheses are not mutually exclusive: the welfare principle may be supported both by theory-building based on alarm-bell responses as well as a distinct set of currency responses. As we argued above, there is ample evidence that a distinction between cognitive and affective processes of moral judgment is warranted. We strongly suspect, however, that when the origins of the cognitive process are understood, we shall find a pervasive influence of affect.

5. Conclusion

As we hope this chapter attests, it no longer makes sense to engage in debate over whether moral judgment is accomplished exclusively by "cognition" as opposed to "affect," or exclusively by conscious reasoning as opposed to intuition. Rather, moral judgment is the product of complex interactions between multiple psychological systems. We have focused on one class of moral judgments: those involving tradeoffs between avoiding larger harms and causing smaller ones. Cases such as these engage at least two distinct systems: an intuitive/affective response prohibiting certain kinds of basic harm, and a conscious/cognitive response favoring the welfare-maximizing response. The underlying psychology of moral judgment in these cases helps to explain why they strike us as particularly difficult moral dilemmas: we are forced to reconcile the conflicting output of competing brain systems.

We have also identified several aspects of this account that are in need of further investigation. First, there is much to be learned about the evaluative processes that operate within each of the systems we have identified. In the case of the intuitive/affective system, we have suggested that one component of the evaluative process mirrors the doctrine of double effect. But the evidence is not conclusive on this point. Moreover, this single principle alone cannot account for the full pattern of data associated with intuitive/affective moral judgments. In the case of the conscious/cognitive system, the data strongly suggest that ordinary people typically reason from a principle favoring welfare-maximizing choices. But there is also good reason to believe that people, at least in some circumstances, explicitly reason from deontological moral principles. Further research in this area will be critical.

Second, the origins of each system of moral judgment remain unknown. In this chapter we have explored two hypotheses concerning the origins of explicit moral principles within individuals, both of which ultimately implicate affective systems. Others have proposed diverse origins for moral principles such as metaphor (Lakoff & Johnson, 1999: 290–334) and construction from social experience (Kohlberg, 1969). A further question is the origin of moral intuitions, which several authors have suggested may have an innate basis (Hauser, 2006: 1; Mikhail, 2007; Greene & Haidt, 2002). Several of these proposals operate at distinct levels of analysis (ontogenetic versus evolutionary) and are specific to one of the two systems we have discussed (cognitive versus affective), and thus may be broadly compatible.

Third, at present we know little about how the intuitive/affective and conscious/cognitive systems interact on-line in the production of moral judgments. This is a topic we have left largely untouched in the present chapter, and somewhat out of necessity. Until the contours of individual systems of moral judgment are better understood, it will be difficult to make much progress towards understanding the interactions between systems. One aspect of this problem that we suspect will be of interest are the standards for the normative plausibility of putative moral principles. Certain factors that reliably shape moral judgments, such as the physical proximity of an agent to a victim, are sometimes rejected as *prima facie* invalid criteria for moral judgment. Others, such as the doctrine of double effect, are more commonly accepted (Cushman et al., 2006). The bases on which particular explicit moral rules are accepted or rejected are poorly understood, and such meta-ethical intuitions are a key area for investigation at the interface between the intuitive/affective and conscious/cognitive systems.

Finally, it remains to be seen how generally the dual-process model developed for harm-based moral dilemmas can be extended to other domains of morality. There are at least two ways that this issue can be framed. On the one hand, we have argued that in the specific case of tradeoffs in harms, conflict between distinct psychological systems gives rise to the phenomenon of a dilemma (Cushman & Young, 2009; Greene, 2007; Sinnott-Armstrong, in preparation). One important question is whether this multi-system account can be employed to understand the phenomenon of a moral dilemma beyond the domain of physically harmful actions. That is, are there distinct systems that give rise to potentially conflicting moral judgments in domains such as the division of economic resources, the establishment of conventional standards of conduct, sexual taboo, and so forth?

On the other hand, we have argued for the operation of two psychological processes: an intuitive/affective response to intentional harms and a conscious/cognitive response favoring welfare maximization. This raises a second question: to what extent do other types of moral judgment depend on the operation of these specific processes? For instance, when evaluating allocations of resources, financial losses could be coded as "harms" and then processed via the operation of one of the systems we have explored in this chapter. Whether these particular systems have such broad applicability is presently unknown.

It is, of course, our hope that the small corner of moral judgment we have explored in this chapter—a corner strictly limited to the occurrence of physical harms and preternaturally concerned with railway operations—will teach lessons with broad applicability. The extent of this applicability remains to be determined, but we feel confident in asserting at least this much: there is no single psychological process of moral judgment. Rather, moral judgment depends on the interaction between distinct psychological systems. Notably, these systems tend to be reflected in the principles characteristic of competing moral philosophies (Greene, 2007).

Acknowledgments

We thank Tim Schroeder for his comments on an earlier version of this chapter. We also thank the members of the Moral Psychology Research Group, and especially John Doris, for their valuable input.

References

Baron, J., & Spranca, M. (1997). Protected values. *Behavior and Human Decision Processes*, 70: 1–16.

Bjorklund, F., Haidt, J., & Murphy, S. (2000). Moral dumbfounding: When intuition finds no reason. *Lund Psychological Reports*, 2: 1–23.

Blair, R. J. R. (1995). A cognitive developmental approach to morality: Investigating the psychopath. *Cognition*, 57: 1–29.

Botvinick, M. M., Braver, T. S., Barch, D. M., Carter, C. S., & Cohen, J. (2001). Conflict monitoring and cognitive control. *Psychological Review*, 108 (3): 624–652.

Ciaramelli, E., Muccioli, M., Ladavas, E., & di Pellegrino, G. (2007). Selective deficit in personal moral judgment following damage to ventromedial prefrontal cortex. *Social Cognitive Affective Neuroscience*, 2: 84–92.

Cushman, F. A., & Young, A. W. (2009). The psychology of dilemmas and the philosophy of morality. *Ethical Theory and Moral Practice*, 12 (1): 9.

Cushman, F. A., Young, L., & Hauser, M. D. (2006). The role of conscious reasoning and intuitions in moral judgment: testing three principles of harm. *Psychological Science*, 17 (12): 1082–1089.

—— (in preparation). Patterns of moral judgment derive from non-moral psychological representations.

Damasio, A. (1994). *Descartes' Error*. Boston, MA: Norton.

Darley, J. M., & Shultz, T. R. (1990). Moral rules—their content and acquisition. *Annual Review of Psychology*, 41: 525–556.

Fischer, J. M., & Ravizza, M. (1992). *Ethics: Problems and Principles*. New York: Holt, Rinehart & Winston.

Foot, P. (1967). The problem of abortion and the doctrine of double effect. *Oxford Review*, 5: 5–15.

Gilligan, C. (1982/1993). *In a Different Voice: Psychological Theory and Women's Development*. Cambridge, MA: Harvard University Press.

Greene, J. D. (2003). From neural 'is' to moral 'ought': what are the moral implications of neuroscientific moral psychology? *Nature Reviews Neuroscience*, 4: 847–850.

—— (2007). The secret joke of Kant's soul. In W. Sinnott-Armstrong (ed.), *Moral Psychology* (Vol. 3). Cambridge, MA: MIT Press, 35–117.

Greene, J. D., & Haidt, J. (2002). How (and where) does moral judgment work? *Trends in Cognitive Science*, 6: 517–523.

Greene, J. D., Cushman, F. A., Stewart, L. E., Lowenberg, K., Nystrom, L. E., & Cohen, J. D. (2009). Pushing moral buttons: The interaction between personal force and intention in moral judgment. *Cognition*, 111 (3): 364–371.

Greene, J. D., Morelli, S. A., Lowenberg, K., Nystrom, L. E., & Cohen, J. D. (2008). Cognitive load selectively interferes with utilitarian moral judgment. *Cognition*, 107: 1144–1154.

Greene, J. D., Nystrom, L. E., Engell, A. D., Darley, J. M., & Cohen, J. D. (2004). The neural bases of cognitive conflict and control in moral judgment. *Neuron*, 44: 389–400.

Greene, J. D., Sommerville, R. B., Nystrom, L. E., Darley, J. M., & Cohen, J. D. (2001). An fMRI investigation of emotional engagement in moral judgment. *Science*, 293: 2105–2108.

Haidt, J. (2001). The emotional dog and its rational tail: A social intuitionist approach to moral judgment. *Psychological Review*, 108: 814–834.

—— (2007). The new synthesis in moral psychology. *Science*, 316 (5827): 998–1002.

Haidt, J., & Hersh, M. (2001). Sexual morality. The cultures and emotions of conservatives and liberals. *Journal of Applied Social Psychology*, 31: 191–221.

Hamlin, K., Wynn, K., & Bloom, P. (2007). Social evaluation by preverbal infants. *Nature*, 450: 557–559.

Hauser, M. D. (2006). *Moral Minds: How Nature Designed a Universal Sense of Right and Wrong*. New York: HarperCollins.

Hauser, M. D., Cushman, F. A., Young, L., Jin, R., & Mikhail, J. M. (2007). A dissociation between moral judgment and justification. *Mind & Language*, 22 (1): 1–21.

Huebner, B., Dwyer, S., & Hauser, M. (2008). The role of emotion in moral psychology. *Trends in Cognitive Science*, 13 (1): 1–6.

Hume, D. (1739/1978). *A Treatise of Human Nature*. In L. Selby-Bigge and P. H. Nidditch (eds.). New York: Oxford University Press.

Kamm, F. M. (1998). *Morality, Mortality: Death and Whom to Save from it*. New York: Oxford University Press.

—— (2006). *Intricate Ethics: Rights, Responsibilities, and Permissible Harm*. New York: Oxford University Press.

Kant, I. (1785/1959). *Foundations of the Metaphysics of Morals*. New York: Macmillan.

—— (1785/1983). *On a Supposed Right to Lie because of Philanthropic Concerns*. Indianapolis, IN: Hackett.

Knutson, B., Taylor, J., Kaufman, M., Peterson, R., & Glover, G. (2005). Distributed neural representation of expected value. *Journal of Neuroscience*, 25 (19): 4806–4812.

Koenigs, M., Young, L., Adolphs, R., Tranel, D., Cushman, F. A., Hauser, M. D., et al. (2007). Damage to the prefrontal cortex increases utilitarian moral judgments. *Nature*, 446: 908–911.

Kohlberg, L. (1969). Stage and sequence: The cognitive-developmental approach to socialization. In D. A. Goslin (ed.), *Handbook of Socialization Theory and Research*. New York: Academic Press, 151–235.

LeDoux, J. (1996). *The Emotional Brain*. New York: Simon & Schuster.

Lombrozo, T. (2008). The role of moral commitments in moral judgment. *Cognitive Science*, 33: 273–286

Lakoff, G., & Johnson, M. (1999). *Philosophy in the Flesh*. New York: Basic Books.

Macmillan, M. (2000). *An Odd Kind of Fame*. Cambridge, MA: MIT Press.

Mendez, M. F., Anderson, E., & Shapria, J. S. (2005). An investigation of moral judgment in frontotemporal dementia. *Cognitive and Behavioral Neurology*, 18 (4): 193–197.

Mikhail, J. M. (2000). Rawls' linguistic analogy: A study of the "generative grammar" model of moral theory described by John Rawls in *A theory of justice*. Unpublished PhD, Cornell University, Ithaca, NY.

—— (2007). Universal moral grammar: Theory, evidence, and the future. *Trends in Cognitive Science*, 11 (4): 143–152.

Miller, E. K., & Cohen, J. D. (2001). An integrative theory of prefrontal cotex function. *Annual Review of Neuroscience*, 24: 167–202.

Phelps, E. A., O'Connor, K. J., Cunningham, W. A., Funayama, E. S., Gatenby, J. C., Gore, J. C., et al. (2000). Performance on indirect measures of race evaluation predicts amygdala activation. *Journal of Cognitive Neuroscience*, 12 (5): 729–738.

Piaget, J. (1965/1932). *The Moral Judgment of the Child*. New York: Free Press.

Pizarro, D. A., Uhlmann, E., & Bloom, P. (2003). Causal deviance and the attribution of moral responsibility. *Journal of Experimental Social Psychology*, 39: 653–660.

Schaich Borg, J., Hynes, C., Van Horn, J., Grafton, S. T., & Sinnott-Armstrong, W. (2006). Consequences, action, and intention as factors in moral judgments: An fMRI investigation. *Journal of Cognitive Neuroscience*, 18 (5): 803–837.

Schnall, S., Haidt, J., Clore, G. L., & Jordan, A. H. (2008). Disgust as embodied moral judgment. *Personality and Social Psychology Bulletin*, 34: 1096–1109.

Schweder, D., & Haidt, J. (1993). The future of moral psychology: truth, intuition, and the pluralist way. *Psychological Science*, 4: 360–365.

Sinnott-Armstrong, W. (2008). Abstract + Concrete = Paradox. In S. Nichols & J. Knobe (eds.), *Experimental Philosophy*. New York: Oxford University Press, 209–230.

Stroop, J. R. (1935). Studies of interference in serial verbal reactions. *Journal of Experimental Psychology*, 12: 643–662.

Tetlock, P., Kristel, O., Elson, S., Green, M., & Lerner, J. (2000). The psychology of the unthinkable. *Journal of Personality and Social Psychology*, 78 (5): 853–870.

Thomson, J. J. (1985). The trolley problem. *The Yale Law Journal*, 279: 1395–1415.

Turiel, E. (1983). *The Development of Social Knowledge: Morality and Convention*. Cambridge: Cambridge University Press.

—— (2005). Thoughts, emotions, and social interactional processes in moral development. In M. Killen and J. Smetana (eds.), *Handbook of Moral Development*. Mahwah, NJ: Lawrence Erlbaum, 1–36.

Valdesolo, P., & DeSteno, D. (2006). Manipulations of Emotional Context Shape Moral Judgment. *Psychological Science*, 17 (6): 476–477.

Waldman, M. R., & Dieterich, J. H. (2007). Throwing a bomb on a person versus throwing a person on a bomb: intervention myopia in moral intuitions. *Psychological Science*, 18 (3): 247–253.

Wheatley, T., & Haidt, J. (2005). Hypnotic disgust makes moral judgments more severe. *Psychological Science*, 16 (10): 780–784.

3

Moral Motivation

TIMOTHY SCHROEDER, ADINA L. ROSKIES, AND
SHAUN NICHOLS

Jen is walking down the street when a homeless man asks her for money. She
stops and gives him a dollar, wishes him well, and walks on. Jen appears to have
done a morally good deed. But now, what motivated her to do it? Perhaps she
was motivated by the thought that the man needed the money more than she
did. Perhaps she was motivated by a desire to look like a nice person to the
people around her. Perhaps she was motivated by an irrational surge of fear at
the thought of what the homeless man might do if not appeased. And on we
could speculate, for every action has many possible motivations.

In this chapter, we begin with a discussion of motivation itself, and use that
discussion to sketch four possible theories of distinctively *moral* motivation:
caricature versions of familiar instrumentalist, cognitivist, sentimentalist, and
personalist theories about morally worthy motivation. To test these theories,
we turn to a wealth of scientific, particularly neuroscientific, evidence. Our
conclusions are that (1) although the scientific evidence does not at present
mandate a unique philosophical conclusion, it does present formidable obstacles
to a number of popular philosophical approaches, and (2) theories of morally
worthy motivation that best fit the current scientific picture are ones that owe
much more to Hume or Aristotle than to Kant.

1. Motivation

Motivation plays a prominent role in discussions of action, practical reason, and
moral psychology. Despite its frequent appearance in philosophical discussions,
philosophers have generally not been clear about what motivation is. In this
first section, we redress this.

Is motivation psychologically real? Is there a state or process that can be
identified as motivation? Some, like Alston (1967), deny that motivation has

psychological reality, suggesting instead that "the concept of motivation is an abstraction from the concept of a motivational explanation, and the task of specifying the nature of motivation is the task of bringing out the salient features of this explanation" (p. 400). But we postulate that motivation is not merely an abstraction, and that it plays a causal role in the production of action.

To get an idea of what motivation as a causally efficacious independent mental state would have to be like, consider some apparent features of motivation.

(I) Motivation is closely related to action, yet distinct from it. When we intentionally perform action A, we are motivated to so act. However, not all motivation results in action: we can be motivated to A, yet fail to A for a variety of reasons.[1]

(II) Motivation is a causally efficacious kind of state. We A because we are motivated to A; that is, our motivational states are causally related to action-production. It might well be that there exist factors that can block motivation from bringing about action (e.g. motivation not to do what one is also motivated to do, habits, phobias, lassitude, etc.) but motivation makes a causal contribution that promotes the production of action.

(III) Motivation is occurrent. If someone has a standing desire for global peace, one might say she is motivated to bring about world peace. But we understand this to mean that, in appropriate circumstances, she would display an occurrent motivation—motivation properly so called—to bring about world peace. Because motivation is occurrent, it is distinct from standing—that is, dispositional and causally inert—desires. And since any desire can be a standing desire (if only briefly), there is something to motivation that is distinct from desire as such. This is obvious with desires such as a desire to create philosophical ideas, for it is often the case that a person with such a desire has it without being motivated at that moment to carry it out.

(IV) Motivation is commonly associated with certain feelings. We have no strong claims to make about these feelings, and nothing hangs on this in what follows, but it seems helpful to acknowledge the potential range of feelings that go with motivation. These feelings cluster around two sorts of cases. In the first sort, one is motivated to achieve some larger goal, and feels "up to the challenge," "bursting with energy," or otherwise

---

[1] Here we focus solely on motivation to act in specific ways, not motivation to refrain from acting. It is likely that neural basis of the latter depends upon a neural system the underlying neurobiology of which is not well understood.

inspired. This first sort of feeling—feeling motivated in general—is non-specific, and feels the same regardless of what one is motivated to do. In the second sort of case, one is motivated to perform some specific action by means of some specific bodily movement. In such cases, one might feel muscular tension preparing one for the action, or have an image of oneself performing it, or experience anticipatory pleasure at the thought of the action, or suffer from one's current non-performance of the action. These feelings are, obviously, much more closely tied to the specific end one is motivated to bring about.

An investigation of moral motivation, then, is first an investigation of motivation: an investigation of an occurrent state, capable of causing actions, and associated with certain feelings. But it is also an investigation of something specifically moral. To the moral side we turn next.

2. Philosophical Approaches to Moral Motivation

Theories of moral motivation are almost as numerous as the number of philosophers writing on the subject. Accordingly, in this section we shall not survey them comprehensively. Instead, our approach will be to sketch caricatures of four familiar approaches, those of the instrumentalist, the cognitivist, the sentimentalist, and the personalist, indicating as we go how these caricatures fit better or worse with the views of particular theorists. We have chosen to sketch our characters as starkly as possible, simplifying away many of the subtle features that would appear in a fleshed-out theory in order to highlight what is fundamentally different in these approaches. These sketches will help make clear the significance of the scientific findings that follow in the next section.[2]

The Instrumentalist

Our instrumentalist holds that people are motivated when they form beliefs about how to satisfy pre-existing desires.[3] Motivation, says the instrumentalist,

[2] It should be noted that each of these four views provides a story about moral motivation, assuming that the judgments or feelings are elicited by a moral situation. We have nothing to say about what sorts of things make judgments or feelings genuine responses to moral facts, features, or situations; to the extent that an account of the moral facts is required, we don't presume to provide a complete characterization of moral motivation. But we take it that a variety of different accounts of moral facts can be added on to our stories about moral motivation, and so we set this issue to one side.

[3] Contrast this with Michael Smith's Humeanism, in which beliefs about what it would be rational to want guide the formation of desires (Smith, 1994). On Smith's Humeanism, belief often precedes desire, rather than vice versa.

begins with intrinsic desires. And desires are intrinsic just in the sense that what is desired is desired for its own sake, and neither merely as a realizer of what was antecedently desired, nor merely as a means to what was antecedently desired. Typical examples of intrinsic desires might include desires for pleasure, for the welfare of loved ones, for the will of God to be done on Earth, for the Montreal Canadians to win the Stanley Cup, and so on (compare Stich et al., Chapter 5, this volume).[4]

Having intrinsic desires is necessary for motivation, holds the instrumentalist, but not sufficient. These desires lurk in the minds of their possessors like buried land mines, waiting for the right conditions in order to explode into occurrent motivation. And the right conditions are conditions of occurrent belief. When a person has an intrinsic desire that P, and then occurrently believes that she can bring it about that P by taking action A, then she becomes motivated to take action A. Becoming so motivated is a matter of forming a new, non-intrinsic pro-attitude toward taking action A. That is, motivation on the instrumentalist's view is a matter of having non-intrinsic desires (or intentions, or the like) to do what is believed to be instrumental to (or a realization of) an intrinsic desire.

The instrumentalist's view is sometimes labeled 'Humean' by philosophers, though many have pointed out that the view is only loosely related to that of Hume himself. Most decision theorists are instrumentalists of our sort or something recognizably related,[5] but relatively few ethicists seem to be. The best-known self-styled neo-Humean at present is perhaps Michael Smith, and Smith's own view of moral motivation is decidedly non-instrumentalist (see Smith, 1994).[6]

On the instrumental view, the story of Jen is straightforward. She desires to do what is right, and forms the belief that by giving the homeless man before her a dollar, she will be doing the right thing.[7] She thus comes to have an occurrent instrumental desire to give the man a dollar. This new desire is her motivation to give the man a dollar. She then acts on her instrumental desire

---

[4] Our instrumentalist thus ignores Hume's own distinction between the calm and the violent passions.

[5] See, e.g., Jeffrey (1990), Sen (1982).

[6] Williams (1981) is often taken to be the starting point for contemporary instrumentalist argument.

[7] There is a substantial literature about what, exactly, the content of Jen's desire and belief must be for her motivation to be morally worthy. Michael Smith has argued that to act on a desire to do what is right as such is to fetishize morality (Smith, 1994), and Nomy Arpaly has argued that one can perform morally worthy actions even while being mistaken about what is right, so long as one's motivating desire has morally relevant content (Arpaly, 2003). In this work we do not mean to take a particular stand on these issues, and will write of desires to do what is right and beliefs about what is right purely for the sake of convenience.

and gives the man a dollar, thereby also acting on her intrinsic desire to do what is right. In so doing, she does what is right because it is right, and acts with moral worth.

The Cognitivist

The cognitivist rejects the thesis that moral motivation begins with desire and the thesis that belief plays a merely instrumental or realizational role in guiding moral action. The cognitivist—our sort of cognitivist, at any rate—is led to this rejection not least because she holds that to desire is merely to be in a state that generates a behavioral impulse. And how, she asks, can a behavioral impulse ever be the source of morally worthy action?[8]

What, then, is left? The cognitivist holds the view that moral motivation begins with occurrent belief. In particular, it begins with beliefs about what actions would be right. The cognitivist holds that, at least in cases of morally worthy action, such beliefs lead to motivation to perform those actions, quite independently of any antecedent desires. The cognitivist is happy to call this motivational state "a desire," but thinks of it as entirely dependent upon the moral belief that created it.

The cognitivist position has recognizable affinities to familiar positions in the philosophical literature (e.g. Korsgaard, 1994; McDowell, 1998: ch. 4; Smith, 1994). These philosophers, of course, hold that much more is going on in the mind of a morally worthy agent than the simple picture painted by our cognitivist.

They generally agree, however, that morally worthy action is not dependent upon antecedent desires, but stems in the first instance from one's judgments.

On the cognitivist's view, Jen's desires are not irrelevant to her action, but they are not the initiating engines of her action either. Instead, her desires are mere data that she considers (perhaps) in coming to be motivated. Given what is available to her, perhaps she comes to believe that it would be right to give the homeless man money, and it never occurs to her to even consider her desires. This consideration of the rightness of giving money to the homeless man motivates Jen to give him some money, and she does. Because she is moved by the right sort of belief, her action has moral worth.

The Sentimentalist

Emotions have not yet been featured in the above accounts of morally worthy action, but they are central to the account given by the sentimentalist.

---

[8] For intimations of this, see, e.g., Korsgaard (1986).

According to all sentimentalists, the emotions typically play a key causal role in motivating moral behavior. Our caricature sentimentalist, like many real sentimentalists, takes a stronger view. Our sentimentalist maintains that an action can't count as being *morally* motivated unless it is driven by certain emotions. Of course it can't be any old emotion. If a person is motivated to save a drowning person only because he hates him and wishes to see him die a slower, more painful death at his own hand, this is emotional motivation, to be sure, but it is hardly *moral* motivation.

Our sentimentalist might opt for several different emotions as the right kind of emotion for producing moral motivation, and compassion is an obvious candidate. When a person is motivated to help an injured child because of a feeling of compassion, that counts as genuine moral motivation. Saying exactly why particular emotion-driven motivations are moral is a controversial issue even among sentimentalists who agree with our sentimentalist, but this needn't detain us here.

The sentimentalist story about Jen is easy to tell. When Jen sees the homeless man, she feels compassion toward him. This feeling of compassion provides the motivation that leads her to treat him kindly. Since sentimentalists typically acknowledge that compassion is a type of emotion that can provide *moral* motivation, Jen's action was morally worthy.

The Personalist

The previous three views have all highlighted specific mental states as central to morally worthy action, but the personalist holds a more holistic position. She holds that morally worthy action stems from good character. Good character involves knowledge of the good, wanting what is good for its own sake, long-standing emotional dispositions that favor good action, and long-standing habits of responding to one's knowledge, desires, and emotions with good actions.

On the view of the personalist, morally worthy action begins with knowledge of the good. This knowledge is unlikely to be retained in a person in the form of an explicit theory, or in the form of a disposition to test one's possible principles of action against particular standards such as universalizability. Instead, it is likely to be retained through a combination of moral heuristics (lying is generally a bad idea, generosity does not require even-handedness, and so on) and a learned sensitivity to particular sorts of situations as calling for one heuristic or another, or for a novel approach that nonetheless extends more familiar moral thought.[9]

---

[9] The personalist can, but need not, hold an explicit theory of right action on which the right action is the one the person of full virtue would perform (Hursthouse, 1999).

This moral knowledge leads through inference (often unconscious) to an occurrent belief that action A is the morally superior action in a given context. But this belief is impotent without a suitably responsive character. Such a character involves long-standing conative dispositions, emotional dispositions, and behavioral dispositions (i.e. habits), with these complexes of dispositions generally being named "virtues." Thus, if action A is one that requires facing a significant threat of harm for a good cause, then the conative emotional and behavioral dispositions required to perform A in a praiseworthy manner[10] will be that complex known as "courage"; if A amounts to telling the truth against one's immediate interests, then the conative, emotional, and behavioral dispositions required will be that complex known as "honesty"; and so on. The personalist holds that neither the emotional dispositions nor the habits that make up good character are reducible to long-standing intrinsic desires, and in this way she opposes the instrumentalist. The personalist's view has affinities to Aristotle's in *Nicomachean Ethics*, and also to contemporary neo-Aristotelians such as Hursthouse and Slote (Aristotle, 2000; Hursthouse, 1999; Slote, 2001).

Jen's story begins with her moral cognitive capacities, on the personalist's account. Although she holds no explicit belief about what is right in every case, her sensitivity to moral patterns and her explicit (if generally unconscious) heuristics lead her to the view that it would be good to give the homeless man a dollar. Because of her character, Jen's moral thoughts engage her standing desires, lead her to feel relevant emotions, and—because of her habits as well—lead her to take the right action, and so she gives the homeless man a dollar. This amounts to the exercise of at least a partial virtue on Jen's part: compassion, as it might be. She thus does what is right for the right reason and is morally worthy.

3. The Neurophysiology of Moral Motivation

The previous section sketched four familiar accounts of doing the right thing with genuinely moral motivations. These accounts, though philosophical, should lead one to make certain empirical predictions. As should already be evident, accounts of moral motivation typically presuppose commitments

---

[10] Like Aristotle in the *Nicomachean Ethics*, the personalist holds that doing what courage requires merely out of love of money, or irrational optimism about one's chances, or the like, does not amount to action out of a virtue.

regarding the nature of psychological states such as beliefs, desires, choices, emotions, and so on, together with commitments regarding the functional and causal roles they play. Observations about the nature and the functional and causal roles of psychological states, it seems to us, are as much empirical as they are philosophical. At least, it is rather obscure *how* such claims are to be understood, if they are not to be understood as involving substantial empirical elements, and we shall not attempt such an exposition here. Instead, we shall adopt what seems to us a more natural and theoretically fertile approach, first laying out what is known from empirical work on the neurophysiology of motivation, then interpreting the neuroscience in psychological terms, and finally examining the consequences of the empirical work for those philosophical accounts we have just described.

To minimize the perils of reliance on cutting-edge scientific work, most of this section will deal in textbook neuroscience. Thus, while we remain aware that neuroscience is as vulnerable to revolution as any science, we also remain moderately confident that the fundamentals of the empirical picture we sketch will remain substantially intact in the future. Our default source for textbook neuroscience is a very standard textbook: Kandel, Schwartz, and Jessell (2000); neuroscientific claims with references not otherwise cited are drawn from this work.

Moral motivation must connect in the right way to voluntary action (or inaction), for no morally worthy action is performed involuntarily. Thus we focus on the neural realization of voluntary movement. The basic fact with which we begin is that, as complex as the brain is, all activity in the brain that eventuates in voluntary movement must eventually stimulate the spinal cord, and to do so must stimulate the parts of the brain that have exclusive control over the spinal cord: the motor cortex and pre-motor cortical areas.[11] Moreover, because the pre-motor cortical areas have control over the motor cortex (except for some minor reflexes), any activity in the brain that eventuates in voluntary behavior must eventually stimulate pre-motor cortex. The pre-motor cortex will thus be the first focus of our interest. (Throughout this section, it will be helpful to refer to Figure 3.1.)

The pre-motor cortex is divided into numerous sub-regions that have control over different sub-regions of the motor cortex, and thus control over different spinal neurons, and thus ultimately control over different possible bodily movements. This control can be thought of as the pre-motor cortex being designed like the keyboards of an organ, with each region capable of

---

[11] We include the cranial motor neurons with the spinal cord for our exegetical purposes.

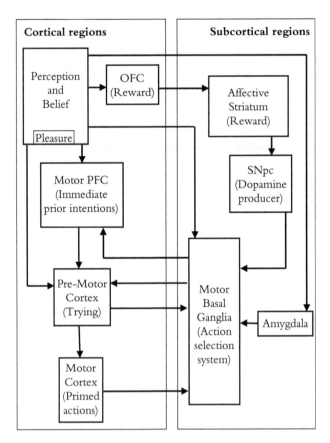

Figure 3.1.

playing "notes" of simple movements and "chords" of slightly more complex movements. Many neuroscientists working on motor and pre-motor cortex write of the different regions of pre-motor cortex as having the ability to issue various motor "commands": commands to the body to move this way or that, for various possible movements (e.g. Jeannerod, 1997). Thus, activity in one part of the pre-motor cortex can cause the utterance of a syllable, while activity in another part can cause a strumming movement, activity in another part can cause the opening of a hand, and so on. Because these possible movements are fairly simple in character, the pre-motor cortex needs to be under higher control if complex actions are to be performed.

What, then, controls the pre-motor cortex? It turns out that almost every part of the brain contributes to such control. There is no uniquely behavioral higher-level control system; instead, a whole host of factors simultaneously bears down upon the pre-motor cortex. These factors can usefully be divided into two categories based on their origins: cortical and sub-cortical.

Cortical inputs to the pre-motor cortex come from perceptual structures in the brain and from higher-level cognitive structures. Perceptual input can be quite simple (input carrying information about touch to the pad of one finger, for instance) or quite complex (input carrying information about whether or not one is looking at something that looks like one's father, for example). Higher-level cognitive structures can have features as complex and diverse as that vague label "higher-level" suggests. For instance, higher-level structures in the brain include those responsible for precisely guiding reaching and grasping movements based on visual, somatic, and proprioceptive inputs. Although this turns out to be a very complex computational task, requiring quite a large region of cortex, it is also not the sort of thing that philosophers are likely to think of as "higher-level," and it will not be the focus of our attention here.[12] More stereotypically higher-level structures in the brain include those responsible for grasping the syntax of sentences one reads, those responsible for grasping the social significance of situations, structures capable of holding motor commands at the ready until some pre-set condition is met, and so on. Neuroscience does not have fully detailed accounts of how the brain realizes complex moral beliefs, moral deliberations, one's principles of action, values, or choices. Nonetheless, if these things are real (as we have no reason to doubt), then they are realized in the higher-level structures of the cortex.[13] And all of these structures, when active, send output to the pre-motor cortex.

Sub-cortical input to the pre-motor cortex comes largely from the motor output structures of the basal ganglia, in the form of global suppression of all activation in the pre-motor cortex, and selective release of that suppression that permits the production of action. Think of the pre-motor cortex as being full of young schoolchildren. Stimulated by cortical centers of perception and higher-level cognition, some of the schoolchildren agitate for doing one thing (producing one movement), others of the schoolchildren agitate for another (producing another movement), and so on. Without further guidance, chaos is the result. Sub-cortical input from the motor basal ganglia prevents this chaos; it is like a teacher, quieting all the children except for a few, who are allowed to "do as they wish." That is, the subcortical input literally blocks

---

[12] See Jeannerod (1997) for more on this sort of input to action production.

[13] Things get complicated if you are a neosentimentalist. If, like Gibbard (1990), you hold that moral beliefs are endorsements of norms for certain emotions, then moral belief will not be realized entirely in higher cortical structures, but rather by a relationship between these structures and conative regions of the brain.

the production of many possible motor commands, but selectively allows certain possible motor commands to go ahead and be turned into bodily movements.

On what basis do the motor basal ganglia selectively release actions? The answer is that four sources of influence combine. First, all the cortical regions that send input to the pre-motor cortex also send input to the motor basal ganglia. Second, the active portions of motor and pre-motor cortex send signals down to the motor basal ganglia. Third, there is input from the brain's reward system. And fourth, there is the internal organization of the motor basal ganglia themselves.

The first source of influence over action selection is simply perception and cognition. There is nothing too surprising here. Obviously, actions cannot be selected unless information about what is going on in the world is provided to the action selection system.

The second source of influence is a little more interesting. Why should active parts of motor and pre-motor cortex send signals down to the brain's action selection system? The answer seems to be that the brain's action selection system responds differentially based upon information about what actions it has released, and what actions are more or less prepared to be performed (what motor commands are even partly activated) in order to select new appropriate actions. Seen in this light, this input is no more surprising than input from perception and cognition.

The third source of influence is input from the brain's reward system. The reward system is identified as such by neuroscientists because it possesses a number of properties: it is selectively activated by what are, intuitively, rewards (food, cooperation from partners in a game of prisoner's dilemma, and so on [see, e.g., Stellar and Stellar, 1985; Rilling et al., 2004]), its signaling properties carry exactly the information required of a reward signal by the mathematical theory of reward learning (Montague, Dayan, & Sejnowski, 1996), it is responsible for reward-based learning but not for other forms of learning (Packard & Knowlton, 2002), its activity causes pleasure (Kandel, Schwartz, & Jessell, 2000), and if allowed to electrically stimulate it, rats have been known to do so to the exclusion of all other activities (Stellar & Stellar, 1985). Because it has these features, we are inclined to follow the scientists in speaking of this system as the "reward system." (There is a natural tendency to think of the reward system as a pleasure-causing system. The reader should suspend this tendency, however; we shall return to the topic below.)

The reward system influences action selection on a moment-to-moment basis. The reward system has a baseline level of activity, but it can increase or reduce its activity. So long as activity is within a biologically normal range, actions can be produced regardless of activity level, but changes in activity level change the likelihood of different actions being performed. Positive reward information in the form of dopamine appears to increase the likelihood of actions being produced in general, and to play an important role in selecting which action is produced in particular (Mink, 1996).

There are two main influences upon reward signals. There are connections from select perceptual and higher cognitive representational capacities that make certain contents into rewards (that I get money, or food, for instance), and other possible contents into punishments (that I get pinched, or that I smell rotting meat, for instance). Representations of the contents exist in perceptual and higher cognitive centers, and send signals forward via the ventromedial portions of prefrontal cortex down to the reward system or to the (hypothesized, but not yet clearly demonstrated) punishment system (Schultz, Tremblay, & Hollerman, 2000). And then there is input to the reward system from the amygdala, a well-known structure that is responsible for many of the brain's strong emotional responses. Its best-studied function is the production of classical fear conditioning, but it is known to be involved in anger and other emotions as well. In the case of fear conditioning, it is the amygdala that learns the association between a previously neutral stimulus (such as the presence of a bee) and an aversive stimulus (being stung), so that when one encounters the previously neutral stimulus again in the future, one's heart rate rises, one sweats, one's stomach churns and tightens, one feels displeasure, and one becomes motivated to avoid the stimulus: that is, one is subject to the familiar syndrome of fear.

Finally, the fourth influence upon the selection of action by the motor basal ganglia is the internal structure of the motor basal ganglia themselves. This internal structure is the locus of our habits and related behavioral inclinations. Scientific research on habit learning and habit retention in human and non-human animals has shown that the internal structure of the basal ganglia is where our unconscious behavioral habits get stored, while consciously retrievable memory (for instance) is localized elsewhere (Knowlton, Mangles, & Squire, 1996; Packard & Knowlton, 2002).

4. Initial Implications of Neurophysiology

Perhaps the above neuroscience has been taxing for the reader. This material is certainly unfamiliar to many moral philosophers, and indeed to many philosophers of any stripe, and as a result it can be pretty tough going. In this section, we hope to repay the reader's patience by interpreting some of the neuroscientific story in terms that make its philosophical significance more apparent.

Implications for Instrumentalism

Consider first what the instrumentalist might make of the neuroscience. The instrumentalist needs there to be intrinsic desires realized somewhere in the neural architecture. But where? The brain's reward system makes an excellent candidate, as has been argued by a pair of philosophers (Morillo, 1990; Schroeder, 2004). When one desires that P intrinsically, one has a representation that P (the content of the desire); by having the desire one both tends to become motivated to bring it about that P and tends to feel pleasure at the prospect of P, or if it comes to be the case that P. The only structure poised to play all of these roles in the brain is the reward system. The reward system also begins with a representation that P (more carefully, a capacity to represent that P), and when triggered (when the representation is occurrent), the reward signals that are caused tend to cause motivational states and to cause pleasure.[14] And further, no other system in the brain could plausibly represent the contents of desires while also causing both motivational states and pleasure. The instrumentalist, then, should hold that intrinsic desires are realized by the reward system.

The instrumentalist holds that intrinsic desires combine with beliefs: beliefs about what actions would be instrumental to satisfying intrinsic desires (or would realize the satisfaction of intrinsic desires). Where will these beliefs be realized? Presumably, in the higher cognitive centers of the brain, for what is a belief if not a higher cognitive state? So the instrumentalist hopes to find brain structures by which the reward system (intrinsic desire) can interact with certain higher cognitions (beliefs about instrumental actions). Fortunately for the instrumentalist, such a structure exists: it is the motor basal ganglia. In the motor basal ganglia, information from higher cognitive centers combines with reward information, and also with information from perception and from current motor commands. Thus the instrumentalist should tentatively accept that the beliefs relevant to motivation are found in higher cognitive centers, for if they are, then they are capable of playing something much like the role he requires, and no other candidates present themselves.

---

[14] Morillo (1990) holds that the reward signal realizes pleasure, rather than causing it. But work published since 1990, much of it summarized in Berridge & Robinson (1998) and Berridge (1999), suggests that the reward signal is rather a crucial normal cause of pleasure.

Furthermore, the instrumentalist holds that intrinsic desires, when combined with relevant beliefs, produce motivational states. Once again, he can be happy with the neuroscience. Intrinsic desires (realized by the reward system) combine with beliefs (in higher cognitive centers) to produce activity in the motor basal ganglia that releases motor commands and ultimately, if all is working normally, produces behavior. So long as the instrumentalist is willing to say that motivation is realized by either activity in the motor basal ganglia, or by activity in its immediate downstream structures, pre-motor or motor cortex, then his picture would seem to be realized very much as he imagined it would be.[15] And there seems to be no good reason for the instrumentalist to deny that motivation is realized in one or more of these structures. These structures have the properties mentioned in Section 1 above: they have occurrent states that are causally real, distinct from intrinsic desires and beliefs, and necessary for the production of voluntary action under normal conditions.

Still, a little more than this is needed. These states of the motor basal ganglia and pre-motor and motor cortex should also have the right contents. Suppose Jesse wants to raise her hand. Activity in the motor basal ganglia will release the appropriate motor program for raising her hand, and so cause her hand to rise. In such a scenario, it would seem reasonable to say both that Jesse was motivated to raise her hand and that the content of the motor basal ganglia state that initiated her hand raising (or the state of her pre-motor cortex that was also crucial to her hand raising, or both) was that she raise her hand. But not every case will go as smoothly. If Jesse has a desire to look good for the party, we might be similarly tempted to say that Jesse is therefore motivated to look good for the party. However, as we have discussed, commands issued by the motor cortex and pre-motor cortex are commands for fairly specific bodily movements or otherwise very simple actions, and looking good for the party is not a simple movement or action. What should the instrumentalist say? We suggest that there is no need to throw out his picture. He can maintain, first, that Jesse is also motivated to thrust her left arm into the sleeve of the sweater she is putting on, motivated because she desires to look good and believes that getting her arm into the sweater will be instrumental to that. This very elemental motivation is one that has a content that can credibly be attributed to motor or pre-motor cortex, or to the motor basal ganglia, for it is the sort of content that is reliably made true by the activity of such structures. Second, the instrumentalist can maintain that any other motivation to bring it about

---

[15] Except insofar as the instrumentalist maintains that instrumental motivation is the only form of moral motivation; in the next section, we address the extent to which the scientific evidence rules out certain views of this sort.

that Q attributable to Jesse on the basis of her intrinsic desire to look good for the party—such as a motivation to wear interestingly contrasting colors—is simply a recognition of the fact that Jesse believes that bringing it about that Q would be instrumental to her intrinsic desire (or a realizer of it) and that Jesse's belief in this instrumentality is in the process of guiding her basic motivations: motivations to thrust this arm into this sleeve, to grasp that pair of pants and this boot, and so on.

Or, the instrumentalist can follow Davidson (1980: ch. 1) in holding that because actions are always "actions under a description," it is correct to maintain that among the proper descriptions of the content of motivational states is the description of their goal, or of the content of the desires that cause them. Thus, although a particular brain state might command for a thrust of an arm, this command might equally be described, in context, as an attempt at "putting on an appealing sweater," and under this description make sense as the motivation to put on an appealing sweater. Whichever route the instrumentalist prefers, it seems that there is a way for the instrumentalist to treat the brain structures that are the immediate causes of bodily movement as the realizers of instrumentalist motivation, which should be just what he wants.

We have so far assumed that what we would ordinarily think of as a motivational state exists either in the motor basal ganglia, or downstream of the motor basal ganglia, in the pre-motor cortex (which seems to realize immediate intentions to act). This assumption is required in order for beliefs and desires to be possible causes of motivation, as the instrumentalist holds: after all, these are the structures that produce actions that are "downstream," so to speak, from association cortex, which realizes belief, and from the reward system, which realizes desire. Can this assumption be defended?

Evidence suggests that localized lesions to parts of the basal ganglia result in the elimination of motivation, both motor and intellectual, in the absence of intellectual impairment. Though imperfect, this is certainly some evidence that we are localizing motivation in the right place. Consider one case of localized bilateral damage to the head of the caudate nucleus (part of the motor basal ganglia). A case report relates:

On admission, [the patient] was clearly hypokinetic with decreased spontaneous movements, facial amimia and Parkinson-like gait. Neurological examination was otherwise normal, except for a moderate limb stiffness. EEG showed mild nonspecific diffuse slowing and CT scan was interpreted as normal for the patient's age. His general behavior was characterized by a dramatic decrease in spontaneous activity. Totally abulic, he made no plans, showed no evidence of needs, will, or desires. He showed obvious lack of concern about relatives' as well as his own condition. When questioned about his mood, he reported no sadness or anxiety. Also noteworthy were a loss of appetite (he never asked for food, even if left more than 24 hours without eating) and food preferences (he would eat with the same apparent satisfaction dishes he did or did not like before). Finally, on every instance he was questioned about the content of his mind, he reported a striking absence of thoughts or spontaneous mental activity. Contrasting with these massive behavioral changes, purely cognitive functions seemed relatively spared.   (Habib, 2004: 511)

In many cases it is difficult to differentiate between motor impairment and motivational impairment. However, this patient with damage to the caudate nucleus of the basal ganglia provides reason to think that severe damage to motor basal ganglia results in a thoroughgoing motivational deficit, encompassing both motivation to act and to think.

Similar profiles have been described in cases of discrete lesions of the globus pallidus, another component of the motor basal ganglia (Strub, 1989; Levy & Dubois, 2006; Vijayaraghavan et al., 2008). Patients with lesions in these regions appear to lack desire and motivation. These case reports are reminiscent of cases of akinetic mutism, in which patients have preserved motor and verbal abilities, but lose the motivation to act in any way. Akinetic mutism is usually caused by bilateral lesions to portions of pre-motor cortex, a target of the output of the motor basal ganglia, but also results from damage to parts of the motor basal ganglia and, more rarely, from lesions to other parts of the fronto-striatal circuit we are considering. All this seems to show fairly clearly that ordinary motivation is massively dependent on the motor basal ganglia.

Implications for Cognitivism

Consider next what the cognitivist might make of the neuroscientific picture. It might seem bleak for her, since the instrumentalist seems to have been given everything he wants. But this impression would be premature, for the cognitivist also has reason to be happy with the neuroscientific picture.

The cognitivist needs for beliefs to have the power to produce motivational states independently of antecedent desires. Given what was just said about motivation, it then seems that the cognitivist needs her beliefs, realized in higher cognitive centers, to directly influence motivational states, realized in the basal ganglia or in the pre-motor or motor cortex. But this is indeed possible. Although the instrumentalist took comfort from the knowledge that intrinsic desires, in the form of reward signals, contribute to motivation, the cognitivist can also take comfort from the knowledge that this contribution made by intrinsic desire is not the only contribution to motivational systems.

In fact, simply looking at Figure 3.1, it is evident that there are direct anatomical connections between the neural realization of higher cognitions and motivational systems, connections that might conceivably by pass the influences of desires. Because of this, the cognitivist and the instrumentalist ought to be ready to agree on the interpretation of the neurophysiology, and simply disagree over how moral action production will proceed in human beings (which is, after all, an empirical question). While the instrumentalist will bet on the pervasive influence of intrinsic desires, the cognitivist will predict that this ancient system, shared with rats and other animals, will by and large be suppressed in human beings in favor of the power of reason, at least in cases of morally motivated behavior. The details of the neural wiring so far canvassed do not decide in favor of either position all on their own.

Implications for Sentimentalism

Consider next the sentimentalist. Emotions are at the center of our sentimentalist's picture of motivation, rather than desires. But there is room in our neuroscientific picture for this, because the reward system gets inputs from brain regions making up the limbic system, thought to be critical neural structures for emotion. For instance, the amygdala receives input from perceptual and cognitive centers, and it can produce a diverse assortment of outputs: it can produce the bodily changes associated with strong emotions (changes in heart rate, breathing, vasoconstriction, digestion, and so on), it can produce bodily changes that are hard to consciously perceive (pupil dilation, galvanic skin response), it influences characteristic emotional facial expressions, it influences felt pleasure and displeasure, and it sends output to the reward system, influencing the release of dopamine (and hence—it would seem—influencing desire).[16] The role of the amygdala in fear has been especially well studied, but it seems to play an important role in other emotions involving fairly consistent patterns of bodily changes, emotions such as anger, disgust, joy, and others. This simple picture will need to be augmented, for it is recognized that a number of brain regions contribute differentially to the various emotions. Some philosophers have been ready to localize certain emotions to the activity of the brain regions themselves (Griffiths, 1997), while others have preferred to identify emotions, following William James, with the feelings of bodily changes that are typically brought about by the amygdala and other brain regions (Prinz, 2004). The sentimentalist might prefer the former account, however, since activity in the limbic system has more direct influence over reward signals, and

---

[16] Kandel et al. (2000), ch. 50.

so behavior, than sensory perceptions of changes in bodily states seem to have. Influence from sensory perceptions of changes in bodily states would seem to influence behavior primarily through connections between such perceptions and the reward system, and so be of a piece with influences on behavior that are central to the instrumentalist's account. To retain a truly distinctive account, our sort of sentimentalist treats the limbic system, especially the amygdala, as central to the emotions.

Implications for Personalism

Consider finally the personalist. Again, there is room for optimism on the personalist's part. Like the instrumentalist and cognitivist, the personalist has a particular idea of what sorts of cognitive inputs drive morally worthy motivation. But once again, because higher cognitive centers in the brain are diverse, there is no reason to doubt that the personalist can find what is needed in this domain. Implicit knowledge of the good, explicit knowledge of heuristics, perceptually driven judgments of the differences between apparently similar situations—all of these can be expected to be realized in perceptual and higher cognitive centers, and all of them can be expected to feed into motivational systems.

The personalist holds that moral perceptions and thoughts combine with morally decent desires and emotions to create moral motivation only in the presence of appropriate habits: that is, only when one has a good character. The personalist will thus be pleased that there is a good candidate for the neural realization of behavioral habits that is poised to take input from perception, thought, desire, and emotion, and deliver motivation as output. This is all possible because the internal structures of the motor basal ganglia are the best candidate realizers for such habits—as discussed in the previous section—and the motor basal ganglia take input from perception and cognition (perceptual and higher cognitive centers), and from emotions (e.g from the amygdala, via the reward signal). On the basis of input plus internal structure, the motor basal ganglia send signals causing the release of motor commands, and these processes constitute motivation. Hence the personalist can for the moment rest content in the knowledge that the brain realizes a system for producing motivation very much in keeping with personalist thinking, with every influence identified by the personalist coming together in action. As things stand, the personalist is in a reasonable position to make an empirical bet with the instrumentalist, cognitivist, and sentimentalist that the story of paradigmatic morally worthy actions will favor the totality of structures central to the personalist story and not the proper subsets of these structures that are held to be uniquely important by the other stories.

5. Some Pressing Questions

At this point, the groundwork has been laid for asking and answering some pressing questions. We shall take up seven: (1) Does neuroscience really bear on the truth of theories of moral motivation? (2) What problems does neuroscience pose for the instrumentalist? (3) What problems does neuroscience pose for the cognitivist? (4) What problems does neuroscience pose for the sentimentalist? (5) What problems does neuroscience pose for the personalist? (6) What does neuroscience reveal about weakness of will? and (7) What does neuroscience reveal about altruism?

Does Neuroscience Bear on the Truth of Theories of Moral Motivation?

We think so. Any theory of moral motivation should include a theory of how moral motivation is instantiated—or at least approximated—in human beings, or provide a compelling argument as to why a theory of moral motivation need not undertake this burden. We know of no such argument, so we shall continue to assume that such theories need to provide an account of psychological phenomena such as moral perceptions, moral beliefs, instrumental beliefs, moral desires, instrumental desires, intentions, moral emotions, and habits. Any plausible theory of moral motivation will thus have to be consistent with what we know about such things as they are instantiated in human beings, and neuroscience has something to say about this.

It might be thought that neuroscience is incapable of imposing significant constraints on moral theorizing, because it is always open to the philosopher to interpret brain activity as she likes. If the instrumentalist sees the motor basal ganglia as combining beliefs and desires, the cognitivist can always interpret it as combining non-moral beliefs and moral beliefs, it might be said. But whatever the merits of this particular idea, we disagree with the claim that there is no limit to such interpretative strategies. This is because philosophical theories of the mental states involved in moral motivation are theories that include causal claims.

Consider pleasure. There are limits to where a reasonable interpretation can localize pleasure in the brain, given the facts about what sorts of damage to the brain provoke and what sorts impede pleasure, given the facts about brain stimulation and pleasure, and so on. Suppose that, for these reasons, one has tentatively localized pleasure to structure P. And now suppose that one has causal claims about desire that can be realized in the brain only by structure D. The question now arises: is structure D a structure that is causally connected to structure P, in a way that supports the observation that desires (when satisfied) are normal causes of pleasure? If it is, then the idea that D realizes desires and P realizes pleasure is consistent, and in fact somewhat confirmed. But if it is not, then something has gone wrong: either P does not realize pleasure, or D does not realize desire, or we were wrong in thinking that desire satisfaction is a common cause of pleasure. If the localization of P is well supported, but the grounds on which D was identified as the realizer of desires are highly contested, then there is going to be good reason to think that the mistake was with identifying D as the realizer of desires.

Of course, if one is absolutely determined to hold on to the idea that D realizes at least some desires, then one can always do so. Perhaps D realizes desires that play all the functional roles of immediate intentions to act, and none of the standard functional roles of desires that differ from those of immediate intentions to act, but nonetheless realizes desires all the same, a theorist might hold. Well, it's always a possibility! But of course this will look like special pleading to most philosophers. And the fact that the interpretation of the brain is as open to special pleading as any other kind of interpretation is no reason to think that there is no constraint on theorizing that comes from neuroscience.

For these sorts of reasons, we are convinced that there are important conclusions to draw from the neuroscience described earlier. We now turn to drawing some of them.

What Problems does Neuroscience pose for the Instrumentalist?

The neuroscience already described seems to make things easy for the instru-mentalist, as one of us has suggested (Schroeder, 2004: ch. 5). Candidate belief structures send output to the same place as candidate desire structures, these converging streams of information then generate candidate immediate intentions to act, and these lead to bodily movement. What more could the instrumentalist want?

One lurking problem for the instrumentalist is the incompleteness of this account. There are more influences on the production of action than recognized by the instrumentalist, and this might prove troublesome. For instance, the intrinsic connections of the motor basal ganglia are important to the production of movement, and one reasonable way to interpret these connections is as realizing habits, according to the research cited earlier. If correct, then it would seem to follow that no action is ever taken entirely independently of one's habits. Similarly, there seem to be influences upon the motor basal ganglia that stem from the amygdala, a candidate for the realizer of certain emotions. If this is correct, then it would seem to follow that actions produced when one is subject to such emotions are not produced independently of such emotions.

What should the instrumentalist make of all this? The instrumentalist might hold that these constant (in the case of habits) or sporadic (in the case of emotions) causal contributors to moral motivation make no contribution to the moral worth of moral motivation. If so, then they can be safely ignored, as much as the details of the neurotransmitters involved can be safely ignored. Pursuing this line of thought, the instrumentalist might hold that motivation that makes one morally worthy is simply moral motivation that stems from a desire to do what is right and a belief that a certain action A is necessary to doing what is right.[17] If this motivation also happens to rely on a weak or strong habit of doing what one takes to be necessary to doing what is right, that makes no difference—positive or negative—to the moral worth of any instance of moral motivation. Likewise, the instrumentalist might hold that a particular instance of moral motivation is neither impugned nor improved by being caused in part by activity in the amygdala realizing stereotypical anger. All that matters, the instrumentalist might hold, is that the right belief and the right desire are at least a part of the cause of the motivation in question.

The instrumentalist might, however, be made queasy by the facts that have come to light about how many different factors are at work in the production of moral motivation. For instance, the idea that habit always plays some role in the production of moral motivation might be in tension with another view she might hold, that moral motivation is only fully worthy when it follows *exclusively* from the right beliefs and desires. This sort of thought might come from thinking about cases of mixed motives: a person who helps a mother struggling with a toddler, a bicycle, and a bag of groceries just because of believing it is the right thing to do and wanting to do the right thing seems like a case of fully worthy moral motivation, whereas a person who is similarly motivated but also partly motivated by wanting to help pretty young women and believing the mother in question to be pretty and young seems rather less fully worthy. If being moved partly by habits is like being moved partly by morally irrelevant desires, then there is a threat in the neuroscientific data that no action will ever be fully morally worthy, because every action is performed partly out of habit (specifically, the habit of doing what seems required to do what is right). And it might not appeal to the instrumentalist to hold this conclusion, if it conflicts with other ideas the instrumentalist had at the outset about moral worth.[18]

---

[17] As noted earlier, there is room for many more subtle specific details about the contents of the desire(s) and belief(s) in question. We continue to set these details aside for ease of exposition.

[18] One theory of moral worth that might be congenial to the instrumentalist in general, but that might hold moral worth to be diminished insofar as an action expresses a mere habit, is found in Arpaly

For at least these reasons, it is not obvious that the instrumentalist should be happy with the details of the neuroscience of moral motivation. But perhaps the instrumentalist need have no worries at all—it seems to depend as much on the details of the particular instrumentalist view as on the neuroscience.

What Problems does Neuroscience pose for the Cognitivist?

Of our four caricature theorists, it is obviously our cognitivist who is most likely to have difficulties accommodating the neuroscientific evidence. Although it was pointed out earlier that the theoretical possibility exists that moral cognition can lead directly to moral motivation independently of the reward system (and so independently of desire), this theoretical possibility proves to be problematic upon closer inspection.

We begin with evidence from Parkinson disease. As will be familiar to many, Parkinson disease is a disorder that results in a number of effects, including tremor, difficulty in initiating movement, and (if taken to its limit) total paralysis. Parkinson disease is caused by the death of the dopamine-producing cells of the substantia nigra pars compacta (the SNpc in Figure 3.1), the very cells that make up the reward system's output to the motor basal ganglia. Thus, on the interpretation of the reward system advocated earlier, Parkinson disease is a disorder in which intrinsic desires slowly lose their capacity to causally influence motivation. As it turns out, Parkinson disease impairs or prevents action regardless of whether the action is morally worthy or not, regardless of whether it is intuitively desired or intuitively done out of duty, regardless of whether the individual trying to act gives a law to herself. Thus Parkinson disease appears to show that intrinsic desires are necessary to the production of motivation in normal human beings, and this would seem to put serious pressure on the cognitivist's position.

The cognitivist might allow that intrinsic desires must exist in order for motivation to be possible, but hold that intrinsic desires normally play no significant role in producing motivation. After all, Parkinson disease shows that intrinsic desires are necessary for motivation, but it does not clearly reveal the role played by intrinsic desires in producing motivation when the desires exist. If sustainable, this would be just a minor concession, and so it is well worth investigating.

What might motivation of the cognitivist's sort look like, if desires play no substantive role in it? It was suggested in the previous section that it might

(2003). Although Arpaly is not focused on the moral significance of habits, this sort of conclusion seems in keeping with her theory of moral worth, since she holds that moral praiseworthiness is proportionate (all else being equal) to the degree to which the act expresses a desire for what is morally good.

look like motivation that stems directly from activity in the higher cognitive centers—like motivation that stems from choosing a law for one's action, in other words. And it turns out that motivation derived from higher cognitive centers independently of desire is possible—but also that the only known model of it is pathological. It is the sort of motivation found in Tourette syndrome.

Tourette syndrome is a disorder characterized by tics: eye blinks, shoulder jerks, barks, obscenities, profanities, and so on. Something like 70–90% of sufferers report that they often voluntarily produce their tics, because the effort of not ticcing is unpleasant and often doomed to failure in any case. But a typical sufferer from Tourette syndrome will also report that tics are quite capable of forcing themselves out regardless of how fiercely they are resisted. Tourette syndrome appears to be caused by a dysfunction in the motor basal ganglia, in which the motor basal ganglia inhibit most motor commands initiated by perceptual and higher cognitive centers, but not quite all. Some motor commands initiated by perceptual or higher cognitive centers get through in spite of the inhibition, and in spite of the fact that reward signals (intrinsic desires) have not released these inhibitions. A tic is the result (Schroeder, 2005). Thus direct causation of motivation by higher cognition via this pathway, quite independently of desire, is the sort of thing that results in a Tourettic tic, but a Tourettic tic is anything but the paradigm of morally worthy action. This seems a very unpromising parallel to be drawn for a cognitivist picture of motivation.

There are other ways to investigate the biological plausibility of our cognitivist's position as well. If reason alone were responsible for moral motivation, one would expect that injuries that spare reason would also spare moral motivation, but there are clinical case studies that suggest otherwise. Damage to the ventromedial (VM) region of prefrontal cortex (located in the OFC in Figure 3.1), a form of brain damage studied extensively by Damasio and colleagues (see, e.g., Damasio, 1994), impairs cognitive input to the reward system, and so alters the output of the reward system to the motor basal ganglia. Such damage seems to render subjects incapable of acting on their better judgments in certain cases—a finding that we think ought to capture the imagination of any moral psychologist.

In a well-known non-moral experimental task, subjects with this sort of injury were asked to draw cards from any of four decks of cards. Each card was marked with a number indicating a number of dollars won or lost, and subjects were asked to draw as they liked from the four decks, attempting to maximize their winnings. Normal control subjects tended to draw at first from two of the decks, which quickly revealed themselves to have high-paying cards when drawn from. But those same decks also had high-costing cards in them, and normal subjects soon enough learned to stay away from these decks and shift to the other two decks, where returns were lower but penalties less punitive (Bechara et al., 1997). Subjects with VM prefrontal injuries—with injuries to structures that are crucial input to the reward system—started their play just as normal subjects did, but strongly tended not to switch to the safer decks, instead staying with the high-paying, high-costing decks until they ran out of money. Fascinatingly, these same subjects sometimes reported being aware of what the better strategy would be, but they nonetheless failed to follow it (Bechara et al., 2000).

This sort of finding should once again give our cognitivist pause, for it suggests that, at least in non-moral contexts, reason alone does not suffice to guide action independently of reward information; it is reasonable to speculate that reason may fail to produce motivation in moral cases as well. Damasio himself interprets these findings as specifically vindicating the role of felt emotional responses in decision-making, a more personalist than instrumentalist conclusion. However, the precise interpretation of the mechanism by which VM prefrontal cortical injury leads to its own peculiar effects is not yet well understood. We return to a discussion of these people with VM damage after exploring the consequences for the cognitivist thesis of another population of people with disorders of moral motivation: psychopaths.

Psychopaths are people who seem cognitively normal, but evince little remorse or guilt for morally wrong actions. Psychopaths are identified by scoring high on a standard psychopathy checklist (Hare, 1991), and seem to be deficient in two respects: (1) emotional dysfunction, and (2) antisocial behavior. Psychopaths seem able to comprehend social and moral rules, and they typically do not seem to have impaired reasoning abilities. (Recent studies suggest that limbic system damage is correlated with psychopathy, and this is consistent with the fact that psychopaths show diminished affective response to cues of suffering in others, but it does not suggest any particularly cognitive impairment [Kiehl, 2006; but see Maibom, 2005].)

As a population apparently capable of making moral judgments but not at all motivated by them, psychopaths present an obvious challenge to the cognitivist. However, research suggests that psychopaths' moral cognition is deficient in at least the following respect: they show a diminished capacity to distinguish moral from conventional violations (Blair, 1995, 1997). For instance, children with psychopathic tendencies are more likely to judge moral violations as authority-dependent (so the morality of hitting another child in a classroom will be held to depend on whether or not the teacher permits it, rather than held to be independent of such rules, as it is by normally developing children). This deficit has led some to argue that psychopaths have impaired moral concepts (Nichols, 2004: 113). Although they are able to say whether an action is right or wrong, permitted or prohibited, philosophers such as these suggest that psychopaths merely mouth the words, or make moral judgments in the "inverted commas" sense: judgments of what is *called* "moral" by others.

The ability of psychopaths to stand as counter-examples to cognitivism rests upon some argument to the effect that psychopaths really do make moral judgments. If psychopaths indeed lack moral concepts or moral knowledge, then their failure to act morally or to appear to lack motivation is no challenge to cognitivism, for it can plausibly be argued that to make moral judgments at all, one must have moral concepts and possess some modicum of moral knowledge (Kennett & Fine, 2007). However, if the ability to make the moral/conventional distinction is not required for moral concepts or moral knowledge, then psychopaths appear to be candidate counter-examples to our cognitivist (see, e.g., Kelly et al., 2007). Although some arguments have been offered to suggest that psychopaths have requisite abilities to make moral judgments (Roskies, 2007), these arguments remain indecisive. On our view, it remains unclear whether psychopaths are competent moral judges.

Many of the objections that have been raised against the psychopath as a challenge to internalism are moot when it comes to people who have sustained damage to their VM frontal cortex (see above). Subjects with VM damage exhibit a fascinating pattern of behavioral deficits often referred to as "acquired sociopathy." Cognitive tests indicate that VM patients have no deficits in reasoning, nor is their knowledge of the world affected by their injury. In particular, on a variety of measures, the moral reasoning of VM patients is unimpaired: they reason at a normal level on Kohlberg's moral reasoning scale (Saver & Damasio, 1991), and make normal moral judgments in a variety of hypothetical scenarios (Koenigs et al., 2007).[19] Nonetheless, case reports suggest that people who had been normal and responsible adults prior to their injury exhibit dramatic changes in their manners and their actions, and among their

---

[19] Koenigs et al. demonstrate that the moral judgments of patients with acquired sociopathy do not exhibit the profile of normals across the board. They are statistically different, in that in situations that Greene et al. (2001, 2004) categorizes as "up close and personal," VM patients make judgments that are more utilitarian than emotionally driven. This result comports with their neurological profile. Nonetheless, we think that this minor difference in moral reasoning does not preclude their inclusion as moral reasoners for two reasons. First, a proportion of normals (and in particular, some moral philosophers!) make moral judgments with this pattern; second, despite the difference in pattern, there is no evidence that the content of their judgment is impaired, so there is no reason to think they are making judgments that don't qualify as moral. If they make moral judgments and are not motivated, our cognitivist is refuted.

deficits is a moral one. The following case study, of patient EVR, illustrates the deficits:

By age 35, in 1975, EVR was a successful professional, happily married, and the father of two. He led an impeccable social life, and was a role model to younger siblings. In that year, an orbitofrontal meningioma was diagnosed and, in order to achieve its successful surgical resection, a bilateral excision of orbital and lower mesial cortices was necessary. EVR's basic intelligence and standard memory were not compromised by the ablation. His performances on standardized IQ and memory tests are uniformly in the superior range (97th–99th percentile). He passes all formal neuropsychological probes. Standing in sharp contrast to this pattern of neuropsychological test performance, EVR's social conduct was profoundly affected by his brain injury. Over a brief period of time, he entered disastrous business ventures (one of which led to predictable bankruptcy), and was divorced twice (the second marriage, which was to a prostitute, only lasted 6 months). He has been unable to hold any paying job since the time of the surgery, and his plans for future activity are defective.   (Damasio et al., 1990)

VM patients with damage late in life exhibit a number of deficits in navigating complex social demands. Although the case reports of these patients do not specifically examine their moral behavior, it has been suggested that among their deficits is a deficit in acting in accord with what they take to be right or best. Although VM patients apparently know what is right and wrong, they do not appear motivated to do what they apparently judge the right thing in a number of quotidian situations. These deficits do not appear to be specifically moral, but this does not impugn them as challenges to cognitivism, since the deficits appear—if anything—broader than those necessary to pose a serious threat to cognitivism. Recently, however, it has been argued that people exhibiting acquired sociopathy do not exhibit moral deficits at all, but that their deficits in non-moral aspects of life merely manifest occasionally in moral situations (Kennett & Fine, 2007). Resolution of this issue must await further studies on these patients, since the available literature does not resolve the question.[20]

Some insight into the role VM cortex plays in moral judgment and motivation can be gained from considering the effects of damage to VM cortex early in life. These people are more like psychopaths in their profile: they are violent and pursue their own ends without regard to others' welfare (Anderson et al., 1999). Therefore it seems that an intact VM cortex is necessary for acquisition but not retention of moral knowledge; the sociopathic behavior of these early damage patients is explained by the fact that they never acquire moral knowledge. Kennett and Fine (2007) have attempted to explain the

---

[20] Roskies (2007) suggests what data are needed to resolve the issue.

differences between the early damage and late damage cases in terms of retained moral motivation in cases in which moral knowledge is preserved: they argue that late damage patients are not violent because they are motivated by their moral judgments. However, alternative explanations of the modest moral infringements characteristic of late damage patients fit better with the psychological profile. Late damage VM patients do not show skin conductance responses (the small changes in the electrical conductivity of the skin caused by changes in sweating) to moral situations, whereas normal people do (Damasio, Tranel, & Damasio, 1990). This is due to the fact that the brain regions involved in making moral judgments are disconnected from regions involved in translating goals into action. In normal people there is a causal connection from regions associated with moral judgment to regions involved in desiring and executing action; this connection is disrupted with VM damage. Late damage patients' lack of violence is perhaps better explained by the absence in these people of immoral motivation and the operation of habit.

In general, the evidence accords with thinking of patients with VM damage as examples of a disconnection syndrome. Recall the picture of motivation sketched above. As we understand it, moral judgment happens in higher cortical regions, either in frontal areas or in areas that project to them. Motivation is due to reward-system-mediated activity being sent to basal ganglia and pre-motor areas. Associations between the cognitive moral judgments and the motivational system are mediated by connections from VM frontal cortex to the basal ganglia: fiber pathways from VM frontal cortex link the output of moral deliberation to the motivational system. The connection between VM cortex and motivation is thus a causal one, and causal connections are contingent. Damage to VM cortex would thus sever the link between the cognitive judgments and motivation, leaving intact the judgment and its content, but not causing motivation that might normally result. Such an effect would establish that moral judgment was not intrinsically or necessarily motivational, but that instead the link between judgment and motivation was contingent and defeasible (Roskies, 2006).

What Problems does Neuroscience pose for the Sentimentalist?

Evidence from psychology and neuroscience indicates that emotions are involved in normal moral behavior, and this is good news for the sentimentalist. Results from brain imaging suggest that at least some moral judgments involve operation of the emotional system (Greene et al., 2001, 2004; Moll et al., 2002). Studies of psychopaths also indicate that emotions play a role in moral behavior, since the moral emotions are blunted in psychopaths (Blair et al.,

1997; see also Blair et al., 2005). But what do these correlations suggest about causation? Are the moral emotions key causes of moral motivation, or are they typically by-products of moral beliefs and moral desires? Or are they something else entirely?

The primary regions of the brain identified as realizing motivation (the motor basal ganglia, pre-motor cortex, and motor cortex) are distinct from those brain structures, such as the amygdala, states of which have been most frequently identified with emotion. As indicated in Figure 3.1, there is input from the amygdala to the reward system and so (indirectly) to the motor basal ganglia, but it seems clear that the basal ganglia as influenced by the reward system can operate independently of the amygdala (a complete amygdalectomy does not prevent motivation, for instance). Upon a second look, then, it might seem as if the situation is just as dire for the sentimentalist as for the cognitivist.

One response available to the sentimentalist here is to claim that while motivation *simpliciter* might be intact in absence of emotions, *moral* motivation will be absent. Sentimentalists who hold that moral judgment depends on the emotions (e.g. Nichols, 2004) might defend sentimentalism about moral motivation by maintaining that moral motivation depends on moral judgment. Alternatively, the sentimentalist might maintain that motivation only counts as moral when it is generated by moral emotions. So if Jen lacks emotions but helps the homeless man, her motivation for doing so isn't properly moral. She can't be feeling compassion, for instance. Or guilt. Perhaps she is helping as a result of rational calculation about the benefits to her reputation. But a sentimentalist might say that this doesn't count as moral motivation. Although this move is available to some sentimentalists, it does require a substantial concession. One of the most important traditional Humean arguments for sentimentalism proceeds as follows: moral considerations motivate; only the passions motivate; therefore moral considerations motivate through the passions. The brain data undercut this traditional argument, for they suggest that motivation does not require emotions. Thus we can't conclude that sentimentalism is true from general considerations about the nature of motivation.

A much different sentimentalist response appeals to general considerations about the nature of the emotions. It is far from clear where one should localize the emotions in the brain. Much hangs on the nature of the emotions themselves. If emotions are, first and foremost, the immediate causes of the changes in heart rate, breathing, gut motility, and so on that we associate with powerful emotions, then emotions might be localized to the amygdala, or perhaps to a system made up of the amygdala, its immediate inputs from perception and cognition, and its immediate outputs to hormonal and visceral systems. On this way of thinking, the fact that massive damage to the amygdala does not seem to impair motivation greatly in general would seem to be a damaging blow to the thesis that moral emotions are crucial to moral motivation—unless there were some special evidence that, while self-protective motivation does not depend on fear, the motivation for restorative justice does depend upon guilt. Being aware of no such evidence, we conclude that prospects are not good for the sentimentalist who holds a purely amygdala-centered theory of the emotions. However, as noted, other limbic and paralimbic areas are also crucial for normal emotional function, and so it is doubtful that the emotions should be localized to the amygdala in the first place.[21]

Some philosophers hold that, rather than being the causes of distinctive bodily changes, emotions are our experiences of these changes (James, 1890; Prinz, 2004). If this is right, then the emotions are perceptual states. In particular, they are perceptions of changes in heart rate, breathing, gut motility, piloerection, and the various other bodily changes we associate with emotions. Should the sentimentalist embrace this view of the emotions as correct for the moral emotions in particular, then it would seem that the moral emotions do their work motivating us through connections from the right perceptual structures to the motor basal ganglia. But this would seem to revive some of the problems that the cognitivist faced. The cognitivist has difficulties explaining moral motivation in part because there appears to be no reasonable pathway from mere perception or cognition through to motivation independently of the reward system (and so, independently of desire). And just as this held for beliefs about rightness, so it would seem to hold for feelings of gut-wrenching guilt. As Figure 3.1 makes clear, there are no important structural differences between the connections that cognition enjoys to motivation and those perception enjoys.

There does seem to be something special about feelings of gut-wrenching guilt, however, that makes them more motivating than the mere belief that one has done wrong, and this is how very unpleasant it is to feel gut-wrenching guilt. As the literature on pain has amply demonstrated, however, the displeasure of a perception of one's body needs to be sharply distinguished from the perception of one's body itself (Dennett, 1978: ch. 11; Hardcastle, 1999). If the unpleasantness of gut-wrenching feelings of guilt is what is so motivating, then this is because displeasure itself is what is so motivating. Note, however, that this need not be inimical to the sentimentalist's view of things. The sentimentalist might hold that the moral emotions are what motivate

---

[21] There are compelling arguments to the effect that it is not possible to have a single, unified localization of the emotions (Griffiths, 1997).

morally worthy behavior, and hold that they do so by involving, as an essential constituent, pleasure or displeasure.

If this is the position of the sentimentalist, then it is unclear how successful the sentimentalist is in accommodating the neuroscientific facts. For it is unclear exactly how important a role pleasure and displeasure play in the production of behavior. Morillo (1990) argues that pleasure is realized by the activity of the reward system, and so pleasure is the immediate cause of much of normal motivation (and likewise, one would assume, for displeasure). But following Berridge (1999) and Schroeder (2004), we have treated pleasure as often *caused by* reward signals rather than identical to them or realized by them. In Figure 3.1, for example, pleasure and displeasure are treated as having the structural properties of perception and cognition, so far as connections to motivation are concerned. If this interpretation of the neuroscience is correct, then again it would seem that there are difficulties for the sentimentalist: if the causal connections of pleasure and displeasure are just those of any perceptual or cognitive state, then they will be subject to all of the problems facing the cognitivist. However, many philosophers hold that pleasure and displeasure have privileged connections to motivation, perhaps necessarily so. If they are correct, then the problems facing the sentimentalist might be less severe.

The position on the emotions that seems most likely to assist the sentimentalist is a form of cognitivism found in, for example, Green (1992), on which the core of any emotion is a combination of a belief and a desire regarding the object of the emotion. On this view, feeling guilty that P entails believing that one did P and desiring not to have done P, for instance. (This is only a necessary condition on guilt, on the view in question. Other factors are required to distinguish guilt from non-moral regret, sadness, etc.) If moral emotions are constituted in whole or in part by combinations of beliefs and desires, then they can produce motivation in just the way that beliefs and desires can produce motivation, and the sentimentalist is at least as well off as the instrumentalist.

What Problems does Neuroscience pose for the Personalist?

Our personalist might seem the best off of all the theorists we have considered, for our personalist holds that a complex combination of factors jointly produces moral motivation, and this might seem to fit the neuroscientific picture better than any more restricted view. Invoking both desires and emotions, the personalist would seem to have the virtues of the instrumentalist and the sentimentalist combined, while lacking the problems of the cognitivist (see, e.g., Casebeer, 2003).

Considering again the details of our personalist's view suggests two changes that might be appropriate, however. One is a form of liberalization. The other change is more conservative.

As we sketched the view, the personalist begins with perceptions and thoughts that might well be unsystematically linked to morality, and eventually reaches a moral belief. Perception of someone crying might lead to the thought that the same person is in distress, for instance. But until a specifically moral belief is formed—that the crying person should be comforted, for instance—no morally worthy action can begin. Is this restriction necessary? As Figure 3.1 suggests, there are dense connections between all of our perceptual and cognitive abilities and our motivational system, both directly and via the reward system. So it is certainly possible to see someone crying, for that perception to be desire frustrating, and so for someone to be moved to offer comfort—all without the intervention of a belief that comfort is what is morally appropriate. Should the personalist hold that this is not an appropriate route to moral motivation?

The issue is difficult. After all, it is not morally worthy to be moved by every tear one perceives—even every genuine tear. Sometimes it is wrong to offer comfort: perhaps it would have been wrong to offer comfort to those convicted at the Nuremberg trials, for instance. This suggests that being moved just by the perception of tears and a desire that others not cry is insufficient to be moved in the morally worthy way.

There are ways of getting more sophisticated without ever arriving at a belief that a certain course of action is morally right, however. For instance, it might be that all the factors perceived and believed in by the subject—all the factors that would justify the belief that a particular action is the morally right one in the context—bear down upon the motivational system, directly and through their connections to the reward system, so as to bring about the action that is, in fact, the right action. This holistic combination of causal influences appears very complex, but there is no reason to be found in Figure 3.1 to think that the motor basal ganglia cannot learn (through processes such as habit formation) to respond with the morally right output to input that *entails* what is morally right even though it does not *explicitly encode* what is morally right. We suggest that philosophers who think of themselves as allied to the personalist should consider keeping their ears open for information that confirms or disconfirms this possibility.

Turning now to the way in which the personalist might need a more conservative view than that sketched: the personalist holds that all three of desires, emotions, and habits are necessary to produce morally worthy motivation. But as we saw in discussing the sentimentalist, it is unclear that the emotions have a privileged role in action production that is distinct from the role accorded to desires. If this is borne out by future research, then the personalist should contract her list from three items to two: it might well be that morally worthy motivation requires only desires and habits as inputs, along with appropriate perceptions and beliefs. Because this was the central issue discussed in the previous section, we shall not belabor the point any further here.

Turning now from our four views of moral motivation, we finish by considering two further topics: weakness of the will and altruism.

How is Weakness of the Will Possible?

It is an old worry in philosophy that it is impossible to act voluntarily in a way that flouts one's considered judgment about the best thing to do. The worry goes as follows. If Andrea says that she thinks it best to skip dessert, but then plunges into the crème brulée, then either she didn't *really* think it best to skip dessert or her action wasn't voluntary. For it seems plausible that one acts voluntarily when and only when one acts from one's considered judgments. There is a voluminous literature that tries either to explain how akratic actions—actions contrary to one's best judgments about the best thing to do—are possible, or to show that the cases of apparent akratic action are only apparent, and that there are no real cases of akratic action.

Considered judgments are, of course, a product of higher cognitive processes, and such judgments are produced in cortical brain regions associated with perception and belief (so we suppose, at least, in the absence of evidence to the contrary). As we stressed earlier, the action selection system (i.e. the motor basal ganglia) is guided by higher cognitive processes, but it is also guided by other, subcortical, factors including the amygdala and the reward system (again, see Figure 3.1). It is worth noticing that the basal ganglia form a relatively ancient system that was presumably involved in action selection prior to the evolution of cortical areas capable of realizing complex deliberative processes. This suggests, first, that it is likely that action selection can sometimes completely bypass considered judgments (perhaps in the case of phobias). Second, it suggests that more primitive pathways are still operative in action selection in normal humans. These subcortical contributors sometimes carry the day, leading to action selection that differs from the action preferred by considered judgment.[22]

Now, somewhat less neutrally, map Andrea's consumption of the crème brulée onto this model. The worry about the possibility of akrasia is, to repeat,

---

[22] Related ideas are explored in depth in Stanovich (2004).

that either it was *not* Andrea's considered judgment to skip dessert or her eating of the crème brulée was not voluntary. To take the first disjunct, on our model there is an obvious way to preserve the claim that it *is* Andrea's considered judgment that it would be best to skip dessert. The higher cognitive processes that go into those judgments are in cortical regions, and we could, no doubt, find numerous signs that Andrea actually has the higher-cognitive judgment that she should skip dessert. Indeed, in light of our model, it strikes us that it would be rather desperate to deny that it is Andrea's considered judgment that it would be best to skip dessert.[23] Of course, there are also subcortical factors that strongly incline Andrea to eat the crème brulée. Sometimes these subcortical factors get integrated into the process of coming to a considered judgment. But it is also the case that the subcortical factors can influence action selection in the basal ganglia in ways that are not routed through cognitively oriented cortical regions. That is, the subcortical mechanisms make *direct* contributions to action selection, unmediated by considered judgments. In such cases it would be strange to identify those subcortical contributors as part of the considered judgment. Why should structures we share with many animals short on considered judgments count as constituting part of our considered judgments just because they move us?

The philosopher who is skeptical of akrasia might opt instead for the view that while Andrea did have the considered judgment that it is best to skip dessert, her consumption of the crème brulée was not *voluntary*. The issue here is more delicate, because the philosophical category of the *voluntary* is far from any neuroscientific category, but we will attempt to integrate the taxonomies. One conceivable way to exclude Andrea's dessert eating from the realm of the voluntary is to maintain that it is a necessary condition on voluntary action that the action is selected *because* it is one's considered judgment. That is, actions are voluntary only when the considered judgment carries the day in the basal ganglia. This would serve to exclude Andrea's dessert eating from the realm of the voluntary, but it is hard to see what the basis would be for such an exclusion. Appeal to folk practice would be no help, for the folk are quick to say that Andrea *chose* to eat the crème brulée and it is her own damn fault if her pants no longer fit!

We think that a more promising approach is to consider again the role of the basal ganglia. It strikes us as a plausible sufficient condition that when an action is selected from among other possible actions (represented in the pre-motor

---

[23] Here we are assuming that judgments about what it is best to do are genuine cognitive states, and not mere expressions of motivational states or complex combinations of these two things.

cortex or motor PFC) by the basal ganglia, then that action is voluntary. Recall from earlier in this section that Tourettic tics are bodily movements produced without the movement being promoted by the basal ganglia. This seems to show that promotion by the basal ganglia is a necessary condition for a movement being voluntary. But we think it is also sufficient, at least barring injury, disease, and the like.[24] For—turning again to our pre-human ancestors—it would seem that other animals are also able to perform voluntary behaviors, even in the absence of beliefs about courses of action being best. (Voluntary in what sense? At least in the senses that (i) these actions are not compelled (not compulsions, fixed action patterns, and the like) or produced by otherwise pathological processes, and (ii) these actions can be evaluated as more or less reasonable given the epistemic and conative standpoint of the animal. And this seems voluntary enough.) And again, actions performed with such spontaneity that there was never any time to consider whether or not the action was best (rapid-fire conversation perhaps best illustrates this phenomenon) are nonetheless performed in part through the action of the basal ganglia, and appear to be as voluntary as any action might be. If these considerations stand up, then Andrea's consumption of the crème brulée is voluntary. Several different actions were available in the motor cortices, and the basal ganglia selected eating the crème brulée from among them.

Thus akratic action can easily be accommodated on our model of motivation. The key fact is that action selection depends on contributions not just from our considered judgments, but also on less exalted psychological factors, like reward, dopamine, and emotions.

What does Neuroscience Reveal about Altruism?

Hedonism is perhaps the most prominent view that denies the existence of altruistic motivation. According to hedonism, all ultimate desires are desires to get pleasure for oneself and avoid one's own pain. If hedonism is true, then an individual's actions will always be ultimately motivated by narrow self-interest—the motivation to seek pleasure and avoid pain. Hence, if hedonism were true, there would be no ultimate desires for the welfare of others. If I am motivated to help a neighbor child with a skinned knee, this motivation ultimately gets traced back to my pursuit of pleasure and flight from pain.

---

[24] One empirical bet we are thus making is that obsessive-compulsive disorder and related disorders will prove to be like Tourette syndrome in that they generate behavior that is not released by the basal ganglia in the normal way we have described.

One of the more interesting implications suggested by the neuroscientific work is that hedonism is false. For as we argued in Section 4, it is plausible that intrinsic desires are realized by the reward system, and it is also plausible that the reward system is distinguishable from the structures that support pleasure and pain. A person can have an intrinsic desire to act in a certain way even in the absence of any pleasure (or pain) signal.

A number of studies have shown that there is significant overlap in the brain regions involved in experiencing pain, imagining pain, and perceiving pain in others (Singer et al., 2004). Since reward signals are involved in governing actions that lessen one's own pain, it is plausible that reward signals (to be distinguished from pleasure) may also be involved in lessening others' pain.

This is hardly the final word on whether altruism exists. For there are non-hedonistic versions of egoism (see Chapter 5 for further discussion). Furthermore, it might turn out that all of our other-regarding desires do derive from connections to pleasure and pain. Nonetheless, if the neuroscience helps to rule out hedonism as a universal account of desire, this will be an important result for the longstanding debate about altruistic motivation.

Summary

Motivation is a causally efficacious, occurrent mental state. An exploration of the neuroscience underlying motivation provides a structure from which to consider the question of what the neural states are that realize morally worthy motivational states. We have characterized four familiar philosophical views of what moral motivation consists in: the instrumentalist's, the cognitivist's, the sentimentalist's, and the personalist's. The instrumentalist's story of desire and belief leading to moral action fits well with the neuroscientific picture, and suggests that motivational states are to be identified with states of the motor basal ganglia or immediate "causally downstream" structures, such as pre-motor or motor cortex, that directly control bodily movement. The neuroscience raises difficulties for the cognitivist's story, since our moral behavior does not appear to be under the control of cognitive states alone, independently of desire. The sentimentalist's view is also under threat, because the emotional system, while closely linked to the system underlying voluntary action, will turn out to be nonetheless distinct from it unless emotions are themselves built in part from desires. The personalist's story, on the other hand, fares relatively well. At this point our understanding of the neuroscience is only partial, and each of the criticisms raised may be countered. However, our understanding of the neurobiological systems underlying complex social cognition are still in their infancy. We suggest that further attention to the actual structure and function of the systems underlying moral motivation and action could serve to constrain future theorizing about the structure of moral agency, as well as have an impact on discussions of other philosophically interesting phenomena, such as weakness of will and altruism.

References

Alston, William. 1967. "Motives and Motivation." In P. Edwards (ed.), *The Encyclopedia of Philosophy*. New York: Macmillan, 399–409.

Anderson, Steven, Bechara, Antoine, Damasio, Hanna, Tranel, Daniel, & Damasio, Antonio. 1999. "Impairment of social and moral behavior related to early damage in human prefrontal cortex." *Nature Neuroscience*, 2: 1032–1037.

Aristotle. 2000. *Nicomachean Ethics*. T. Irwin (trans.). Indianapolis, IN: Hackett.

Arpaly, Nomy. 2003. *Unprincipled Virtue: An inquiry into moral agency*. New York: Oxford University Press.

Bechara, A., Damasio, H., & Damasio, A. R. 2000 "Emotion, decision making and the orbitofrontal cortex." *Cerebral Cortex*, 10: 295–307.

Bechara, A., Damasio, H., Tranel, D., & Damasio, A. R. 1997. "Deciding Advantageously Before Knowing the Advantageous Strategy." *Science*, 275: 1293–1295.

Berridge, K. C. 1999. "Pleasure, pain, desire, and dread: hidden core processes of emotion." In D. Kahneman, E. Diener, & N. Schwarz (Eds.), *Well-Being: Foundations of Hedonic Psychology*. New York: Russell Sage Foundation, 527–559.

Berridge, K. C., & Robinson, T. E. 1998. "What is the role of dopamine in reward: hedonic impact, reward learning, or incentive salience?" *Brain Research Reviews*, 28: 309-369.

Blair, R. 1995. "A Cognitive Developmental Approach to Morality: Investigating the Psychopath," *Cognition*, 57: 1–29.

—— 1997. "Moral Reasoning and the Child with Psychopathic Tendencies," *Personality and Individual Differences*, 26: 731–739.

Blair, R., Jones, L., Clark, F., & Smith, M. 1997. "The Psychopathic Individual: A Lack of Responsiveness to Distress Cues?" *Psychophysiology*, 34: 192–198.

Blair, R., Mitchell, D., & Blair, K. 2005. *The Psychopath: Emotion and the Brain*. New York: Wiley-Blackwell.

Casebeer, W. 2003. *Natural Ethical Facts*. Cambridge, MA: MIT Press.

Damasio, Antonio. 1994. *Descartes' Error: Emotion, Reason, and the Human Brain*. New York: Putnam's.

Damasio, Antonio, Tranel, Daniel, & Damasio, Hanna. 1990. "Individuals with Sociopathic Behavior Caused by Frontal Damage Fail to Respond Autonomically to Social Stimuli." *Behavioral Brain Research*, 41: 81–94.

Davidson, Donald. 1980. *Essays on Actions and Events*. Oxford: Clarendon Press.

Dennett, Daniel. 1978. *Brainstorms*. Cambridge, MA: MIT Press.

Gibbard, Alan. 1990. *Wise Choices, Apt Feelings*. Cambridge, MA: Harvard University Press.

Green, O.H. 1992. *The Emotions*. Dordrecht: Kluwer.

Greene, Josh, Sommerville, R. B., Nystrom, L. E., Darley, J. M., & Cohen, J. D. 2001. "An FMRI Investigation of Emotional Engagement in Moral Judgment." *Science*, 293: 2105–2108.

Greene, Josh, Nystrom, L. E., Engell, A. D., Darley, J. M., & Cohen, J. D. 2004. "The Neural Bases of Cognitive Conflict and Control in Moral Judgment." *Neuron*, 44: 389–400.

Griffiths, Paul. 1997. *What Emotions Really Are: The Problem of Psychological Categories*. Chicago, IL: Chicago University Press.

Habib, Michel. 2004. "Athymhormia and Disorders of Motivation in Basal Ganglia Disease." *Journal of Neuropsychiatry and Clinical Neuroscience*, 16: 509–524.

Hardcastle, Valerie. 1999. *The Myth of Pain*. Cambridge, MA: MIT Press.

Hare, R. (1991). *The Hare Psychopathy Checklist-Revised*. Toronto: Multi-Health Systems.

Hursthouse, Rosalind. 1999. *On Virtue Ethics*. Oxford: Oxford University Press.

James, William. 1890. *Principles of Psychology*. New York: Henry Holt.

Jeannerod, Marc. 1997. *The Cognitive Neuroscience of Action*. Cambridge, MA: Blackwell.

Jeffrey, Richard. 1990. *The Logic of Decision: 2nd ed*. Chicago, IL: University of Chicago Press.

Kandel, Eric, Schwartz, James, & Jessell, Thomas. 2000. *Principles of Neural Science: 4th ed*. New York: McGraw-Hill.

Kelly, D., Stich, S., Haley, K. J., Eng, S., & Fessler, D. M. T. 2007. "Harm, affect, and the moral/conventional distinction." *Mind & Language*, 22: 117–131.

Kennett, Jeanette, & Fine, C. 2007. "Internalism and the Evidence from Psychopaths and 'Acquired Sociopaths'." In Walter Sinnott-Armstrong (ed.), *Moral Psychology Vol. 3: The Neuroscience of Morality*. Cambridge, MA: MIT Press, 173–190.

Kiehl, K. 2006. "A cognitive neuroscience perspective on psychopathy: evidence for paralimbic system dysfunction." *Psychiatry Research*, 142: 107–128.

Koenigs, M., Young, L., Adolphs, R., Tranel, D., Cushman, F., Hauser, M., et al. 2007. "Damage to the prefrontal cortex increases utilitarian moral judgments." *Nature*, 446: 908–911.

Knowlton, B., Mangels, J., & Squire, L. 1996. "A Neostriatal Habit Learning System in Humans." *Science*, 273: 1399–1402.

Korsgaard, Christine. 1986. "Skepticism about Practical Reason." *Journal of Philosophy*, 83: 5–25.

Levy, R., & Dubois, B. 2006. "Apathy and the Functional Anatomy of the Prefrontal Cortex-Basal Ganglia Circuits." *Cerebral Cortex*, 16: 916–928.

Maibom, H. 2005. "Moral Unreason: The case of psychopathy." *Mind & Language*, 20: 237–257.

McDowell, John. 1998. "Are Moral Requirements Hypothetical Imperatives?" In J. McDowell, *Mind, Value, and Reality*. Cambridge, MA: Harvard University Press, 77–94.

Mink, Jonathan. 1996. "The basal ganglia: focused selection and inhibition of competing motor programs." *Progress in Neurobiology*, 50: 381–425.

Moll, J., de Oliveriera-Souza, R., Eslinger, P. J., Bramati, I. E., Mourao-Miranda, J., Andreiuolo, P. A., et al. 2002. "The neural correlates of moral sensitivity: A functional magnetic resonance imaging investigation of basic and moral emotions." *Journal of Neuroscience*, 22: 2730–2736.

Montague, Read, Dayan, Peter, & Sejnowski, Terrence. 1996. "A Framework for Mesencephalic Dopamine Systems Based on Predictive Hebbian Learning." *Journal of Neuroscience*, 16: 1936–1947.

Morillo, Carolyn. 1990. "The Reward Event and Motivation." *Journal of Philosophy* 87: 169–186.

Nichols, Shaun. 2004. *Sentimental Rules: On the Natural Foundations of Moral Judgment*. New York: Oxford University Press.

Packard, M., & Knowlton, B. 2002. "Learning and Memory Functions of the Basal Ganglia." *Annual Review of Neuroscience*, 25: 563–593.

Prinz, Jesse. 2004. *Gut Reactions: A Perceptual Theory of Emotion*. New York: Oxford University Press.

Rilling, J., Sanfey, A., Aronson, J., Nystrom, L., & Cohen, J. 2004. "Opposing BOLD Responses to Reciprocated and Unreciprocated Altruism in Putative Reward Pathways." *Neuroreport*, 15: 2539–2543.

Roskies, A.L. 2006. "Patients with ventromedial frontal damage have moral beliefs," *Philosophical Psychology*, 19 (5): 617–627.

—— 2007. "Internalism and the evidence from pathology." In Walter Sinnott-Armstrong (ed.), *Moral Psychology Vol. 3: The Neuroscience of Morality*. Cambridge, MA: MIT Press, 191–206.

Saver, J. L., & Damasio, Antonio. 1991. "Preserved access and processing of social knowledge in a patient with acquired sociopathy due to ventromedial frontal damage." *Neuropsychologia*, 29: 1241–1249.

Schroeder, Timothy. 2004. *Three Faces of Desire*. New York: Oxford University Press.

—— 2005. "Moral Responsibility and Tourette Syndrome." *Philosophy and Phenomenological Research*, 71: 106–123.

Schultz, Wolfram, Tremblay, Leon, & Hollerman, Jeffrey. 2000. "Reward Processing in Primate Orbitofrontal Cortex and Basal Ganglia." *Cerebral Cortex*, 10: 272–283.

Sen, Amartya. 1982. *Choice, Welfare, and Measurement*. Cambridge, MA: MIT Press.

Singer, T., Seymour, B., O'Doherty, J., Kaube, H., Dolan, R., & Frith, C. 2004. "Empathy for Pain Involves the Affective but not Sensory Components of Pain." *Science*, 303: 1157–1162.

Slote, Michael. 2001. *Morals from Motives*. Oxford: Oxford University Press.

Smith, Michael. 1994. *The Moral Problem*. Oxford: Blackwell.

Stanovich, Keith. 2004. *The Robot's Rebellion: Finding Meaning in the Age of Darwin.* Chicago, IL: University of Chicago Press.

Stellar, Elliot & Stellar, Jim. 1985. *The Neurobiology of Reward and Punishment.* New York: Springer-Verlag.

Strub, R. L. 1989. "Frontal lobe syndrome in a patient with bilateral globus pallidus lesions," *Archives of Neurology,* 46(9): 1024–1027.

Vijayaraghavan, Lavanya, Vaidya, Jatin G., Humphreys, Clare T., Beglinger, Leigh J., & Paradiso, Sergio. 2008. "Emotional and motivational changes after bilateral lesions of the globus pallidus." *Neuropsychology,* 22 (3): 412–418.

Williams, Bernard, 1981. "Internal and External Reasons." In *Moral Luck.* New York: Cambridge University Press, 101–113.

4

Moral Emotions*

JESSE J. PRINZ AND SHAUN NICHOLS

Within Western philosophy, it's widely recognized that emotions play a role in moral judgment and moral motivation. Emotions help people see that certain actions are morally wrong, for example, and they motivate behavioral responses when such actions are identified. Philosophers who embrace such views often present them at a high level of abstraction and without empirical support. Emotions motivate, they say, but they don't explain how they motivate or why (e.g. Ayer, 1936; McDowell, 1985; Dreier, 1990). We think that empirical moral psychology is essential for moving from imprecise formulations into more detailed explanations.

We shall address several questions. First, we shall survey empirical evidence supporting the conjecture that emotions regularly occur when people make moral judgments. We shall describe several models of moral judgment that are consistent with these data, but we won't adjudicate which is right, since all these models agree that emotions are important for moral psychology. Then we shall turn to the question of *which* emotions are involved in moral judgment, and offer some suggestions about how to distinguish moral emotions from non-moral emotions. And, finally, we shall discuss two moral emotions that are central to moral thought and action: anger and guilt. We shall discuss other moral emotions in passing, but anger and guilt are arguably the most prevalent, at least in Western morality, and a careful analysis of how they function will help to underscore why they are so important. Indeed, we shall conclude by suggesting that these moral emotions may be necessary for morality in some sense.

1. The Role of Emotions in Moral Cognition

Almost all major ethical theories in Western philosophy implicate the emotions in one way or another. On some of these theories, emotions are essential to

* We are grateful to John Doris and Dan Kelly for comments on a previous draft of this chapter.

morality, and in others they are not. But, even those authors who deny that emotions are essential usually find a place for them in moral psychology. This is true even for Kant, who is notorious for arguing that morality depends on reason rather than sentiment. In Kant's (1997: 43) system, reason tells us that we follow the moral law, but acting from the moral law begins with respect for the law, which is constituted by respect for persons, which is a natural consequence of recognizing the dignity of each person as a law-governed agent. In addition to respect, Kant (1996: 160) claims that moral judgments are accompanied by moral feelings. It is difficult to find a philosopher who does not think emotions are important to morality.

Despite this consensus, there is considerable disagreement about the exact role that emotions are supposed to play. In addition, even where moral philosophers have invoked emotions, they seldom attend carefully to the psychological characteristics of the emotions to which they appeal. Indeed, it would be hard to exaggerate the extent to which philosophers, even self-described sentimentalists, have neglected psychological research on the moral emotions. This chapter is intended as a partial corrective.

We shall begin by considering two ways in which emotions have been alleged to contribute to morality. Then we shall go on to discuss how empirical work on specific emotions might be used to characterize these contributions with greater detail and accuracy.

1.1. *Motivation*

It is widely assumed that emotions play a role in moral motivation. This is hardly surprising, because emotions are thought to be major sources of motivation in general. Some philosophers conjecture that reasons can be motivating in the absence of emotions, but even they would likely admit that emotions can motivate when present.

There are two contexts in which the link between emotions and moral motivation are often explicitly discussed. The first is in discussions of prosocial behaviors. In the social sciences, several lines of research explore that link. In developmental psychology, there is research on correlations between emotions and good deeds. Children are more likely to engage in various praiseworthy behaviors if they have certain emotional responses (Chapman et al., 1987; Eisenberg, 2000). For example, when children show concern in response to the distress of others, they are likely to engage in consolation behaviors (Zahn-Waxler et al., 1992). Psychologists have also investigated the relationship between emotions and good deeds in adults. For example, Isen and Levin (1972) show that induction of positive affect dramatically increases the likelihood that a person will help a stranger pick up some papers that have fallen on the street. There is also work looking at the role of emotion in promoting cooperative behavior in prisoner's dilemmas and other economic games (Batson & Moran, 1999). Positive emotions and affiliative feelings may promote cooperation. Of course, cooperative behavior might be motivated by self-interest and emotions, such as greed. One topic of current debate is whether genuine altruism must be motivated by certain emotional states, such as sympathy, concern, empathy, or care (see Chapter 5; and, for a less optimistic view, see also Prinz, forthcoming).

In all these examples, emotions play a role in promoting prosocial behavior. But it is important to notice that one can engage in prosocial behavior without judging that it is good. This is true even in many cases of altruistic motivation. You might help someone who is drowning, for example, without first thinking to yourself that doing so would be what morality demands. The term "moral motivation" is ambiguous between motivation to act in a way that (as a matter of fact) *fits* with the demands of morality and motivation to act in a way because one judges that morality demands such action. Research on altruism, cooperation, and prosocial behavior in children typically falls in the former category. But helping because you care is different, psychologically speaking, from helping because you think it is what morality demands. Both forms of motivation should be distinguished, and both can be empirically investigated.

Like altruistic motivation, the motivation to do something because it is what morality demands is also widely thought to involve emotions. Doing something because it is demanded by morality requires making a moral judgment. A moral judgment is a judgment that something has moral significance. In expressing moral judgments we use terms such as *right* and *wrong*, *good* and *bad*, *just* and *unjust*, *virtuous* and *base*. Typically, when people judge that something has moral significance they become motivated to behave in accordance with those judgments. Emotions are widely believed to contribute to that motivation. This conjecture has been widely discussed within philosophy. There is a raging debate about whether moral judgments are intrinsically motivating (see Frankena, 1973; Brink, 1989; Smith, 1994). Motivation internalists claim that we cannot make moral judgments without thereby being motivated to act in accordance with them. To make this case, they sometimes suppose that moral judgments are constituted, at least in part, by emotions. Judgments are mental states, and to say that they are partially constituted by emotions is to say that the mental state of judging, for example, that killing is immoral is constituted by a mental representation of killing along with an emotional state directed toward that represented act. Externalists argue that judgments can be made without motivation, but they often agree with internalists that, when motivation accompanies a judgment, it derives from an emotional state. In other words, internalists and externalists usually agree that emotions contribute to moral motivation for those individuals who are motivated to act in accordance with their moral judgments.

In sum, emotions motivate or impel us to act morally, and they can do so in the absence of a moral judgment or as a consequence of a moral judgment. But this leaves open numerous questions. When emotions motivate as a consequence of moral judgments, it may be because they are somehow contained in those judgments or because they are elicited by those judgments (a dispute that won't concern us here). In addition, the emotions involved in prosocial behavior may vary. Buying Girl Scout cookies to support the Scouts may involve different emotions than saving someone who is drowning or attending a rally to protest government injustice. We shall not discuss this issue here. Instead we shall focus on the emotions that arise when people make moral judgments, and, as we shall see in Section 2, these too may vary significantly.

1.2. *Moral Judgment*

In recent years, empirical research has been used to demonstrate that emotions arise in the context of moral judgment. This may seem obvious, but empirical work is needed to confirm casual observation and to clarify the specific roles that emotions play.

Some research suggests that emotions can serve as moral "intuitions." The basic idea is that, under some circumstances, we do not come to believe that something is, say, morally wrong by reasoning about it. Rather, we have an emotion, and the emotion leads us to judge that it is wrong. This model has been gaining momentum in psychology. One version of it has been developed by Jonathan Haidt (2001). He and his collaborators have shown that one can influence moral judgments by manipulating emotions. In one study, Schnall et al. (2008) placed subjects at either a clean desk or a filthy desk and had them fill out questionnaires in which they were asked to rate the wrongness of various actions, such as eating your pet dog for dinner after killing it accidentally. Subjects at the filthy desk gave higher wrongness ratings than subjects at the clean desk. The same effect was obtained using disgusting films and "fart spray." In another study, Wheatley and Haidt (2005) used hypnosis to cause subjects to feel disgusted whenever they heard a neutral word, such as "often." Then they asked subjects to morally assess the actions of various characters. Subjects gave more negative ratings when the disgust-eliciting word was included in the description of those actions. They even gave more negative moral appraisals when the action was neutral. For example, disgust-induced subjects gave more negative appraisals to a student body representative after reading that he "often" invites interesting speakers to campus. Wheatley and Haidt conclude that the pang of disgust causes subjects to make a negative moral judgment. Of course, in ordinary life, our emotions are not usually induced hypnotically, and they may lead to more consistent and defensible intuitions. If you see someone kick a dog, for example, that might disgust you, and the feeling of disgust might lead you to say the perpetrator has done something terribly wrong.

Haidt thinks that emotional intuitions are the basis of most moral judgments. Others argue that emotions play a role only when making specific kinds of moral judgments, but not others. For example, Joshua Greene (2008) argues that there are two ways people arrive at moral decisions: through reason and through passion. He argues further that people who apply consequentialist principles may be guided by cool reason, and people who make deontological judgments may use their emotions. To test this, he and his collaborators present subjects in a functional magnetic resonance imaging (fMRI) scanner with moral dilemmas that require killing one person to save several others. In some dilemmas people tend to make judgments that conform to "deontological" prohibitions (don't kill, regardless of the consequences), while, in others, people make consequentialist judgments (do what ever maximizes the number of lives saved). When brain activity is examined, the deontological judgments are associated with stronger activation in areas associated with emotion.

The results of Greene et al. invite the view that consequentialist judgments may not involve emotion at all, but their data just show that emotions are less active, and working memory is more active. It is possible, therefore, that these are cases where the emotional intuition is overridden by reasoning. Alternatively, the two cases may involve different kinds of emotions: a negative feeling associated with transgression may guide deontological judgments, while a positive feeling that motivates helping may guide consequentialist judgments. Indeed, other studies of moral judgment using fMRI have consistently shown emotional activation. Moll and colleagues have shown that emotions are active when we judge sentences to express something morally wrong and when we look at pictures of moral transgressions (Moll et al., 2002, 2003). Heekeren et al. (2003) found evidence of emotional activations as people assessed sentences for moral, as opposed to semantic, correctness. Sanfey et al. (2003) found a similar pattern when people made judgments of unfairness during economic games. Just about every fMRI study of moral judgment has shown emotional activations. Collectively such results show that emotions arise in making moral judgments at least some, and perhaps even all, of the time.

The data we have been reviewing strongly suggest that emotions are regularly and reliably active during episodes of moral cognition. Emotions seem to arise no matter what the moral task, and induction of emotions prior to moral evaluation can influence responses, suggesting that the link between emotion and moral cognition is not merely correlational or epiphenomenal.

Still, the data we have reviewed are consistent with several different models of how emotions and moral judgment relate. We shall briefly describe these here, though we shall not adjudicate. We think that on any of these models the study of moral emotions will be of considerable importance.

The first model, which we shall call affective rationalism, combines what we shall call judgment rationalism with motivation emotionism. As we shall define these terms, judgment rationalism combines the following two views:

- Rational genesis: the judgment that something is moral or immoral is typically arrived at through a process of reasoning that can occur without emotions.
- Rational essence: when emotions arise in the context of moral judgment, they are contingent in the sense that a token of the very same judgment could have occurred in the absence of those emotions.

The affective rationalist accepts this, but also adds:

- Emotional motivation: emotions play a central and reliable role in motivating people to act in accordance with their moral judgments.

For the affective rationalist, we need only reason to recognize the moral law, but we may need emotion to care about the moral law. Since most of us care, emotions normally arise when we make moral judgments. Affective rationalists must also admit that emotions can influence moral judgments (as the data clearly demonstrate), but they chalk this up to a more general phenomenon of emotional influence: emotions can have an impact on judgment quite generally and, when this happens, it is usually a form of bias or noise that we should try to guard against.

The second model is Haidt's social intuitionism. According to Haidt, we do not typically arrive at moral judgments through reasoning, so he rejects rational genesis. Rather, we typically arrive at moral judgments through "intuitions" which are gut feelings that lead us to conclude that something is right or wrong:

- Emotional genesis: the judgment that something is moral or immoral is typically arrived at as a consequence of emotional feelings.

Haidt probably also accepts emotional motivation, but his stance on rational essence is a bit hard to determine. He sometimes implies that a moral judgment is a cognitive state that could, in principle, arise without emotions, even if this happens only rarely in practice.

The next model we will consider is Nichols's (2004) "sentimental rules" theory. Nichols argues that healthy moral judgment involves two different components: a normative theory and systems of emotion. The normative theory specifies rules and the emotions alter their character and give them motivational force. Nichols thus endorses emotional motivation. He also says that moral judgments can arise through the influence of either affect or reasoning, and characteristically involve an element of both; so he accepts both emotional and rational genesis. The most distinctive feature of the sentimental rules theory is the rejection of the rational essence principle. Nichols argues that moral rules have a characteristic functional role, which includes being regarded as very serious and authority independent, and being justified by appeal to the suffering of victims. These features usually result from emotional responses. The concern we have for victims infuses our judgments with feelings, which influences both our justificatory patterns and our sense that moral rules are serious. Emotions also lead us to feel that moral judgments are, in some sense, independent of authority. Even if authorities approve of cruelty, for example, is still just feels wrong. Thus, for Nichols, the characteristic role of moral judgments depends crucially on emotions. One can make a moral judgment without emotions, but it would be a moral judgment of an unusual and perhaps pathological kind, because it would not have the characteristic functional role. Thus Nichols would reject rational essence as formulated above. In its place, he would say:

- Emotional essence: when emotions arise in the context of moral judgment, they are necessary in the sense that a token of the very same judgment would not have occurred in the absence of those emotions.

Nichols is *not* saying that moral judgments are impossible without emotions, just that these would be abnormal. The normative theory component can function when emotions are absent. In this respect, his view about the role of emotions can be regarded as a *causal* model, meaning that moral judgments can occur with emotions and, when this happens, those emotions influence the role of the judgment in a way that significantly affects it functional profile, making it a judgment of a very distinctive kind (an emotion-backed judgment). This idea can be captured by an elaboration of emotional essence:

- Emotional essence (causal): when emotions arise in the context of moral judgment, they are necessary in the sense that they causally influence the functional role of those judgments such that they become judgments of a different type than they would be were the emotions absent.

The final model we shall consider is the "emotional constitution model", one version of which can be found in the "constructive sentimentalism" of

Prinz (2007). On this account, token instances of moral concepts, such as MORAL and IMMORAL, literally contain emotions in the way that tokens of the concept FUNNY might contain amusement. When one applies these concepts, one is having an emotional response. One judges that a joke is funny by being amused, and one judges that something is immoral by being outraged. Thus the emotional constitution model embraces emotional essence but in a somewhat different way than the sentimental rules model. To wit:

- Emotional essence (constitution): emotions are necessary to moral judgments because they are essential parts: moral judgments are psychological states that include emotional states as parts, and a judgment would not qualify as moral if these emotional states were absent.

We think that empirical research can be used to adjudicate between these models. Some of the research already mentioned may even be helpful in this regard, but most of these findings really leave all the models as open possibilities. Our goal here is not to advocate one or another. Rather, we want to point out that they all share a crucial feature. They all say that emotions generally arise in the context of making moral judgments. Therefore defenders of all the models should welcome research on moral emotions. They can find common ground in investigating *which* emotions arise in the context of moral judgment, *what* information those emotions convey, and *how* those emotions influence behavior. Answering these questions in detail is crucial for a fully developed account of how emotions contribute to moral judgment. These details can be illuminated empirically, and we shall analyze two specific moral emotions below. First, we need to gain a bit more clarity on what moral emotions are.

2. The Moral Emotions

Any complete account of the relationship between emotions and morality must say something about the nature of emotions and the nature of moral emotions in particular. This is not the place to survey theories of emotion, much less to present evidence in favor of any one theory (see Prinz, 2004). But we offer a few remarks.

Theories about the nature of emotions divide into two classes. Some researchers claim that emotions are essentially cognitive. On these views, every emotion necessarily has a cognitive component. That cognitive component is usually presumed to be an evaluative judgment or "appraisal" (e.g. Lazarus, 1991; Scherer, 1997). "Sadness," for example, might comprise the judgment that there has been an irrevocable loss, together with a distinctive feeling and motivational state. In Lazarus's terminology, each emotion has a core relational theme: a relation between organism and environment that occasions the onset of the emotion. When we judge that there has been a loss, we become sad; when we judge that we are in danger, we become afraid; and when we judge that our goals have been fulfilled, we become happy.

Other researchers argue that emotions can occur without cognitive components. The feeling of sadness might occur, they claim, without any explicit judgment to the effect that there has been a loss. Defenders of such non-cognitive theories agree with defenders of cognitive theories that each emotion has a specific range of eliciting conditions. They agree that sadness occurs in contexts of loss. They simply deny that one must judge that there has been a loss (Prinz, 2004). Perhaps it is enough merely to see a loved one depart on a train, or grow distant in demeanor. On the non-cognitive view, each emotion has a core relational theme, but the relevant relations are sometimes registered without judgment. A sudden loss of support can directly trigger fear, and a noxious smell can instill disgust.

We do not wish to resolve this debate here. Both sides agree that each emotion has a characteristic class of eliciting conditions, and that these conditions must ordinarily be recognized or internally represented for an emotion to occur. For a cognitive theorist, recognition takes the form of an explicit appraisal (e.g. a judgment that there has been a loss). For the non-cognitive theories, recognition will often consist in a representation of an event that happens to be an instance of a particular category without explicit recognition of its membership in that category (e.g. a perception of a loved one leaving); the emotional feeling itself constitutes the appraisal (e.g. I feel sad when you depart). For both theories, emotions are elicited by the same kinds of events (e.g. sadness is elicited by loss). To remain neutral about this, we shall use the term "elicitor" when talking about the events that serve to elicit emotional responses.

Let's turn now to a more important question for this chapter: what makes an emotion qualify as moral? One possibility is that there is no distinction between moral and non-moral emotions, either because all emotions are intrinsically moral (that seems unlikely—consider fear of heights), or because no emotions are moral. On this latter view, it may happen that emotions can occur in the context of moral judgments, but the emotions that do so are not special in any way; perhaps any emotion could participate in moral cognition. Another possibility is that moral emotions contain moral judgments. This could be the case only if cognitive theories of emotion were correct. A further pair of possibilities is that moral emotions are emotions that are either constitutive of moral judgments or causally related to moral judgments in a special way (they reliably give rise to such judgments or are caused by such judgments). Finally, moral emotions might be defined as emotions that promote moral behaviors. Some of these definitions are compatible. One could define one class of moral emotions as the emotions that promote moral behaviors, and another class as the ones that are either constitutively or causally related to moral judgments.

Notice that these ways of defining moral emotions will work only if we can find some way of defining morality, because the definition builds in the concept *moral*. In philosophy, morality is concerned with norms, where norms are construed as rules about how we should act or what kind of people we should be. But this is, at best, a necessary condition for qualifying as moral. Not all norms have moral content. There are norms of etiquette, for example, and norms of chess playing (Foot, 1972). Psychologists try to narrow down the moral domain by drawing a distinction between moral and conventional rules (Turiel, 1983; Smetana, 1993; Nucci, 2001). If we can define morality by appeal to moral, as opposed to conventional, rules, then we can define moral emotions as those that promote behavior that accords with moral rules or those that play a causal or constitutive role in mentally representing such rules. Of course, this will avoid circularity only if we can cash out the concept of moral rules without using the concept *moral*. On the standard approach in psychology, moral rules are operationalized as being distinctive in three ways. We have already alluded to this operationalization in sketching Nichols's sentimental rules model above. In comparison to conventional rules, moral rules are regarded as more serious, less dependent on authority, and more likely to be justified with reference to empathy and the suffering of others (Turiel, 1983). The attempt to use these features to define the notion of morality has been challenged (Shweder et al., 1987; Kelly et al., 2007). For example, there may be moral rules that are authority contingent and don't involve suffering (e.g. rules prohibiting consensual incest with birth control), and conventional rules that are very serious (e.g. driving on the right-hand side of the road). Moreover, researchers persuaded by moral relativism believe that all rules may depend on convention (Prinz, 2007). We find these objections compelling. Nevertheless, we think the evidence from this tradition is getting at important differences in the way people think about different classes of violations. Many people seem to have strong intuitions about whether certain rules (say, prohibitions against joy killing) are moral or merely conventional. We think such intuitions must ultimately be explained.

Here we mention two ways of trying to make sense of people's intuitions about a moral/conventional distinction. One option is to define moral rules negatively as rules that are not believed to depend on any specific social conventions. The idea is that, when people construe a norm as conventional, they know that it depends on the opinions or practices of others. With moral rules, people presume this is not the case. This straightforward suggestion may be workable, but there are a few concerns. One is that some moral rules may be construed as depending on others, such as the rule that one should follow the ways of one's elders or the rule that one should obey dietary customs. These rules are sometimes construed morally in some cultures. Another concern is that this formulation implies that a rule's status as moral or conventional depends on how we think about its ultimate source or justification. This is intellectually demanding. It's not implausible that we acquire both moral and conventional rules before having any beliefs about how they are justified or where they come from. Young children may be sensitive to the moral/conventional distinction without having a concept of social conventions. A third concern is that there may be non-moral norms that do not depend on conventions, such as personal norms or prudential norms. A fourth concern is that, if relativism is right, moral rules may depend on conventions, but people who embrace relativism need not deny that moral rules exist.

Another strategy for defining moral norms makes reference to the emotions. There is evidence that moral norms are associated with different emotions than conventional norms (Arsenio & Ford, 1985; Tangney et al., 1996; Takahashi et al., 2004; see also Grusec & Goodnow, 1994, for indirect evidence). If one violates a rule of etiquette, one might feel embarrassed, but one is unlikely to feel guilty or ashamed. On this approach, moral norms are defined as norms whose violation tends to elicit moral emotions. This definition overcomes many of the worries we have been discussing, but it is problematic in the present context. We were trying to define moral emotions in terms of moral norms, and now we are defining moral norms in terms of moral emotions. One could break out of it by simply listing the moral emotions. Moral norms could be defined as norms that implicate the emotions on that list. On this view, moral norms are defined in terms of moral emotions, and moral emotions are simply stipulated.

Perhaps one of these approaches to the moral/conventional distinction can be made to float. Perhaps other options are available. We shall not take a stand. When we invoke the moral/conventional distinction in what follows, we shall try to rely on uncontroversial examples of each (e.g. the assassination of Martin Luther King was morally wrong, and eating with a hat on is merely conventionally wrong). We'll rely on these folk intuitions, which are confirmed—at least among North America respondents in the literature on moral development. The fact that people have strong intuitions about whether certain rules are moral or conventional suggests that there is some psychological basis for the distinction.

Until there is an uncontroversial definition of what makes a norm count as moral, it may be easiest to define moral emotions as those that are associated with paradigm cases of moral rules (e.g. emotions that arise in the context of killing, stealing, and giving to charity). Following other authors, we find it useful to distinguish several different families (see, e.g., Ben-Ze'ev, 2000; Haidt, 2003). First, there are prosocial emotions, which promote morally good behavior by orienting us to the needs of others. These include empathy, sympathy, concern, and compassion. It's possible that empathy and sympathy are not emotions in their own right, but rather capacities to experience other people's emotions vicariously. Second, there are self-blame emotions, such as guilt and shame. Third, there are other-blame emotions, such as contempt, anger, and disgust.

One might wonder why there are so many different moral emotions. Why isn't there just a single emotion of disapprobation, for example, rather than multiple ways of experiencing blame? The obvious answer is that each moral emotion has a different functional role. This, we think, is an important feature of moral emotions, which has been underappreciated in philosophy. Consider the emotions of other-blame: contempt, anger, and disgust. Rozin et al. (1999) have argued that these three emotions play different roles corresponding to three different kinds of moral norms. They build on the work of the anthropologist Richard Shweder (e.g. Shweder et al., 1999), who argues that three different kinds of moral rules, or "ethics," crop up cross-culturally. Rozin et al. map the emotions of other-blame onto Shweder's taxonomy, by asking subjects in Japan and the United States to indicate which of these emotions they would likely feel in a range of circumstances corresponding to Shweder's three kinds of norms. Here is what they find. Contempt arises when people violate *community* norms, such as norms pertaining to public goods or social hierarchies. Anger arises when people violate *autonomy* norms, which are norms prohibiting harms against persons. Disgust arises, in non-secular societies, when people violate *divinity* norms, which require that people remain pure; in secular societies, people also have norms about purity, but they construe violations of these norms as crimes against nature, rather than as crimes against gods. Coincidentally, the research reveals pairings of contempt and community, anger and autonomy, and disgust and divinity. Therefore, Rozin et al. call this the CAD model.

In addition to prosocial emotions, self-blame emotions, and other-blame emotions, there may be a variety of other emotions that have moral significance even though they have not been extensively studied in that context. There are emotions such as self-righteousness, gratitude, admiration, and elevation, which may serve as rewards for good behavior. There are emotions such as loyalty, affection, and love, which create and promote morally relevant commitments (for a useful survey, see Fessler & Haley, 2003 and Haidt, 2003). These are clearly worthy of further investigation.

We cannot possibly review the research on each moral emotion here. We leave aside prosocial emotions (but see Preston & de Waal, 2002 and Hoffman, 2000). We focus instead on emotions associated with blame, and, more specifically, on anger and guilt. These illustrate the other-blame and self-blame categories respectively, and have been extensively studied by researchers interested in morality. We choose anger and guilt because they are associated with violations of autonomy norms, which are perhaps the most familiar kinds of moral norms. Autonomy norms are ones that regulate how we treat individual persons, and canonical violations of autonomy norms involve harming another person. Sometimes the person is physically hurt; sometimes property is taken. In other cases, nothing is taken, but the person doesn't get what they deserve or are entitled to. In still others, a person is prevented from doing something even though the prevention is unwarranted. Most broadly, autonomy norms are characteristically construed in terms of harms or rights. Someone is harmed when they are hurt or lose property. Someone's rights are violated when they are not given certain benefits or allowances.

Autonomy norms are privileged in Western philosophy and Western culture. Most normative ethical theories in the West (with the possible exception of virtue ethics) focus on autonomy in one way or another. Even utilitarianism counts as an autonomy-focused theory, on the technical definition used in psychology, because it focuses on benefits and harms to persons (as opposed to, say, status hierarchies or victimless sexual acts that strike members of traditional societies as impure). Patterns of justification in the West tend to focus on how a victim has been affected. If asked whether a certain sexual behavior is wrong, for example, Westerners often try to determine whether it was harmful. Victimless behaviors such as masturbation are considered morally permissible in contemporary Western societies because no one is harmed, although, in earlier times, masturbation (or onanism) was viewed as a crime (Tissot, 1766). In contrast, bestiality and incest are regarded as wrong by contemporary Westerners, because they assume that one party does not consent. Westerners do moralize some acts that have no unwilling victims, such as consensual incest (Haidt, 2001). But they seem to exhibit discomfort or puzzlement in not being able to provide a victim-based justification. Members of non-Western cultures and people with low socioeconomic status are often more comfortable with saying that there can be victimless crimes (Haidt et al., 1993). This tendency may also be found to some degree in Westerners who are politically conservative (Haidt, 2007). Traditional value systems regulate everything from sex to dress and diet. Those who endorse traditional values may be more willing than modern Western liberals to condemn behavior that is not harmful to anyone. Moral theories in modern Western philosophy shift away from traditional values and try to identify norms that may be more universal. Norms regulating harm are purported to have this status (although their universality may be challenged; Prinz, 2008). By focusing on the emotions that arise in response to violations of autonomy norms, we present those that are most directly relevant to Western ethical theories. But we don't mean to imply that these emotions, anger and guilt, are exclusively Western. They may be culturally widespread emotions with deep biological roots.

3. Anger

Of all the emotions that look to play a prominent role in moral psychology, anger is the one most commonly thought to have clear analogues in lower mammals (e.g. Panksepp, 2000). Indeed, anger has been explored extensively by biologically oriented emotion theorists. It is included on most lists of "basic emotions." Basic emotions, as they are understood in contemporary emotion research, are evolved emotions that do not contain other emotions as parts. They are usually associated with distinctive elicitors, physiological responses, action tendencies, and expressive behaviors. This is certainly true of anger. It is associated with a distinctive facial expression (furrowed brow, thin lips, raised eyelids, square mouth) (Ekman, 1971), and it is physiologically differentiated from other basic emotions (high heart rate and high skin temperature) (Ekman et al., 1983: 1209). In infants, anger is thought to be triggered by goal obstructions (Lemerise & Dodge, 2008). Affective neuroscientific work indicates that anger is associated with activations in the amygdala, the hypothalamus, and the periaqueductal gray of the midbrain (Panksepp, 1998: 187, 195–196). And already with Darwin, we get a proposal about the adaptive function of anger: it serves to motivate retaliation. Darwin writes: "animals of all kinds, and their progenitors before them, when attacked or threatened by an enemy, have exerted their utmost powers in fighting and in defending themselves. Unless an animal does thus act, or has the intention, or at least the desire, to attack its enemy, it cannot properly be said to be enraged" (1872: 74).

Because anger seems to be present in all mammals, and because weasels are perhaps not typically regarded as having *moral* emotions, it is tempting for the moral psychologist to restrict attention to "moral anger" or "moral outrage" (cf. Fessler & Haley, 2003; Gibbard, 1990). But we want to begin our discussion of anger without explicitly restricting it to moral anger.

3.1. *Psychological Profile of Anger*

In the recent moral psychological literature on anger, the familiar characterization of the profile of anger is that it's caused by a judgment of transgression and it generates an inclination for aggression and retributive punishment. Thus we find Averill claiming that "the typical instigation to anger is a value judgment. More than anything else, anger is an attribution of blame" (1983: 1150). Lazarus (1991) maintains that the "core relational theme" for anger is "a demeaning offence against me and mine." Similarly, Ortony and Turner suggest that "the appraisal that an agent has done something blameworthy . . . is the principal appraisal that underlies anger" (Ortony & Turner, 1990: 324). Relatedly, according to the CAD model of Rozin et al. (see Section 2), anger is triggered by violations of "autonomy" norms.

Much of the evidence for this profile comes from work in social psychology over the last two decades. The dominant method in this research has been to ask subjects to recall a past situation in which they were angry, then to elaborate in various ways on the details of the situation and the experience (e.g. Averill, 1983; Baumeister et al., 1990; Ellsworth & Smith, 1988; Scherer, 1997; Shaver et al., 1987; Smith & Ellsworth, 1985). In these sorts of surveys, investigators have consistently found that people tend to give examples of feeling anger in which they report that (i) the cause was an injustice and (ii) the effect was a motivation to retaliate.

Drawing on self-reports of anger episodes, Shaver et al. maintain that the prevailing cognitive antecedent is the "judgment that the situation is illegitimate, wrong, unfair, contrary to what ought to be" (1987: 1078). This is present in 95% of the cases (p. 1077). More recently, Scherer reports the results of a large cross-cultural study in which subjects were asked to recall episodes in which they felt each of several emotions (sadness, joy, disgust, fear, shame, anger, and guilt) and also to rate the situation along several dimensions. Across cultures, subjects tended to assign high ratings of unfairness to the anger-inducing situation. Indeed, overall, anger-inducing situations got the highest rating of unfairness out of all the emotions (1987: 911). Furthermore, when people are asked to recall an event in which they were treated unjustly, the most common emotion reported is anger/rage/indignation (Mikula, 1986).

Shaver et al. also found that people tended to report similar kinds of reactions to anger-inducing situations: "the angry person reports becoming stronger . . . in order to fight or rail against the cause of anger. His or her responses seem designed to rectify injustice—to reassert power or status, to frighten the offending person into compliance, to restore a desired state of affairs" (1987: 1078). This, of course, nicely fits the standard profile on which anger generates a motivation for retaliation.

Another line of research in social psychology explicitly tries to induce anger by presenting subjects with scenarios or movies that seem to depict injustice. In these cases, too, anger is the dominant emotion that people feel (or expect to feel) in response to the unjust situation (Mikula, 1986; Clayton, 1992; Sprecher, 1992). Furthermore, presenting subjects with apparently unjust scenarios generates behavioral effects associated with anger. For instance, Keltner and colleagues (1993) had subjects imagine a scenario in which they were treated unfairly. Then they were presented with another scenario, this time describing an awkward social situation. Subjects who were first exposed to the unjust scenario were more likely than control subjects to blame the situation on other people (p. 745). So it seems that presentations of unjust scenarios trigger emotions that increase blame attributions. In a related study, Lerner and colleagues showed subjects in one condition, the *anger* condition, a video clip of a bully beating up a teenager; in the other condition, the *neutral emotion* condition, subjects watched a video clip of abstract figures (Lerner et al., 1998: 566). After this emotion-induction condition, subjects were presented with an unrelated scenario in which a person's negligence led to an injury. Subjects were asked "To what extent should the construction worker . . . be punished for not preventing your injury, if at all?" (p. 567). Lerner and colleagues found that subjects who had been shown the bully video were more punitive than control subjects.

The punitive impulses that emerge from injustice-induced anger are apparently not *de dicto* desires to improve society. This is beautifully illustrated in a study by Haidt and Sabini (ms) in which they showed subjects film clips that depicted injustices, and then subjects were asked to rate different possible endings. Subjects were not satisfied with endings in which the victim dealt well with the loss and forgave the transgressor. Rather, subjects were most satisfied when the perpetrator suffered in a way that paralleled the original injustice. That is, subjects preferred the ending in which the perpetrator *got the comeuppance he deserved*. Perceived injustice thus seems to generate a desire for retribution.

Some of the most interesting recent evidence on anger comes from experimental economics. One familiar experimental paradigm in the field is the ultimatum game, played in pairs (typically anonymously). One subject, the "proposer," is given a lump of money to divide with the other subject, the "responder." The proposer's offer is communicated to the responder, who also knows the total amount of money to be divided. The responder then decides whether to accept or reject the offer. If he rejects the offer, then neither he nor the proposer gets any of the money. The consistent finding (in most cultures, but see Henrich et al., 2004) is that low offers (e.g. 20% of the total allocation) often get rejected. That is, the responder often decides to take nothing rather than a low offer.

Over the last several years, evidence has accumulated that suggests that anger plays an important role in leading to rejections in these sorts of games. In one of the earliest published findings on the matter, Pillutla and Murninghan (1996) had subjects play an ultimatum game after which they were invited to give open-ended responses to two questions: "How did you react when you received your offer? How did you feel?" (p. 215). Independent coders rated the responses for anger and perceived unfairness. Reports of anger and perceived unfairness were significantly correlated. Anger (which was almost always accompanied by perceived unfairness) was a strong predictor of when a subject would reject an offer. Unfairness alone also predicted rejections, but more weakly than anger. Pillutla and Murninghan's suggestion is straightforward: when subjects view the offer as unfair, this often leads to anger, and this response increases the tendency to reject the offer (p. 220).

Using somewhat different economic games, other researchers have also found that perceived unfairness in offers generates anger, which leads to retaliatory actions (Bosman & van Winden, 2002: 159; Hopfensitz & Reuben, forthcoming, ms: 13–14). But there is one finding, using public-goods games, that deserves special mention. In a public-goods game, anonymous participants are each allotted a sum of money that they can invest in a common pool. Their investment will lead to increased overall wealth for the group, but the payoff for the investing individual will always be a loss. So, for instance, for each $1 a person invests, each of the four group members will get $0.40, so that the investor will get back only 40% of his own investment. Fehr and Gächter (2002) had subjects play a series of public-goods games in which it was made clear that no two subjects would be in the same game more than once. After each game, subjects were given an opportunity to punish people in their group—for each 1 monetary unit the punisher pays, 3 monetary units are taken from the punishee. Since the subjects know that they will never again interact with any agent that they are allowed to punish, punishing apparently has no future economic benefit for the punisher. Nonetheless, punishment was in fact frequent in the experiment. Most people punished at least once, and most punishment was directed at free-riders (individuals who contributed less than average) (Fehr & Gächter 2002: 137).

Why do subjects *pay* to punish even when they presumably know it is not in their financial self-interest? *Anger*, according to Fehr and Gächter. To support this hypothesis, they asked their subjects how they would feel in the following situation: "You decide to invest 16 francs to the project. The second group member invests 14 and the third 18 francs. Suppose the fourth member invests 2 francs to the project. You now accidentally meet this member. Please indicate your feeling towards this person" (Fehr & Gächter, 2002: 139). As predicted, subjects indicated high levels of anger toward this person. Fehr and Gächter maintain that this finding, together with the pattern of punishment responses, fits very well with the hypothesis that negative emotions like anger provide the motivation to punish free-riders. Furthermore, as with Haidt and Sabini's findings, it seems that the motivation is for *retributive* punishment, not for rehabilitation or other happy endings.

Thus far, we've been summarizing evidence that anger is elicited by injustice. That may not be the only elicitor, however. In the social psychological literature mentioned initially, the empirical strategy is rather striking: subjects are asked to give a single example of an episode of anger from their own life (Averill, 1983; Baumeister et al., 1990; Ellsworth & Smith, 1988; Scherer, 1997; Shaver et al., 1987; Smith & Ellsworth, 1985). It is an important finding that people tend to volunteer injustice-related episodes. But it would obviously be rash to draw conclusions about the representativeness of these examples. Perhaps injustice-induced anger is just especially salient, but not especially common. One of the most illuminating studies on the matter is also one of the oldest. Hall (1898) did a mammoth survey study, collecting detailed reports from over 2000 subjects, and he reproduces numerous examples offered by the subjects, which enables us to see something of the range of what people take to be typical elicitors of anger. References to injustice abound in Hall's sample of subjects' reports of the causes of their anger: "Injustice is the worst and its effects last longest"; "injustice to others"; being "accused of doing what I did not do"; "injustice"; "self gratification at another's expense, cruelty, being deceived" (pp. 538–539). This fits well with the suggestion that perceived injustice is a central trigger for anger.

Thus, subjects do mention injustice, both in the recent social psychological work and in Hall's nineteenth-century surveys. However, while recent work tends to ask subjects to recall a single experience of anger, Hall asks subjects more open-ended questions about their experience with anger and to list things that cause them to feel anger. As a result, his data have the potential to reveal a richer range of causes of anger. That potential is abundantly realized. Most of the sample quotations he gives concerning causes of anger include situations in which judgments of injustice seem not to be involved. Here are some examples of typical causes of anger offered by a range of people from schoolchildren to adults:

"unpleasant manners and looks";

"narrow mindedness";

"girls talking out loud and distracting me in study hours";

"being kept waiting, being hurried, having my skirt trodden on, density in others";

"If I am hurrying in the street and others saunter, so that I cannot get by . . . or when given a seat in church behind a large pillar";

"Frivolity in others, asking needless questions, attempting to cajole or boot-lick the teachers";

"An over tidy relative always slicking up my things";

"slovenly work, want of system, method and organization";

"late risers in my own house, stupidity";

"when I see a girl put on airs, strut around, talk big and fine. I scut my feet and want to hit her, if she is not too big" (pp. 538–539)

None of these examples obviously invokes considerations of injustice, and for some of them, it seems rather implausible that perceived injustice is at the root of the anger. Perhaps if you squint, you can see all of them as involving perceived injustice. But we are somewhat skeptical about the methodological propriety of squinting.

That anger is frequently triggered by something other than perceived injustice should not be surprising if, as seems likely, the anger system is evolutionarily ancient. On the contrary, if anger (or a close analogue) reaches deep into our mammalian ancestry, it would be surprising if it turned out that the only activator for anger is an appraisal of unfairness. In older phyla, the homologues of anger may be more typically elicited by physical attacks by conspecifics or the taking of resources (battery or theft). Similar responses may also arise in hierarchical species, when an animal that is not dominant tries to engage in dominant behavior or take a privilege reserved for dominant individuals. This is the furry equivalent, perhaps, of seeing a girl put on airs, strut around, talking all big and fine.

The common denominators here for eliciting anger seems to relate to challenges to the individual's autonomy (as discussed in Section 2). So it is perhaps not surprising that, in humans, anger gets triggered by violations of autonomy norms. When a person aggresses against another, that causes harm, and violates the victim's entitlement to be left in peace. Theft is a harm that violates a victim's entitlement to possessions. Putting on airs is a way of acting superior, which harms others by placing them in a position of subordination or inequitable distribution and insulting them by treating them as inferior. Being annoying or disruptive, thwarting goals, violating

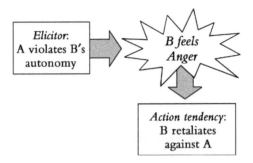

Figure 4.1. The psychological profile of anger

personal possessions of space, being insulting or offensive—all these things have a negative impact on a victim, and thus fail to respect individual rights or autonomy. Injustice is just one special and prevalent case. When people fail to cooperate or take more than is just for themselves, they treat others as inferior or less deserving. In our society, where presumptions of equality are strongly emphasized, that is seen as a harm. This is especially true in cases of free-riding. If one party incurs a cost for a benefit, and another takes the benefit without incurring the cost, then the person who incurs the cost is, in effect, incurring the cost for two. This is a form of harm, because it takes advantage of the victim. In summary, then, many of the various elicitors of anger can be regarded as violations of autonomy norms, with injustice being a paradigm case. This profile is represented in Figure 4.1.

Typically, anger will be experienced by the victim. In the economic games, one player gets angry at another and retaliates. It is worth noting, however, that the anger can also be experienced by third parties who observe the transgression. Sometimes the victim of an autonomy norm violation is passive, indifferent, oblivious, or even dead. Third parties who empathize with the victim or have norms against the offending behavior may incur the cost of retaliating. This has rarely been observed in non-human animals, but it is relatively common in humans, as when Western liberals rally for the end of foreign wars or when PETA activists intervene to protect animals.

3.2. Anger and Moral Motivation

Does anger play an important role in moral motivation? There's little reason to think that anger plays a direct internal role in motivating us to save drowning children, give money to Oxfam, or refrain from stealing, killing, and raping. But anger serves to underwrite external enforcement of morally valued

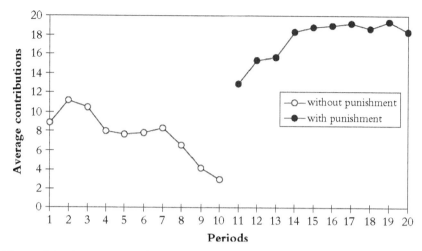

Figure 4.2. Average contributions without and with punishment (from Fehr & Gächter, 2000)

behaviors. And the awareness of anger serves to provide further motivation for prosocial behaviors.

In the previous section, we noted that free-riding in public-goods games generates anger and a corresponding motivation to punish the free-rider by paying to deplete his funds. What we didn't mention is that punishment is remarkably powerful in shaping behavior in these games. Over a number of experiments, Fehr and his colleagues have consistently found that when punishment is an available option in public-goods games, cooperation increases dramatically (Fehr & Gächter, 2000; Fehr & Fischbacher, 2004). Perhaps the most impressive illustration of this occurs when subjects first play several rounds in which punishment is not an option. In one such experiment (Fehr & Gächter, 2000), ten rounds are played in which punishment is not an option; by the tenth round the average contribution dropped to very low levels (below 20%). Punishment becomes available for the eleventh round, and the average contribution skyrockets. By the fourth round in which punishment is available, average contributions are at 90%! (see Figure 4.2). If Fehr and Gächter are right that this punishment is driven by anger, then anger is a formidable force for motivating cooperation.

Since cooperation is a morally valued behavior, and since punishment in public-goods games is plausibly driven by anger, it seems that anger plays a powerful role to the good. For anger apparently secures cooperation by motivating punishment. In addition, there's a second indirect role for anger in moral motivation. In Fehr and Gächter's experiments, as soon as subjects are told that punishment is available, there is already a huge leap in cooperation (see Figure 4.2). Why is this? Fehr and Gächter suggest that it is because subjects realize that, if they defect, others will become angry and punish them. While this is a plausible explanation for the dramatic leap in average contributions between the tenth and eleventh trials, it isn't the only possible explanation. Another possibility is that people are more willing to contribute when they know that they can punish. We suspect that both factors contribute to the effect and that anticipation of anger-driven retaliation does contribute to the motivation to cooperate.

So far we have argued that anger facilitates good behavior *in others*, because it motivates people to avoid angry responses. This kind of good behavior can be explained simply in terms of self-interest. But it's important to note that anger can motivate good behavior that can't be assimilated to a simple self-interest story. For instance, Fehr & Fischbacher (2004) found that third-party observers would pay to punish people who defect in a prisoner's dilemma. The motivation here seems not to be simple self-interest, but, rather, to rectify an injustice. In this case, the motivation looks to be more properly *moral*. Thus anger apparently serves to motivate moral behavior in multiple ways.

4. Guilt

Guilt is perhaps the quintessential moral emotion. No other emotion is more directly associated with morality. As we pointed out, it's plausible that anger can occur in non-moral contexts. By contrast, guilt almost always plays a moral role and, arguably, guilt occurs in non-moral contexts only when people take a moral stance toward something that does not warrant such a stance. If you feel guilty about breaking your diet, for example, you may be unwittingly moralizing weight ideals and self-control. Guilt is also closely associated with the idea of conscience. It is construed as a guide that tells us when an action is wrong. Guilt may play important roles in moral development, moral motivation, and moral judgment.

4.1. *Psychological Profile of Guilt*

Guilt has long been regarded as an important emotion in psychology, especially in the clinical tradition. Freud thought that neuroses sometimes resulted from guilt about suppressed desires, including the desires associated with the Oedipal complex. For both Freud and some later psychoanalytic theorists, guilt is regarded as a kind of inner conflict between components of the self, and is often negatively regarded as an emotion that does more harm than good. In recent years, conceptions of guilt have been changing, and it is now widely regarded as a fundamentally social emotion, which plays a positive prosocial role. We shall focus on this emerging conception of guilt (for a useful overview, see Baumeister et al., 1994).

As we noted in Section 2, emotions can be distinguished by their "core relational themes" (Lazarus, 1991). The core relational theme for guilt seems to be transgression of moral rules. But this simple formulation cannot distinguish guilt from shame, or, for that matter, from anger. There are several different emotions that arise when rules are violated. One obvious difference between guilt and anger is that we typically feel anger at other people when they violate rules. By contrast, if I feel guilty, it is typically when I myself have violated a rule. There may also be cases where I feel *angry* at myself, but that may be most common when thinking of the self in the second person (as in the familiar [to us] self-recrimination, "You idiot!"). We suspect such self-directed anger plays a different role than guilt. People get angry at themselves when they behave stupidly, but guilt arises when people violate norms. In fact guilt arises only for a specific class of norms. I don't feel guilty about jay-walking, and many people don't feel any guilt about cheating on their taxes, although they may feel afraid of getting caught. Guilt is especially likely to arise when we cause harm to another person, and the likelihood and intensity increase if that person is close to us in some way. We feel more guilty about harming members of the in-group than of the out-group, and guilt is most intense when the victim of our transgression is a loved one. This finding leads Baumeister et al. (1994) to conclude that guilt is an emotion that arises especially when there is a threat of separation or exclusion. When you jay-walk or cheat on your taxes, it is unlikely that you will be socially ostracized, much less that your primary relationship partners will abandon you. In contrast, when you harm someone close to you, you potentially undermine the attachment relation that you have with that person and with other members of your social group.

As a first pass, then, the core theme for guilt is something like: I have harmed someone whose well-being is a matter of concern to me. But it is important to note that the person who experiences guilt is not always actually responsible for harming anyone. As Baumeister et al. (1994) point out in their review, people feel guilty when they fare better than other people, even if they are not responsible for the inequity. The most famous and troubling example of this is survivor guilt. People who survived the Holocaust, the nuclear attack on Hiroshima, the AIDS epidemic among gay men, and other great catastrophes often report feeling guilty about surviving, especially if friends and family members were killed. Guilt is also experienced by those who keep their jobs when others are laid off, those who receive greater benefits than someone who worked just as hard, and even those who are recipients of unrequited love.

In the face of all these examples, one might be inclined to conclude that guilt has no special connection to transgression, but is rather an emotion whose core relational theme is: I am the recipient of a benefit that others whom I care about did not receive. But this proposal is difficult to reconcile with the fact that we often feel guilty about *causing* harm. It would seem that there are two forms of guilt: one elicited by causing harm and the other elicited by inequitable benefits. This is inelegant; it doesn't explain why people use the term "guilt" to describe these seemingly different cases. We are inclined to think that survivor guilt and other cases of guilt without transgression are actually over-extensions of cases involving transgression. People who experience survivor guilt feel responsible for the misery of others. They sometimes say that they should have done more to help. It seems that survivors erroneously believe that they have violated a norm; they think they were obligated to protect their loved ones and in a position to do so. In cases of guilt stemming from inequity, people often think, I didn't deserve this. The idea of desert, again, implies responsibility. People who feel guilty about, say, earning more than someone else who works equally hard may believe that they have violated a norm that says we should share our benefits with anyone who is equally deserving. Even if I am not the cause of an inequity, I am in a position to do something about it; I can protest it. Our conjecture is that all these cases hinge crucially on the fact that the people who experience guilt think that they are responsible for harming others. The difference between these cases and core cases is that the responsibility comes from omission rather than commission. If you feel guilty about cheating on your lover, then, in effect, you feel guilty about causing harm, and if you feel guilty about earning more than the person in the next cubicle, then you feel guilty about failing to prevent harm (e.g. failing to protest the unequal distribution).

In light of the foregoing, we conclude that the core relational theme for guilt is something like: someone I am concerned about has been harmed and I have responsibility for that in virtue of what I have done or failed to do. Guilt also, of course, has characteristic effects. Guilt is an unpleasant emotion, and, when it is experienced, people try to get rid of it in various ways. The most common coping strategies are confession, reparation, self-criticism, and punishment. The last of these was once believed to be especially central to guilt. Psychoanalysts thought that guilt would lead people to seek punishment from others, but evidence suggests that this tendency is not especially common (Baumeister et al., 1994). It more common for guilty people to try to clear

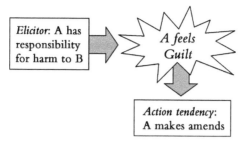

Figure 4.3. Psychological profile of guilt

their conscience by either apologizing or doing something to compensate for the harm they have caused. We return to this issue below. The story so far is summarized in Figure 4.3.

We are now in a position to see some of the ways that guilt differs from shame. For one thing, they have different core relational themes. Guilt occurs when we are responsible for causing harm to others. Shame differs from this in two respects. First, it doesn't always involve harm: one might feel ashamed about masturbating, for example. Jones et al. (1995) demonstrated that people feel guilty when they commit relational transgressions (harming another person), but not when they commit non-relational transgressions (e.g. masturbating or smoking marijuana). In non-relational cases, shame is more likely. Second, shame doesn't require a sense of control. We feel guilty in cases where we think we could have prevented some bad outcome, but shame sometimes arises in cases where we don't think we could have done otherwise. One might feel ashamed of oneself for compulsively having nasty thoughts about other people or for lacking the talent required to live up to others' expectations. Guilt and shame also differ in their effects. Guilty parties typically try to make up for what they have done by confessing or making amends. Shame is more likely to lead to withdrawal. People hang their heads in shame, and they avoid social contact. In studies of toddlers, psychologists exploit these differences to operationalize the distinction between guilt and shame. In one study, Barrett et al. (1993) had 2-year-olds play with a doll that had been rigged to break. Some of the toddlers showed the broken doll to adults apologetically, and others simply avoided looking at adults after the mishap. Following the differences noted above, reparative behavior is interpreted as indicating guilt and gaze avoidance is interpreted as indicating shame. Shame and guilt also differ in another way. People usually feel guilty about what they do or fail to do; but people feel ashamed about what they are or what they fail to be. In other words, guilt is action-directed, and shame is self-directed. Actions may lead one to feel ashamed, but in feeling ashamed, one feels like a bad or corrupt person. One can feel guilty without feeling like a bad person.

The contrast between guilt and shame is reminiscent of the contrast between anger and disgust. Anger tends to be associated with actions. We think it is likely that one can be angry at a person for doing something wrong without feeling as if that person is intrinsically bad. Disgust, in contrast, tends to transfer from action to person. If someone does something that you find repellent (a sexually perverse act, for example), you might find that person repellent thereafter. A person who does something disgusting becomes a disgusting person, but a person that does something irksome does not necessarily qualify as irksome thereby. These parallels suggest that guilt and shame might be first-person analogues of anger and disgust respectively (Prinz, 2007). We saw in Rozin et al.'s (1999) CAD model that anger occurs when someone violates an autonomy norm and disgust occurs when someone commits an unnatural act. These emotions are other-directed. If you yourself violate someone's autonomy, that qualifies as a form of harm, and if you harm someone, you are likely to feel guilty. If you perform an unnatural act, you are more likely to feel ashamed.

Both guilt and shame are sometimes regarded as basic emotions (Ekman, 1994). It is not implausible that they both evolved to play roles in regulating social behavior. But another possibility is that these emotions are learned by-products of other emotions that are more fundamental. We will not explore this idea with respect to shame, but consider guilt (both are discussed by Prinz, 2004). On the face of it, guilt has striking similarities to other emotions. In particular, it has much in common with sadness and, to a lesser extent, fear. Like sadness, guilt is often associated with feeling downtrodden. Excessive guilt is a core symptom of clinical depression (American Psychiatric Association, 1994); young children who score high in sadness ratings, also score high in guilt (Eisenberg, 2000); when adults recall events that caused them to feel intense guilt, they also report feeling sadness (Shin et al., 2000); and when asked to select facial expressions to associate with guilt vignettes, people tend to select frowning faces (Prinz, unpublished study). The relation between guilt and fear may be a little weaker, but fear is correlated with guilt in children (Kochanska et al., 2002). One explanation for these findings is that guilt is actually a form of sadness, or sadness mixed with a little anxiety. It might be acquired as follows. When young children misbehave, parents withdraw love. Love withdrawal threatens the attachment relationship that children have with their parents, and losing attachments is a paradigm cause of sadness. It can also cause anxiety, insofar as attachment relations are a source of security. The threat of losing love leads children to associate sadness with transgression. Initially, they are sad about losing their parents' affection, but, through associative learning, sadness becomes associated with the transgressions themselves. The anxiety-tinged sadness about wrongdoing is then labeled "guilt." This would help explain why guilt is so linked with transgressions that involve harm. Harming another person is especially likely to threaten that relationship. If a child is caught breaking a rule that does not involve harm (e.g. taking off clothing in public), parents may react differently (e.g. scolding or displaying disgust). This story would also explain why guilt leads people to make amends. If guilt arises in contexts of potential loss, those all-important relationships can be repaired by apology or confession. And it also explains the fact that we feel guilt about harming people even when the harm was not intended, because inadvertent harm can also threaten attachment relations.

4.2. Guilt and Moral Motivation

We have already touched on ways in which guilt contributes to moral motivation. When people feel guilty, they confess, make reparations, criticize themselves, or, less frequently, seek punishment. Notice that these behaviors are all attempts to make up for misdeeds. Guilt probably plays an important role motivating us to compensate for harming others (Baumeister et al., 1994). Guilt may play a second and related motivational role as well. Guilt is unpleasant, and people may resist doing things when they anticipate feeling guilty about them. In our discussion of anger, we noted that people may obey rules to avoid the ire of others. People may also obey rules to avoid feeling guilty later. Indeed, guilt avoidance may play a more powerful role in rule conformity than anger avoidance. Anger is associated with aggression, and anticipating aggression causes fear. But fear is thought to be a comparatively weak moral motivator (Caprara et al., 2001). For example, power assertion is known to be a less effective tool in moral education than love withdrawal, which causes guilt. Guilt is more correlated with good behavior than is fear.

Evolutionary game theorists have argued that anticipatory guilt promotes cooperative behavior by adding an emotional cost to defection (Trivers, 1971; Frank, 1988). In terms of actual material gain, in many economic games, defection is a dominant strategy: defectors do better than cooperators regardless of whether their trading partners defect or cooperate. But this fact makes it rational for both parties to defect, even though mutual defection is worse than mutual cooperation in many of these games. Trivers (1971) speculates that evolution has promoted the emergence of guilt because it makes defection less attractive. People may gain materially from defecting, but guilt makes them suffer emotionally, and that leads them to cooperate. Frank (1988) notes that this tendency is so deeply engrained that people even avoid defection in cases where the other party is not a likely partner in future exchanges. For example, people leave good tips in roadside restaurants even though they are unlikely to ever encounter the waitstaff again. Both Trivers and Frank assume that guilt is the result of biological evolution, and this would support the hypothesis that guilt is a basic emotion. But it is equally possible that guilt emerged under cultural pressure as a tool for ensuring that people cooperate. Cross-cultural variation in economic games suggests that culture may contribute to how people construe fairness. The Machiguenga of Peru, for example, seem to accept very inequitable offers as fair, even when North Americans would judge otherwise (Henrich & Smith, 2004). In their slash−and-burn economy, the Machiguenga do not depend much on strangers, so cultural pressure has not led them to morally condemn those who hoard resources rather than dividing them equitably.

The forms of moral motivation that we have mentioned so far relate to transgression; guilt motivates us to make up for misdeeds, and it deters us from behaving badly. What about good behavior? When we introduced the topic of moral motivation, we suggested that emotions might lead people to behave prosocially. It's not obvious that guilt should play a role in prosocial behavior. Folk psychology would have us believe that we do nice things for people out of empathy or concern. There is evidence, however, that guilt can promote good deeds as well. Carlsmith and Gross (1969) demonstrated that guilt can promote altruistic behavior. They set up a situation similar to the one used by Stanley Milgram in his famous obedience studies. Subjects were asked to administer electric shocks to another person, ''the learner,'' whenever he failed to answer questions correctly. The learner was introduced as a volunteer for the study, but he was actually a confederate in the experiment. Afterwards, the subject was asked to make phone calls on behalf of an environmental organization. In one condition, subjects are asked to make the calls by the learner, in another condition subjects are asked by a witness who observes the whole affair, and in a third control condition the subject is never asked to administer electric shocks. Subjects who are asked by the learner to make the calls are not more likely to do so than subjects in the control condition. This suggests that people are not inclined to be more altruistic as a way of making amends to victims of their transgressions. But subjects who are asked to make the calls by a witness make dramatically more calls than in the other two conditions. This suggests that, when people feel guilty, they are more inclined to engage in altruism when the request comes from a third-party witness. This implies that while good deeds might not serve as form of restitution, they can mitigate the aversive effects of guilt.

The Carlsmith and Gross study shows that guilt can promote prosocial behavior. Subsequent work has shown that it is most likely to do so when individuals have no other way of coping with their guilt. In an ingenious study, Harris et al. (1975) set up a donation stand for the March of Dimes in a Catholic church. They solicited donations from people who were either just coming from confession or on their way to confession. Almost 40% of those who were on their way to confess made a donation, but under 20% of those who had already confessed made a donation. The likely interpretation is that, once confessions are made, guilt is reduced, and that leads to the reduction in altruism. Guilt may promote altruistic behavior by default, but that disposition drops precipitously if people can cope with their guilt in a less costly way. Shame may play a role in this study too, but guilt is more likely to be doing the work: guilt is behaviorally associated with both confession and making amends, whereas shame tends to promote inward focus, and it is not easily assuaged by confession.

Another limitation of guilt is that it may not promote prosocial behavior toward members of an out-group. As noted above, guilt mostly arises when harm comes to someone we care about. With out-groups, care is mitigated. We often find strong popular support for government programs that bring immense suffering to citizens of other nations. Guilt is especially unlikely if we construe the victim as an enemy or, in some other respect, undeserving of our concern. Studies have show that when we harm a member of an out-group, there is a tendency to justify the transgression by denigrating the victim. In a chilling Milgram-style study, Katz et al. (1973) had white males administer electric shocks to a "learner" before and after filling out a questionnaire to assess the learner's personality. The responses to the personality questionnaires did not change when the learner was white, but, after administering strong shocks to a black learner, subjects tended to dramatically lower the assessment of his personality. Subjects would denigrate the black man after treating him cruelly. One explanation is that the subjects felt more guilt about harming a black man, given the history of injustice toward that group. To diminish the guilt, they confabulate a justification for their actions, by implying that the black man somehow deserved to receive shocks. It is unclear from these findings whether subjects felt guilty and assuaged those feelings through denigration, or whether the denigration prevented the onset of guilt. In any case, the intensity and duration of guilt seem to depend on attitudes toward the victim.

In summary, guilt can play a significant role in promoting prosocial behavior, although that role may be limited. Those who want to expand the impact of guilt must find ways to broaden the range of people for whom we feel a sense of responsibility and concern.

5. Concluding Question: Morality without Anger and Guilt?

In this chapter, we have been looking at ways in which emotion relates to morality. We began with the observation that emotions typically arise when people make moral judgments, and went on to observe that the emotions in question are ones that involve self- or other-directed blame. The actual moral emotion that arises on any occasion will depend on what kind of transgression has taken place. We looked at two of these emotions in some detail: anger and guilt. We suggested that these emotions are particularly important in Western morality, because they arise in response to autonomy norm violations, and autonomy norms are central in Western morality. But we do not mean to imply that autonomy is an exclusively Western concern. Indeed, we want to conclude by asking whether morality is even possible in the absence of anger and guilt.

Let us compare anger and guilt to another pair of moral emotions, disgust and shame. As we have seem, disgust tends to arise when actions are construed as crimes against nature, and shame tends to arise with unwelcome attention from others. They are related because crimes against nature bring unwelcome attention. In this light, it is plausible to think of the disgust/shame dyad as functioning to shape the social self. By "social self" we mean those aspects of personal behavior that define oneself as a member of a social group. If there are behaviors that bring negative attention from the group, we avoid them. We act in ways that are approved of by our communities. Among these behaviors are those that are construed as natural. Natural behaviors are characteristically bodily in nature: how we dress, diet, and sexual conduct are all paradigm cases. There may also be norms about how we stand, move, breathe, and digest (whether we can spit, where we defecate, and what to do when we belch, for example). Each social group seems to have a set of behaviors that are considered natural. These are expressed in dietary rules (don't eat bugs or horses), sexual mores (don't have sex with animals), and countless norms regulating self-presentation (wear shirts in public).

Norms that construct the social self are extremely important for identity and group membership. They also regulate many of our day-to-day activities and crucial life choices, such as whom we can marry. So it would be a terrible oversight to neglect such norms, as has too often been the case in Western moral philosophy. But norms that are enforced by anger and guilt may be even more important for morality, in some sense. Notice that norms pertaining to the social self could be replaced by something like customs and conventions that are not regarded moralistically. They would be regarded as optional forms of self-expression and group affiliation rather than norms that must be followed. There is evidence that this trend has occurred in the West, where, for example, victimless sexual perversions are not seen as morally wrong, at least by high SES groups (Haidt et al., 1993). But we can't so easily replace the norms associated with anger and guilt. These are autonomy norms, and their violation leads to harms. If these were treated as optional, harms might proliferate and social stability would be threatened. Norms pertaining to the social self may be important for identity, but norms pertaining to harm are important for preservation of life. They are, therefore, less dispensable.

Now one might argue that we can preserve our autonomy norms while dropping the concomitant emotions. There are several reasons for thinking this won't work. First, it may be that these norms are constituted by the emotions, as suggested by constitution models (Prinz, 2007), or depend on such emotions for their characteristic moral profile, as suggested by the sentimental rules theory (Nichols, 2004). Second, even if this is not the case, the emotions may play a crucial role in maintaining the norms and acting on them. Recall that anger promotes retaliation (as when we punish free-riders), and retaliation leads to norm conformity. Anticipation of guilt leads to norm conformity even when retaliation won't arise (as when we can get away with being free-riders). When we anticipate the wrath of others or our own guilt, this can defeat the temptation to engage in harmful behavior. If these costs were removed, then norm conformity might drop off dramatically.

We think this lesson follows from the empirical research. Those who regard emotions as inessential to morality—or even as disruptive to morality—should study the roles that these emotions play before recommending their elimination. In our view, anger and guilt may play roles that are especially important. Whether or not moral judgments essentially involve emotions, as the authors of this chapter have argued elsewhere, emotions may be essential for the preservation and practice of morality. If anger and guilt are not core ingredients of a moral outlook, they may still be the *sine qua non*.

References

American Psychiatric Association (1994). *Diagnostic and Statistical Manual of Mental Disorders*, 4th ed. Washington, DC: American Psychiatric Association.

Arsenio, W. & Ford, M. (1985). The role of affective information in social-cognitive development: Children's differentiation of moral and conventional events. *Merrill–Palmer Quarterly*, 31: 1–17.

Averill, J. (1983). Studies on anger and aggression: Implications for theories of emotion, *American Psychologist*, 38: 1145–1160.

Ayer, A. (1936). *Language, Truth, and Logic*. London: Gollancz.

Barrett, K. C., Zahn-Waxler, C., & Cole, P. M. (1993). Avoiders versus amenders: implications for the investigation of guilt and shame during toddlerhood? *Cognition and Emotion*, 7: 481–505.

Batson, D. & Moran, T. (1999). Empathy-induced altruism in a prisoner's dilemma. *European Journal of Social Psychology*, 29: 909–924.

Baumeister, R. F., Stillwell, A. M., & Heatherton, T. F. (1994). Guilt: An interpersonal approach. *Psychological Bulletin*, 115: 243–267.

Baumeister, R. F., Stillwell, A., & Wotman, S. R. (1990). Victim and perpetrator accounts of interpersonal conflict: Autobiographical narratives about anger. *Journal of Personality and Social Psychology*, 59: 994–1005.

Ben-Ze'ev, A. (2000). *The Subtlety of Emotions*. Cambridge, MA: MIT Press.

Bosman, R. & van Winden, F. (2002). Emotional hazard in a power to take experiment. *The Economic Journal*, 112: 147–169.

Brink, D. (1989). *Moral Realism and the Foundation of Ethics*. Cambridge, UK: Cambridge University Press.

Caprara, G., Barbaranelli, C., Pastorelli, C., Cermak, I., & Rosza, S. (2001). Facing guilt: Role of negative affectivity, need for reparation, and fear of punishment in leading to prosocial behaviour and aggression. *European Journal of Personality*, 15: 219–237.

Carlsmith, J. M. & Gross, A. E. (1969). Some effects of guilt on compliance, *Journal of Personality and Social Psychology*, 11: 232–239.

Chapman, M., Zahn-Waxler, C., Cooperman, G., & Iannotti, R. (1987). Empathy and responsibility in the motivation of children's helping. *Developmental Psychology*, 23: 140–145.

Clayton, S. D. (1992). The experience of injustice: Some characteristics and correlates. *Social Justice Research*, 5: 71–91.

Darwin, C. (1872). *The Expression of the Emotions in Man and Animals*. London: John Murray.

Dreier, J. (1990). Internalism and speaker relativism. *Ethics*, 101: 6–26.

Eisenberg, N. (2000). Emotion, regulation, and moral development. *Annual Review of Psychology*, 51: 665–697.

Ekman, P. (1971). Universals and cultural differences in facial expressions of emotion. *Nebraska Symposium on Motivation*, J. Cole (ed.). Lincoln, NE: University of Nebraska Press, 207–283.

—— (1994). All emotions are basic. In P. Ekman & R. Davidson (eds.), *The Nature of Emotion*. New York: Oxford University Press, 15–19.

Ekman, P., Levenson, R. W., & Friesen, W. V. (1983). Autonomic nervous system activity distinguishes among emotions. *Science*, 221 (4616): 1208–1210.

Ellsworth, P. C. & Smith, C. A. (1988). From appraisal to emotion: Differences among unpleasant feelings. *Motivation and Emotion*, 12: 271–302.

Fehr, E. & Fischbacher, U. (2004). Third party punishment and social norms. *Evolution and Human Behavior*, 25: 63–87.

Fehr, E. & Gächter, S. (2000). Cooperation and punishment in public goods experiments. *American Economic Review*, 90: 980–994.

—— (2002). Altruistic punishment in humans. *Nature*, 415: 137–140.

Fessler, D. & Haley, K. (2003). The strategy of affect. In P. Hammerstein (ed.), *Genetic and Cultural Evolution of Cooperation*. Cambridge, MA: MIT Press, 7–36.

Foot, P. (1972). Morality as a system of hypothetical imperatives, *The Philosophical Review*, 81: 305–316.

Frank, R. (1988). *Passions Within Reason*. New York: W. W. Norton.

Frankena, W. (1973). *Ethics*, 2nd ed. Englewood Cliffs, NJ: Prentice Hall.

Gibbard, A. (1990). *Wise Choices, Apt Feelings*. Cambridge, MA: Harvard University Press.

Greene, J. (2008). The secret joke of Kant's soul. In W. Sinnott-Armstrong (ed.), *Moral Psychology, Vol. 3*. Cambridge, MA: MIT Press, 35–80.

Grusec, J. E. & Goodnow, J. J. (1994). Impact of parental discipline methods on the child's internalization of values: A reconceptualization of current points of view. *Developmental Psychology*, 30: 4–19.

Haidt, J. (2001). The emotional dog and its rational tail: A social intuitionist approach to moral judgment. *Psychological Review*, 108: 814–834.

—— (2003). The moral emotions. In R. Davidson et al. (eds.), *The Handbook of Affective Sciences*. Oxford: Oxford University Press, 852–870.

—— (2007). The new synthesis in moral psychology. *Science*, 316: 998–1002.

Haidt, J. & Sabini, J. (ms). What exactly makes revenge sweet?

Haidt, J., Koller, S., & Dias, M. (1993). Affect, culture, and morality, or is it wrong to eat your dog? *Journal of Personality and Social Psychology*, 65: 613–628.

Hall, G. S. (1898). A study of anger. *The American Journal of Psychology*, 10: 516–591.

Harris, M., Benson, S., & Hall, C. (1975). The effects of confession on altruism. *Journal of Social Psychology*, 96: 187–192.

Heekeren, H., Wartenburger, I., Schmidt, H., Schwintowski, H., & Villringer, A. (2003). An fMRI study of simple ethical decision-making. *Neuroreport*, 14: 1215–1219.

Henrich, J. & Smith, N. (2004). Comparative experimental evidence from Machiguenga, Mapuche, Huinca, and American populations. In J. Henrich et al., *Foundations of Human Sociality*. New York: Oxford University Press, 125–167.

Henrich, J., Boyd, R., Bowles, S., Camerer, C., Fehr, E., & Gintis, H. (2004). *Foundations of Human Sociality*. New York: Oxford University Press.

Hoffman, M. L. (2000). *Empathy and Moral Development*. New York: Cambridge University Press.

Hopfensitz, A., & Reuben, E. (forthcoming). The importance of emotions for the effectiveness of social punishment. Downloaded 20 September 2005 from http://www.fee.uva.nl/creed/pdffiles/HR05.pdf.

Isen, A. M. & Levin, P. F. (1972). The effect of feeling good on helping: Cookies and kindness. *Journal of Personality and Social Psychology*, 21: 384–388.

Jones, W. H., Kugler, K., & Adams, P. (1995). You always hurt the one you love: Guilt and transgressions against relational partners. In K. Fisher & J. Tangney (eds.), *Self-conscious Emotions*. New York: Guilford, 301–321.

Kant, I. (1996). *The Metaphysics of Morals*. M. J. Gregor (trans.). Cambridge: Cambridge University Press.

——(1997). *Groundwork of the Metaphysics of Morals*, ed. Mary Gregor. Cambridge: Cambridge University Press.

Katz, I., Glass, D., & Cohen, S. (1973). Ambivalence, guilt, and the scapegoating of minority group victims. *Journal of Experimental Social Psychology*, 9: 423–436.

Kelly, D., Stich, S., Haley, K., Eng, S., & Fessler, D. (2007). Harm, affect and the moral/conventional distinction. *Mind & Language*, 22: 117–131.

Keltner, D., Ellsworth, P. C., & Edwards, K. (1993). Beyond simple pessimism: Effects of sadness and anger on social perception. *Journal of Personality and Social Psychology*, 64: 740–752.

Kochanska, G., Gross, J., Lin, M., & Nichols, K. (2002). Guilt in young children: Development, determinants, and relations with a broader system of standards. *Child Development*, 73: 461–482.

Lazarus, R. (1991). *Emotion and Adaptation*. New York: Oxford University Press.

Lemerise, E. & Dodge, K. (2008). The development of anger and hostile reactions. In Michael Lewis et al. (eds.), *Handbook of Emotions*, 3rd edn. New York: Guilford Press, 730–741.

Lerner, J., Goldberg, J., & Tetlock, P. (1998). Sober second thought: The effects of accountability, anger, and authoritarianism on attributions of responsibility, *Personality and Social Psychology Bulletin*, 24: 563–574.

McDowell, J. (1985). Values and secondary qualities. In T. Honderich (ed.), *Morality and Objectivity*. London: Routledge & Kegan Paul, 110–129.

Mikula, G. (1986). The experience of injustice: toward a better understanding of its phenomenology. In *Justice in Social Relations*, H. W. Bierhoff, R. L. Cohen, & J. Greenberg (eds.). New York: Plenum, 103–124.

Moll, J., de Oliveira-Souza, R., & Eslinger, P. J. (2003). Morals and the human brain: A working model. *Neuroreport*, 14: 299–305.

Moll, J., de Oliveira-Souza, R., Bramati, I., & Grafman, J. (2002). Functional networks in emotional moral and nonmoral social judgments. *NeuroImage*, 16: 696–703.

Nichols, S. (2004). *Sentimental Rules: On the Natural Foundations of Moral Judgment*. New York: Oxford University Press.

Nucci, L. (2001). *Education in the Moral Domain*. Cambridge: Cambridge University Press.

Ortony, A. & Turner, J. (1990). What's basic about basic emotions? *Psychological Review*, 97: 315–331.

Panksepp, J. (1998). *Affective Neuroscience*. New York: Oxford University Press.

——(2000). Emotions as natural kinds within the mammalian brain. In M. Lewis & J. Haviland (eds.) *Handbook of Emotions*, 2nd ed. New York: Guilford Press, 87–107.

Pillutla, M. & Murnighan, J. (1996). Unfairness, anger and spite. *Organizational Behavior and Human Decision Processes*, 68: 208–224.

Preston, S. & de Waal, F. (2002). Empathy: Its ultimate and proximate bases. *Behavioral and Brain Sciences*, 25: 1–20.

Prinz, J. (2002). *Furnishing the Mind: Concepts and Their Perceptual Basis*. Cambridge, MA: MIT Press.

—— (2004). *Gut Reactions: A Perceptual Theory of Emotion*. New York: Oxford University Press.

—— (2007). *The Emotional Construction of Morals*. Oxford: Oxford University Press.

—— (2008). Is morality innate? In W. Sinnott-Armstrong (ed.), *Moral Psychology, Volume 1: The Evolution of Morality: Adaptations and Innateness*. Cambridge, MA: MIT Press, 367–406.

—— (forthcoming). Is empathy necessary for morality? In P. Goldie & A. Coplan (eds.), *Empathy: Philosophical and Psychological Perspectives*. New York: Oxford University Press.

Rozin, P., Lowry, L., Imada, S., & Haidt, J. (1999). The CAD triad hypothesis. *Journal of Personality and Social Psychology*, 76: 574–586.

Sanfey, A., Rilling, J., Aronson, J., Nystrom, L., & Cohen, J. (2003). The neural basis of economic decision-making in the ultimatum game. *Science*, 300: 1755–1758.

Scherer, K. R. (1997). The role of culture in emotion-antecedent appraisal. *Journal of Personality and Social Psychology*, 73: 902–922.

Schnall, S., Haidt, J., & Clore, G. (2008). Disgust as embodied moral judgment. *Personality and Social Psychology Bulletin*, 34: 1096–1109.

Shaver, P., Schwartz, J., Kirson, D., & O'Connor, C. (1987). Emotion knowledge: Further exploration of a prototype approach. *Journal of Personality and Social Psychology*, 52: 1061–1086.

Shin, L. M., Dougherty, D., Macklin, M. L., Orr, S. P., Pitman, R. K., & Rauch, S. L. (2000). Activation of anterior paralimbic structures during guilt-related script-driven imagery. *Biological Psychiatry*, 48: 43–50.

Shweder, R., Mahapatra, M., & Miller, J. (1987). Culture and moral development. In J. Kagan & S. Lamb (eds.), *The Emergence of Morality in Young Children*. Chicago, IL: University of Chicago Press, 1–83.

Shweder, R., Much, N., Mahapatra, M., & Park, L. (1999). The "Big Three" of morality (autonomy, community, divinity) and the "Big Three" explanations of suffering. In A. Brandt & P. Rozin (eds.), *Morality and Health*. New York: Routledge, 119–169.

Smetana, J. (1993). Understanding of social rules. In M. Bennett (ed.), *The Development of Social Cognition: The Child as Psychologist*. New York: Guilford Press, 111–141.

Smith, C. A. & Ellsworth, P. C. (1985). Patterns of cognitive appraisal in emotion. *Journal of Personality and Social Psychology*, 48: 813–838.

Smith, M. (1994). *The Moral Problem*. Oxford: Blackwell.

Sprecher, S. (1992). How men and women expect to feel and behave in response to inequity in close relation. *Social Psychology Quarterly*, 55: 57–69.

Sripada, C. & Stich, S. (2006). A framework for the psychology of norms. In P. Carruthers, S. Laurence, & S. Stich (eds.), *The Innate Mind: Culture and Cognition*. New York: Oxford University Press.

Stark, R. (1997). *The Rise of Christianity*. New York: HarperCollins.

Stevenson, C. (1944). *Ethics and Language*. New Haven, CT: Yale University Press.

Takahashi, H., Yahata, N., Koeda, M., Matsuda, T., Asai, K., & Okubo, Y. (2004). Brain activation associated with evaluative processes of guilt and embarrassment: An fMRI study. *NeuroImage*, 23: 967–974.

Tangney, J. P., Miller, R. S., Flicker, L., & Barlow, D. H. (1996). Are shame, guilt, and embarrassment distinct emotions? *Journal of Personality and Social Psychology*, 70: 1256–1269.

Tissot, S. A. D. (1766). *A Treatise on the Crime of Onan, Illustrated with a Variety of Cases Together with the Method of Cure*. London: B. Thomas.

Trivers, R. (1971). The evolution of reciprocal altruism, *Quarterly Review of Biology*, 46: 35–57.

Turiel, E. (1983). *The Development of Social Knowledge: Morality and Convention*, Cambridge: Cambridge University Press.

Wheatley, T. & Haidt, J. (2005). Hypnotically induced disgust makes moral judgments more severe. *Psychological Science*, 16: 780–784.

Zahn-Waxler, C., Radke-Yarrow, M., Wagner, E., & Chapman, M. (1992). Development of concern for others, *Developmental Psychology*, 28: 126–136.

Zelazo, P., Helwig, C., & Lau, A. (1996). Intention, act, and outcome in behavioral prediction and moral judgment, *Child Development*, 67: 2478–2492.

5

Altruism

STEPHEN STICH, JOHN M. DORIS, AND ERICA
ROEDDER

1. Philosophical Background

People sometimes behave in ways that benefit others, and they sometimes do this while knowing that their helpful behavior will be costly, unpleasant, or dangerous. But at least since Plato's classic discussion in the second book of the *Republic*, debate has raged over *why* people behave in these ways. Are their motives altruistic, or is their behavior ultimately motivated by self-interest? According to Thomas Hobbes, who famously advocated the latter option,

> No man giveth but with intention of good to himself, because gift is voluntary; and of all voluntary acts, the object is to every man his own good; of which, if men see they shall be frustrated, there will be no beginning of benevolence or trust, nor consequently of mutual help. (Hobbes, 1651/1981: ch. 15)

This selfish or *egoistic* view of human motivation has had no shortage of eminent advocates, including La Rochefoucauld (1665/2007), Bentham (1824: 392–393), and Nietzsche (1881/1997: 148).[1] Egoism is also arguably the dominant view of human motivation in much contemporary social science, particularly in economics (see Grant, 1997; Miller, 1999). Dissenting voices, though perhaps fewer in number, have been no less eminent. Butler (1726: esp. *Sermon* XI), Hume (1751/1975: 272, 298), Rousseau (1754/1985) and Adam Smith (1759/1853) have all argued that, sometimes at least, human motivation is genuinely *altruistic*.

Although the issue that divides egoistic and altruistic accounts of human motivation is substantially empirical, competing answers may have profound

---

[1] Interpretation of historical texts is, of course, often less than straightforward. While there are passages in the works of each of these philosophers that can be interpreted as advocating egoism, scholars might debate whether these passages reflect the author's considered option. Much the same is true for the defenders of altruism mentioned below.

consequences for moral theory.[2] For example, Kant (1785: sec. 1, para. 12) famously argued that a person should act "not from inclination but from duty, and by this would his conduct first acquire true moral worth." But egoism maintains that *all* human motivation is ultimately self-interested, and if so, people *can't* act "from duty" in the way that Kant urged. Thus, if egoism were true, Kant's account would entail that *no* conduct has "true moral worth."[3] The same difficulty obtains for Aristotle's insistence, in *Nicomachean Ethics* ii 4, that acting virtuously requires choosing the virtuous action "for its own sake." Once again, if all actions are ultimately self-interested, it is unclear how any action can meet Aristotle's criterion, and we must consider the possibility of skepticism about virtuous action.

Whether or not such difficulties can be ameliorated, there can be little doubt that they resonate widely. It is easy to find philosophers who suggest that altruism is required for morality or that egoism is incompatible with morality—and easier still to find philosophers who claim that *other* philosophers think this. In the standard reference work we consulted (LaFollette, 2000a), examples abound:

Moral behavior is, at the most general level, altruistic behavior, motivated by the desire to promote not only our own welfare but the welfare of others. (Rachels, 2000: 81)

[O]ne central assumption motivating ethical theory in the Analytic tradition is that the function of ethics is to combat the inherent egoism or selfishness of individuals. Indeed, many thinkers define the basic goal of morality as "selflessness" or "altruism." (Schroeder, 2000: 396)

Philosophers since Socrates worried that humans might be capable of acting only to promote their own self-interest. But if that is all we can do, then it seems morality is impossible. (LaFollette, 2000b: 5)

If these philosophers are right, and egoism is true, moral skepticism may be in order.

Additionally, if egoism is true, then we face a dilemma in answering the venerable question, "Why should I be moral?" If this question requests a justification that can actually motivate an agent to act morally, then egoism

---

[2] A note on terminology: we shall use the terms "egoism" and "altruism" for views about the nature of human motivation that will be explained in more detail below. Other authors prefer to call these views "psychological egoism" and "psychological altruism" to distinguish them from normative claims about how people should behave, and from an evolutionary notion of altruism that we'll discuss in Section 3. Since both evolutionary altruism and psychological altruism will be considered in Section 3, we'll use "psychological altruism" for the latter notion in that section.

[3] Kant appears to consider this possibility: "A cool observer, one that does not mistake the wish for good, however lively, for its reality, may sometimes doubt whether true virtue is actually found anywhere in the world" (Kant, 1785: sec. 2.)

poses strong constraints on how it can be answered: the answer will have to ground moral motivation in the agent's self-interest. On the other hand, the question "Why should I be moral?" might be construed as inquiring after a merely theoretic justification—one that might or might not motivate a person to act morally. If the question is construed in this way, and if egoism is true, then there may well be a disconnect between moral theory and moral motivation. Our best moral theories may well answer the question "Why be moral?" by appealing to symmetry between the self and other or ideals of social harmony. Unfortunately, these appeals—while perhaps enlightening—will be motivationally moot.

Yet another cluster of issues surrounds the principle *"ought" implies "can."* Depending on the modal strength of egoism, it could turn out that persons simply cannot be motivated by anything other than self-interest. If this is true, and if "ought" implies "can," then it cannot be said that humans *ought* to be motivated by anything other than self-interest.

There are related implications for political philosophy. If the egoists are right, then the *only* way to motivate prosocial behavior is to give people a selfish reason for engaging in such behavior, and this constrains the design of political institutions intended to encourage civic-minded behavior. John Stuart Mill, who like Bentham before him was both a utilitarian and an egoist, advocated a variety of manipulative social interventions to engender conformity with utilitarian moral standards.[4]

Since the empirical debate between egoists and altruists appears to have such striking implications, it should come as no surprise that psychologists and other scientists have done a great deal of work aimed at determining which view is correct. But before we turn to the empirical literature, it is important to get clearer on what the debate is really about. We shall begin, in Section 2, with a brief sketch of a cluster of assumptions about human desires, beliefs, actions, and motivation that are widely shared by historical and contemporary authors on both sides in the debate. With this as background, we'll be able to offer a more sharply focused account of the debate.[5] In Section 3, our focus will be on links between evolutionary theory and the egoism/altruism debate. There is a substantial literature employing evolutionary theory on each side of the

---

[4] For example, Mill suggests instilling "hope of favor and the fear of displeasure from our fellow creatures or from the Ruler of the Universe" (Mill, 1861/2001: ch. 3). Another proposal was to instill a feeling of conscience: "a pain, more or less intense, attendant on violation of duty . . . . This feeling [is] all encrusted over with collateral associations . . . derived from . . . fear; from all the forms of religious feeling; from self-esteem . . . and occasionally even self-abasement" (ibid.).

[5] For more on the history of the debate between egoists and altruists, see Broad (1930); MacIntyre (1967); Nagel (1970); Batson (1991), chs. 1–3; Sober & Wilson (1998), ch. 9.

issue. However, it is our contention that neither camp has offered a convincing case. We are much more sanguine about recent research on altruism in social psychology, which will be our topic in Section 4. Although we don't think this work has resolved the debate, we shall argue that it has made illuminating progress—progress that philosophers interested in the question cannot afford to ignore.

2. Desires and Practical Reasoning

As we understand it, the egoism/altruism debate is typically structured by three familiar assumptions about the nature of desire and practical reasoning. First, parties to the debate typically assume that genuine actions are caused by desires. If Albert wants (or desires) to raise his hand, and if this desire causes his hand to go up, then this behavior counts as an *action*.[6] If, by contrast, Beth has no desire to raise her hand but it goes up anyway because of a nervous tic, or because Albert lifts it, then this behavior does not count as an action. Within this debate the term "desire" is used in a very inclusive way; it is a general term covering many motivational states. Donald Davidson (1963: 685–686) famously characterized all such motivational states as *pro-attitudes* (we prefer the term *desires*) and emphasized that this was meant to include states such as wantings, urges, promptings, and yens, enduring character traits like a taste for loud company, and passing fancies like a sudden desire to touch a woman's elbow!

A second assumption is that desires and beliefs can interact to generate a chain of new desires via a process that is often called *practical reasoning*. Thus, for example, if Cathy wants an espresso, and if she acquires the belief that the Starbucks on Main Street is the best place to get an espresso, this may cause her to desire to go to the Starbucks on Main Street. If she believes that the best way to get to Main Street is to take the number 43 bus, this, along with the newly formed desire to go to Starbucks, may cause a desire to take the number 43 bus. And so on.[7] Cathy's desire to take the bus and her desire to go to Starbucks are *instrumental* desires. She has them only because she wants that espresso.

But, and this is the final assumption, not all desires can be instrumental desires. If we are to avoid circularity or an infinite regress, there must be some

---

[6] Actually, not just any causal link between the desire and the behavior will do, and a great deal of philosophical work has been devoted to specifying the appropriate connection. See Grice (1971); Davidson (1980); Bratman (1987); Velleman (1989); Wilson (2002).

[7] For a classic statement of this conception of action, see Goldman (1970).

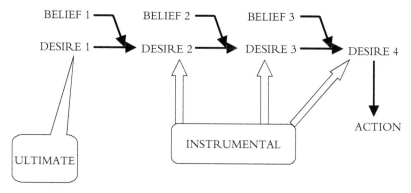

Figure 5.1. Practical reasoning
A causal process in which pre-existing desires and beliefs interact to generate a
chain of new instrumental desires

desires that are *not* generated by our belief that satisfying them will facilitate
satisfying some other desire. These are our "ultimate" desires; the states of
affairs that will satisfy them are desired, as is often said, *for their own sake*.
Figure 5.1 depicts all this in a format that will come in handy later on.

With this background in place, it can be seen that the debate between
egoists and altruists is a debate about *ultimate* desires. Egoists maintain that *all*
of our ultimate desires are selfish, and although altruists concede that some of
our ultimate desires are selfish, they insist that people can and do have ultimate
desires for the well-being of others. However, this account of the debate leaves
a number of sticky issues yet to be addressed.[8]

One of these concerns the distinction between ultimate and instrumental
desires. Our explanation of the distinction suggests that all desires fall into one
category or the other, but it certainly seems to be possible for some desires
to be both. Consider, for example, the desire to avoid pain. This is often
cited as a paradigm case of an ultimate desire. But now suppose that David
is in pain and desires not to be. Suppose too that David believes his mother
is deeply distressed by the fact that he is in pain, and that David *also* wants
his pain to end in order to alleviate his mother's distress. Should we count
this desire as ultimate or instrumental? It seems to be both. In the context
of the egoism/altruism debate we think that both sides should agree that a

---

[8] This account of the debate raises interesting questions about the role of emotions. There are
complex issues here. However, in this chapter we shall be assuming that, for any emotion, if that
emotion is to serve as the origin of action, it must cause some ultimate motivational state (i.e. an
ultimate desire), or include some motivational component (again, an ultimate desire). We can then ask
whether that ultimate desire is self- or other-oriented. This, in turn, will determine whether the action
is egoistic or altruistic.

desire counts as ultimate if it has *any* ultimate "component" and that desires like David's clearly have an ultimate component. So if people's desires for the well-being of others ever have an ultimate component, then the altruist wins. But this still leaves us with the problem of saying more precisely what this talk about "ultimate components" amounts to.

Some progress can be made by appealing to counterfactuals: a person's desire has an ultimate component if she would continue to have the desire even if she no longer believed that satisfying the desire would lead to the satisfaction of some other desire. This is only a first pass, since, as clever philosophy majors know, it is easy to construct counter-examples to simple counterfactual analyses like this one.[9] For our purposes, however, no more nuanced account is required.

Another issue is how we are to interpret the notion of *self-interested* desires and desires *for the well-being of others*. According to one influential version of egoism, often called *hedonism*, there are only two sorts of ultimate desires: the desire for pleasure and the desire to avoid pain.[10] Another, less restrictive, version of egoism allows that people may have a much wider range of ultimate self-interested desires, including desires for their own survival, power, and prestige.[11] While these desires are unproblematically self-interested, there are lots of other examples whose status is less clear. Is a desire for friendship self-interested? How about a desire to be involved in a mutually loving relationship? Or a desire to discover the cure for AIDS? Whether or not people have ultimate desires for any of these things is an open question. If they do, then hedonism is simply mistaken, since hedonism claims that there are only two sorts of ultimate desires. But what about non-hedonistic egoism; would it be refuted if people have ultimate desires like these? Given the conceptual uncertainties, we're inclined to think that egoism is vague. And similarly for altruism: if Albert has an ultimate desire that Beth be happy or that Cathy be cured of AIDS, then clearly the altruists are right and the egoists are wrong, since ultimate desires like these, if they exist, surely count as desires for the well-being of others. But suppose Albert has the ultimate desire that he and Beth be involved in a mutually loving relationship, or that *he* (as opposed to his rival in the next lab) cure Cathy of AIDS. Would *these* ultimate desires

---

[9] Martin (1994); Lewis (1997).

[10] Perhaps the most famous statement of hedonism is found in the first two sentences of Jeremy Bentham's *An Introduction to the Principles of Morals and Legislation* (1798/1996: 11): "Nature has placed mankind under the governance of two sovereign masters, *pain* and *pleasure*. It is for them alone to point out what we ought to do, as well as to determine what we shall do."

[11] Hedonists do not deny that many people desire such things, but they insist that these are not *ultimate* desires. According to the hedonist, people want wealth, power, and the rest only because they believe that being wealthy, powerful, etc. will lead to more pleasure and less pain.

suffice to show that altruism is right and egoism is wrong? Here again there is no clear and well-motivated answer. So altruism, like egoism, is vague. Fortunately, this vagueness need not be an insuperable problem in evaluating the competing theories, since there is no shortage of clear cases on both sides. If all ultimate desires are *clearly* self-interested, then the egoists are right. But if there are any ultimate desires that are clearly for the well-being of others, then the altruists are right and the egoists are wrong.

Before we turn to the empirical literature, there is one final complication that needs to be discussed. Despite the vagueness of the categories of self-interested desires and desires for the well-being of others, there seems to be a wide range of desires that clearly fall into *neither* category. Examples include the desire that great works of art be preserved and the desire that space exploration be pursued. Perhaps more interesting for moral theory are examples like the desire to do one's moral duty and the desire to obey God's commandments. Whether anyone holds these as *ultimate* desires is debatable. But if people do, then egoism is mistaken, since these desires are not self-interested. Interestingly, however, if ultimate desires like these exist, it would *not* show that altruism is true, since these desires are not desires for the well-being of others. Of course, a person who held the ultimate desire to do his moral duty might also believe that it was his duty to alleviate the suffering of the poor, and that belief might generate a desire to alleviate the suffering of the poor, which *is* a clear example of a desire for the well-being of others. But this lends no support to altruism, because the *ultimate* desire, in this case, is not for the well-being of others.

The topography has gotten a bit complicated; Figure 5.2 may help keep the contours clear. In that figure, we've distinguished four sorts of desires. Hedonism maintains that all ultimate desires fall into category 1. Egoism maintains that all ultimate desires fall into category 2, which has category 1 as

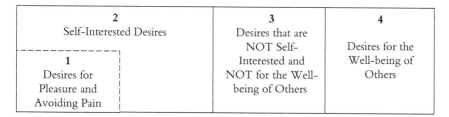

Figure 5.2. Four sorts of desires
Hedonism maintains that all ultimate desires are in category 1; egoism maintains that all ultimate desires are in category 2; altruism maintains that some ultimate desires are in category 4.

a subset. Altruism claims that *some* ultimate desires fall into category 4. Finally, if there are ultimate desires that fall into category 3 but none that fall into category 4, then both egoism and altruism are mistaken.

3. Altruism and Evolution

Readers familiar with some of the popular literature on the evolution of morality that has appeared in the last few decades might suspect that contemporary evolutionary biology has resolved the debate between egoists and altruists. For some readers—and some writers—seem to interpret evolutionary theory as showing that altruism is "biologically impossible." However, we maintain that the large literature on evolution and altruism has done very little to advance the philosophical debate. In this section, we shall make the case for this claim. We'll begin with arguments that purport to show that considerations drawn from evolutionary theory make altruism unlikely or impossible (except, perhaps, in a very limited range of cases). We'll then turn to a cluster of arguments, offered by Elliott Sober and David Sloan Wilson, that try to establish the opposite conclusion: evolutionary theory makes it appear quite likely that psychological altruism is true.

3.1. *Evolutionary Arguments against Altruism*

In discussions of evolution and altruism it is important to bear in mind a crucial distinction between two very different notions of altruism, which (following Sober and Wilson) we'll call *evolutionary altruism* and *psychological altruism*. Psychological altruism is the notion that has been at center stage in philosophical debates since antiquity. In most of this chapter, when we use the word "altruism," we are referring to psychological altruism. But in this section, to avoid confusion, we'll regularly opt for the longer label "psychological altruism." As we explained in Section 2, an organism is psychologically altruistic if and only if it has ultimate desires for the well-being of others, and a behavior is psychologically altruistic if and only if it is motivated by such a desire. By contrast, a behavior (or a behavioral disposition) is *evolutionarily altruistic* if and only if it reduces the inclusive fitness of the organism exhibiting the behavior and increases the inclusive fitness of some other organism. Roughly speaking, inclusive fitness is a measure of how many copies of an organism's genes will exist in subsequent generations.[12] Since an

---

[12] Attempting a more precise account raises difficult issues in the philosophy of biology (e.g. Beatty, 1992); fortunately, our purposes do not require greater precision.

organism's close kin share many of its genes, an organism can increase its inclusive fitness either by reproducing or by helping close kin to reproduce. Thus many behaviors that help kin to reproduce are *not* evolutionarily altruistic, even if they are quite costly to the organism doing the helping.[13]

It is important to see that evolutionary altruism and psychological altruism are logically independent notions—neither one entails the other. It is logically possible for an organism to be evolutionarily altruistic even if it is entirely devoid of mental states and thus can't have any ultimate desires. Indeed, since biologists interested in evolutionary altruism use the term "behavior" very broadly, it is possible for paramecia, or even plants, to exhibit evolutionarily altruistic behavior. It is also logically possible for an organism to be a psychological altruist without being an evolutionary altruist. For example, an organism might have ultimate desires for the welfare of its own offspring. Behaviors resulting from that desire will be psychologically altruistic but not evolutionarily altruistic, since typically such behaviors will increase the inclusive fitness of the parent.

Evolutionary altruism poses a major puzzle for evolutionary theorists, since if an organism's evolutionarily altruistic behavior is heritable, we might expect that natural selection would replace the genes implicated in evolutionarily altruistic behavior with genes that did not foster evolutionarily altruistic behavior, and thus the evolutionarily altruistic behavior would disappear. In recent years, there has been a great deal of discussion of this problem. Some theorists have offered sophisticated models purporting to show how, in appropriate circumstances, evolutionary altruism could indeed evolve,[14] while others have maintained that evolutionary altruism is extremely unlikely to evolve in a species like ours, and that under closer examination all putative examples of altruistic behavior will turn out not to be altruistic at all. In the memorable words of biologist Michael Ghiselin (1974: 247), "Scratch an 'altruist' and watch a 'hypocrite' bleed."

What is important for our purposes is that, even if the skeptics who doubt the existence of evolutionary altruism are correct, this would not resolve the philosophical debate over egoism and altruism since, as we have noted above, it entails nothing at all about the existence of psychological altruism. Unfortunately, far too many writers, including perhaps Ghiselin himself, have

[13] Some writers, including Sober and Wilson, define evolutionary altruism in terms of *individual* fitness (a measure of how many descendants an individual has) rather than inclusive fitness. For present purposes, we prefer the inclusive fitness account, since it facilitates a more plausible statement of the evolutionary argument aimed at showing that psychological altruism is possible only in very limited domains.

[14] See, for example, Sober & Wilson (1998), Part I.

made the mistake of assuming that the arguments against evolutionary altruism show that the sort of altruism that is of interest to moral theorists does not exist.

Although these considerations show that evolutionary theorists have no reason to deny that organisms can be psychological altruists, some authors have suggested that evolutionary theory permits psychological altruism only in very limited domains. The reasoning proceeds as follows: there are only two ways that a disposition to engage in behavior that helps other organisms but lowers one's own chance of survival and reproduction can evolve. One of these is the case in which the recipients of help are one's own offspring, or other close kin. Kin selection theory, pioneered by W. D. Hamilton (1963, 1964a, 1964b) makes it clear that in appropriate circumstances, genes leading to costly helping behavior will tend to spread throughout a population, provided that the recipients of the help are relatives, since this sort of helping behavior increases the number of copies of those genes that will be found in future generations. The other way in which a disposition to help can evolve requires that episodes of helping behavior are part of a longer-term reciprocal strategy in which the organism that is the beneficiary of helping behavior is subsequently disposed to help its benefactor. Building on ideas first set out in Trivers's (1971) classic paper on "reciprocal altruism," Axelrod and Hamilton (1981) described a simple "tit-for-tat" strategy, in which an organism helps on the first appropriate opportunity and then helps on subsequent opportunities if and only if the partner helped on the previous appropriate opportunity. They showed that tit-for-tat would be favored by natural selection over many other strategies, including a purely selfish strategy of never offering help but always accepting it. Since psychological altruism will lead to helping behavior, it is argued, psychological altruism can evolve only when a disposition to helping behavior can. So it is biologically possible for organisms to have ultimate desires to help their kin, and to help non-kin with whom they engage in ongoing reciprocal altruism. But apart from these special cases, psychological altruism can't evolve.

Versions of this influential line of thought can be found in many places (see, e.g., Nesse, 1990; Wright, 1994: chs. 8 & 9; Rachels, 1990: ch. 4). However, we think there is good reason to be very skeptical about the crucial assumption, which maintains that dispositions to helping behavior can evolve *only* via kin selection or reciprocal altruism. It has long been recognized that various sorts of group selection, in which one group of individuals leaves more descendants than another group, can lead to the evolution of helping behavior. Until recently, though, the reigning orthodoxy in evolutionary biology has been that the conditions under which group selection can act are highly unlikely to occur in natural breeding populations, and thus group selection is unlikely to have played a substantial role in human evolution. This view has been boldly challenged by Sober and Wilson (1998), and while their views are very controversial, we think that the extent to which group selection played a role in human evolution is very much an open question.

Much less controversially, Boyd and Richerson (1992) have developed models demonstrating that helping behavior (and, indeed, just about *any* sort of behavior) can evolve if informal punishment is meted out to individuals who do not help in circumstances when they are expected to. In such circumstances, psychological altruism could be favored by natural selection. More recently, Sripada (2007) has argued that ultimate desires for the well-being of others could evolve via a rather different route. As Sripada observes, there are many situations in which people are better off if they act in a coordinated way, but where no specific way of acting is best. Driving on the right (or the left) is an obvious example: it matters not a whit whether the convention is to drive on the right or left, but failure to adopt *some* convention would be a disaster. In these situations several different "coordination equilibria" may be equally adaptive. To enable groups to reap the benefits of acting in a coordinated way, Sripada argues, natural selection may well have led to the evolution of a psychological mechanism that generates ultimate desires to adhere to locally prevailing customs or practices. And since some of those locally prevailing customs may require helping others, some of the ultimate desires produced by that psychological mechanism might well be psychologically altruistic. If Boyd and Richerson and Sripada are right, and we believe they are, then evolutionary theory gives us no reason to suppose that psychological altruism must be restricted to kin or to individuals involved in reciprocal exchanges. So, contrary to the frequently encountered presumption that evolutionary biology has resolved the debate between psychological egoists and psychological altruists in favor of egoism, it appears that evolutionary theory offers little succor to the egoists.

3.2. *Evolutionary Arguments for Altruism*[15]

In stark contrast with writers who think that evolutionary arguments show that psychological altruism is unlikely or impossible, Sober and Wilson (1998) believe that there are evolutionary arguments *for* the existence of psychological altruism. "Natural selection," they maintain, "is unlikely to have given us

---

[15] Much of this section is based on Stich (2007). We are grateful to Elliott Sober and Edouard Machery for helpful comments on this material.

purely egoistic motives."[16] While granting that their case is "provisional" (8), they believe that their "analysis . . . provides evidence for the existence of psychological altruism" (12).

In setting out their arguments, Sober and Wilson adopt the wise strategy of focusing on the case of parental care. Since the behaviors that organisms exhibit in taking care of their offspring are typically *not* altruistic in the evolutionary sense, we can simply put aside whatever worries there may be about the existence of evolutionary altruism. Given the importance of parental care in many species, it is all but certain that natural selection played a significant role in shaping that behavior. And while different species no doubt utilize very different processes to generate and regulate parental care behavior, it is plausible to suppose that in humans *desires* play an important role in that process. Sober and Wilson believe that evolutionary considerations can help us determine the nature of these desires:

> Although organisms take care of their young in many species, human parents provide a great deal of help, for a very long time, to their children. We expect that when parental care evolves in a lineage, natural selection is relevant to explaining why this transition occurs. Assuming that human parents take care of their children because of the desires they have, we also expect that evolutionary considerations will help illuminate what the desires are that play this motivational role.   (301)

Of course, as Sober and Wilson note, we hardly need evolutionary arguments to tell us about the content of some of the desires that motivate parental care. But it is much harder to determine whether these desires are instrumental or ultimate, and it is here, they think, that evolutionary considerations can be of help.

> We conjecture that human parents typically *want* their children to do well—to live rather than die, to be healthy rather than sick, and so on. The question we will address is whether this desire is merely an instrumental desire in the service of some egoistic ultimate goal, or part of a pluralistic motivational system in which there is an ultimate altruistic concern for the child's welfare. We will argue that there are evolutionary reasons to expect motivational pluralism to be the proximate mechanism for producing parental care in our species.   (302)

Since parental care is essential in humans, and since providing it requires that parents have the appropriate set of desires, the processes driving evolution must have solved the problem of how to assure that parents would have the requisite

---

[16] Sober & Wilson (1998: 12). For the remainder of this section, all quotes from Sober & Wilson (1998) will be identified by page numbers in parentheses.

desires. There are, Sober and Wilson maintain, three kinds of solutions to this evolutionary problem.

A relatively direct solution to the design problem would be for parents to be psychological altruists—let them care about the well-being of their children as an end in itself. A more indirect solution would be for parents to be psychological hedonists[17]—let them care only about attaining pleasure and avoiding pain, but let them be so constituted that they feel good when their children do well and feel bad when their children do ill. And of course, there is a pluralistic solution to consider as well—let parents have altruistic *and* hedonistic motives, both of which motivate them to take care of their children.   (305)

"Broadly speaking," they continue, "there are three considerations that bear on this question" (ibid.). The first of these is *availability*; for natural selection to cause a trait to increase in frequency, the trait must have been available in an ancestral population. The second is *reliability*. Since parents who fail to provide care run a serious risk of never having grandchildren, we should expect that natural selection will prefer a more reliable solution over a less reliable one. The third consideration is *energetic efficiency*. Building and maintaining psychological mechanisms will inevitably require an investment of resources that might be used for some other purpose. So, other things being equal, we should expect natural selection to prefer the more efficient mechanism. There is, Sober and Wilson maintain, no reason to think that a psychologically altruistic mechanism would be less energetically efficient than a hedonist mechanism, nor is there any reason to think that an altruistic mechanism would have been less likely to be available. When it comes to reliability, on the other hand, they think there is a clear difference between a psychologically altruistic mechanism and various possible hedonistic mechanisms: an altruistic mechanism would be more reliable, and thus it is more likely that the altruistic mechanism would be the one that evolved.

To make their case, Sober and Wilson offer a brief sketch of how hedonistic and altruistic mechanisms might work, and then set out a variety of reasons for thinking that the altruistic mechanism would be more reliable. However, we believe that in debates about psychological processes, the devil is often in the details. So rather than relying on Sober and Wilson's brief sketches, we shall offer somewhat more detailed accounts of the psychological processes that might support hedonistic and psychologically altruistic parental behavior.

---

[17] Sober and Wilson cast their argument as contest between altruism and *hedonism* because "[b]y pitting altruism against hedonism, we are asking the altruism hypothesis to reply to the version of egoism that is most difficult to refute" (297). For expository purposes, we shall follow their lead here, although we are not committed to their evaluation of hedonism.

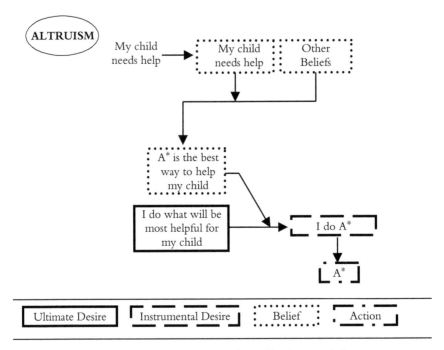

Figure 5.3. The process underlying psychologically altruistic behavior

After setting out these accounts, we'll go on to evaluate Sober and Wilson's arguments about reliability.

Figure 5.3 is a depiction of the process underlying psychologically altruistic behavior. In Figure 5.3, the fact that the agent's child needs help (represented by the unboxed token of "My child needs help" in the upper left) leads to the belief *My child needs help*. Of course, formation of this belief requires complex perceptual and cognitive processing, but since this part of the story is irrelevant to the issue at hand, it has not been depicted. The belief *My child needs help*, along with other beliefs the agent has, leads to a belief that a certain action, A*, is the best way to help her child. Then, via practical reasoning, this belief and the *ultimate* desire, *I do what will be most helpful for my child*, leads to the desire to do A*. Since in this altruistic account the desire, *I do what will be most helpful for my child*, is an ultimate desire, it is not itself the result of practical reasoning.

The hedonistic alternatives we shall propose retain all of the basic structure depicted in Figure 5.3, but they depict the desire that *I do what will be most helpful for my child* as an instrumental rather than an ultimate desire. The simplest way to do this is via what we shall call *future pain hedonism*, which maintains that the agent believes she will feel bad in the future if she does not help her

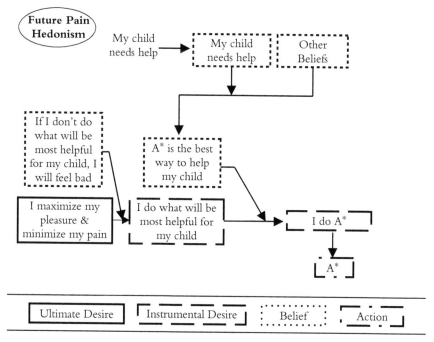

Figure 5.4. The process underlying future pain hedonism

child now. Figure 5.4 is our sketch of future pain hedonism. In it, the content of the agent's ultimate desire is hedonistic: *I maximize my pleasure and minimize my pain*. The desire, *I do what is most helpful for my child*, is an instrumental desire, generated via practical reasoning from the ultimate hedonistic desire along with the belief that *If I don't do what is most helpful for my child I will feel bad*.

Figure 5.5 depicts another, more complicated, way in which the desire, *I do what is most helpful to my child*, might be the product of hedonistic practical reasoning, which we'll call *current pain hedonism*. On this account, the child's need for help causes the parent to feel bad, and the parent believes that if she feels bad because her child needs help and she does what is most helpful, she will stop feeling bad. This version of hedonism is more complex than the previous version, since it includes an affective state—feeling bad—in addition to various beliefs and desires, and in order for that affective state to influence practical reasoning, the parent must not only experience it, but know (or at least believe) that she is experiencing it, and why.

In their attempt to show that natural selection would favor an altruistic process over the hedonistic alternatives, Sober and Wilson offer a number

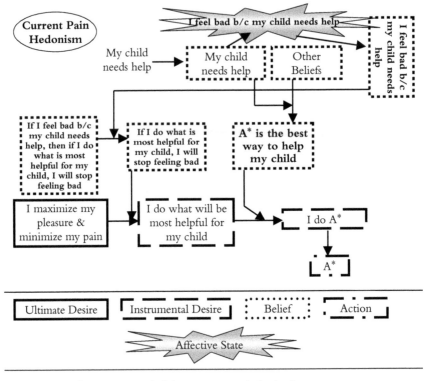

Figure 5.5. The process underlying current pain hedonism

of arguments, all of them focused on the more complicated current pain hedonism, although they think that "the argument would remain the same if we thought of the hedonist as acting to avoid future pain" (318). In discussing these arguments, we shall start with three that we don't find very plausible; we'll then take up one that we think poses a serious challenge to hedonism and leads to some important questions about how, exactly, psychological egoism and psychological altruism should be understood.

A first pair of arguments focuses on the causal link between believing that one's child needs help and feeling an appropriate level of distress or pain. The worry raised by the first argument is that the link could occasionally fail.

If the fitness of hedonism depends on how well correlated the organism's pleasure and pain are with its beliefs about the well-being of its children, how strong is this correlation apt to be? (315) . . . [W]e think it is quite improbable that the psychological pain that hedonism postulates will be *perfectly* correlated with believing that one's children are doing badly. One virtue of . . . [altruism] . . . is that its reliability does not depend on the strength of such correlations." (316, emphasis in the original)

The second argument focuses on the fact that, to do its job appropriately, the mechanism underlying the belief-to-affect link must not only produce pain or distress; it must produce *lots* of it.

Hedonism assumes that evolution produced organisms—ourselves included—in which psychological pain is strongly correlated with having beliefs of various kinds. In the context of our example of parental care, the hedonist asserts that whenever the organism believes that its children are well off, it tends to experience pleasure; whenever the organism believes that its children are doing badly, it tends to feel pain. What is needed is not just that *some* pleasure and *some* pain accompany these two beliefs. The amount of pleasure that comes from seeing one's children do well must exceed the amount that comes from eating chocolate ice cream and from having one's temples massaged to the sound of murmuring voices. This may require some tricky engineering . . . To achieve simplicity at the level of ultimate desires, complexity is required at the level of instrumental desires. This complexity must be taken into account in assessing the fitness of hedonism.[18]   (315)

Sober and Wilson are certainly right that current pain hedonism requires the affect generated by the belief that one's child is doing well or badly be of an appropriate magnitude, and that this will require some psychological engineering that is not required by the altruist process. They are also right that the mechanism responsible for this belief-to-affect link will not establish a perfect correlation between belief and affect; like just about any psychological mechanism, it is bound to fail now and then.

However, we don't think that either of these facts offers much reason to believe that natural selection would favor the altruistic process. To see why, let's first consider the fact that the belief-to-affect link will be less than perfectly reliable. It seems that natural selection has built lots of adaptively important processes by using links between categories of belief and various sorts of affective states. Emotions like anger, fear, and disgust, which play crucial roles in regulating behavior, are examples of states that are often triggered by different sorts of beliefs. And in all of these cases, it seems (logically) possible to eliminate the pathway that runs via affect, and replace it with an ultimate desire to behave appropriately when one acquires a triggering belief. Fear, for example, might be replaced by an ultimate desire to take protective action when you believe that you are in danger. Since natural selection has clearly opted for an emotion mediation system in these cases rather than relying on an

---

[18] It is perhaps worth noting that, *pace* Sober and Wilson, neither of these arguments applies to future pain hedonism, since that version of hedonism does not posit the sort of belief-to-affect link that Sober and Wilson find suspect. We should also note that for the sake of simplicity, we'll ignore the pleasure engendered by the belief that one's child is well off and focus on the pain or distress engendered by the belief that one's child is doing badly.

ultimate desire that avoids the need for a belief-to-affect link, we need some further argument to show that natural selection would not do the same in the case of parental care, and Sober and Wilson do not offer any.

The second argument faces a very similar challenge. It will indeed require some "tricky engineering" to be sure that beliefs about one's children produce the right amount of affect. But much the same is true in the case of other systems involving affect. For the fear system to work properly, seeing a tiger on the path in front of you must generate quite intense fear—a lot more than would be generated by your belief that if you ran away quickly you might stub your toe. While it no doubt takes some tricky engineering to make this all work properly, natural selection was up to the challenge. Sober and Wilson give us no reason to think natural selection was not up to the challenge in the case of parental care as well. Edouard Machery has pointed out to us another problem with the "tricky engineering" argument. On Sober and Wilson's account, altruists will have many ultimate desires in addition to the desire to do what will be most helpful for their children. So to ensure that the ultimate desire leading to parental care usually prevails will *also* require some tricky engineering.

A third argument offered by Sober and Wilson is aimed at showing that natural selection would likely have preferred a system for producing parental care, which they call "PLUR" (for *pluralism*), in which *both* hedonistic motivation and altruistic motivation play a role, over a "monistic" system that relies on hedonism alone. The central idea is that, in many circumstances, two control mechanisms are better than one.

PLUR postulates two pathways from the belief that one's children need help to the act of providing help. If these operate at least somewhat independently of each other, and each on its own raises the probability of helping, then the two together will raise the probability of helping even more. Unless the two pathways postulated by PLUR hopelessly confound each other, PLUR will be more reliable than HED [hedonism]. PLUR is superior because it is a *multiply connected control device*. (320, emphasis in the original)

Sober and Wilson go on to observe that "multiply connected control devices have often evolved." They sketch a few examples, then note that "further examples could be supplied from biology, and also from engineering, where intelligent designers supply machines (like the space shuttle) with backup systems. Error is inevitable, but the chance of disastrous error can be minimized by well-crafted redundancy" (Ibid.).

Sober and Wilson are surely right that well-crafted redundancy will typically improve reliability and reduce the chance of disastrous error. They are also right that both natural selection and intelligent human designers have produced lots of systems with this sort of redundancy. But, as the disaster that befell the Columbia space shuttle and a myriad of other technical catastrophes vividly illustrate, human engineers also often design crucial systems *without* backups. So too does natural selection, as people with damaged hearts or livers, or with small but disabling strokes, are all too well aware. One reason for lack of redundancy is that redundancy almost never comes without costs, and those costs have to be weighed against the incremental benefits that a backup system provides. Since Sober and Wilson offer us no reason to believe that, in the case of parental care, the added reliability of PLUR would justify the additional costs, their redundancy argument lends no support to the claim that natural selection would prefer PLUR to a monistic hedonism, or, for that matter, to a monistic altruism.[19]

Sober and Wilson's fourth argument raises what we think is a much more troublesome issue for the hedonistic hypothesis.

Suppose a hedonistic organism believes on a given occasion that providing parental care is the way for it to attain its ultimate goal of maximizing pleasure and minimizing pain. What would happen if the organism provides parental care, but then discovers that this action fails to deliver maximal pleasure and minimal pain? If the organism is able to learn from experience, it will probably be less inclined to take care of its children on subsequent occasions. Instrumental desires tend to diminish and disappear in the face of negative evidence of this sort. This can make hedonistic motivation a rather poor control device. (314) . . . [The] instrumental desire will remain in place only if the organism . . . is trapped by an unalterable illusion. (315)

Sober and Wilson might have been more careful here. When it turns out that parental care does not produce the expected hedonic benefits, the hedonistic organism needs to have some beliefs about *why* this happened before it can effectively adjust its beliefs and instrumental desires. If, for example, the hedonist portrayed in Figures 5.4 or 5.5 comes to believe (perhaps correctly) that it was mistaken in inferring that A* was the best way to help, then it will need to adjust some of the beliefs that led to that inference, but the beliefs linking helping to the reduction of negative affect will require no modification. But despite this slip, we think that Sober and Wilson are onto something important. Both versions of hedonism that we've sketched rely quite crucially on beliefs about the relation between helping behavior and affect. In the case of future pain hedonism, as elaborated in Figure 5.4, the

---

[19] Even if there were some reason to think that natural selection would prefer a redundant system, this would not, by itself, constitute an argument for altruism. Redundancy can exist in an entirely hedonistic system, for instance one that includes both current and future pain hedonism.

crucial belief is: *If I don't do what will be most helpful for my child, I will feel bad*. In the version of current pain hedonism sketched in Figure 5.5, it's: *If I feel bad because my child needs help, then if I do what is most helpful for my child, I will stop feeling bad*. These beliefs make empirical claims, and like other empirical beliefs they might be undermined by evidence (including misleading evidence) or by more theoretical beliefs (rational or irrational) that a person could acquire by a variety of routes. This makes the process underlying parental care look quite vulnerable to disruption and suggests that natural selection would likely opt for some more reliable way to get this crucial job done.[20] The version of altruism depicted in Figure 5.3 fits the bill nicely. By making the desire, *I do what will be most helpful for my child* an ultimate desire, it sidesteps the need for empirical beliefs that might all too easily be undermined.

We think this is an original and powerful argument for psychological altruism. Ultimately, however, we are not persuaded. To explain why, we'll have to clarify what the altruist and the egoist are claiming. Psychological altruists, recall, maintain that people have ultimate desires for the well-being of others, while psychological egoists believe that all desires for the well-being of others are instrumental, and that all of our ultimate desires are self-interested. As depicted in Figure 5.1, an instrumental desire is a desire that is produced or sustained entirely by a process of practical reasoning in which a desire and a belief give rise to or sustain another desire. In our discussion of practical reasoning (in Section 2), while a good bit was said about desire, nothing was said about the notion of *belief*; it was simply taken for granted. At this point, however, we can no longer afford to do so. Like other writers in this area, including Sober and Wilson, we tacitly adopted the standard view that beliefs are inferentially integrated representational states that play a characteristic role in an agent's cognitive economy. To say that a belief is *inferentially integrated* is to say (roughly) that it can be both generated and removed by inferential processes that can take any (or just about any) other beliefs as premises.

While inferentially integrated representational states play a central role in many discussions of psychological processes and cognitive architecture, the literature in both cognitive science and philosophy also often discusses

---

[20] Note that the vulnerability to disruption we're considering now is likely to be a much more serious problem than the vulnerability that was at center stage in Sober and Wilson's first argument. In that argument, the danger posed for the hedonistic parental care system was that "the psychological pain that hedonism postulates" might not be "*perfectly* correlated with believing that one's children are doing badly" (316, emphasis in the original). But, absent other problems, a hedonistic system in which belief and affect were highly—though imperfectly—correlated would still do quite a good job of parental care. Our current concern is with the stability of the crucial belief linking helping behavior and affect. If that belief is removed, the hedonistic parental care system simply crashes, and the organism will not engage in parental care except by accident.

belief-like states that are "stickier" than this. Once they are in place, these "stickier" belief-like states are hard to modify by acquiring or changing other beliefs. They are also often unavailable to introspective access. In Stich (1978), they were termed *sub-doxastic states*.

Perhaps the most familiar example of sub-doxastic states are the grammatical rules that, according to Chomsky and his followers, underlie speech pro-duction, comprehension, and the production of linguistic intuitions. These representational states are clearly not inferentially integrated, since a speaker's explicit beliefs typically have no effect on them. A speaker can, for example, have thoroughly mistaken beliefs about the rules that govern his linguistic processing without those beliefs having any effect on the rules or on the linguistic processing that they subserve. Another important example is the *core beliefs* posited by Carey and Spelke (Carey & Spelke, 1996; Spelke, 2000, 2003). These are innate representational states that underlie young children's inferences about the physical and mathematical properties of objects. In the course of development, many people acquire more sophisticated theories about these matters, some of which are incompatible with the innate core beliefs. But, if Carey and Spelke are correct, the core beliefs remain unaltered by these new beliefs and continue to affect people's performance in a variety of experimental tasks.

Although sub-doxastic states are sticky and hard to remove, they do play a role in *inference-like* interactions with other representational states, although their access to other representational premises and other premises' access to them is limited. In *The Modularity of Mind*, Fodor (1983) notes that representational states stored in the sorts of mental modules he posits are typically sub-doxastic, since modules are "informationally encapsulated." But not all sub-doxastic states need reside in Fodorian modules.

Since sub-doxastic states can play a role in inference-like interactions, and since practical reasoning is an inference-like interaction, it is possible that sub-doxastic states play the belief-role in some instances of practical reasoning. So, for example, rather than the practical reasoning structure illustrated in Figure 5.1, some examples of practical reasoning might have the structure shown in Figure 5.6. What makes practical reasoning structures like this important for our purposes is that, since SUB-DOXASTIC STATE 1 is difficult or impossible to remove using evidence or inference, DESIRE 2 will be reliably correlated with DESIRE 1.

Let's now consider whether DESIRE 2 in Figure 5.6 is instrumental or ultimate. As we noted in Section 1, the objects of ultimate desires are typically characterized as "desired for their own sakes" while instrumental desires are those that agents have only because they think that satisfying the desire will

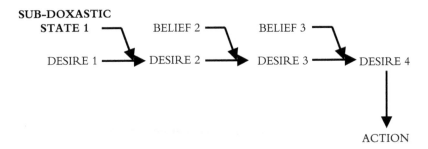

Figure 5.6. An episode of practical reasoning in which a sub-doxastic state plays a role

lead to the satisfaction of some other desire. In Figure 5.6, the agent has DESIRE 2 only because he thinks that satisfying the desire will lead to the satisfaction of DESIRE 1. So it looks as if the natural answer to our question is that DESIRE 2 is instrumental; the only ultimate desire depicted in Figure 5.6 is DESIRE 1.

If this is right, if desires like DESIRE 2 are instrumental rather than ultimate, then Sober and Wilson's evolutionary argument for psychological altruism is in trouble. The central insight of that argument was that both versions of hedonism rely on empirical beliefs that might all too easily be undermined by other beliefs the agent might acquire. Suppose, however, that in Figures 5.4 and 5.5, the representations

If I don't do what will be most helpful for my child, I will feel bad

and

If I feel bad because my child needs help, then if I do what is most helpful for my child, I will stop feeling bad

are not beliefs but sticky sub-doxastic states. If we grant that desires like DESIRE 2 in Figure 5.6, which are produced or sustained by a desire and a sub-doxastic state, count as instrumental desires, not ultimate desires, then the crucial desire whose presence Sober and Wilson sought to guarantee by making it an ultimate desire, i.e.

I do what will be most helpful for my child

is no longer at risk of being undermined by other beliefs. Since the crucial desire is reliably present in both the altruistic model and in both versions of the hedonist model, natural selection can't prefer altruism because of its greater reliability in getting a crucial job done.

As we've seen, Sober and Wilson contend that when an instrumental desire does not lead to the expected hedonic payoff, the "desire will remain in place only if the organism . . . . is trapped by an unalterable illusion" (315). But as a number of authors have noted, some illusions—or as we would prefer to put it, some belief-like representational states that are not strictly true—are conducive to fitness (Stich, 1990; Plantinga, 1993; Sober, 1994; Godfrey-Smith, 1996). In a variety of domains, it appears that natural selection has used sub-doxastic states and processes that have some of the features of mental modules to ensure that those representations stay put and are not undermined by the systems that revise beliefs. Since natural selection often exploits the same trick over and over again, it is entirely possible that, when faced with the problem of assuring that parents were motivated to care for their children, this was the strategy it selected. Our conclusion, of course, is *not* that parental care is subserved by an egoistic psychological process, but rather that Sober and Wilson's argument leaves this option quite open. Their analysis does not "provide . . . evidence for the existence of psychological altruism" (12).

Our central claim in this section has been that evolutionary theory offers little prospect for movement in philosophical debates between psychological egoism and psychological altruism. In 3.1 we saw that evolutionary considerations don't rule out psychological altruism or restrict its scope, and in 3.2 we've argued that Sober and Wilson's arguments—by far the most sophisticated attempt to make an evolutionary case *for* psychological altruism—are not convincing.

4. The Social Psychology of Altruism

We now turn from theoretical considerations purporting to make the existence of altruism seem likely (or unlikely) to attempts at directly establishing the existence of altruism through experimental observation. The psychological literature relevant to the egoism vs. altruism debate is vast, but in this section we shall focus primarily on the work of Daniel Batson and his associates, who have done some of the most important work in this area.[21] Batson, along with many other researchers, begins by borrowing an idea that has deep roots in philosophical discussions of altruism. Although the details and the terminology

---

[21] For useful reviews of the literature see Piliavin & Charng (1990); Batson (1991,1998); Schroeder et al. (1995); Dovidio et al. (2006). We are grateful to Daniel Batson for helpful discussion of the material in this section.

differ significantly from author to author, the central idea is that altruism is often the product of an emotional response to another's distress.

For example, Aquinas maintains that "mercy is the heartfelt sympathy for another's distress, impelling us to succour him if we can."[22] And Adam Smith tells us that "pity or compassion [is] the emotion we feel for the misery of others, when we either see it, or are made to conceive it in a very lively manner" and these emotions "interest [man] in the fortunes of others, and render their happiness necessary to him, though he derives nothing from it except the pleasure of seeing it."[23] While different writers have used different terms for the emotional response in question, Batson (1991: 58) labels it "empathy," which he characterizes as "an other-oriented emotional reaction to seeing someone suffer," and he calls the traditional idea that empathy leads to altruism the *empathy—altruism hypothesis.*

In this section we shall begin, in 4.1, by introducing Batson's account of empathy, and discussing some problems with that account. In 4.2, we'll evaluate Batson's claims about the causal pathway leading from perspective-taking to empathy and from empathy to helping behavior. In the remainder of the section, we'll look carefully at some of Batson's experiments that are designed to test the empathy—altruism hypothesis against a variety of egoistic alternatives. In a number of cases, we believe, the experiments have made important progress by showing that versions of egoism that have loomed large in philosophical discussion are not very promising. But in other cases we'll argue that Batson's experiments have not yet succeeded in undermining an egoistic alternative.

While the Batson group's experimental program is novel, the dialectical space is one, we dare say, that has exercised generations of introductory philosophy students: for many examples of helping behavior, the egoist and altruist can both offer psychological explanations consistent with their hypothesis, and the ensuing arguments concern which explanation is most plausible. Unfortunately, as generations of introductory philosophy students have found out, such arguments are bound to end in inconclusive speculation—so long as the competing explanations are not empirically evaluated. By showing how such evaluation may proceed, the Batson group has enabled progress in a shopworn debate.

4.1. *Empathy and Personal Distress*

Since there is no standardized terminology in this area, Batson's choice of the term "empathy" to label the emotion, or cluster of emotions, that plays

---

[22] Aquinas (1270/1917, II–II, 30, 3).   [23] Smith (1759/1853: I, I, 1. 1).

a central role in his theory is inevitably somewhat *stipulative*—he might have chosen "compassion" or "sympathy" or even "pity" for the term of art he needs. Because of this, we are not concerned with the question of whether he uses "empathy" in ways consistent with common usage. However, we do think his characterization of empathy is neither as clear nor as detailed as one might hope. Much of what Batson says is aimed at contrasting empathy with a different cluster of affective responses to other people's suffering, which Batson calls "personal distress." According to Batson, empathy "includes feeling sympathetic, compassionate, warm, softhearted, tender, and the like, and according to the empathy–altruism hypothesis, it evokes altruistic motivation" (1991: 86). Personal distress, by contrast, is "made up of more self-oriented feelings such as upset, alarm, anxiety, and distress" (ibid.: 117). Elsewhere, he tells us that personal distress "includes feeling anxious, upset, disturbed, distressed, perturbed, and the like, and evokes egoistic motivation to have the distress reduced" (ibid.: 86). While these characterizations may suffice for designing experiments aimed at testing the view that empathy leads to altruistic motivation, they leave a number of important issues unaddressed.

One of these issues is often discussed under the heading of "congruence" or "homology." Sometimes when an observer becomes aware that another person (the "target" as we'll sometimes say) is experiencing an emotion, this awareness can cause a similar emotion in the observer. If, for example, you are aware that Ellen is frightened of the man walking toward her, you may also become frightened of him; if you learn that your best friend is sad because of the death of his beloved dog, this may make you sad as well. In these cases, the emotion evoked in the observer is said to be *congruent* or *homologous* to the emotion of the target. Since Batson describes empathy as a "vicarious emotion that is congruent with but not necessarily identical to the emotion of another" (1991: 86), it is tempting to suppose that he thinks empathic emotions are always at least similar to an emotion the target is experiencing (or similar to what the observer believes the target's emotion to be). But as both Sober and Wilson (1998: 234–5) and Nichols (2004: 32) have noted, *requiring* congruence in the emotion that allegedly gives rise to altruistic motivation may be unwise. Accident victims who are *obviously* unconscious sometimes evoke an "other-oriented emotional reaction" that might be characterized as "compassionate, warm, softhearted, tender, and the like," and people who feel this way are sometimes motivated to help the unconscious victim. But if empathy requires congruence, then the emotion that motivates people to help in these cases *can't* be empathy, since unconscious people aren't experiencing any emotions. We're inclined to give Batson the benefit of the doubt here, and interpret him—charitably, we believe—as holding that empathy is sometimes, or often, a congruent emotion, but that it need not always be. Presumably personal distress is also sometimes congruent, as when one person's anxiety or alarm evokes anxiety or alarm in an observer. So empathy and personal distress cannot be distinguished by reference to congruence.

Another issue of some importance is whether empathy is always unpleasant or, as psychologists often say, aversive. According to Batson (1991: 87), "empathy felt for someone who is suffering will likely be an unpleasant, aversive emotion," and of course this is just what we would expect if empathy were often a congruent emotion. But as Sober and Wilson (1998: 235) note, we sometimes talk about empathizing with another person's pleasant emotions, and when the term is used in this way, one can have empathic joy as well as empathic sadness. Although Sober and Wilson are certainly right that ordinary language allows us to talk of empathizing with people's positive emotions as well as with their negative emotions, we think Batson is best understood as *stipulating* that, as he uses the term, empathy is a response to the belief that the target is suffering, and that it is typically aversive. Since personal distress is typically—or perhaps always—unpleasant, the distinction between them cannot be drawn by focusing on aversiveness.

That leaves "self-orientedness" vs. "other-orientedness" as the principal dimension on which personal distress and empathy differ. Thus the distinction is doing important theoretical work for Batson, although he does not tell us much about it. We believe that the distinction Batson requires becomes sufficiently clear when operationalized in his experimental work, and we shall not further tarry on the conceptual difficulty. But more conceptual and empirical work aimed at clarifying just what empathy and personal distress are would certainly be welcome.[24]

4.2. *Empathy, Perspective-Taking and Helping Behavior*

In order to put the empathy–altruism hypothesis to empirical test, it is important to have ways of inducing empathy in the laboratory. There is, Batson maintains, a substantial body of literature suggesting that this can indeed be done. For example, Stotland (1969) showed that subjects who were instructed to imagine how a target person felt when undergoing what subjects believed to be a painful medical procedure reported stronger feelings of empathy and showed greater physiological arousal than subjects who were instructed to watch the target person's movements. Krebs (1975) demonstrated that subjects who observe someone *similar to themselves* undergo painful experiences show

---

[24] Both Sober & Wilson (1998: 231–237) and Nichols (2004: ch. 2) have useful discussions, though we think much more remains to be done.

more physiological arousal, report identifying with the target more strongly, and report feeling worse while waiting for the painful stimulus to begin than do subjects who observe the same painful experiences administered to someone who is not similar to themselves. Additionally, Krebs (1975) found subjects more willing to help at some personal cost when the sufferer was similar to themselves.

There is also evidence that the effects of empathy are focused on the specific distress that evokes it. Stotland's technique for manipulating empathy by instructing subjects to take the perspective of the person in distress was used by Dovidio et al. (1990) to induce empathy for a young woman, with subjects focusing on one of two quite different problems that the young woman faced. When given an opportunity to help the young woman, subjects in whom empathy had been evoked were more likely to help than subjects in a low empathy condition, and the increase in helping was specific to the problem that had evoked the empathy.

On the basis of these and other experiments, Batson concludes that the process of perspective-taking plays a central role in arousing empathy. According to Batson, "adopting the needy person's perspective involves imagining how that person is affected by his or her situation" (1991: 83), and "adopting the needy person's perspective seems to be a *necessary condition* for arousal of empathic emotion" (ibid.: 85, emphasis added). He goes on to assemble a list of ways in which perspective-taking, and thus empathy, can be induced.

[A] perspective-taking set, that is, a set to imagine how the person in need is affected by his or her situation . . . may be induced by prior experience in similar situations, by instructions, or by a feeling of attachment to the other. In the psychology laboratory perspective taking has often been induced by instructions . . . In the natural stream of behavior also, perspective taking may be the result of instructions, including self-instructions (e.g., "I should walk a mile in his moccasins"), but it is more often the result either of prior similar experience ("I know just how you must feel") or of attachment." (Ibid.: 84)

Figure 5.7 is a sketch of the causal pathways that, on Batson's account, can lead to empathy.

Although we are prepared to believe that Figure 5.7 depicts a number of possible routes to empathy, we are, for two reasons, skeptical about Batson's claim that perspective-taking is a *necessary condition* for arousing empathy. First, while the experimental evidence Batson cites makes it plausible that attachment and similarity to self can indeed lead to empathy, it does not rule out the possibility that these processes bypass perspective-taking and lead *directly* to empathy. Second, we know of no literature that takes on the task of showing that there are no *other* routes to empathy, so the existence of quite different

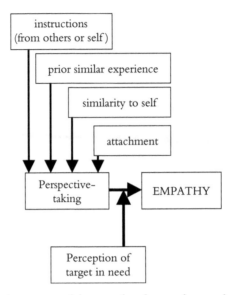

Figure 5.7. Batson's account of the causal pathways that can lead to empathy

causal pathways leading to empathy is largely unexplored. Neither of these reservations poses a major challenge to Batson's project, however, since what he really needs is the claim that—whatever the mechanism may be—the four factors at the top of Figure 5.7 can be used to induce empathy in experimental subjects. And we think that both the pre-existing literature and many of Batson's own experiments provide compelling support for that claim.

With this element in place, Batson's next step is to make the case that empathy leads to helping behavior. Here again, he relies in part on work by others, including the Krebs (1975) and Dovidio et al. (1990) studies cited earlier. Many of Batson's own experiments, some of which we'll describe below, also support the contention that empathy and empathy-engendering experimental manipulations increase the likelihood of helping behavior. Another important source of support for this conclusion is a meta-analysis of a large body of experimental literature by Eisenberg and Miller (1987). On the basis of these and other studies, Batson (1991: 95) concludes that "there is indeed an empathy-helping relationship; feeling empathy for a person in need increases the likelihood of helping to relieve that need."

4.3. *The Empathy–Altruism Hypothesis*

It might be thought that establishing a causal link between empathy and helping behavior would be bad news for egoism. But, as Batson makes clear, the fact that empathy leads to helping behavior does not resolve the dispute between egoists and altruists, since it does not address the nature of the *motivation* for the helping behavior that empathy evokes. Egoists, of course, do not deny that people engage in helping behavior. Nor need they deny that seeing other people in distress can cause emotions like empathy or that these emotions can lead to helping behavior. The crucial question dividing egoists from altruists is: *how* does the emotion engender helping behavior?

The *empathy–altruism hypothesis* asserts that empathy causes a genuinely altruistic desire to help—an ultimate desire for the well being of the sufferer. It is important to note that the empathy–altruism hypothesis does *not* predict that agents who feel empathy for a target person will *always* help the target; people typically have various and conflicting desires, and not all conflicts are resolved in favor of empathy's urgings. Moreover, even when there are no conflicting desires, it will sometimes be the case that the agent simply does not know how to help. What the empathy–altruism hypothesis claims is that empathy evokes an ultimate desire that the target's distress be reduced. In favorable cases, this ultimate desire, along with the agent's background beliefs, will generate a plan of action. That plan will compete with other plans generated by competing, non-altruistic desires. When the altruistic desire is stronger than the competing desires, the altruistic plan is chosen and the agent engages in helping behavior. It is also important to keep in mind that the empathy–altruism hypothesis does not entail that people who feel little or no empathy will not want to help and will not engage in helping behavior, since an instrumental desire to help can be produced by a variety of processes in which empathy plays no role.

So the empathy–altruism hypothesis offers one account of the way in which empathy can lead to helping behavior. But there is also a variety of egoistic alternatives by which empathy might lead to helping behavior without generating an ultimate desire to help. Perhaps the most obvious of these is that empathy might simply be (or cause) an unpleasant experience, and that people are motivated to help because they believe that helping is the best way to *stop* the unpleasant experience that is caused by someone else's distress. Quite a different family of egoistic possibilities focuses on the rewards to be expected for helping and/or the punishments to be expected for withholding assistance. If people believe that others will sanction them if they fail to help in certain circumstances, or reward them if they do help, and if they believe that the feeling of empathy marks those cases in which social sanctions or rewards are most likely, then we would expect people to be more helpful when they feel empathy, even if their ultimate motivation is purely egoistic. A variation on this theme focuses on rewards or punishments that are self-generated or self-administered. If people believe that helping may make them feel good, or that failing to help may make them feel bad, and that these feelings will be most likely to occur in cases where they feel empathy, then once again we would expect people who empathize to be more helpful, although their motives may be not at all altruistic.

For more than twenty-five years, Batson and his associates have been systematically exploring these and other options for explaining the link between empathy and helping behavior. Their strategy is to design experiments in which the altruistic explanation, which maintains that empathy leads to an ultimate desire to help, can be compared to one or another *specific* egoistic alternative. If the strategy succeeds, it does so by eliminating plausible egoistic competitors one at a time and by generating a pattern of evidence that is best explained by the empathy–altruism hypothesis. Batson (1991: 174) concludes, albeit tentatively, that the empathy–altruism hypothesis is correct.

In study after study, with no clear exceptions, we find results conforming to the pattern predicted by the empathy–altruism hypothesis, the hypothesis that empathic emotion evokes altruistic motivation. At present, there is no egoistic explanation for the results of these studies . . . . Pending new evidence or a plausible new egoistic explanation for the existing evidence, the empathy–altruism hypothesis, however improbable, seems to be true.

Reviewing all of these studies would require a very long chapter indeed.[25] Rather than attempt that, we shall take a careful look at some of the best known and most influential experiments aimed at putting altruism to the test in the psychology laboratory. These will, we hope, illustrate both the strengths and the challenges of this approach to the egoism vs. altruism debate.

4.4. *The Empathy–Altruism Hypothesis vs. the Aversive-Arousal Reduction Hypothesis*

Of the various egoistic strategies for explaining helping behavior, among the most compelling is what Batson calls the "aversive-arousal reduction hypothesis." The simplest version of this idea claims that seeing someone in need causes an aversive emotional reaction—something like Batson's *personal distress*—and this leads to a desire to eliminate the aversive emotion. Sometimes the agent will believe that helping is the easiest way to eliminate the aversive emotion, and this will lead to an *instrumental* desire to help, which then leads to helping behavior.[26] However, this simple version of the aversive-arousal

---

[25] For excellent overviews of this research, see Batson (1991,1998).

[26] This idea, which is widely discussed in the social sciences, has venerable philosophical roots. In *Brief Lives*, written between 1650 and 1695, John Aubrey (1949) describes an occasion on which

reduction hypothesis cannot explain the strong effect that empathy-inducing factors have on helping behavior (as discussed in Section 4.2). To accommodate that effect, a more sophisticated version of the hypothesis must be constructed. A plausible suggestion is that the distress felt when we see someone in need is significantly greater when we also feel empathy. This increased distress might be explained by the fact that empathy itself is aversive, or it might be because personal distress is increased when we feel empathy, or perhaps both factors play a part. Whatever the cause, the egoist will insist that the increased helping in situations that evoke empathy is due to an ultimate desire to alleviate the increased distress. By contrast, the empathy–altruism hypothesis maintains that when people feel empathy, this evokes an ultimate desire to help, and that, in turn, sometimes leads to genuinely altruistic behavior.

Batson argues that manipulating *difficulty of escape* allows us to compare these two hypotheses experimentally. The central idea is that if a subject is motivated by an ultimate desire to help the target, that desire can be satisfied only by helping. However, if a subject is motivated by a desire to reduce his own distress, that desire can be satisfied either by helping *or* by merely escaping from the distress-inducing situation—for example, by leaving the room so that one is no longer confronted by the needy target. Assuming that subjects do whatever is easier and less costly, the aversive-arousal reduction hypothesis thus predicts that even subjects experiencing empathy will simply leave the needy target, provided escape is made easy enough.

Since the experimental designs are rather complex, it will be helpful to graphically illustrate the claims made by both the empathy–altruism hypothesis and the aversive-arousal reduction hypothesis. If a subject feels little or no empathy for a target, then Figure 5.8 depicts the processes underlying the subject's behavior according to *both* the aversive-arousal reduction hypothesis and the empathy–altruism hypothesis. In this low-empathy situation, personal distress is the only emotional reaction engendered by the perception of the target in need, and both helping and leaving are live options for reducing this distress.

Although the empathy–altruism hypothesis and the aversive-arousal reduction hypothesis agree about the case in which a subject feels no empathy for a target, the two hypotheses differ where a subject feels a significant amount of empathy for a target. Figure 5.9 depicts the processes underlying the subject's behavior according to Batson's version of the empathy–altruism hypothesis.

Thomas Hobbes gave alms to a beggar. Asked why, Hobbes replied that by giving alms to the beggar, he not only relieved the man's distress but he also relieved his own distress at seeing the beggar's distress.

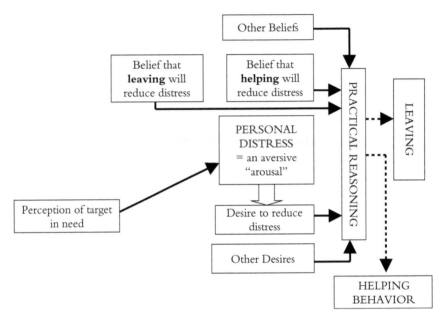

Figure 5.8. Low-empathy subject on both the empathy–altruism hypothesis and the aversive-arousal reduction hypothesis

Here, perception of the target's need leads to empathy and that produces an ultimate desire to help. Since leaving is not an effective strategy for satisfying this desire, helping is the likely behavior—although, of course, the subject might have some *other* desire that is stronger than the ultimate desire to help, so helping is not the only possible outcome.[27] The aversive-arousal reduction hypothesis, by contrast, depicts the processes underlying a high-empathy subject as in Figure 5.10. While the perception of the target in distress leads to empathy in this case too, the empathy simply heightens the subject's personal

---

[27] Since Batson holds that empathy is typically aversive, one might wonder why the egoistic motivation to reduce this aversive arousal plays no role in motivating helping behavior in Figure 5.9. The answer is that, for strategic reasons, Batson focuses on a "strong" version of the empathy–altruism hypothesis which maintains "not only that empathic emotion evokes altruistic motivation but also that all motivation to help evoked by empathy is altruistic . . . It is easy to imagine a weaker form of the empathy–altruism hypothesis, in which empathic emotion evokes both egoistic and altruistic motivation . . . The reason for presenting the strong form . . . is not because it is logically or psychologically superior; the reason is strategic. The weak form has more overlap with egoistic explanations of the motivation to help evoked by empathy, making it more difficult to differentiate empirically from these egoistic explanations" (1991: 87–88). Although it is not depicted in Figure 5.9, Batson's version of the empathy–altruism hypothesis would presumably also maintain that in many cases perception of a target person in distress would also generate some personal distress even in an agent who strongly empathizes with the target. And when the agent believes that leaving is the easiest way to reduce that personal distress, this will generate some motivation to leave.

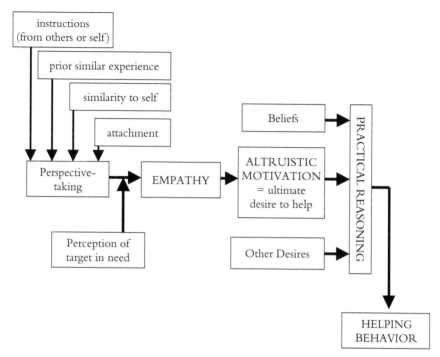

Figure 5.9. High-empathy subject on the empathy–altruism hypothesis

distress and thus strengthens his desire to reduce the distress. Since the subject believes that either helping or leaving will reduce distress, both of these actions are live options, and the subject will select the one that he believes to be easiest.

In designing experiments to compare the empathy–altruism hypothesis with the aversive-arousal reduction hypothesis, Batson must manipulate two distinct variables. To determine whether empathy is playing a role in producing helping behavior, he has to compare the behavior of low-empathy and high-empathy subjects. To determine whether ease of escape has any effect on the likelihood of helping behavior, he must arrange things so that leaving is significantly more costly for some subjects than for others. So there are four experimental conditions: low-empathy subjects where escape is either (1) easy or (2) hard, and high-empathy subjects where leaving is either (3) easy or (4) hard. Batson summarizes what he takes to be the predictions made by the aversive-arousal reduction hypothesis and by the empathy–altruism hypothesis in Tables 5.1 and 5.2 (Batson, 1991: 111). The crucial difference is in the upper-right quadrants, where escape is easy and empathy is high. Under these conditions, Batson maintains, the egoistic aversive-arousal reduction hypothesis predicts a

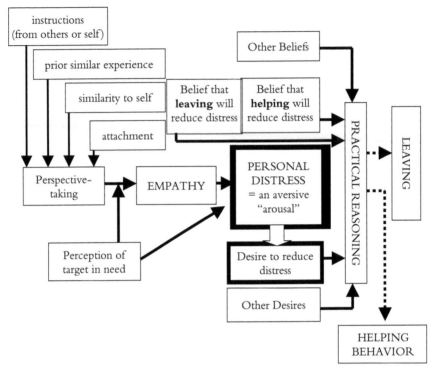

Figure 5.10. High-empathy subject on the aversive-arousal reduction hypothesis

Table 5.1. Predictions from the aversive-arousal reduction hypothesis for the rate of helping in an escape × empathy design

	Empathy	
Escape	Low	High
Easy	Low	**Low**
Difficult	High	High/Very High

low level of helping behavior, while the empathy–altruism hypothesis predicts that the rate of helping will be high.

To test these predictions, Batson and his colleagues conducted a total of six experiments. In one of these (Batson et al., 1981: experiment 1), student subjects were required to watch, via what they believed to be closed-circuit TV, as another student subject, Elaine, attempted to perform a task while receiving electric shocks at random intervals. Observer subjects were told that their task would be to form and report an impression of how Elaine

Table 5.2. Predictions from the empathy–altruism hypothesis for the rate of helping in an escape × empathy design

| | Empathy | |
Escape	Low	High
Easy	Low	**High**
Difficult	High	High

performs under aversive conditions. Actually, what the subjects were viewing was a videotape. On the tape, Elaine is clearly finding the shocks very uncomfortable, and after her second trial at doing the task, she explains to Martha, the assistant overseeing the experiment, that she is unusually sensitive to mild electric shocks because of a childhood trauma. Martha then suggests that perhaps the observer subject might be willing to help Elaine by taking her place, and the experimenter asks whether the subject is willing to do that. To manipulate ease of escape, some subjects are told that if they decide not to take Elaine's place, they will be required to watch eight additional trials, while other subjects are told that if they decide not to take Elaine's place, they will be free to go, although Elaine will have to endure eight more trials. To manipulate the level of empathy that subjects feel for Elaine, subjects are given a copy of a personal values and interests questionnaire, allegedly filled out by Elaine, in order to help them form an impression of her performance. In the high-empathy condition, Elaine's values and interests are very similar to the subject's (which had been determined in a screening session several weeks before), while in the low-empathy condition, they are very different. The results, given in Table 5.3, clearly exhibit the pattern that Batson thinks is predicted by the empathy–altruism hypothesis, not the pattern that Batson thinks is predicted by the aversive-arousal reduction hypothesis.

In four additional experiments, Batson and his associates used a total of four different techniques to create the low- and high-empathy conditions, two

Table 5.3. Proportion of subjects agreeing to take shocks for Elaine (Batson et al., 1981: experiment 1)

| | Empathy Condition | |
Escape Condition	Low (Dissimilar Victim)	High (Similar Victim)
Easy	.18	.91
Difficult	.64	.82

techniques for manipulating ease of escape, and two different need situations.[28] The results in all of these experiments exhibited the same pattern. Intriguingly, in a sixth experiment, Batson attempted to break the pattern by telling the subjects that the shock level they would have to endure was the highest of four options, "clearly painful but not harmful." They reasoned that, in these circumstances, even if high-empathy subjects had an ultimate desire to help, this desire might well be overridden by the desire to avoid a series of very painful shocks. As expected, the pattern of results in this experiment fit the pattern in Table 5.1.

These are, we think, truly impressive findings. Over and over again, in well designed and carefully conducted experiments, Batson and his associates have produced results that are clearly compatible with what Batson has argued are the predictions of the empathy–altruism hypothesis, as set out in Table 5.2, and clearly incompatible with the predictions of the aversive-arousal reduction hypothesis, as set out in Table 5.1. Even the "clearly painful shock" experiment, which produced results in the pattern of Table 5.1, is comfortably compatible with the empathy–altruism hypothesis since, as we noted in our discussion of Figure 5.9, the empathy–altruism hypothesis allows that high-empathy subjects may have desires that are stronger than their ultimate desire to help the target, and the desire to avoid a painful electric shock is a very plausible candidate.

There is, however, a problem to be overcome before we conclude that the aversive-arousal reduction hypothesis cannot explain the findings that Batson has reported. In arguing that Table 5.1 reflects the predictions made by the aversive-arousal reduction hypothesis, Batson assumes that escape will alleviate personal distress (and the aversive component of empathy) in both low- and high-empathy situations, and that subjects *believe* this, although the belief, along with many other mental states and processes posited in Figures 5.8, 5.9, and 5.10, may not be readily available to introspection. We might call this the *out of sight, out of mind* assumption.[29] But, elaborating on an idea suggested by Hoffman (1991) and Hornstein (1991), an advocate of egoism might propose that although subjects do believe this when they have little empathy for the target, *they do not believe it when they have high empathy for the target.* Perhaps high-empathy subjects believe that if they leave the scene they will continue to be troubled by the thought or memory of the distressed target and thus that

---

[28] The experiments are reported in Batson et al. (1981), Toi & Batson (1982), and Batson et al. (1983).

[29] As Batson himself remarks, "[T]he old adage, 'Out of sight, out of mind,' reminds us that physical escape often permits psychological escape as well" (1991: 80).

physical escape will not lead to psychological escape. Indeed, in cases where empathy is strong and is evoked by attachment, this is just what common sense would lead us to expect. (Do you suppose that if you abandoned your mother when she was in grave distress, you would no longer be troubled by the knowledge of her plight?) But if the high-empathy subjects in Batson's experiments believe that they will continue to be plagued by distressing thoughts about the target even after they depart, then the egoistic aversive-arousal reduction hypothesis predicts that these subjects will be inclined to help in both the easy physical escape and the difficult physical escape conditions, since helping is the only strategy they believe will be effective for reducing the aversive arousal.[30] So neither the findings reported in Table 5.3 nor the results of any of Batson's other experiments would give us a reason to prefer the empathy–altruism hypothesis over the aversive-arousal reduction hypothesis, because both hypotheses would make the same predictions.

Is it the case that high-empathy subjects in experiments like Batson's believe that unless they help they will continue to think about the target and thus continue to feel distress, and that this belief leads to helping because it generates an egoistic instrumental desire to help? This is, of course, an empirical question, and until recently there was little evidence bearing on it. But a cleverly designed experiment by Stocks and his associates (Stocks et al., 2009) suggests that, in situations like those used in Batson's experiments, a belief that they will continue to think about the target does *not* play a significant role in causing the helping behavior in high-empathy subjects. The first phase of the experiment was a "psychological escape" manipulation. Half the subjects were told that they would soon be participating in a "deleting memories" training session that would permanently delete their memories of an audiotaped news segment that they were about to hear. The remaining subjects were told that they would soon be participating in a "saving memories" training session designed to permanently enhance the memories of the news segment they were about to hear. Then, using stimulus materials that we shall see in various of Batson's experiments, the experimenters played subjects a fictional college radio news segment about the plight of a fellow student, Katie Banks, whose parents have recently been killed in an automobile accident, leaving her to care for her younger brother and sister. In the interview, Katie mentions that she has begun a fundraising campaign to raise money for her college tuition and for living expenses for her siblings. If she is not successful, she

---

[30] The point emerges clearly in Figure 5.10. If the *Belief that leaving will reduce distress* is eliminated, then LEAVING is no longer a way to satisfy the *Desire to reduce distress*. So HELPING BEHAVIOR is the only way to satisfy this desire.

Table 5.4. Proportion of subjects agreeing to help Katie Banks (Stocks et al., under review: experiment 1)

Psychological Escape	Empathy	
	Low	High
Easy—memory deleted	.08	.67
Difficult—memory enhanced	.42	.58

will be forced to drop out of school and put her brother and sister up for adoption. Empathy for Katie was manipulated by using the Stotland-inspired technique—instructing some participants to imagine how Katie felt and others to try to remain as objective and detached as possible. After hearing the tape, subjects completed two questionnaires, one designed to assess the success of the empathy manipulation, the other designed to test the effectiveness of the psychological escape manipulation. Both manipulations were successful: crucially, subjects reported being quite confident that the memory training session would enhance or delete their memory of the Katie Banks interview they had just heard. Finally, subjects were given an unexpected opportunity to help Katie with her child care and home maintenance chores.

Stocks and his associates reasoned that if high-empathy subjects in the Batson experiments recounted earlier are egoists who help because they believe that they will continue to have distressing thoughts about the victim, then in this experiment high-empathy subjects who believed their memories of Katie would be enhanced by the training session would be highly motivated to help, while subjects who believed that their memories of Katie would soon be deleted would have little motivation to help. If, by contrast, empathy generates altruistic motivation, there should be little difference between those high-empathy subjects who believe their memories of Katie will be enhanced and those who believe that their memories of her will soon be deleted. The results, shown in Table 5.4, provide impressive confirmation of the prediction based on the empathy–altruism hypothesis.[31]

We believe that Batson's work on the aversive-arousal reduction hypothesis, buttressed by the Stocks et al. finding, is a major advance in the egoism vs. altruism debate. No thoughtful observer would conclude that these experiments

---

[31] Both the aversive-arousal reduction hypothesis and the empathy–altruism hypothesis predict that low-empathy subjects will behave egoistically, and thus that they will be less inclined to help when they believe that their memories of Katie will be deleted than when they believe their memories will linger. The fact that this prediction is confirmed is a further indication that the psychological escape manipulation was successful.

show that altruism is true, since, as Batson himself emphasizes, the aversive-arousal reduction hypothesis is just one among many egoistic alternatives to the empathy−altruism hypothesis, although it has been one of the most popular egoistic strategies for explaining helping behavior. But the experimental findings strongly suggest that in situations like those that Batson has studied, the empathy−altruism hypothesis offers a much better explanation of the subjects' behavior than the aversive-arousal reduction hypothesis (Batson, 1991: 127).

4.5. *The Empathy−Altruism Hypothesis vs. The Empathy-Specific Punishment Hypothesis*

As noted earlier, thinkers in the egoist tradition have proposed many alternatives to the hypothesis that empathy engenders genuine altruism. Although aversive-arousal reduction may be the most popular of these, another familiar proposal maintains that people engage in helping behavior because they fear they will be punished if they do not help. On one version of this view, the punishments are socially administered. If I don't help, the agent worries, people will think badly of me, and this will have negative effects on how they treat me. On another version, which to our mind is both more plausible and more difficult to assess experimentally, the punishments that people are worried about are self-administered. If she doesn't help, the agent believes, she will suffer the pangs of guilt, or shame, or some other aversive emotion. As they stand, neither of these egoist accounts can explain the fact that empathy increases the likelihood of helping, but more sophisticated versions are easy to construct.[32] They need only add the assumption that people think either social sanctions or self-administered sanctions for not helping are more likely when the target engenders empathy. We'll take up the social and self-administered variants in turn. We believe that currently available evidence supports the conclusion that the social version is incorrect, but we shall argue that the evidence regarding the self-administered version is inconclusive.

Following Batson, let's call the social variant of this hypothesis (the one that maintains that subjects believe socially administered sanctions to be more likely when the target engenders empathy) the *socially administered empathy-specific punishment hypothesis*. To test it against the empathy−altruism hypothesis, Batson and his associates designed an experiment in which they manipulated both the level of empathy that the subject felt for the target and the likelihood that anyone would know whether or not the subject had opted to help a

---

[32] The problem is similar to the one confronting the simple version of the aversive-arousal reduction hypothesis discussed at the beginning of 4.4, as is the solution.

Table 5.5. Predictions about the amount of helping on the socially administered empathy-specific punishment hypothesis

Would the helping choice be private or public?	Empathy	
	Low	High
Public	Low	High
Private	Low	**Low**

Table 5.6. Predictions about the amount of helping on the empathy–altruism hypothesis

Would the helping choice be private or public?	Empathy	
	Low	High
Public	Low	High
Private	Low	**High**

person in need. Obviously, if your decision is secret, you need have no fear of social sanctions. Thus the socially administered empathy-specific punishment hypothesis predicts that high-empathy subjects will be more likely to help when others will know whether or not they decide to help. On the empathy–altruism hypothesis, by contrast, high-empathy subjects are motivated by an ultimate desire to help, and thus their helping levels should be high whether or not others will know if they decided not to help. In the low-empathy condition, both hypotheses predict that levels of helping will be low. These predictions are summarized in Tables 5.5 and 5.6.

Subjects in the experiment were told that they were participating in an impression-formation study, and that they had been randomly assigned to the role of "listener" who would read confidential notes from another student participant, the "communicator." The listeners were given two notes from a fictional communicator, "Janet Arnold," an out-of-state freshman who reveals that she is very lonely and hoping to find a friend. After completing a form on which subjects indicated their impressions of Janet and their emotional responses to her note, they were presented with an unexpected opportunity to befriend Janet by volunteering to take part in a study of long-term relationships which would involve an initial meeting with Janet and periodic phone interviews about the development of their friendship. Participants who were willing to help were asked how much time they were willing to spend with Janet during the next month.

To manipulate empathy, Batson and his associates used the Stotland technique. Subjects assigned to the low-empathy condition were instructed to "Read the information in the communicator's notes carefully, trying to be as objective as possible. Try to focus on the techniques used to get the communicator's message across." Subjects assigned to the high-empathy condition were instructed to "Read the information in the communicator's notes carefully, trying to take the perspective of the individual writing the notes. Try to imagine how this individual feels about what he or she writes" (1991: 132).

Four steps were taken to manipulate the perceived potential for negative social evaluation. In the *low-potential* condition, where the subjects' choices were private (Batson 1991: 132):

(1) Subjects were told that they would be the only person ever to read the communicator's notes, and the notes were delivered in a sealed envelope.
(2) Subjects were assured that the questionnaires reporting their reactions to Janet's note would be anonymous.
(3) Subjects' responses to the invitation to participate in the long-term relationship study were returned to the professor in a sealed envelope, so no one would know if they did not want to help Janet. (Since they believed the professor had not read Janet's note, they could be expected to surmise that he would not know that Janet needed a friend.)
(4) In the letter inviting them to participate in the relationship study, subjects were told that Janet would be contacted "only if you want a meeting; if you do not, then we will not contact the communicator and he or she will not know that you were ever asked about actually meeting."

In the *high-potential* condition where the subjects' choices were public (Batson, 1991: 133):

(1) Subjects were told that the experimenter would (a) read the communicator's notes, (b) collect the subject's completed questionnaire, and (c) compare the content of the notes with the content of the questionnaire.
(2) No envelope was provided for their response to the invitation to participate in the long-term relationship study, so subjects could infer that the experimenter would know about Janet's need for a friend, about their emotional reaction to Janet, and would also know whether or not they had agreed to help Janet.
(3) Subjects were told that Janet would know if they decided not to help.

As Batson states, or perhaps understates, procedures in the high-potential (public) condition "were designed to highlight the possibility of negative social evaluation if the participant decided not to volunteer to spend time with Janet" (1991: 133).

Table 5.7. Amount of help offered Janet (Fultz et al., 1986: study 2)

Would the helping choice be private or public?	Empathy	
	Low	High
Public	.67	1.71
Private	1.29	2.44

The results, given in Table 5.7, indicate that the socially administered empathy-specific punishment hypothesis did not fare well. On the basis of this experiment and a similar experiment in which empathy for Janet was not manipulated but was measured by self-report, Batson concludes that the socially administered empathy-specific punishment hypothesis is not consistent with the experimental findings.

Contrary to what the social-evaluation version of the empathy-specific punishment hypothesis predicted, eliminating anticipated negative social evaluation in these two studies did not eliminate the empathy-helping relationship. Rather than high empathy leading to more help only under high social evaluation, it led to more helping under both low and high social evaluation. This pattern of results is not consistent with what would be expected if empathically aroused individuals are egoistically motivated to avoid looking bad in the eyes of others; it is quite consistent with what would be expected if empathy evokes altruistic motivation to reduce the victim's need. (1991: 134)

Although two experiments hardly make a conclusive case, we are inclined to agree with Batson that these studies make the socially administered empathy-specific punishment hypothesis look significantly less plausible than the empathy–altruism hypothesis. High-empathy subjects were more likely to help *whether or not* they could expect their behavior to be socially scrutinized. So another popular egoist hypothesis has been dealt a serious blow. At least in some circumstances, empathy appears to facilitate helping independently of the threat of social sanction.[33]

There is, however, another version of the empathy-specific punishment hypothesis that must be considered, and we are less sanguine about Batson's

---

[33] These studies do not address a variant of the socially administered empathy-specific punishment hypothesis that might be called the "*divinely* administered empathy-specific punishment hypothesis." It is very plausible that subjects in the private low potential for social evaluation condition believed that no ordinary person would know if they declined to help someone in need. But these subjects might believe that *God* would know, that *He* would punish them for their failure to help, and that God's punishment would be particularly severe when they failed to help someone for whom they felt empathy. To the best of our knowledge, the divinely administered empathy-specific punishment hypothesis is a version of egoism that has not been explored empirically.

attempts to defend the empathy–altruism hypothesis against this version. According to the *self-administered* empathy-specific punishment hypothesis, people are motivated to help because they believe that if they don't help they will experience some negative self-regarding emotion, such as guilt or shame. As Batson (1991: 98) explicates the view, "we learn through socialization that empathy carries with it a special obligation to help and, as a result, an extra dose of self-administered shame or guilt if we do not. When we feel empathy we think of the impending additional self-punishments and help in order to avoid them . . . To test whether self-punishment underlies the empathy-helping relationship," Batson (1991: 134–135) notes, "high-empathy individuals must anticipate being able to escape . . . from negative self-evaluation." But, one might wonder, how is that possible? Here is the crucial passage in which Batson addresses the question and sets out his strategy.

[I]f expectations of self-punishment have been internalized to the degree that they are automatic and invariant across all helping situations, then providing escape seems impossible. It seems unlikely, however, that many people—if any—have internalized procedures for self-punishment to such a degree. Even those who reflexively slap themselves with guilt and self-recrimination whenever they do wrong are likely to be sensitive to situational cues in determining when they have done wrong . . . And given the discomfort produced by guilt and self-recrimination, one suspects that most people will not reflexively self-punish but will, if possible, overlook their failures to help. They will dole out self-punishments only in situations in which such failures are salient and inescapable.

If there is this kind of leeway in interpreting failure to help as unjustified and hence deserving of self-punishment, then expectation of self-punishment may be reduced by providing some individuals with information that justifies not helping in some particular situation. The justifying information probably cannot be provided directly by telling individuals not to feel guilty about not helping. Calling direct attention to the failure may have the reverse effect; it may highlight the associated punishments. The information needs to be provided in a more subtle, indirect way.   (1991: 135)

Before considering how Batson and his associates designed experiments that attempt to implement this strategy, we want to emphasize a subtle but very important concern about the passage we've just quoted. In that passage, Batson slips back and forth between claims about people's *expectations* about self-punishment and their internalized procedures for administering it. The latter are claims about what people will actually feel if they fail to help in various circumstances, while the former are claims about what people *believe* they will feel. The distinction is an important one because in the debate between egoists and altruists it is the *beliefs* that are crucial. To see this, recall what is at issue. Both egoists and altruists agree that people sometimes desire to help

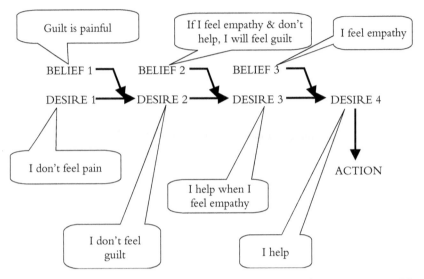

Figure 5.11. The self-administered empathy-specific punishment account of the practical reasoning leading to the instrumental desire to help

others, but egoists insist that these desires are always instrumental desires, while altruists maintain that, sometimes at least, these desires are not instrumental but ultimate. As we saw in Section 1, instrumental desires are desires that are produced or sustained via practical reasoning, a process in which desires and beliefs lead to new desires. So an egoist who advocates the self-administered empathy-specific punishment hypothesis would maintain that the desire to help is generated by an episode of practical reasoning something like the one in Figure 5.11. In that diagram, BELIEF 2 (*If I feel empathy and don't help, then I will feel guilty*) plays a central role, since it is this belief that is supposed to capture the agent's expectations about self-punishment. That belief may or may not be accurate—perhaps the agent won't actually feel guilty. But the accuracy of the belief is not relevant to the debate between egoists and altruists. What is crucial is just that the subject has some belief that, together with her desire not to feel guilt (DESIRE 2), will generate DESIRE 3 (*I help when I feel empathy*). The importance of all this will emerge as we review Batson's experiments and how he interprets them.

In designing experiments to test the empathy–altruism hypothesis against the self-administered empathy-specific punishment hypothesis, Batson's strategy is to provide some subjects with a justification for not helping. By doing this, Batson's goal is to alter his subjects' beliefs; he expects that subjects who have been given a justification for not helping will be less likely to believe that they will feel guilty if they do not help. In one experiment, subjects were asked to listen to a tape of what they were told was a pilot broadcast of a campus radio show. The show is an interview with Katie Banks, whom we met earlier in our discussion of the Stocks et al. experiment. She is a student on their campus struggling to stay in school and keep her family together after her parents are killed in an automobile accident. To manipulate levels of empathy, the investigators again used the Stotland procedure. After listening to the tape, subjects are given an opportunity to pledge time to help Katie. To manipulate the justification that subjects have for not helping, some are given a sign-up sheet on which five of seven previous "participants" in the study have agreed to help, while others are given a sign-up sheet on which only two of the previous seven participants have agreed to help. By getting the second group to believe that most previous participants had not been willing to help, Batson and his associates intend to be providing just the sort of "subtle, indirect" justification for not helping that their strategy requires.[34]

According to Batson, in the low-empathy condition, both the empathy–altruism hypothesis and the self-administered empathy-specific punishment hypothesis will make the same prediction: helping will be high in the low-justification condition (where subjects have little justification for not helping), and low in the high-justification condition (where subjects have a lot of justification for not helping).[35] In the high-empathy condition, however, Batson maintains that the two hypotheses make different predictions. Empathy–altruism claims that empathy will lead to an ultimate desire to help, and thus it predicts that helping should be high whether or not the subject has good justification for not helping. Self-administered empathy-specific punishment, on the other hand, predicts that having or lacking a justification will affect the likelihood of helping. Helping will be high when there is little justification for not helping, but low when there is good justification for not helping. This is because in the former case subjects will believe they will feel very guilty if they do not help, but in the latter case they do not believe this.

The results in the Katie Banks experiment are given in Table 5.8. They conform, quite dramatically, to the "three high and one low" empathy–altruism

[34] One might worry, here, that the sign-up-sheet manipulation could have just the opposite effect. If lots of other people have already signed up to help Katie, some subjects might come to believe that they are justified in *not* helping, since she already has plenty of help.

[35] In order to derive this prediction for the low-justification condition, Batson must assume that, even without empathy, subjects "should be egoistically motivated to avoid general shame and guilt associated with a failure to help" (1991:136). So, as Batson is interpreting the self-administered empathy-specific punishment hypothesis, it maintains that even low-empathy individuals believe they will feel *some* guilt if they fail to help without justification, and high-empathy individuals believe they will feel significantly more guilt if they fail to help without justification.

Table 5.8. Proportion of participants volunteering to help Katie Banks (Batson et al., 1988: study 3)

Justification condition	Empathy Condition	
	Low	High
Low justification for not helping	.55	.70
High justification for not helping	.15	.60

hypothesis prediction. Moreover, "there was no evidence of the significant effect of the justification manipulation in the high-empathy condition predicted by the self-punishment version of the empathy-specific punishment hypothesis" (1991: 138). In a pair of additional experiments, Batson and his associates varied the helping opportunity, the justification manipulation and the empathy manipulation. In those experiments, too, "the pattern of helping was very much as predicted by the empathy–altruism hypothesis" (ibid.: 140). Once again, it appears there is good reason to prefer the empathy–altruism hypothesis over an egoistic empathy-specific punishment alternative. But we are not convinced.

Our concerns are not focused on the details of Batson's experiments, but on his account of what the self-administered empathy-specific punishment hypothesis predicts. To make the point, let's return to the practical reasoning diagram in Figure 5.11. In that diagram, BELIEF 2 portrays the agent believing: *If I feel empathy and don't help, I will feel guilt.* But if Batson is right, that account of BELIEF 2 needs to be modified, since if the agent really believed that, then the justification manipulation would have no effect. In order for the justification manipulation to disrupt the process portrayed in Figure 5.11, BELIEF 2 would have to be something like: *If I feel empathy & don't help, I will feel guilt UNLESS there is justification for not helping.* That belief, along with DESIRE 2 (*I don't feel guilt*), would lead to DESIRE 3 with the content: *I help when I feel empathy UNLESS there is justification for not helping*, and that is just what Batson needs to derive his predictions about what agents are likely to do in high-empathy situations, if the self-administered empathy-specific punishment hypothesis is correct. Suppose, however, that instead of this candidate for BELIEF 2, what agents actually believe is: *If I feel empathy & don't help, I will feel guilt EVEN IF there is justification for not helping.* In that case, DESIRE 3 would be: *I help when I feel empathy EVEN IF there is justification for not helping*, and the self-administered empathy-specific punishment hypothesis would predict high levels of helping in high-empathy subjects whether or not there is justification for not helping. Since this is just what the empathy–altruism hypothesis predicts, Batson's experiments would not be able to distinguish between the two hypotheses. So clearly the content of agents' beliefs about the link between empathy and guilt is playing a crucial role in Batson's argument.

What grounds does Batson offer for assuming that subjects believe: *If I feel empathy & don't help, I will feel guilt UNLESS there is justification for not helping*, rather than: *If I feel empathy & don't help, I will feel guilt EVEN IF there is justification for not helping*? As best we can tell, the long passage we quoted earlier is his only attempt to justify the assumption. But that passage offers no evidence for the claims it makes about people's "internalized procedures for self-punishment." Moreover, even if Batson's speculations about those procedures are true, it would not justify the claim he really needs, namely that people have accurate *beliefs* about these internalized procedures. The prediction that Batson derives from the egoistic hypothesis requires assuming that people typically have a specific sort of belief about what they will feel if they fail to help when there is justification for not helping. That is an empirical assumption, of course, but it is one for which Batson offers no evidence. Batson might be able to protect his argument from our critique by showing that subjects really do have the belief that his prediction assumes. But until that is done, the experiments we have discussed give us no good reason to reject the self-administered empathy-specific punishment hypothesis.

The findings we have discussed so far are not, however, the only ones that Batson relies on in his critique of the self-administered empathy-specific punishment hypothesis. In another version of the Katie Banks experiment, Batson and his associates attempted to determine *what participants were thinking* when they made their decisions about whether to offer help. Here is Batson's explanation of the motivation for this experiment:

The empathy-specific punishment hypothesis and the empathy–altruism hypothesis each postulate a different goal for the helping associated with feeling empathy: The goal is avoiding punishment in the former; the goal is relieving the victim's need for the latter. Each hypothesis assumes that the empathically aroused individual, when deciding to help, has one of these goals in mind. If this is true, then cognitions relevant to one of these goals should be associated with empathy-induced helping.   (1991: 143)

So if we can find some way to determine what empathically engaged individuals are thinking about, Batson argues, we may be able to provide evidence for one or another of these hypotheses. Simply asking subjects what they were thinking about is methodologically problematic, first because the relevant thoughts might not have been fully conscious, and second because subjects might be unwilling, or otherwise unable, to provide accurate self-reports. But, as it happens, the well-known Stroop procedure provides a way of determining what people are thinking about without directly asking them. In the Stroop procedure, subjects are shown words typed in various colors. Their task is to name the color of the type, and to do so as quickly as possible. Previous research had shown that the time taken to respond for a particular word (the "latency" in psychologists' jargon) will increase whenever a subject has been thinking about something related to that word (Geller & Shaver, 1976).

In the experiment, which for the most part repeated the Katie Banks procedure, the experimenter paused after telling subjects that they would be given an opportunity to sign up to help Katie, and administered a Stroop test. Some of the words used, like DUTY, GUILT, SHAME, SHOULD, were taken to be "punishment-relevant"; other words, including HOPE, CHILD, NEEDY, FRIEND, were classified as "victim-relevant"; and still other words, LEFT, RAPID, LARGE, BREATH, were classified as neutral. Here is Batson's account of the results and his interpretation of them:

[T]he only positive association in the high-empathy condition was a correlation between helping and color-naming latency for the victim-relevant words . . . This was the correlation predicted by the empathy–altruism hypothesis. Contrary to the prediction of the empathy-specific punishment hypothesis, there was no evidence of a positive correlation in the high-empathy condition between helping and color-naming latency for the punishment-relevant words.

In the low-empathy condition, in which empathic feelings had not been explicitly aroused, there was not a positive correlation between helping and latency for the victim-relevant words. This finding suggests that the positive correlation for victim-relevant words in the high-empathy condition was not due to some general characteristic of these words or their association with helping. The relationship seemed to be empathy specific.   (1991: 147)

Although this is an ingenious experiment with intriguing results, we are again skeptical that the results favor one hypothesis over the other. To make the case for our skepticism, we'll argue that the self-administered empathy-specific punishment hypothesis can be plausibly construed in a way that it *does not* predict, of the agent, that she will be thinking punishment-relevant thoughts. Instead, it predicts exactly what Batson found: the agent thinks only victim-relevant thoughts.

Let's begin by returning to the quotation, two paragraphs back, in which Batson explains the motivation for the experiment. According to Batson, "The empathy-specific punishment hypothesis and the empathy–altruism hypothesis each postulate a different goal for the helping associated with feeling empathy: The goal is avoiding punishment in the former; the goal is relieving the victim's need for the latter" (1991: 143). It is important to see that this claim is plausible only if "goal" is understood to mean *ultimate desire*, and is clearly false if "goal" refers to any desire that may play a role in the process leading to helping behavior. On the empathy-specific punishment hypothesis, although the ultimate desire is avoiding punishment (or the pain that punishment engenders), this leads to an *instrumental* desire to relieve the victim's need. So it is misleading for Batson to claim that "each hypothesis assumes that the empathically aroused individual, when deciding to help, has one of these goals in mind" (1991: 143), since the empathy-specific punishment hypothesis maintains that the empathically aroused individual has *both* desires in mind—one as an ultimate desire and the other as in instrumental desire. This suggests that the empathy-specific punishment hypothesis should predict that high-empathy subjects have a longer latency for *both* punishment-relevant words and victim-relevant words.

If this is right, then we've located a slip in what Batson claims about the prediction of the empathy-specific punishment hypothesis. However, it might be thought that this does no serious harm to Batson's case, since the experimental results also contradict this new prediction. On the new prediction, high-empathy subjects should be thinking both punishment-relevant and victim-relevant thoughts. But they aren't. They are thinking only victim-relevant thoughts, which is what the empathy–altruism hypothesis predicts.

This is not the end of the story, however. For we believe that on one very natural interpretation of the empathy-specific punishment hypothesis, it will *not* predict that agents think punishment-relevant thoughts. To set out this interpretation, we'll need to introduce the idea of a *long-standing instrumental desire*. Consider what happens when you get your monthly electric bill. Typically, we'll assume, you pay it. Why? Well, because you have a desire to pay it. This is, to be sure, an instrumental desire, not an ultimate desire. You want to pay your electric bill because you believe that if you don't, they will turn off your electricity, and that would lead to lots of other unpleasant consequences which you want to avoid. The lights would go out; the heat or air conditioning would go off; your computer would stop working; it would be a real pain in the neck. But are any of these consequences on your mind when you reach for the checkbook to pay the electricity bill? Quite typically, we think, the answer is no. Rather, what happens is that you have a *long-standing desire* to pay the electric bill on time whenever it comes. This is an instrumental desire; there is nothing intrinsically desirable about paying the bill. So, like other instrumental desires, it was formed via a process of practical reasoning. But that was a long time ago, and there is no need to revisit that process every time you pay your bill. Most people, we think, have *lots* of desires like that. They are enduring desires that were formed long ago via practical reasoning. When the circumstances are appropriate, they are activated, they generate further instrumental desires, and ultimately they lead to action. And all of this happens without either consciously or unconsciously revisiting the practical reasoning that led to the formation of the long-standing desire.

Let's return, now, to Figure 5.11, which sketches the motivational structure underlying helping behavior on one version of the empathy-specific punishment hypothesis. On the interpretation of the hypothesis that we are proposing, DESIRE 3 is a long-standing instrumental desire. It was originally formed via the egoistic process of practical reasoning sketched on the left side of Figure 5.11. But there is no need to repeat that process every time the desire is activated, any more than there is a need to reflect on the lights going out every time you pay your electric bill. On this interpretation of the empathy-specific punishment hypothesis, the agent will not activate thoughts about guilt and punishment when she decides to help. Instead, the only thoughts that need be activated are thoughts about the victim and how to help her. So, on this interpretation, the results of Batson's Stroop experiment are just what the empathy-specific punishment hypothesis would predict. Thus the experiment gives us no reason to prefer empathy–altruism over empathy-specific punishment.

In this section we have looked at two versions of the egoistic empathy-specific punishment hypothesis. We've argued that Batson's work poses a serious challenge to the version on which the punishment is delivered by others. But Batson's experiments do not make a convincing case against the version on which the punishment is *self-inflicted*, via guilt or some other aversive emotion. To address the problems we've elaborated, Batson needs to provide more convincing evidence about the beliefs that subjects invoke when they are making their decision about helping Katie Banks, and about the processes that generate and sustain the desires involved in that decision. This is a tall order, since it is no easy matter to get persuasive evidence about either of these. The need for such evidence makes it clear how challenging empirical work in this area can be. But, as illustrated by Batson's own work, as well as the Stocks et al. study discussed in the previous section, cleverly designed experiments can go a long way toward resolving issues that at first appear intractable. So the gap in Batson's case against the empathy-specific punishment hypothesis certainly gives us no reason to be skeptical about the experimental approach to the egoism vs. altruism debate.

4.6. The Empathy–Altruism Hypothesis vs. The Empathy-Specific Reward Hypothesis

In the previous section our focus was on the venerable idea that helping is motivated by fear of punishment. In this section, we'll take a brief look at the equally venerable idea that helping is motivated by the expectation of reward. Like punishment, reward can come from two sources: others can reward us in various ways for our helpful actions, or we can reward ourselves—helping others can make us feel good. But just as in the case of punishment, the simple theory that people help others because they believe they will be rewarded offers no explanation for the fact that empathy increases helping behavior. To remedy this problem, the egoist can propose that "helping is especially rewarding when the helper feels empathy for the person in need" (Batson, 1991: 97). This is the view that Batson calls *the empathy-specific reward hypothesis*. Although the idea can be spelled out in a variety of ways, we'll begin with the version that claims "that we learn through socialization that *additional rewards* follow helping someone for whom we feel empathy; these rewards most often take the form of extra praise from others or a special feeling of pride in ourselves. When we feel empathy, we think of these additional rewards, and we help in order to get them" (ibid.).

To motivate an ingenious experiment designed to test this hypothesis against the empathy–altruism hypothesis, Batson notes that it is only one's own helping, or attempts to help, that make one eligible for the rewards that helping engenders; if someone else helps the target before you get around to it, the rewards are not forthcoming. This is plausible both in the case where the rewards are provided by others and in the case where the rewards are provided by our own self-generated feeling of pride. For surely we don't typically expect others to praise us because someone else has helped a person in distress, nor do we expect to feel pride if the target's distress is alleviated by a stranger, or by chance. So on the version of the empathy-specific rewards hypothesis that we are considering, we should predict that an empathically aroused agent will be pleased when he gets to help the target (either because he is feeling a jolt of pride or because he is looking forward to the rewards that others will provide), but he will not be pleased if he is unable to help the target.

For reasons that will emerge shortly, Batson distinguishes two cases in which the agent is unable to help. In the first, there is just nothing he can do to relieve the target's distress; in the second, someone (or something) else relieves the target's distress before the agent gets a chance to act. In both cases, Batson maintains, the egoistic reward-seeking agent has nothing in particular to be pleased about. Finally, Batson suggests that we can determine whether an agent is pleased by using self-report tests to assess changes in his mood—the more the mood has improved, the more pleased the agent is.

If the empathy–altruism hypothesis is correct, then agents are motivated by an ultimate desire that the target's distress be alleviated. So on this hypothesis, it shouldn't matter *how* the target's distress is alleviated. No matter how it is accomplished, the agent's altruistic ultimate desire will be satisfied. If we assume that people are pleased when their ultimate desires are satisfied, then the empathy–altruism hypothesis predicts that empathically aroused individuals should be pleased—and thus have elevated moods—whenever the target is helped. They should be displeased, and exhibit a lower mood, only in the case where the target's distress is not alleviated.

To see which of these predictions was correct, Batson and his associates designed an experiment in which participants were told that they would likely have the chance to perform a simple task that would reduce the number of electric shocks that a peer would receive (Batson et al., 1988: study 1). Somewhat later, half of the participants learned, by chance, that they would not be performing the helping task after all, and thus that they could not help the other student. This divided the participants into two experimental conditions, "perform" and "not perform." Subsequently, half of the participants in each condition learned that, by chance, the peer was not going to get the shocks, while the other half learned that, by chance, the peer would still have to get the shocks. This yielded two more experimental conditions, "prior relief." and "no prior relief". All participants were also asked to self-report their level of empathy for the peer, so that high- and low-empathy participants could be distinguished. To assess mood change, the moods of all participants were measured both before and after the experimental manipulation. As we saw above, the version of the empathy-specific reward hypothesis that we're considering predicts that participants in the perform + no prior relief condition should indicate an elevated mood, since they were able to help the peer; it also predicts that participants in all the other conditions should not have an elevated mood, since for one reason or another they were unable to help, and thus were ineligible for the reward. The empathy–altruism hypothesis, by contrast, predicts an elevated mood in all three conditions in which the peer escaped the shocks: perform + no prior relief, perform + prior relief, and not perform + prior relief. The only condition in which empathy–altruism predicts low mood is the one in which the peer gets the shocks: not perform + no prior relief. In fact, the results fit the pattern predicted by the empathy–altruism hypothesis, not the pattern predicted by empathy-specific reward.

We are inclined to agree with Batson that this experiment shows that the version of the empathy-specific reward hypothesis we've been considering is less plausible than the empathy–altruism hypothesis.[36] However, there's

---

[36] Batson and colleagues (Batson et al., 1988) also did a Stroop experiment aimed at testing this version of the empathy-specific reward hypothesis. But for the reasons discussed in the previous section, we don't think the Stroop procedure is useful in this context.

another way of elaborating the self-administered version of the empathy-specific reward hypothesis that the experiment does not address. On the version of the empathy-specific reward hypothesis we've been considering, the self-administered rewards come from something like a "jolt of pride" that the empathically aroused agent feels when he helps the target. And, as Batson rightly notes, it is unlikely that an agent would expect to get *this* reward if he were in no way involved in the relief of the target's distress. But the jolt of pride story is not the only one that an egoist can tell about the self-administered reward an empathically aroused agent might anticipate when confronted with an opportunity to help; another option focuses on the vicarious *pleasure* that empathically aroused agents might expect to feel when the target's distress is alleviated. This account, the *empathic-joy hypothesis*, maintains that empathically aroused individuals "help to gain the good feeling of sharing vicariously in the needy person's joy at improvement" (Batson et al., 1991: 413). On this story, the actor's ultimate goal is egoistic; the desire to help is just instrumental.

There have been a number of experiments aimed at testing the empathic-joy hypothesis. All of them rely on manipulating subjects' expectations about the sort of *feedback* they can expect about the condition of the target. The central idea in two of these experiments[37] was that if the empathic-joy hypothesis is correct, then high-empathy subjects should be more highly motivated to help when they expect to get feedback about the effect of their assistance on the target's well-being than when they have no expectation of learning about the effect of their assistance. In the latter ("no-feedback") condition subjects won't know if the target's situation has improved and thus they can't expect to experience vicarious joy. On the empathy–altruism hypothesis, by contrast, high-empathy subjects are motivated by an ultimate desire for the well-being of the target, so we should not expect those anticipating feedback to be more likely to help than those not anticipating feedback. In both experiments, the Stotland technique was used to manipulate empathy, and in both cases the subjects who were instructed to imagine how the target felt failed to show a higher level of helping in the feedback condition than in the no-feedback condition. This looks like bad news for the empathic-joy hypothesis, but for two reasons, the situation is less than clear-cut. First, doubts have been raised about the effectiveness of the Stotland manipulation in these experiments.[38] Second, in one experiment there was an unexpected finding: while high-empathy subjects helped more than low-empathy subjects in the no-feedback condition, they actually helped *less* in the feedback condition.

[37] Smith et al. (1989) and Batson et al. (1991), experiment 1.
[38] For discussion, see Smith et al. (1989) and Batson et al. (1991).

In an effort to buttress the case against the empathic-joy hypothesis, Batson and his colleagues designed two additional experiments in which the rationale was rather different.[39] If the empathic-joy hypothesis is true, they reasoned, then if high-empathy subjects listen to a taped interview detailing the plight of a troubled target in the recent past and are then offered a choice between getting an update on how the target is doing and hearing about another person, there should be a linear relationship between the probability that the target has improved and the likelihood of choosing to get an update on the target, since the more likely it is that the target has improved, the more likely it is that the subject will get to experience the vicarious joy that he seeks. In both experiments, subjects were given what were alleged to be experts' assessments of the likelihood that the target would improve in the time between the first and second interviews. Neither experiment showed the sort of linear relationship that the empathic-joy hypothesis predicts.

We agree with Batson and colleagues' contention that these results "cast serious doubt on the empathic-joy hypothesis" (1991: 425). But as they go on to note, the experiments were not designed to test the empathic-joy hypothesis *against* the empathy–altruism hypothesis, since the latter hypothesis makes no clear prediction about the scenarios in question. Therefore, Batson and colleagues (1991: 425) are appropriately cautious, observing that the experiments "did not provide unequivocal support" for empathy–altruism. The bottom line, as we see it, is that while the empathic-joy hypothesis does not look promising, more evidence is needed before coming to a final judgment.

4.7. *The Social Psychology of Altruism: Summing Up*

Batson concludes that the work we have reviewed in this section gives us good reason to think that the empathy–altruism hypothesis is true.

Sherlock Holmes stated: "When you have eliminated the impossible, whatever remains, *however improbable*, must be the truth." If we apply Holmes's dictum to our attempt to answer the altruism question, then I believe we must, tentatively, accept the truth of the empathy–altruism hypothesis. It is impossible for any of the three major egoistic explanations of the empathy-helping relationship—or any combination of these—to account for the evidence reviewed.   (Batson, 1991: 174)

Although we don't believe that this conclusion is justified, we think it is clear that Batson and his associates have made important progress. They have shown that one widely endorsed account of the egoistic motivation underlying helping

---

[39] Batson et al. (1991), experiments 2 and 3.

behavior, the aversive-arousal reduction hypothesis, is very unlikely to be true in the sorts of cases used in their studies. They have also dealt a serious blow to both the socially administered empathy-specific punishment hypothesis and to several versions of the empathy-specific reward hypothesis. However, we think the jury is still out on the self-administered empathy-specific punishment hypothesis, and that the case against the empathy-specific reward hypothesis is not yet conclusive.

A worry of another sort emerges when we focus on Batson's claim that no "combination" of the three major egoistic explanations could explain the experimental data. An egoistic thesis that might be labeled *disjunctive* egoism maintains that when empathically aroused people try to help, they have a variety of egoistic motivations—they are sometimes motivated by the desire to reduce aversive arousal, sometimes by the desire to avoid socially or self-administered punishment and sometimes by the desire for socially or self-administered reward. Since all of Batson's experiments are designed to test empathy–altruism against *one or another* specific egoistic hypothesis, none of these experiments rules out this sort of disjunctive egoism. For it might be the case that in each experiment subjects are motivated by one of the egoistic goals that the experiment is *not* designed to rule out. We're not sure how seriously to take this concern, since it seems to require that nature is playing a shell game with the investigators, always relying on an egoistic motivation that the experiment is not designed to look for. But we do think the idea deserves more explicit attention than it has so far received in the literature.[40] Clearly, there is still much important work to be done on the social psychology of altruism.

5. Conclusion

Readers might be tempted to think, at this point, that our concluding section must be rather inconclusive. After all, we haven't claimed to have resolved the philosophically venerable egoism vs. altruism debate, and the scientific record appears somewhat equivocal, as indeed we've been at pains to show. But before we offer refunds, we should enumerate what we think we *have* learned.

Our first lesson is negative: contrary to what some writers have asserted, appeal to evolutionary theory does not generate movement in the philosophical debate about altruism. This may seem disappointing, especially given

---

[40] This worry about Batson's one-at-a-time strategy was noted, albeit briefly, in Cialdini (1991). For a helpful discussion, see Oakberg (unpublished ms.).

the fecundity of recent explications of philosophical ethics in the light of evolutionary theory (e.g. Joyce, 2006: Machery & Mallon, Chapter 1, this volume). Fortunately, our conclusions regarding the philosophical impact of experimental social psychology are rather more inspiring. Batson and associates have shown quite conclusively that the methods of experimental psychology can move the debate forward; it now looks as though certain venerable renderings of psychological egoism are not true to the contours of human psychology. Indeed, in our view, Batson and his associates have made more progress in the last three decades than philosophers using the traditional philosophical methodology of *a priori* arguments buttressed by anecdote and intuition have made in the previous two millennia. Their work, like other work recounted in this volume, powerfully demonstrates the utility of empirical methods in moral psychology.

References

Aquinas, T. (1270/1917). *The Summa Theologica* (Vol. 2, Part II). New York: Benziger Brothers.

Aubrey, J. (1949). *Aubrey's Brief Lives*, ed. Oliver Lawson Dick. Boston, MA: David R. Godine. Aubrey's sketch of Hobbes is available online at: http://www-groups.dcs.st-and.ac.uk/~history/Societies/Aubrey.html

Axelrod, R. & Hamilton, W. D. (1981). The evolution of cooperation. *Science*, 211: 1390–1396.

—— (1991). *The Altruism Question: Toward a Social-Psychological Answer*. Hillsdale, NJ: Lawrence Erlbaum Associates.

Batson, C. D. (1998). Altruism and prosocial behavior. In D. T. Gilbert & S. T. Fiske (eds.), *The Handbook of Social Psychology*, Vol. 2. Boston, MA: McGraw-Hill, 282–316.

Batson, C. D., Duncan, B., Ackerman, P., Buckley, T., & Birch, K. (1981). Is empathic emotion a source of altruistic motivation? *Journal of Personality and Social Psychology*, 40: 290–302.

Batson, C. D., O'Quin, K., Fultz, J., Vanderplas, M., & Isen, A. (1983). Self-reported distress and empathy and egoistic versus altruistic motivation for helping. *Journal of Personality and Social Psychology*, 45: 706–718.

Batson, C. D., Dyck, J., Brandt, R., Batson, J., Powell, A., McMaster, M., & Griffitt, C. (1988). Five studies testing two new egoistic alternatives to the empathy–altrusim hypothesis. *Journal of Personality and Social Psychology*, 55: 52–77.

Batson, C. D., Batson, G., Slingsby, J., Harrell, K., Peekna, H., & Todd, R. M. (1991). Empathic joy and the empathy–altruism hypothesis. *Journal of Personality and Social Psychology*, 61: 413–426.

Beatty, J. (1992). Fitness. In E. Keller & L. Lloyd (eds.), *Keywords in Evolutionary Biology*. Cambridge, MA: Harvard University Press.

Bentham, J. (1789). *An Introduction to the Principles of Morals and Legislation*, ed. J. H. Burns & H. L. A. Hart, with a new introduction by F. Rosen. Oxford: Oxford University Press, 1996.

——(1824). *The Book of Fallacies*. London: Hunt.

Boyd, R. & Richerson, P. (1992). Punishment allows the evolution of cooperation (or anything else) in sizable groups. *Ethology and Sociobiology*, 13: 171–195. Reprinted in R. Boyd & P. Richerson, *The Origin and Evolution of Cultures*. Oxford: Oxford University Press, 2005.

Bratman, M. (1987). *Intention, Plans, and Practical Reasoning*. Cambridge, MA: Harvard University Press.

Broad, C. D. (1930). *Five Types of Ethical Theory*. New York: Harcourt, Brace.

Butler, J. (1726). *Fifteen Sermons Preached at the Rolls Chapel*. Sermons I, II, III, XI, XII, reprinted in S. Darwall (ed.), *Five Sermons Preached at the Rolls Chapel and A Dissertation Upon the Nature of Virtue*. Indianapolis, IN: Hackett, 1983.

Cialdini, R. B. (1991). Altruism or egoism? That is (still) the question. *Psychological Inquiry*, 2: 124–126.

Carey, S. & Spelke, E. (1996). Science and core knowledge. *Philosophy of Science*, 63 (4): 515–533.

Davidson, D. (1963). Actions, reasons, and causes. *Journal of Philosophy*, 60 (23): 685–700.

——(1980). Agency. In *Essays on Actions and Events*. Oxford, Clarendon Press, 43–61.

Dovidio, J., Allen, J., & Schroeder, D. (1990). The specificity of empathy-induced helping: Evidence for altruistic motivation. *Journal of Personality and Social Psychology*, 59: 249–260.

Dovidio, J., Piliavin, J., Schroeder, D., & Penner, L. (2006). *The Social Psychology of Prosocial Behavior*. Mahwah, NJ: Lawrence Erlbaum Associates.

Eisenberg, N. & Miller, P. (1987). Empathy and prosocial behavior. *Psychological Bulletin*, 101: 91–119.

Fodor, J. (1983). *The Modularity of Mind*. Cambridge, MA: Bradford Books/MIT Press.

Fultz, J., Batson. D., Fortenbach, V., McCarthy, P., & Varney, L. (1986). Social evaluation and the empathy-altruism hypothesis. *Journal of Personality and Social Psychology*, 50, 761–769.

Geller, V. & Shaver, P. (1976). Cognitive consequences of self-awareness. *Journal of Experimental Social Psychology*, 12: 99–108.

Ghiselin, M. (1974). *The Economy of Nature and the Evolution of Sex*. Berkeley, CA: University of California Press.

Godfrey-Smith, P. (1996). *Complexity and the Function of Mind in Nature*. Cambridge: Cambridge University Press.

Goldman, A. (1970). *A Theory of Human Action*. Englewood-Cliffs, NJ: Prentice-Hall.

Grant, C. (1997). Altruism: A social science chameleon. *Zygon*, 32 (3): 321–340.

Grice, H. P. (1971). Intention and certainty. *Proceedings of the British Academy*, 57: 263–279.

Hamilton, W. D. (1963). The evolution of altruistic behavior. *American Naturalist*, 97: 354–356.

——(1964a). The general evolution of social behavior I. *Journal of Theoretical Biology*, 7: 1–16.

——(1964b). The general evolution of social behavior II. *Journal of Theoretical Biology*, 7: 17–52.

Hobbes, T. (1981). *Leviathan*. Edited with an introduction by C. B. Macpherson. London: Penguin Books. First published 1651.

Hoffman, M. (1991). Is empathy altruistic? *Psychological Inquiry*, 2: 131–133.

Hornstein, H. (1991). Empathic distress and altruism: Still inseparable. *Psychological Inquiry*, 2: 133–135.

Hume, D. (1975). *Enquiry Concerning the Principles of Morals*, ed. L. A. Selby-Bigge, 3rd ed. revised by P. H. Nidditch. Oxford: Clarendon Press. Originally published 1751.

Joyce, R. (2006). *The Evolution of Mind*. Cambridge, MA: MIT Press.

Kant, I. (1785/1949). *Fundamental Principles of the Metaphysics of Morals*, trans. Thomas K. Abbott. Englewood Cliffs, NJ: Prentice-Hall/Library of Liberal Arts.

Krebs, D. (1975). Empathy and altruism. *Journal of Personality and Social Psychology*, 32: 1134–1146.

LaFollette, H. (2000a) (ed.). *The Blackwell Guide to Ethical Theory*. Oxford: Blackwell.

——(2000b). Introduction. In LaFollette (2000a), 1–12.

La Rochefoucauld, F. (2007). *Collected Maxims and Other Reflections*, trans. E. H. Blackmore, A. M. Blackmore, & Francine Giguère. New York: Oxford University Press. Originally published 1665.

Lewis, D. (1997). Finkish dispositions. *Philosophical Quarterly*, 47: 143–158.

MacIntyre, A. (1967). Egoism and altruism. In P. Edwards (ed.), *The Encyclopedia of Philosophy*, Vol. 2. New York: Macmillan, 462–466.

Martin, C. B. (1994). Disposition and conditionals. *Philosophical Quarterly*, 44: 1–8.

Mill, J. S. (1861/2001). *Utilitarianism*. Indianapolis, IN: Hackett.

Miller, D. T. (1999). The Norm of Self-Interest. *American Psychologist*, 54: 1053–1060

Nagel, T. (1970). *The Possibility of Altruism*. Oxford: Oxford University Press.

Nesse, R. (1990). Evolutionary explanations of emotions. *Human Nature*, 1: 261–289.

Nichols, S. (2004). *Sentimental Rules: On the Natural Foundations of Moral Judgment*. Oxford: Oxford University Press.

Nietzsche, F. (1997). *Daybreak: Thoughts on the Prejudices of Morality*, trans. R. J. Hollingsdale, ed. M. Clark & B. Leiter. Cambridge: Cambridge University Press. Originally published 1881.

Oakberg, T. (unpublished ms). A critical review of Batson's project and related research on altruism.

Piliavin, J. & Charng, H. (1990). Altruism—A review of recent theory and research. *Annual Review of Sociology*, 16: 27–65.

Plantinga, A. (1993). *Warrant and Proper Function*. Oxford: Oxford University Press.

Rachels, J. (2000). Naturalism. In LaFollette (2000a), 74–91.

Rousseau, J. J. (1985). *A Discourse on Inequality*. New York: Penguin. Originally published 1754.

Schroeder, D., Penner, L., Dovidio, J., & Piliavin, J (1995). *The Psychology of Helping and Altruism*. New York: McGraw-Hill.

Schroeder, W. (2000). Continental ethics. In LaFollette (2000a), 375–399.

Smith, A. (1759/1853). *The Theory of Moral Sentiments*. London: Henry G. Bohn.

Smith, K., Keating, J., & Stotland, E. (1989). Altruism revisited: The effect of denying feedback on a victim's status to emphatic witnesses. *Journal of Personality and Social Psychology*, 57: 641–650.

Sober, E. (1994). The adaptive advantage of learning and *a priori* prejudice. In *From a Biological Point of View*. Cambridge: Cambridge University Press.

Sober, E. & Wilson, D. S. (1998). *Unto Others: The Evolution and Psychology of Unselfish Behavior*. Cambridge, MA: Harvard University Press.

Spelke, E. (2000). Core knowledge. *American Psychologist*, 55: 1233–1243.

——(2003). Core knowledge. In N. Kanwisher & J. Duncan (eds.), *Attention and Performance, vol. 20: Functional neuroimaging of visual cognition*. Oxford: Oxford University Press, 29–56.

Sripada, C. (2007). Adaptationism, culture and the malleability of human nature. In P. Carruthers, S. Laurence, & S. Stich (eds.), *Innateness and the Structure of the Mind: Foundations and the Future*. New York: Oxford University Press, 311–329.

Stich, S. (1978). Beliefs and sub-doxastic states, *Philosophy of Science*, 45(4): 499–518.

——(1990). *The Fragmentation of Reason*. Cambridge, MA: MIT Press.

——(2007). Evolution, altruism and cognitive architecture: A critique of Sober and Wilson's argument for psychological altruism, *Biology & Philosophy*, 22 (2): 267–281.

Stocks, E., Lishner, D., & Decker, S. (2009). Altruism or psychological escape: Why does empathy promote prosocial behavior? *European Journal of Social Psychology*, 39: 649–665.

Stotland, E. (1969). Exploratory studies of empathy. In L. Berkowitz (ed.), *Advances in Experimental Social Psychology*, Vol. 4. New York: Academic Press, 271–313.

Toi, M. & Batson, C. D. (1982). More evidence that empathy is a source of altruistic motivation. *Journal of Personality and Social Psychology*, 43: 281–292.

Trivers, R. (1971). The evolution of reciprocal altruism. *Quarterly Review of Biology*, 46: 35–57.

Velleman, D. (1989). *Practical Reflection*. Princeton, NJ: Princeton University Press.

Wilson, G. (2002). Action. In *The Stanford Encyclopedia of Philosophy*. Edward N. Zalta (ed.), URL = <http://plato.stanford.edu/archives/sum2002/entries/action/>.

Wright, R. (1994). *The Moral Animal*. New York: Pantheon Books.

6

Moral Reasoning

GILBERT HARMAN, KELBY MASON, AND WALTER
SINNOTT-ARMSTRONG

Jane: "Hi, Kate. Do you want to grab a quick bite? I'm tired, but I feel like eating something before I go to bed."
Kate: "I can't. I'm desperate. You know that big philosophy paper that's due tomorrow? I haven't even started it. I spent all evening talking to Eleanor about breaking up with Matt."
Jane: "Wow, that's too bad. My paper took me a long time. I had to write two versions. The first one wasn't any good, so I started all over."
Kate: "Really? Hmm. Did you show anybody the first one?"
Jane: "No."
Kate: "Was it really bad?"
Jane: "Not that bad, but I want to get an 'A.' It's my major, you know."
Kate: "Well, then, do you think you could email me your first paper? I could polish it up and hand it in. That would really save my life. I don't know how else I could finish the assignment in time. And I'm doing really bad in the course, so I can't afford to mess up this paper. Please."
Jane: "Well, uhh . . . you've never asked me anything like that before. [Pause] No. I can't do that. Sorry."
Kate: "Why not? Nobody'll find out. You said you didn't show it to anybody. And I'm going to make changes. We are friends, aren't we? Please, please, please."
Jane: "Sorry, but that's cheating. I just can't do it. Good luck, though. I hope you write a good one."
Kate: "Thanks a lot."

In this simple example, Jane forms a moral judgment. Did she engage in moral reasoning? When? What form did it take? That depends partly on which processes get called moral reasoning.

Jane started with an initial set of moral and non-moral beliefs that were or could become conscious. She ended up with a new set of such beliefs, including the moral belief that she morally ought not to send her paper to Kate, a belief that she had not even thought about before. In addition, Jane started with a set of intentions and added a new intention, namely, an intention to refuse to send her paper to Kate, which she had not formed before. In some contexts, forming new beliefs and intentions in this way is described as moral reasoning.

How did Jane form her new moral belief and new intention? At first, Jane just took in information about the situation, which she then analyzed in the light of her prior beliefs and intentions. Her analysis might have been unconscious in the way that her auditory system unconsciously broke down the verbal stimulus from Kate and then inferred the meaning of Kate's utterances. In this case her analysis may be described as an instance of unconscious moral reasoning, even if it appears to her as a direct *moral intuition* or emotional reaction that seems at a conscious level to involve no inference at all. (On moral intuitions, see Sinnott-Armstrong, Young, & Cushman, Chapter 7 in this volume.)

Later, when Kate asks, "Why not?" Jane responds, "that's cheating. I just can't do it . . . " This response suggests an argument: "For me to email you my first paper would be cheating. Cheating is wrong, except in extreme circumstances. But this is not an extreme circumstance. Therefore, it would be wrong for me to email you my first paper. I can't do what I know is wrong. So I can't email you my first paper." Jane probably did not go through these steps explicitly before Kate asked her "Why not?" However, Jane still might have gone through some of these steps or some steps like these explicitly before she uttered the sentences that suggest this argument. And Jane did utter public sentences that seem to fit into some such form. Conscious thinking as well as public assertions of *arguments* like this are also often called moral reasoning.

Now suppose that Jane begins to doubt that she did the right thing, so she goes and asks her philosophy professor what counts as cheating, whether cheating is wrong, and why. Her professor might argue for a theory like rule utilitarianism, talk about the problems that would arise if cheating were openly and generally permitted, and infer that cheating is morally wrong. Her professor might then define cheating, apply the definition to Jane's case, and conclude that it would have been morally wrong for Jane to email her first paper to Kate. This kind of *reflective* argument may occur relatively rarely outside of settings like a philosophy classroom, but, when it does, it is often included under "moral reasoning."

Thus at least three kinds of processes might be called moral reasoning. First, unconscious information processing, possibly including emotions, can lead to a new moral judgment without any consciousness of any steps in any inference. Second, when faced with a moral issue, people might consciously go through steps by thinking of and endorsing thoughts whose contents fit into standard patterns of deductive arguments or inductive inferences. Third, when they have enough time, some people sometimes engage in more extensive reflection and infer moral conclusions, even surprising moral conclusions, from consciously articulated thoughts.

While theories of moral reasoning often address all or some of these kinds of moral reasoning, different theories may emphasize different kinds of reasoning, and theories also differ in their goals. Accounts of reasoning can be either *descriptive* psychological theories, attempting to characterize something about how people actually reason, or *normative* theories, attempting to say something about how people ought to reason or to characterize certain aspects of good or bad reasoning.

Most of this chapter will focus on one popular theory of moral reasoning, which claims that moral reasoning does and should fit the form of deductive arguments. We shall argue that such a deductive model is inadequate in several ways. Later we shall make some tentative suggestions about where to look for a better model. But first we need to clarify what moral reasoning is.

1. Kinds of Moral Reasoning

1.1. *Internal versus External Reasoning*

We distinguish *internal* or *intrapersonal* reasoning—reasoning something out by oneself, inference or personal deliberation—from *external* or *interpersonal* reasoning—bargaining, negotiation, argument, justification (to others), explanation (to others), and other sorts of reasoning done for or together with other people. The two types of reasoning often intersect; for instance, when two people argue, they will also be doing some internal reasoning, deciding what to say next, whether their opponent's conclusions follow from their premises and so on (again, this internal reasoning might well be unconscious). In the other direction, we sometimes use external reasoning to aid our internal reasoning, as when talking through an issue with somebody else helps us see it in a new light. Nonetheless, the two types of reasoning are clearly different, involving different sorts of processes—various mental operations in the one case, and various public acts in the other. In this chapter, we shall be concerned with moral reasoning of the internal kind.

1.2. *Theoretical versus Practical Reasoning*

It is useful to distinguish "theoretical" reasoning or inference from "practical" reasoning or deliberation in roughly the following way. Internal *practical* reasoning is reasoning that in the first instance is apt to modify one's decisions, plans, or intentions; internal *theoretical* reasoning is reasoning that in the first instance is apt to modify one's beliefs ("apt" because of limiting cases in which reasoning leaves matters as they are, without any effect on one's beliefs or intentions).

One way to distinguish the two types of reasoning is by looking at how their conclusions are expressed. The results of theoretical reasoning are typically expressed in declarative sentences, such as "Albert went to the late show at the Garden Theater." By contrast, the results of practical reasoning are typically expressed with imperatives, such as "Let's go to the late show at the Garden."

Much internal reasoning is a mixture of practical and theoretical reasoning. One reasons about what is the case in order to decide what to do; one's decision to do something can influence what one believes will happen. Moral reasoning can be either theoretical or practical, or a mixture. It is theoretical to the extent that the issue is (what to believe) about what someone morally ought to do, or what is morally good or bad, right or wrong, just or unjust. Moral reasoning is practical to the extent that the issue is what to do when moral considerations are or might be relevant.

What Practical and Theoretical Reasoning have in Common Internal reasoning of both sorts can be goal directed, conservative, and coherence seeking. It can be directed toward responding to particular questions; it can seek to make minimal changes in one's beliefs and decisions; and it can try to avoid inconsistency and other incoherence and attempt to make one's beliefs and intentions fit together better.

So, for example, one might seek to increase the positive coherence of one's moral views by finding acceptable moral principles that fit with one's opinions about particular cases and one might try to avoid accepting moral views that are in conflict with each other, given one's non-moral opinions. We discuss empirical research specifically directed to this model of internal reasoning later in this chapter.

How Internal Practical and Theoretical Reasoning Differ Despite the commonalities between them, and the difficulty of sharply demarcating them, there are at least three important ways in which internal practical and theoretical reasoning differ, having to do with wishful thinking, arbitrary choices, and "direction of fit." First, the fact that one wants something to occur can provide a reason to decide to make it occur, but not a reason to believe it has occurred. Wishful thinking is to be pursued in internal practical reasoning—in the sense that we can let our desires determine what we decide to do—but avoided in internal theoretical reasoning—in the sense that we typically shouldn't let our desires guide what we believe.

Second, internal practical reasoning can and often must make arbitrary choices, where internal theoretical reasoning should not. Suppose there are several equally good routes to where Mary would like to go. It may well be rational for Mary arbitrarily to choose one route and follow it, and it may be irrational for her not to do so. By contrast, consider Bob, who is trying to determine which route Mary took. It would not be rational for Bob to choose one route arbitrarily and form the belief that Mary took that route instead of any of the others. It would not be irrational for Bob to suspend belief and form neither the belief that Mary took route A nor the belief that Mary took route B. Bob might be justified in believing that Mary took either route A or route B without being justified in believing that Mary took route A and without being justified in believing that Mary took route B, even though Mary can be justified in deciding to take either route A or route B and then arbitrarily deciding which to take.

A third difference is somewhat difficult to express, but it has to do with something like the "direction of fit" (Austin, 1953). Internal theoretical reasoning is part of an attempt to fit what one accepts to how things are. Internal practical reasoning is an attempt to accept something that may affect how things are. Roughly speaking, theoretical reasoning is reasoning about how the world already is, and practical reasoning is reasoning about how, if at all, to change the world. Evidence that something is going to happen provides a theoretical reason to believe it will happen, not a practical reason to make it happen (Hampshire, 1959). This way of putting things is inexact, however, because changes in one's beliefs can lead to changes in one's plans. If Mary is intending to meet Bob at his house and then discovers that Bob is not going to be there, she should change her plans (Harman, 1976). Even so, the basic idea is clear enough.

Internal reasoning (theoretical or practical) typically leads to (relatively small) changes in one's propositional attitudes (beliefs, intentions, desires, etc.) by addition and subtraction. Of course, there are other ways to change one's propositional attitudes. One can forget things, or suffer from illness and injuries leading to more drastic changes. These processes don't appear to be instances of reasoning. However, it is not easy to distinguish processes of internal reasoning from such other processes.

For one thing, there appear to be rational ways of acquiring beliefs as "direct" responses to sensation and perception. Are these instances of reasoning? The matter is complicated because unconscious "computation" may occur in such cases, and it is difficult to distinguish such computation from unconscious reasoning (as we discuss in Section 1.3). It is not clear whether these and certain other changes in belief should be classified as reasoning.

In any case, inferences are supposed to issue in conclusions. Ordinary talk of what has been "inferred" is normally talk of a new conclusion that is the result of inference, or perhaps an old conclusion whose continued acceptance is appropriately reinforced by one's reasoning. We do not normally refer to the discarding of a belief in terms of something "inferred," unless the belief is discarded as a result of accepting its negation or denial. But there are cases in which reasoning results in ceasing to believe something previously believed, without believing its negation. In such a case it is somewhat awkward to describe the result of internal reasoning in terms of what has been "inferred." Similarly, when reasoning leads one to discard something one previously accepted, it may be awkward to talk of the "conclusion" of the reasoning.

To be sure, it might be said that the "conclusion" of one's reasoning in this case is *to stop believing (or intending) X* or, maybe, *that one is (or ought) to stop believing or intending X*. And, although it is syntactically awkward to say that what is "inferred" in such a case is *to stop believing (or intending) X* (because it is syntactically awkward to say that *Jack inferred to stop believing (or intending) X*), it might be said that what is "inferred" is *that one is (or ought) to stop believing (or intending) X*.

These ways of talking might also be extended to internal reasoning that leads to the acceptance of new beliefs or intentions. It might be said that the "conclusion" of one's reasoning in such a case is *to believe (or decide to) Y* or *that one is (or ought) to believe (or decide to) Y* and that what one "infers" is *that one ought to believe (or decide to) Y*.

One of these ways of talking might seem to imply that all internal reasoning is practical reasoning, reasoning about what to do—*to stop believing (or intending) X* or *to believe (or decide to) Y* (cf. Levi, 1967). The other way of talking might seem to imply that all reasoning is theoretical reasoning, reasoning about what is the case—*it is the case that one is (or ought) to stop believing (or intending) X* or *it is the case that one ought to believe (or decide to) Y* (cf. Nagel, 1970).

Such reductive proposals have difficulty accounting for the differences between internal theoretical and practical reasoning. A reduction of internal theoretical reasoning to practical reasoning would seem to entail that there is nothing wrong with arbitrary choice among equally good theoretical conclusions. A reduction of internal practical reasoning to internal theoretical reasoning simply denies that there is such a thing as internal practical reasoning, in the sense of reasoning that results in decisions to do things and otherwise potentially modifies one's plans and intentions. Since neither reduction seems plausible to us, we continue to suppose that internal theoretical and practical reasoning are different, if related, kinds of reasoning.

1.3. *Conscious and Unconscious Moral Reasoning*

Finally, internal reasoning may be conscious or unconscious. Although some accounts of moral judgment identify reasoning with conscious reasoning (Haidt, 2001), most psychological studies of reasoning have been concerned with unconscious aspects of reasoning. For example, there has been controversy about the extent to which reasoning about deduction makes use of deductive rules (Braine & O'Brien, 1998; Rips, 1994) as compared with mental models (Johnson-Laird & Byrne, 1991; Polk & Newell, 1995). All parties to this controversy routinely suppose that such reasoning is not completely conscious and that clever experiments are required in order to decide among these competing theories.

Similarly, recent studies (Holyoak & Simon, 1999; Simon et al., 2001; Simon, 2004; Thagard, 1989, 2000) investigate ways in which scientists or jurors reason in coming to accept theories or verdicts. These studies assume that the relevant process of reasoning (in contrast with its products) is not available to consciousness, so that evidence for theories of reasoning is necessarily indirect. (We discuss some of this literature below.)

Indeed, it is unclear that one is ever fully conscious of the *activity* of internal reasoning rather than of some of its intermediate and final *upshots*. Perhaps, as Lashley (1958) famously wrote, "No activity of mind is ever conscious." To be sure, people are conscious of (aspects of) the *external* discussions or arguments in which they participate and they can consciously imagine participating in such discussions. But that is not to say that they are conscious of the internal processes that lead them to say what they say in those discussions. Similarly, people can consciously and silently count from 1 to 5 without being able to be conscious of the internal processes that produce this conscious sequence of numbers in the right order.

Since external arguments are expressed in words, imagined arguments will be imagined as expressed in words. This does not imply that internal reasoning is itself ever in words as opposed to being reasoning about something expressed in words (Ryle, 1979) and does not imply that internal reasoning is ever conscious.

When theorists refer to "conscious reasoning," they may be referring either to such externally expressed or imagined arguments or to other upshots of internal reasoning.

Finally, Gibbard (1990) and Scanlon (1998) argue that moral thinking is concerned with finding ways of acting that can or could be justified to others. In that case, internal moral reasoning might always involve thinking about external moral reasoning to others and so might always or typically involve conscious envisioning of external reasoning. But the internal reasoning processes about such external reasoning would not themselves normally be conscious.

1.4. *Section Summary*

To summarize this section: reasoning can be characterized along three dimensions, namely practical/theoretical; internal/external; and, when internal, conscious/unconscious. The sort of moral reasoning we shall discuss in this chapter is internal, and may be practical or theoretical, and conscious or unconscious.

2. The Deductive Model of Moral Reasoning

Assuming this understanding of what moral reasoning is, we can now ask how it works, what form it takes, and when it is good. One popular model of moral reasoning gives distinctive answers to all three questions. We call this *the deductive model* of moral reasoning.

On the deductive model, a person's reasoning might start from a very general moral rule or principle, such as the principle of utility, the categorical imperative, the doctrine of double effect, or some claim about abstract rights or social contracts. However, if the person is not a philosopher, the reasoning is usually thought to start with a mid-level moral principle, such as that it is wrong to kill, lie, steal, or hurt other people. In Jane's case, the argument might be something like this:

(P1) Cheating is always morally wrong except in extreme circumstances.
(P2) This act is cheating.
(P3) This circumstance is not extreme.
Therefore, (C) this act is morally wrong.

Background arguments might be added to support these premises. The moral reasoning is then seen as good only if it is deductively valid, only if the premises are justified, and only if the argument commits no fallacies, such as equivocation or begging the question.

Proponents of the deductive model usually make or assume several claims about it:

(1) Deductive arguments make people justified in believing the conclusions of those arguments.
(2) A person's beliefs in the premises cause that person to believe the conclusion.
(3) The premises are independent, so the universal premise (P1) contains all of the moral content, and the other premises are morally neutral.
(4) The terms in the argument fit the so-called classical view of concepts (as defined by necessary and sufficient conditions for class inclusion).

Not everyone who defends the deductive model makes all of these claims, but they are all common. (1) is clearly a normative claim about the justification relation between the premises and conclusions of a deductive moral argument. By contrast, (2)–(4) are most naturally interpreted as descriptive claims about the way people actually morally reason. Someone could make them as normative claims—claiming that one's moral reasoning *ought* to conform to them—but we'll discuss them under the more natural descriptive interpretation.

The deductive model can be applied universally or less broadly. Some philosophers seem to claim that all moral reasoning (or at least all good moral reasoning) fits this model. Call this the *universal deduction claim*. Others suggest the weaker claim that much, but not all, moral reasoning fits this deductive model. Call that the *partial deduction claim*. Most philosophers do not commit themselves explicitly to either claim. Instead, they simply talk and write as if moral reasoning fits the deductive model without providing details or evidence for this assumption.

Although it has not often been explicitly stated, this deductive model has been highly influential throughout the history of philosophy. For example, Stich (1993) attributes something like this view (or at least the claim about concepts) to Plato's *Republic* and other dialogues. The Socratic search for necessary and sufficient conditions makes sense only if our moral views really are based on concepts with such conditions, as the classical view proposes. When Kant first introduces the categorical imperative, he says, "common human reason does not think of it abstractly in such a universal form, but it always has it in view and uses it as the standard of its judgments" (Kant, 1785: 403–404). To keep it "in view" is, presumably, to be conscious of it in some way, and Kant "uses" the categorical imperative in deductive arguments when he applies it to examples. Similarly, Mill attributes the deductive model to opponents of utilitarianism who posit a natural "moral faculty": "our moral faculty . . . supplies us only with the general principles of moral judgments; it is a branch of our reason, not of our sensitive faculty; and must be looked to for the abstract doctrines of morality, not for perception of it in the concrete" (Mill, 1861/2001: 2). Our "moral faculty," on such a view, delivers to us moral principles from which we must deductively argue to the morality of specific cases.

In the twentieth century, Hare says, "the only inferences which take place in [moral reasoning] are deductive" (1963: 88) and "it is most important, in a verbal exposition of an argument about what to do, not to allow value-words in the minor premise" (1952: 57). Rule-utilitarians also often suggest that people make moral judgments about cases by deriving them from rules that are justified by the utility of using those rules in conscious moral reasoning that is deductive in form (cf. Hooker & Little, 2000: 76, on acceptance of rules). When Donagan analyzes common morality in the Hebrew–Christian tradition, he claims, "every derived precept is strictly deduced, by way of some specificatory premise, either from the fundamental principle or from some precept already derived" (1977: 71). He does add that the specificatory premises are established by "unformalized analytical reasoning" (ibid.: 72), but that does not undermine the general picture of a "simple deductive system" (ibid.: 71) behind common people's moral judgments. More recently, McKeever and Ridge argue that "moral thought and judgment presuppose the possibility of our having available to us a set of unhedged moral principles (which go from descriptive antecedents to moral consequents) which codifies all of morality available to us" (2006: 170). The principles are unhedged and their antecedents are descriptive so that moral conclusions can be deduced from the principles plus morally neutral premises, as the deductive model requires. Principles that enable such deductions are claimed to be an intrinsic goal of "our actual moral practice" (ibid.: 179).

Traditional psychologists also sometimes assume a deductive model. The most famous studies of moral reasoning were done by Lawrence Kohlberg (1981). Kohlberg's method was simple. He presented subjects (mainly children and adolescents) with dilemmas where morally relevant factors conflicted. In his most famous example, Heinz could save his dying wife only by stealing a drug. Kohlberg asked subjects what they or the characters would or should do in those dilemmas, and then he asked them why. Kohlberg found that children from many cultures typically move in order through three main levels, each including two main stages of moral belief and reasoning:

Level A: Preconventional
    Stage 1 = Punishment and Obedience
    Stage 2 = Individual Instrumental Purpose

Level B: Conventional
   Stage 3 = Mutual Interpersonal Expectations and Conformity
   Stage 4 = (Preserving) Social Order

Level C: Postconventional and Principled Level
   Stage 5 = Prior Rights and Social Contract or Utility
   Stage 6 = Universal Ethical Principles

Kohlberg's theory is impressive and important, but it faces many problems. First, his descriptions of his stages are often imprecise or even incoherent. Stage 5, for example, covers theories that some philosophers see as opposed, including utilitarianism and social contract theory. Second, Kohlberg's Stage 6 is questionable because his only "examples of Stage 6 come either from historical figures or from interviews with people who have extensive philosophic training" (Kohlberg, 1981: 100). Third, even at lower levels, few subjects gave responses completely within a single stage, although the percentage of responses within a single stage varied, and these variations formed patterns. Fourth, psychologists have questioned Kohlberg's evidence that all people move through these same stages. The most famous critique of this sort is by Gilligan (1982), who pointed out that women and girls scored lower in Kohlberg's hierarchy, so his findings suggest that women are somehow deficient in their moral reasoning. Instead, Gilligan claims, women and girls engage in a different kind of moral reasoning that Kohlberg's model misses. (For a recent, critical meta-analysis of studies of Gilligan's claims, see Jaffe & Hyde, 2000.)

Whether or not Kohlberg's theory is defensible, the main point here is that he distinguishes levels of moral reasoning in terms of principles that could be presented as premises in a deductive structure. People at Stage 1 are supposed to reason like this: "Acts like this are punished. I ought not to do what will get me punished. Therefore, I ought not to do this." People at Stage 2 are supposed to reason like this: "Acts like this will defeat or not serve my purposes. I ought to do only what will serve my purposes. Therefore, I ought not to do this." And so on. The last two stages clearly refer to principles that, along with facts, are supposed to entail moral judgments as conclusions in deductive arguments. This general approach, then, suggests that all moral reasoning, or at least the highest moral reasoning, fits some kind of deductive model.

However, Kohlberg's subjects almost never spelled out such deductive structures (and the only ones who did were trained into the deductive model). Instead, the deductive gloss is added by coders and commentators. Moreover, Kohlberg and his colleagues explicitly asked subjects for reasons. Responses to such questions do not show either that the subjects thought of those reasons back when they made their judgments or that those reasons caused the judgments or that people use such reasons outside of such artificial circumstances.

More generally, it is not clear that Kohlberg's method can really show much, if anything, about internal moral reasoning. Even if people in a certain group tend to cite reasons of certain sorts when trying to explain and justify their moral beliefs, the context of being asked by an experimenter might distort their reports and even their self-understanding. Consequently, Kohlberg's method cannot show why people hold the moral beliefs they do.

Hence Kohlberg's research cannot support the universal deduction claim. It cannot even support a partial deduction claim about normal circumstances. The most that this method can reveal is that people, when prompted, come up with different kinds of reasons at different stages of development. That is interesting as a study in the forms of public rhetoric that people use at different points in their lives, but it shows nothing about the internal processes that led to their moral judgments.

As far as we know, there is no other empirical evidence that people always or often form moral judgments in the way suggested by the deductive model. Yet it seems obvious to many theorists that people form moral judgments this way. In fact, there is some evidence that children are sometimes capable of reasoning in accord with the deductive model (e.g. Cummins, 1996; Harris & Núñez, 1996). What these studies show is that, given an artificial rule, children are capable of identifying violations; and a natural explanation of their performance here is that they are reasoning in accord with the deductive model, i.e. using the rule as a premise to infer what the person in a scenario ought to be doing and concluding that the person is breaking the rule (or not). But this does not show that children normally accord with the deductive model when they are morally reasoning in real life, and not considering artificial rules contrived by an experimenter. *A fortiori*, this does not show that adults generally reason in accord with the deductive model when they reason morally. Thus there is so far little or no empirical evidence that the deductive model captures most real situated moral reasoning in adults.

Moreover, there are many reasons to doubt various aspects of the deductive model. We shall present four. First, the deductive model seems to conflate inferences with arguments. Second, experimental results show that the premises in the deductive model are not independent in the way deductivists usually suppose. Third, other experimental results suggest that moral beliefs are often not based on moral principles, even when they seem to be. Fourth, the deductive model depends on a classical view of concepts that is questionable. The next four sections will discuss these problems in turn.

3. Do Deductive Arguments Justify Conclusions?

Defenders of the deductive model often claim or assume that good arguments must conform to standards embodied in formal logic, probability theory, and decision theory. This claim depends on a confusion between formal theories of validity and accounts of good reasoning.

3.1. *Logic, Probability, and Decision Theory*

To explain this claim, we need to say something about the relevance of logic, probability, and decision theory to reasoning by oneself—inference and deliberation—and to reasoning with others—public discussion and argument. The issue is somewhat complicated, because the terms "logic," "theory of probability," and "decision theory" are used sometimes to refer to formal mathematical theories of implication and consistency, sometimes to refer to theories of method or methodologies, and sometimes to refer to a mixture of theories of these two sorts.

On the formal mathematical side, there is formal or mathematical logic, the mathematical theory of probability, and mathematical formulations of decision theory in terms of maximizing expected utility. An obvious point, but one that is often neglected, is that such formal theories are by themselves neither descriptive theories about what people do nor normative theories about what people ought to do. So they are not theories of reasoning in the sense in which we are here using the term "reasoning."

Although accounts of formal logic (e.g. Goldfarb, 2003) sometimes refer to "valid arguments" or examples of "reasoning" with steps that are supposed to be in accord with certain "rules of inference," the terms "reasoning" and "argument" are then being used to refer to certain abstract structures of propositions and not to something that people do, not to any concrete process of inference or deliberation one engages in by oneself or any discussion among two or more people. The logical rules in question have neither a psychological, nor a social, nor a normative subject matter. They are rules of implication or rules that have to be satisfied for a structure to count as a valid formal argument, not rules of inference in the sense in which we are here using the term "inference."

The logical rule of *modus ponens* says that a conditional and its antecedent jointly imply the consequent of the conditional. The rule does not say that, if one believes or otherwise accepts the conditional and its antecedent, one must or may also believe or accept the consequent. The rule says nothing about belief in the consequent, and nothing about what may or may not be asserted in an argument in our sense.

There may be corresponding principles about what people do or can or should rationally believe or assert, but such principles would go beyond anything in formal logic. Indeed, it is nontrivial to find corresponding principles that are at all plausible (Harman, 1986: ch. 2). It is certainly not the case that, whenever one believes a conditional and also believes its antecedent, one must or may rationally believe its consequent. It may be that one also already believes the negation of the consequent and should then either stop believing the conditional or stop believing its antecedent.

A further point is that inference takes time and uses limited resources. Given that any particular set of beliefs has infinitely many logical consequences, it is simply not true that one rationally should waste time and resources cluttering one's mind with logical implications of what one believes.

Similar remarks apply to consistency and coherence. Formal logic, probability theory, and decision theory characterize consistency of propositions and coherence of assignments of probability and utility. Such formal theories do not say anything about what combinations of propositions people should or should not assert or believe, or what assignments of probability and utility they should accept. There may be corresponding principles connecting consistency and coherence with what people should not rationally believe or assert, but again those principles go beyond anything in formal logic, probability theory, and decision theory, and again it is nontrivial to find such principles that are at all plausible.

Given limited resources, it is not normally rational to devote significant resources to the computationally intractable task of checking one's beliefs and probability assignments for consistency and coherence. Furthermore, having discovered inconsistency or incoherence in one's beliefs and assignments, it is not necessarily rational to drop everything else one is doing to try to figure out the best way to eliminate it. The question of what to do after having discovered inconsistency or incoherence is a practical or methodological issue that can be addressed only by a normative theory of reasoning. The answer is not automatically provided by formal logic, probability theory, and decision theory.

As we mentioned earlier, the terms "logic," "probability theory," and "decision theory" can be used not only for purely formal theories but also for methodological accounts of how such formal theories might be relevant to rational reasoning and argument (Mill, 1846; Dewey, 1938). Our point is that these methodological proposals are additions to the purely formal theories and do not follow directly from them.

3.2. *Application to Moral Reasoning*

These general points have devastating implications for normative uses of the deductive model of moral reasoning. The deductive model suggests that a believer becomes justified in believing a moral claim when that person formulates an argument with that moral claim as a conclusion and other beliefs as premises. The argument supposedly works if and only if it is deductively valid.

This picture runs into several problems. First, suppose Jane believes that (C) it is morally wrong to send her first paper to Kate, she also believes that (P1) cheating is always morally wrong and that (P2) sending her old paper to Kate would be cheating, and she knows that the latter two beliefs entail the former. Add also that her belief in the conclusion is causally based on her belief in the premises. According to the deductive model, the fact that she formulates this argument and bases her belief on it makes her justified in believing her moral conclusion.

But this can't be right. When Jane believes the premises, formulates the argument, and recognizes its validity, she still has several options. The argument shows that Jane cannot consistently (a) believe the premises and deny the conclusion. If that were the only other alternative, then Jane would have to (b) believe the premises and believe the conclusion. Still, Jane could instead deny a premise. She could (c) give up her belief that all cheating is morally wrong and replace it with the vague belief that cheating is usually wrong or with the qualified belief that all cheating is wrong except when it is the only way to help a friend in need. Alternatively, Jane could (d) give up her belief that sending her paper to Kate would be cheating, if she redefines cheating so that it does not include sharing paper drafts that will later be modified.

How can Jane decide among options (b)−(d)? The deductively valid argument cannot help her decide, since all that argument does is rule out option (a) as inconsistent. Thus, if reasoning is change of belief or intention, as discussed above, then the deductive argument cannot tell Jane whether to change her beliefs by adding a belief in the conclusion, as in (b), or instead to change her beliefs by removing a belief in some premise, as in (c) and (d). Since moral reasoning in this case involves deciding whether or not to believe the conclusion, this moral reasoning cannot be modeled by the deductive argument, because that deductive argument by itself cannot help us make that decision.

This point is about epistemology: formulating and basing one's belief on a deductively valid argument cannot be sufficient to justify belief in its conclusion. Nonetheless, as a matter of descriptive psychology, it still might be true that people sometimes believe premises like P1 and P2, then notice that the premises entail a conclusion like C, so they form a new belief in C as a result. The facts that they could give up one of the premises in order to avoid the conclusion and that they might be justified in doing so do not undermine the claim that people often do in fact accept conclusions of deductive arguments in order to maintain consistency without giving up their beliefs in the premises. Some of the psychological pressure to add the conclusion to one's stock of beliefs might come from a general tendency not to give up beliefs that one already holds (a kind of doxastic conservatism). The remaining question, of how often moral beliefs are actually formed in this way, is a topic for further study in empirical moral psychology.

4. Are the Premises Independent?

Many philosophers who use the deductive model seem to assume that some of its premises are morally loaded and others are morally neutral. Recall, again,

(P1) Cheating is always morally wrong except in extreme circumstances.
(P2) This act is cheating.
(P3) This circumstance is not extreme.
Therefore, (C) this act is morally wrong.

Premise P1 is definitely a moral principle, but premise P2 might seem to be a morally neutral classification of a kind of act. However, it is difficult to imagine how to define "cheating" in a morally neutral way; "cheating" seems to be a morally loaded concept, albeit a "thick" one (Williams, 1985). One of us has a golfing buddy who regularly kicks his ball off of tree roots so that he won't hurt his hands by hitting a root. He has done this for years. Is it cheating? It violates the normal rules of golf, but people who play with him know he does it, and he knows that they know and that they will allow it. Groups of golfers often make special allowances like this, but he and his friends have never made this one explicit, and it sometimes does affect the outcomes of bets. Although it is not clear, it seems likely that people who think that he should not kick his ball will call this act cheating, and people who think there is nothing wrong with what he does will not call it cheating. If so, the notion of cheating is morally loaded, and so is premise P2.

This point applies also to lying: even if a person already accepts a principle, such as "Never lie," she or he still needs to classify acts as lying. Are white lies lies? You ask me whether I like your new book. I say "Yes," when I really think it is mediocre or even bad. Is that a lie? Those who think it is dishonest and immoral will be more likely to call it a lie. It is not clear whether people call an act immoral because they classify it as a lie or, instead, call it a lie because they see it as immoral. Which comes first, the classification or the judgment? Maybe sometimes a person considers an act, realizes that it is (or is not) a lie on some morally neutral definition, applies the principle that lying is always wrong, and concludes that the act is wrong. But it is not clear how often that kind of moral reasoning actually occurs.

One case is particularly important and, perhaps, surprising. A common moral rule or principle says that it is morally wrong to kill intentionally without an adequate reason. Many philosophers seem to assume that we can classify an act as killing (or not) merely by asking whether the act causes a death, and that we can determine whether an act causes a death independently of any moral judgment of the act. (Causation is a scientific notion, isn't it?) Many philosophers also assume that to say an act was done intentionally is merely to describe the act or its agent's mental state. (Intentions are psychological states, aren't they?)

These assumptions have been questioned, however, by recent empirical results. First, Alicke (1992) has shown that whether an act is picked out as the cause of a harm depends in at least some cases on whether the act is judged to be morally wrong. Second, Knobe (2003) reported results that are often interpreted as suggesting that whether a person is seen as causing a harm intentionally as opposed to unintentionally also depends on background beliefs about the moral status of the act or the value of its effects. More recently, Cushman, Knobe, and Sinnott-Armstrong (2008) found that whether an act is classified as killing as opposed to merely letting die also depends on subjects' moral judgments of the act. All of these experiments suggest that people do not classify an act as intentional killing independently of their moral judgments of that act.

Defenders of the deductive model could respond that, even if classifications like cheating, lying, and killing as well as cause and intention are not morally neutral, other classifications of acts still might be morally neutral. The problem is that neutral classifications would be difficult to build into unhedged moral principles that people could apply deductively. Even if this difficulty could be overcome in theory, there is no evidence that people actually deduce moral judgments from such neutral classifications. Instead, moral reasoners usually refer to the kinds of classifications that seem to be already morally loaded—like cheating, lying, and killing.

These results undermine the deductive model's assumption that common moral reasoning starts from premises that classify acts independently of moral judgments. Without that assumption, the deductive arguments postulated by the deductive model cannot really be what lead people to form their moral judgments. We do not classify acts as causing harm, as intentional, or as killing and then reach a moral conclusion later only by means of applying a moral principle. Instead, we form some moral judgment of the act before we classify the act or accept the minor premise that classifies the act. The argument comes after the moral judgment. Moreover, anyone who denies the conclusion will or could automatically deny one of the premises, because that premise depends on a moral judgment of the act, perhaps the very moral judgment in the conclusion. This kind of circularity undermines the attempt to model real moral reasoning as a deductive structure.

5. Are Moral Judgments based on Principles?

Sometimes it seems obvious to us that we judge an act as morally wrong because we have already classified that act as killing. However, this appearance might well be an illusion. One recent study suggests that it is an illusion in some central cases.

Sinnott-Armstrong, Mallon, McCoy, and Hull (2008) collected moral judgments about three "trolley problems," a familiar form of philosophical thought experiment that has lately been exploited in empirical work. In the *side track* case (see Figure 6.1), a runaway trolley will kill five people on a main track unless Peter pulls a lever that will deflect the trolley onto a side track where it will kill only one and then go off into a field.

In the *loop track* case (see Figure 6.2), a runaway trolley will again kill five people on a main track unless Peter pulls a lever that will deflect the trolley

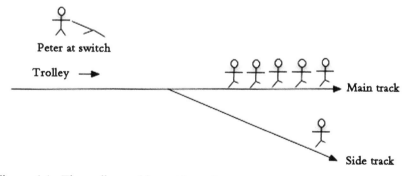

Figure 6.1. The trolley problem: side track case

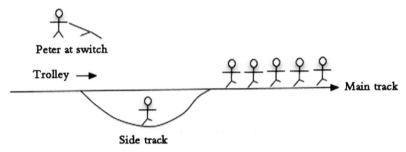

Figure 6.2. The trolley problem: loop track case

onto a side track, but this time the side track loops back and rejoins the main track so that the trolley would still kill the five if not for the fact that, if it goes onto the side track, it will hit and kill one person on the loop track, and that person's body will slow the trolley to a stop before it returns to the main track and hits the five.

The third case is *combination track* (see Figure 6.3). Here Peter can save the five on the main track only by turning the runaway trolley onto a side track that loops back onto the main track just before the five people (as in the loop track case). This time, before this loop track gets back to the main track, a second side track splits off from the loop track into an empty field (as in the side track case). Before the trolley gets to this second side track, Peter will be able to pull a lever that will divert the trolley onto the second side track and into the field. Unfortunately, before the trolley gets to the second side track, it will hit and kill an innocent person on the looped side track. Hitting this person is not enough to stop the trolley or save the five unless the trolley is redirected onto the second side track.

The two factors that matter here are intention and timing. In the loop track case, subjects judge that Peter intentionally kills the person on the side track,

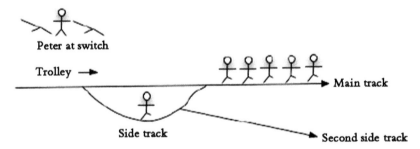

Figure 6.3. The trolley problem: combination track case

because Peter's plan for ending the threat to the five will fail unless the trolley hits the person on the side track. In contrast, in the side track and combination track cases, Peter's plan to save the five will work even if the trolley misses the person on the side track, so subjects judge that Peter does not intentionally kill the person on the side track in either the side track case or the combination track case.

Next consider timing. In the side track case, the bad effect of the trolley hitting the lone person occurs *after* the good effect of the five being saved, because the five are safe as soon as the trolley enters the side track. In contrast, in the loop track and combination track cases, the bad effect of the trolley hitting the person occurs *before* the good effect of the five being saved, since that good effect occurs only when the trolley slows down in the loop track case and only when the trolley goes off onto the second side track in combination track.

Comparing these three cases allows us to separate effects of intention and timing. Sinnott-Armstrong et al. asked subjects to judge not only whether Peter's act was morally wrong but also whether Peter killed the person on the side track. They found that subjects' moral judgments of whether Peter's act was wrong *did* depend on *intention*, because these moral judgments were different in the case where the death was intended (the loop track case) than in the cases where the death was not intended (the side track and combination track cases). However, these moral judgments did *not* depend on *timing*, because they were statistically indistinguishable in the case where the good effect occurred first (side track) and the cases where the bad effect occurred first (the loop track and combination track cases). The opposite was found for classifications of Peter's act as killing. Whether subjects classified Peter's act as killing did *not* depend on *intention*, because subjects' classifications were statistically indistinguishable in the case where the death was intended (the loop track case) and the cases where the death was not intended (the side track and combination track cases). However, subjects' classifications as killing did depend on *timing*, because these classifications were statistically different in the case where the good effect occurred first (the side track case) than in the cases where the bad effect occurred first (the loop track and combination track cases). In short, intention but not timing affects judgments of moral wrongness, whereas timing but not intention affects classifications as killing.

This comparison suggests that these subjects did not judge the act to be morally wrong simply because it is killing (or intentional killing). If moral judgments really were based on such a simple rule about killing, then what affects classifications as killing would also affect moral judgments of wrongness. Since temporal order affects what subjects classify as killing, temporal order would also indirectly affect subjects' moral judgments. However, temporal order *did* affect classifications as killing, but temporal order did *not* affect subjects' moral judgments. Thus their moral judgments in such cases must not be based on deduction from any simple rule about killing.

These subjects did, however, often externally justify their moral judgments by saying that it is morally wrong to kill. They seemed to think that they were deducing their moral judgments from a moral principle against killing. This shows that, at least in some central cases, when moral judgments seem to be based on deductive arguments, this appearance is an illusion. It is not clear whether this result generalizes to other cases, but, if it does, then this result would be a serious problem for the deductive model as a description of actual moral reasoning.

The lesson is not that moral reasoning *never* works by classification and deduction. Moral reasoning still might fit the deductive model in other cases. That seems plausible, for example, in cases when someone reasons that an otherwise neutral act is illegal and, hence, is morally wrong (although the source of moral judgment is not clear even in that case). At least we can reach this conclusion: moral reasoning sometimes does not work by deducing moral judgments from intuitive, consciously accessible moral principles, even when it seems to. This weak conclusion might be all that we can say, because there is no reason to think that all actual moral reasoning must fit into any specific form or model.

6. Against the Classical View of Concepts

Moral reasoning seems to involve, at the very least, some manipulation of one's prior moral beliefs. To understand the nature of moral reasoning, then, we must understand how the mind stores and uses these prior moral beliefs, including, among other things, beliefs about moral norms and about the rightness or wrongness of particular actions or types of action.

According to the deductive model, our moral beliefs are stored in the form of general principles, and we reason about particular cases by applying these general principles to specific cases. The general principles might be very complex, but they are nonetheless genuine principles, as opposed to, say, a disjunctive list of specific instances.

In this section, following Stich's (1993) lead, we shall discuss several different theories of how mental content is stored and manipulated, and how these theories relate to the deductive model and broader debates in moral philosophy.

We start with computationalism and the so-called classical view of concepts, and then move on to views that are progressively less friendly to the deductive model.

6.1. *What are Concepts?*

The dominant account of mental processes in cognitive science is *computationalism*, according to which the brain is a sort of computer, and mental processes are computations (e.g. Haugeland, 1978; Newell & Simon, 1976). In its orthodox version, computationalism is typically combined with the *representational theory of mind* (RTM). According to RTM, mental computations involve the manipulation of stored mental representations, which are like sentences in natural language. Just as sentences are composed of simpler elements (words) that contribute their semantic value to the overall semantic value of the sentence, so thoughts are composed of simpler representations that, likewise, contribute their semantic value to the overall semantic value of thoughts. These simpler mental representations are *concepts*. Concepts are the constituents of thought, and thoughts inherit their content from the concepts they contain. Like words, concepts can represent kinds, properties, sets, individuals, relations, and so on.

According to orthodox computationalism, then, mental information is generally stored as strings of mental representations—sentences in Mentalese, so to speak, composed from concepts. When Jane makes the new moral judgment that it would be wrong to email Kate her first paper, she comes to stand in a new relationship to a complex representation with the content "it would be wrong to email Kate my first paper." That representation is itself composed of simpler representations, concepts like KATE, EMAIL and WRONG ACTION (we follow the convention of representing concepts in small caps). Jane's moral knowledge consists in her having representations like these, and their standing in certain relationships to one another. To understand the nature of moral knowledge, then, we further need to understand the nature of concepts.[1]

6.2. *The Classical View of Concepts*

One theory of concepts has been so influential that it is called the *classical view* (Laurence & Margolis, 1999). According to the classical view, all or most concepts have definitions in terms of necessary and sufficient conditions.

---

[1] For far more expansive reviews of the literature on concepts and many of the theoretical details we omit here, see Margolis & Laurence (1999) and Murphy (2002).

UNCLE, for example, might be defined as BROTHER OF A PARENT. The concepts contained in the definitions are themselves defined in terms of simpler concepts (MALE and SIBLING), which, in turn, are defined in still simpler concepts, and so on, down to a bedrock of basic, undefined elements.

In one particularly common formulation of the view, which Laurence and Margolis (1999) call the *containment model*, complex concepts are literally *composed* of the elements in their definitions. In that case, UNCLE would be literally made up of the "simpler" concepts BROTHER and PARENT, which themselves would be made up of still simpler concepts. On an alternative formulation, the *inferential* model, complex concepts are not *literally* composed of the concepts in their definitions, but rather stand in an inferential relation to them. UNCLE would then be inferentially related to the concepts BROTHER and PARENT in a way that represents the belief that uncles are (necessarily) brothers of parents.

The classical view of concepts is so called because, in either the containment or inferential version, it was predominant in philosophy until the mid-twentieth century. As already noted, when Plato presents Socrates' search for necessary and sufficient conditions for justice and right action, for instance, he seems to be assuming the classical view. Similarly, Locke fairly explicitly endorses the containment model when he claims that the "*Idea* of the *Sun*" is "an aggregate of those several simple *Ideas*, Bright, Hot, Roundish, having a constant regular motion, at a certain distance from us, and, perhaps, some other" (Locke, 1700/1975: 298–299). And Kant endorses a containment version of the classical view when he characterizes analytic judgments as those where we judge the predicate to be "(covertly) contained" in the subject (Kant, 1787/1929: 48).

The classical view gives rise to a very clear picture of how categorization works. First we categorize an object or event as falling under various basic concepts, and then simply build up more complex concepts from those. So Locke might claim that, when we look up into the sky and see the sun, we first recognize it as BRIGHT, HOT, ROUNDISH, and so on. On the containment model, we've thereby categorized it as the sun, for the concept SUN just *is* the aggregate of those simpler concepts. On the inferential model, we may have to engage in some further inference from those basic concepts to the complex concept of which they are a definition.

6.3. *Challenges and Revisions to the Classical View*

The classical view was long the dominant theory of concepts in philosophy and psychology. But in the 1970s, a series of empirical problems emerged, the most important of which were the so-called *typicality effects* (e.g. Rips et al., 1973; Rosch & Mervis, 1975). For any given concept, people can judge how typical an item is of that concept, and there is high inter-subject agreement on these judgments. For instance, American subjects consider a robin a more typical instance of the concept BIRD than a chicken is. More typical items are categorized faster than less typical items and are more often named when subjects are asked for instances of the concept. Finally, typical items are not necessarily the most frequent or familiar items in the list. A robin is judged to be a more typical bird than a chicken, even though many people have fewer encounters with robins than with chickens (albeit dead ones). What makes an instance a typical item for a concept is, rather, that it has lots of features in common with other instances of the same concept and few features in common with non-instances. Thus robins fly, sing, lay eggs, are small, nest in trees and eat insects—common features in birds. Chickens, by contrast, don't fly, don't sing, don't nest in trees, and aren't small—and therefore chickens aren't typical birds.

Strictly speaking, these empirical effects aren't incompatible with the classical view, but *prima facie* it is hard to see why classically defined concepts would produce them. If BIRD has a definition in terms of necessary and sufficient conditions, then presumably chickens and robins meet those conditions equally well. And since robins aren't more frequent or familiar than chickens, there is nothing in the classical theory to explain why robins are categorized as birds more quickly than chickens, why they are judged more typical, and so on.

There were two main responses to these results: the first was to retain the basic idea of the classical view that concepts have definitions, but add a separate *identification procedure* that could account for the typicality effects; second, to account for the typicality effects directly, by building typicality into the very structure of concepts and therefore rejecting the classical view entirely. On the first response, sometimes called a *dual theory* of concepts, concepts still have a definitional *core* of necessary and sufficient conditions that an item must meet to count as an instance of that concept. But in addition to their core, concepts also have an associated set of non-definitional features that can be used in quick-and-dirty categorization; these are the identification procedure.[2] For the concept BIRD, these features might include features like flies, sings, etc. Since these features are used in quick identification, robins will be categorized as birds more quickly than chickens will. But since chickens meet the core conditions for the concept BIRD, subjects will also agree that chickens are nonetheless birds as well.

---

[2] For examples of dual theories, see Armstrong et al. (1983); Osherson & Smith (1981).

Few psychologists, however, chose to pursue dual theories in the 1980s and 1990s. The more common response was, rather, to develop new theories of concepts, of which two are particularly relevant here: prototype and exemplar theories.

6.4. *Alternatives to the Classical View*

Prototype Theories   In the *Philosophical Investigations*, Wittgenstein (1953) introduced the idea that many concepts could not be defined in terms of necessary and sufficient conditions. He illustrated this with the concept GAME. Rather than any shared set of features, what makes board-games, card-games, ball-games, etc. all instances of GAME are *family resemblances* between the instances. Some board-games have some things in common with some card-games, other board-games have other things in common with ball-games, and so on. What makes these all instances of GAME is that each instance has enough features in common with enough other instances. Concepts like GAME are also sometimes called *cluster concepts* (Gasking, 1960) since they have a cluster of common features, none of which is necessary to be an instance of the concept.

In response to the typicality effects they had discovered, Rosch and Mervis (1975) developed Wittgenstein's ideas into a psychological theory of concepts. According to prototype theories, a concept is a *prototype*—a summary representation of information about a category, something like a weighted list of (representations of) features generally shared by instances of the concept. The weights for each feature determine how important that feature is to the concept but, as with cluster concepts, in general no single feature is necessary. An item is an instance of the concept if it shares enough of the weighted features.

Thus, for instance, the concept BIRD might contain the following features (among others): flies, sings, lays eggs, is small, nests in trees, eats insects (Smith, 1995). And these features will each be weighted; perhaps "lays eggs" has high weight, "flies" and "eats insects" slightly lower, and "is small" not very much weight at all.

On a prototype theory, categorization is a comparison of an item to various feature lists. We can think of the comparison as calculating how many "points" the item scores on different lists. For every feature on a given list that the item shares, it gains "points"; for every feature that the item lacks, it loses points. The number of points lost and gained for each feature depends on that feature's weight. The item is categorized as an instance of whichever concept gives it the most points. There are various models for the underlying calculations, which give rise to various more specific prototype theories.

According to prototype theorists, this calculation of "points" is really a calculation of the "similarity" between two types of mental representation. On the one hand, there is the representation of the item to be categorized. On the other hand are the various concepts under which it could be categorized. Categorization is a comparison of the first sort of representation with the second sort; the item is categorized as an instance of whichever concept its representation is most similar to.

Exemplar Theories   There are also exemplar theories of concepts (e.g. Medin & Schaffer, 1978). Like prototype theories, exemplar theories claim that concepts don't have definitional cores. But exemplar theories go one step further than prototype theories, denying that concepts contain any kind of summary representation about instances of the concept. Instead, a concept just *is* a set of stored (representations of) instances. The concept BIRD just is a set of representations of birds.

As with prototype theories, categorization in exemplar theories is a measurement of similarity. To categorize an item, agents measure the similarity of (their representation of) that item to the various representations constituting different concepts, using some similarity metric or other. (As with prototype theories, various exemplar theories differ in the details of these similarity metrics.) An item is categorized as an instance of BIRD just in case it is similar enough to one's representations or *exemplars* of previously encountered birds.

Nearest Neighbor Pattern Classification   Issues of categorization are also addressed under the heading of "pattern recognition" or "pattern classification" in statistical learning theory and machine learning (e.g. Duda et al., 2001; Harman & Kulkarni, 2007). In the basic framework, the task is to use certain features of an item to assign a category or label to it. Features can have many possible values and are taken to be real valued. If there are D features, there is a D-dimensional *feature space* with a dimension for each feature. Each point in the feature space represents an assignment of values to each of the D features.

In the basic framework, it is assumed that there is an unknown background statistical probability distribution determining probabilistic relations between features and labels and the probabilities that items with various features and labels will be encountered. Data for classification are represented as a set of labeled points in feature space.

A 1-nearest neighbor classification assumes a metric on the feature space and assigns to any unlabeled point the same label as its nearest labeled point. A k-nearest neighbor classification assigns to any unlabeled point the label of a majority of its k nearest points. A k_n-nearest neighbor classification assigns to an unlabeled point the label of a majority of its k_n nearest points, where k_n is a function of n such that as $n \rightarrow \infty$: $k_n \rightarrow \infty$ but $\frac{k_n}{n} \rightarrow 0$. Clearly, there is a resemblance between such nearest neighbor classifications as studied in statistical learning theory and exemplar theories as studied in psychology.

Statistical learning theory is concerned with finding classification rules that minimize expected error and not with finding rules that model human psychology. But the rules that statistical learning theory endorses may provide suggestive models for psychology.

6.5. *Categorization and Moral Principles*

The Classical View, the Deductive Model, and Moral Generalism Of all the theories of mental representation, the theory most amenable to the deductive model is the classical view. If the classical view is correct, then moral concepts have definitions in terms of necessary and sufficient conditions, and so moral categorization consists of testing cases against those definitions. It seems fair enough to construe this process as the application of moral principles, the principles being embodied by the definitions of moral concepts.

To make things a bit more concrete: if moral concepts have classical structure, then a concept such as RIGHT ACTION has a definition. Suppose (what is probably false, but it doesn't matter) that the definition is ACTION THAT MAXIMIZES EXPECTED UTILITY. When we decide whether or not an action is right, we test it against this definition. And this looks very much like the application of the principle "an action is right if and only if it maximizes expected utility." So the classical view of concepts looks like a straightforward implementation of the deductive model.

We need not suppose that a "definition" in this sense captures the *sense* of the concept. The "definition" does not have to be *a priori*. It is enough that it captures one's current *conception*, one's current rule for determining whether the concept applies in a given case. Hare (1952) supposes that although one has such a rule at any given moment for *morally ought*, an account of the meaning of *morally ought* is not provided by that rule but rather by the theory that *morally ought* is used to express universalizable prescriptions, and Hare emphasizes that one may change one's rule without changing what one means by *morally ought*.

What would it mean if the deductive model did correctly describe our moral reasoning? Well, one natural thought might be that this gives some support to moral generalism in its debate against moral particularism.[3] First, however,

---

[3] For examples of this debate, see Dancy (1993), Hooker & Little, (2000), McKeever & Ridge (2006), Sinnott-Armstrong (1999), and Väyrynen (2004).

some crucial terminology. We should distinguish between particularism and generalism as claims about moral *psychology* and as claims about moral *right and wrong*. As a claim about moral psychology, particularism is the view that human moral judgment does not involve the application of moral principles. Call this view *psychological particularism*. As a claim about what is morally right or wrong, particularism is the view that there really aren't any general principles that capture the difference between right and wrong. Call this view *normative particularism*.[4] By contrast, generalism is simply the view denied by particularism. Hence psychological generalism: moral judgment *does* involve the application of moral principles. And normative generalism: there really are general moral principles governing right and wrong.

If the deductive model is correct, then *psychological* generalism seems to be correct. There is a very natural sense in which categorization, in the classical view of concepts, involves the application of principles embodied in the definitions of concepts. But note that the principles might not resemble anything like the principles sought by most generalists. The classical view makes no specific predictions about the definitions for any particular concept, or even about which concepts an agent will have. For all the classical view claims, an agent's concept of RIGHT ACTION *might* have the utilitarian definition just given. Or it might have a massively disjunctive definition consisting of a list of particular right actions: an action is right if and only if it helps the poor in such-and-such a way and it's Tuesday, or it fulfills a promise to call home on Wednesday without hurting anyone, or . . . . Or an agent might not have a single concept of RIGHT ACTION, but instead a long list of different concepts for different types of right action: an action is RIGHT$_1$ if and only if it maximizes utility; an action is RIGHT$_2$ if and only if it is performed out of duty; and so on.[5]

In either of these two latter cases, there is a sense in which moral reasoning would be the application of moral principles (namely, the definitions of the moral concepts), and so the deductive model would be correct. It is not clear whether this would vindicate the sort of moral generalism theorists like Rawls defend, since the "principles" embodied in our moral concepts would be highly specific. On the other hand, Hare (1952: 56–78) expressly allows

---

[4] This distinction is related to, but different from, Sinnott-Armstrong's (1999) distinction between *analytic* and *metaphysical* particularism. Analytic particularism is a claim about the *content* of moral judgments, i.e. that they are about particular cases and not principles. By contrast, psychological particularism is a claim about the *mental processes* that produce moral judgments. These two claims could come apart. Moral judgments could be *about* particular cases (and so analytic particularism true) but produced by the application of moral principles (and so psychological particularism false).

[5] Of course, to motivate the claim that such an agent had several different concepts, rather than one disjunctive concept, we would need a good theory of concept individuation. And that's a whole other can of worms.

for implicitly accepted general moral principles that one cannot formulate in words. So perhaps some versions of generalism have room for even such highly specific moral concepts.

Of course even if *psychological* generalism is true, this tells us very little about the truth or falsity of *normative* generalism. It might be that our moral reasoning works by applying general principles, but that it is mistaken to do so. It is well known that our intuitive reasoning about probability and statistics often goes awry, leading us to make mathematical judgments that conflict with our best mathematical theories (Kahneman et al., 1982). So too may our moral psychology conflict with our best meta-ethical theory, if moral psychology happens to work by applying moral principles but we come to decide (for whatever reason) that the best meta-ethical theory is particularism.

Similarity-Based Theories and Moral Particularism   Conversely, it has been argued that, if the classical view is false and one of the similarity-based theories correct, then psychological particularism must be true (Churchland, 1996, 2000; Casebeer, 2003). We just discussed how testing items against definitions (as in the classical view) could be construed as a type of application of principles, but can the same move be made for categorization in similarity-based theories? Recall how categorization works in these theories. In prototype theories, we categorize by counting weighted features and judging whether an item has enough of the important features in common with other instances of the concept. In exemplar theories, we categorize by calculating the similarity between (our representation of) an item and stored representations of instances of the concept. In either case, it may not seem felicitous to describe the process as the application of principles.

Such a description may be more felicitous under *some* specifications of prototype theories, for prototypes are still summary representations of instances of the concept. If the features constituting the concept are few enough, and sufficiently recognizable as moral, then there is a sense in which we can describe categorization as the application of principles—they just happen not to be the sort of the principles we were expecting. Suppose, for instance, the concept of MURDER had three features, all of them weighted heavily: intentional killing; against the victim's will; without official legal sanction. In that case, there is a sense in which the agent follows a principle in categorizing an action as murder, the principle being something like "an action is a murder if and only if it is calculated as passing a certain threshold with respect to those three features." Such a principle, although different from what moral principles are generally taken to be, is still not that far off from a more familiar principle like "an action is a murder if and only if it is an intentional killing against the victim's will without official legal sanction."[6] If moral concepts were prototypes, but were simple in this way, then there's a reasonable sense in which psychological particularism would be false and the deductive model correct.

Notice that Churchland supposes that the *moral principles* referred to in the issue between particularism and generalism are limited to principles that resemble the kinds of principles that people invoke in *external* discussion and argument with others, so "that our internal representations and cognitive activities are essentially just hidden, silent versions of the external statements, arguments, dialogues, and chains of reasoning that appear in our overt speech and print" (Churchland, 2000: 293). This is actually an odd restriction when the topic is whether *internal* moral reasoning depends on principles. It would rule out the complex implicit moral principles that Hare (1952: 56–78) alludes to, and it is difficult to take similar restrictions seriously in other intellectual disciplines. For example, it would be bizarre to limit linguistic principles to those that ordinary people appeal to in ordinary discussions about language. Drawing an analogy between moral and linguistic knowledge, Rawls made just this point: linguistic principles are "known to require theoretical constructions that far outrun the ad hoc precepts of our explicit grammatical knowledge" and a "similar situation presumably holds in moral philosophy" (Rawls, 1971: 47). But, for the sake of unpacking Churchland's view, let us continue our discussion of generalism and particularism on the odd assumption that moral principles have to be simple and relatively familiar.

The point then is that prototype concepts need not be simple. The feature list, set of weights, and calculation of similarity might be extremely complex, so complex that they baffle easy characterization. This is the possibility that Casebeer and Churchland have in mind when they suggest that prototype theory entails particularism—the possibility that the "principles" embodied by prototypes are so utterly unlike familiar moral principles that they don't deserve to be called "principles." Thus, it is not so much their endorsement of prototype theory that leads them to psychological particularism, but their endorsement of prototype theory along with some specific claims about what moral prototypes are like.[7]

---

[6] Needless to say (but we'll say it anyway), we're not actually endorsing this as the correct characterization of MURDER.

[7] To his credit, Casebeer is much more explicit than Churchland about the need for this extra premise and is open to the possibility that the premise might be false (cf. Casebeer, 2003: 114–115).

Andy Clark describes this view of moral prototypes as follows: "our moral knowledge [as represented by our moral prototypes] may quite spectacularly outrun anything that could be expressed by simple maxims or moral rules" (Clark, 2000a: 271). At first blush, Clark's (2000a, 2000b) responses to Churchland seem to deny that this view of moral prototypes entails psychological particularism. But Clark seems to agree that the entailment holds; what he actually denies is that people's moral knowledge *is* entirely embodied in these kinds of prototypes.[8] Instead, Clark claims, people also encode moral principles—and if they encode and reason with moral principles, then psychological particularism is false.

Similarly, if moral concepts have exemplar structure, then we lose any hope of giving an informative characterization to the processes underlying moral categorization in terms of moral principles. For exemplar theories do away with summary representation altogether and construe concepts as just a set of representations of instances. The only principle that an agent could be applying in categorization, therefore, would be an extremely uninformative one: "an action is morally right if and only if it sufficiently resembles my representations of other morally right actions."

So it seems basically right to claim that psychological particularism is entailed by exemplar theories, or by prototype theories along with certain assumptions about the structure of the prototype.[9] Some versions of similarity-based theories do entail psychological particularism. But, as with the argument from classical theories to psychological generalism, it is important to see that this conclusion does not appear to have direct implications for ethics. The conclusion is psychological, not normative, particularism. The truth of the former (supposing it is true) is no argument for the latter, for the same reason that the analogous argument wouldn't hold in other domains like mathematics. Suppose, for example, that a view analogous to particularism were true for human mathematical reasoning—suppose, that is to say, that most of our judgments of numerosity, comparative size, and so on didn't involve the application of simple and familiar rules or principles. Clearly we shouldn't infer from this fact about human psychology any claims about mathematics.

Someone might argue, however, that the relationship between moral psychology and moral right and wrong is distinctive, and that therefore an

---

[8] E.g. "the marginalization of summary linguistic formulations and sentential reason [by Churchland] is a mistake. Summary linguistic formulations are not . . . mere tools for the novice. Rather, they are . . . crucial and (as far as we know) irreplaceable elements of genuinely moral reason" (Clark, 2000a: 274).

[9] Our points in this and the preceding subsection are very similar to those made in Stich (1993).

argument from psychological to normative particularism would go through in the moral case. We think such an argument faces problems, but it might be developed as follows:

Suppose that psychological particularism really is true. This would mean that, when we make moral judgments or engage in other moral reasoning, we aren't applying moral principles. Perhaps this is because our moral concepts are exemplars, or prototypes of a certain kind.

Now, how do we discover what is right or wrong? Through our moral judgments and other moral reasoning. But if we don't use moral principles in our actual moral judgment, then we can never discover general principles of right and wrong through moral judgment. Contrast this with the case of mathematics. What makes us justified in thinking there is a gap between mathematical reasoning and mathematical reality is that the former is not our only guide to the latter. We can discover mathematical reality through more general processes of reasoning—logic, formal proofs, etc.

But our only guide to moral right and wrong is our moral psychology itself. So even if there really are moral principles, we are epistemically blocked from them. Moreover, since we are thus forced to build an account of right and wrong which doesn't include moral principles, it would seem otiose to postulate that there really are moral principles all the same, lurking mysteriously in the background, ever out of our epistemic reach. Given our epistemic situation, metaphysical moral particularism is more parsimonious than metaphysical moral generalism.

This argument relies on two problematic premises. First, it assumes that if moral judgment doesn't involve the application of moral principles, then moral judgment can't be *described* by moral principles. But in general a process can be governed by principles even if it doesn't involve the principles represented anywhere in the process. The behavior of a billiard-ball physical system might be governed by a simple set of physical laws, even though the billiard balls themselves don't "apply" those laws. Similarly, human moral judgment might be following moral principles that aren't explicitly represented in human minds.

Second, the argument assumes that our intuitive moral psychology is our only guide to moral right and wrong. And there seems ample room to deny that, by claiming that we can also use more general processes of reasoning to discover moral right and wrong. We certainly use such general processes in other cases, such as mathematics, and there's no obvious reason to deny that we can use them in the moral case as well. We discuss reasoning toward narrow or wide reflective equilibrium below. In the present case we might use such reasoning to come up with a set of moral principles that captures most of our judgments. We might also expand the input into this equilibrium beyond moral judgment to more general considerations, such as theoretical simplicity and so on. Such a wide reflective equilibrium gives even more opportunity for rejecting particular moral judgments, and therefore even greater space between moral reality and moral psychology.

In short, just as we saw in the previous section that psychological generalism does not entail normative generalism, so do we now see that psychological particularism does not entail normative particularism. It would only do so on the further assumptions that (1) if moral agents don't represent and apply moral principles, then their moral judgments aren't governed by moral principles, and (2) our only guide to the correct moral view is our intuitive moral judgments. The first assumption is unmotivated, and the second relies on a contentious moral epistemology. Thus, even if our moral concepts are exemplars or (the relevant kind of) prototypes, there is still some hope for generalism as a claim about right and wrong.

7. Reflective Equilibrium

There are, therefore, several good reasons to suppose that the deductive model is not an adequate model. All of the four claims made by the deductive model appear to be false or, at least, to have little evidential support for most moral reasoning. We now briefly discuss an alternative model, already mentioned. On this alternative model, internal reasoning takes the form of making mutual adjustments to one's beliefs and plans, in the light of one's goals, in pursuit of what Rawls (1971) calls a "reflective equilibrium."

Thagard (1989, 2000) develops models of this process using connectionist "constraint satisfaction." The models contain networks of nodes representing particular propositions. Nodes can receive some degree of positive or negative excitation. There are two sorts of links among nodes, mutually reinforcing and mutually inhibiting. Positive links connect nodes with others such that as one of the nodes becomes more excited, the node's excitation increases the excitation of the other nodes and, as one such node becomes less excited or receives negative excitation, excitation of the other nodes is reduced. Negative links connect nodes such that as one node receives more excitation, the others receive less and vice versa. Excitation, positive and negative, cycles round and round the network until it eventually settles into a relatively steady state. Nodes in the steady state that have a positive excitation above a certain threshold represent beliefs. Nodes in the final state that have a negative excitation beyond a certain threshold represent things that are disbelieved. Nodes in the final state with intermediate excitation values represent things that are neither believed nor disbelieved. The resulting state of the network represents a system of beliefs in some sort of equilibrium.

It has often been noted that a connectionist network provides a possible model of certain sorts of Gestalt perception, for example, of a Necker cube (Feldman, 1981). A given vertex might be perceived either as part of the near surface or part of the back surface. This can be modeled by using nodes in a connectionist network to represent vertices and by setting up positive links among the vertices connected by horizontal or vertical lines and negative links between vertices connected by diagonal lines, where the degree of excitation of a vertex is used to represent how near it seems to the perceiver. As excitation on a given vertex is increased, this increases the excitation on the three other vertices of that face and drives down the excitation of the vertices on the other face. The result is that one tends to see the figure with one or the other face in front and the other in back. One tends not to see the figure as some sort of mixture or as indeterminate as to which face is in front.

Thagard (1989) uses his constraint satisfaction connectionist network to model the reasoning of jurors trying to assess the guilt of someone in a trial. The model makes certain predictions. For example, a juror might begin with a view about the reliability of a certain sort of eye-witness identification, a view about whether posting a message on a computer bulletin board is more like writing something in a newspaper or more like saying something in a telephone conversation, and so forth. Suppose the case being decided depends in part on an assessment of such matters. Then Thagard's model predicts that a juror's general confidence in this type of eye-witness identification should increase if the juror judges that in this case the testimony was correct and should decrease if the juror judges that in this case the testimony was not correct. The model predicts a similar effect on the juror's judgment about what posting on a computer network is more similar to, and so forth. The model also predicts that, because of these effects, the juror's resulting reflective equilibrium will lead to the juror's being quite confident in the verdict he or she reaches.

Experiments involving simulated trials confirm this prediction of Thagard's model (Simon, 2004). In these experiments, subjects are first asked their opinions about certain principles of evidence about certain sorts of eyewitness identifications, resemblances, etc. Then they are given material about difficult cases involving such considerations to think about. The subjects' final verdicts and their confidence in their verdicts and in the various principles of evidence are recorded.

One result is that, as predicted, although subjects may divide in their judgment of guilt at the end, with some saying the defendant is guilty and others denying this, subjects are very confident in their judgments and in the considerations that support them. Furthermore, also as predicted, there are also changes in subjects' judgments about the value of that sort of eye-witness identification, about whether posting on a computer bulletin board is more like writing in a newspaper or having a private conversation, and so forth.

The model implies that judgments in hard cases are sometimes fragile and unreliable under certain conditions. When there is conflicting evidence, there is considerable tension among relevant considerations, just as there is a certain sort of tension among the nodes representing vertices in the Necker cube problem. If some nodes acquire even slightly increased or decreased excitation, the relevant inhibitory and excitatory connections can lead to changes in the excitation of other nodes in a kind of chain reaction or snowballing of considerations leading to a clear verdict, one way or the other, depending on the initial slight push, just as happens in one's perception of a Necker cube. After the Gestalt shift has occurred, however, the case may seem quite clear to the juror because of ways the juror's confidence has shifted in response to the positive and negative connections between nodes.

One upshot of this is that the slight errors in a trial that look like "harmless errors" can have a profound effect that cannot be corrected later by telling jurors to ignore something. By then the ignored evidence may have affected the excitation of various other items in such a way that the damage cannot be undone. Similarly, the fact that the prosecution goes first may make a difference by affecting how later material is evaluated.

This fragility of reflective equilibrium casts doubt on using the method of reflective equilibrium to arrive at reliable opinions. This sort of problem has been noted in discussions of Rawls's claim that justification of views about justice consists in getting one's judgments into reflective equilibrium. It is sometimes suggested that the problem might be solved by trying to find a "wide" rather than a "narrow" reflective equilibrium, where that involves not only seeing how one's current views fit together, but also considering various other views and the arguments that might be given for them, and trying to try to avoid the sorts of effects that arise from the order in which one gets evidence or thinks about an issue (Daniels, 1979). One needs to consider how things would have appeared to one if one had gotten evidence and thought about issues in a different order, for example. In this way one tries to find a *robust* reflective equilibrium that is not sensitive to small changes in one's starting point or the order in which one considers various issues.

Experimenters have shown that if subjects acting as jurors are instructed to try for this sort of wide, robust reflective equilibrium, they are less subject to the sorts of effects that occur when they are not so instructed (Simon, 2004). But the effects do not completely go away. So it is still not clear whether this model succeeds as a normative theory of reasoning by jurors or by people forming moral judgments.

8. Conclusion

We have made a number of distinctions, between theoretical and practical reasoning; between internal personal reasoning, leading to changes in one's beliefs and intentions, and external social reasoning or argument with others; and between conscious and unconscious reasoning. Where philosophers tend to suppose that reasoning is a conscious process and that theories of reasoning can be assessed against introspection, most psychological studies of reasoning treat it as a largely unconscious process whose principles can be studied only indirectly with clever experiments.

We then described what we take to have been a particularly influential model of internal moral reasoning throughout the history of philosophy (and, to a lesser extent, of psychology)—namely, the deductive model. This model can be found, either in part or wholly, in Plato, Kant, Mill, Hare, rule-utilitarians (like Hooker), natural-law theorists (like Donagan), Kohlberg, and others. The deductive model is characterized by four claims: (1) deductive arguments make people justified in believing the conclusions of those arguments; (2) people's conscious belief in the premises of arguments makes them believe the conclusions of those arguments; (3) the premises in the arguments are independent; and (4) the terms in the arguments are classically defined.

What we have argued, over the second half of this chapter, is that all four of these premises are confused, false, or seriously in need of empirical support as claims about most moral reasoning. Against the first claim, it is no trivial matter to derive normative claims about how one *should* reason from formal theories of validity, so it cannot be assumed that deductive arguments produce justification for their conclusions. We also cannot assume that moral judgments are causally produced by beliefs in the premises of such arguments. Third, we presented evidence that people's moral reasoning isn't produced by arguments with independent premises, at least in some cases. We also presented some evidence that people's moral judgments can't be based on the principles that they actually adduce in their support. Finally, we discussed the substantial empirical problems with the classical view of concepts, described three alternatives, and discussed the implications of those alternatives.

Although many options remain available that we haven't ruled out, nonetheless it seems to us that the deductive model is implausible as a model for most moral reasoning, in light of the evidence. So what other games are there in town? We discussed only one alternative model here, reflective equilibrium. And, as we saw, even if they turn out to be descriptively accurate models of actual moral reasoning, reflective equilibrium models have potentially worrying normative implications due to their fragility (at least in some models). This is obviously just the tip of the iceberg. Much more could be said, for instance, about the potential psychological and philosophical relevance of developments in machine learning (Harman & Kulkarni, 2007), or alternatives to classical computationalism such as mental models (Johnson-Laird, 2006) or connectionism. It would thus be an understatement to conclude that more work remains to be done in order to understand moral reasoning. The truth is, a *lot* more work remains to be done.

References

Alicke, M. D. 1992. "Culpable Causation," *Journal of Personality and Social Psychology* 63: 368–378.

Armstrong, S., Gleitman, L., & Gleitman, H. 1983. "What some concepts might not be," *Cognition* 13: 263–308.

Austin, J. L. 1953. *How to Do Things with Words*. Oxford: Oxford University Press.

Braine, M. D. S. & O'Brien, D. P. (eds.). 1998. *Mental Logic*. Mahwah, NJ: Lawrence Erlbaum Associates.

Casebeer, W. 2003. *Natural Ethical Facts: Evolution, Connectionism, and Moral Cognition*. Cambridge, MA: MIT Press.

Churchland, P. M. 1996. "The Neural Representation of the Social World." In L. May, M. Friedman & A. Clark (eds.), *Mind and Morals*. Cambridge, MA: MIT Press, 91–108.

—— 2000. "Rules, Know-How and the Future of Moral Cognition," *Canadian Journal of Philosophy* supplementary vol. 26: 291–306.

Clark, A. 2000a. "Word and Action: Reconciling Rules and Know-How in Moral Cognition," *Canadian Journal of Philosophy* supplementary vol. 26: 267–289.

—— 2000b. "Making Moral Space: A Reply to Churchland," *Canadian Journal of Philosophy* supplementary vol. 26: 307–312.

Cummins, D. 1996. "Evidence for the innateness of deontic reasoning," *Mind & Language* 11: 160–190.

Cushman, F. A., Knobe, J., & Sinnott-Armstrong, W. A. 2008. "Moral Judgments Affect Doing/Allowing Judgments," *Cognition* 108: 281–289.

Daniels, N., 1979. "Wide Reflective Equilibrium and Theory Acceptance in Ethics," *Journal of Philosophy* 76: 256–282.

Dancy, J. 1993. *Moral Reasons*. Oxford, Blackwell.

Dewey, J. 1938. *Logic: The Theory of Inquiry*. New York: Holt, Rinehart and Winston.

Donagan, A. 1977. *The Theory of Morality*. Chicago, IL: University of Chicago Press.

Duda, R. O., Hart, P. E., & Stork, D. G. 2001. *Pattern Classification*. New York: Wiley.

Feldman, J. A. 1981. "A Connectionist Model of Visual Memory." In G. E. Hinton & J. A. Anderson (eds.), *Parallel Models of Associative Memory*. Hillsdale, NJ: Erlbaum, 49–81.

Gasking, D. 1960. "Clusters," *Australasian Journal of Philosophy* 38: 1–36.

Gibbard, A. 1990. *Wise Choices, Apt Feelings: A Theory of Normative Judgment*. Cambridge, MA: Harvard University Press.

Gilligan, C. 1982. *In a Different Voice*. Cambridge, MA: Harvard University Press.

Goldfarb, W. 2003. *Deductive Logic*. Indianapolis, IN: Hackett.

Haidt, J. 2001. "The Emotional Dog and Its Rational Tail: A Social Intuitionist Approach to Moral Judgment," *Psychological Review* 108: 814–834.

Hampshire, S. 1959. *Thought and Action*. London: Chatto and Windus.

Hare, R. M. 1952. *Language of Morals*. Oxford: Clarendon Press.

—— 1963. *Freedom and Reason*. Oxford: Clarendon Press.

Harman, G. 1976. "Practical Reasoning," *Review of Metaphysics* 29: 431–463.

—— 1986. *Change in View*. Cambridge, MA: MIT Press.

Harman, G. & Kulkarni, S. 2007. *Reliable Reasoning: Induction and Statistical Learning Theory*. Cambridge, MA: MIT Press.

Harris, P. & Núñez, M. 1996. "Understanding of Permission Rules by Preschool Children," *Child Development* 67: 1572–1591.

Haugeland, J. 1978. "The Nature and Plausibility of Cognitivism," *Behavioral and Brain Sciences* 2: 215–226.

Holyoak, K. J. & Simon, D. 1999. "Bidirectional Reasoning in Decision Making by Constraint Satisfaction," *Journal of Experimental Psychology: General* 128: 3–31.

Hooker, B. & Little, M. 2000. *Moral Particularism*. New York: Oxford University Press.

Jaffe, S. & Hyde, J. S. 2000. "Gender Differences in Moral Orientation: A Meta-Analysis," *Psychological Bulletin* 126: 703–726.

Johnson-Laird, P. N. 2006. *How We Reason*. Oxford: Oxford University Press.

Johnson-Laird, P. N. & Byrne, R. M. J. 1991. *Deduction*. Hillsdale, NJ: Lawrence Erlbaum Associates.

Kahneman, D., Slovic, P., & Tversky, A. (eds.) 1982. *Judgement Under Uncertainty: Heuristics and Biases*. Cambridge: Cambridge University Press.

Kant, I. 1785/1993. *Grounding for the Metaphysics of Morals* (trans. J. Ellington, 3rd ed.). Indianapolis, IN: Hackett.

—— 1787/1929. *Critique of Pure Reason* (trans. N. K. Smith). London: Macmillan Press.

Knobe, J. 2003. "Intentional Action and Side Effects in Ordinary Language," *Analysis*, 63: 190–193.

Kohlberg, L. 1981. *Essays on Moral Development, Volume 1: The Philosophy of Moral Development*. New York: Harper & Row.

Lashley, K. S. 1958. "Cerebral Organization and Behavior." In H. C. Solomon, S. Cobb, & W. Penfield (eds.), *The Brain and Human Behavior*, Vol. 36. Association for Research in Nervous and Mental Disorders, Research Publications. Baltimore, MD: Williams and Wilkin, 1–18.

Laurence, S. & Margolis, E. 1999. "Concepts and Cognitive Science." In Margolis and Laurence (eds.), *Concepts: Core Readings*, Cambridge, MA: MIT Press, 3–81.

Levi, I. 1967. *Gambling with Truth*. New York: Knopf.

Locke, J. 1700/1975. *An Essay Concerning Human Understanding*. Oxford: Oxford University Press.

Margolis, E. & Laurence, S. 1999. *Concepts: Core Readings*. Cambridge, MA: MIT Press.

Medin, D. & Schaffer, M. 1978. "Context theory of classification learning." *Psychological Review* 85: 207–238.

McKeever, S. & Ridge, M. 2006. *Principled Ethics: Generalism As a Regulative Ideal*. Oxford: Oxford University Press.

Mill, J. S. 1846. *A System of Logic, Ratiocinative and Inductive: Being a Connected View of the Principles of Evidence and the Methods of Scientific Investigation*. New York: Harper.

—— 1861/2001. *Utilitarianism*. Indianapolis, IN: Hackett.

Murphy, G. L. 2002. *The Big Book of Concepts*. Cambridge, MA: MIT Press.

Nagel, T. 1970. *The Possibility of Altruism*. Oxford: Oxford University Press.

Newell, A. & Simon, H. 1976. "Computer Science As Empirical Inquiry: Symbols and Search." Reprinted in J. Haugeland (ed.), *Mind Design II*, Cambridge, MA: MIT Press, 1997, 81–110.

Osherson, D. & Smith, E. 1981. "On the Adequacy of Prototype Theory as a Theory of Concepts." *Cognition* 9: 35–58.

Polk, T. A. & Newell, A. 1995. "Deduction as Verbal Reasoning," *Psychological Review*, 102: 533–566.

Rawls, J. 1971. *A Theory of Justice*. Cambridge, MA: Harvard University Press.

Rips, L. J. 1994. *The Psychology of Proof*. Cambridge, MA: MIT Press.

Rips, L., Shoben, E., & Smith, E. 1973. "Semantic Distance and the Verification of Semantic Relations," *Journal of Verbal Learning and Verbal Behavior* 12: 1–20.

Rosch, E. & Mervis, C. 1975. "Family resemblances: studies in the internal structure of categories." *Cognitive Psychology* 7: 573–605.

Ryle, G. 1979. *On Thinking*, Totowa, NJ: Rowman and Littlefield.

Scanlon, T. M. 1998. *What We Owe To Each Other*. Cambridge, MA: Harvard University Press.

Simon, D. et al. 2001. "The Emergence of Coherence over the Course of Decision Making," *Journal of Experimental Psychology: Learning, Memory, and Cognition* 27: 1250–1260.

Simon, D. 2004. "A Third View of the Black Box: Cognitive Coherence in Legal Decision Making," *University of Chicago Law Review* 71: 511–586.

Sinnott-Armstrong, W. 1999. "Varieties of Particularism," *Metaphilosophy* 30: 1–12.

Sinnott-Armstrong, W., Mallon, R., McCoy, T., & Hull, J. (2008). "Intention, Temporal Order, and Moral Judgments," *Mind & Language* 23: 90–106.

Smith, E. 1995. "Concepts and Categorization." In E. Smith and D. Osherson (eds), *Thinking: An Invitation to Cognitive Science* vol. 3, 2nd ed. Cambridge, MA: MIT Press, 3–33.

Stich, S. 1993. "Moral Philosophy and Mental Representation," in M. Hechter, L. Nadel, & R. Michod (eds.), *The Origin of Values*. New York: Aldine de Gruyter, 215–228.

Thagard, P. 1989. "Explanatory Coherence," *Behavioral and Brain Science* 12: 435–467.

——2000. *Coherence in Thought and Action*. Cambridge, MA: MIT Press.

Väyrynen, P. 2004. "Particularism and Default Reasons," *Ethical Theory and Moral Practice* 7: 53–79.

Williams, B. 1985. *Ethics and the Limits of Philosophy*. London: Fontana.

Wittgenstein, L. 1953. *Philosophical Investigations*, trans. G. E. M. Anscombe. Oxford: Blackwell.

7

Moral Intuitions

WALTER SINNOTT-ARMSTRONG, LIANE YOUNG,
AND FIERY CUSHMAN

Card players often find themselves in positions where they could cheat with little or no risk of being caught, but they don't cheat, because cheating strikes them as immoral. Similarly, needy customers are often able to steal an item that they want and cannot afford to buy, but they choose to go home empty-handed, because they see stealing as immoral. Many everyday decisions like these are based on moral intuitions.

So are moral theories. It is hard to imagine any way to develop a moral theory without relying on moral intuitions at all. How could you choose among consequentialism, Kantianism, contractarianism, and virtue theories without appealing to moral intuitions at some point in some way? Most contemporary moral theorists use something like the method of reflective equilibrium, which in effect systematizes moral intuitions, so they must admit that they rely on moral intuitions.

Because moral intuitions are crucial to everyday life and moral theory, they have attracted a great deal of attention from both philosophers and psychologists (as well as neuroscientists, more recently). Still, there is little agreement or conversation between philosophers and psychologists about moral intuitions. When they do discuss moral intuitions, it is not clear that they are talking about the same topic, since they often disagree about what counts as a moral intuition.

When we refer to *moral intuitions*, we mean strong, stable, immediate moral beliefs. These moral beliefs are *strong* insofar as they are held with confidence and resist counter-evidence (although strong enough counter-evidence can sometimes overturn them). They are *stable* in that they are not just temporary whims but last a long time (although there will be times when a person who has a moral intuition does not focus attention on it). They are *immediate* because they do not arise from any process that goes through intermediate steps of conscious reasoning (although the believer is conscious of the resulting moral belief).

Such moral intuitions can be held about specific cases (e.g. a person, A, morally ought to keep this promise to this person, B), about general types of cases (e.g. whenever anyone promises to do anything, she or he morally ought to do it unless there is an adequate reason not to do it), or about very abstract principles (e.g. if A ought to do X, and A cannot do X unless A does Y, then A ought to do Y). We focus on moral intuitions about specific cases, because so little empirical research has been done on general or abstract moral intuitions.

Philosophers tend to ask *normative* questions about such intuitions: are they justified? When? How? Can they give us moral knowledge? Of what kinds? And so on. In contrast, psychologists tend to ask *descriptive* questions: how do moral intuitions arise? To what extent does culture influence moral intuitions? Are moral intuitions subject to framing effects? How are they related to emotions? And so on.

Until the last decade of the twentieth century, philosophers and psychologists usually engaged in their enterprises separately. This was unfortunate, because it is hard to see how to determine whether certain moral intuitions are justified without any understanding of the processes that produce those intuitions. We are not claiming that psychological findings alone entail philosophical or moral conclusions. That would move us too quickly from "is" to "ought." Our point is different: moral intuitions are unreliable to the extent that morally irrelevant factors affect moral intuitions. When they are distorted by irrelevant factors, moral intuitions can be likened to mirages or seeing pink elephants while one is on LSD. Only when beliefs arise in more reputable ways do they have a fighting chance of being justified. Hence we need to know about the processes that produce moral intuitions before we can determine whether moral intuitions are justified. That is what interests us in asking how moral intuitions work.

There are several ways to answer this question. One approach is neuroscience (Greene et al., 2001, 2004). Another uses a linguistic analogy (Hauser et al., 2008). Those methods are illuminating, and compatible with what we say here, but they are discussed elsewhere in this volume. (See Chapters 2 and 8 in this volume.) Here we want to discuss a distinct, though complementary, research program. This approach is taken by psychologists who study heuristics and claim that moral intuitions are, or are shaped and driven by, heuristics.

A few examples of non-moral heuristics will set the stage. Then, after identifying a general pattern, we can return to ask whether moral intuitions fit that pattern.

1. Non-Moral Heuristics

How many seven-letter words whose sixth letter is "n" (____n_) occur in the first ten pages of Tolstoy's novel, *War and Peace*? Now, how many seven-letter words ending in "ing" (____ing) occur in the first ten pages of *War and Peace*? The average answer to the first question is several times lower than the average answer to the second question. However, the correct answer to the first question cannot possibly be lower than the correct answer to the second question, because every seven-letter word ending in "ing" is a seven-letter word whose sixth letter is "n." Many subjects make this mistake even when they are asked both questions in a single sitting with no time pressure. Why? The best explanation seems to be that their guesses are based on how easy it is for them to come up with examples. They find it difficult to produce examples of seven-letter words whose sixth letter is "n" when they are not cued to think of the ending "ing." In contrast, when asked about seven-letter words ending in "ing," they easily think up lots of examples. The more easily they think up examples, the more instances of the word-type they predict in the ten pages. This method is called *the availability heuristic* (Kahneman et al., 1982, chs. 1, 11–14). When subjects use it, they base their beliefs about a relatively inaccessible attribute (the number of words of a given type in a specified passage) on a more accessible attribute (how easy it is to think up examples of such words).

A second classic heuristic is *representativeness*. Kahneman et al. (1982: ch. 4) gave subjects this description of a graduate student:

Tom W. is of high intelligence, although lacking in true creativity. He has a need for order and clarity and for neat and tidy systems in which every detail finds its appropriate place. His writing is rather dull and mechanical, occasionally enlivened by somewhat corny puns and by flashes of imagination of the sci-fi type. He has a strong drive for competence. He seems to have little feel and little sympathy for other people and does not enjoy interacting with others. Self-centered, he nonetheless has a deep moral sense.

Subjects were given a list of nine fields of graduate study. Subjects in one group were then asked to rank those fields by the degree to which Tom "resembles a typical graduate student" in each field (and, hence, is representative of that field). Subjects in another group were asked to rank the fields by the likelihood that Tom is in each field. Both groups of subjects were also asked to estimate the percentage of graduate students in each of the nine fields. These estimates varied from 3% to 20%, and Tom's description fit the stereotype of the smaller fields, such as library science, but not larger fields, such as English.

These percentage estimates should have big effects on subjects' probability rankings, because any given graduate student is less likely to be in a field that is smaller. Nonetheless, subjects' percentage estimates had almost no effect on their probability rankings. Instead, the answers to the questions about representativeness and probability were almost perfectly correlated (0.97). This suggests that these subjects neglected the baseline percentage and based their probability estimates almost totally on their judgments of representativeness. As before, they substituted a relatively accessible attribute (representativeness) for a relatively inaccessible attribute (probability).[1]

A third example is the *recognition heuristic*, studied by Gigerenzer et al. (1999: chs. 2–3). When asked which US city (San Diego or San Antonio) or which German city (Berlin or Munich) is larger, people tend to guess cities they recognize. This heuristic makes sense on the reasonable assumption that people hear more about bigger cities. Still, this heuristic can also be misleading. Gigerenzer's group found that subjects followed the recognition heuristic regularly (median 100%, mean 92%), even after they received information that should lead them to stop following this decision rule, such as information about which cities have professional soccer teams (1999: 50–52). Again, these subjects seem to base their beliefs about a relatively inaccessible attribute (population) on an accessible attribute (recognition) rather than on other available information that is known to be relevant.

1.1. *Battle of the Titans*

We included examples from both Kahneman and Gigerenzer because their research programs are often seen as opposed. Gigerenzer and his colleagues emphasize that simple heuristics can make us smart, whereas Kahneman, Tversky, and their colleagues study how heuristics and biases can lead to mistakes. However, this difference is largely a matter of emphasis (Samuels, Stich, & Bishop, 2002). Both sides agree that our heuristics lead to accurate enough judgments in most cases within typical environments. Otherwise, it would be hard to understand why we evolved to use those heuristics. Both sides also agree that heuristics can lead to important mistakes in unusual environments, and they agree that which heuristics lead to mistakes in which environments is a matter for empirical research.

Kahneman and Gigerenzer might still seem to disagree about rationality. Gigerenzer argues that it is rational to employ heuristics because heuristics

---

[1] A better-known example of representativeness is Linda the feminist bank teller (Kahneman et al., 1982: ch. 6). This example is controversial, because some critics claim that, in a list with "feminist bank teller," "bank teller" alone might be interpreted as "non-feminist bank teller." We will avoid the controversy by discussing the case of Tom, which is not subject to this objection.

provide the best method available in practice. In contrast, Kahneman suggests that people who use heuristics exhibit a kind of irrationality insofar as their responses violate rules of logic, mathematics, and probability theory. Again, however, we doubt that this disagreement is deep, since the apparently conflicting sides use different notions of rationality, and neither can legitimately claim that their notion of rationality is the only defensible one. If a heuristic is the best available method for forming true beliefs, but sometimes it leads people to violate the rules of logic, math, or probability, then it is rational in Gigerenzer's practical sense to use the heuristic even though this use sometimes leads to irrationality in Kahneman's formal sense. They can both be correct.

Gigerenzer and his followers also complain that Kahneman's heuristics are not specified adequately. They want to know which cues trigger which particular heuristic, which computational steps run from input to output, and how each heuristic evolved. We agree that these details need to be spelled out. We apologize in advance for our omission of such details here in this initial foray into a heuristic model of moral intuition. Still, we hope that the general model will survive after such details are specified. Admittedly, that remains to be shown. Much work remains to be done. All we can do now is try to make the general picture attractive and show its promise.

1.2. *Heuristics as Unconscious Attribute Substitutions*

What is common to the above examples that makes them all heuristics? On one common account (Sunstein, 2005), heuristics include any mental short-cuts or rules of thumb that generally work well in common circumstances but also lead to systematic errors in unusual situations. This definition includes explicit rules of thumb, such as "Invest only in blue-chip stocks" and "Believe what scientists rather than priests tell you about the natural world." Unfortunately, this broad definition includes so many diverse methods that it is hard to say anything very useful about the class as a whole.

A narrower definition captures the features of the above heuristics that make them our model for moral intuitions. On this narrow account, which we shall adopt here, all heuristics work by means of unconscious attribute substitution (Kahneman & Frederick, 2005).[2] A person wants to determine whether an object, X, has a target attribute, T. This target attribute is difficult to detect

---

[2] This pattern is not shared by all methods that are called "heuristics" by psychologists. Some exceptions, such as anchoring, still resemble paradigm heuristics in specifiable ways (Kahneman & Frederick, 2005: 272). Other so-called heuristics enable action or decision without belief. Gigerenzer discusses the gaze heuristic that baseball outfielders follow to catch a fly ball: fixate your gaze on the ball, start running, and adjust your speed so that the angle of gaze remains constant (2008: 7). Outfielders who use this heuristic rarely form any belief about the heuristic, about why they use it, about what the

directly, often due to the believer's lack of information or time. Hence, instead of directly investigating whether the object has the target attribute, the believer uses information about a different attribute, the heuristic attribute, H, which is easier to detect.[3] The believer usually does not consciously notice that he is answering a different question: "Does object, X, have heuristic attribute, H?" instead of "Does object, X, have target attribute, T?" The believer simply forms the belief that the object has the target attribute, T, if he detects the heuristic attribute, H.

In the above case of availability, the target attribute is the rate of occurrence of certain words, and the heuristic attribute is how easy it is for this person to think up examples of such words. In the above case of representativeness, the target attribute is the probability that Tom is studying a certain field, and the heuristic attribute is how representative Tom's personal attributes are of each field. In the above case of recognition, the target attribute is a city's population, and the heuristic attribute is ease of recognizing the city.

In some of these cases, what makes the heuristic attribute more accessible is that it is an attribute of the person forming the belief rather than an attribute of the object. How easy it is for someone to think up certain words or to recognize the name of a city is a property of that person. In contrast, the target attribute is not an attribute of the person. In our examples, it is an attribute of words, cities, and Tom. Thus the heuristic attribute need not be an attribute of the same thing as the target attribute.

Nonetheless, these heuristic attributes are contingently and indirectly related to their target attributes. In some cases, the heuristic attribute is even a part of the target attribute. For example, in "one-reason" decision-making (Gigerenzer et al. 1999: chs. 4–8), we replace the target attribute of being supported by the best reasons overall with the heuristic attribute of being supported by a single reason. When people buy cars in this way, they might focus on fuel efficiency alone instead of trying to think about all of the pros and cons of all available cars at once. Why do people focus on a single reason? It is too difficult to consider all of the many and varied considerations that are relevant, and too much information can be confusing or distracting, so people are often more accurate when they consider only one reason. Then they base their decision on the simpler heuristic attribute rather than on the more complex target attribute.

---

angle is, and so on. This heuristic helps them catch balls, not form beliefs. In contrast, we shall focus on heuristics that help people form beliefs or judgments.

[3] To say that subjects substitute one attribute for another is not to say that they would treat them identically in all respects if explicitly probed. The point is just that subjects answer a question about the target attribute by means of answering a question about the heuristic attribute.

Heuristics come in many forms, but all of the heuristics discussed here involve unconscious attribute substitution. This account applies to a wide variety of heuristics from Kahneman, Gigerenzer, and others (such as Chaiken, 1980, who discusses the I-agree-with-people-I-like heuristic, and Laland, 2001, who adds the do-what-the-majority-does heuristic). Unconscious attribute substitution is what makes them all heuristics in the narrow sense that will concern us here.

1.3. *Heuristics are not just Old-Fashioned Inferences from Evidence*

Such unconscious attribute substitution might seem to involve some form of inference. The believer moves from a belief that the object has the heuristic attribute to a belief that the object has the target attribute. This process starts with a belief and adds a new belief, so it might seem to be an inference. The heuristic attribute might even seem to be evidence for the target attribute.

We have no objection to these labels. Still, they should not hide the important differences between heuristics and what is commonly seen as evidence.

First, heuristics normally operate unconsciously. Some people might consciously appeal to availability, representativeness, or recognition in order to answer a question. However, most characteristic uses of heuristics are unconscious. This is shown in several ways. Subjects in the reported experiments usually do not mention the heuristic attribute when asked to explain how they arrived at their answers. In contrast, imagine the description said that Tom W. reads books about library science. Then subjects would, presumably, cite his reading habits as evidence when they are asked why they believe that Tom W. is in library science. If they did not report his reading habits, this omission would suggest that they did not use his reading habits as evidence for their beliefs, assuming they had no special reason to avoid mentioning this evidence. Similarly, when subjects do not mention the heuristic attribute of representativeness, that omission suggests that subjects do not use that attribute as evidence in the same way as they would use his reading habits as evidence.

Furthermore, unconscious processes are disturbed less by concurrent cognitive loads on working memory (such as distracting irrelevant tasks) than conscious processes are. Thus, if heuristics are unconscious but can be monitored and corrected by conscious processes, as dual-process models suggest, then subjects with greater cognitive loads will deviate less from the heuristic even when it is obviously mistaken. That's exactly what is found in experiments (Kahneman & Frederick, 2005: 268, 273, 285). In contrast, concurrent cognitive loads would seem to increase deviations from inferences based on evidence. All of that suggests that heuristics do not operate consciously in the way that normal inferences and evidence do.

Second, partly because heuristics are unconscious, they are not easily corrected when they go astray. Sure enough, researchers find that even experts on probability make the mistakes predicted by the various heuristics. When the experimental design makes the mistakes obvious enough, and there is no concurrent cognitive load, then experts do make fewer salient mistakes (Kahneman & Frederick, 2005: 273, 278–279, 287). Still, the persistence of heuristics is remarkable. In contrast, experts find it easier to correct misleading evidence, partly because the evidence exerts its effects through conscious reasoning.

Third, attribute substitution plays a role that normal evidence does not, insofar as attribute substitution silences or excludes or distracts from opposing evidence. If Tom W. is reported to wear a hat emblazoned with "Milton Matters," subjects would presumably weigh this evidence against his personal attributes and reduce their estimates of the probability that Tom W. is in library science instead of English. In contrast, when representativeness is substituted for probability in Kahneman's case of Tom, for example, representativeness is not weighed against the other evidence coming from subjects' percentage estimates. Instead, the baseline percentages are overlooked, and the judgment is based almost completely on the heuristic attribute of representativeness. Gigerenzer got similar results for his recognition heuristic, as discussed above. This silencing of other considerations might be appropriate: sometimes too much information can increase rates of errors. In any case, their role as silencers shows that heuristics have a force that normal evidence (such as Tom's hat) lacks.

Some philosophers allow unconscious evidence and exclusionary reasons, so they still might insist on calling the heuristic attribute evidence. We do not want or need to argue about whether heuristic attributes really are or are not evidence. If heuristic attributes are evidence, they are a special kind of evidence that operates in a special way with a special force. That is what matters here.

1.4. *Do we use Non-Moral Heuristics?*

Whether or not we classify heuristics as inferences or as evidence, the important questions are when, in which ways, and to what extent heuristics guide our beliefs. How can we tell?

The most direct evidence for attribute substitution comes from correlations between answers to questions about the target attribute and about the heuristic attribute. In the case of the representativeness heuristic, as we said, subjects' answers to questions about representativeness and probability were almost perfectly correlated (0.97). The near-perfection of this correlation strongly suggests that these subjects substituted the heuristic attribute of representativeness for the target attribute of probability in answering questions about the target attribute.

If subjects were answering a question about probability and using representativeness only as standard evidence for probability, then their answers would reflect other factors, including counter-evidence against their probability estimates. This counter-evidence might be overridden, but it would not be silenced in the sense of removing all of its force. In particular, their answers would be expected to vary with baseline percentages, since baseline percentages affect probabilities. But then the correlation between judgments of representativeness and of probability would not be as high as they are, because probability would vary with baseline percentage but representativeness would not. The near perfection of the observed correlations thus suggests that subjects do not simply treat heuristic attributes as one bit of evidence among others.

Instead, these high correlations suggest that subjects do not even distinguish the questions of probability and representativeness. If subjects were answering questions about representativeness, then they would be expected to ignore baseline percentages, because representativeness is not affected by how many students are in a field. The observed high correlation would, thus, be expected if subjects answered a question about representativeness when asked about probability. By substituting one question for another, they silence all of the factors or counter-evidence that affect the target attribute but not the heuristic attribute. The attribute substitution hypothesis thus explains the observed high correlations.

The attribute substitution hypothesis also explains some framing effects. When several heuristic attributes might be substituted for a given target attribute, when those different heuristics would lead to different beliefs about the target attribute, and when contextual framing affects which of these heuristic attributes gets substituted for the target attribute, then contextual framing will affect subjects' beliefs about the target attribute (Kahneman & Frederick, 2005: 269) Subtle wording and order differences can trigger different heuristics and thereby lead to different judgments. This mysterious phenomenon of framing thus receives a natural explanation from the hypothesis that these beliefs are driven by heuristics.

Much more could be said in favor of an attribute substitution account of non-moral heuristics, but the general pattern should be clear, and there is abundant evidence that this pattern is common outside morality. The next question is whether the use of heuristics in the form of attribute substitution also occurs inside the domain of morality.

2. Moral Heuristics

Moral intuitions fit the pattern of heuristics, in our "narrow" sense, if they involve (a) a target attribute that is relatively inaccessible, (b) a heuristic attribute that is more easily accessible, and (c) an unconscious substitution of the target attribute for the heuristic attribute. We shall discuss these elements in turn.

2.1. Is the Target Attribute Inaccessible?

The target attribute in a moral judgment is simply the attribute that the person who makes the judgment ascribes to the act, correctly or not.[4] When someone judges that an act is morally wrong, the target attribute for that judgment is moral wrongness. When judging that someone is morally virtuous, the target attribute for that judgment is moral virtue.[5] Similarly for judgments of moral goodness, rights, and so on. Each of these target attributes is relatively inaccessible in its own way, but in the interest of streamlining our discussion, we shall focus on moral wrongness as a target attribute.

Many people seem to think that they have easy and direct access to moral wrongness. They claim to see that acts are wrong. However, that's also what people think when they feel confident that Tom is more likely to be in library science than in English because he is more representative of the former type of graduate student. A target attribute (such as probability) can be difficult to access directly, even if it seems easily accessible to people who confuse it with a heuristic attribute that is easily accessible. Analogously, any impression that we can easily access moral wrongness by means of direct moral intuition might be explicable as a confusion of the target attribute with its heuristic. Thus apparent accessibility cannot show that moral wrongness has real accessibility.

To determine whether moral wrongness really is accessible, we need to ask what accessibility is and what moral wrongness is. With regard to heuristics, the relevant notion of accessibility is accessibility in practice, with realistic constraints on time and information. After all, the point of heuristics is to be fast and frugal enough to be useful in real life.

---

[4] In this general sense, even expressivists who are quasi-realists can talk about target attributes.

[5] Consider moral virtue. Evidence for situationism is sometimes said to make improbable the existence of robust character traits, such as virtues (Doris, 2002; Harman, 1999; Merritt, 2000; Merritt et al., Chapter 11, this volume). We need not go so far in order to recognize that it is no simple matter to tell who has a moral virtue or vice. Such judgments depend not only on how agents would act in circumstances that they have never faced but also on their internal motivations, which are hard to tell from the outside (and often from the inside).

To determine whether moral wrongness is accessible in this way, we need to ask what moral wrongness is. Luckily, we do not need to commit ourselves to any particular account of moral wrongness, for all the plausible candidates suggest that moral wrongness is not accessible in the relevant way.[6] Consider the consequentialist view that whether an act is morally wrong depends only on whether some alternative has better consequences overall. It is notoriously hard to tell which act maximizes pleasure and pain, much less the good. This requires knowing far into the future, and nobody has the information or capacity required to calculate the total or average. Thus, if the attribute of moral wrongness is the attribute of failing to maximize the good, then this target attribute is definitely inaccessible.[7] It does not help much to make moral wrongness depend only on expected value, since it is also often hard to tell whether a real agent reasonably believes that an act will maximize the good.

Kantianism might seem to make moral wrongness easier to access in real life, but it doesn't. The ongoing debates about Kant's first formula of the categorical imperative show that it is hard to tell what the maxim of an act is, what it means for an act to be universalizable or not, and whether a given maxim is universalizable. It is also hard to say exactly what it is to treat someone as a means only, as prohibited by Kant's second formula, and whether the act would violate the rules of a kingdom of ends, as prohibited by Kant's third formula. The general point is that such theoretically delicate notions are too complex and unwieldy for moral decisions by common folk in normal situations.

The same goes for contractarianism, as in Rawls (1971) and Scanlon (1999). If to judge an act wrong is to judge that it violates rules that all rational impartial people would accept or, instead, rules that no reasonable person could reject, then it will be very hard for any ordinary person in real life, likely to be both

---

[6] Although we focus on substantive moral theories in the text, meta-ethical theories support the same conclusion. "Cornell" moral realists (e.g. Brink, 1989) argue that moral wrongness is a natural kind, just as water is H_2O. The chemical compositions of liquids are not accessible directly, so we need to use their phenomenal properties to identify liquids in everyday life. If moral wrongness is analogous, we shall not have direct access to the natural property that is moral wrongness. Cornell realists usually say that moral wrongness is a homeostatic cluster and is discovered by a complex process of reflective equilibrium, both of which suggest inaccessibility in everyday life. Inaccessibility is also suggested by "Canberra" moral realists, who analyze moral wrongness as the property that best explains a large set of shared platitudes about moral wrongness (e.g. Jackson, 1998: chs. 5–6). It would clearly be very difficult for common people to think so systematically about moral wrongness when making moral judgments in everyday life. Admittedly, moral realists could claim that moral wrongness is a simple non-natural property that is accessible directly (e.g. Ross, 1930). But how is it accessed? And why adopt such a queer metaphysics and epistemology?

[7] This inaccessibility in practice is not a problem for consequentialists if they claim only a theoretical standard or criterion of rightness instead of a practical guide or decision procedure (see Bales, 1971).

irrational and partial, to determine directly whether any act is morally wrong. Experts might be able to apply such abstract theories after long reflection, but that cannot be what is going on in everyday life.

Social moral relativism might seem to aid access to moral wrongness, if it makes moral wrongness depend on the actual conventions of society (Harman, 1996). However, it is not easy or quick for someone judging a particular act to determine which conventions are essential to the moral wrongness of this act and also whether those conventions are in place in this society, because which conventions exist in a society depends on patterns of action and motivation for many people other than the person making the moral judgment.

There are many other possibilities, but, in the end, the only theories that make moral wrongness easily accessible are those that identify moral wrongness with the judger's own emotional reactions or preferences. However, such subjectivism is totally implausible, as was shown long ago, because of its inability to account for interpersonal disagreements and other common features of morality. Thus no plausible theory will make moral wrongness accessible in practice without heuristics.

2.2. *Which Moral Heuristic?*

Inaccessibility creates the need for a heuristic attribute. If moral wrongness were easily accessible, we would not need to substitute any heuristic attribute in order to judge whether an act is morally wrong. Because moral wrongness is so hard to access directly, we need to substitute a more easily accessible heuristic attribute in order to be able to judge whether an act is morally wrong.

Which heuristic attribute? A heuristic attribute must be easily and quickly accessible (like availability, representativeness, or recognition). Heuristics are supposed to be fast and frugal, after all, and reliable, at least in common situations. A heuristic attribute must, therefore, be related somehow to the target attribute. Otherwise, it would be a mystery why we evolved to substitute that heuristic. Still, there are lots of relevant accessible attributes that people might substitute for the inaccessible attribute of moral wrongness.

One possibility, as Gigerenzer (2008: 9) puts it, is that "Heuristics that underlie moral actions are largely the same as those for underlying behavior that is not morally tinged. They are constructed from the same building blocks in the adaptive toolbox. That is, one and the same heuristic can solve both problems that we call moral and those we do not." Heuristics that guide non-moral beliefs, decisions, and actions clearly also affect moral beliefs, decisions, and actions. Gigerenzer mentions Laland's (2001) do-what-the-majority-does heuristic: if you see the majority of peers behave in a certain way, do the same.

We could add Chaiken's (1980) I-agree-with-people-I-like heuristic. These heuristics affect moral and non-moral beliefs alike. However, it seems unlikely that all moral beliefs and actions can be explained completely in terms of general heuristics that apply outside as well as inside morality. Morality sometimes leads us to criticize the majority as well as people we like, and moral judgments are not entailed simply by factual beliefs that ordinary heuristics enable, so there must be additional heuristics behind at least some moral intuitions.

Another suggestion is that the heuristic attributes behind common moral judgments are the attributes mentioned in common moral rules and principles, such as don't kill, disable, cause suffering, lie, cheat, steal, or break promises, at least without an adequate justification. People might seem to use these categories to reach judgments about moral wrongness. Instead of directly asking whether an act is morally wrong, they might seem to classify the act as killing, say, and then infer that it is morally wrong because it is killing.

However, recent experimental evidence suggests that people do not form moral judgments by applying a rule about killing or by checking whether the act has the attribute of being a killing (Sinnott-Armstrong et al., 2008; described in Chapter 6 in this volume). Other studies suggest that we often cannot apply the notion of causation, which is central to several of the common moral rules, without presupposing some prior moral judgment (Alicke, 1992). If we cannot apply common moral rules without prior moral judgments, then an account of moral intuitions needs to explain those prior moral judgments and not just the way that they get used in applying common moral rules.

More generally, this approach is too indeterminate. You can view any moral principle as a heuristic. Just-war theory, for example, includes a principle that forbids preventive war as opposed to preemptive war. On this view, the property of being preventive is what makes a war immoral. In contrast, this principle can be reconceived as a heuristic where the target attribute is moral wrongness and the heuristic attribute is being preventive war. On this heuristic view, the property of being preventive does not itself make war wrong but instead is substituted for the separate target property of wrongness. So, which is it: principle or heuristic? There is no solid basis for either claim without substantive moral assumptions about what makes wrong acts wrong. This problem generalizes to other principles. Sunstein (2005) writes, "what a utilitarian sees as a moral heuristic (never lie!) might be regarded as a freestanding moral principle by a deontologist." Deontologists can even see the basic principle of utility as a heuristic that usually works well but leads us astray in exceptional cases. There seems to be no way to tell which is a moral principle and which is a heuristic without making assumptions about what is morally wrong and why. Scientists need a more neutral way to study heuristics.

Finally, these principles might be heuristics in the broad sense mentioned above, but they are normally conscious, so they are crucially different from the narrow heuristics that concern us here. Subjects who use the availability heuristic are rarely conscious of applying any rule like, "If you can think of lots of examples, then guess that there will be lots more." That makes it misleading to see the features in conscious moral rules as heuristic attributes.

A third set of heuristic attributes is proposed by Sunstein (2005):

Cold-heart Heuristic: "Those who know they will cause a death and do so anyway are regarded as cold-hearted monsters." (This is supposed to explain widespread opposition to cost–benefit analysis.)

Fee Heuristic: "People should not be permitted to engage in wrongdoing for a fee." (This is supposed to explain opposition to emissions trading.)

Betrayal Heuristic: "Punish, and do not reward, betrayals of trust." (This is supposed to explain opposition to safer airbags that cause some deaths.)

Nature Heuristic: "Don't tamper with nature" (a.k.a. "Don't play God"). (This is supposed to explain some opposition to genetic engineering and cloning.)

Action Heuristic: "Don't do harmful acts." (This is supposed to explain why people see doing harm as worse than allowing harm, as in active *vs.* passive euthanasia and in vaccination policies.)

These might all count as heuristics under Sunstein's broad definition. However, just as with the common moral rules mentioned above, there is no morally neutral way to tell whether these are heuristics or new deontological rules. Also, Sunstein's heuristics cannot be moral heuristics in our narrow sense, because they typically operate consciously rather than unconsciously.

Some other moral principles do seem to operate unconsciously. Subjects often make moral judgments in a pattern prescribed by the doctrine of double effect without being able to cite that principle as a justification and, presumably, without being conscious of using that principle (Hauser et al., 2008; Cushman et al., 2006; Mikhail, 2002). The attribute that makes an act violate the doctrine of double effect is that its agent intends harm as a means. This attribute might, therefore, operate much like heuristic attributes. That's why moral judgments that fit that pattern and are based on that principle are classified as moral intuitions, in contrast to moral judgments that are inferred from conscious rules.

Other factors also unconsciously affect our moral intuitions. Most people, for example, are more likely to judge harmful acts as morally wrong when their agents touch the victim and less likely to judge acts morally wrong when the victim is at some physical distance. When asked whether contact and physical distance are morally important, they often deny that it is important or at least admit that they cannot say why it is important (Cushman et al., 2006). This suggests that contact and physical distance might be operating as heuristic attributes for the target attribute of moral wrongness.

However, the attribute of intention as a means is not so easy to access. And recent research (Greene et al., 2009) suggests that the contact principle needs to be reformulated as a less accessible principle of personal force that applies when one transfers energy to another directly by the force of one's muscles. This inaccessibility makes these attributes bad candidates for heuristic attributes, which are supposed to be easily accessible.

One promising approach tries to account for a variety of moral intuitions, as well as the grab bag of moral heuristics proposed above, as instances of a general *affect heuristic* (Kahneman & Frederick, 2005: 271b, 283; cf. Slovic et al., 2002). We shall sketch this approach here and discuss evidence for it in a subsequent section (2.4). Unlike the aforementioned moral heuristics, which caution against specific acts or act-types, the affect heuristic is content-free. All the affect heuristic says is, roughly: if thinking about the act (whatever the act might be) makes you feel bad in a certain way, then judge that it is morally wrong. The point, of course, is not that everyone consciously formulates this conditional. The claim is only that people unconsciously substitute how the act makes them feel for the target attribute of moral wrongness and then judge the act morally wrong on the basis of how it makes them feel.[8]

The relevant bad feelings are diverse: if you consider doing the act yourself, you might feel compunction in advance or anticipate guilt and/or shame afterwards. If you imagine someone else doing the act to you, then you might feel anger or indignation. If you imagine someone else doing the act to a third party, then you might feel outrage at the act or the agent. (The outrage heuristic of Sunstein, 2005 is, thus, a part of the larger affect heuristic.) And different kinds of negative affect might accompany judgments in different areas of morality: anger in moral judgments about harm, contempt in the moral judgments about hierarchy, and disgust in moral judgments about impurity. (Cf. Haidt & Joseph, 2004 on the CAD hypothesis and Kass, 1997 on the "wisdom of repugnance.") In all these cases, some kind of negative affect accompanies some kind of moral judgment. The affect operates as a heuristic

---

[8] The affect need not be felt every time the judgment is made. Instead, it could be made in some cases and then generalized into a rule, or it could be felt in paradigm cases and then lead us to judge other cases wrong because they resemble the paradigm cases.

attribute if (but only if) people reach the moral judgment by unconsciously substituting the affect for the target attribute of moral wrongness.

This affect heuristic might underlie the other moral heuristics. If people feel worse when they imagine causing harm intentionally than when they imagine causing harm unintentionally (cf. Schaich Borg et al., 2006), then the hypothesis that people follow an affect heuristic predicts that moral judgments will display the pattern prescribed by the doctrine of double effect. Similarly, if we feel worse when we imagine causing harm to someone we contact (or exert personal force on), then the hypothesis that we follow an affect heuristic predicts that our moral judgments will follow the pattern predicted by the contact (or personal force) heuristic. Similarly for other heuristics. And people do seem to feel bad when they imagine acts that violate such heuristics. Thus the affect heuristic might explain what is common to all (or many) of the other postulated moral heuristics.

Much work needs to be done in order to determine which cues trigger which emotions and, thereby, which moral judgments. As long as the process works by means of emotion or affect, however, it will be illuminating to see moral intuitions as based on an affect heuristic.

2.3. *Moral Heuristics and Biological Adaptation*

The preceding accounts of moral heuristics as attribute substitutions might seem to presuppose that moral wrongness is a real attribute or property. Hardened skeptics, however, might deny that moral wrongness is any property of events to begin with. They might complain that moral intuitions cannot operate as heuristics, because there is no objective moral truth for them to approximate. They might add that there is no moral reality beyond moral intuitions as psychological objects. In this section we suggest that moral intuitions can be fruitfully understood as heuristics even on such a skeptical view. In doing so, we rely on the assumption that moral intuitions have an important functional role as biological adaptations.

Many of the above examples of non-moral heuristics apply in cases where an individual is attempting to establish some sort of factual representation, such as the number of words of a particular type in a text, the probability of a person possessing a set of attributes, or the population of a city. In each of these cases, the output of the heuristic is a mental representation of some feature of the world.

One purpose of representing the world, of course, is to guide action. Thus we might substitute attributes ("he has a shaved head, spiked leather chains, and lots of tattoos") for a target property ("he is dangerous") in order to produce the most appropriate course of action ("move away from him"). Importantly, we can sometimes construct heuristics in such a way that they move directly from the substitute attribute to the appropriate course of action without ever representing the target property. We might, for instance, tell our children "Avoid men with tattoos" without bothering to explain that we are substituting certain visual correlates for the underlying target property of dangerousness. For the sake of clarity, let's call heuristics of this second type "motivational heuristics" and contrast them with "representational heuristics." Representational heuristics output representations of some fact about the world, while motivational heuristics output the appropriate course of action.

Natural selection makes abundant use of motivational heuristics. Bad-tasting food directly motivates an avoidance response without any direct representation of the underlying probability of toxic or pathogenic qualities. Good-looking people directly motivate an approach response without any direct representation of the underlying probability of fecundity or fitness. Moreover, there is a sense in which "bad-tasting" or "good looking" do not refer to a property of foods or people in any objective sense at all. These psychologically constructed attributions guide behavior around very real costs and benefits, but do so by providing heuristic motivations ("eat yummy food") rather than by providing heuristic beliefs ("yummy food is nutritious").

Moral intuitions could be understood in much the same way. Moral judgment motivates a host of behaviors: do this, don't do that; punish him, reward her; shun her, affiliate with him. Prosocial behaviors are adaptive because they help individuals to reap the payoffs of cooperative interactions, to avoid sanctions, and to enforce prosociality among social partners. People often perform behaviors motivated by moral intuitions without directly representing the underlying reason why the behavior is adaptively favorable.

One of the most compelling cases for adaptive moral heuristics is incest avoidance. Taboos against sexual intercourse between first-degree relatives come as close to cross-cultural universality as any social psychological phenomenon (Wilson, 1998). Indeed, reproduction between first-degree relatives is uncommon among most sexually reproducing species. There is an obvious adaptive explanation for this behavior: reproduction between first-degree relatives tends to produce less biologically fit offspring, especially over successive generations. Our moral intuition that incest is wrong is not a representational heuristic for estimating the fitness consequences of reproduction, but it can be fruitfully understood as a motivational heuristic for behavior that tends to have fitness-enhancing consequences.

We're now in a position to re-evaluate whether skepticism about moral facts threatens our proposal to understand moral intuitions as heuristics. If we regard moral intuitions as representational heuristics—in particular, if we regard moral intuitions as heuristic devices for estimating the moral truth in a computationally efficient manner—then the moral skeptic will have little use for our proposal. On the other hand, if we regard moral intuitions as a motivational heuristic for producing adaptive behaviors, skepticism about moral facts is not threatening at all. We may regard moral intuitions as subjective psychological states that exist because they motivate fitness-enhancing behaviors in a computationally efficient manner.

2.4. *Do we use Moral Heuristics?*

Of course, it is easy to postulate and hard to prove. We need evidence before we can conclude that we really do follow the affect heuristic or any other heuristic when we form moral judgments. Since heuristics are unconscious attribute substitutions, the evidence comes in two stages: we need evidence that the process is attribute substitution. Then we need evidence that the process is unconscious. We also need some reason to believe that the heuristic attribute is related in a significant way to the target attribute in order to understand why that heuristic arose.

What is the evidence for attribute substitution? As with non-moral heuristics, the most direct evidence of attribute substitution would be strong correlations between answers to questions about the target and heuristic attributes. Which heuristics are at work will be revealed by which correlations hold.

Consider the affect heuristic. When subjects presented with various harmful acts were asked (a) how "outrageous" the act was and also (b) how much the agent should be punished, the correlation between their two answers was a whopping 0.98 (Kahneman et al., 1998). The term "outrageous" might not signal emotion, but a later study by Carlsmith et al. (2002) asked subjects how "morally outraged" they were by the act and then how severe the crime was and how much the agent should be punished. The correlations between outrage and severity and between outrage and sentence, respectively, were 0.73 and 0.64 in their study 2 and 0.52 and 0.72 in their study 3. These correlations, though significant and high, are not as high as in Kahneman et al., but that reduction might be because the crimes in Carlsmith et al. were milder. In any case, these high correlations are striking because people often refer to consequences, such as deterrence, when asked abstractly why societies should punish, but such consequences seem to have little effect on their judgments of how much to punish in concrete cases. This conflict suggests that people might have both an unconscious emotional system that drives their concrete moral judgments and a conscious consequentialist system that drives their abstract moral judgments (see Greene et al., 2001, 2004, 2008; Cushman et al., 2006 proposes a similar view; see also Chapter 2 in this volume). This dichotomy in moral judgments seems analogous to subjects' tendency to say that the baseline is crucial to probability when asked abstractly but then to overlook baseline percentages and focus solely on representativeness when asked to make a probability judgment in a concrete case.

A correlation between affect and moral judgment has also been found in a different area of morality. Haidt et al. (1993) presented their subjects with offensive actions, including eating one's pet dog who had died in an accident, masturbating in a chicken carcass and then eating it, and so on. Then they asked whether such acts are harmful, whether they are morally wrong, and whether it would bother them to witness the action. In the groups that tended to judge these acts morally wrong, the correlation between this moral judgment and predictions of bothersome affect was 0.70 (which was higher than the correlation with their answers to the harm question). This relation held across cultures (Brazil and Philadelphia). In contrast, moral judgments were more highly correlated with judgments of harm than with judgments of bothersome affect in those groups (especially higher socioeconomic Philadelphians) that tended to judge that these offensive acts are not morally wrong. On the assumption that people in these groups are better educated, this variation might reflect a greater tendency to control the unconscious emotional system with the less emotional conscious system, just as better-educated subjects tended to make fewer mistakes in the experiments with non-moral heuristics. Again, moral intuitions resemble non-moral heuristics in important respects.

Others have found many more correlations with affect. See Sunstein (2005), Kahneman and Frederick (2005: 271b, 283), and the neuroimaging studies of Greene et al. (2001, 2004) and Schaich Borg et al. (2006). Still, these are only correlations. All of these studies leave open the possibility that emotion is an after-effect of moral judgment. However, that possibility is undermined by a steadily increasing number of studies using diverse methods from both psychology and neuroscience.

One approach is to manipulate the extent of emotional engagement during moral judgment. For example, Haidt and colleagues have boosted emotional engagement by either hypnosis or priming. Wheatley and Haidt (2005) showed that when highly hypnotizable individuals were given a posthypnotic suggestion to experience disgust upon encountering an arbitrary word, they made harsher judgments of both morally relevant actions (e.g. eating one's dead pet dog, shoplifting) and morally irrelevant actions (e.g. choosing topics for academic discussion) specifically when these actions were described in vignettes including the disgust-inducing word.

Governed by the same logic, a second study (Schnall et al., 2008) probed subjects' responses to moral scenarios featuring morally relevant actions such as eating one's dead pet dog while priming subjects to feel disgusted. In one experiment, subjects filled out their questionnaires while seated at either a clean desk or a disgusting desk, stained and sticky and located near an overflowing waste bin containing used pizza boxes and dirty-looking tissues. Subjects who were rated as highly sensitive to their own bodily state were more likely to condemn the actions when seated at the disgusting desk than at the clean desk. Such studies suggest that emotion is not epiphenomenal when it comes to moral judgments but can instead causally affect moral judgments.

Greene and colleagues (2008) employed a more indirect manipulation of emotion via cognitive load, thought to interfere with "controlled cognitive processes," and therefore to result in a relative increase in the emotional contribution to moral judgment. As predicted, cognitive load slows down consequentialist responses but has no effect on nonconsequentialist responses, suggesting that affect plays a causal role in at least some moral judgments, specifically, nonconsequentialist responses.

In contrast to the previous studies, Valdesolo and DeSteno (2006) sought to *reduce* affect, specifically, negative affect, by presenting short comedic film clips to subjects before they produced moral judgments. Reducing negative affect was found to result in a greater proportion of consequentialist judgments, supporting the proposal that (negative) affect is not merely associated with but critically drives nonconsequentialist judgments.

Finally, studies of clinical populations have provided similar support for the affect heuristic or at least the crucial role of affect in some moral judgments. Mendez and colleagues (2005) showed that patients with frontotemporal dementia and resulting blunted affect produce more consequentialist moral judgments as compared to healthy subjects. Koenigs, Young, and colleagues (2007) and Ciaramelli and colleages (2007) found a similar pattern of heavily consequentialist moral judgments among patients with severe emotional deficits due to ventromedial prefrontal lesions. Lesion studies such as these indicate the causal nature of the relationship between affect and moral judgment. Although much related work remains to be done, the existing body of evidence from multiple disciplines converges on the notion that moral judgments are not just correlated with emotion but result from emotion, as demanded by our account of the affect heuristic.

In addition, indirect evidence of attribute substitution comes from explanatory power. Attribute substitution can explain why common moral rules are defeasible, and also why it is so hard to specify when common moral rules are defeated. It is easy to say "don't break your promise unless there is an adequate reason to break it," but it is hard to specify explicit rules that can be used to determine which promises may be broken. The affect heuristic view suggests that we consult our emotions or affect in order to determine when promises may be broken. That would explain why the rule against promise-breaking has exceptions and also why it is hard to specify what those exceptions are.

The heuristic hypothesis also explains why people seem able to answer complex moral questions surprisingly quickly, since attribute substitution would reduce reaction times—they are fast as well as frugal. It is hard to imagine any better explanation of such observations, given the inaccessibility of moral wrongness (discussed above, Section 2.1), so the best explanation seems to be that moral intuitions are attribute substitutions.

We still need evidence that this process is unconscious, but we already saw some. Both Hauser et al. (2008) and Mikhail (2002) found that subjects' moral judgments fit the doctrine of double effect, but very few subjects cited that doctrine when asked to justify their judgments. Additional evidence of unconsciousness comes from subjects' tendency to reject certain moral heuristics on reflection. When subjects become conscious that their moral judgments are affected by physical contact, for example, they often deny that contact really affects moral wrongness (Cushman et al., 2006). Since they reject the heuristic when asked to explain themselves, it seems unlikely that they were conscious of it at the earlier time when they formed their moral judgment. Subjects (and indeed many kinds of philosophers) also seem reluctant to endorse other heuristics, such as when they deny that their moral judgments are based on affect, so the same argument suggests that those other heuristics also operate unconsciously.

Finally, if moral heuristics are unconscious in the same way as non-moral heuristics, we would expect both to be partly but not wholly correctable by slower conscious reflection. In studies of the representativeness heuristic, subjects made fewer mistakes about Tom's field of study when they not only use the heuristic attribute of representativeness but also took time to consciously reflect on the additional information about the relative populations in various fields (Kahneman & Frederick, 2005). Analogously, when asked whether an act is morally wrong, people who initially use the affect heuristic can later correct their initial impressions if they take time to reflect on additional features, such as the consequences of actions. A neat example is Bentham's (1978) apparent disgust at gay sex while his utilitarian theory enables him to override that feeling and judge that gay sex is not morally wrong. See also Greene et al. (2004) on more recruitment of brain regions for abstract reasoning among those who choose to smother the crying baby. In such cases, moral heuristics seem unconscious but consciously correctable in much the same way as non-moral heuristics.

Although moral intuitions resemble non-moral heuristics in all of these ways, there are differences as well. First, with one exception, none of the correlations between candidates for a heuristic attribute and moral wrongness is close to the 0.97 correlation that Kahneman et al. (1982) found with non-moral heuristics. However, the moral cases are more complex. Several different moral heuristics could operate on a single case. The availability of alternative heuristics, along with cultural overlays and other complications, should reduce correlations between moral wrongness and any one heuristic attribute in moral cases.

Moral heuristics are also more intractable than non-moral heuristics. When someone points out that every seven-letter word ending in "ing" has "n" in its sixth place, most people quickly admit that they made a mistake. People seem much more resistant to giving up their moral judgments even when they admit the analogies to heuristics. Why? One reason might be that they are not caught in an explicit inconsistency, as they are in the case of availability, so it is much harder to show them that their moral judgment is mistaken. People have a tendency to stick by their heuristics unless proven inconsistent or incorrect, which is harder to do in moral cases.[9]

Another reason for resistance is that giving up the heuristic has more costs in the moral case. People stick by their moral intuitions because they would feel uncomfortable without them, and because they know that others would be less comfortable with them if they did not share their moral views. None of that applies to cases like Tom the graduate student, the number of seven-letter words in a passage, or which German cities have soccer teams. In addition, some of our most valued social practices and institutions depend on using heuristics such as don't let your friends down. Without the tendency to stand by our friends even when doing so has bad consequences, our friendships would be very different and might not even count as friendships at all. That gives people extra incentive to resist giving up their heuristic-based moral judgments.[10]

Of course, numerous serious complications remain.[11] Many more kinds of moral intuitions need to be tested. Much more empirical work needs to be done. Nonetheless, this research project seems promising in psychology.[12]

---

[9] In this way, moral target attributes are even less accessible than non-moral target attributes.

[10] This introduces a kind of partiality into moral intuitions insofar as those moral intuitions depend our personal interests and desires.

[11] Moral heuristics might contain several levels or be used in chains. We might usually follow conscious rules and turn to heuristics, such as the affect heuristic, only when rules run out. Some heuristics might be hardwired by biology, although culture still might affect which heuristics we use.

[12] One promise is to explain adolescents. Adolescents tend to use non-moral heuristics less than adults do, so the view of moral intuitions as heuristics suggests that adolescents would also not have

3. Some Philosophical Implications

We have not, of course, come close to showing that *all* moral intuitions fit the heuristic model. As we said at the start, we have been talking only about a subclass of moral intuitions—intuitions about specific cases. Only a small subclass of that subclass has been tested experimentally. Still, it is worthwhile to ask what would follow if the heuristic model turned out to hold for all moral intuitions. On that assumption, the heuristic model of moral intuitions might have several important philosophical implications.

3.1. *Direct Insight*

First, if moral intuitions result from heuristics, moral intuitionists (cf. Stratton-Lake, 2003) must stop claiming direct insight into moral properties. This claim would be as implausible as claiming direct insight into probability or numbers of seven-letter words, based on how we employ the representativeness and availability heuristics. Heuristics often *seem* like direct insight, but they never really *are* direct insight, because they substitute attributes. If moral judgments are reached through mediating emotions or affect, then they are not reached directly.

Some moral intuitionists might respond that they claim direct insight only *after* reflection (Audi, 2004). However, subjects also reflect when they use non-moral heuristics, like representativeness and availability, to estimate probabilities and numbers of words. Thus the presence of reflection does not show either that no heuristic is employed or that the insight is direct.

3.2. *Reliability*

Second, the view that moral intuitions result from heuristics raises doubts about whether and when we should trust moral intuitions. Just as non-moral heuristics lack reliability in unusual situations, so do moral intuitions, if they are based on moral heuristics. It would be interesting and important (though challenging) to do the empirical work needed to determine which moral intuitions are reliable in which circumstances, just as Gigerenzer and his colleagues are trying to do for non-moral heuristics.

Of course, just as disagreements abound over whether the use of heuristics is rational or not in the non-moral domain (see Gigerenzer & Kahneman),

---

fully-formed moral intuitions of some kinds. This would explain both crazy behavior by adolescents and also moral relativism among adolescents (cf. Nichols, 2004).

similar concerns will arise for moral intuitions. Which specific moral intuitions are products of heuristics? Are heuristic-driven intuitions especially unreliable? If so, in what circumstances? Should the mechanisms by which heuristics exert their effects inform our answers to the previous questions? For instance, if the affect heuristic turns out indeed to be the master heuristic (in place of or in addition to a set of heuristics concerning specific and apparently morally relevant acts, such as lying or killing), should we alter our attitude towards the resultant intuitions? All of these questions can stimulate new philosophical thinking about morality.

3.3. Counter-Examples and Consequentialism

Finally, this account of moral intuitions helps to defend consequentialism and other moral theories against simple counter-examples. Critics often argue that consequentialism can't be accurate, because it implies moral judgments that are counter-intuitive, such as that we are morally permitted to punish an innocent person in the well-known example where this is necessary to stop riots and prevent deaths. With the heuristic model in hand, consequentialists can respond that the target attribute is having the best consequences, and any intuitions to the contrary result from substituting a heuristic attribute.

Of course, consequentialists can't just assert these claims without support. They need to explain how these heuristic attributes are related to the target attribute in order to understand why we evolved with these heuristics rather than with others. But that's not too hard, because the usual heuristic attributes do seem to be good indicators of the best consequences in common circumstances (Baron, 1994). That is why rule-utilitarians can support common moral intuitions (Hooker, 2000).

If moral intuitions reflect normal consequences, and if that is why they evolved, then moral intuitions in unusual circumstances have no more force against consequentialism than folk intuitions about Tom have against probability theory. Consequentialists can go on to admit that moral intuitions are useful and even necessary as a practical guide or decision procedure, as long as the standard or criterion of right remains the target attribute of having the best consequences (Bales, 1971). This nice fit between consequentialism and the heuristic model of moral intuitions does not give any positive support for either, but it does help to defend consequentialism against common objections, and it shows that the heuristic model is relevant to normative issues.

Similar moves are also available for other moral theories, as long as they make moral wrongness inaccessible in practice and can explain why the heuristic attributes are good indicators of moral wrongness. Many moral theories can do that, so the heuristic account of moral intuitions is neutral among those moral theories. The lesson is not about which moral theory is true but, instead, about which method to use in choosing among moral theories. The heuristic model suggests that moral philosophy cannot be done simply by means of counter-examples and accusations that opposing theories are counter-intuitive. Instead, we need to consider how those contrary moral intuitions arose, via which heuristic or set of heuristics. In this and other ways, the heuristic model of moral intuitions has important implications for methodology in moral philosophy.

References

Alicke, M. D. 1992. Culpable Causation. *Journal of Personality and Social Psychology, 63*: 368–78.

Audi, Robert. 2004. *The Good in the Right: A Theory of Intuition and Intrinsic Value.* Princeton, NJ: Princeton University Press.

Bales, R. E. 1971. Act-utilitarianism: account of right-making characteristics or decision-making procedures? *American Philosophical Quarterly*, 8: 257–65.

Baron, J. 1994. Nonconsequentialist Decisions. *Behavioral and Brain Sciences, 17*: 1–10.

Bentham, J. 1978. Offences Against One's Self. *Journal of Homosexuality*, 3 (4): 389–405, and 4 (1): 91–107.

Bentham, J. 1823. *An Introduction to the Principles of Morals and Legislation.* London: Pickering.

Brink, D. 1989. *Moral Realism and the Foundations of Ethics.* Cambridge and New York: Cambridge University Press.

Carlsmith, K. M., Darley, J. M., & Robinson, P. H. 2002. Why do we punish? Deterrence and just deserts as motives for punishment. *Journal of Personality and Social Psychology, 83*: 284–299.

Chaiken, S. 1980. Heuristic versus Systematic Information Processing and the Use of Source versus Message Cues in Persuasion. *Journal of Personality and Social Psychology, 39*: 752–766.

Ciaramelli, E., Muccioli, M., Làdavas, E., & di Pellegrino, G. 2007. Selective deficit in personal moral judgment following damage to ventromedial prefrontal cortex. *Social Cognitive and Affective Neuroscience*, 2 (2): 84–92.

Cushman, F., Young, L., & Hauser, M. 2006. The Role of Conscious Reasoning and Intuition in Moral Judgments: Testing Three Principles of Harm. *Psychological Science, 17*: 1082–1089.

Doris, J. 2002. *Lack of Character: Personality and Moral Behavior.* Cambridge: Cambridge University Press.

Gigerenzer, G. 2008. Moral Intuition = Fast and Frugal Heuristics? In *Moral Psychology, Volume 2: The Cognitive Science of Morality*, W. Sinnott-Armstrong (ed.), pp. 1–26. Cambridge: MIT Press.

Gigerenzer, G., Todd, P., & the ABC Research Group. 1999. *Simple Heuristics that Make us Smart.* New York: Oxford University Press.

Greene, J. D., Lindsell, D., Clarke, A. C., Lowenberg, K., Nystrom, L. E., & Cohen, J. D. 2009. Pushing moral buttons: The interaction between personal force and intention in moral judgment. *Cognition, 111 (3)*: 364–371.

Greene, J. D., Morelli, S. A., Lowenberg, K., Nystrom, L. E., & Cohen, J. D. 2008. Cognitive load selectively interferes with utilitarian moral judgment. *Cognition, 107 (3)*: 1144–1154.

Greene, J. D., Nystrom, L. E., Engell, A. D., Darley, J. M., & Cohen, J. D. 2004. The neural bases of cognitive conflict and control in moral judgment. *Neuron, 44*: 389-400.

Greene, J. D., Sommerville, R. B., Nystrom, L. E., Darley, J. M., and Cohen, J. D. 2001. An fMRI investigation of emotional engagement in moral judgment. *Science, 293*: 2105–2108.

Haidt, J., Koller, S. H., & Dias, M. G. (1993). Affect, culture, and morality, or is it wrong to eat your dog? *Journal of Personality and Social Psychology, 65*: 613–628.

Haidt, J., & Joseph, C. 2004. Intuitive Ethics: How Innately Prepared Intuitions Generate Culturally Variable Virtues. *Daedalus*: 55–66.

Harman, G. 1996. Moral Relativism. In *Moral Relativism and Moral Objectivity*, G. Harman & J. J. Thomson, pp. 1–64. Oxford: Blackwell.

—— 1999. Moral philosophy meets social psychology: Virtue ethics and the fundamental attribution error. *Proceedings of the Aristotelian Society 99*: 315–331.

Hauser, M., Young, L., & Cushman, F. 2008. Reviving Rawls' Linguistic Analogy: Operative Principles and the Causal Structure of Moral Action. In *Moral Psychology, Volume 2: The Cognitive Science of Morality*, W. Sinnott-Armstrong (ed.), pp. 107–143. Cambridge: MIT Press.

Hooker, Brad. 2000. *Ideal Code, Real World: A Rule-Consequentialist Theory of Morality*. New York: Oxford University Press.

Jackson, F. 1998. *From Metaphysics to Ethics: A Defense of Conceptual Analysis*. Oxford: Clarendon Press.

Kahneman, D., & Frederick, S. 2005. A Model of Heuristic Judgment. In *The Cambridge Handbook of Thinking and Reasoning*, K. J. Holyoak & R. G. Morrison (eds.), pp. 267–293. New York: Cambridge University Press.

Kahneman, D., Schkade, D., & Sunstein, C. R. 1998. Shared outrage and erratic rewards: The psychology of punitive damages. *Journal of Risk and Uncertainty, 16*: 49–86.

Kahneman, D., Slovic, P., & Tversky, A. 1982. *Judgement Under Uncertainty: Heuristics and Biases*. Cambridge: Cambridge University Press.

Kass, Leon. 1997. The Wisdom of Repugnance. *The New Republic, 2*, 17–26.

Koenigs, M., Young, L., Adolphs, R., Tranel, D., Cushman, F., Hauser, M., & Damasio, A. 2007. Damage to the prefrontal cortex increases utilitarian moral judgments. *Nature, 446*: 908–911.

Laland, K. 2001. Imitation, Social Learning, and Preparedness as Mechanisms of Bounded Rationality. In *Bounded Rationality: The Adaptive Toolbox*, G. Gigerenzer and R. Selten (eds.), pp. 233–248. Cambridge: MIT Press.

Mendez, M. F., Anderson, E., & Shapira, J. S. 2005. An Investigation of Moral Judgment in Frontotemporal Dementia. *Cognitive Behavioral Neurology, 18* (4): 193–197.

Merritt, M. 2000. Virtue ethics and situationist personality psychology. *Ethical Theory and Moral Practice, 3*: 365–383.

Mikhail, J. 2002. Aspects of a Theory of Moral Cognition: Investigating Intuitive Knowledge of the Prohibition of Intentional Battery and the Principle of Double Effect. Downloadable at http://ssrn.com/abstracts=762385

Nichols, Shaun. 2004. *Sentimental Rules: On the Natural Foundations of Moral Judgment.* New York: Oxford University Press.

Rawls, J. 1971. *A Theory of Justice.* Cambridge, MA: Harvard University Press.

Ross, W. D. 1930. *The Right and the Good.* Oxford: Clarendon Press.

Samuels, R., Stich, S., & Bishop, M. 2002. Ending the Rationality Wars: How to Make Disputes about Human Rationality Disappear. In *Common Sense, Reasoning and Rationality*, R. Elio (ed.), pp. 236–268. New York: Oxford University Press.

Scanlon, T. M. 1999. *What We Owe to Each Other.* Cambridge, MA: Belknap Press.

Schaich Borg, J., Hynes, C., Grafton, S., & Sinnott-Armstrong, W. 2006. Consequences, Action, and Intention as Factors in Moral Judgments: An fMRI Investigation. *Journal of Cognitive Neuroscience* 18 (5): 803–817.

Schnall, S., Haidt, J., Clore, G., & Jordan, A. 2008. Disgust as embodied moral judgment. *Personality and Social Psychology Bulletin* 34: 1096–1109.

Sinnott-Armstrong, W., Mallon, R., McCoy, T., & Hull, J. 2008. Intention, Temporal Order, and Moral Judgments. *Mind & Language* 23 (1): 90–106.

Slovic, P., Finucane, M., Peters, E., & MacGregor, D. G. 2002. The Affect Heuristic. In *Heuristics and Biases: The Psychology of Intuitive Judgment*, T. Gilovich, D. Griffin, & D. Kahneman (eds.), pp. 397–420. New York: Cambridge University Press.

Stratton-Lake, P., (ed.) 2003. *Ethical Intuitionism: Re-evaluations.* New York: Oxford University Press.

Sunstein, Cass. 2005. Moral Heuristics. *Behavioral and Brain Sciences* 28: 531–73.

Valdesolo, P., & DeSteno, D. 2006. Manipulations of Emotional Context Shape Moral Judgments. *Psychological Science* 17 (6): 476–477.

Wheatley, T., & Haidt, J. 2005. Hypnotic disgust makes moral judgments more severe. *Psychological Science* 16: 780–784.

Wilson, E. O. 1998. *Consilience: The Unity of Knowledge.* New York: Knopf.

8

Linguistics and Moral Theory[1]

ERICA ROEDDER AND GILBERT HARMAN

Analogies are often theoretically useful. Important principles of electricity are suggested by an analogy between water current flowing through a pipe and electrical current "flowing" through a wire. A basic theory of sound is suggested by an analogy between waves caused by a stone being dropped into a still lake and "sound waves" caused by a disturbance in air. At the very least, analogies suggest questions and shape the direction of research; at most, analogies may be crucial to explaining and understanding natural phenomena (Holyoak & Thagard, 1995). Of course, principles suggested by such analogies need to be confirmed by relevant evidence. Even where analogies are fruitful, they are only partial. Sound waves and electricity are not wet; electricity does not spill out when a wire is cut.

In this chapter we consider what is suggested by taking seriously an analogy between language and morality. Recently there have been a number of striking claims made about such a linguistic analogy—claims that, if true, have profound implications for longstanding debates in moral philosophy about the innateness of moral capacities, and the existence of moral universals. (For example, the title of Hauser, 2006 is *Moral Minds: How Nature Designed a Universal Sense of Right and Wrong*.) We shall indicate what support pursuit of the linguistic analogy might provide for such claims. Perhaps more importantly, we shall discuss implications the linguistic analogy might have for the methodology and structure of moral theory.

1. Moral Grammar

Rules of morality have sometimes been described as analogous to rules of grammar, with the occasional further suggestion that moral theory may be at least in some respects analogous to linguistic theory.

---

[1] We have benefited from comments on an earlier version of this chapter from members of our moral psychology research group at a workshop in Pittsburgh November 2007 and more recently from detailed comments from Stephen Stich.

Adam Smith appeals to this analogy when he says, "The rules of justice may be compared to the rules of grammar; the rules of the other virtues, to the rules which critics lay down for the attainment of what is sublime and elegant in composition" (Smith, 1817: 281).[2]

More recently, starting in the 1950s (Chomsky, 1957, 1965), a few moral theorists began to see analogies between moral theory and generative linguistic theory. According to John Rawls,

[O]ne may think of moral theory at first (and I stress the provisional nature of this view) as the attempt to describe our moral capacity; or, in the present case, one may regard a theory of justice as describing our sense of justice. . . . A conception of justice characterizes our moral sensibility when the everyday judgments we do make are in accord with its principles. . . . We do not understand our sense of justice until we know in some systematic way covering a wide range of cases what these principles are.

A useful comparison here is with the problem of describing the sense of grammaticalness that we have for the sentences of our native language [here Rawls refers to Chomsky, 1965: 3–9]. In this case the aim is to characterize the ability to recognize well-formed sentences by formulating clearly expressed principles which make the same discriminations as the native speaker. This undertaking is known to require theoretical constructions that far outrun the ad hoc precepts of our explicit grammatical knowledge. A similar situation presumably holds in moral theory. There is no reason to assume that our sense of justice can be adequately characterized by familiar common sense precepts, or derived from the more obvious learning principles. A correct account of moral capacities will certainly involve principles and theoretical constructions which go much beyond the norms and standards cited in everyday life . . .   (Rawls, 1971: sec. 9)

Moreover, the appeal of the linguistic analogy has not been limited to philosophers in the Western "analytic tradition." Pope Benedict XVI uses a similar analogy in his message for the 2007 World Day of Peace:

The transcendent "grammar," that is to say the body of rules for individual action and the reciprocal relationships of persons in accordance with justice and solidarity, is inscribed on human consciences, in which the wise plan of God is reflected. As I recently had occasion to reaffirm: "we believe that at the beginning of everything is the eternal word, reason and not unreason." Peace is thus also a task demanding of everyone a personal response consistent with God's plan. The criterion inspiring this response can only be respect for the "grammar" written on human hearts by the divine creator.   (Benedict, 2006)[3]

The authors above are explicitly concerned with analogies between principles of grammar and principles of justice. In addition, other authors invoke an analogy between rules of grammar and more general moral principles.

---

[2] We are indebted here to Richard Holton.   [3] Here we are indebted to Liberman (2006).

For instance, three years before Rawls (1971), Nozick (1968) offered an account of "moral complications and moral structures" in general, not limited to principles of justice. Nozick (1997: 4–5) reports that one "model [for the 1968 paper] was Noam Chomsky's *Syntactic Structures*, and I meant 'Moral Complications' to begin to uncover the structure underlying our moral judgments." Nozick (1968) mentions that "one needs a distinction similar to that which linguists make between linguistic competence and linguistic performance," referring to Chomsky (1965), a distinction we discuss below.

As another example, Kamm (2007) describes the methodology she uses in that book and in Kamm (1992, 1993, 1996) as follows:

[P]eople who have responses to cases are a natural source of data from which we can isolate the reasons and principles underlying their responses. The idea [is] that the responses come from and reveal some underlying psychologically real structure, a structure that was always (unconsciously) part of the thought processes of some people. Such people embody the reasoning and principles (which may be thought of as an internal program) that generates these responses. . . . (Unlike the deep structure of the grammar of a language, at least one level of the deep structure of moral intuitions about cases seems to be accessible upon reflection by those who have intuitive judgements . . .) If the same "deep structure" is present in all persons—and there is growing psychological evidence that this is true (as in the work of Professor Marc Hauser)—this would be another reason why considering the intuitive judgements of one person would be sufficient, for each person would give the same response. (Kamm, 2007: 8)

We return below to the issue whether the same moral deep structure is present in all persons. At the moment we are content to point to Kamm's acceptance of an analogy between the grammar of a language and an individual's moral principles.

Finally, Mikhail (2000, 2007) provides an account of "universal moral grammar," based on legal categories. We eventually return to the idea of a *universal* moral grammar. But we want first to consider what proposals about "moral grammar" are suggested by the analogy with the grammar of a language, appealing to developments in contemporary linguistics starting with Chomsky (1957, 1965).

I-grammar

The primary object of study of linguistics so conceived is not language in the ordinary sense in which English, German, Mohawk, and Chinese are languages. Any ordinary language in this sense has different dialects that blend into one another in ways that do not correspond to national or geographical boundaries. There is a well-known saying that "a language (in the ordinary sense) is a dialect with an army and a navy." What counts as a dialect of French rather than Flemish is a social or political issue, not an issue in the science of language. It may be that any two speakers have at least somewhat different dialects, with at least somewhat different vocabularies. Chomsky (2000) and other linguists (e.g. Freidin, 1992; Isac and Reiss, 2008) are concerned with language as a property of a particular person, assumed to be abstractly specifiable by an internal grammar, or I-grammar.

This is one of a number of significant idealizations or abstractions linguistics makes in the course of arriving at a theoretically useful account of an otherwise unwieldy phenomenon. Others include the distinction, mentioned below, between "competence" and "performance" and a more controversial distinction some linguists make between "core" and other aspects of grammar.

In pursuing possible analogies between linguistics and moral theory, we might consider whether similar idealizations or abstractions are theoretically useful to moral theory. Should moral theory be in the first instance concerned with an individual's I-morality—that *particular* person's moral standards? This might be captured by some sort of (possibly unconscious) abstract representation, an I-moral-grammar. I-morality in this sense would be distinguished from the principles or conventions of a social group; it would also be distinguished from the correct moral principles, if there are any.

"Generative" Grammar

A generative grammar of a language (a generative I-grammar) would fully and explicitly characterize the relevant linguistic properties of expressions of the language (Chomsky, 1965; Freidin, 1992). It is very important to recognize that the word "generative" is here used as a technical term. There is no implication that the principles of a generative grammar are followed by speakers in generating (in a more ordinary sense) what they say. To suppose that there is a passive "transformation"—a function that associates the structure underlying an active sentence like *Bill gave Mabel a book* with the structure underlying a passive sentence like *Mabel was given a book by Bill*—is not necessarily to suppose that a speaker first forms the active structure and then, by some causal process, converts it into the passive structure.

A generative grammar of a particular person's language would specify the linguistic *structure* of expressions of that language, indicating the nouns, verbs, adjectives, prepositions, etc., as well as the phrases of which these are the "heads," as when a noun is the head of a noun phrase and a preposition the head of a prepositional phrase. A generative grammar might specify important aspects of the meanings of expressions, depending on how the expressions are structured and possibly indicating the scope of quantifiers and other such operators. The grammar would also specify aspects of the pronunciation of expressions (for spoken languages—something similar would be true of the grammar of a sign language). So, a generative grammar would relate pronunciations of expressions to possible interpretations, in this way indicating certain sound–meaning (phonetic–semantic) relationships.

An analogous moral grammar would attempt explicitly to characterize an individual's moral standards. Just as a grammar specifies the structure of a well-formed linguistic sentence by using a specialized linguistic vocabulary, an I-moral grammar might specify the structure of impermissible actions, using a specialized moral vocabulary.[4] That is, just as English grammar might specify how a noun phrase and verb phrase combine to form a grammatical sentence, an I-moral grammar might specify that that certain actions, in virtue of their structure, are impermissible, e.g. intentional harm directed towards an innocent person without reason. In this way, an I-moral grammar might specify certain action-assessment relationships—or, indeed, character-assessment or situation-assessment relationships. Thus the rules of an I-moral-grammar would generate a set of impermissible actions, just as a linguistic grammar generates a set of grammatical sentences. An I-moral grammar would have to specify the relevant structures of the objects of moral assessment (e.g. acts, character traits, situations, etc.) using a specialized moral vocabulary, perhaps including terms like ought, obligation, duty, justice, fairness, right, wrong, responsibility, excuse, justification, etc.

Relatedly, principles of generative grammar specify how the structure of a sentence might be transformed, grammatically, into another. For instance, the structure underlying a declarative sentence *The book is on the chair* is transformable into the structure underlying a question, *What is on the chair?* Characterized abstractly, such principles allow the theoretician to move from the known grammaticality of one sentence structure to the grammaticality of a transformed sentence structure. Similarly, there might be found certain transformative principles within I-morality; we suggest an example of such a principle below.

Given such a picture, it may be tempting to assume certain causal structures. However, this would be a mistake. For instance, let us assume that the moral grammar specifies action-assessment relationships. If this is right, one might

---

[4] Mikhail (2000; see also 2007) suggests that relevant aspects of structure may be arrived at through using Goldman's (1970) theory of action and legal concepts of battery, end, means, side effect, intention, etc. Abstractly considered, the resulting structures are somewhat similar to the phrase structures that figure in linguistic theory.

assume the following causal structure: first, some non-moral brain system assigns a structural description of the action. Second, the structural description is provided as input to the moral system, and the moral system generates a moral assessment. As in the linguistic case, however, there is no guarantee that the brain's causal pathway parallels that of the grammatical principles. While the existence of such a moral grammar guarantees that there is, in a mathematical sense, a mapping of action to assessments, the brain's method of processing information may be quite different. (Cf. Marr's [1982] distinction between computational and algorithmic descriptions of mental processing.)

This point about the non-causal character of moral grammars is important for at least two reasons, which we discuss immediately below. The first reason is a theoretical point about recursive embedding; the second reason draws on some recent empirical studies.

Recursive Embedding

The rules of a generative grammar specify recursive embedding of grammatical structures. For example, a larger sentence can contain a smaller sentence within it, which can contain another even smaller sentence, and so on without limit:

> Jack told Betty that Sally believes that Albert no longer thinks Arnold wants to leave Mabel.

Similarly, the rules of grammar imply that a noun phrase can contain a noun phrase within it, which can contain another noun phrase, and so on:

> the man next to the girl near the door with the broken hinge.

So, a particular generative grammar might imply rules that could be represented as follows:

$$S \Rightarrow NP + (V + S)$$
$$NP \Rightarrow Art + N + (P + NP)$$

This point about linguistic recursive embedding is a point about grammatical rules. It is not just that a sentence can occur within a larger sentence or a noun phrase within a larger noun phrase. This sort of "recursion" is common enough: many artifacts can contain smaller things of the same kind, e.g. a large raft can be made of smaller rafts which have been tied together.[5] Thus there is a sense in which recursion is not particularly uncommon. However, there is a

---

[5] We thank Jesse Prinz for bringing this point to our attention and John Doris for the specific example.

substantial difference between recursion found in linguistic grammars and this sort of everyday "recursion." In the case of linguistics, recursion is an explicit feature of rules that have proved theoretically useful. In contrast, recursion is not explicitly implied by theoretically fruitful rules either for artifacts in general, or for rafts in particular. Were we to construct rules to answer the question, "What objects count as rafts?" the answer would presumably focus on how the object functions (it bears weight as it floats on water), its similarity to certain prototypes, etc. without making use of recursion.

The analogy between morality and language suggests that a "generative moral grammar" might also imply recursive embedding. It might, for example, imply that *it is wrong to encourage someone to do something that is wrong*, which is recursive in the sense that it implies that it is wrong to encourage someone to encourage someone to do something that is wrong, etc. Similarly, a generative moral grammar might imply that it is wrong to promise to do something that it would be wrong to do.[6]

There are two points to be made about recursive embedding. First, true recursion—as opposed to the natural embedding that occurs with rafts—is an important feature of grammatical rules. This recursive character allows a relatively small number of rules to generate a potentially infinite set of sentences. Recursion is an important, and perhaps distinctive, feature of generative grammars; thus if moral judgments can only be modeled using a recursive theory, that is a point in favor of the linguistic analogy.

Second, recursive embedding emphasizes that, in a generative I-moral grammar, the normative evaluation assigned to structural descriptions can depend on normative evaluations embedded within those structural descriptions. The point does not yet by itself rule out a processing model that first constructs nonnormative action and situation descriptions in terms of causes and effects, ends and means, distinguishing what is done intentionally or not, etc., and then, when that is done, adds normative labels to various parts of the structure, perhaps starting with smaller parts, and then labeling larger parts to handle the recursive aspects of the I-moral grammar. But such a processing model faces the further worry that seemingly nonnormative aspects of relevant descriptive structure themselves seem to depend on normative considerations.

Structural Dependence on Normative Assessments

There is considerable evidence (summarized in Knobe, 2008) that whether people accept certain seemingly descriptive claims can depend on whether

---

[6] Such principles are famously problematic for expressivist theories that try to explain the meaning of *wrong* simply by saying the word is used to express disapproval (Geach, 1965).

they accept certain normative claims about side effects of actions. For example, suppose Tom increases his profits by doing something that, as a side effect, either (a) harms or (b) helps the environment, where Tom does not care either way about the effect on the environment. People who think that it is good to help the environment and bad to harm it tend to say (a) that in so acting Tom intentionally harmed the environment but will tend not to say (b) that in so acting Tom intentionally helped the environment (Knobe, 2003; for further discussion, see Knobe & Doris, Chapter 10 in this volume).

They also tend to say (a) that Tom increased profits *by* harming the environment but tend not to say (b) that he increased profits *by* helping the environment. They tend to say (a) that Tom harmed the environment *in order to* increase profits but tend not to say (b) that he helped the environment *in order to* increase profits (Knobe, 2007). And they are more inclined to say (a) that the harming of the environment *was the same thing* as the implementing of the policy than they are to say (b) that the helping of the environment *was the same thing* as the implementing of the policy (Ulatowski, 2008).

Furthermore, sometimes whether one will judge that a particular person *caused* a certain result can depend on whether one judges that the person is morally at fault for doing what he or she did (Mackie, 1955; Dray, 1957; Alicke, 1992; Thomson, 2003). For example, whether one judges that Tom's omitting to water the plants caused their death can depend in part on whether one thinks Tom was obligated to water the plants.

So, it seems that relevant structural descriptions of the situations or actions must themselves sometimes involve normative assessments.

Categorization versus Grammar

Many moral judgments offer a moral categorization of an action, person, or situation. So, instead of drawing an analogy between moral theory and generative grammar, some theorists (e.g. Stich, 1993) propose instead to draw an analogy between moral theory and psychological theories of categorization, especially theories in which an instance to be categorized is compared with a number of standard prototypes (or exemplars) of various categories and is then assigned the category of the prototype to which it is most similar (theories of this sort are described in section 6 in Harman, Mason, & Sinnott-Armstrong, Chapter 6, this volume).

We can offer two preliminary comments on the categorization proposal: first, it is not clear that a categorization approach competes with a moral grammar approach. The two approaches may be apples and oranges. Categorization is a mental process, i.e. the term refers to a form of cognitive processing. In contrast, the proposal that there is a mental grammar is not, first and foremost, about mental processes at all. Rather, it is a proposal about the structures of the contents of moral assessments, just as a linguistic grammar is a proposal about the structures of linguistic expressions. It might both be true that there is a moral grammar, and that we make moral judgments by applying certain prototypes. This might be the case if, for instance, all of a person's "murder" prototypes shared certain basic features, e.g. intentional harm of an innocent.

Second, modern theories of concepts and categorization often emphasize the multi-faceted nature of concepts: they are not just prototypes; they also embedded in theories (Murphy, 2004; Machery, 2009). Prototypes and exemplars alone seem insufficient to explain certain features of categorization. If moral concepts also have a theoretical component, as seems likely to be demonstrated empirically, then that would leave the door open to a moral grammar approach as part of a theory of mental processing.

"Competence–Performance Distinction"

In developing a theory of linguistic grammar, Chomsky (1965) distinguishes between "competence" and "performance"—where these are technical terms that are not used in their ordinary senses. By "competence" Chomsky means an individual's internalized grammar. He uses the term "performance" to refer to all other factors that may affect the use of language. In Chomsky's framework, an individual's linguistic intuitions may or may not reflect the individual's competence, in Chomsky's sense.

For example, compare the following sentences:

This is the cheese that the mouse that the cat that the dog that the man owns bothered chased ate.

This is the man that owns the dog that bothered the cat that chased the mouse that ate the cheese.

Intuitively, the first sentence is hard to understand—deviant in some way—while the second is much easier to understand. The relative deviance of the first sentence appears to be the result of "center embedding." When this center embedding is made explicit, it can appear that the semantic content of the two sentences is similar:

This is the cheese that the mouse ate.
This is the cheese that the mouse that the cat chased ate.
This is the cheese that the mouse that the cat [that the dog bothered] chased ate.
This is the cheese that the mouse that the cat [that the dog (that the man owns)] bothered chased ate.

The intuitive deviance of the first sentence may fail to reflect something about one's linguistic competence in the sense of an internalized grammar. It may instead be due, for example, to limitations of one's parsing strategies, in which case it may be purely the result of performance limitations. The sentence may fit one's I-grammar, but performance factors affect one's ability to comprehend the sentence as fully grammatical.

The linguistic analogy suggests that it might be fruitful to suppose that there is a distinction between moral competence and performance in something like Chomsky's technical sense of the terms "competence" and "performance." As in the linguistic case, we might suppose that other considerations beyond one's assumed I-morality affect moral intuitions. In addition to memory and other processing limitations, moral intuitions might be affected by "heuristics and biases" (Gilovich, Griffin, & Kahneman, 2002; see Sinnott-Armstrong et al., Chapter 7 in this volume; also Sunstein, 2004; Horowitz, 1998; Doris & Stich, 2005; Sinnott-Armstrong, 2008), prejudices, emotional responses, self-interest, etc.[7] For example, utilitarians such as Greene (2008) have argued that intuitions that appear to conflict with utilitarianism are due to morally irrelevant emotional factors (see also Baron, 1993).

Of course, in most cases, performance factors are not distorting; they are an integral part of proper functioning. One needs an internal parsing strategy in order to comprehend what others say, so that strategy is not necessarily distorting, as it may be in the above example. Similarly, *pace* Greene, emotions like disgust may play an important role in getting one to appreciate the moral character of a situation—even though, in other cases, they can lead one astray. Someone with full moral "competence" (that is, with an internalized moral grammar) who is unable to experience relevant emotions may have trouble with moral evaluations in the same way that someone with full linguistic "competence" but with a damaged parser might be unable to understand other speakers. Here we have in mind work on so-called "psychopaths" or other brain-damaged patients who do not exhibit normal emotive responses. Research has shown that such individuals make abnormal moral judgments (Blair, 1995, 1997; Koenigs et al., 2007). Some of these patients might possess moral "competence" (an internalized moral grammar) but lack certain critical performance capabilities. Of course, whether or not this is a useful way to understand such patients depends on future empirical work. We offer this only as an example of how the distinction between performance and competence might be put into play.

---

[7] Of course, there is an ongoing debate whether such "biases" should or should not be thought of as bad reasoning. See, for instance, Gigerenzer (2007).

More generally, our point is that in moral theory, as in linguistics, we can consider whether it makes sense to postulate a distinction between an individual's internal moral grammar or moral "competence" in contrast with various other factors that determine the person's intuitions and actions. For linguistics, the corresponding assumption has been theoretically fruitful and illuminating. With respect to moral theory, the assumption amounts to assuming that there is a distinctive moral competence or I-moral-grammar. A contrary view is that one's morality is determined entirely by performance factors, so that for example one's emotional responses are actually constitutive of one's moral view rather than merely enabling or distorting performance factors.

It may be that a distinction between competence and performance applies only to certain parts of morality and not other parts. We come back to this possibility below in considering whether to distinguish aspects of morality we share with other animals and aspects that are distinctively human.

Summary of Suggested Issues about Generative Moral Grammar

We have so far discussed one idea from linguistics that might be relevant to the theory of morality, namely, generative grammar—an explicit specification of the grammatical properties of expressions of a language. The conception of grammar as generative or explicit in this way has proved quite productive for the study of language and some moral theorists try to see an analogous conception of moral grammar that might be productive for the study of morality.

Among the issues such an analogy raises for moral theory are (1) whether the useful unit of analysis for moral theory is an individual's I-grammar, in contrast, for example, with the moral conventions of a group; (2) whether and how such a moral grammar might associate structural descriptions of actions, situations, etc. with normative assessments; (3) whether and how the rules of such a moral grammar might involve recursive embedding of normative assessments; and (4) whether it is useful to distinguish moral "competence" from moral "performance," using these terms in the technical senses employed in linguistic theory.

2. Universal Morality

We now turn to a related issue about linguistic and moral universals. Features of language are universal if they occur in all natural human languages that children can acquire as first languages. Universal grammar is concerned in part with such linguistic universals and also with limits on ways in which natural human languages can differ. To what extent might it be fruitful to develop an analogous universal moral theory which would seek to describe common features of any moralities children can acquire as first moralities—along with an account of how moralities can differ?

Some people believe that various familiar moral principles are universal in the sense that they are cross-culturally accepted: "You should not steal." "It is wrong to murder or harm others." "You should not tell lies." "You should do your part in useful group activities." "You should help those worse off than yourself." "You should not treat others as you would not want to be treated." "You should do unto others what you would want them to do unto you."

Instead of directly discussing whether such *familiar principles* are universally accepted, we shall focus on two other sorts of universality suggested by the analogy with linguistics. (That is, we shall not discuss whether everyone, cross-culturally, believes that it is wrong to murder; instead, we shall consider universality of the sort that linguists find.) The first sort of universality is the existence of universal *constraints* on possible I-moral grammars; the second is the notion of universal *parameters* (with local variance in parameter settings).

Constraints on Linguistic Grammars

Universal linguistic grammar is concerned in part with constraints on the rules of particular I-grammars. Such grammars might contain two sorts of rules—*phrase structure* rules for forming phrases out of their parts and *transformations* or *movement* rules for reorganizing these parts (Chomsky, 1957, 1965; Freidin, 1992; van Riemsdijk & Williams, 1986).

For example, an adjective like *green* can combine or "merge" with a noun like *apple* to form a noun phrase *green apple*; a determiner like *a* or *the* can merge with a noun phrase to form a determiner phrase like *a green apple*; a preposition like *from* can merge with a determiner phrase to form a prepositional phrase like *from a green apple*; and so on. These are instances of phrase structure rules. Universal grammar places constraints on the phrase structure rules for a given I-language. One such constraint implies that, if there are prepositions and so prepositional phrases in which prepositions appear before their objects, then the same must be true of verb phrases and noun phrases: verbs must appear before their objects and nouns before their objects. On the other hand, if instead of prepositions there are postpositions and postpositional phrases in which postpositions appear after their objects, then the same must be true of verb phrases and noun phrases: verbs and nouns must appear after their objects.

Transformations allow items in phrase structures to be rearranged. For example, a transformation (*wh*-movement) might allow the derivation of the structure underlying a relative clause like (2) from something like the structure underlying (1).

(1) *Bob gave which to Bill.*
(2) *which Bob gave to Bill.*

A different transformation (topicalization) might allow the derivation of the structure underlying (4) from something like the structure underlying (3).

(3) *Bob gave a book to Bill.*
(4) *A book, Bob gave to Bill.*

Chomsky (1964) observed that there must be constraints of various sorts on such transformations. He proposed an "*A* over *A*" constraint that would rule out moving an item of a given type *A* from a larger phrase of type *A*. That turned out to be overly simple and Ross (1967) proposed to replace it with a number of more specific "island constraints," where "islands" are structures that items cannot be moved out of. Ross's constraints include a "coordinate structure constraint" and a "complex *NP* constraint," among others; here we describe only his coordinate structure constraint.

Coordinate structures are special cases of the *A* over *A* principle in which an item of type *A* immediately contains two or more coordinate items of type *A*, as in the noun phrase: *a man, a woman, and a child*; or the verb phrase: *kissed Jack or hugged Harry*. These larger phrases themselves immediately contain smaller coordinate phrases of the same type.

Ross's coordinate structure constraint prevents transformations from moving any coordinate item out of a coordinate structure and also prevents transformations from moving anything contained in a coordinate item out of that item. Suppose, for example, there is a transformation of topicalization that starts with (5) and moves *a book* to the front to yield (6):

(5) *Bob gave a book to Bill.*
(6) *A book, Bob gave to Bill.*

Ross's constraint would prevent topicalization from moving *a book* from a position in a coordinate structure like (7) to yield (8).

(7) *Bob gave a record and a book to Bill.*
(8) * *A book, Bob gave a record and to Bill.*

Observe that it is unclear how a coordinate structure constraint of this sort could be learned by children either from explicit instruction or by trial and error. No one had heard about this constraint before Ross (1967), so no one could have told children about it before that time. Furthermore, children never seem to make errors that consist in violating the constraint, so they don't seem to acquire it by trial-and-error learning.

One way to explain the above facts about acquisition is to postulate that children are predisposed towards certain linguistic constraints. If there is such a predisposition, however, it would be present in all normally developing children.

Of course, it is possible to invent and use an artificial language that is not subject to the constraint. But such a language might not be easily acquired as a first language by children. We might expect them to acquire a variant that is subject to the constraint. Furthermore, we might expect that children not exposed to human language (e.g. because they were deaf) who developed a language among themselves (presumably a sign language) would develop a language that was subject to the constraint. There is evidence that this expectation is correct. Padden (1988) claims that coordinate clauses in American Sign Language (ASL) adhere to the coordinate structure constraint.

Constraints on Moralities?

A number of moral philosophers (Foot, 1978; Quinn, 1993) have suggested that ordinary moral intuitions obey certain non-obvious rules. For instance, it may be that moral intuitions reflect some version of the Principle of Double Effect. Here is one version of that principle:

> *Double Effect:* It is worse knowingly to harm one person X in saving another Y when the harm to X is intended as part of one's means to saving Y as opposed to when the harm to X is merely a foreseen unintended side-effect of one's attempt to save Y.

For another example, Thomson (1978) suggests that some ordinary moral intuitions might reflect a principle of the following sort:

> *Deflection:* It is better to save a person X by deflecting a harmful process onto another person Y than by originating a process that harms Y.

As with Ross's coordinate structure constraint, these principles are not generally recognized and it is therefore unlikely that they are explicitly taught to children. If children do acquire moralities containing such principles, it would seem that they must be somehow predisposed to do so. If so, we might expect such principles to be found in all moralities that children naturally acquire.[8]

As in the linguistic case, even if there are such constraints, it may be possible to construct more or less artificial moral systems not subject to them—utilitarian moralities, for example. But we might then expect that children of utilitarians would not easily and naturally acquire their parents' morality but would acquire a version subject to those constraints. John Stuart Mill (1859, 1863, 1873) might be an example. His version of utilitarianism appears to incorporate various principles that do not fit with the version taught him by his father, James Mill (1828). In particular, John Stuart Mill's views about the importance of personal creativity, self-development, and personal liberty led him to adopt a distinction between higher and lower qualities of pleasure that conflicts with the purely quantitative conception of amount of pleasure accepted by Bentham and James Mill.

Linguistic Principles and Parameters

We now turn to a discussion of linguistic principles and parameters and possible analogies for moral theory.

Baker (2001) begins a highly readable account of current linguistic theory with the story of eleven Navajo Code Talkers. During World War II, Allied forces in the Pacific were in difficulty because Japanese cryptographers were able to decode all their messages. The US Marine Corps solved the problem by using the Code Talkers to transmit and receive military communications in Navajo. Japanese cryptographers were unable to "decode" these messages.

Baker notes that this illustrates two important points about languages. On the one hand, Navajo is sufficiently different from English and Japanese that skilled cryptographers were unable to decode the Navajo messages. On the other hand, Navajo is sufficiently similar to English that the Code Talkers could immediately translate messages from English into Navajo and from Navajo back into English. How can we account for both the similarities and the differences? Indeed, how can we account for the fact that a child exposed to a language when young will easily acquire that language, when the best cryptographers are unable to make head or tail of it?

Part of the answer why a child can so easily learn a language may be that the child is somehow prepared to acquire a language whose syntax is largely determined by the setting of a small number of parameters—a parameter that

---

[8] The linguistic analogy suggests that this remark is too strong. As we shall explain, a principles and parameters approach of the sort we are about to discuss allows for other possibilities.

indicates whether a sentence must have a subject as in English, or not as in Italian; a parameter that indicates whether the head of a phrase precedes its complements, as in English, or follows, as in Japanese; and so on. Baker suggests that it may be possible to give something like a structured periodical table of languages, much as there is a structured periodical table of chemical elements. (Hence his title, *The Atoms of Language*.)

A child picks up language from its interactions with others; there is no need for explicit teaching. According to the principles and parameters theory, the child uses its limited experience to set a relatively small number of parameters and acquire the "core" syntax of a language. Other "non-core" aspects of syntax, perhaps involving stylistic variation, are learned as exceptions.

Universal grammar includes an account of principles and parameters. To repeat a point mentioned above in connection with universal constraints on rules, it is possible to devise and use a language that is not in accord with the principles and parameters of universal grammar, and people can learn to use that language. But children will not naturally acquire that language in the way they acquire languages that are in accord with universal grammar.

Another aspect of the principles and parameters universal grammar approach in linguistics is that a theorist's conception of the generative grammar of a given language can be affected by considerations involving other languages and ease of language acquisition. The task of the child learner is easier to the extent that as much as possible of grammar is part of universal grammar and so is built into the child's innate language faculty. So, for example, instead of detailed rules for noun phrases, verb phrases, adjective phrases, and prepositional or postpositional phrases, the basic theory of phrase structure might become part of universal grammar, perhaps with a single phrase structure rule (*merge* X with something to form a phrase), so that the grammar of a particular language like English would be limited to such matters as whether the head of a phrase (noun, verb, adjective, preposition or postposition) comes before or after its complement. The grammar of a particular language like English might contain no special rearrangement or transformational rules; instead there might be a single rule of universal grammar (*move* X somewhere) that says something can be moved anywhere, subject to universal constraints (Chomsky, 1981; van Riemsdijk & Williams, 1986).

One possible parameter might be whether or not the grammar allows such movement or rearrangement. At least one currently existing language appears not to allow this, the Amazonian Pirahã (Everett, 2005). Bolender (2007) argues that all or most languages existing more than 40,000 years ago would probably not have allowed such movement.

The linguistic analogy suggests considering whether it is possible to develop a universal theory of *morality* involving relevant principles and parameters.

How Moralities Differ: Principles and Parameters?

Moralities differ about abortion and infanticide, about euthanasia, about slavery, about the moral status of women, about the importance of chastity in women and in men, about caste systems, about cannibalism, about eating meat, about how many wives a man can have at the same time, about the relative importance of equality versus liberty, the individual versus the group, about the extent to which one is morally required to help others, about duties to those outside one or another protected group, about the importance of religion (and which religion is important), about the importance of etiquette (and which standards of etiquette), about the relative importance of personal virtues, and so on.

What are the prospects of a principles and parameters approach to explaining these and other moral differences? Perhaps all moralities accept principles of the form: avoid harm to members of group G, share your resources with members of group F, etc., where G and F are parameters that vary from one morality to another. However, Prinz (2008) points out that such parameters would differ from those envisioned in linguistics by having many possible values, whereas the parameters in linguistics have a small number of values, typically two.

Dworkin (1993) argues that all intuitive moralities take human life to have what he calls a "sacred value" that increases during pregnancy and in childhood, reaching a maximum at the beginning of adulthood, and slowly declining thereafter, so that the death of 20-year-old person is worse ("more tragic") than the death of an infant or someone who has reached old age. However, according to Dworkin, individual moralities differ concerning whether an early embryo or fetus has significant sacred value. Dworkin argues that this difference is what lies behind ordinary (as opposed to theoretical) disagreements about abortion. Perhaps there are different settings of a "sacred value" parameter. In this case there might be only two relevant settings, indicating whether there is significant sacred value in the embryo or fetus immediately after conception.

A somewhat different appeal to parameters can perhaps be found in the work of certain anthropologists who see a small number of ways of organizing societies, with differences in which ways organize which aspects. Fiske (1991, 1992) distinguishes four general types of social organization: communal sharing, authority ranking, equality matching, and market pricing. Shweder et al. (1997) distinguish the "big three" of morality: autonomy, community, and divinity. In these cases, the relevant "parameters" might determine which models fit which aspects of organization in a given society.

However, we shall need to have more explicit generative accounts of a variety of moralities before being able to think clearly about moral principles and parameters.

Does Morality have to be Taught?

Acquisition of language does not require explicit instruction. Children pick it up from the locals even if parents do not know the local language. The linguistic analogy suggests we consider whether morality is like that.

How does a child acquire an I-morality? Does the child pick up morality from others in something like the way in which language is picked up? Does morality have to be taught? Can it be taught?

Perhaps all normal children pick up the local morality much as they pick up the local dialect, whether or not they receive explicit instruction in right and wrong. Children with certain brain defects might have trouble acquiring morality, just as children with certain other brain defects have trouble acquiring language.

Prinz (2008) suggests that moral conventions can be picked up in the way other conventions are, with no need for moral universals, principles and parameters, and other aspects of moral grammar. Similar suggestions were raised as objections against universal grammar in linguistics in the 1960s (e.g. Harman, 1967, later retracted in Harman, 1973). But today universal grammar is a central part of contemporary linguistics (Baker, 2001).

Core Morality?

As mentioned above, some linguists distinguish "core" aspects of grammar from other "peripheral" aspects. In their view, the "core" grammar of an I-language is constituted by those aspects of grammar acquired just by setting parameters. Peripheral aspects of the I-language are special language-specific rules and exceptions that are acquired in other ways. Examples might include irregular verbs and special "constructions" as in the sentence *John sneezed the tissue across the table*, where the normally intransitive verb *sneeze* is used in a special way. However, the distinction between core and peripheral aspects of grammar is controversial, with some linguists (Newmeyer, 2005) treating it as a matter of degree and others rejecting it altogether (Culicover and Jackendoff, 2005; Goldberg, 1995).

The linguistic analogy suggests there might be a similar controversy within moral theory about the usefulness of a distinction between core and peripheral aspects of morality, where the core aspects are universal or are anyway acquired via parameter setting and other aspects are acquired in other ways. For example, it might be that people explicitly accept certain moral principles on the basis of authority, much as they might accept certain grammatical principles on the basis of authority. Where some people accept, purely on the basis of authority, that it is ungrammatical to end an English sentence with a preposition, others might accept, purely on the basis of authority, that euthanasia is always wrong even to prevent prolonged terrible suffering when someone is dying. This is just an example; we do not know whether a distinction between core and peripheral moral principles will prove to be theoretically useful in thinking about morality.

Humans and Other Animals

Certain aspects of language are similar to aspects of communication systems in other animals—the use of certain sounds and gestures, for example. Other aspects are particular to human language, arguably the existence of recursive embedding rules of grammar of the sort discussed above. An analogy between language and morality suggests that it might be useful to consider what aspects of morality are shared with animals and what aspects are specific to human moralities.

Recall Fiske's four models of social relations: communal sharing, authority ranking, equality ranking, and market pricing. Bolender (2003) notes that the first three of these models, or something like them, can be found among non-human social animals. Furthermore, only two of Fiske's models, communal sharing and egalitarian equality matching, seem to have existed in most groups of hunter-gatherers, a mode of life "which represents over ninety-nine percent of human existence" (Bolender, 2003: 242). Bolender offers "evidence that humans do not need hierarchy in groups of 150 or less" (245) so that this form of social relation "was little used before the advent of plowing . . . [which] forced people to allocate meager resources in large groups" (245). Similarly, there was no previous need for market pricing.

Some questions arise here. Are the moralities of humans who use only these two models (communal sharing and egalitarian equality matching) significantly different from the moralities of social animals who use these models? Do such humans have moralities with anything like the recursive properties mentioned above, so that they accept such principles as that it is wrong to encourage someone to do something that it is wrong to do? (Do non-human animals accept such principles?)

One way to test speculation in this area might be to look at the morality of the Pirahã mentioned above, a small group of people with limited contact with others until recently. The Pirahã have a very limited sense of absent items; their language does not appear to use any sort of quantification or other constructions that involve variable binding operators (Everett, 2005; Bolender, 2003, 2007). Presumably they cannot even express in their language the principle that it is wrong to encourage someone to do what is wrong. A Pirahã infant who was removed from that culture and brought up by adoptive parents in New Jersey would acquire normal human language, an ability to use quantification, and similar moral principles to those accepted by others in New Jersey. On the other hand, nothing similar is true of a non-human social animal.

3. Conclusion

In this chapter, we have described various issues suggested by the analogy between morality and linguistics. In the first part of the chapter, we discussed what might be involved in a generative "moral grammar." In the second part we discussed what might be involved in a *universal* moral grammar that parallels universal linguistic grammar.

We believe that the issues suggested by such analogies are worth pursuing. In particular, we think that looking at the developed science of linguistics suggests new sorts of research that might be useful in thinking about the complicated structure of morality. First, if moral theory is modeled on linguistics, its primary focus would be on an individual's I-morality. Second, it may be useful to distinguish performance and competence. Third, as in linguistics, moral theory may benefit by distinguishing between the principles characterizing a moral grammar and the algorithms actually used in the mental production of grammatical sentences. Fourth, the linguistic analogy suggests ways to think systematically about how moralities differ from each other and whether there are moral universals. Finally, the analogy frames fruitful questions regarding innateness of morality, the existence of a core morality, and the comparison of human and animal morality.

In summary, linguistics has successfully developed into a mature science of human language. In considering the linguistic analogy, then, we have been exploring one possible way to develop a mature science of human morality.

References

Alicke, M. D. (1992). "Culpable Causation," *Journal of Personality and Social Psychology* 63: 368–378.

Benedict XVI, Pope (2006). "The Human Person, the Heart of Peace," Vatican City. Available online at <http://www.catholic.org/international/international_story.php?id=22342>.

Baker, M. C. (2001). *The Atoms of Language: The Mind's Hidden Rules of Grammar*. New York: Basic Books.

Baron, J. (1993). "Heuristics and biases in equity judgments: a utilitarian approach." In B. A. Mellers and J. Baron (eds.), *Psychological Perspectives on Justice: Theory and Applications*. New York: Cambridge University Press, 109–137.

Blair, Robert James (1995). "A Cognitive Developmental Approach to Morality: Investigating the Psychopath," *Cognition* 57: 1–29.

——(1997). "Moral Reasoning and the Child with Psychopathic Tendencies," *Personality and Individual Differences* 26: 731–739.

Bolender, J. (2003). "The Genealogy of the Moral Modules," *Minds and Machines* 13: 233–255.

——(2007). "Prehistoric Cognition by Description: A Russellian Approach to the Upper Paleolithic," *Biology and Philosophy* 22: 383–399.

Chomsky, N. (1957). *Syntactic Structures*. The Hague: Mouton.

——(1964). *Current Issues in Linguistic Theory*. The Hague: Mouton.

——(1965). *Aspects of the Theory of Syntax*. Cambridge, MA: MIT Press.

——(1981). *Lectures on Government and Binding*. Dordrecht: Foris.

——(2000). *New Horizons in the Study of Language and the Mind*. Cambridge: Cambridge University Press.

Culicover, P. W. & Jackendoff, R. (2005). *Simpler Syntax*. New York: Oxford University Press.

Doris, J. M. & Stich, S. P. (2005). "As a Matter of Fact: Empirical Perspectives on Ethics." In F. Jackson & M. Smith (eds.), *The Oxford Handbook of Contemporary Philosophy*. Oxford: Oxford University Press, 114–152.

Dray, W. (1957) *Laws and Explanation in History*. London: Oxford University Press.

Dworkin, R. (1993). *Life's Dominion: An Argument about Abortion, Euthanasia, and Individual Freedom*. New York: Knopf.

Everett, D. (2005). "Cultural Constraints on Grammar and Cognition in Pirahã," *Current Anthropology* 46: 621–634.

Fiske, A. P. (1991). *Structures of Social Life: The Four Elementary Forms of Human Relations*. New York: Free Press.

——(1992). "The Four Elementary Forms of Sociality: Framework for a Unified Theory of Social Relations," *Psychological Review* 99: 689–723.

Foot, P. (1978). *Virtues and Vices and Other Essays in Moral Philosophy*. Berkeley, CA: University of California Press; Oxford: Blackwell.

Freidin, R. (1992). *Foundations of Generative Syntax*. Cambridge, MA: MIT Press.

Geach, P. T. (1965). "Assertion," *Philosophical Review* 69: 449–465.

Gilovich, T., Griffin, D., & Kahneman, D. (eds.) (2002). *Heuristics and Biases*. Cambridge: Cambridge University Press.

Gigerenzer, Gerd (2007). *Gut Feelings*. New York: Viking Penguin.

Goldberg, A. (1995). *Constructions: A Construction Grammar Approach to Argument Structure*. Chicago, IL: University of Chicago Press.

Goldman, A. I. (1970). *A Theory of Human Action*. Englewood Cliffs, NJ: Prentice-Hall.

Greene, J. (2008). "The Secret Joke of Kant's Soul." In W. Sinnott-Armstrong (ed.), *Moral Psychology, Vol. 3: The Neuroscience of Morality: Emotion, Disease, and Development*. Cambridge, MA: MIT Press, 35–79.

Harman, G. (1967). "Psychological aspects of the theory of syntax," *Journal of Philosophy* 64: 75–87.

—— (1973). Review of Noam Chomsky, *Language and Mind, Revised Edition*, in *Language* 49: 453–464.

Hauser, M. (2006). *Moral Minds: How Nature Designed a Universal Sense of Right and Wrong*. New York: Ecco Press/HarperCollins.

Holyoak, K. J. & Thagard, P. (1995). *Mental Leaps: Analogy in Creative Thought*. Cambridge, MA: MIT Press.

Horowitz, T. (1998). "Philosophical Intuitions and Psychological Theory." In M. DePaul & W. Ramsey (eds.), *Rethinking Intuition*. Lanham, MD: Rowman & Littlefield, 143–160.

Isac, D. & Reiss, C. (2008). *I-Language: An Introduction to Linguistics as a Cognitive Science*. New York: Oxford University Press.

Kamm, F. (1992). *Creation and Abortion*. New York: Oxford University Press.

—— (1993). *Morality, Mortality, Vol. 1: Death and Who to Save from It*. New York: Oxford University Press.

—— (1996). *Morality, Mortality, Vol. 2: Rights, Duties, and Status*. New York: Oxford University Press.

—— (2007). *Intricate Ethics: Rights, Responsibilities, and Permissible Harm*. New York: Oxford University Press.

Knobe, J. (2003). "Intentional Action and Side Effects in Ordinary Language," *Analysis* 63: 190–193.

—— (2007). "Reason Explanation in Folk Psychology." *Midwest Studies in Philosophy* 31: 90–106.

—— (2008). "Action Trees and Moral Judgment." Unpublished manuscript. University of North Carolina–Chapel Hill.

Koenigs. M., Young, L., Adolphs, R., Tranel, D., Hauser, M., Cushman, F., & Damasio, A. (2007). "Damage to the prefrontal cortex increases utilitarian moral judgments." *Nature*, 19.

Liberman, M. (2006). "Chomsky and the Pope: Separated at Birth?" Posting on *Language Log*, 20 December 2006 at <http://itre.cis.upenn.edu/~myl/languagelog/archives/003940.html>.

Machery, E. (2009). *Doing Without Concepts*. New York: Oxford University Press

Mackie, J. L. (1955). "Responsibility and Language." *Australasian Journal of Philosophy* 33: 143–159.

Marr, D. (1982). *Vision: A Computational Approach*. San Francisco, CA: Freeman.

Mikhail, J. (2000). *Rawls' Linguistic Analogy: A Study of the "Generative Grammar" Model of Moral Theory Discussed by John Rawls in A Theory of Justice*. PhD dissertation in Philosophy, Cornell University.

——(2007). "Universal Moral Grammar: Theory, Evidence, and the Future," *Trends in Cognitive Sciences* 11: 143–152.

Mill, J. (1828). *Essays on Government*. London: J. Innes.

Mill, J. S. (1859). *On Liberty*. London: J. W. Parker.

——(1863). *Utilitarianism*. London: Parker, Son & Bourn.

——(1873). *Autobiography*. London: Longmans, Green, Reader, & Dyer.

Murphy, Gregory M. (2004). *The Big Book of Concepts*. Cambridge, MA: MIT Press.

Newmeyer, F. J. (2005). *Possible and Probable Languages*. Oxford: Oxford University Press.

Nozick, R. (1968). "Moral Complications and Moral Structures," *Natural Law Forum* 13: 1–50.

——(1997). *Socratic Puzzles*. Cambridge, MA: Harvard University Press.

Padden, C. A. (1988). "Grammatical Theory and Signed Languages." In F. Newmeyer (ed.), *Linguistics: The Cambridge Survey* (Vol. II). Cambridge & New York: Cambridge University Press.

Prinz, J. (2008). "Is Morality Innate?" *Moral Psychology, Volume 1: The Evolution of Morality: Adaptations and Innateness*, W. Sinnott-Armstrong (ed.). Cambridge, MA: MIT Press, 367–406.

Quinn, W. (1993). *Morality and Action*. Cambridge: Cambridge University Press.

Rawls, J. (1971). *A Theory of Justice*. Cambridge, MA: Harvard University Press.

van Riemsdijk, H. & Williams, E. (1986). *Introduction to the Theory of Grammar*. Cambridge, MA: MIT Press.

Ross, J. R. (1967). *Constraints on Variables in Syntax*. Cambridge, MA: MIT PhD Dissertation. (Published as *Infinite Syntax*, Ablex, 1986.)

Shweder, R. A., Much, N. C., Mahapatra, M., & Park, L. (1997). "The 'Big Three' of Morality (Autonymy, Community, and Divinity) and the 'Big Three' Explanations of Suffering as Well." In A. Brandt & P. Rozen (eds.), *Morality and Health*. New York: Routledge, 119–169.

Sinnott-Armstrong, W. (2008). "Framing Moral Intuitions." In W. Sinnott-Armstrong (ed.), *Moral Psychology, Volume 2: The Cognitive Science of Morality*. Cambridge, MA: MIT Press, 47–76.

Smith, A. (1817). *The Theory of Moral Sentiments*. Philadelphia, PA: Anthony Finley.

Stich, S. (1993). "Moral Philosophy and Mental Representation." In M. Hechter, L. Nadel, & R. Michod (eds.), *The Origin of Values*. New York: Aldine de Gruyter, 215–228.

Sunstein, C. (2004). "Moral Heuristics and Moral Framing," *Minnesota Law Review* 88:1556.

Thomson, J. J. (1978). "Killing, Letting Die, and the Trolley Problem," *Monist* 59: 204–217.

—— (2003). "Causation: Omissions," *Philosophy and Phenomenological Research* 66: 81–103.

Ulatowski, J. (2008). "Action Under a Description." Unpublished manuscript. University of Wyoming.

9

Rules

RON MALLON AND SHAUN NICHOLS

Is it wrong to torture prisoners of war for fun? Is it wrong to yank on someone's hair with no provocation? Is it wrong to push an innocent person in front of a train in order to save five innocent people tied to the tracks? If you are like most people, you answered "yes" to each of these questions. A venerable account of human moral judgment, influential in both philosophy and psychology, holds that these judgments are underpinned by internally represented principles or rules and reasoning about whether particular cases fall under those rules. Recently, this view has come under sustained attack from multiple quarters, and now looks to be in danger of being discarded. In this chapter we consider this evidence, and find that it does not support the elimination of rules from moral psychology.

1. Moral Rules and Moral Reasoning

Long traditions in religion, law, philosophy, and psychology connect moral judgment to moral rules. According to traditional rule-based accounts of morality, an action is wrong if it violates a moral rule. According to "rule utilitarians" (e.g. Brandt, 1985), it is morally wrong to violate a rule that is justified by a balance of good consequence, while deontologists hold that there are rules—such as the prohibition against treating another person as a means to one's own end—that are wrong to violate whatever the consequences (Kant, 1785/1964; Ross, 1930). The central thread of these traditional approaches is *prescriptive*. For instance, deontologists maintain that murdering one innocent person to save two others really is wrong. It shouldn't be done. But for the purposes of this chapter, our interests are entirely on the proper *descriptive* characterization of moral judgments. And there is a closely related *descriptive* claim that is also suggested by traditional rule-based accounts: the way a person actually comes to form a moral judgment depends on the person's application of a rule. An action is judged to be morally impermissible if the action violates a moral rule that is embraced by the judge.

In addition to the rich philosophical tradition of rule-based accounts of morality, there is a rich empirical tradition that adverts to rules as essential to certain normative judgments. In the literature on the moral/conventional distinction, it's widely agreed that at least for judgments of "conventional" violations (e.g. talking during class), these judgments depend on knowledge of local rules (see, e.g., Turiel et al., 1987). Thus there is reason to think that people make at least some normative judgments by drawing on their knowledge of rules. In addition, by appealing to agents' knowledge of local rules, we get an obvious explanation for cross-cultural differences in normative judgments. For example, people in the US but not people in China would think it wrong not to tip servers in local restaurants. The obvious explanation for this difference is that people in the US embrace a rule about tipping (in the US) and people in China do not embrace that rule about tipping (in China). Thus there is independent reason to think that rules do play a role in at least some normative judgments.

Our aim here is not to defend the view that moral rules are the only factor in generating moral judgment, but rather to insist that moral rules are *one* crucial factor in the psychological processes that lead to moral judgments. In particular, we are defending an *internal* account of rules on which such rules are mentally represented and play a causal role in the production of judgment and behavior.[1] Such rules come into play when they are thought to apply to a situation, i.e. when features of the situation instantiate properties that are represented in the rule, and one kind of rule we are concerned with represents properties traditionally considered to be of moral relevance (e.g. intention, injury). Consider, for example, the considerable evidence that judgments of moral responsibility for an act's consequences are sensitive to the intention with which the act was performed (e.g. Shultz et al., 1981; Shultz & Wright, 1985; Shultz et al., 1986). A plausible explanation for this sensitivity is that judgments of responsibility typically require the satisfaction of rules that specify the relevance of intention. And this is exactly the kind of explanation that is offered in detail in "information-processing" theories of moral cognition (see Darley & Shultz, 1990 for a review).

In arguing for the importance of moral rules, we follow influential traditions in both philosophy and psychology. In philosophy, much work on moral judgment can be seen as including an attempt to decide which properties and

---

[1] Such a view therefore assumes that certain connectionist views of the mind, on which the mind is entirely comprised of nonrepresentational networks, are false.

principles we ordinarily think of as morally relevant. Similarly, the tradition of information-processing approaches to moral psychology can be seen also as attempting to discern which properties and rules give rise to moral judgments and behaviors (again, see Darley & Shultz, 1990). Despite these influential traditions, moral rules have recently come to seem retrograde, a relic of best-discarded views of moral judgment.

2. Rules and Social Intuitions

A recent and provocative challenge to a rule-based approach to moral judgment is Jonathan Haidt's (2001) "social intuitionist" model. Haidt argues against a prominent role for moral reasoning in the production of moral judgment. Rather, he writes, "[Understanding of moral truths occurs] not by a process of ratiocination and reflection, but rather by a process more akin to perception, in which one 'just sees without argument that they are and must be true' (Harrison, 1967, p. 72)" (2001: 814). In place of processes of reasoning, Haidt argues that moral judgments are typically caused by moral intuitions (including moral emotions) that are "a kind of cognition" but "not a kind of reasoning" (ibid.).

Since all of the theories that are being considered are, effectively, causal models of moral judgment, it is useful to depict them with flow charts in which the boxes represent psychological mechanisms and the arrows represent causal relations. We might then depict a "rationalist" model as in Figure 9.1. This is the model that Haidt has in his sights. In place of the rationalist model, Haidt offers a complex *social intuitionist* model, a crucial part of which we have illustrated in Figure 9.2.

Haidt marshals an impressive array of considerations to support his intuitionist model. Here, it might be helpful to focus on one sort of evidence that nicely

Figure 9.1. Rationalist model of moral judgment

Figure 9.2. Intuitionist model of moral judgment

illustrates his position: cases of moral dumbfounding. Haidt and colleagues presented the following case to subjects:

Julie and Mark are brother and sister. They are traveling together in France on summer vacation from college. One night they are staying alone in a cabin near the beach. They decide that it would be interesting and fun if they tried making love. At the very least, it would be a new experience for each of them. Julie was already taking birth control pills, but Mark uses a condom too, just to be safe. They both enjoy making love, but they decide not to do it again. They keep that night as a special secret, which makes them feel even closer to each other. What do you think about that? Was it okay for them to make love?   (2001: 814)

Haidt reports that subjects presented with such cases and asked for a moral judgment typically answer "immediately" that the action was "wrong," and begin "searching for reasons" (ibid.). Only, these cases have been designed by Haidt and colleagues to undermine the most obvious reasons for a moral judgment (e.g. the risks and harms are eliminated, *ex hypothesi*). Thus many subjects find themselves unable to provide reasons that justify their judgment. When faced with this dumbfounding, do subjects give up? No. They simply insist that their judgment is correct in the absence of reasons.

   The conclusion Haidt draws from this and other evidence is that reasoning typically plays no role in the production of moral judgment. While Haidt allows that reasoning sometimes plays a role in moral judgment and behavior, he holds (*contra* the rationalist model) that most moral reasoning is *post facto*, not causing moral judgment but rather being deployed in the process of justifying one's moral responses to others—just as the subjects in the dumbfounding case search for reasons for their judgments. If this is so, then why do we think we know the reasons for our judgments? Our ignorance is readily explained by a host of experimental evidence (some of it reviewed in Nisbett and Wilson's seminal [1977]; see Wilson, 2002 and Stanovich, 2004 for more recent coverage) that (i) people are not consciously aware of the processes that connect their mental states to the causal effects of those states and (ii) people routinely confabulate explanations for their behavior.

   Haidt is relying here on what are sometimes called "dual-process" models of cognition (Chaiken & Trope, 1999), the fundamental idea of which is that cognition is subserved by two very different kinds of mechanisms. On the one hand, there are mechanisms characterized by conscious control, in which the "reasoner searches for relevant evidence, weighs evidence, coordinates evidence with theories, and reaches a decision" (Haidt, 2001: 818). Call these *controlled* processes. On the other, there are processes that operate "quickly, effortlessly, and automatically, such that the outcome but not the process is accessible to consciousness" (ibid.). Call these *intuitive* processes. Haidt's move is, then, to suggest (on the basis of a range of evidence) that most moral judgment results from this second kind of system, and so he concludes that it is not a kind of reasoning.

There is a variety of ways to question Haidt's account of moral judgment without relying on what Haidt (2001: 815) calls philosophers' "worship of reason." Indeed, one of the best-developed dual-process literatures within social psychology—that of implicit social attitudes—looks to provide an empirical basis for doubting Haidt's view.

Consider the substantial literature documenting unconscious (implicit) racial attitudes. It is a hallmark of this literature that a person can, on various indirect measures (e.g. the "Implicit Association Test" or IAT), exhibit racial biases, while on explicit measures (like self-report) that same individual is not racially prejudiced.[2] In the most common version of the task, pictures of faces (black or white) are paired with positively or negatively valenced words in a sorting task. In such a test, subjects typically find it easier to perform the task when white faces are paired with good words and black faces with bad words than vice versa. And this effect occurs even when subjects appear to have explicit nonracist attitudes on paper-and-pencil questionnaires (e.g. Greenwald et al., 1998). The literature fits nicely within the dual-process framework, with the automatic, implicit processes producing one set of outcomes while consciously controlled processes produce another. But which processes are "in charge"? On Haidt's model, what drives moral responses are, in the first place, implicit, intuitive processes, and the reasoning processes come along after the fact. Is that what goes in the literature on racial attitudes? We suggest not.

Instead, the literature seems to show that conscious controlled processes exert substantial control over explicit verbal responses and behavior, and that, as these processes become overtaxed or exhausted (e.g. by increasing cognitive load or by so-called "ego depletion"), verbal responses and behavior come to align more and more closely with implicit attitudes. For example, Richeson and Shelton (2003) found that white subjects demonstrating an anti-black/pro-white IAT effect and then interacting with an African American confederate subsequently performed worse on tasks requiring effort and attention (i.e. a Stroop task).[3] The suggestion is that interacting with the African American confederate required additional control resources (to suppress automatic anti-black responses), thereby depleting a resource that would be needed on

---

[2] Greenwald et al. (1998); see Nosek et al. (2007) for a review, and Kelly et al. (Chapter 13 in this volume) for more discussion.

[3] Richeson et al. (2003) present brain-imaging data suggesting that executive control inhibits the expression of implicit processes.

subsequent tasks. And Bartholow et al. (2006) show that alcohol consumption interferes with the capacity to intentionally regulate implicit biases, an effect they link to a compromise of control mechanisms.

This is an important research program, and one that has revealed a startling array of implicit attitudes that may exert surprising effects on behavior. But the program does not show that intuitions run the show, only to be served by *ex post facto* reasoning. Rather, the correct model here seems quite a bit more like Plato's image of the soul as the charioteer (*Phaedrus* 246–254e) who must hold the reigns of the spirited horses (the automatic processes) closely so as to control them. When the charioteer becomes exhausted or drunk, the horses go wild, but that hardly shows that this is the typical case. Rather, it seems that where controlled processes maintain their integrity, connections between intuitions and behavior may be checked. At least the dual-process research on racial cognition provides a substantial body of evidence that in an important domain of real-world moral behavior, implicit racial bias processes are checked by controlled processes.[4] We take these to provide substantial reason to doubt that Haidt's general model of moral judgment is correct.

Still, this is far from definitive. Perhaps racial cognition is the exception with respect to the role of controlled processes. Perhaps elsewhere in moral cognition, conscious control plays little role.[5]

In truth, no one has made any serious attempt to count moral judgments in ordinary life. Nor is it obvious how one might approach such a daunting task. It is therefore difficult to find evidence that would definitively answer the question of whether moral judgments are typically caused in a particular way.

But even if intuitions do predominate to the extent that Haidt thinks they do, it doesn't settle the question of whether moral rules or moral reasoning figure in the production of moral judgment. This is because the distinction Haidt

[4] Why not think that the implicit biases literature shows a competition between two automatic or intuitive processes—one generating anti-racist moral intuitions and one generating evaluative racial biases? The question for this alternate model is why compromising control (e.g. via exhaustion or drunkenness) alters the balance of power among intuitions (e.g. leaving anti-racist intuition weaker than evaluative racial bias, when normally it is stronger). An account that pits control against the automatic processes explains this, but an account that pits automatic processes against one another does not.

[5] Haidt produces a range of evidence to argue that the failure of introspective access on display in his dumbfounding cases is a typical feature of moral reasoning. One sort of response to Haidt, provided by Pizarro & Bloom (2003), is to question whether it matters if reflective reasoning typically plays little role in moral judgment. Pizarro and Bloom maintain that Haidt undersells the role of reasoning in moral judgment, for even one-off reasoning can have an enduring significance for an individual when it results in a lasting change to the individual's motivational make-up. For instance, many individuals reason to the conclusion that it is immoral to eat mammals, and this often has long-term ramifications for the individual's behavior. Even if Haidt has succeeded in showing that reasoning rarely drives judgment, this wouldn't be a great problem for defenders of the relevance of reasoning and moral rules. For defenders could, like Pizarro and Bloom, insist on the importance of these (numerically rare) cases.

(following the dual-process orientation) offers between conscious "reasoning" processes as opposed to automatically produced "moral intuitions" is simply the distinction between processes that are under direct conscious control, and those that are not.[6] And this distinction cross-cuts the category of inferential, rule-based processes that are at the core of the view we defend. To see this, consider that Haidt's case against the relevance of moral reasoning to moral judgment hangs largely on his characterization of reasoning processes as conscious or introspectively accessible. It is because, for example, the dumbfounded subjects seemingly employed no reflective reasoning to reach their moral judgments, and were unable to employ it to defend these judgments, that Haidt claims reasoning plays no role.

One might think that this is an odd way to characterize "reasoning" processes—indeed, Nisbett and Wilson's (1977) seminal work reports a variety of results involving complex cognitive processes—processes that are tempting to characterize as examples of reasoning—that seem to fail to be introspectible. For example, Storms and Nisbett (1970) experimented with insomniac subjects by placing them into three groups: arousal, relaxation, and control. Subjects in the first and second conditions were given placebo pills to take 15 minutes before bed on two consecutive nights, but the arousal condition subjects were told that the placebo would produce "rapid heart rate, breathing irregularities, bodily warmth, and alertness—symptoms, in other words, of insomnia" (Nisbett & Wilson, 1977: 237). In contrast, relaxation subjects were told just the opposite, that the pill would produce "lowered heart rate, breathing rate, body temperature, and a reduction in alertness" (ibid.: 238). According to the subjects' reports, arousal subjects got to sleep significantly faster and relaxation subjects took significantly longer to get to sleep (with no change in control subjects).

The explanation Storms and Nisbett offered for this effect was simply that arousal condition subjects reattributed their insomnia symptoms to action of the pill, while relaxation condition subjects assumed their arousal must be particularly intense since they still felt their symptoms despite having taken a pill that would relax them. Nisbett and Wilson (1977: 238) are particularly struck by the fact that in post-experimental interviews, subjects "almost uniformly insisted that after taking the pills they had completely forgotten about them." That is, although the resulting behavior appears to be the result of a process of reasoning involving the comparison of an introspective assessment of one's

---

[6] This is a little quick, for Haidt thinks unconscious processes typically share a host of other properties, including features of computational architecture. So Haidt (2001) suggests that unconscious processes are computed nonsequentially and nonsymbolically (perhaps in a connectionist network). Because we see no reason to think that rule-based processes must be conscious, and because we have doubts that this aspect of dual-process theorizing is well motivated, we ignore this here.

arousal states with the an expected state, the subjects cannot recover this process of reasoning when asked later.

One explanation for this failure—the one that parallels Haidt's explanation of his dumbfounding subjects—is that the reasoning processes involved are subserved by automatic, unconscious processes.[7] Suppose that is true. Then these processes would not be reasoning in Haidt's sense, even though they seem to involve complex inferences, determinations of relevant information, and other features characteristic of intelligent cognition. The right thing to conclude from this is that Haidt's use of "reasoning" excludes mental processes that may nonetheless be inferential, rule-based, and highly "intelligent." For example, Haidt's moral dumbfounding cases show nothing about whether moral rules or inferential processes were involved in the production of the moral judgments. They show only that whatever these processes are, they either (a) fail to be introspectively accessible shortly after completion or (b) fail to "deactivate" quickly in the face of countervailing evidence. Option (a) seems the right explanation of at least some of the classic data regarding failures of self-knowledge—for example, the Nisbett and Storms data reviewed above. There is good reason to think an inferential process is occurring, but for whatever reason (because it is implicit, or because it is not well encoded in memory) this process cannot be recovered in response to questioning soon after. Option (b) might also explain Haidt's dumbfounding results: after all, the subjects do produce reasons for their judgments, but these reasons are refuted by the experimenter. It's only after this process of refutation that the subjects are dumbfounded, but perhaps once the judgment is made it is not quickly abandoned.

Having said all this, we are now in a position to simply stipulate that moral rules may play an important causal role in inferences without that process being consciously accessible, and therefore without being "reasoning" in Haidt's sense. Because Haidt's attack on conscious reasoning leaves the door wide open to rational, rule-governed inference at the unconscious level, his critique doesn't address whether moral rules play a role in moral judgment.

3. Rules and the Moral/Conventional Distinction

A more direct challenge to the importance of moral rules comes from James Blair's (1995) explanation of performance on the moral/conventional task (e.g.

---

[7] Another possibility is that the subjects simply cannot remember the contents of (what was) a conscious process.

Nucci, 2001; Smetana, 1993; Turiel, 1983). Blair's work, like Haidt's, stresses the importance of relatively automatic mechanisms underlying moral responses. But while Haidt discusses the relatively broad class of what he calls intuitions (which includes moral emotions), Blair emphasizes the special importance of emotional response in moral judgment and behavior.

Blair offers a sophisticated account of the mechanisms underlying moral judgments in the moral conventional task. In order to appreciate this model, it will be useful to review features of the moral/conventional task. Previous researchers found that a wide range of populations—adult and child, developmentally delayed and developmentally normal, autistic and nonautistic—seem to treat "moral" violations (e.g. unprovoked hitting) differently than "conventional" violations (e.g. standing up during story time) (see, e.g., Blair, 1995; Nichols, 2002; Nucci, 2001; Turiel et al., 1987). Subjects tend to appeal to harm to the victim in explaining why a moral violation is wrong; for example, children say that pulling hair is wrong because it hurts the person. By contrast, children's explanations of why conventional transgressions are wrong often proceed in terms of social acceptability; standing up during story time is wrong because it's rude or impolite, or because "you're not supposed to." Further, conventional rules, unlike moral rules, are viewed as dependent on authority: if the teacher at another school has no rule against chewing gum, children will judge that it's not wrong to chew gum at that school, but even if the teacher at another school has no rule against hitting, children claim that it's still wrong to hit.[8]

Blair maintains that the capacity to draw the moral/conventional distinction derives from the activation of a Violence Inhibition Mechanism (VIM). The idea for VIM comes from Konrad Lorenz's (1966) suggestion that social animals like canines have evolved mechanisms to inhibit intra-species aggression: when a conspecific displays submission cues, the attacker stops. Blair suggests that there's something analogous in our cognitive systems, the VIM, and that this mechanism is the basis for our capacity to distinguish moral from conventional violations.

According to Blair, VIM is activated by displays of distress and results in a withdrawal response (1995: 4). Moreover, VIM activation generates an aversive experience.[9] On Blair's view, it is this feeling of aversiveness that generates the responses to the moral items on the moral/conventional task.

---

[8] Kelly et al. (2007) launch an important critique of the moral/conventional distinction. We won't draw on their critique here, however. Rather, we shall argue that Blair's theory doesn't work even if the moral/conventional distinction is viable.

[9] Blair's theory has a further wrinkle. VIM-activation initially simply produces a withdrawal response. This VIM-activation becomes aversive through "meaning analysis": "the withdrawal response following the activation of VIM is experienced, through meaning analysis, as aversive" (1995: 7). But Blair (1995) does not elaborate on what the "meaning analysis" comes to. Moreover,

Thus stated, Blair's account of VIM is an importantly incomplete account of moral judgment, for people are wont to make moral judgments in cases where they witness no distress displays. For example, we suspect many people are likely to make a moral judgment upon hearing that in Salt Lake City during the summer of 2003, Mark Hacking shot his wife Lori in her sleep, disposed of her body in a trash dumpster, reported her missing, and personally led thousands of volunteers in a week-long search for signs of her, all to conceal the fact that he had lied to family and friends that he had been admitted to medical school. But in hearing this story, we witness the distress of neither Lori Hacking nor her family and community. Similarly, in canonical presentations of the moral/conventional task, there are no displays of distress.

Blair extends the VIM model to these cases via classical conditioning:

During normal development, individuals will witness other individuals displaying distress cues resulting in the activation of VIM. On many occasions the observers may role take with the distressed victims; they will calculate representations of the victim's internal state (e.g. "she's suffering"; "what a poor little boy"; "he must be cold and hungry"). There will thus be pairings of distress cues activating VIM with representations formed through role taking. It is suggested here that the representations formed through role taking will become, through classical conditioning, trigger stimuli for VIM. . . . Thus, an individual may generate empathetic arousal to just the thought of someone's distress (e.g. "what a poor little boy") without distress cues being actually processed.   (1995: 4–5)

On the Blair model, then, there are two processes important to the development of typical moral response, with the former ontogenetically prior to the latter:

Distress Cues → VIM
Role taking → Representations of Distress → VIM

His explanation of the moral/conventional distinction is, then, simply that the violation of moral rules gives rise (via role taking) to representations of a victim's distress. And these representations activate VIM (in normally developed individuals).

Blair's account competes with the moral rules account we defend, because it proposes to account for all moral judgment via the association of moral violations with victims' distress, mediated by an aversive emotion-like response. For present purposes, it's useful to simplify the model as an "emotionist" model, as depicted in Figure 9.3.

---

our critique will apply regardless of whether the notion of "meaning analysis" is invoked. Hence, in our discussion of Blair we will simplify and say that VIM causes the experience of aversion.

Figure 9.3. Emotionist model of moral judgment

This model offers a clear and radical alternative to a rule-based or rationalist account of moral judgment.[10] For Blair's emotionist model maintains that moral judgment is caused by a particular kind emotional response that is caused by cues of suffering. In contrast, the moral rules account we want to defend suggests that assessing situations for the presence of more theoretical properties (like "intention," "right," "injury" and so forth) is crucial to the activation of moral judgment.

So which account is right? We think it is clear that Blair's account will not explain moral judgment because distress, and the representation of distress, are not sufficient for judgments that an act (or act type) is "wrong." Perhaps the easiest way to illustrate this is by exploiting the venerable distinction between judging something *bad* and judging something *wrong*. Many occurrences that are regarded as bad are not regarded as wrong. Toothaches, for instance, are bad, but they aren't wrong. The moral/conventional task gets its interest primarily because it gives us a glimpse into judgments of *wrong*. This is reflected by the fact that the items in the moral/conventional task are explicitly *transgressions*, and the very first question in standard moral/conventional tasks checks for the *permissibility* of the action. As we'll see, the problem with Blair's account is that, while the proposal might provide an account of judging something bad (in a certain sense), it does not provide an account of judging something wrong (Nichols, 2002, 2004).

If Blair's theory is right, VIM leads to a distinctive aversive response. As with toothaches, we might regard the stimuli that prompt this aversive response as "bad." Furthermore, it might be important to treat stimuli that produce VIM-based aversion as "bad" in a distinctive way. Now, what is the class of stimuli that are bad in this sense? Well, anything that reliably produces VIM-activation. Distress cues will be at the core of this stimulus class (Blair, 1995, 1999). The class of stimuli that will be accordingly aversive will include distress cues from victims of natural disasters and accidents and even distress cues in paintings and drawings. Thus the class of stimuli that VIM will lead us to regard as "bad" includes natural-disaster victims, accident victims,

---

[10] Indeed, Blair's more recent work offers a less radical model of moral judgment (see, e.g., Blair, 2008). We focus on his original theory because it provides such a delightfully clear and testable emotionist model of moral judgment.

and superficial distress cues. But it is quite implausible that these things are regarded as *wrong*. Natural disasters are, of course, bad. But, barring theological digressions, natural disasters aren't regarded as *wrong*. Similarly, if a child falls down, skins her knee, and begins to cry, this will produce aversive response in witnesses through VIM. Yet the child's falling down doesn't count as a moral transgression. This was put to the test in a recent experiment by Leslie, Mallon, and Dicorcia (2006). Children were presented with a scenario in which a child exhibited distress cues, but only because the child was a "crybaby." Children were told a story in which two characters, James and Tammy, were eating their lunch. Each of them had a cookie, but James wanted Tammy's cookie as well as his own. Their teacher says, "In this school, anybody can eat their own cookie if they want to. Anybody can eat their own cookie." This makes Tammy very happy and she eats her cookie, but that makes James unhappy, and he cries. When presented with this scenario, both 4-year-old children and children with autism thought that it was perfectly okay for Tammy to eat her cookie, even though it made James cry. So the mere fact that Tammy's action led to James's distress wasn't enough to generate a judgment of a moral transgression.

Thus, while Blair's theory might provide an account of how people come to judge things as *bad* in a certain sense, it does not provide an adequate account of moral judgments of *wrong* on the moral/conventional task. The natural explanation for why the problem arises for Blair's account is that the account fails to include *rules* in the processes that generate moral judgment. If we invoke rules, then we can easily explain why it isn't judged wrong to have a toothache, fall off your bike, or eat your own cookie (knowing full well that it will make Jimmy cry). None of these are judged wrong because they don't violate the internally represented rules. Now there is a variety of detailed ways that Blair's account might be amended. For example, rather than pairing representations of distress with VIM-activation, Blair might pair transgression types (e.g. intentional harm) with VIM-activation. Alternatively, Blair might hold that in some of these cases other cognitive mechanisms, or what he calls "executive functions," may override the connection between VIM and moral judgment. But we suggest that these emendations to Blair's account, to the extent they are successful, are simply ways of supplementing the account with internally represented rules.

4. Rules and Moral Dilemmas

The final important threat to rules comes from an emerging body of work on the psychological factors involved in assessing moral dilemmas. As with Blair's work, one of the important results from research on dilemmas has been to show how emotions can impact moral judgment (Greene et al., 2001). And this gives rise to an emotion-based account of moral judgment that threatens to displace a rule-based account. However, again, we shall argue that moral rules play a vital role in the psychology underlying the assessment of moral dilemmas.

This recent work on moral dilemmas grows out of a large body of research in philosophy that draws out our intuitions about a wide range of dilemmas and attempts to determine a set of principles that captures our intuitions about the cases.[11] The most intensively studied dilemmas are the "trolley cases," which serve to isolate different factors that might affect our intuitions. In the *bystander* case, we are asked to imagine that a person sees a train approaching that will kill five innocents on the track, and the only way to prevent the deaths of these five is to flip a switch that will divert the train to a side track. Diverting the train to the side track will lead to the death of the person on the side track, but it is the only way to save the five people on the main track. Philosophers have maintained that the intuitive position is that it is acceptable to flip the switch to divert the train, leading to the death of one instead of five (e.g. Thomson, 1976). In the *footbridge* case, the situation is quite similar except that there is no side track, and the only way for the protagonist to save the five is to push a large stranger off of a footbridge in front of the oncoming train, which will kill the stranger. In this case, philosophers maintain that the intuitive position is that it is wrong to push the stranger (Foot, 1967; Quinn, 1989; Thomson, 1976). This can seem puzzling since, on a simple utilitarian calculus, the cases seem quite parallel: five lives can be saved for the price of one. One goal of the philosophical investigations has been to develop a unified normative theory that will accommodate intuitions about such cases. This goal has been exceedingly difficult to meet, and few would maintain that philosophers have succeeded in finding a unified normative theory that fits with the full range of our intuitions about moral dilemmas.

This work in philosophy was unapologetically *a priori*, but recently researchers have conducted interview and survey experiments with these sorts of cases (Petrinovich & O'Neill, 1996; Mikhail, 2000; Greene et al., 2001; Hauser et al., 2007). The results have largely confirmed what philosophers maintained about the bystander and footbridge cases: most people have the

---

[11] In addition to this descriptive philosophical project, there is a related *prescriptive* project that attempts to characterize the normative theory that *should* guide our judgments in these cases. Some of this literature seems to take the view that identifying our intuitive responses to dilemma cases (which is in some sense a descriptive question) will provide important input for characterizing the normative theory that *should* guide our judgments (e.g. Thomson, 1976).

intuition that it is acceptable to flip the switch in *bystander* but that it is not acceptable to push the stranger in *footbridge*. The interesting subsequent question concerns the psychological underpinnings of these judgments. Why do people judge pushing the stranger as inappropriate but turning the train as appropriate?

In an important recent discussion, Joshua Greene proposes that the response in footbridge-style cases is generated by the fact that these actions are "personal" and such actions generate greater emotional engagement than "impersonal" actions. The personal/impersonal distinction is drawn as follows:

A moral violation is personal if it is: (i) likely to cause serious bodily harm, (ii) to a particular person, (iii) in such a way that the harm does not result from the deflection of an existing threat onto a different party . . . A moral violation is impersonal if it fails to meet these criteria. . . . Pushing someone in front of a trolley meets all three criteria and is therefore "personal," while diverting a trolley involves merely deflecting an existing threat, removing a crucial sense of "agency" and therefore making this violation "impersonal." (Greene & Haidt, 2002: 519)[12]

Thus Greene maintains that footbridge cases elicit inappropriateness judgments because they trigger emotional responses, and they trigger emotional responses because they are *personal*. In support of this account, Greene and colleagues provide evidence that emotional processing plays a key role when people consider footbridge cases (Greene et al., 2001; Greene et al., 2004). The proposal is that the key difference between footbridge and bystander—the difference that generates the different response—is that footbridge is *personal* and bystander is *impersonal*.

Greene incorporates this distinction into a dual process approach to moral judgment, as depicted in Figure 9.4.

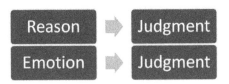

Figure 9.4. Dual-process model of moral judgment

---

[12] One aspect of Greene's description requires some clarification. What is meant by "moral violation" in this passage? It doesn't seem to mean *transgression* because diverting the trolley in the bystander case is cast as an "impersonal moral violation," but it's doubtful that that action is a transgression at all. Indeed, if transgressions are measured by judgments of permissibility, the available evidence indicates that diverting the train isn't a transgression—in all of the extant studies, a majority of participants judge it to be permissible (Greene et al., 2001; Hauser et al., 2007; Mikhail, 2000). Since "violation" is easily confused with "transgression," we shall set aside this terminology in characterizing Greene's account.

According to Greene, impersonal dilemmas tend to activate the "reason" path, whereas personal dilemmas run through the "emotion" path. Like Haidt's, Greene's model suggests that we can arrive at moral judgments either through reasoning or through emotions. But unlike Haidt, Greene never suggests that our reasoning-based judgments are rare. He does, however, suggest that reason-based judgments are characteristically utilitarian.

Greene's focal cases are dilemmas like *bystander* and *footbridge*, but of course, if his theory aims merely to provide a theory of judgments about trolley cases, it is of limited interest. Greene's approach is particularly interesting and provocative if it is taken to suggest a general account of moral judgment. That is, one might maintain that, quite generally, personal acts generate moral condemnation through the emotional pathway in the dual-process model. However, if we take this as a general account of moral judgment, there are numerous *prima facie* counter-examples, cases in which manifestly personal (and emotionally salient) acts are not judged impermissible. Just as Blair's account runs afoul of cases in which distress is insufficient for moral judgment, the appeal to "personal" acts runs afoul of cases in which acts are personal but permissible. For example, some acts of self-defense, war, and punishment are plausibly personal and emotional, but regarded as permissible nonetheless. For instance, many people think that spanking their own child is permissible, even though it is obviously personal and emotional. Similarly, there is cultural variation in the harms that are judged impermissible. Among Yanomamö men, wife-beating is judged permissible, despite being personal and emotional (Chagnon, 1992). Closer to home, in much of Western culture, male circumcision is permissible though obviously personal. So the idea that actions are judged to be wrong when they're personal faces *prima facie* concerns.

Greene does discuss situations in which being personal is insufficient to result in a moral judgment of wrongness. Thus he allows for cases in which an action may be judged appropriate despite being personal. However, the cases he discusses in which the personal is insufficient to generate moral judgment are cases in which the utilitarian calculus is obviously in favor of acting. For instance, in one dilemma, the "crying baby" case, you have to decide whether it's permissible to smother your baby in order to prevent the Nazis from discovering and killing your entire family (including the baby). Greene maintains that although such cases involve personal acts, many people draw on utilitarian considerations to reach the judgment that the actions are permissible. This explanation comports well with the general account he offers in which each of the two systems (emotions, utilitarian reasoning) in his dual-process model are in competition with one another. Taking these examples and Greene's model together, Greene's model (generalized as an account of moral judgment) suggests the following two regularities obtain:

(a) If an action is personal, it must maximize utility to be permitted (e.g. crying baby)

(b) If an action maximizes utility, it must be personal to be prohibited (e.g. footbridge)

We agree with Greene that something like utilitarian considerations can play an important role in reasoning about these kinds of dilemmas, but we doubt that regularity (a) obtains and that this model is complete.[13] For we doubt that the appeal to utilitarian considerations could explain the permissibility of the cases above. For instance, it's implausible to maintain that the reason people think it's okay to punish people is because it maximizes utility (cf. Haidt & Sabini, 2000; Fehr & Gächter, 2002; see Prinz & Nichols, Chapter 4 in this volume for a brief presentation of these results). If this is correct, then Greene's appeal to personal acts together with utilitarian considerations fails to provide an adequate account of moral judgment.

Even if one concedes that the appeal to personal acts doesn't explain moral judgment generally, one might maintain that it explains the asymmetry in judgments in footbridge and bystander trolley cases. However, we think that even in this restricted domain, the appeal to personal acts and utilitarian considerations is inadequate to explain the phenomena. The reader will not be surprised to learn that we think that rules provide a critical supplement to the factors that Greene invokes. Unlike the appeal to *personal acts*, the rule-based approach with which we began has an obvious explanation for why personal acts like self-defense, punishment, and circumcision are not judged impermissible. The judge doesn't embrace a rule against them. Thus, once again, we find that the traditional rule-based account gives a very natural explanation for some obvious facts about people's moral judgments.[14]

---

[13] In fact, we also doubt that (b) is correct, for we suspect subjects may judge a utility-maximizing lie to be morally wrong, at least in some cases. Of course, it may be that such cases show the limits of generalizing Greene's explanation beyond the tightly circumscribed moral dilemmas (e.g. trolley cases) characteristic of this literature.

[14] One important response to our view is that the culturally specified rules act as *overrides* to the natural moral judgment, which itself is a basic and universal emotional reaction. We regard it as an open question whether the rules act as "overrides" to a basic emotion. But we do maintain that if we identify "moral judgment" with this basic emotional response, then we have no longer provided an account of moral judgment that answers to the primary question at hand, which concerns why people think what they do about morally fraught situations. The standard measures here have been, of course, their spontaneous judgments about scenarios. Some of the scenarios are difficult moral dilemmas; others, like the scenarios in the moral/conventional task, involve less conflict but still generate spontaneous judgment. Our point is that even if rules provide an "override" to the emotional response, this override is typically already factored in to the spontaneous judgments that we are trying to explain.

We suggest that rules play an important role, not just in judgments about the problematic cases we've pressed, but also in judgments about the moral dilemmas that dominate this literature.

The rule-based approach does owe an answer to the original challenge, however. Why do people judge that choosing five over one is acceptable in the bystander case but not in the footbridge case? The traditional answer is that the different status of these actions is explained by what the rules do and do not forbid. One important proposal is that a rule like "Do not kill persons" forbids one from intending to bring about a person's death, but it does not necessarily forbid acting in a way that brings about a person's death as an unintended but foreseen side effect. Hence, in the bystander case, it is permissible to divert the trolley even though it has an effect (the killing of an innocent) that it would be impermissible to intend. There has been protracted debate on how exactly to characterize what moral rules do and do not forbid (Foot, 1967; Thomson, 1976; Quinn, 1989). Sorting all this out has been enormously complicated and has not produced any consensus, but we need not delve into this debate. For the important point is simply that the traditional advocate of rule-based moral judgment maintains that we can explain the intuitions about the trolley cases in terms of what the rules do and do not forbid.

The rule-based approach offers an alternative to the emotion-based explanation of the asymmetry between the footbridge and bystander cases. However, in light of the apparent failure of philosophers to achieve consensus on how to characterize what the rules do and do not forbid, the rule-based explanation of the asymmetry between the footbridge cases and bystander cases may seem ad hoc. Is there an independent way to support the claim that the asymmetry between the footbridge cases and the bystander cases is explained by what the rules do and do not forbid? Our hypothesis is that it is a common feature of many rules, not specific to personal contexts, that they exhibit the asymmetry reflected in the footbridge and bystander cases. We recently conducted a set of experiments on adults to test this hypothesis (Nichols & Mallon, 2006).

The idea behind the experiments was to create cases that parallel the footbridge and bystander cases, but which do not count as personal. We did this by altering the scenarios such that the possible human victims were replaced with teacups. Here are the two central cases.

Impersonal Bystander Case

> When Billy's mother leaves the house one day, she says "you are forbidden from breaking any of the teacups that are on the counter." Later that

morning, Billy starts up his train set and goes to make a snack. When he returns, he finds that his 18 month old sister Ann has taken several of the teacups and placed them on the train tracks. Billy sees that if the train continues on its present course, it will run through and break five cups. Billy can't get to the cups or to the off-switch in time, but he can reach a lever which will divert the train to a side track. There is only one cup on the side track. He knows that the only way to save the five cups is to divert the train to the side track, which will break the cup on the side track. Billy proceeds to pull the lever and the train is diverted down the side track, breaking one of the cups.

Did Billy break his mother's rule?   YES   NO

Impersonal Footbridge Case

When Susie's mother leaves the house one day, she says "you are forbidden from breaking any of the teacups that are on the counter." While Susie is playing in her bedroom, her 18 month old brother Fred has taken down several of the teacups and he has also turned on a mechanical toy truck, which is about to crush 5 of the cups. As Fred leaves the room, Susie walks in and sees that the truck is about to wreck the cups. She is standing next to the counter with the remaining teacups and she realizes that the only way to stop the truck in time is by throwing one of the teacups at the truck, which will break the cup she throws. Susie is in fact an excellent thrower and knows that if she throws the teacup at the truck she will save the five cups. Susie proceeds to throw the teacup, which breaks that cup, but it stops the truck and saves the five other teacups.

Did Susie break her mother's rule?   YES   NO

The results were clear. In two different experiments, most subjects said that the rule was broken in the impersonal footbridge case, but fewer than half said that the rule was broken in the bystander case. The difference between the responses was highly significant (see Figure 9.5).

These results support the rule-based interpretation of the results on the original trolley cases. For it seems that, even in impersonal cases, subjects distinguish footbridge-style cases from bystander-style cases. This provides independent reason to think that traditional rule-based accounts illuminate the asymmetric responses on the original bystander and footbridge cases. Namely, the judgment of impermissibility in the footbridge cases is guided by a moral rule that is not violated in the bystander cases.

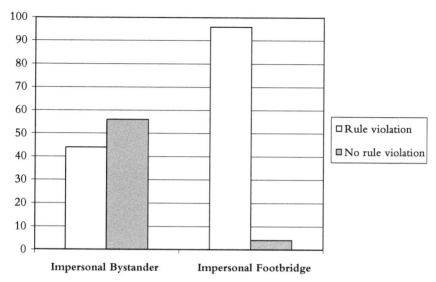

Figure 9.5. Responses to impersonal moral dilemmas (Nichols & Mallon, 2006: experiment 2)

5. Rule Violations and All-in Permissibility

In the previous sections, we have tried to beat back the emotion-based attacks on moral rules in recent moral psychology. However, it is not clear that we can wring a complete account of moral judgment from the appeal to rules alone. The results discussed above leave open the possibility that people might judge that an action violates a rule and also judge that the action is acceptable, *all things considered*. For instance, stealing bread violates a rule, but if a person is starving, we might think that it is okay for him to steal the bread, *all things considered*.

In the impersonal footbridge case, we know that participants tend to regard the action as a rule violation ("it breaks her mother's rule"). But we don't yet know whether participants would regard the action as impermissible in the all-in sense. So in addition to the rule violation question, we also asked a question to get at judgments of all-in permissibility:

All things considered, was it okay for Susie to throw the teacup?   YES NO

Most participants said Yes to the all-in question on the impersonal footbridge case. Indeed, most subjects said both that Susie broke her mother's rule and that what she did was, all things considered, okay.

So, participants recognize a distinction between breaking a rule and all-in impermissibility, at least in the case of some rules. But perhaps this complication doesn't arise in the case of moral rules. In philosophical ethics, one important view, absolutist deontology, maintains that if an action violates a moral rule, it is thereby the wrong thing to do, all things considered (e.g. Fried, 1978). In addition, some rule-utilitarians (e.g. Brandt, 1985) also endorse the primacy of moral rules, even in the face of consequences that favor breaking the rule. On such views, breaking a moral rule is (at least typically) sufficient for all-in impermissibility. If either account is a correct view of the role of moral rules in actual moral judgments, then we have a very plausible explanation of the original footbridge results. In those cases, the action violates a moral rule, and violating a moral rule suffices for generating a judgment of all-in impermissibility.

However, there is now converging evidence from several different methodologies that suggests that emotions do make a critical contribution to moral judgment (e.g. Blair, 1995; Greene et al., 2004, Valdesolo & DeSteno, 2006; Koenigs et al., 2007). In particular, judgments of "all-in permissibility" are plausibly influenced by emotional activity. This suggests that no adequate account of moral judgment can be given in terms of rules alone. But of course this doesn't mean that we should give up rules altogether. On the contrary, we've spent this entire chapter arguing that an adequate account of moral judgment cannot ignore the role of rules. A natural proposal at this stage is that emotions contribute to the salience and importance of the rules. That is what elevates certain rules, and certain applications of rules, above other morally relevant considerations (Nichols & Mallon, 2006).

It's important to note that, although this model of non-utilitarian moral judgments invokes separate processes, it does so in a way that is quite different from typical dual-process models offered in recent moral psychology (e.g. Greene & Haidt, 2002). Typical dual-process accounts depict two systems vying for control: the rational versus the emotional; the smart versus the stupid; the slow versus the quick. As we noted above, this is especially clear in Greene's account of what happens in moral dilemmas. The rational system votes for pushing the man in front of the footbridge, the emotional system votes against pushing the man, and the stronger signal carries the day. Like Greene, we think that utilitarian considerations contribute to judgments of all-in permissibility. Furthermore, we would allow that utilitarian considerations can be in competition with non-utilitarian patterns of thought. Indeed, that's what makes the dilemmas vexing in the first place. But we have a different view of the psychological character of *non-utilitarian* judgment. Our model of non-utilitarian judgment invokes separate factors—rules and emotions—but they are not in competition with each other. Rather, the emotions and

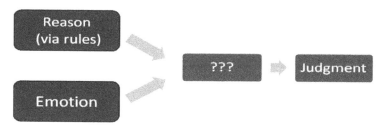

Figure 9.6. Dual-vector model of (non–utilitarian) moral judgment

the rules combine to produce the judgment. Of course there might still be competition when these judgments are pitted against other considerations. But the explanation for why people judge, for example, that it's wrong to push the man in footbridge appeals to multiple systems working together to produce the judgment. In particular, it depends on the integration of emotional reactions and internally represented rules. Thus, instead of thinking of this as a dual-*process* model, on which moral judgment comes from either reason or emotion, we promote a dual *vector* model of non-utilitarian moral judgment. This is depicted in Figure 9.6.

When people make non-utilitarian moral judgments, as in the footbridge case and the moral transgressions in Turiel-style cases, both emotional and rule-based processes are implicated. As reflected in the figure, however, it remains quite unclear how the emotions and rules interact to generate the judgment.

To reinforce the point that rules are critical to such cases of moral judgment, we want to consider one last experiment that has been recently celebrated (e.g. Kelly, forthcoming; Nado et al., forthcoming). In an experiment involving emotion induction, Wheatley and Haidt gave participants a case that involved "no violation of any kind" (2005: 782):

> Dan is a student council representative at his school. This semester he is in charge of scheduling discussions about academic issues. He [tries to take/often picks] topics that appeal to both professors and students in order to stimulate discussion.

The trick was that the subjects had received hypnotic instructions that would lead them to feel disgust at the mention of a certain word (either "often" or "take"), and the experiment was set up so that half of the subjects would get their disgust trigger and the other half wouldn't. What they found was that subjects in the disgust condition did give significantly higher ratings on a scale of moral wrongness (p. 783). However, it is critical to pay attention to the actual numbers here. On a scale from 1 ("not at all morally wrong") to 100 ("extremely morally wrong"), the mean rating for disgust-subjects was still only 14. And that is obviously well on the side of "not morally wrong." Thus, in the one data point we have in which emotion is induced in the absence of a rule, we find that moral condemnation does *not* emerge.

6. Conclusion

The recent wave of research showing a role for emotions in moral judgment has generated a great amount of interest, and we think that this is entirely justified. The discovery and elucidation of the important role that emotions play is perhaps the most exciting pattern of results in moral psychology. However, we should not let our enthusiasm for the emotion-based results lead us into thinking that moral judgment (or even just "deontological" moral judgment) can be identified with an emotional response. Rather, the capacity for moral judgment is rich and complex. The evidence suggests that emotions are one important part of the story, but rule-based accounts also capture an important element of the psychological underpinnings of moral judgment. While we think this much is clear, we think it remains unclear how rules interact with emotions to produce the patterns of moral judgments that we see.

References

Bartholow, B. D., Dickter, C. L., & Sestir, M. A. 2006. Stereotype Activation and Control of Race Bias: Cognitive Control of Inhibition and Its Impairment by Alcohol. *Journal of Personality and Social Psychology*, 90: 272–287.

Blair, J. (1995). A cognitive developmental approach to morality: investigating the psychopath. *Cognition*, 57: 1–29.

—— (2008). Comment on Nichols. In W. Sinnott-Armstrong (ed.), *Moral Psychology vol. 2.* Cambridge, MA: MIT Press, 275–278.

Blair, R. (1999). Responsiveness to Distress Cues in the Child with Psychopathic Tendencies. *Personality and Individual Differences*, 27: 135-145.

Brandt, R. (1985). *A Theory of the Good and the Right*, Oxford: Clarendon Press.

Chagnon, N. (1992). *Yanomamö*, 4th ed. New York: Harcourt Brace Jovanovich.

Chaiken, S. & Trope, Y. (eds.) (1999). *Dual Process Theories in Social Psychology*. New York: Guilford.

Darley, J. M. & Shultz, T. R. (1990). Moral rules: Their content and acquisition. *Annual Review of Psychology*, 41, 525–556.

Fehr, E. & Gächter, S. (2002). Altruistic punishment in humans. *Nature*, 415: 137–140.

Foot, P. (1967). The problem of abortion and the doctrine of the double effect. *Oxford Review*, 5. Reprinted in P. Foot, *Virtues and Vices, and Other Essays in Moral Philosophy*. New York: Oxford University Press, 19–32.

Fried, C. (1978). *Right and Wrong*. Cambridge, MA: Harvard University Press.

Greene, J. & Haidt, J. (2002). How (and where) does moral judgment work? *Trends in Cognitive Science*, 612: 517–523.

Greene, J., Sommerville, R., Nystrom, L., Darley, J., & Cohen, J. (2001). An fMRI investigation of emotional engagement in moral judgment, *Science*, 293: 2105–2108.

Greene, J., Nystrom, L., Engell, A., Darley, J., & Cohen, J. (2004). The Neural Bases of Cognitive Conflict and Control in Moral Judgment. *Neuron*, 44: 389–400.

Greenwald, A., McGhee, D., & Schwartz, J. 1998. Measuring Individual Differences in Implicit Cognition: The Implicit Association Test, *Journal of Personality and Social Psychology*, 74 (6): 1464–1480.

Haidt, J. (2001). The emotional dog and its rational tail. *Psychological Review*, 108: 814–834.

Haidt, J. & Sabini, J. (2000). What exactly makes revenge sweet? Unpublished manuscript, University of Virginia.

Hauser, M., Cushman, F., Young, L., Jin, R., & Mikhail, J. (2007). A dissociation between moral judgments and justifications. *Mind & Language*, 22: 1–21.

Kant, I. (1785/1964). *Groundwork of the Metaphysics of Morals*, trans. H.J. Paton. New York: Harper & Row.

Kelly, D. (forthcoming). Moral Disgust and Tribal Instincts: A Byproduct Hypothesis. *Connected Minds: Cognition and Interaction in the Social World. Proceedings of Cognitio Conference 2007.*

Kelly, D., Stich, S., Haley, K., Eng, S., & Fessler, D. (2007). Harm, Affect and the Moral/Conventional Distinction. *Mind & Language*, 22: 117–131.

Koenigs, M., Young, L., Adolphs, R., Tranel, D., Cushman, F., Hauser, M., Damasio, A. 2007. Damage to the prefrontal cortex increases utilitarian moral judgments. *Nature*, 446: 908–911.

Leslie, A., Mallon, R., & Dicorcia, J. (2006). Transgressors, victims, and cry babies: Is basic moral judgment spared in autism? *Social Neuroscience*, 1: 270–283.

Lorenz, K. (1966). *On Aggression*. New York: Harcourt Brace Jovanovich.

Mikhail, J. (2000). Rawls' Linguistic Analogy. Unpublished PhD thesis, Cornell University.

Nado, J., Kelly, D., and Stich, S. (forthcoming). Moral judgment. In *Routledge Companion to the Philosophy of Psychology*, John Symons & Paco Calvo (eds.).

Nichols, S. (2002). Norms with feeling: Towards a psychological account of moral judgment, *Cognition*, 84: 221–236.

—— (2004). *Sentimental Rules: On the Natural Foundations of Moral Judgment*. New York: Oxford University Press.

Nichols, S., & Mallon, R. (2006). Moral dilemmas and moral rules. *Cognition*, 100: 530–542.

Nisbett, R. & Wilson, T. (1977). Telling More Than We Can Know: Verbal Reports on Mental Processes. *Psychological Review*, 84: 231–259.

Nosek, B. A., Greenwald, A. G., & Banaji, M. R. (2007). The Implicit Association Test at age 7: A methodological and conceptual review. In J. A. Bargh (ed.), *Automatic Processes in Social Thinking and Behavior*. New York: Psychology Press, 265–292.

Nucci, L. (2001). *Education in the Moral Domain*. Cambridge: Cambridge University Press.

Petrinovich, Lewis & O'Neill, Patricia (1996). Influence of Wording and Framing Effects on Moral Intuitions. *Ethology and Sociobiology* 17: 145–171.

Pizarro, D. A. & Bloom, P. (2003). The intelligence of the moral intuitions: A reply to Haidt (2001). *Psychological Review*, 110: 193–196.

Quinn, W. (1989). Actions, intentions, and consequences: The doctrine of double effect, *Philosophy and Public Affairs*, 18: 334–351.

Richeson, J., Baird, A., Gordon, H., Heatherton, T., Wyland, C., Trawalter, S., & Shelton, N. (2003). An fMRI investigation of the impact of interracial contact of executive function, *Nature Neuroscience*, 6 (12): 1323–1328.

Richeson, J. A. & Shelton, J. N. (2003). When prejudice does not pay: Effects of interracial contact on executive function. *Psychological Science*, 14: 287–290.

Ross, W. (1930). *The Right and the Good*. Oxford: Clarendon Press.

Smetana, J. (1993). Understanding of social rules. In M. Bennett (ed.), *The Development of Social Cognition: The Child as Psychologist*. New York: Guilford Press, 111–141.

Shultz, T. R., Schleifer, M., et al. (1981). Judgments of causation, responsibility, and punishment in cases of harm-doing. *Canadian Journal of Behavioral Science*, 13 (3): 238–253.

Shultz, T. R. & Wright, K. (1985). Concepts of negligence and intention in the assignment of moral responsibility. *Canadian Journal of Behavioral Science*, 17: 97–108.

Shultz, T. R., Wright, K., et al. (1986). Assignment of Moral Responsibility and Punishment. *Child Development*, 57: 177–184.

Stanovich, K. (2004). *The Robot's Rebellion*. Chicago, IL: University of Chicago Press.

Storms, M. & Nisbett, R. (1970). Insomnia and the attribution process. *Journal of Personality and Social Psychology*, 2: 319–328.

Thomson, J. (1976). Killing, letting die, and the trolley problem, *The Monist*, 59: 204–217.

Turiel, E. (1983). *The Development of Social Knowledge: Morality and Convention*. Cambridge: Cambridge University Press.

Turiel, E., Killen, M., & Helwig, C. (1987). Morality: Its structure, functions, and vagaries. In J. Kagan & S. Lamb (eds.), *The Emergence of Morality in Young Children*. Chicago, IL: University of Chicago Press.

Valdesolo, P., and DeSteno, D. (2006). Manipulations of Emotional Context Shape Moral Judgment. *Psychological Science*, 17: 476–477.

Wheatley, T., & Haidt, J. (2005). Hypnotically Induced Disgust Makes Moral Judgments More Severe. *Psychological Science*, 16: 780–784.

Wilson, T. (2002). *Strangers to Ourselves*. Cambridge, MA: Harvard University Press.

10

Responsibility[1]

JOSHUA KNOBE AND JOHN M. DORIS

Much of the agenda for contemporary philosophical work on moral responsibility was set by P. F. Strawson's (1962) "Freedom and Resentment." In that essay, Strawson suggests that we focus not so much on metaphysical speculation about the nature of freedom and determinism as on understanding the actual practices surrounding the assignment of praise and blame. If progress can be made on empirical questions regarding how this practice works and what role it serves in people's lives, it is hoped, progress can be made on the apparent philosophical paradoxes surrounding the notion of moral responsibility.

Although many of the philosophers working on moral responsibility today would disagree with the substantive conclusions Strawson reached in that early essay, almost all have been influenced to some degree by his methodological proposals. Thus a great many participants in the contemporary debate about moral responsibility make some appeal to "ordinary practice," particularly to the ordinary practices associated with praise and blame. Each side tries to devise cases in which the other side's theory yields a conclusion that diverges from ordinary practice, and to the extent that a given theory actually is shown to conflict with people's ordinary judgments, it is widely supposed that there is at least some reason to reject the theory itself.

It seems to us that this philosophical effort to understand the ordinary practice of moral responsibility judgment has in some ways been a great success and in other ways a dismal failure. We have been extremely impressed with the ingenuity philosophers have shown in constructing counter-examples to each other's theories, and we think that a number of participants in the debate have

[1] Thanks to audiences at Stanford University; University of Memphis; University of Missouri, Columbia, and the Society for Empirical Ethics for valuable feedback. Special thanks to Michael Bratman, David Henderson, Jonathan Kvanvig, Ken Taylor, Deb Tollefsen, and Peter Vallentyne. We are grateful to our colleagues in the Moral Psychology Research Group, especially Ron Mallon, who provided in-depth comments on all aspects of the present manuscript. This paper was previously circulated under the title "Strawsonian Variations"; the content is unchanged.

been successful in coming up with cases in which their opponents' theories yield conclusions that conflict with ordinary practice. But we have been less impressed with attempts to actually develop theories that accord with ordinary judgments. It seems that each side has managed to show that the other falls prey to counter-examples, resulting in a kind of mutual annihilation or, as Fischer (1994: 83–5) calls it, a "dialectical stalemate."

We want to offer a diagnosis for this persistent difficulty. We suggest that the problem can be traced back to a basic assumption that has guided almost all philosophical discussions of moral responsibility. The assumption is that people should apply the *same* criteria in *all* of their moral responsibility judgments. In other words, it is supposed to be possible to come up with a single basic set of criteria that can account for all moral responsibility judgments in all cases—judgments about both abstract questions and concrete questions, about morally good behaviors and morally bad behaviors, about close friends and complete strangers. Apparently, it is supposed to be completely obvious, and hence in need of no justification or argument, that we ought to apply the same criteria in all cases rather than applying different criteria in different cases. This assumption is so basic that it has never even been given a name. We shall refer to it as the assumption of *invariance*.

The question now is whether it is possible to reconcile this assumption of invariance with the aim of developing a theory that captures what is most important about our ordinary practice. That is, the question is whether one can develop a theory that does an acceptable job of fitting with the ordinary practice (perhaps revising that practice here and there but nonetheless holding on to its essential character) and yet relies only on invariant principles for responsibility attribution.

In our view—and in the view of increasing numbers of philosophers (Alexander & Weinberg, 2006; Knobe & Nichols, 2008; Nadelhoffer & Nahmias, 2007)—the best way to test an assumption about people's ordinary judgments is to conduct systematic experimental studies. Recent years have seen numerous studies of responsibility attribution along these lines, and the results collectively suggest a surprising new hypothesis. It seems that people do not make moral responsibility judgments by applying invariant principles. Instead, it appears that people tend to apply quite different criteria in different kinds of cases. Thus, if one wants to understand why people make the judgments they do, it is no use looking for a single basic set of criteria that fits all of people's ordinary judgments. A more promising approach would be to look at how and why people may adopt different criteria in different cases, depending on the way an issue is framed, whether the agent is a friend or a stranger, and so on.

This discovery in empirical psychology leaves us with a stark choice in moral philosophy. One option would be to hold on to the goal of fitting with people's ordinary judgments and thereby abandon the assumption of invariance. The other would be to hold on to the assumption of invariance and thereby accept a quite serious divergence from people's ordinary judgments. But it seems that one cannot have it both ways. As we shall see, a growing body of experimental results points to the view that it is not possible to capture all of people's ordinary judgments with a theory that applies the very same criteria in every case.

1. Invariantist Theories in Philosophy

We begin by briefly reviewing some of the major invariantist theories of moral responsibility. Our aim here is not to represent individual theories in detail, but simply to introduce some of the themes that we shall be discussing in more depth in the sections to come.

Before reviewing the major theories, however, a few words are in order about what we mean by "invariantism". A theory counts as invariantist if it applies the same basic criteria in all cases where people are making moral responsibility judgments. Thus, an invariantist theory might say:

(1) "No matter who we are judging, no matter what the circumstances are, always make moral responsibility judgments by checking to see whether the agent meets the following criteria . . ."

Note that the criteria given by an invariantist theory need not involve strict necessary and sufficient conditions. The criteria could just as easily involve prototypes, exemplars, or whatever cognitive scientists think up next. What makes a theory invariantist is not the specific character of the criteria themselves but the fact that the theory applies the *same* criteria in all cases.

It would, however, be a rejection of invariantism to say:

(2) "If the agent is a friend, use the following criteria . . . but if the agent is a stranger, use these other, slightly different criteria . . ."

It is important to emphasize that the rejection of invariantism does not entail the rejection of a search for clear and definite principles. Rule (2) does give us a definite principle; it's just that this principle does not have the property of being invariantist. Instead of telling us to apply the same criteria in all cases, it tells us how to apply different criteria in different cases.

Now, to really explain what it is for a rule to be invariantist, we would have to say more precisely what it means to "apply the same criteria in all cases." Needless to say, this would be a daunting task. (For example, there is a rather trivial sense in which the person who follows rule (2) is applying the same criteria in all cases—namely, that in all cases he or she is applying rule (2).) The technical problems here are thorny, and philosophers of science have been wrestling with them for decades.[2] But in this case, as so often, we think it is possible to make important philosophical progress without first stepping into the swamp of technicalities necessary to "define one's terms." The best way to make it clear what counts as an invariantist theory is just to take a look at a few of the major theories from the existing philosophical literature. All of these theories truly do proceed by applying the same criteria to all cases. Our approach, then, will be ostensive: we'll describe a few of the most influential philosophical theories and then ask whether it is really possible to capture ordinary responsibility judgments using the invariantist approach they all share.[3]

Of the theories we will be discussing, the oldest and most well known is *incompatiblism* (e.g. Kane, 1996; Pereboom, 2001; van Inwagen, 1983). Incompatiblism is the claim that moral responsibility is incompatible with determinism. In other words, incompatibilists say that an agent can never be morally responsible for a behavior if that behavior was a deterministic consequence of certain initial conditions and physical laws. For example, incompatibilists endorsing the Principle of Alternate Possibilities insist that the agent is responsible *only if* she could have done otherwise, a condition allegedly incompatible with causal determinism, and these incompatibilists are committed to the view that in *no case* where the agent was unable to do otherwise can the agent be legitimately attributed responsibility. Recent years have seen an increasingly sophisticated debate about whether the incompatibilist thesis is warranted, but we shall not be discussing the nuances of that debate here. Instead, we simply want to emphasize that the many incompatibilist theories on current offer are invariantist views. That is, these theories claim that moral

---

[2] Initially, one might think that it is possible to explain what makes a rule like (2) turn out not to be invariantist just by adverting to its logical form. But things are not quite that simple. Thus, suppose we define the predicate *franger* by saying that a person is "franger" if she is either a friend who meets criterion *x* or a stranger who meets criterion *y*. Then someone could say: "I apply the same basic criterion to all cases. No matter who a person is, I always determine whether or not she is morally responsible by checking to see whether she is franger." In such a case, it seems clear that the person is *not* really applying the same criterion in each case—he is applying one criterion to friends, another to strangers—but it has proven extraordinarily difficult to say precisely how rules like this one differ from rules that do legitimately apply the same criteria to every case (see, e.g., Goodman, 1954).

[3] For more comprehensive reviews, see Eshleman (2004) and Fischer (1999).

responsibility is *always* incompatible with determinism. No incompatibilist we know of suggests that the incompatibilist thesis might apply only to very close friends or that it might apply only to certain particular types of behaviors. Rather, the thesis is that, for all possible behaviors and all possible contexts, moral responsibility is incompatible with determinism.

Those who reject the incompatibilist thesis are known as *compatibilists*. Thus compatibilists say that it is possible for a person to be morally responsible even in a deterministic universe. But compatibilists are no less invariantist than the incompatibilists they argue against. Compatibilists typically say that determinism is *never* relevant to moral responsibility in any way. They then put forward some other invariant principle that is supposed to serve as a criterion for moral responsibility judgments in all possible contexts. A wide variety of such criteria has been proposed. We shall be concerned here with two of the most influential.[4]

First, the *real self view*. The key claim behind this view is that people are morally responsible only for behaviors that stem from a specific part of the self or a specific type of mental state. Hence it may be suggested that people are morally responsible only for behaviors that stem from the part of their selves with which they are "identified" (Frankfurt, 1988: 53–54) or that they are responsible only for behaviors that accord with their values (Watson, 1975).

A second major compatibilist position might be called the *normative competence theory*. This theory says that people are morally responsible only for behaviors that were produced by a process that is appropriately sensitive to reasons (Fischer & Ravizza, 1998; Wolf, 1990). Proponents of this theory have been especially explicit in claiming that a single basic criterion can be applied to all possible behaviors. Indeed, much of the intellectual excitement surrounding the normative competence theory stems from the ingenious ways in which researchers have been able to derive an apparently diverse array of moral responsibility judgments from an underlying principle that is extremely simple and unified. To put it in the present lexicon, such approaches appeal in part because of the success they appear to have in deploying an invariantist standard.

Debate between these rival views often appeals to "ordinary practice." Each side tries to come up with cases in which people's judgments conflict with the conclusions that follow from the other side's theory. So, for example, incompatibilists try to devise cases in which people would ordinarily say that an agent is not morally responsible for her behavior but in which the major compatibilist positions (real self, normative competence, etc.) all yield the

---

[4] The two approaches need not be incompatible. Doris (2002: ch. 7) considers a position that appears to combine elements of both views.

conclusion that she actually is responsible (e.g. Pereboom, 2001). Conversely, compatibilists try to find cases in which people would ordinarily say that an agent is morally responsible but in which all of the major incompatibilist positions yield the conclusion that she is not (e.g. Frankfurt, 1969).

Our claim is that this is a conflict in which *both* sides endure unacceptable casualties. That is, each side can show that the other's views conflict with seemingly entrenched judgments in certain kinds of cases. The problem, we suggest, is that people simply do not have invariant criteria for making moral responsibility judgments. Thus, whenever a theory offers an invariant criterion, it will be possible to come up with cases in which people's judgments conflict with conclusions that can be derived from the theory. If one really wants to develop a theory that accords with the ordinary practice, one needs to abandon the search for invariant criteria and try instead to examine the ways in which people end up using different criteria in different cases.

Here we shall be concerned with three kinds of factors that appear to influence the criteria people use—the abstractness or concreteness of the question, the normative status of the behavior itself, and the relationship between the person making the judgment and the agent being judged.

2. Abstract vs. Concrete

It is essential to distinguish between different ways of checking to see whether a given principle is in accord with ordinary people's judgments. One approach would be to present people with an explicit statement of the principle itself and ask them whether or not they agree with it. Another would be to look at people's judgments regarding particular cases and see whether these judgments fit the criteria derived from the principle. The usual view seems to be that both of these approaches are relevant when we are evaluating proposed criteria for moral responsibility.

One of the chief lessons of contemporary cognitive science, however, is that these two approaches quite often lead to different conclusions. It can easily happen that the principles people put forward in abstract conversations have almost nothing to do with the criteria they actually use when considering concrete cases. Thus most linguists agree that people's grammatical intuitions about concrete cases are based on a complex competence that is almost entirely unrelated to the principles they are able to apply when asked more abstract, theoretical questions (e.g. Chomsky, 1986). Similarly, social psychologists have uncovered numerous factors that appear to influence people's judgments in concrete cases but which people regard as irrelevant when asked in the abstract (e.g. Wicker, 1969). There is good reason to expect that judgments about moral responsibility will show a similar pattern. That is, one should expect to find that people's judgments in concrete cases do not match up perfectly with the principles they endorse in more abstract discussions.

One particularly striking example arises in the debate over whether ordinary people are compatibilists or incompatibilists. The most common view among philosophers is that most people have strongly incompatibilist inclinations:

Beginning students typically recoil at the compatibilist response to the problem of moral responsibility.   (Pereboom, 2001: xvi)

. . . we come to the table, nearly all of us, as pretheoretic incompatibilists.   (Ekstrom, 2002: 310)

In my experience, most ordinary persons start out as natural incompatibilists . . . Ordinary persons have to be talked out of this natural incompatibilism by the clever arguments of philosophers.   (Kane, 1999: 218)

When ordinary people come to consciously recognize and understand that some action is contingent upon circumstances in an agent's past that are beyond that agent's control, they quickly lose a propensity to impute moral responsibility to the agent for that action.   (Cover & O'Leary-Hawthorne, 1996: 50)

Clearly, these are empirical claims, but it has traditionally been assumed that there is no need to test them using systematic experimental techniques. After all, philosophers are continually engaged in a kind of informal polling.[5] They present material in classes and listen to how their students respond. What they typically find, it seems, is that students lean strongly toward incompatibilism, and this is customarily taken to indicate that folk morality, as practiced outside the confines of philosophy classrooms, is itself incompatibilist. But when researchers began examining these questions more systematically, their findings did not confirm the claims that philosophy professors had been making about their students. In fact, the results pointed strongly in the opposite direction: people's judgments, over a range of stimulus materials, appeared to be strongly *compatibilist*.

The first study to arrive at this surprising conclusion was conducted by Viney and colleagues (1982, 1988). The researchers used an initial questionnaire to distinguish between subjects who believed that the universe was deterministic

---

[5] Jackson (1998) is a rare philosopher who makes this methodology explicit. For the difficulties Jackson faces, see Doris & Stich (2005).

and those who did not. All subjects were then given questions in which they had an opportunity to provide justifications for acts of punishment. The key finding was that determinists were no less likely than indeterminists to offer retributivist justifications. This finding provided some initial evidence that most determinists were predominately compatibilists.

Woolfolk, Doris, and Darley (2006) arrived at a similar conclusion using a very different methodology. They ran a series of experiments in which subjects were given short vignettes about agents who operated under high levels of constraint. In one such vignette, a character named Bill is captured by terrorists and given a "compliance drug" to induce him to murder his friend:

> Its effects are similar to the impact of expertly administered hypnosis; it results in total compliance. To test the effects of the drug, the leader of the kidnappers shouted at Bill to slap himself. To his amazement, Bill observed his own right hand administering an open-handed blow to his own left cheek, although he had no sense of having willed his hand to move. The leader then handed Bill a pistol with one bullet in it. Bill was ordered to shoot Frank in the head . . . Bill thought he noticed his finger moving on the trigger, but could not feel any sensations of movement. While he was observing these events, feeling like a puppet, passively observing his body moving in space, his hand closed on the pistol, discharging it and blowing Frank's brains out.

The researchers also manipulated the degree to which the agent was portrayed as *identifying* with the behavior he has been ordered to perform. Subjects in one condition were told that Bill did not want to kill Frank; those in the other condition were told that Bill was happy to have the chance to kill Frank. The results showed that subjects were more inclined to hold Bill morally responsible when he identified with the behavior than when he did not. In other words, people assigned more responsibility when there were higher levels of identification *even though the agent's behavior was entirely constrained*. (A manipulation check indicated that subjects, quite sensibly, recognized the strength of the "compliance drug" constraint.) The study therefore provides strong evidence for the view that people are willing to hold an agent morally responsible for a behavior even when that agent could not possibly have done otherwise.

Finally, Nahmias, Morris, Nadelhoffer, and Turner (2006) ran a series of experiments in which subjects were given stories about agents who performed immoral behaviors in deterministic worlds. Subjects were then asked to say whether these agents were morally responsible for what they had done. In one such experiment, subjects were given the following case:

> Imagine that in the next century we discover all the laws of nature, and we build a supercomputer which can deduce from these laws of nature and from the current state of everything in the world exactly what will be happening in the world at any future time. It can look at everything about the way the world is and predict everything about how it will be with 100% accuracy. Suppose that such a supercomputer existed, and it looks at the state of the universe at a certain time on March 25th, 2150 A.D., twenty years before Jeremy Hall is born. The computer then deduces from this information and the laws of nature that Jeremy will definitely rob Fidelity Bank at 6:00 PM on January 26th, 2195. As always, the supercomputer's prediction is correct; Jeremy robs Fidelity Bank at 6:00 PM on January 26th, 2195.

Subjects were then asked whether Jeremy was morally blameworthy. The vast majority (83%) said yes, indicating that they thought an agent could be morally blameworthy even if all of his behaviors were determined by natural laws. The researchers conducted three experiments—using three quite different ways of explaining determinism—and always found a similar pattern of responses.

Looking at these results, it may seem mysterious that any philosopher could have thought that ordinary people were incompatibilists. How could philosophers have concluded that people were incompatibilists when they so readily give compatibilist answers in systematic psychological studies? Are philosophy professors just completely out of touch with what their undergraduates really think? We suspect that something more complex is going on: perhaps people tend to give compatibilist answers to *concrete* questions about particular cases but incompatibilist answers to *abstract* questions about general moral principles. Then the divergence between the findings from psychological studies and the conclusions of philosophers teaching classes might simply be due to a difference between two ways of framing the relevant question.

Nichols and Knobe (2007) conducted an experiment to test this hypothesis. All subjects were given a story about a universe ("Universe A") in which events always unfold according to deterministic laws. Subjects in the "abstract condition" were then given the question:

> In Universe A, is it possible for a person to be fully morally responsible for their actions?

Subjects in the "concrete condition" were given the question:

In Universe A, a man named Bill has become attracted to his secretary, and he decides that the only way to be with her is to kill his wife and 3 children. He knows that it is impossible to escape from his house in the event of a fire. Before he leaves on a business trip, he sets up a device in his basement that burns down the house and kills his family.

Is Bill fully morally responsible for killing his wife and children?

The results were dramatic. A full 72% of subjects in the concrete condition said that the agent was fully morally responsible, but less than 5% of subjects in the abstract condition said that it was possible to be fully morally responsible in a deterministic universe.

If this pattern of results is replicated in further experiments, we shall have good reason to believe that no invariantist theory of moral responsibility can capture all of people's ordinary judgments. Traditional incompatibilist theories diverge from people's judgments in more concrete cases, whereas traditional compatibilist theories diverge from people's judgments about more abstract principles. The only kind of theory that could consistently accord with people's judgments would be a theory that generated different conclusions depending on whether the question at hand was abstract or concrete.

3. Variance due to Differences in Normative Status

As we explained above, the ambition of invariantist accounts of moral responsibility is to find a single system of criteria that can be used to assess moral responsibility for all possible behaviors. One is not supposed to end up with one criterion for morally good behaviors and another, slightly different criterion for morally bad behaviors. The aim is rather to find a single system of underlying principles from which all moral responsibility judgments can be derived.

This approach certainly has a strong intuitive appeal. It seems that moral responsibility is one thing and the goodness or badness of the behavior is something else. If we put together a judgment of moral responsibility with a judgment about whether the behavior itself is good or bad, we can determine whether or not the agent deserves praise or blame. But—it might be claimed—we do not need to assess the goodness or badness of the behavior itself before determining whether or not the agent is responsible for performing it.

Adherents of normative competence theories, for example, have sometimes argued that it is possible to find a single set of criteria that can be applied to all behaviors, regardless of their moral status. The claim is that we can use this same set of criteria to make moral responsibility judgments for morally good behaviors, morally bad behaviors, and even behaviors that are morally neutral (e.g. Fischer & Ravizza, 1998). This is a claim at the level of philosophical theory, but one will want to ask, inasmuch as one follows the philosophically familiar course of taking conformity to actual practice as a theoretical desideratum, how well it accords with people's practice. Our task now is to figure out whether or not it is possible to capture people's ordinary judgments by setting forth a single basic set of criteria that apply to all kinds of behavior.

A growing body of evidence suggests that it is not. In fact, there appear to be at least five distinct asymmetries whereby the criteria for moral responsibility depend in part on the moral status of the behavior itself.

3.1. *The Side-Effect Asymmetry*

It is widely agreed that an agent can be morally responsible for a behavior only if she stands to that behavior in a certain kind of psychological relation. Still, there has been considerable disagreement about precisely which sort of psychological relation is necessary here. Some authors suggest that the agent needs only to have certain *beliefs* about what she is doing (e.g. Fischer & Ravizza, 1998); others say that the agent needs to *identify* herself with the behavior (e.g. Frankfurt, 1988; Doris, 2002: ch. 7); and a number of researchers have suggested that there is an important link between moral responsibility and the notion of acting *intentionally* (e.g. Wallace, 1994). In general, participants in this debate have tried to find a single type of psychological relation that would be necessary for moral responsibility in all cases. What we want to suggest here is that things may not be quite so simple. Perhaps different psychological relations prove relevant depending on whether the behavior itself is good or bad.

Consider people's judgments of moral responsibility in cases of *foreseen side-effects*. These are cases in which an agent performs a behavior because she wants to bring about one effect (the desired effect) but is aware that she will also be bringing about some other effect that she does not specifically desire (the foreseen side-effect). The question is whether people will feel that the agent is responsible for bringing about the foreseen side-effects of her behaviors. As you may have guessed, the answer appears to be that it depends on whether the side-effects themselves are morally good or morally bad.

One way to get at this phenomenon is to conduct studies in which subjects are randomly assigned to receive either a vignette about a morally good side-effect or a morally bad side-effect. In one such study (Knobe, 2003), subjects in one condition were given a vignette about an agent who harms the environment:

> The vice-president of a company went to the chairman of the board and said, "We are thinking of starting a new program. It will help us increase profits, but it will also harm the environment."
>
> The chairman of the board answered, "I don't care at all about harming the environment. I just want to make as much profit as I can. Let's start the new program."
>
> They started the new program. Sure enough, the environment was harmed.

Subjects in the other condition received a vignette that was almost exactly the same, except that the word "harm" was replaced with "help." The vignette thus became:

> The vice-president of a company went to the chairman of the board and said, "We are thinking of starting a new program. It will help us increase profits, and it will also help the environment."
>
> The chairman of the board answered, "I don't care at all about helping the environment. I just want to make as much profit as I can. Let's start the new program."
>
> They started the new program. Sure enough, the environment was helped.

As expected, people's moral judgments showed a marked asymmetry. Most subjects who had been given the vignette about environmental harm said that the chairman deserved blame, but very few subjects who had been given the vignette about environmental help said that the chairman deserved praise. Subsequent research has found similar effects using other vignettes (Knobe, 2003; Sverdlik, 2004). There appears to be a general tendency whereby people are given blame for bad side-effects but are *not* given praise for good side-effects. Thus, if we wanted to know whether a given effect was the sort of thing for which an agent would be said to deserve praise or blame, it would not be enough merely to know about the agent's psychological relation to the effect. We would also have to know whether the effect itself was good or bad.

How is this effect to be explained? It might at first be thought that the effect here is due to a quite general "negativity bias" (e.g. Rothbart & Park, 1986: 137; Richey et al., 1975, 1982; Reeder & Coovert, 1986; Skowronski & Carlston, 1989)—i.e. that people simply have a general tendency to be "stingier" with praise than they are with blame. The asymmetry we see here could then be understood as just one manifestation of an across-the-board disposition to apply more stringent criteria for moral responsibility in cases where a behavior is morally good. But, as we shall see, things are not so simple. There does not appear to be a general effect whereby people are always stingier with praise than with blame. Rather, it appears that there is a complex interaction between the goodness or badness of the behavior and the criteria for moral responsibility.

3.2. *The Emotion Asymmetry*

The complexity of people's responses emerges especially clearly when we consider the role that the attribution of emotional states plays in judgments of moral responsibility. Sometimes an agent is so overwhelmed by emotion that she cannot resist performing a particular behavior. On such "heated" occasions, will people assign less praise or blame than they would have if the agent had decided to perform the behavior after a period of calm deliberation?

Pizarro, Uhlmann, and Salovey (2003) set out to determine whether the impact of emotion might depend on the moral status of the behavior itself. They began by constructing a series of vignettes about agents who perform behaviors as a result of overwhelming emotion. Some of the vignettes featured morally good behaviors; others featured morally bad behaviors. Here is an example of a vignette with a morally good behavior:

> Because of his overwhelming and uncontrollable sympathy, Jack impulsively gave the homeless man his only jacket even though it was freezing outside.

And here is one with a morally bad behavior:

> Because of his overwhelming and uncontrollable anger, Jack impulsively smashed the window of the car parked in front of him because it was parked too close to his.

For each of these vignettes, the researchers then constructed a contrast case in which the agent acted calmly and deliberately. So, for example, the contrast case for the morally good behavior described above was:

> Jack calmly and deliberately gave the homeless man his only jacket even though it was freezing outside.

And the contrast case for the morally bad behavior was:

> Jack calmly and deliberately smashed the window of the car parked in front of him because it was parked too close to his.

When the researchers gave these vignettes to subjects, they found a striking asymmetry. Subjects gave the agent considerably less blame for morally bad behaviors when those behaviors were the result of overwhelming emotion than when they were the result of calm deliberation. But, for morally good behaviors, there was no corresponding effect. Subjects assigned just as much praise when the agent acted on overwhelming emotion as when the agent acted after calm deliberation. Apparently, emotion diminishes attributions of responsibility only in cases of transgression.

Putting the side-effect asymmetry together with the emotion asymmetry, we see the beginnings of a complex pattern. It seems that the fact that an outcome was merely a foreseen side-effect reduces the responsibility attributed for morally good behaviors but not for morally bad ones, whereas the fact that a behavior was the product of overwhelming emotion reduces the responsibility attributed for morally bad behaviors but not for morally good ones.

3.3. The Intention/Action Asymmetry

As if this were not complicated enough, we now turn to people's attributions of responsibility for unfulfilled intentions. Suppose an agent forms an intention but never actually gets a chance to perform the corresponding action. Will people assign praise or blame for the mere forming of the intention? Here again, the answer appears to depend on whether the behavior in question is good or bad.

To confirm this hypothesis, Malle and Bennett (2004) constructed pairs of sentences—with each pair consisting of one sentence that described an action and one that described the corresponding intention. Some of the pairs described actions and intentions that were morally good; others described actions and intentions that were morally bad. One of the morally good pairs was:

[*action*] helped a neighbor fix his roof.
[*intention*] intends to help a neighbor fix his roof.

One of the morally bad pairs was:

[*action*] sold cocaine to his teenage cousin.
[*intention*] intends to sell cocaine to his teenage cousin.

Subjects were given a list of such sentences and asked to make moral judgments. Some subjects were given sentences about actions; others were given sentences about mere intentions. In either case, subjects were asked how much praise or blame the agent deserved. This "between-subjects" design allowed the researchers to measure the *difference* between the amount of praise or blame given for an action and the amount given for the corresponding intention.

As expected, there was a significant asymmetry between the morally good cases and the morally bad cases. Specifically, the difference between the amount of praise for morally good actions vs. morally good intentions was far greater than the difference in blame for morally bad actions vs. morally bad intentions. (Indeed, the effect size of the difference for morally good pairs was *twice* as high as the effect size for morally bad pairs.) In other words, people were given almost as much blame for bad intentions as they were for bad actions, but they were not given nearly as much praise for good intentions as they were for good actions. Apparently, even if good intentions don't always pave the road to hell, neither do they grease the rails to heaven.

3.4. *The Moral Ignorance Asymmetry*

It is often supposed that an agent is not morally responsible for her behavior when that behavior is the product of non-culpable ignorance. Thus, consider the agent who asks a question that ends up hurting someone's feelings. It seems that this agent is not morally responsible unless there was some way she could have guessed that she was bringing up a touchy subject.

The issue becomes considerably more complex, however, when the ignorance in question is concerned only with *moral* considerations. Suppose that an agent knows all of the relevant non-moral facts but suffers from a kind of ignorance that makes her unable to see that a particular action is wrong. Is she still morally responsible for her action?

Unfortunately for those who think that this question admits of an easy answer, Shoemaker (2007) has gathered data that raise some interesting and difficult new philosophical issues. First, he presented subjects with the case of a dictator named JoJo. (The case closely follows an example from Wolf, 1987.)

> JoJo is the favorite son of Jo the First, an evil and sadistic dictator of a small, undeveloped country, entirely cut off from the outside world. Because of his father's special feelings for the boy, JoJo is given a special education and is allowed to accompany his father and observe his daily routine. In light of this treatment, little JoJo, who worships his father (as most boys do), takes his father as a role model and develops values just like his dad's. As an adult, JoJo does the same sorts of things his father did, including sending people to prison or to death or to torture chambers on the basis of whim. He does these things because he sincerely believes they are morally right, and he is aware of no reason to think otherwise. One day, a peasant sneezes as JoJo walks by, so JoJo heads over to the peasant and punches him in the face, just like his father would have done. He feels no guilt afterwards.

Other subjects were presented with a case exactly like this one except that it described JoJo as having all of the relevant moral knowledge. Just as one might expect, subjects thought that JoJo was less morally blameworthy when they were told that he suffered from moral ignorance than they were when they were told that he had the relevant moral knowledge.

Now comes the surprising part. In another condition, Shoemaker presented subjects with a story in which JoJo's action is morally *praiseworthy*. This story began much like the first one but then ended with the words:

> As he's pulling back his fist, though, he suddenly feels compassion and discovers that he can't bring himself to punch the peasant, even though he still believes it's the right thing to do. He thus backs away and lets the peasant go free, even though he believes that doing so is immoral, and he feels quite guilty afterwards.

Here again, the intuitions of subjects who received this story could be compared with intuitions of subjects who received a story that was almost exactly the same except that JoJo had all of the relevant knowledge. But this time, there was no difference in moral judgments. Subjects thought that JoJo was *no less praiseworthy* when he didn't know he was doing the right thing as when he did know (cf. Arpaly, 2003).

In other words, there seems to be an asymmetry such that moral ignorance makes people think an agent is less blameworthy but does not make people think the agent is less praiseworthy. Will it be possible to explain this asymmetry and all of the others using a single invariant system of criteria? The prospects are looking dimmer and dimmer.

3.5. *The Severity Asymmetry*

Finally, consider cases in which the harm is due entirely to an accident. For any given accident, it will almost always be possible to find some way in which some agent could have taken precautions that would have prevented it, but one does not always conclude that such agents are responsible for the harm that results. Quite often, one feels that the agents did all that they could reasonably be expected to do and that they are therefore not responsible for the accidents that eventually occurred. So it seems that people are able to establish a vague sort of threshold, such that one can say: "As long as the agent's degree of care does not fall below this threshold, she is not responsible for the harm that results." The key question now is whether people always draw that threshold at the same point or whether the precise location of the threshold actually depends on the goodness or badness of the outcome that transpires.

Four decades of research on this topic points unequivocally to the conclusion that the location of the threshold actually depends on the nature of the outcome itself. People are willing to say that an agent is responsible for a severe harm even when that agent's behavior was only very slightly negligent, whereas they refused to say that an agent is responsible for mild harms unless the agent was very negligent indeed.[6]

The severity asymmetry was first detected in a classic study by Walster (1966) and has since been replicated in a broad array of additional experiments. In Walster's original study, all subjects were given a story about a man who parks his car at the top of a hill. They were told that the man remembered to put on his brakes but that he neglected to have his brake cables checked. The car rolls down the hill and ends up causing an accident. In one condition, subjects were told that the resulting harm was *mild* (a damaged fender); in the other condition, subjects were told that the resulting harm was *severe* (serious injury to an innocent child). All subjects were then asked whether the agent had acted carelessly and whether he was responsible for the accident. There was no difference between conditions in subjects' judgments as to whether the agent acted carelessly, but subjects were significantly more likely to say that the agent was responsible for the accident in the condition where the harm was described as severe than they were in the condition where the harm was described as mild.[7]

This result was regarded as surprising, since it was initially assumed that people's responsibility judgments would depend only on the agent's level of negligence and not on the level of harm that ended up resulting. But the effect obtained in Walster's original study has subsequently been replicated in a number of additional studies using quite different methodologies, and a recent meta-analysis of 75 studies on the topic leaves little doubt that the effect is real (Robbennolt, 2000).

3.6. *Summing Up*

Thus far, we have presented data from five studies on people's assignment of praise and blame. These five studies all used the same basic structure. People

---

[6] Note that this asymmetry is different in form from the four asymmetries discussed above. The asymmetry here is not between good outcomes and bad outcomes but rather between mildly bad outcomes and severely bad outcomes.

[7] Note that this result goes beyond the phenomena usually discussed under the heading of "moral luck" (Nagel, 1976; Williams, 1981). It is not simply that people assign more blame when the outcome is severe than they do when the outcome is mild (which would not be a very surprising experimental result); rather, the key finding is that subjects actually think that the agent is morally responsible for the severe harm but that he or she is not morally responsible for the mild harm.

were presented with behaviors that differed in their moral status but seemed highly similar in every other relevant respect. It was then shown that people ascribed a lot of praise or blame to one of the behaviors but not to the other. The key question now is whether these results indicate that the folk practice of responsibility attribution is not invariantist or whether there is some way to explain the results even on the assumption that people are applying the very same criteria in all cases.

It might be argued, for example, that the asymmetries obtained in the studies are not really showing us anything about people's attributions of moral responsibility. Maybe people regard the agents in both conditions as morally *responsible*; it's just that they don't assign *praise or blame* in one of the conditions because they do not feel that the agent in that condition truly did anything good or bad. This explanation might be plausible for the intention/action asymmetry, but it does not seem plausible for any of the others on our list. Subjects can be reasonably supposed to believe that helping the environment is something good and smashing a car window is something bad. To the extent that people do not assign praise or blame for these behaviors, it is presumably because they do not take the agent to be morally responsible.

A second possible strategy would be to argue that there is a single, more or less unified criterion for moral responsibility and that all of the apparent asymmetries we have discussed can be derived in some way from this one criterion. So, for example, Wolf (1990) has argued that what we have called the "emotion asymmetry" can actually be derived in a straightforward way from the normative competence theory. Recall that the normative competence theory says that an agent is morally responsible if and only if she is capable of doing the right thing for the right reasons. But this unified theory seems to lead immediately to different judgments in cases of different emotions. After all, it does seem that overwhelming and uncontrollable anger might render a person incapable of doing the right thing for the right reasons but that overwhelming and uncontrollable sympathy does not have the same effect.

Given the actual data gathered about the emotion asymmetry, it is not at all clear that this theory accords with the overall pattern of people's intuitions. (Note that Pizarro and colleagues [2003: study 2] found that subjects were reluctant to praise an agent who acted out of compassion but who wished that he could become less compassionate.) But that is not the real problem. The real problem is that the theory does not even begin to explain the various other asymmetries (e.g. the side-effect asymmetry). To show that the folk practice is invariantist in the relevant sense, it would be necessary to find a single system of criteria that can explain all of the asymmetries described in this section.

It certainly would be an instructive and valuable effort to look for a single invariant system of criteria from which all of these apparent asymmetries can be derived, and we wish future researchers the best of luck in this effort. But to be frank, we don't think it is very likely that they will have much success.

4. Variance in the Antecedents of Responsibility Judgments

At this point, it might be thought that we have located some variantist elements in certain peripheral aspects of the practice of responsibility attribution but that there still remains a kind of "core" of the practice that is entirely invariantist. Hence, someone might say: "Look, you've convinced me that at least *some* aspects of the criteria vary, but let's not get carried away. It certainly does seem that many central aspects of the criteria always remain exactly the same. No matter whether the outcome is good or bad, we will always be concerned with questions about whether the agent *caused* that outcome and whether she brought it about *intentionally*. These aspects of the criteria, at least, appear to be perfectly invariant."

Our response to this objection will be a somewhat surprising one. It is at least possible that people always base responsibility judgments on antecedent judgments about causation and intentional action, but we want to suggest that these antecedent judgments *themselves* are not invariant. It may be, for example, that people always ask themselves whether the agent *caused* the outcome and whether the agent acted *intentionally*, but there is evidence to suggest that people do not have invariant criteria for assigning causation and intentional action. Instead, it appears that people use different criteria depending on whether the behavior itself is good or bad.

Consider first the claim that responsibility judgments are always sensitive to judgments as to whether or not the agent acted intentionally. How can this claim be reconciled with the hypothesis (presented above) that the relevant psychological relation depends on whether the behavior itself is good or bad? The answer is simple. People always ask whether the agent acted intentionally, but their judgments as to whether or not the agent acted intentionally sometimes depend on whether the behavior itself was good or bad.

This point comes out clearly in the experiment described above (Knobe, 2003). Recall that all subjects were given a vignette about an agent who brings about a foreseen side-effect, but some subjects received a vignette in which the side-effect was morally bad and others received a vignette in which the side-effect was morally good. The surprising result was that subjects in these different conditions had different intuitions about whether or not the agent acted intentionally. Most subjects in the harm condition said that the corporate executive *intentionally* harmed the environment, but most subjects in the help condition said that the agent *unintentionally* helped the environment.[8] Here we find an asymmetry in people's views about whether the agent acted intentionally even though all of the relevant psychological features appear to be the same in the two conditions. The chief difference seems to lie in the moral status of the behavior performed.

These results are puzzling, and a number of competing hypotheses have been proposed to explain them (Adams & Steadman, 2004; Knobe, 2003; Machery, 2006; Malle, 2006; Nadelhoffer, 2006; Nichols & Ulatowski, forthcoming). We shall not be defending a specific hypothesis here. Instead, we want simply to point to the surprising mesh between the criteria used for assessing moral responsibility and the criteria used for determining whether or not an agent acted intentionally. We noted above that moral responsibility judgments rely on different psychological states depending on whether the behavior itself is good or bad. In particular, it seems that foresight is often sufficient when the behavior is morally bad but that actually aiming at the relevant effect is usually necessary when the behavior is morally good. We now see exactly the same pattern in people's judgments as to whether the agent acted intentionally. Here again, it seems that foresight is sufficient when the behavior is morally bad but that actually aiming at the effect is necessary when the behavior is morally good.

Similar remarks apply to people's judgments of causation. It may well be that judgments of causation play an important role whenever people are trying to assess moral responsibility, but the evidence suggests that causal judgments themselves are not derived using invariant criteria. Instead, it appears that the criteria used in causal judgments vary depending on the moral status of the behavior itself.

This point comes out especially clearly in a well-known study by Alicke (1992). All subjects were given a story about an agent who is driving home 10 miles per hour above the speed limit. In one condition, the agent needs to get home swiftly so that he can hide the present he just bought for his parents. In

---

[8] This effect appears to be remarkably robust. It continues to emerge when the vignettes are translated into Hindi and run on Hindi-speaking subjects (Knobe & Burra, 2006), when subjects are only four years old (Leslie et al., 2006), and even when subjects have deficits in emotional processing due to frontal lobe damage (Young et al., 2006). For further replications and extensions, see Adams & Steadman (2004), Feltz & Cokely (2007), Nadelhoffer (2006), Malle (2006), McCann (2005), and Nichols & Ulatowski (forthcoming).

the other, he needs to get home so that he can hide his stash of cocaine. Either way, he then ends up getting into an accident. The key dependent variable was subjects' judgments about the degree to which the agent *caused* the accident by driving too fast. By now, you have probably guessed the result. Subjects were significantly more inclined to say that the agent caused the accident when he was driving home to hide his cocaine than when he was driving home to hide the present (Alicke, 1992). Similar results have been obtained in a variety of other studies (Alicke, 2000; Alicke et al., 1994; Solan and Darley, 2001). The consensus among social psychologists appears to be that, collectively, these studies provide strong evidence for the view that moral considerations have a powerful impact on people's causal judgments.

Nonetheless, most social psychologists assume that moral considerations do not actually play any role in people's underlying *concept* of causation. Instead, the usual view distinguishes between multiple levels. First, there is the competence that people use to assess causation. This competence is taken to be a purely descriptive mechanism (perhaps something along the lines suggested by Kelly's 1967 theory of 'the person as scientist'), and it is assumed that moral considerations play no role in it. Then, second, there is some additional process by which moral considerations can "bias" or "distort" people's causal judgments, leading them away from what the underlying competence itself would have proposed.

In recent years, however, a number of philosophers have proposed more radical views according to which the observed effects of moral considerations are showing us something fundamental about the concept of causation itself (Dray, 1957; Hitchcock, 2007; Knobe & Fraser, forthcoming; Mackie, 1955; McGrath, 2005; Thomson, 2003). These philosophers argue that the connection between moral judgments and causal judgments is not, in fact, due to a performance error. Rather, people's moral judgments influence their causal judgments because moral features actually figure in people's concept of causation.

Perhaps the best way to get a sense for what these philosophers are suggesting is to consider the kinds of cases they typically discuss. Here is one representative case:

> The receptionist in the philosophy department keeps her desk stocked with pens. The administrative assistants are allowed to take the pens, but faculty members are supposed to buy their own.
>
> The administrative assistants typically do take the pens. Unfortunately, so do the faculty members. The receptionist has repeatedly emailed them reminders that only administrative assistants are allowed to take the pens.

On Monday morning, one of the administrative assistants encounters Professor Smith walking past the receptionist's desk. Both take pens. Later that day, the receptionist needs to take an important message . . . but she has a problem. There are no pens left on her desk.

Faced with this case, most subjects say that Professor Smith *did* cause the problem but that the administrative assistant *did not* cause the problem (Knobe & Fraser, forthcoming). And yet the two agents seem to have performed almost exactly the same behavior in almost exactly the same circumstances; the principal difference between the two behaviors appears to lie in their differing *moral* statuses. In cases like these, it seems plausible to suppose that moral considerations could really be playing some fundamental role in the basic competence by which we assess causation.

Of course, it might be true that causal judgments always have the same impact on judgments of moral responsibility, regardless of whether the behavior itself is morally good or morally bad. But the moral goodness or badness of the behavior still ends up influencing moral responsibility judgments in an indirect way. It influences people's causal judgments, which in turn play a role in their judgments of moral responsibility.

5. Variance due to Relationships

Philosophical discussions of moral responsibility are often concerned in an essential way with our ordinary practice of responsibility attribution, and philosophers therefore frequently appeal to ordinary people's judgments about particular cases. But the cases described in these philosophical discussions almost always take a somewhat unusual form. They are almost always hypothetical cases involving entirely *imaginary* characters. So, for example, Frankfurt's (1969) famous argument about alternate possibilities relies on a story about a man named Jones being controlled by a nefarious neurosurgeon named Black. When one sees that most people agree about whether or not the characters in these stories are morally responsible, it is easy to get the sense that there must be some invariant criterion for moral responsibility that almost everyone is using.

But, clearly, ordinary attributions of moral responsibility do not usually work like these philosophical examples. Most ordinary attributions of responsibility are not about complete strangers; they are about people to whom we stand in certain *relationships* (friends, spouses, coworkers, etc.). If we want to know whether there really is an invariant criterion for responsibility judgments, we need to look at cases involving a wide variety of relationships and see whether it is possible to identify a single criterion underlying them all.

The best way to address this question is to look at the psychological literature on moral responsibility. Unfortunately, though, most of this literature uses the very same methodology that the philosophical literature does. Indeed, a recent review (Pearce, 2003) found that 77% of psychological studies on blame used hypothetical scenarios, and 65% used scenarios in which the transgressor was an entirely fictional character. So although the empirical literature does provide a few fascinating insights into the connection between personal relationships and attributions of moral responsibility, it also leaves a number of important questions unanswered. Here we discuss a few highlights of the existing literature and then pose a number of questions that still remain unaddressed.

We begin with Arriaga and Rusbult's (1998) study of perspective taking and blame. The phrase "perspective taking" refers here to a disposition to try to imagine how a situation might appear from another person's position. The researchers wanted to know whether this disposition would be associated with low levels of blame attribution. So they proceeded in the obvious way. They gave all subjects a questionnaire designed to assess an overall disposition for perspective taking. Then they presented subjects with hypothetical stories and asked them how much blame the agents in these stories deserved. The key research question was whether or not there would be a correlation between level of perspective taking and level of blame. As it happened, there was no significant correlation: high levels of perspective taking were not positively associated with low levels of blame attribution.

But the researchers also introduced an interesting variation on the usual experimental paradigm. Subjects were asked questions designed to assess the degree to which they showed perspective taking *specifically in relation to their spouses*. Instead of being asked general questions about their personalities, subjects were asked to specify their level of agreement with sentences about how they normally thought of their partner (e.g. "When I'm upset or irritated by my partner, I try to imagine how I would feel if I were in his/her shoes."). After answering these initial questions, each subject was presented with a hypothetical scenario concerning his or her spouse. For example:

> You feel neglected by your partner, who has been very busy lately. You nevertheless make dinner plans for an approaching evening, to which the partner reluctantly agrees. Your partner arrives for dinner half an hour late, not ready to dine, explaining that he or she must cancel dinner because of a course project that is due the next day.

Subjects were then asked how much blame the spouse would deserve if this scenario had actually taken place. As predicted, there was a significant correlation whereby subjects who were high in perspective taking in relation to their spouses tended to assign lower levels of blame. In other words, people's attributions of blame to an agent seemed to depend on their relationship to that particular agent, with people assigning lower amounts of blame to those agents whose perspectives they were especially likely to take.

Similar results were obtained in a study by Fincham, Beach, and Baucom (1987). The aim of the study was to compare blame attributions among ordinary couples with attributions from "distressed" couples who had chosen to come in for counseling. Members of each of these groups received two kinds of questions:

(1) They were told to imagine that their *spouses* had performed particular behaviors and then asked how much praise or blame the spouses would deserve.

(2) They were told to imagine that *they themselves* had performed certain behaviors and were asked how much praise or blame they themselves would deserve.

The key question was whether subjects in each group would assign different levels of blame depending on whether the agent was the self or the spouse.

Members of distressed couples showed an asymmetry between judgments about the self and judgments about the spouse. They assigned more credit to themselves than to their spouses and more blame to their spouses than to themselves. This result is hardly surprising. The surprising results came from the normal couples (couples who had not specifically come in for counseling). Members of these couples also showed an asymmetry—but in the opposite direction. They assigned more credit to their spouses than they did to themselves. In other words, members of normal couples were in a state of systematic disagreement with each other. Each of them thought that the other was the one who deserved more praise.

Of course, a number of questions arise about how to interpret these results. It is possible (at least in principle) that the results could be obtained even if people's relationships had no effect at all on their attributions of blame and praise. For example, it could be that some factor that has nothing to do with people's relationships is causing certain couples to show higher levels of blame. This high blame might then cause the relationship to become distressed, thereby producing the correlation found in the study. But the experimental evidence suggests that the process does not actually work like this (e.g. Harvey et al., 1978). Instead, it appears that attributions and marital satisfaction affect each other in a cyclical fashion, with high levels of satisfaction leading to low levels of blame and low levels of satisfaction leading to high levels of blame.

Still, a question arises about precisely how marital satisfaction impacts attributions of blame. In particular, one wants to know whether marital satisfaction is actually having any impact on the fundamental criteria underlying people's moral judgments or whether it only affects moral judgments indirectly by first affecting people's judgments regarding particular matters of fact (what their spouses are trying to do, how much control they have over certain outcomes, etc.).

The studies of Madden and Janoff-Bulman (1981) help us to address this question. Women exhibiting varying levels of marital satisfaction were presented with hypothetical stories involving their spouses. They were then asked to make judgments about both (a) certain purely factual aspects of the stories (e.g. how much control the spouse would have had over particular outcomes) and (b) the amount of blame the spouse would deserve if the fictitious events had actually happened.

As in earlier studies, there was a correlation whereby people with lower levels of marital satisfaction showed higher levels of blame. In this study, however, it was also possible to get a handle on the specific mechanisms whereby marital satisfaction and blame were related. In particular, it was possible to test the hypothesis that marital satisfaction only influenced blame attributions indirectly—i.e. that marital satisfaction influenced judgments about specific matters of fact, which then influenced attributions of blame. The results indicated that this is not, in fact, how the effect arises. It seems that the relationship between marital satisfaction and blame is entirely direct, unmediated by specific factual judgments.

We began this section by noting that philosophical discussions of moral responsibility often try to make contact with our ordinary practice of responsibility attribution. The most common method for investigating this practice is to look at people's judgments concerning particular cases. However, the studies we have presented seem to indicate that people's judgments about particular cases can vary dramatically depending on their relationship to the agent. Thus people may arrive at different attributions depending on whether the agent is a beloved partner, a bitter enemy, or a complete stranger. This conclusion sheds new light on the methods usually used in philosophical discussions. It seems that these discussions have been concerned with attributions to one particular type of agent—namely, attributions to agents with whom one has no prior relationship.

Here it might be argued that the absence of any prior relationship gives us an especially pure glimpse into the nature of responsibility attributions. It might be thought, for example, that people's relationships to the agent serve as a kind of "distortion," leading them to violate norms that they themselves accept. This is an interesting hypothesis, which needs to be investigated empirically. One wants to know whether information about personal relationships actually figures in the fundamental competence underlying ascriptions of moral responsibility or whether it impacts the process only by increasing the probability of various performance errors.

On a related note, it would be helpful to know how people who stand in different relationships to the agent conceive of the difference between their perspectives. Take the case of a woman who cheats on her husband. Here we might find that her husband regards her as blameworthy but her friends do not. What remains to be seen is how people make sense of the divergence of attitudes in cases like this one. One possibility would be that both sides agree that there is a single objective answer to the question as to whether the woman is blameworthy or not and that they simply disagree about what this answer actually is. Another possibility would be that neither side believes that there is any real disagreement. That is, both sides might feel that different standards are appropriate depending on one's relationship to the woman in question, and everyone might therefore agree that she is worthy of being blamed by her husband but not by her friends. If we did obtain this result, we would have evidence that people explicitly reject the idea of invariant criteria for the ascription of moral responsibility.

6. Conclusion

Thus far, we have been marshaling evidence for the claim that the ordinary practice of responsibility attribution is pervasively variantist. People's ordinary responsibility judgments do not appear to follow from a single system of criteria that can be applied in all cases. Instead, it seems that people use different sorts of criteria depending on the case at hand.

In this final section, we assume that the evidence presented above is sufficient to warrant this basic claim and then go on to examine its implications for psychology and for moral philosophy. One of our key claims will be that these two sorts of implications should be understood as *separate*. The correct psychological theory cannot by itself settle the relevant moral questions, nor can the correct moral theory tell us what we need to know about the psychological questions.

Psychological Implications[9]

From a psychological perspective, the most important remaining questions are about how to explain the various results we have been reviewing here. Clearly, the only way to answer these questions would be to go through each of the different effects and consider in detail the various hypotheses one might offer to explain it. Here, however, our aim is not so much to pursue this project in detail as to make some general comments about how such a research program might proceed.

To begin with, it is customary to distinguish between two different aspects of the psychological mechanism underlying people's moral judgments:

- The *competence* underlying a person's judgments of moral responsibility consists of that person's own representation of the criteria for moral responsibility.
- A person's *performance systems* are the systems that enable that person to figure out whether a given agent fulfills the criteria given by his or her underlying competence.

Note that the notion of competence employed here is a straightforwardly psychological one. The suggestion is that we posit a "competence" as part of an empirical theory that, taken as a whole, enables us to predict and explain certain observable phenomena. The decision to posit a competence as part of such a theory should be regarded as independent of the various philosophical debates surrounding concepts, conceptual analysis, analyticity, and so forth.

Instead, the point is simply that it can prove helpful to distinguish between different sorts of psychological factors that play a role in generating moral judgments. Thus, suppose that people observe an agent performing a behavior and want to know whether or not this agent is responsible. They may have certain criteria about the conditions this agent needs to meet before he or she can be considered morally responsible (the underlying competence) and then certain capacities that allow them to apply those criteria to the case at hand (performance systems). Together, these two factors could generate a judgment as to whether or not the agent actually is morally responsible.

Corresponding to these two aspects of our psychology are two possible hypotheses about why any given factor might impact people's intuitions. One

---

[9] We are grateful to Ron Mallon for extremely helpful comments on the material presented here.

possible hypothesis would be that our competence actually represents this factor as being relevant to moral responsibility; the other would be that the factor simply interferes with the performance systems that would normally enable people to apply their competence correctly. Each of these hypotheses offers a plausible account of the various asymmetries we have been documenting here. Thus, consider the impact that relationships appear to have on attributions of responsibility. One way to explain this impact would be to say that relationships actually play a role in our underlying criteria for moral responsibility judgments; the other would be to say that the feelings we have as a result of these relationships are simply interfering with our ability to correctly apply our own criteria.

One of the most exciting developments in the study of these phenomena over the past few years has been the construction of detailed models that say precisely how the competence and performance systems together generate the patterns we have been discussing (e.g. Alicke, 2008; Malle, 2006; Nadelhoffer, 2006; Nahmias, 2006). These models bring up a variety of fascinating theoretical questions, and we cannot possibly do justice to them here. Instead, we simply want to say something about their epistemic status. Specifically, we want to emphasize that the claim that these effects are due to performance errors is an *empirical* claim. The best way to assess such a claim is to use the existing models to generate specific predictions and then put these predictions to the test in further experiments. If the predictions do not pan out, we shall have good reason to reject the claims about performance errors.

This basic approach should be contrasted with an alternative that might initially seem appealing but that, we believe, ultimately serves only to hinder the progress of research in this area. On this alternative approach, one appeals directly to people's intuitions about which considerations can plausibly be considered relevant to the underlying competence. For example, one might say: "It's just *obvious* that moral judgments can't be playing a role in the fundamental competence underlying the concept of causation." Or perhaps: "The severity of a harm couldn't *possibly* be playing any role in the competence underlying judgments of moral responsibility." Tempting though this approach may be, we think that it does not truly have any place in a legitimate scientific study of these phenomena. The fact that a particular view strikes certain people as obvious does not show us anything about the nature of the competence underlying ordinary attributions of responsibility. What would show us something about that competence is a specific, testable model that accounts for the existing data and can then be used to generate new predictions that can be examined in further studies.

Above all, it is important not to confuse the distinction between competence and performance (a psychological distinction) with the distinction between getting the right answer and getting the wrong answer (a normative distinction). When researchers say that a given intuition is not due to any performance error, all they mean is that this intuition was generated by correctly working out the implications of people's own criteria. The question as to whether those criteria themselves are correct is a quite separate question, which can only be resolved by doing serious moral philosophy.

Moral Implications

Suppose now that the basic competence underlying people's attributions of responsibility actually does turn out to be variantist. We shall then face a new question, namely: *but are they right?* That is, if we learn that people are variantists, we shall have to answer the question as to whether variantism is truly correct or whether people are making some kind of mistake.

In discussions of questions like this one, it is often helpful to distinguish two basic viewpoints. *Conservatives* believe that the criteria we employ are more or less correct as they are, while *revisionists* believe that the criteria we now employ are seriously mistaken and therefore in need of revision. (For further discussion, see Vargas, 2005.) Of course, most plausible views will lie somewhere on the continuum between extreme conservativism and extreme revisionism. On one hand, it seems unlikely that everything about our existing practices is perfectly fine just the way it is; on the other, it seems unlikely that everything about these practices is fundamentally flawed and in need of revision. Presumably, we shall find that some aspects of our practices are now correct while others need to be revised.

The key question for present purposes, however, is not about the extent to which we should revise our practices in general but rather about whether we should specifically revise these practices in such a way that they become invariantist. In other words, the question is whether we should remove all of the variantist elements from these practices, so that we end up applying precisely the same criteria in all cases. This question brings up a number of complex issues, and we have discussed it in detail elsewhere (Doris et al., 2007). Our aim here is just to make a few quick remarks about how the issue ought to be understood.

It has sometimes been suggested to us that invariantism is obviously correct and that any trace of variantism just *has* to involve some sort of moral error. This conclusion, we believe, is a bit too hasty. Although invariantism may ultimately turn out to be correct, its correctness is far from obvious. To see the complexity here, it may be helpful to look at the sorts of value judgments we make in other domains. Thus, consider the enormous variety of cases in which we might say that an outcome is 'good'—cases in which the outcome is morally good, cases in which it is aesthetically good, and so forth. Here it certainly seems plausible to suggest that we do not need to find a single fundamental system of criteria from which these two different types of judgments can be derived. One might simply say: "Moral judgments and aesthetic judgments are very different sorts of things. There is no reason why there has to be a single system of criteria for both." And, of course, a similar suggestion might be made about the relationship between moral blame and moral praise. Suppose that someone said: "Moral blame and moral praise are just two very different things. There is no reason why we need a single system of criteria for both." It should be clear that this view is a coherent one; the only question now is whether it is actually correct.

In our view, that latter question still remains open. At any rate, one cannot help but be struck by how difficult it has been to develop an invariantist theory that does not fall prey to counter-examples. Perhaps it is time to give variantism a try.

References

Adams, F., & Steadman, A. (2004). Intentional Action in Ordinary Language: Core Concept or Pragmatic Understanding? *Analysis*, 64: 173–181.

Alexander, J., & Weinberg, J. (2006). Analytic Epistemology and Experimental Philosophy. *Philosophy Compass*, 2 (1): 56–80.

Alicke, M. D. (1992). Culpable causation. *Journal of Personality and Social Psychology*, 63: 368–378.

——(2000). Culpable control and the psychology of blame. *Psychological Bulletin*, 126: 556–574.

——(2008). Blaming Badly. *Journal of Cognition and Culture*, 8: 179–186.

Alicke, M. D., Davis, T. L., & Pezzo, M. V. (1994). A posteriori adjustment of a priori decision criteria. *Social Cognition*, 12: 281–308.

Arpaly, N. (2003). *Unprincipled Virtue: An Inquiry into Moral Agency*. Oxford: Oxford University Press.

Arriaga, X., & Rusbult, C. (1998). Standing in my partner's shoes: Partner perspective taking and reactions to accommodative dilemmas. *Personality and Social Psychology Bulletin*, 9: 927–948.

Chomsky, N. (1986). *Knowledge of Language: Its Origin, Nature and Use*. New York: Praeger.

Cover, J. A., & O'Leary-Hawthorne, J. (1996). Free agency and materialism. In *Faith, Freedom and Rationality*, J. Jordan & D. Howard-Snyder (eds.). Lanham, MD: Roman and Littlefield, 47–71.

Doris, J. M. (2002). *Lack of Character: Personality and Moral Behavior*. Cambridge: Cambridge University Press.

Doris, J. M., Knobe, J., & Woolfolk, R. (2007). Variantism about responsibility. *Philosophical Perspectives*, 21: 184–214.

Doris, J. M.,& Stich, S. (2005). As a Matter of Fact: Empirical Perspectives on Ethics. In F. Jackson & M. Smith (eds.), *The Oxford Handbook of Contemporary Analytic Philosophy*. Oxford: Oxford University Press, 114–152.

Dray, W. (1957). *Laws and Explanation in History*. London: Oxford University Press.

Ekstrom, L. (2002). Libertarianism and Frankfurt-style cases. In R. Kane (ed.), *The Oxford Handbook of Free Will*. New York: Oxford University Press, 309–322.

Eshleman, A. (2004). Moral responsibility. *The Stanford Encyclopedia of Philosophy* (Fall ed.), E. N. Zalta (ed.), URL = <http://plato.stanford.edu/archives/fall2004/entries/moral-responsibility/>.

Feltz, A., & Cokely, E. (2007). An Anomaly in Intentional Action Ascription: More Evidence of Folk Diversity. In *Proceedings of the Cognitive Science Society*. Mahwah, NJ: Lawrence Erlbaum, 1748.

Fincham, F., Beach, S., & Baucom, D. (1987). Attribution processes in distressed and nondistressed couples: 4. Self-partner attribution differences. *Journal of Personality and Social Psychology*, 52: 739–748.

Fischer, J. M. (1994). *The Metaphysics of Free Will*. Cambridge, MA: Blackwell.

——(1999). Recent work on moral responsibility. *Ethics*, 110: 93–139.

Fischer, J., & Ravizza, M. (1998). *Responsibility and Control: A Theory of Moral Responsibility*. New York: Cambridge University Press.

Frankfurt, H. (1969). Alternate possibilities and moral responsibility. *Journal of Philosophy*, 66: 829–39.

——(1988). *The Importance of What We Care About*. Cambridge: Cambridge University Press.

Goodman, N. (1954). *Fact, Fiction, and Forecast*. London: Athlone Press.

Harvey, J. H., Wells, G. L., & Alvarez, M. D. (1978). Attribution in the context of conflict and separation in close relationships. In J. H. Harvey, W. J. Ickes, & R. F. Kidd (eds.), *New Directions in Attribution Research* (Vol. 2). New York: Lawrence Erlbaum Associates, 235–266.

Hitchcock, C. (2007). Three concepts of causation. *Philosophy Compass*, 2/3: 508–516.

van Inwagen, P. (1983). *An Essay on Free Will*. Oxford: Oxford University Press.

Jackson, F. (1998). *From Metaphysics to Ethics: A Defense of Conceptual Analysis*. New York: Oxford University Press.

Kane, R. (1996). *The Significance of Free Will*. New York: Oxford University Press.

——(1999). Responsibility, luck, and chance: Reflections on free will and indeterminism. *Journal of Philosophy*, 96: 217–240.

Kelly, H. H. (1967). Attribution theory in social psychology. In D. Levine (ed.), *Nebraska Symposium on Motivation*. Lincoln, NE: University of Nebraska Press, 129–238.

Knobe, J. (2003). Intentional action and side effects in ordinary language. *Analysis*, 63: 190–193.

Knobe, J., & Burra, A. (2006). The folk concepts of intention and intentional action: A cross-cultural study. *Journal of Culture and Cognition*, 6: 113–132.

Knobe, J., & Fraser, B. (2008). Causal judgment and moral judgment: Two experiments. In W. Sinnott-Armstrong, *Moral Psychology Volume 2: The Cognitive Science of Morality: Intuition and Diversity*. Cambridge, MA: MIT Press, 441–448.

Knobe, J., & Nichols, S. (2008). *Experimental Philosophy*. New York: Oxford University Press.

Leslie, A., Knobe, J., & Cohen, A. (2006). Acting intentionally and the side-effect effect: "Theory of mind" and moral judgment. *Psychological Science*, 17: 421–427.

Machery, E. (2006). The folk concept of intentional action: Philosophical and experimental issues. *Mind & Language*, 23(2): 165–189.

Mackie, J. L. (1955). Responsibility and Language. *Australasian Journal of Philosophy*, 33: 143–159.

Madden, M., & Janoff-Bulman, R. (1981). Blame, control, and marital satisfaction: Wives' attributions for conflict in marriage. *Journal of Marriage and the Family*, 43: 663–674.

Malle, B. (2006). Intentionality, morality, and their relationship in human judgment. *Journal of Cognition and Culture*, 6: 87–113.

Malle, B., & Bennett, R. (2004). People's praise and blame for intentions and actions: Implications of the folk concept of intentionality. Unpublished manuscript. University of Oregon.

McCann, H. (2005). Intentional action and intending: Recent empirical studies. *Philosophical Psychology*, 18: 737–748.

McGrath, S. (2005). Causation by omission. *Philosophical Studies*, 123: 125–148.

Nadelhoffer, T. (2006). Bad acts, blameworthy agents, and intentional actions: Some problems for jury impartiality. *Philosophical Explorations*, 9 (2): 203–220.

Nadelhoffer, T., & Nahmias, E. (2007). The Past and Future of Experimental Philosophy. *Philosophical Explorations*, 10: 123–150.

Nagel, T. (1976). Moral luck. *Proceedings of the Aristotelian Society*, Supplementary vol. 50: 137–155.

Nahmias, E. (2006). Folk Fears about Freedom and Responsibility: Determinism vs. Reductionism. *Journal of Cognition and Culture*, 6 (1–2): 215–237.

Nahmias, E., Morris, S., Nadelhoffer, T., & Turner, J. (2006). Is incompatibilism intuitive? *Philosophy and Phenomenological Research*, 73 (1): 28–53. Reprinted in *Experimental Philosophy*, S. Nichols & J. Knobe (eds.), Oxford: Oxford University Press, 2008.

Nichols, S., & Knobe, J. (2007). Moral Responsibility and Determinism: The Cognitive Science of Folk Intuitions. *Noûs*, 41: 663–685.

Nichols, S., & Ulatowski, J. (forthcoming). Intuitions and Individual Differences: The Knobe Effect Revisited. *Mind & Language*.

Pearce, G. (2003). The psychology of everyday blame. Doctoral dissertation. University of Oregon.

Pereboom, D. (2001). *Living Without Free Will*. Cambridge: Cambridge University Press.

Pizarro, D., Uhlmann, E., & Salovey, P. (2003). Asymmetry in judgments of moral blame and praise: The role of perceived metadesires. *Psychological Science*, 14: 267–272.

Reeder, G. D., & Coovert, M. D. (1986). Revising an Impression of Morality. *Social Cognition*, 4: 1–17.

Richey, M. H., Koenigs, R. J., Richey, H. W., & Fortin, R. (1975). Negative Salience in Impressions of Character: Effects of Unequal Proportions of Positive and Negative Information. *Journal of Social Psychology*, 97: 233–241.

Richey, M. H., Bono, F. S., Lewis, H. V., & Richey, H. W. (1982). Selectivity of Negative Bias in Impression Formation. *Journal of Social Psychology*, 116: 107–118.

Robbennolt, J. (2000). Outcome severity and judgments of "responsibility": A meta-analytic review. *Journal of Applied Social Psychology*, 30: 2575–2609.

Rothbart, M., & Park, B. (1986). On the Confirmability and Disconfirmability of Trait Concepts. *Journal of Personality and Social Psychology*, 50: 131–142.

Shoemaker, D. (2007). Autonomy and responsibility. Manuscript in preparation. Bowling Green State University.

Skowronski, J. J., & Carlston, D. E. (1989). Negativity and Extremity Biases in Impression Formation: A Review of Explanations. *Psychological Bulletin*, 105: 131–142.

Solan, L. M., & Darley, J. M. (2001). Causation, contribution, and legal liability: An empirical study. *Law and Contemporary Problems*, 64: 265–298.

Strawson, P. F. (1962). Freedom and resentment. *Proceedings of the British Academy*, 48: 187–211.

Sverdlik, S. (2004). Intentionality and moral judgments in commonsense thought about action. *Journal of Theoretical and Philosophical Psychology*, 24: 224–236.

Thomson, J. (2003). Causation: Omissions, *Philosophy and Phenomenological Research*, 66: 81.

Vargas, M. (2005). The revisionist's guide to responsibility. *Philosophical Studies*, 125: 399–429.

Viney, W., Waldman, D., & Barchilon, J. (1982). Attitudes toward Punishment in Relation to Beliefs in Free Will and Determinism. *Human Relations*, 35: 939–949.

Viney, W., Parker-Martin, P., & Dotten, S. D. H. (1988). Beliefs in Free Will and Determinism and Lack of Relation to Punishment Rationale and Magnitude. *Journal of General Psychology*, 115: 15–23.

Wallace, R. J. (1994). *Responsibility and the Moral Sentiments*. Cambridge, MA: Harvard University Press.

Walster, E. (1966). Assignment of responsibility for an accident. *Journal of Personality and Social Psychology*, 3: 73–79.

Watson, G. (1975). Free agency. *Journal of Philosophy*, 72: 205–220.

Wicker, A. W. (1969). Attitudes vs. actions: The relationship of verbal and overt behavioural responses to attitude objects. *Journal of Social Issues*, 22: 41–78.

Williams, B. (1981). *Moral Luck*. New York: Cambridge University Press.

Wolf, S. (1987). Sanity and the metaphysics of responsibility. In Ferdinand Schoeman (ed.), *Responsibility, Character, and the Emotions*. Cambridge: Cambridge University Press, 46–62.

—— (1990). *Freedom Within Reason*. Oxford: Oxford University Press.

Woolfolk, R. L., Doris, J. M., & Darley, J. M. (2006). Identification, situational constraint, and social cognition: Studies in the attribution of moral responsibility. *Cognition*, 100: 283–301.

Young, L., Cushman, F., Adolphs, R., Tranel, D., & Hauser, M. (2006). Does emotion mediate the effect of an action's moral status on its intentional status? Neuropsychological evidence. *Journal of Cognition and Culture*, 6: 291–304.

11

Character

MARIA W. MERRITT, JOHN M. DORIS, AND GILBERT
HARMAN[1]

1. Introduction

On the one hand, the burgeoning tradition of modern virtue ethics centrally
involves discussions of moral psychology, where it is often claimed that
character-based ethical theories manifest greater "psychological realism" than
their competitors (Anscombe, 1958: 1, 15; Williams, 1985: 206; Flanagan,
1991: 182; Hursthouse, 1999: 19–20). On the other hand, much research
in personality and social psychology appears to unsettle familiar notions of
character; although it was not much noticed until recently, philosophers
and psychologists had been talking about the same things for decades. The
philosophers who first exploited this synchronicity advanced views that were,
in varying degrees, skeptical of philosophical approaches to character current
in virtue ethics (e.g. Flanagan, 1991; Doris, 1998, 2002, 2005; Harman, 1999,
2000; Merritt, 2000; Vranas, 2005). Subsequently, this skepticism drew spirited
replies from defenders of virtue ethics (e.g. Appiah, 2008; Adams, 2006: chs.
8–12; Annas, 2005; Arpaly, 2005; Montmarquet, 2003; Kamtekar, 2004; Miller,
2003; Kupperman, 2001; Sabini & Silver, 2004, 2005; Solomon, 2003, 2005;
Sreenivasan, 2002; Webber, 2006; 2007a, b; Swanton, 2003: 30–31). While
some of these respondents (e.g. DePaul, 1999) have denied that virtue ethics
makes empirical claims of sufficient strength to be troubled by the critique,
they have more often eschewed such empirical modesty, and acknowledged
that virtue ethics ought to make use of the empirical literature (e.g. Swanton,
2003: 30–33). It is this strain of the discussion that we shall take up here, in

[1] For valuable research assistance, Maria Merritt thanks Daryl Cameron, whose work was supported
by a Chappell Undergraduate Fellowship from the Charles Center at the College of William and Mary.
Some of Maria Merritt's work on this chapter was supported by a 2005–06 Faculty Fellowship at the
Edmond J. Safra Foundation Center for Ethics at Harvard University, where Dennis F. Thompson,
Arthur I. Applbaum, Renee M. Jones, and other members of the 2005–06 Faculty Fellows seminar
offered helpful comments and discussion.

exploring some of the avenues available to, and the difficulties faced by, an empirically sensitive character psychology. We consider virtue-ethical ideals of practical rationality, as well as certain basic moral norms, in light of the picture of human cognition now emerging in the cognitive sciences. We interpret some of the classic psychological experiments as evidence that morally consequential behavior is pervasively influenced by cognitive processes that resist intentional direction, and are at best insensitive to personal, reflectively endorsed moral norms, if not contrary to them. Lastly, on the basis of this understanding, we survey the prospects for using empirical results to seek remedies for such adverse influences on moral thinking and behavior. But before (re)entering the fray, we had better describe it.

2. Skepticism about Character

The dispute concerns the extent to which there are *robust character traits*. As we understand this presumption, "a person [who] has a robust trait can confidently be expected to display trait-relevant behavior across a wide variety of trait-relevant situations, even where some or all of these situations are not optimally conducive to such behavior" (Doris, 2002: 18; cf. Merritt, 2000: 365–366). The virtues are paradigmatic examples of such traits: if one possesses the virtue of courage, for example, one is expected to behave *consistently* courageously when it is ethically appropriate to do so, despite the presence of inducements to behave otherwise. This seems intuitive enough, and evidence abounds, both in the philosophical literature (see Doris, 2002: ch. 2; Harman, 1999) and in psychological research on social perception (Jones, 1990; Ross & Nisbett, 1991; Gilbert & Malone, 1995; Kunda, 1999) that many find it so. Indeed, there is a strong tendency for people—at least Western people[2]—to attribute seemingly unusual actions of any sort to such robust character traits rather than to the situations of agents.

The trouble comes in the form of a long "situationist" experimental tradition in social psychology.[3] Consider some examples familiar in the philosophical literature:

- Isen and Levin (1972: 387) discovered that subjects who had just found a dime were 22 times more likely to help a woman who had dropped some papers than subjects who did not find a dime (88% vs. 4%).

[2] Numerous studies indicate that the conception of character at issue is considerably less prominent in other cultures, notably East Asian ones (see Nisbett, 2003; Doris, 2002: 105–106, 2005).

[3] For summaries of this 80-year research tradition, see Ross & Nisbett (1991); Kunda (1999); Doris (2002); Vranas (2005).

- Haney et al. (1973) describe how college students role-playing as guards in a simulated prison rapidly descended to pervasive cruelty and abuse.
- Darley and Batson (1973: 105) report that passersby not in a hurry were 6 times more likely to help an unfortunate who appeared to be in significant distress than were passersby in a hurry (63% vs. 10%).
- Milgram (1974) found that subjects would repeatedly "punish" a screaming "victim" with realistic (but simulated) electric shocks at the polite request of an experimenter.
- Mathews and Cannon (1975: 574–575) reported that subjects were 5 times more likely to help an apparently injured man who had dropped some books when ambient noise was at normal levels than when a power lawnmower was running nearby (80% vs. 15%).

These experiments, some of which will be further discussed below, are not aberrational, but *representative*: social psychologists have *repeatedly* found that the difference between good conduct and bad appears to reside in the situation more than in the person; both disappointing omissions and appalling actions are *readily* induced through seemingly minor situations. What makes these findings so striking is just how *insubstantial* the situational influences that produce troubling moral failures seem to be; it is not that people fail standards for good conduct, but that people can be induced to do so with such ease. At the same time, as Mischel (1968) observed in his famous critique of trait theory, research predicated on the attribution of character and personality traits has enjoyed uneven success in the prediction of behavior; standard measures of personality traits have very often been found to be only tenuously related to behavior in particular situations where the expression of those traits is expected.[4] In short, situational influences often appear to do their work with little regard to the characters of the people in the situation. Viewing this (very substantial) empirical record, we should begin to question whether behavior is perspicuously understood as "flowing" from robust traits.

The skeptical argument pressed by the empirical record may be formulated as a *modus tollens*:[5]

(1) If behavior is typically ordered by robust traits, systematic observation will reveal pervasive behavioral consistency.

---

[4] There is a history of personality psychologists expressing doubts about notions of personality traits like that at issue here (e.g. Vernon, 1964; Peterson, 1968; Mischel, 1968, 1999; Pervin, 1994). For criticism of this critical view, see Funder (1991) and Goldberg (1993, 1995). Doris (2002: ch. 4) attempts an adjudication of this heated dispute.

[5] Alternatively, think of the argument as abductive (Harman, 1999; Doris, 2002: 26): The variousness of human behavior is best explained by reference to the hypothesis that robust traits are rarely instantiated in human beings.

(2) Systematic observation does *not* reveal pervasive behavioral consistency.

(3) Behavior is *not* typically ordered by robust traits.

If this argument is sound, a central presupposition of ordinary thinking about character is seriously undermined and character-based moral psychology is threatened—to the extent that it constitutes an extrapolation from ordinary thinking about character, and so long as it is committed to empirically assessable descriptive claims. Now we think this argument, or something in the immediate vicinity, is sound, but some defenders of virtue ethics will be quick to disagree. So far as we can tell, the observation embodied by premise (2) is not much in dispute; while there may be differences of degree, all parties agree that situational variability is a pervasive feature of human behavior, at least when that behavior is systematically sampled. Instead, one important response to the skeptical argument can be seen as addressing premise (1), and it is here that we shall begin.

The conditional in (1) reflects the following thought: to justify the attribution of robust traits, we require evidence in the form of consistent behavior. The conditional further assumes a notion of "overt" behavior, having to do with (in principle) publicly observable performances like helping someone with some dropped papers, or refusing to torture animals (or people!) in the name of science. While the notion of overt behavior may seem unproblematic, even the skeptics allow that it is a slippery one (see Doris, 2005). Defenders of virtue ethics, for their part, think it is a recipe for missing the point. According to Swanton (2003: 30–31), to contend that the experimental literature "demonstrates the empirical inadequacy of virtue ethics, because there is a lack of cross-situational consistency in *behavior*, betrays a lack of understanding of the virtue ethicist's concept of virtue."[6] Apparently, trait attributions are warranted (or not) by reference to evidence of a different sort; namely, by characteristic inner states. Webber (2006: 205) advocates a conception of traits as "long-term dispositions to have inclinations of certain strengths to behave in certain ways in response to certain kinds of stimuli"—e.g. the inclination to respond with physical violence to insults—together with a theory of how such dispositions combine to issue in behavior (ibid.: 204–205): "One's overt behavior is the result of the relative strengths of one's competing inclinations." Whereas Webber does not specify the normative criteria for a virtuous resolution of competition among inclinations, Swanton (2003: 30–31) emphasizes the emotional propensities characteristic of virtue, while Annas (2005)

---

[6] Similar observations have been offered in psychology; Allport (1966: 1) insisted that "[a]cts, and even habits, that are inconsistent with a trait are not proof of the non-existence of the trait."

emphasizes rational propensities. According to Annas (2005), for example, the reliability associated with virtue is "a firmness in intelligent deliberation." Adams (2006: 115–136) develops a careful distinction between "direct behavioral dispositions" identified strictly as dispositions to produce behavior (e.g. for the disposition of talkativeness, the behavior is talking) and virtue as a *well-motivated* disposition to do what is right," which must be understood in terms of the person's desires, commitments, "experiences, sensitivities, and disciplines of reasoning." Adams (2006) ultimately argues for a subtle account of virtuous dispositions, so understood, as "fragmentary" and "frail" but nonetheless having great moral importance; the situationist need not disagree.

Even at its most conciliatory, it seems to us, the line of response emphasizing virtuous inner states does not eliminate the difficulty. In particular, cognitive functioning has itself been shown to be highly susceptible to situational variation, and a wealth of empirical work indicates that people experience remarkable difficulty "transferring" cognitive skills across even closely related domains, such as from job training to actual work situations (Detterman, 1993; Ceci, 1996). Additionally, quantities of experimental work indicate that even slight variations in problem formulation may impact solutions. Perhaps most famous are the "framing effects" documented by Tversky and Kahneman (1981); in their well-known "Asian Disease" case, couching proposed public health interventions in terms of numbers expected to be "saved" or numbers expected to "die" affected subject judgments as to which interventions were best, even though the fatality estimates for the different "framings" of the problem were *identical*. Such framing differences look to be ethically irrelevant influences on ethical responses, just as whether or not one found a dime looks to have nothing to do whether one is morally obligated to help.[7] Another suggestive line of research indicates that the salience of different values is highly sensitive to seemingly minor variations in the cognitive environment. For example, Gardner, Gabriel, and Lee (1999; cf. Brewer & Gardner, 1996; Gardner, Gabriel, & Hochschild, 2002) found that subjects "primed" by searching for first person *plural* pronouns (e.g. *we, our*) in a writing sample were more likely to report that "interdependent" values (belongingness, friendship, family security) were a "guiding principle in their lives" than were subjects primed by searching for first person *singular* pronouns (e.g. *I, my*). Apparently, what people say matters to them can be influenced by things that don't matter very much.

---

[7] Some authors (e.g. Baron, 1994) have argued that the distorting influences of "heuristics and biases" like those uncovered in recent cognitive psychology are widespread in everyday ethical reflection. For overviews of the relevant psychological literature, see Nisbett & Ross (1980); Kahneman et al. (1982); Baron (2001).

Of course, "reason" and "behavior" cannot be easily disentangled; indeed, the situational variability of cognitive processes can be invoked to explain behavioral variability. For example, Darley and Batson (1973: 107–108) observe that some of their hurried subjects may have failed to help not because of callousness or indifference, but because haste impaired their ability to *see the situation* as an "occasion for ethical decision." How people respond to their environment depends on how they "code" it, and this coding is itself highly dependent on environmental factors. The empirical research suggests that reason is no less situationally susceptible than overt behavior; the suggestion we must consider is that notions of rationality operative in traditional understandings of character are themselves empirically inadequate.[8]

3. Character and Practical Rationality

Rationality in the form of practical wisdom (*phronesis*) is central to the traditional Western philosophical conception of virtue shared by Plato, Aristotle, and the Stoics, as contemporary proponents like Kamtekar (2004) and Annas (2005) affirm. Practical wisdom, "the ability to reason correctly about practical matters" (Hursthouse 1999:154), is what organizes the virtuous person's conduct of his life amidst the complex, dynamic unfolding of particular situations in the world. On occasions for action when multiple considerations are in play (i.e. most of the time), a high degree of motivational integration and reflective oversight is necessary in order to act well on one's knowledge of what is worth caring about. In a canonical neo-Aristotelean account, John McDowell (1997: 144) brings out the importance of such integration when he speaks of virtue as "a single complex sensitivity," a general "ability to recognize requirements which situations impose on one's behavior."[9] Another sympathetic contemporary expositor, Richard Kraut (2008: abstract), summarizes the Aristotelean ethical ideal as follows:

[8] Webber's (2006: 205) response to situationism develops an understanding of traits in terms of a person's characteristic, often competing behavioral inclinations. Webber construes such inclinations as inner events that mediate between stimuli and overt behavior, so that not only overt behavior but also these inner events themselves may be experimentally manipulated and measured. Unlike Annas (2005), Webber does not strongly emphasize reason-responsiveness, so his position is not a central target of the critique we shall develop here.

[9] According to McDowell (1997: 144), talk of specific virtuous dispositions like courage or generosity is a useful device for tracking the many "manifestations" of virtue in various situations, but such talk should not mislead us into regarding these specific dispositions as "a batch of independent sensitivities." Similarly, Hursthouse (1999: 154) holds that practical wisdom "does not exist in discrete, independent packages."

What we need, in order to live well, is a proper appreciation of the way in which such goods as friendship, pleasure, virtue, honor and wealth fit together as a whole. In order to apply that general understanding to particular cases, we must acquire, through proper upbringing and habits, the ability to see, on each occasion, which course of action is best supported by reasons.[10]

The exercise of this ability may be reconstructed in terms of practical reasoning.[11] For a very loosely expressed example:

1. It is shameful to induce physically degrading states in myself.
2. Here's a group of people asking me to take a nausea-inducing drug so that they can observe what happens.

   Conclusion: I will not take the drug.

Premise 1 states a standing concern that derives from a general conception of how one should live (cf. McDowell, 1997: 156). Premise 2 identifies the present situation as one in which the object of that concern is in play.[12] The conclusion is a resolution to act (or to refrain from acting). The conclusion can be derived from the premises so long as no other relevant considerations enter the picture. But because life usually teems with other considerations, practical reasoning had better be defeasible: it may be altered by countervailing considerations. A countervailing consideration identifies the present situation as an instance of one or more other standing concerns also accepted by the agent. Registering the countervailing consideration, a different line of reasoning will now track the concerns in play more sensitively than the initial one.[13] Continuing with our example:

1.* It's good to help others when given the opportunity.
2.* Here's a group of people asking me to take a nausea-inducing drug so that they can observe what happens, as part of a clinical trial meant to help cancer patients cope with chemotherapy.

   Conclusion★: I will take the drug.

---

[10] Kraut (2008: sec. 5.2) explicates the metaphor of "seeing" as "simply a way of registering the point that the good person's reasoning does succeed in discovering what is best in each situation."

[11] Some discussions of virtue ethics (e.g. McDowell, 1997: 154–158; Millgram, 2005: 134) revive the Aristotelean theoretical apparatus known as the "practical syllogism." (For an exegetically informed discussion of Aristotle's practical syllogism, see Broadie, 1968.) Strictly speaking, we find it better to refer to practical reasoning rather than the practical syllogism. A syllogism has to do with logic, but, as discussed elsewhere in this volume (Chapter 6 on moral reasoning), logic is not best conceived of as a theory of reasoning.

[12] For an account of what distinguishes this type of reasoning from means-end reasoning, see Millgram (2005: 158, n. 5).

[13] Cf. McDowell (1997: 157): "Acting in the light of a conception of how to live requires selecting and acting on the right concern."

Whereas taking the drug may be prohibitively shameful in the situation of, say, participating in a reality-TV contest, it is *ceteris paribus* less shameful, and reasonably understood as not prohibitively shameful, to take it in the situation of participating in a clinical trial designed to help cancer patients.

Given the importance of recognizing potentially countervailing considerations, practical wisdom crucially involves "being implicitly aware of the relevance of all of one's other concerns to the problem at hand" (Millgram, 2005: 146). It is important to emphasize that for the purposes of ethical conduct, this all-encompassing rational sensitivity is an *interpersonal* sensitivity. The virtuous person is aware, implicitly or explicitly, of what all those she encounters need and deserve from her, in whatever situation she encounters them. She is thus liable to feel the appropriate emotional responses to the various social circumstances in which she finds herself, and she is able to reflect and deliberate effectively on what each situation ethically requires. For example, Hursthouse (1999: 128) imagines the sorts of reasons that motivate acts of courage ("I could probably save him if I climbed up there"), temperance ("I'm driving"), generosity ("He needed help"), friendship ("I can't let him down"), honesty ("It was the truth"), and justice ("She has the right to decide").[14]

As we shall see later (in Sections 6 through 8 below), this picture of practical rationality, taken together with the picture of human cognition being developed in cognitive science, indicates that good practical reasoning is often difficult: a fact that should concern those advocates of virtue-as-practical-rationality who aspire to psychological realism. Of course, as we've said before, character psychologists need not be in the business of articulating a widely applicable psychological theory, in which case it is possible to insist that the classic situationist experiments show only that their subjects are defective practical reasoners.[15] This line of argument is not implausible, but its plausibility depends upon the *distance* between the philosophical virtue ethicist's model of human cognition and the model emerging in the cognitive sciences. If the philosophical model is *radically unlike* the scientific model—say, because it does not allow for cognitive processes that play a central or dominant role in the production of behavior—it faces pointed questions: should people aspire to curtail or eliminate the operation of such processes in their cognition

---

[14] Hursthouse (1999: chs. 5–7) offers a searching account of emotion, motivation, and reasons for action in the life of the virtuous agent. Grappling with the problems of navigating among different and sometimes conflicting considerations, Swanton (2003: chs. 5–7) delineates virtue as the integration of a complex array of "modes of moral acknowledgment": love for others and self, respect for others and self, and creativity (2003: 99).

[15] Millgram (2005: 162, n. 31) entertains a response along these lines. See also Annas (2005).

and behavior? If so, how? To answer such questions, accounts of practical rationality will have to be informed by a detailed familiarity with the relevant cognitive science.

4. Defective Rationality

As we've noted, the experimental record shows that morally arbitrary situational factors, even seemingly minor ones, exert a disproportionately powerful influence on morally important behavioral outcomes. Of particular philosophical interest are experiments in which individual subjects' behavior fails to comply with moral norms of the sort the subjects can be reasonably supposed to accept: the obligation not to inflict significant harm on an innocent person against his will, say, or the obligation to help others in an emergency if you are easily able to help, you don't have more important, conflicting obligations, and no one else will help if you don't. Since the subjects' demeanor often indicates that they (at some level) endorse the norms that their behavior contravenes, we suggest the label *moral dissociation* as shorthand for such phenomena.[16]

Stanley Milgram's widely replicated obedience studies are the classic example:[17]

A person comes to a psychological laboratory and is told to carry out a series of acts that come increasingly into conflict with conscience. The main question is how far the participant will comply with the experimenter's instructions before refusing to carry out the actions required of him.   (Milgram, 1974: 3)

The unwitting subjects agreed to serve as "teacher" in a purported study of punishment and learning. Teachers were asked by the experimenter to give a remotely administered "test" to an experimental confederate "learner" hidden from their view in another room, and to punish wrong answers with realistic-seeming simulated shocks. Subjects were directed to increase the shock voltage with each wrong answer, and as these "punishments" increased in intensity, the learner responded with increasingly vehement

---

[16] This coinage is meant to dramatize the separation or divergence between subjects' morally important behavior in the situations of interest, and the moral values that subjects endorse (or would endorse) under reflection. We do *not* mean for our expression to take on the clinical connotations of the term "dissociation" as used in psychiatry (the pathological, individualized splitting off of traumatic thoughts, feelings, sensations or other mental processes from the mainstream of a person's consciousness).

[17] For more detailed discussion than we are able to provide here, see Doris (2002: ch. 3); Miller (1986); Miller et al. (1995); and Blass (2000, 2004).

protests (Milgram, 1974: 56). When subjects balked, the experimenter firmly but politely responded to teacher/subjects' requests to stop with a series of scripted prompts that increased in urgency if the subject continued to resist: "Please continue," "The experiment requires that you continue," "It is absolutely essential that you continue," "You have no other choice, you *must* go on" (ibid.: 21). For those subjects who continued to protest beyond the end of the scripted sequence, the experimenter agreed to stop. Yet in standard permutations, approximately two-thirds of subjects were fully obedient: they complied with the experimenter's directives—even though many also felt bad and protested verbally—until they were asked to stop administering shocks.[18] Subsequent research has obtained similar rates of obedience, in both men and women, and across cultures in Europe, South Africa, and Jordan.[19]

These results diverge radically from the way people expect themselves and most others to behave (Milgram, 1974: 27–31). Behavioral experts and laypeople alike, surveyed by Milgram, predicted that no more than 1% or 2% of subjects—a "pathological fringe"—would obey the experimenter to the end, and 100% of respondents predicted that they themselves would defy the experimenter, were they a subject (ibid.: 14–16). Given this, it is unsurprising that many subjects displayed great emotional strain—sweating, trembling, and repeated pleas for the experiment to be terminated (ibid.: 161–162). It is therefore very plausible to suppose that most of Milgram's subjects had internalized a prohibition against inflicting harm on innocents; with respect to basic moral commitments, there is no reason to think these "postal clerks, high school teachers, salesmen, engineers, and laborers" were much different from the rest of us (ibid.: 16).

It is of course possible that while the obedient subjects did not represent a pathological fringe, they did represent a pathological *center*; perhaps *most of us* are more than a little prone to inflict harm on others. Fortunately, this unhappy thought is squelched by reflection on Milgram's "free-choice" condition, where the experimenter told subjects they could set the shock level wherever they liked when the protocol called for them to deliver a shock. Almost all of the subjects in this condition behaved in accordance with a straightforward prohibition against harming an innocent person against his will. Out of 40 subjects, three "limited their shocks to the very lowest on

[18] E.g. Experiment 5, Milgram (1974: 56–57, 60). On subjects' bad feelings and attempts to resist, see Milgram (1974: 10): "Many of the people studied in the experiment were in some sense against what they did to the learner, and many protested even while they obeyed." For sample transcripts recording the words of obedient but protesting subjects, see Milgram (1974: 73–80).

[19] Fiske (2003: 519); Miller et al. (1995).

the board, 28 went no higher than the first indication of discomfort, and 38 did not go beyond the point where the learner vehemently protested" (Milgram, 1974: 70–72). The enormous increase in rates of obedience from the free-choice condition to the standard or "baseline" condition is plausibly attributable not to personal differences among the subjects, but to the main situational factor that is varied between conditions: how the experimenter instructs subjects to proceed.

In order to suggest the challenge this result poses for philosophical accounts of practical rationality, we shall offer a somewhat artificial reconstruction of the practical reasoning of obedient subjects in the baseline condition (Experiment 5):

1. It is good to contribute to society by participating in scientific research.
2. My role as a participant in the present research is to obey the instructions of the experimenter.
   Conclusion: I'll go on obeying the experimenter.

Early on in the trial, at the 150-volt shock level, the learner protests:

Ugh!!! Experimenter! That's all. Get me out of here. I told you I had heart trouble. My heart's starting to bother me now. Get me out of here, please. My heart's starting to bother me. I refuse to go on. Let me out.   (Quoted in Milgram, 1974: 56)

Here any subject who endorses a harm-prohibition (as most subjects appeared to) ought to recognize a countervailing consideration identifying the situation at hand as an instance of morally impermissible harm.

1.* It is wrong to inflict harm (discomfort, pain, suffering, injury) on an innocent person against his will.
2.* The learner says these shocks are harming him and he refuses to go on.
   Conclusion*: I'll stop.

Given the widely endorsed moral prohibition on harming innocents against their will, one expects the second line of reasoning to trump easily, just as Milgram's survey respondents predicted. But when it should have become evident to subjects that in order to obey the experimenter they had to harm the learner against his will, a clear majority somehow failed to pull the rational pieces together and treat the harmfulness of their continued obedience as a decisive reason to stop.[20] Out of 40 subjects, 33 went on past the learner's

---

[20] Cf. Swanton (2003: 31): "it is clear from Milgram's account that the anguished saw themselves as operating under a rather severe virtue dilemma. A benevolent agent may also possess the virtues of respect for authority, trust, honouring commitments (fidelity), and appreciation of (the value of) knowledge. All of these virtues were in play during the experiment." The difficulty, of course, is why they experienced it as a dilemma, when the proper behavior appears so clear to outside observers.

first explicit protest, and 26 of those kept right on going through his agonized screams, hysterical pleading, and (finally) unresponsive silence. To couch it in the philosophical lexicon, they failed to recognize that the countervailing consideration should have defeated the initial line of reasoning.

There is no way to prettify this result by talking about obedient subjects' inner states.[21] However terrible the obedient subjects might have felt about continuing to harm the learner, they did not put the prohibition on harm into practice at the level of a resolution to act. The right conclusion was, "I'll stop." The wrong one was, "I'll go on obeying the experimenter." The atrocious one was, "I'll go on and on and on . . ." The learner's predicament is the same whether the subject's conclusion is "I'll go on . . ." or "I feel terrible anguish but I'll go on." For a person who accepts the moral prohibition on harm, continuing to obey the experimenter even one step beyond the learner's explicit protest, let alone all the way to the end, is a clear failure of practical rationality—as we put it, a case of moral dissociation.

Such failures are hardly confined to the laboratory. During the Rwanda genocide of 1994, as Hutus inflamed by militant propaganda took 100 days to hack to death 800,000 of their Tutsi and moderate Hutu neighbors, officials in the UN, Europe, and the United States rebuffed—repeatedly—the expertly informed, impassioned, and increasingly desperate pleas of Romeo Dallaire, commander of the UN peacekeeping mission in Rwanda, for permission to intervene.[22] Any officials who responded with anguish or tension seem to have diverted their feelings into the institutional equivalent of hand-wringing, leaving the victims' plight unrelieved.

A . . . feature of the response that helped to console U.S. officials at the time was the sheer flurry of Rwanda-related activity. Government officials involved in policy met constantly and remained, in bureaucratic lingo, "seized of the matter"; they neither appeared nor felt indifferent. Although little in the way of effective intervention emerged from midlevel meetings in Washington and New York, an abundance of memoranda and other documents did.   (Power, 2002: 384)

As one frustrated US official wrote in his personal journal, "just don't ask us to do anything—agonizing is our specialty" (ibid.: 385).

It may be said that the person who feels terrible anguish, yet fails to act in accordance with it, is by some increment more virtuous or less vicious than the person who feels no anguish, *ceteris paribus*. But it is morally hazardous to employ such nice distinctions in one's own case. Seizing upon the consolations of one's

---

[21] For a compelling argument against such prettification, see Vranas (2005: 21–22).
[22] For a powerfully observant account of the Rwanda genocide, see Gourevitch (1998).

exquisitely sensitive feelings is a tempting and all-too-easy way to distance oneself from the real impact of one's actions or omissions.[23] This phenomenon is awkward for accounts of virtue that emphasize the moral importance of inner states as contrasted with overt behavior (Adams, 2006; Swanton, 2003).

5. Explaining Moral Dissociation

The difficulty is to explain moral dissociation. Psychologists John Sabini and Maury Silver (2005) have recently taken up the explanatory project. They identify a single response tendency—roughly, *fear of embarrassment*—and purport to explain experimentally observed moral dissociation entirely in terms of the interaction between this tendency and situations in which the subject confronts unanimous or authoritative opposition. According to them, when individuals find themselves alone in their perception of what it makes sense to believe or to do, so that in order to act accordingly they would need to take a solitary stand against other people whose views appear firmly opposed to their own, they are "confused and inhibited by the anticipation of embarrassment" (559). In such situations people "cannot be trusted to follow the dictates of their own conscience . . . against the commands of an authority or group" (555). Sabini and Silver propose that this process suffices to explain all the studies they take to represent the most important social influences data, including the Milgram paradigm.[24] If fear of embarrassment explains these results, they argue, then there is nothing in the data to support the skeptic's claim that morally important behavior is typically subject to a great number and variety of morally inconsequential situational factors. Since fear of embarrassment is sensitive to a readily identifiable type of situational factor (although many things cause embarrassment), and plausibly thought to be remediable through the agent's intentional efforts, results like Milgram's emerge as less unsettling than they initially appear.

Call such approaches *rationalizing explanations*, which attempt to describe a respect in which the problematic behavior *made sense* to the actor. If such a

---

[23] Milgram (1974: 10) remarks on this point as follows: "[S]ubjective feelings are largely irrelevant to the moral issue at hand so long as they are not transformed into action. . . . The attitudes of guards at a concentration camp are of no consequence when in fact they are allowing the slaughter of innocent men to take place before them. Similarly, so-called 'intellectual resistance' in occupied Europe—in which persons by a twist of thought felt that they had defied the invader—was merely indulgence in a consoling psychological mechanism."

[24] Sabini & Silver (2005: 544–559) centrally rely on Milgram's (1974) obedience studies, the Darley & Batson (1973) Samaritanism study, the Latané & Darley (1970) group effect studies, and the Asch (1955) conformity studies.

strategy is successful, it takes much of the bite from the skeptic's challenge. One of the reasons that the situationist experiments are so disconcerting is that the subjects' behavior seems *irrational*. But rationalizing explanations, if successful, eliminate this appearance of irrationality; we can see why the actor thought it reasonable, all things considered, to do what she did. Of course Milgram's obedients did not act for the *best* reason—after all, they behaved egregiously—but they acted for a reason: the avoidance of the embarrassment attendant upon contradicting authorities.

Sabini and Silver are in the business of damage control, rounding up many of the situational factors revealed by the social influences data and corralling them into the confines of a single, corrigible aspect of interpersonal relations. The fear-of-embarrassment predicament they portray is an extreme version of a reassuringly non-mysterious experience; while the resulting behavior may not be admirable, it is certainly intelligible. Since the actors in such cases are reason-responsive, even if not optimally reason-responsive, we can nurture the hope that their defective reasoning is ameliorable through the right sort of intervention. For Sabini and Silver (2005: 562), the remedy is clear: be vigilant when you find your moral perceptions opposed by others, and "understand both that it is hard and that it is possible to confront other people who are doing wrong." As they conclude, comfortingly, the "disturbance to our conception of character is local, not global" (ibid.: 561).

Sabini and Silver's strategy bears the risk of all ambitious unifying explanations: a single explanatory factor is being asked to do *a lot* of work. Even if the embarrassment explanation were a good one for the studies they cite, there are *many* relevant studies, as they are well aware, and we doubt that they can all be neatly packaged under the unifying rubric of embarrassment. Consider Isen and Levin's "phone booth" experiment, where finding a dime is associated with helping someone pick up their dropped papers, and failure to find a dime is associated with not helping.[25] Or Mathews and Cannon's "lawnmower" study, where the noise from a power mower reduced the likelihood that subjects would help an apparently injured man with some dropped books. These effects do not look in the first instance to be social, as they are in the cases on which Sabini and Silver rely. If anything, one would expect embarrassment to be implicated in *helping* in some of these scenarios; mightn't one feel embarrassed (or ashamed) under the reproachful eye (real or imagined) of the victim one is tempted to ignore? Sabini and Silver are right to demand a

---

[25] Sabini & Silver (2005) reject the significance of the Isen and Levin study. Whatever one thinks of the particular study, it is representative of a large literature on the effect of mood on prosocial behavior, and Sabini and Silver, we think, owe a full account of how their embarrassment hypothesis fares on it.

fuller explanatory story than the character skeptics have to date provided, but their own explanation, as apt as it is for some cases, will be only a part of the story.

Some versions of rationalizing explanations are even more ambitious than Sabini and Silver's; these explanations attempt to show that ostensibly disturbing behavior is actually *compatible* with virtue, instead of merely rationalizable (Sreenivasan, 2002). The basic move in these *sanitizing explanations* is to reinterpret subjects' supposedly virtue-inconsistent behavior as being consistent with the overall psychological economy of a virtuous character. This strategy seems most promising for situations that one might reasonably construe as morally ambiguous, such as that encountered by subjects in Darley and Batson's Good Samaritan study, where degree of hurry strongly influenced prosocial behavior. Darley and Batson (1973: 102) set the stage with deliberate ambiguity: "the victim should appear somewhat ambiguous—ill-dressed, possibly in need of help, but also possibly drunk or even potentially dangerous."[26] Moreover, the general moral obligation to help others in need has limits, and people may reasonably disagree about where, in principle, to draw them. In fact, many moral theories recognize "imperfect duties" and allow wide latitude for personal discretion over whether and when to help. As regards the particular case, conscientiousness about keeping appointments is not in general morally irrelevant, and it may be that conscientiousness trumped helpfulness in the reasoning of some subjects. Taking into account all the relevant moral considerations as they might reasonably figure in a hurried subject's long-term goals and policies, one can see how an acceptable all-things-considered moral judgment could permit passing by. Thus construed, the omission should not count as evidence against a person's possession of virtuous character, understood as a unified guiding constellation of long-term values, goals, policies, and sensibilities.

Quite obviously, such stories will not be equally apt to all cases. While sanitizing explanations of Darley and Batson's (1973) results may have some appeal (*contra* Doris, 2002: 34), they almost certainly do not in a case like Milgram, where familiarity with the experiment makes it clear that the obedient subjects acted in a virtue-contrary fashion, perhaps deplorably so (see Vranas, 2005: 5–9). More significantly, both sanitizing and other rationalizing explanations suffer a general difficulty: the picture of human cognition they invoke is very likely to be empirically inadequate. These explanations suppose that the actor acted on what he took (or on reflection would take) to be a reason,

---

[26] Situational ambiguity has been repeatedly shown to be negatively associated with helping behavior (e.g. Shotland & Stebbins, 1980: 519; Clark & Word, 1972, 1974; DeJong et al., 1980).

but a large body of empirical work indicates that this may relatively seldom be the case. Conceptions of practical rationality may still perform important theoretical work, such as underwriting the ethical evaluation of action, but they are unlikely to play a central role in an empirically sophisticated account of moral cognition and behavior. In the following three sections, we shall explain why this is so.

6. Another Perspective

To recap: well-established observations of moral dissociation confront anyone interested in ethics with the problem of explaining what goes wrong. A person brings to an occasion for action some set of pre-existing evaluative commitments, which may include reflectively endorsed moral norms. Ideally, moral cognition is supposed to orchestrate a smooth transition from pre-existing moral norms to a choice of action in line with them, through the appropriate uptake of information about the actor's present circumstances. When moral dissociation occurs, something fouls up the transition.

How to explain the foul-up? An oversimplified version of the debate goes like this. Virtue-ethicists invoke shortcomings in practical rationality, while their opponents invoke the power of situational factors, such as those that social psychologists can manipulate to influence the behavior of experimental subjects. But in order to improve the clarity and precision of the debate, all parties should acknowledge that what is really at issue is how to explain *interactions* between morally arbitrary situational factors and people's tendencies to respond to them. This is why we shall devote extensive discussion, here and in the following two sections, to the cognitive processes that mediate such interactions.

In contrast to the philosophical virtue-ethicist's preoccupation with personal dispositions that embody subjects' attempts to exercise practical rationality, our discussion will track *depersonalized* response tendencies, which function largely independently of actors' evaluative commitments. A response tendency is depersonalized to the degree that when activated by a situational factor to which it responds, it leads to highly predictable behavior, through cognitive processes on which individuals' personal, reflectively endorsed values have relatively little influence. Real-life exposure to moral dissociation increases so far as such cognitive processes are not only indifferent to personal values, but also resistant to intentional direction. When depersonalized response tendencies are recalcitrant in this way, they may be beyond the reach of individual practical rationality.

The evidence we have been discussing up to this point matters for ethics and moral philosophy because it involves interpersonal encounters that bring basic moral commitments into play: primarily, the prohibition on harm against innocents, and the obligation to help. Since the focus of moral concern is, in both cases, *how the other person is doing*, acting rightly calls for orienting one's attention to the other person's standpoint. Accordingly, we shall suggest that part of the explanation for experimentally observed moral dissociation is the subliminal inhibition or misdirection of subjects' other-oriented attention. Because the same types of response tendencies are exposed to similar factors across real-life situations of many kinds, experimentally observed moral dissociation indicates a serious challenge to the highly integrated model of deliberation that Aristoteleans presuppose.

We develop our proposal about breakdowns in other-oriented attention in several stages. In Section 7, we present empirical support for the claim that many important cognitive and motivational processes proceed without intentional direction, and result in cognitive and behavioral outcomes inconsistent with the agent's (often reflectively affirmed) evaluative commitments. In Section 8, we consider empirical studies suggesting that other-oriented attention is often influenced by such unsupervised processes. Through these processes, morally arbitrary situational factors can determine whether and how fully a subject's other-oriented attention is activated, and which particular person's standpoint will attract its focus. We then take a second look at some of the situationist experiments discussed earlier, in order to illustrate how the inhibition and misdirection of other-oriented attention may figure in moral dissociation. Finally, in Section 9, we discuss the range of possibilities for remedial measures that might protect morally important cognition from such disruptions.

We emphasize that we offer our proposal by way of suggesting a *partial* explanation. We have no aspirations to neatly unified theory; on the contrary, we would expect a comprehensive exploration to turn up multiple, and disparate, explanatory factors. It is beyond the scope of this chapter to attempt a complete account here. Our aim is to consider other-oriented attention as one aspect of moral cognition, in order to illustrate the explanatory potential of accounts focusing on the cognitive processes that mediate between situation and behavior.

7. Automaticity and Incongruency

From the 1970s onward, much cognitive science has investigated the extent to which cognitive processes, for example those that influence judgments and behavior, tend to operate without intentional direction. The main concepts used to organize research into these highly influential "dual-process" theories are *control* and *automaticity*.[27] If a cognitive process were fully controlled, it would be completely responsive to intentional direction. If a cognitive process were fully automatic, it would be completely *un*responsive to intentional direction.

To the extent that cognitive processes are controlled, they make intensive demands on limited cognitive resources: they require effort and can be disturbed by a diversion or restriction of conscious attention. To the extent that cognitive processes are automatic, they make low demands on cognitive resources: they are effortless, efficient, and capable of occurring in parallel with other (sometimes more controlled) processes. The extent to which an activity demands cognitive effort can vary with conditions from moment to moment. When it does demand effort, its execution will suffer in proportion to the degree of surrounding cognitive distraction. If you were driving a car while talking on your cell phone, you might be able to carry on nicely so long as traffic was light. But in heavy traffic you would be advised to "hang up and drive" so as to dedicate all of your attention to the road.[28]

It is inadvisable to sort cognitive processes rigidly between two mutually exclusive categories, "controlled" and "automatic," because control and automaticity are not mutually exclusive in the actual operation of cognitive processes. Few processes governing social judgments and behavior are either fully controlled or fully automatic. As Wegner and Bargh (1998: 484) note, "the larger portion of mental processes, including those involved in social life, are characterized by mixtures, transformations, and relations between control and automaticity."[29] Imagine meeting a friend over coffee to discuss a paper you've been working on. You open with an informal summary of the material you have prepared to talk about. Your cognitive activity, to begin with, demands the intentional, highly effortful direction of your attention. As your friend responds with questions and objections, you find yourself replying spontaneously, effortlessly, with fresh thoughts that arise unbidden, until you have to stop and ransack your mind (through a process that again draws on

---

[27] For helpful overviews, see Bargh & Chartrand (1999); Wegner (2002); Wilson (2002); Stanovich (2004); Haidt (2006); Hassin et al. (2005). The details of dual-process theory are treated differently by different investigators; we limit our observations to ones that we believe would seem relatively uncontroversial to most psychologists working in the field.

[28] McEvoy et al. (2005) surveyed 456 drivers who used or owned mobile phones and had been in car crashes that sent them to the hospital. They found that cell phone use increased the risk of crashing fourfold. Using a hands-free phone was no safer than using a hand-held phone.

[29] Cf. Kunda (1999: 267); Bargh (1989, 1994, 1996); Fiske (1992, 1993, 2003: 158); Jones & Thibaut (1958).

the effortful direction of your attention) to recall exactly how the argument went in that article you read last night. While the degree of effort and directed attention involved in your talking may wax and wane, your talking remains, at least in part, continually open to your supervision: you can correct yourself if you make a grammatical mistake, or censor yourself to avoid saying something your friend might take as an insult. All the while, your coffee-drinking may proceed with little effort, directed attention, or supervision: you go through the motions of raising the cup to your lips, sipping or gulping, and lowering the cup again without much noticing. But the processes underlying both talking and coffee-drinking, even though they can become automatic in several respects, are not at any point fully automatic, since they remain partially responsive to intentional direction.

For our purposes, the main point of interest is that many cognitive processes typically influencing behavior are substantially automatic. Particularly striking is the degree to which cognitive processes are resistant to introspective access, even when subjects are encouraged to reflect on the reasons for their behavior (Nisbett & Wilson, 1977; Wilson, 2002; Kunda, 1999: 269). For example, it has been shown repeatedly that the greater the number of bystanders on the scene of an emergency, the less likely each individual is to offer help (see Latané & Nida, 1981), yet experimental subjects may insist that the number of bystanders has nothing to do with their behavior, as Latané and Darley (1970: 124) report on their subject debriefings:

We asked this question every way we know how: subtly, directly, tactfully, bluntly. Always we got the same answer. Subjects persistently claimed that their behavior was not influenced by the other people present. This denial occurred in the face of results showing that the presence of others did inhibit helping.

Such disconnects between reflective understanding and determinative stimuli appear to be commonplace, as the experimental literature on automaticity indicates.

A series of experiments by Bargh, Chen, and Burrows (1996) is illustrative. The experiments first induced nonconscious activation—"priming"—of subjects' mental constructs for certain trait characteristics or demographic stereotypes. Subjects next encountered a situation artificially designed (unbeknownst to them) to elicit behavior related to the construct for which they had been primed. One experiment tested for the behavioral outcome of priming subjects' constructs for *rude* and *polite*. Subjects were primed by means of a "scrambled sentence test" (Srull & Wyer, 1979) in which they were asked to compose a grammatical four-word sentence from a string of five randomly ordered words. By random assignment, subjects took one of three tests: one to prime the trait-construct *rude*, another to prime the trait-construct *polite*, and a third (the neutral control condition) to prime neither construct. Fifteen out of thirty items in each test included words whose meaning was related to the target construct for that test, or, in the case of the neutral control, unrelated to either target construct. For instance, if the target construct was *rude*, a scrambled sentence would read "they her *bother* see usually," whereas if the target construct was *polite*, the counterpart scrambled sentence would read "they her *respect* see usually," and in the neutral test, it would read "they her *send* see usually" (our italics). In the second stage of the experiment, subjects who had taken the test were to go to another room and ask the experimenter for further instructions. There they found the experimenter engaged in conversation with another subject (actually a confederate). The measure of rudeness or politeness in the behavior of subjects who had just taken the priming test was the amount of time they would wait before interrupting the conversation: subjects exposed to the *rude* priming condition interrupted significantly earlier than those exposed to the *polite* or neutral priming conditions. Upon debriefing, no subjects thought that the scrambled-sentence test might have influenced their behavior. In a second experiment, the scrambled-sentence prime included words evoking the stereotype *elderly* (e.g. "old," "lonely," "grey," "bingo," "retired," "wrinkle"), while the control condition contained only stereotype neutral words (e.g. "thirsty," "clean") in place of the elderly-stereotype words. After completing the test, subjects in the *elderly* priming condition walked to the elevator more slowly than subjects in the control condition. Again, subjects were asked whether they thought the scrambled-sentence test might have affected them, and whether they had noticed that it contained *elderly*-stereotype words. No subject said they had noticed the stereotypical words, and no subject thought that taking the test had affected his or her behavior.

Of particular ethical interest is a third experiment, which involved activation of a racial stereotype. There, "non-black" subjects subliminally primed with a photograph of a "Black" male face manifested more hostility in response to a frustrating computer failure than subjects subliminally primed with a "White" male face. Afterwards, subjects were asked to fill out two questionnaires designed to measure racial attitudes, with the cover story that the questionnaires were only "part of a pilot pretest in preparation for some future experiments" and were not connected with the computer task the subjects had just done (Bargh et al., 1996: 239).[30] Subjects who scored low on the self-report

---

[30] The questionnaires were the Racial Ambivalence Scale (Katz & Hass, 1988) and the Modern Racism Scale (McConahay, 1986).

measures for racist attitudes toward African Americans were *just as likely* as those who scored high to express hostility after being primed with the subliminal images. While interpretation of the self-report measures employed is difficult (see Kelly et al., Chapter 13 in this volume), it seems reasonable to infer that the subliminal stimuli influenced behavior in a manner that was substantially independent of subjects' introspectively accessible attitudes about race. Comparable discrepancies between subjects' conscious attitudes about race and their automatic tendencies have been repeatedly found elsewhere (Devine, 1989; Fazio et al., 1995; Chen & Bargh, 1997). The tendency appears to be quite general: related studies have revealed other implicit biases, cued by such factors as ethnicity, age, obesity, and socioeconomic status, that conflict with subjects' introspectively accessible values.[31]

The empirical evidence on automatic biases in social cognition suggests that, in many instances, behavior is influenced by cognitive processes that, if they were accessible to reflection, the actor would not endorse as acceptable reasons for action. This *incongruency*, as we shall call it, involves a relation between (1) automatic processes likely to influence a subject's behavior on normatively significant occasions of action, and (2) normative commitments of the subject, such that (3) if the subject knew about (1), he or she would reject (1) in light of (2). Introspective awareness is, at best, only partially reliable and often misleading as a guide to the actual determinants of our behavior; as a consequence, introspective monitoring is unreliable as a way to ensure that our behavior remains under the control of our evaluative commitments (Kunda, 1999: 307).

To the extent that incongruency is pervasive, it renders the virtue-ethical model of practical rationality problematic. Most obviously, incongruency unsettles notions of well-integrated deliberation, such as, for example, that which Wiggins (1980: 234) attributes approvingly to Aristotle:

The man of highest practical wisdom is the man who brings to bear upon a situation the greatest number of genuinely pertinent concerns and genuinely relevant considerations commensurate with the importance of the deliberative context.

Furthermore, incongruency challenges the model of virtuous practical rationality—i.e. practical wisdom—as the harmonious interrelation of reflective deliberation and habitual sensibilities. On many occasions of action, practical wisdom requires a swiftness of response—in perception, feeling, judgment, and behavior—that could be subserved only by the automatic aspects of

---

[31] E.g. ethnicity: Florack et al. (2001); age: Nosek et al. (2002); obesity: Teachman et al. (2003); socioeconomic status: Rudman et al. (2002).

cognitive processes.[32] It is this kind of well-trained automaticity that supports the habitual sensibilities central to Aristotelean virtue; automatic aspects of the virtuous agent's responses should be reliably governed by her reflectively held normative commitments.[33] But this is not the picture emerging from empirical work: a considerable gap separates this Aristotelean model of moral cognition from the type of model emerging in contemporary cognitive science.

If there is such a gap, is it only a manifestation of the rarity and difficulty of virtue? Take the example of incongruent racist tendencies. People's behavior isn't determined by the automatic activation of racist or other derogatory stereotypes unless they already have the stereotypes in their cognitive repertoire. That so many people do have them, even despite reflective commitments to the contrary, is the unfortunate result of long-term and continuing immersion in cultural surroundings that perpetuate stereotypical attitudes. This is only to say, as Aristoteleans often do, that good upbringing is psychologically necessary for the inculcation of virtue, not least for the acquisition of the right habitual sensibilities.[34] With respect to the ideal of practical wisdom, if people can get their habitual sensibilities right, then they don't need to be capable of using introspection to monitor them, nor do they need to be capable of effectively deciding to start or stop them at the moment of action.

The widespread operation of this or that particular implicit bias in a given culture might indeed be a matter of parochial sensibilities, a defect ameliorable in principle by a sufficiently enlightened social regime. But evidence from cross-cultural studies, and comparison with non-human primates closely related to humans, supports the claim that some form of in-group orientation is a near-universal feature of human cognitive functioning (Haidt & Graham, 2007: 105).[35] To be sure, this is compatible with some people's achieving an enlightened cosmopolitanism. Yet even if it were possible for a super-enlightened culture (or individual) to transcend every form of prejudice and

---

[32] "Automatic" does not entail "incongruent."

[33] On occasions when even Aristoteleans would hold that it is better to act immediately, so that very little "governing" goes on (e.g. jumping to push a child out of the way of an onrushing vehicle), one's responses should at least be *in sync* with reflectively held commitments. Thanks to Walter Sinnott-Armstrong for prompting this clarification.

[34] See, e.g., Hursthouse (1999: 113–118) and Broadie (1991: 109–110, 271–274).

[35] Haidt & Graham (2007: 105) characterize the in-group orientation as "special social-cognitive abilities backed up by strong social emotions related to recognizing, trusting, and cooperating with members of one's co-residing ingroup while being wary and distrustful of members of other groups." As Haidt and Graham take pains to point out, the in-group orientation is not in itself morally objectionable: it may be expressed in such virtues as friendship, loyalty, and courage. Nonetheless, morally objectionable forms of cognition such as prejudice and stereotyping are perhaps best explained as regrettable manifestations of the in-group orientation.

stereotyping that might arise from the in-group orientation, implicit bias is only one form of cognition that may be incongruent with subjects' reflectively endorsed values. Conflict of interest, for example, is another ubiquitous site of incongruency, in this case between self-interest (which is "automatic, viscerally compelling, and often unconscious") and people's personal or professional obligations to others (Jones, 2006; Moore & Loewenstein, 2004).

Consider physicians' prescribing practices as influenced by pharmaceutical promotions. A review of 29 empirical studies (Wazana, 2000) supports the generalization that such promotions—e.g. small gifts, free drug samples, meals, continuing medical education—result in aggregate patterns of prescribing behavior that significantly raise expenditure on drugs, with no justifying benefit to patients. Yet large majorities of physicians surveyed deny that pharmaceutical promotions influence their own prescribing behavior (ibid.: 375, 378).[36] On the other hand, large majorities of physicians surveyed also believe that the prescribing behavior of most other physicians is influenced by pharmaceutical promotions (Dana & Loewenstein, 2003: 254). This is exactly what we should expect for a bias that operates automatically. However readily individual physicians recognize the operation of self-interested bias in the prescribing behavior of their peers, they do not actually experience it in their own decision-making, so they sincerely deny its influence on their own actions.

The empirical record strongly suggests that moral incongruency in many forms is routine, and prevalent even among well-meaning, sensitive, intelligent people (Bazerman & Banaji, 2004). More broadly, the empirical record strongly suggests that behavior-influencing processes that bypass introspection and intentional direction, thereby using limited cognitive resources efficiently, are ubiquitous in human cognition (Stanovich, 2004). We have good reason to think that this feature of cognitive functioning is both deeply entrenched and widely instantiated: that is, we would expect it to operate in biologically normal individuals across many environments and many circumstances. While automaticity by itself is not enough for incongruency, the extensive reach of automaticity in human cognition provides ample opportunity for incongruency to occur.

---

[36] In a representative study, Orlowski & Wateska (1992) asked physicians who were planning to attend sponsored symposia at luxury resorts whether they expected any effect on their prescribing behavior. Out of 20 physicians interviewed, 17 were convinced that there would be no influence: "They appeared to sincerely believe that any decision to prescribe a drug is based on scientific data, clinical experience, and patient needs, rather than on promotion by pharmaceutical companies" (ibid.: 271). In fact, subsequent prescribing patterns for the group showed significant increases in usage of the new drugs as compared with previous practice in their home institution and contemporaneous practice at similar medical facilities nationwide.

8. Other-Oriented Attention and Moral Incongruency

In this section, we entertain a set of hypotheses to the effect that many experimental and real-life cases of moral dissociation result from the kind of incongruencies we have just described, specifically through the misdirection or inhibition of subjects' *other-oriented attention* by predominantly automatic response tendencies. We will first clarify what we mean by "other-oriented attention," referring to the experimental literature to indicate suggestive findings about its causal role in morally important behavior. We then formulate and entertain a set of hypotheses linking particular situational factors (physical position and social status) to moral incongruency in helping and harming behavior, through automatic aspects of cognitive processes that mediate other-oriented attention. We shall trace these hypotheses through a fresh examination of key variations in Milgram's obedience studies. Our aim in this exercise is not to demonstrate that the hypotheses entertained are correct. That would require extensive experimentation! However, we contend that our hypotheses are viable, based on what is currently known. If true, our hypotheses make considerable difficulty for the Aristotelian model of deliberation as highly integrated. For this reason, we contend, it is incumbent on defenders of that model to either discredit our hypotheses or modify the model. The needed work is just beginning, of course; our present aim is to stimulate further research, both philosophical and empirical, on the automatic processes that may help to account for morally troubling incongruencies.

8.1. *Other-Oriented Attention*

Orienting one's attention around the standpoint of other people involves imagining, or trying to imagine, what it is like for them to experience the situation at hand. In order to discuss this kind of cognitive activity, which may have affective dimensions, we shall need to employ some terms whose use in both philosophy and psychology is poorly standardized: "empathy," "sympathy," and the like. We shall simply stipulate our uses of these terms for the purposes of the present chapter. For the sake of consistent exposition, we shall use these terms only as stipulated when we describe experimental designs and results, rather than attempt to follow the sometimes divergent usage of study authors (contrast Stich et al., in this volume).

In an encounter between two persons, A and B, *empathic response* (we stipulate) is a feeling on A's part that mimics more or less accurately B's affective state. Empathic response is a subset of A's overall response to B. Call A the *subject* of empathic response. Call B the *target* of empathic response.[37]

A typical sequence of processes by which situational factors can trigger empathic response runs as follows. Seeing the facial expression of another person (the potential target of empathic response) activates a mimicking reaction in the facial muscles of the subject: for example, happy to happy, pained to pained. Some muscular mirroring occurs even when subjects are asked to suppress their facial reactions. Consequent neural activity in the facial muscles can cause the subject to experience the affective state normally coincident with a facial expression like the one displayed by the target. When the subject's empathic response to the target's facial expression is caused in this manner, it bears all the hallmarks of automaticity: it occurs without the subject's conscious awareness or intentional direction, quickly and effortlessly, and through processes that go on even if the subject is trying to stop them.[38]

When the target's affective state is some form of suffering (e.g. fear, pain, anguish), the subject's empathic response may lead in either of two directions. On the one hand, it may expand into *sympathy*, which (we continue to stipulate) is a benevolent sense of fellow-feeling for the target, accompanied by the other-oriented cognitive activity of appreciating what it is like for the target to experience the situation. On the other hand, the subject's empathic response may give rise to *personal distress*, a feeling of aversion to the target's standpoint and affective state. In personal distress, the subject reverts to a self-oriented pattern of attention at odds with continuing to imagine what it is like for the target to experience the situation (Fiske, 2003: 339).

When operationalized for experimental purposes roughly as we have stipulated above, sympathy and personal distress are each correlated with distinct patterns of physiological arousal, motivation, and overt behavior. Sympathy correlates with a decelerated heart-rate, while personal distress correlates with an accelerated heart-rate (Eisenberg et al., 1989; Fiske, 2003: 339–340). Batson and colleagues (1983) found that subjects who reported feeling *sympathetic*, *moved*, or *compassionate* toward a distressed target were about equally likely to

---

[37] Labeling the subject as "A" should present no confusion in our discussion of experimental studies, since the "subjects" observed in the relevant studies are at the same time the "subjects" of the empathic responses of interest.

[38] Hansen & Hansen (1994); Bush et al. (1989); Dimberg (1988); Adelmann & Zajonc (1989); Levenson & Ruef (1992); Hodges & Wegner (1997: 316). See also Niedenthal (2007) and Chartrand & Bargh (1999). Some degree of affective mimicking can also be activated by tone of voice even when the speaker is not present. In one study, different groups of subjects listened to an abstract philosophical speech read in a happy, sad, or neutral tone of voice. Afterwards subjects' ratings of their mood corresponded to the tone of the speech they had heard (Neumann & Strack, 2000).

help in situations both with and without an easy escape route, that is, an option to refrain from helping with little or no penalty. By contrast, they found, subjects who reported feeling *alarmed, grieved, worried, disturbed,* or *perturbed* in response to a distressed target behaved differently depending on the availability of an escape route. Those who could choose an easy escape option helped less than those who were stuck without one. On the standard interpretation of such results (Batson, 2002: 95; Fiske, 2003: 340), escape-independent helping behavior is a marker of comparatively other-oriented motivation: subjects take the relief of the target's distress as an end worth pursuing for its own sake. Helping behavior that depends on subjects' having no easy escape is considered a marker of comparatively self-oriented motivation. If subjects' primary end is to relieve their own personal distress, one means to that end is to escape the situation. When no easy escape is available, acting to relieve the target's distress becomes more salient as a goal instrumental to the primary end of self-relief.

Perspective-sharing is a salient example of a mediating cognitive factor that can automatically influence whether a subject's empathic response will be converted into other-oriented or self-oriented motivation. In one study that is representative of the literature on this point, Batson and colleagues (1981) asked several groups of subjects, all female, to watch a female confederate receive the first two electric shocks of a ten-shock protocol. The subjects were then offered an opportunity to help her by receiving the other shocks in her place. Subject groups differed across two variables: extent of shared perspective and availability of escape. The extent of shared perspective was manipulated by telling subjects the extent to which the confederate shared their personal values (e.g. the genre of their favorite magazines: *Cosmopolitan* and *Seventeen* vs. *Time* and *Newsweek*, or whether they preferred urban to rural living). Availability of escape was manipulated by telling some subjects they could leave after seeing the confederate receive first two shocks, and telling others they would have to remain present for all ten. Among subjects who believed the confederate's values matched their own, most traded places with the confederate even if they had an easy escape, while those who believed their values diverged from the confederate's values opted for the easy escape if they could take it. Presumably, it is not that subjects explicitly reasoned, "She's a city girl just like I am, so I should care more about her suffering," but, rather, that subjects who happened to share the perspective of the target were prone to automatically experience the situation in greater sympathy with her, and to act accordingly.

8.2. *Physical Position, Social Status, and Helping/Harming: Milgram revisited*

A large body of empirical work suggests that, in general, subjects' behavior will display predictable regularities as a dependent variable in response to certain attributes of other persons in a social situation, when these attributes are manipulated as independent variables (Latané, 1981). One such attribute is "immediacy," understood as "closeness in space or time and absence of intervening barriers or filters" (ibid.: 344). *Physical position* in an interpersonal situation is an obvious determinant of immediacy. Another type of attribute, termed "strength," is the "salience, power, importance, or intensity" that one person may project in the eyes of others in a social situation (ibid.). A typical determinant of strength is *social status*, e.g. institutional authority. Apparent social status can be manipulated in various ways, such as the wearing of an official-looking uniform in the context of a generally respected institutional setting (Sedikides & Jackson, 1990).

How do physical position, social status, other-oriented attention, and morally important behavior interact? Consider the following hypotheses:

(a) The physical position and social status of others in relation to a subject influences the activation and direction of subjects' other-oriented attention.

Hypothesis (a) predicts that the activation and direction of subjects' other-oriented attention will vary depending on either the physical position, or the social status, or both, of other individuals in an interpersonal situation.

(b) The activation and direction of subjects' other-oriented attention influences the extent to which they engage in overt harming/nonharming or helping/nonhelping behavior.

Hypothesis (b) predicts that the extent of subjects' engagement in overt harming/nonharming behavior, or helping/nonhelping behavior, will vary depending on the activation and direction of their other-oriented attention. Taken together, (a) and (b) entail the following prediction: the extent of subjects' engagement in overt harming/nonharming or helping/nonhelping behavior will vary depending on the physical position, or social status, or both, of other persons in the situation.

We suggest further that an important type of mediating causal mechanism can be found in the cognitive processes, such as perspective-sharing, that activate, direct, or inhibit subjects' other-oriented attention. These mediating cognitive processes often have two features. First, they typically operate without the subject's intentional direction. Second, their deliverances may be incongruous with the subject's (often reflectively affirmed) evaluative commitments. Accordingly, we offer a third hypothesis:

> (c) For some instances in which the extent of subjects' overt harming/nonharming or helping/nonhelping behavior varies depending on the physical position, or social status, or both, of other persons in the situation, the causal interaction is mediated by cognitive processes that operate outside subjects' intentional direction and may result in behavior contrary to their reflectively affirmed moral commitments.

With this set of hypotheses in view, we now re-examine some key findings of Stanley Milgram's (1974) obedience studies.

In Milgram's baseline condition, as the victim's protests grow more and more anguished, most obedient subjects behave as if their attention is oriented primarily to some combination of their own rising distress and the standpoint of the experimenter, who appears coolly indifferent. As Milgram reports, "The cries of pain issuing from the learner strongly affected many participants, whose reaction to them is immediate, visceral, and spontaneous" (1974: 155). Milgram also reports "numerous signs of stress" such as "sweating, trembling, and . . . anxious laughter" (161). We noted above that similar patterns of affective and physiological arousal are correlated with personal distress, as opposed to sympathy. Avoidance behaviors on the part of many subjects express strong aversion and an urge to escape.[39] To test the hypothesis that subjects in the baseline condition are more likely to respond to the victim's suffering with personal distress than with sympathy, experimental variations could compare behavior between groups of subjects who were offered different combinations of distinct options to trade places with the learner midcourse, or to quit and walk away.[40]

At best, the obedient subjects seem to orient their attention only intermittently, incompletely, and ineffectually to the standpoint of the victim. Assuming

---

[39] Some subjects turn their heads "in an awkward fashion to avoid seeing the victim suffer" (in variations where the victim is visible to the subject), some "deliberately read the word pairs in a loud, overpowering voice, thus masking the victim's protests," some withdraw their attention from the victim and confine it to "the mechanics of the experimental procedure" (158–161).

[40] Given that the Milgram-type electric-shock protocol is ethically dubious by the standards of contemporary guidelines for research with human subjects, our suggested variations would have to be translated into an analogous but less physically brutal protocol. As a step in this direction, see Meeus & Raaijmakers (1995).

they would reflectively endorse the basic moral prohibition against harming an innocent person against his will, this is a case of moral incongruency. How does it come about?

Initially, the subject may straightforwardly come to share the experimenter's perspective on the proceedings, taking up the ostensible goals of his scientific inquiry, perhaps partly through semantic priming. In the experimenter's short faux-academic presentation on theories about "the effect of punishment on learning," the word "punishment" is used at least six times, once with emphasis. The words "learn," "learning," or "learner" are used at least a dozen times, often in close proximity to "punishment" (Milgram 1974: 18–19; cf. 59). The frequent repetition of these words resembles the priming exercises used by researchers on automaticity, as in the Bargh, Chen, and Burrows (1996) study of behavioral effects of priming with the elderly stereotype (see above, Section 7). In light of findings by Bargh and others, it is reasonable to hypothesize that when the subject is assigned to the role of teacher, he or she will have been primed to mimic the attitude of the experimenter, more or less automatically regarding the learner as a fitting object of punishment for purposes of the experiment. This hypothesis could be tested by keeping all other variables constant save the initial orientation speech, so that one group of subjects hears the baseline speech, while another group hears a speech featuring a more sympathetic set of embedded semantic primes, and dwelling on what it will be like, from the learner's point of view, to be strapped into a chair and shocked as punishment for wrong answers on a test.

In order to highlight the role of physical position and social status as factors that influence subjects' other-oriented attention, and through it, their helping/harming behavior, let us now consider several dramatic variations in Milgram's obedience studies. Experiments 14–16 introduced *role permutations* to isolate distinct situational factors that might differentially elicit subjects' obedience to the demand to go on delivering shocks. We shall focus here on two factors: the social status of the experimenter as an institutional authority, and the physical position of the experimenter in the interpersonal situation (Milgram, 1974: 99–112).

In Experiment 14, with the experimenter placed in the role of learner (seated out of view in an adjoining cubicle), and someone who was supposedly an ordinary fellow-subject, named "Mr. March," giving the orders to continue (seated in the same room as the subject), every subject respected the experimenter-learner's demands to stop.

Mr. March's instructions to shock the experimenter were totally disregarded. . . . At the first protest of the shocked experimenter, every subject broke off, refusing to administer even a single shock beyond this point. There is no variation whatsoever in response. Further, many subjects literally leapt to the aid of the experimenter, running into the other room to unstrap him. Subjects often expressed sympathy for the experimenter, but appeared alienated from the common man, as if he were a madman. (Milgram, 1974: 103)

Behavior in Experiment 14 was far more actively sympathetic toward the victim of the shocks than in any other variation. Not content to rest with the relatively passive nonharming behavior of discontinuing the shocks, subjects immediately seized control of the situation and rushed to rescue the experimenter.

On the face of it, the overt behavior of these subjects looks to be the very picture of congruency between immediate cognitive processes and the concern for others' good that a morally well-meaning person would reflectively endorse. It is perhaps how some of us like to imagine we would act in a similar situation, so sure of the right response that we hardly need to stop and think. And indeed, sympathetic overt behavior is accompanied by self-reports of sympathetic motivation:

Many subjects explained their prompt response on humane grounds, not recognizing the authority aspect of the situation. . . . When asked what they would do if a common man were being shocked, these subjects vehemently denied that they would continue beyond the point where the victim protests.   (Milgram, 1974: 103–104)

Behavior in other conditions indicates that such self-reported understandings are in all likelihood inaccurate. In fact, not only are people likely to mistreat a layperson cast by chance in the role of learner in the baseline condition; they are equally likely to mistreat an authority cast by chance in the role of learner, if the man giving the orders is an authority too. Experiment 16 presents the subject with two experimenters, "alike in appearance and apparent authority." A coin flip determines which of the two will participate in the session with the naïve subject, and the usual rigged drawing assigns the role of learner to the experimenter-participant. From the adjoining cubicle, he follows the same script and schedule of protests as the usual victim, while the second experimenter remains in the room with the subject and follows the script insisting that the experiment go on. As in the baseline condition, two-thirds of subjects obey the nonlearner experimenter and continue to the end.

The remoter physical position of the protesting experimenter in Experiment 16 may have influenced obedient subjects' behavior, as suggested by the results of Experiment 15. Here, two experimenters of equal initial status both remain positioned as in the baseline "experimenter" role, in the same room with the subject, with the usual layperson as learner in the enclosed cubicle. At the point when the learner begins to protest explicitly, the two experimenters openly disagree with each other about whether to go on, and give contradictory instructions to the subject. Out of 20 subjects, 19 did not go beyond that point, and the remaining subject stopped one step later.

In both Experiments 15 and 16, subjects can in a sense choose between two ways to "obey" as soon as the two authorities disagree between themselves. Yet when the instruction to stop comes from an experimenter in the physical position of the learner, his social status as an institutional authority makes little impact, perhaps in part because it is undermined by his more remote location. When an instruction to stop comes from an experimenter who remains in the room with the subject and the other experimenter, all subjects readily orient their attention around the standpoint of the dissenting experimenter, who conveys sympathy for the learner ("The subject is in pain. We cannot go on with the experiment." Milgram, 1974: 106.)[41]

8.3. *Recap*

In sum, response tendencies cued by relative physical position and social status could have directed subjects' other-oriented attention, and through it their behavior, differently across Milgram's many experimental permutations. At one behavioral extreme, when a single experimenter's unchallenged social status is bolstered by his physical presence a few feet away (baseline condition), subjects' attention is strongly directed to the standpoint of the experimenter, inhibiting their ability to share the learner's perspective and sympathize with his suffering. Subjects are then most likely to obey the experimenter and continue harming the learner. At the other behavioral extreme, when an ordinary person gives the commands and the experimenter occupies the "learner" role (Experiment 14), subjects' empathic response to the experimenter's predicament could be readily converted to sympathy by his uniquely authoritative social status, leading them to stop harming him and even to try to rescue him—despite his more remote physical position. In between, open disagreement between two experimenters of comparable status induces behavioral outcomes that diverge sharply depending on other factors, including the experimenters' respective physical positions.

Remember that several straightforward, self-interested incentives that lead many people to obey authorities in real life, presumably through rational

---

[41] Additional evidence for the importance of physical position comes from Experiment 7 (Milgram 1974: 59–62), in which obedience decreases markedly from baseline (to below 25%) with decreased physical proximity of the experimenter to the subject, and a series of permutations (ibid.: 33-40) in which the physical proximity of the learner to subjects was gradually increased, producing rates of obedience gradually declining from 65% to 30%.

calculations of self-interest, can be ruled out in the obedience studies. The experimenter does not control any future distribution of resources valued by the subject. He does not wield any special power to inflict damage on the subject. Experimenter and subject have no long-term social relationship, nor do they have any kind of civic relationship that would entitle the experimenter to intervene in how the subject's life goes at some later time. (Contrast the relationship between a police officer and a citizen pulled over for a speeding violation.) The only power the experimenter holds, initially, is power the subject agrees to cede to him, with the option (in principle) of revoking it at any point.[42] The subject's act of volunteering to participate in the study, in response to a newspaper ad or direct mail solicitation, might well be governed by some more or less explicitly rational thought process. But as soon as subject and experimenter make their first in-person contact, factors of comparative physical position and social status can influence the subject's behavior. These factors appear to operate over and above subjects' rational sense of obligation to the experimenter ("I said I would help"), continuing to influence behavior well beyond the point when any such obligation should have been overridden by the moral prohibition against harming the protesting learner.

Let us again emphasize that we have entertained this set of hypotheses about physical position and social status by way of suggesting a *partial* explanation for observed moral dissociation. Other social factors, or nonsocial situational factors such as ambient noise (Mathews & Cannon, 1975: 574–575), could be substituted for physical position and social status to form hypotheses with empirically testable implications. Very likely, there are many different response tendencies whose sensitivity to situational factors may produce moral incongruency, and one would expect these multiple tendencies to operate in various combinations.

Bystander intervention (Latané & Darley, 1970) makes a good example. Each experimental subject witnesses what appears to be an emergency: in one study, an epileptic seizure; in another study, billowing smoke. When each subject believes that he or she alone is available to deal with the emergency, a large majority (85% and 75%, respectively) respond appropriately. But when other, unresponsive bystanders are (or are believed to be) present, subjects are less likely to behave appropriately, i.e. to help the "seizure victim" and to report the smoke. Extensive subsequent research has shown that the decrease

---

[42] As the experiment progresses, in most permutations, subjects find it difficult to exercise this option. That very difficulty is what is under study. But at least the situation is not one of brute coercion, like a robbery at gunpoint.

in individual response with increasing numbers of nonresponsive bystanders is a predictable regularity.[43] Perhaps fear of embarrassment, as sketched by Sabini & Silver (2005), leads each individual to look to the others, erring on the side of caution. Then, seeing no response on the part of others, subjects receive no cues to feel urgent pressure to act. If anything, what individuals would mimic in this situation, based on their perceptions of each other, is the extinguishing of affect in cool indifference, countering any stray feelings of either personal distress or sympathy that might be evoked by the victim's plight. Each subject's other-oriented attention, then, is misdirected in that they look to their fellow bystanders, rather than to the victim, to supply their cognitive anchor-point in the situation.

The important point here is that the cognitive processes apparently at work in classic experimental observations of moral dissociation do not bear much resemblance to philosophical models of reflective deliberation or practical reasoning, processes that are expected to be governed, to a considerable extent, by the actor's evaluative commitments.[44] Instead, the determinative cognitive processes occur unreflectively and automatically, cued by morally arbitrary situational factors. In this sense, we suggest, many of the processes implicated in moral functioning—or dysfunctioning—are likely to be largely unaffected by individuals' personal, reflectively endorsed values.

9. Remedial Measures

The normative ideal of virtue ethics places a heavy executive burden on agents' reflective supervision of their behavior. Too heavy, we suggest, to be effectively borne by human cognitive equipment on many morally important occasions for action.[45] The virtue-ethical model emphasizes selecting the right reason on which to act, such as "She needs help," or "It's hurting him, this has got to stop" (cf. Hursthouse, 1999: 128). This requires being able "to see, on each occasion, which course of action is best supported by reasons" (Kraut, 2008). But the trouble with moral dissociation, on the explanation we have proposed, is that it occurs largely through cognitive processes that bypass

---

[43] Situations studied include explosions, falling bookcases, spilled groceries, people needing an ambulance, theft of personal items in a library, shoplifting, and intervening with a peer's intention to drive drunk. See Fiske (2003: 320, 336), Latané & Nida (1981).

[44] See Bok (1996: 180–183).

[45] To be sure, there may also be many occasions that are not very cognitively demanding, such that people are able to arrive at the right action through conscious reflection, or the automatic aspects of moral cognition lead them to choose the right action. Of course, we do not claim that morally decent behavior never occurs. Thanks to Walter Sinnott-Armstrong for prompting this clarification.

the type of reflective supervision that is supposed to characterize acting for reasons.[46]

Recall that the rationalizing explanations discussed in Section 5 above (e.g. Sabini and Silver, 2005; Sreenivasan, 2002) portray experimentally observed moral dissociation as primarily a matter of defective practical reasoning, in principle remediable by better practical reasoning. So far as this portrayal presupposes that the kinds of cognitive processes that play a dominant role in producing morally important behavior are capable of figuring directly in reflective deliberation, empirical findings about automaticity and moral incongruency are bad news. However, there is a more empirically plausible alternative. To the extent that behavior-determining cognitive processes can be brought under the influence of reflective deliberation somehow, even if they don't figure in it directly, there is still an important role for practical reason to play. For example, the proactive formulation of personal goals and policies, explicitly targeting situational factors pre-identified as problematic, may on the occasion of action diminish the influence of unwelcome automatic tendencies.

An important body of empirical work within the automaticity literature is dedicated to exploring such mechanisms of self-control (e.g. Trope & Fishbach, 2005). Some of this work seeks to identify techniques for individual cognitive retraining, as well as intergroup communication, to weaken implicit bias (e.g. Dovidio et al., 2000; Blair, 2002). Another option of interest is to identify specific mediating mechanisms between implicit attitudes and prejudicial behavior that may be open to self-monitoring and self-control, so that people who realize that bias is possible can try to correct it in their behavior (Dasgupta, 2004: 157–160; Dasgupta & Rivera, 2006).

By way of remediation, then, the traditional virtue-ethical approach can prescribe, in effect, an agenda of deliberate self-improvement: e.g. "Note to self: pay better attention to how the other person is doing" or, "If I encounter someone in distress and other bystanders are around, do not look to the others to figure out what to do". But given the ubiquity and power of behavior-influencing cognitive processes that may resist reflective supervision, and the limitations on the cognitive resources required to implement such supervision, there is good reason to doubt whether a program of deliberate

---

[46] Since the cognitive processes at issue resist introspective awareness, people's *ex post facto* readiness to explain their reasons for action is no evidence that they really acted for the stated reasons or indeed for any reason. Moreover, it is an established finding of cognitive psychology that part of normal human cognitive functioning is the confabulation of self-rationalizing narratives that misrepresent the actual causal history of behavior (e.g. Nisbett & Wilson, 1977; Wilson, 2002; Johansson et al., 2005, 2006).

self-improvement will alone suffice to alleviate tendencies toward moral dissociation. Fortunately, reflective deliberation on the part of the individual agent is not the only remedial resource available.

One way to get ourselves to pay better attention to, for example, how other people are doing is to create and sustain regularly recurring social contexts likely to activate automatically the desired aspects of moral cognition, and likely to channel them in the desired directions. This would turn automaticity to the advantage of moral sensitivity. Merritt (2000, 2009) develops a modified virtue-ethical approach that can accommodate empirical findings in the psychology of interpersonal processes, including interpersonal impacts on moral cognition. With respect to many morally important response tendencies, the behavioral consistency that people may achieve is often due to their inhabiting climates of social expectation that elicit and support the consistency in question.[47] Second, behavioral consistency sustained in this manner can be motivationally deep, relatively enduring, and responsive to reasons, along the lines celebrated in virtue ethics. It is not merely a matter of commonplace social restraint, as when you have a prudential reason, in the immediate presence of your friends or colleagues, not to do things you know they would disapprove of. The point is rather that over time, the cumulative effect of maintaining your interpersonal relationships or fulfilling your social role is formative: it helps to sustain consistent response tendencies, some of them morally important, in your cognition and behavior.[48]

However, it is necessary to guard against complacent overreliance on shared values that people may take for granted in their close relationships (Merritt, 2009). Adherence to some external standard of conduct should supplement routine engagement with recurrent social settings, lest familiarity breed laziness. Empirical work on decision-making and accountability suggests that when people believe they will need to justify their decisions to unknown third parties, their thinking is significantly more careful, systematic, and self-critical, and they are less vulnerable to a wide variety of cognitive biases, such as oversensitivity to the order in which information appears (Lerner & Tetlock, 1999; Pennington & Schlenker, 1990). Although it is not obvious how individuals might best bring this sort of discipline to bear in private life, the point applies quite clearly to organizational and institutional governance.

---

[47] For reviews of the psychological literature supporting this claim, see: S. Chen et al. (2006); Banaji & Prentice (1994); Markus & Cross (1990); Leary (2001); and Schlenker & Weigold (1992). See also Drigotas et al. (1999). For further philosophical discussion, see Merritt (2009).

[48] For an example of suggestive experimental work along these lines, see Fitzsimmons & Bargh (2003).

For example, as noted by Merritt (2009: 45), in the wake of twentieth-century scandals involving medical research with human subjects, the protection of subjects' rights and welfare is no longer entrusted entirely to the personal character (however sterling) of the scientists conducting the research. Under international guidelines, and under the law of the United States and other countries, medical research with human subjects must undergo prospective and ongoing independent review, prompting scientists to think more sensitively and systematically about how to protect the rights and welfare of research subjects.[49] Similarly, to reduce the risk of catastrophic ethical failures like the 2001 Enron debacle, regulatory mechanisms under corporate law can be designed, in ways informed by empirical research in social psychology, to promote greater accountability in corporate governance (Jones, 2006; Darley, 2005).

In hierarchical institutions, it is the moral responsibility of individuals in leadership positions to establish and maintain accountability for members of the groups they lead. This responsibility is perhaps nowhere more important than in law enforcement and the military, the institutions that exercise the state's monopoly on the legitimate use of force. Regarding the military, so far as its existence and activities are morally justified, individual soldiers are licensed to transgress ordinary moral prohibitions on using force and committing harm—but only in circumscribed cases, and acting only in their institutional role, accountable to a clear chain of command. Strict institutional discipline is necessary to keep harm and the use of force in check, by constantly clarifying individuals' understanding of what they are and are not permitted to do. When such discipline breaks down, and especially when individuals confront ambiguous situations under extreme stress, atrocity is, tragically, to be expected (Doris & Murphy, 2007; Minow, 2007).

An infamous example is the "numerous instances of sadistic, blatant, and wanton criminal abuses" found to have been "intentionally perpetrated" by US forces at Abu Ghraib prison in Iraq (Taguba, 2004). This disastrous breakdown in military discipline can be plausibly traced all the way to the top of the US Department of Defense (Hersh, 2004). Consider a telling episode of decision-making behavior on the part of then-Secretary of Defense Donald Rumsfeld, as reported by *New Yorker* correspondent Jane Mayer (2006: 35–36). "On December 2nd [2002], Secretary of Defense Rumsfeld gave

---

[49] Beecher (1966); Brandt (1978); National Commission for the Protection of Human Subjects of Biomedical and Behavioral Research (1979); United States Code of Federal Regulations Title 45, part 46; Council for International Organizations of Medical Sciences (2002).

formal approval for the use of 'hooding,' 'exploitation of phobias,' 'stress positions,' 'deprivation of light and auditory stimuli,' and other coercive tactics ordinarily forbidden by the Army Field Manual." In a handwritten addendum to his formal memorandum of December 2nd, Rumsfeld "asked why detainees could be forced to stand for only four hours a day, when he himself often stood 'for 8–10 hours a day.' " Field commanders could have read such a handwritten marginal note—making light even of the few limits ostensibly acknowledged by the formal text—as a signal for "Anything goes."

It said, 'Carte blanche, guys,' . . . 'That's what started them down the slope. You'll have My Lais then. Once you pull this thread, the whole fabric unravels.'   (Mayer, 2006: 36)[50]

The anything-goes detention policy, initially developed for interrogating suspects like those captured in Afghanistan and held at the Guantanamo Bay detention facility, eventually made its way to Abu Ghraib. This top-down unraveling of military discipline opened the door to atrocious behavior by individuals at the lowest levels of the hierarchy. The removal of organizational constraints quite predictably gave free rein to automatic response tendencies, such as those involving physical position and social status, likely to issue in the abuse of prisoners by guards (cf. Haney et al., 1973).

Minow (2007) develops an empirically informed, constructive proposal for building moral and legal safeguards into the organizational life of the military. One of her most striking recommendations is that legal analysis of problematic situations should be integrated into military operations at every level, right down to platoon leaders (ibid.: 51–53). Because the platoon leader is "closest to the ordinary soldier," he or she "should carry special responsibility for knowing and applying the law of war in assessing commands from above and framing decisions for action" (ibid.: 52). Noting the literature in experimental psychology on conformity (e.g. Asch, 1955), Minow (2007: 53) even suggests that platoon leaders might sometimes be charged with "the specific job of playing devil's advocate in order to reduce the groupthink and conformity surrounding a superior officer." Redefining the roles and responsibilities of platoon leaders in these ways might plausibly turn to moral advantage their social status (carrying official institutional authority to critically scrutinize orders from above) and their physical position (typically in closer proximity than any superior officer) with respect to soldiers under their command.

---

[50] Quoting Colonel Lawrence Wilkerson, "a retired military officer who was a chief of staff to former Secretary of State Colin Powell" (Mayer, 2006: 36).

10. Conclusion

We have proposed an explanation for the disconcerting phenomenon of moral dissociation, and have briefly indicated directions that remedies might take. We have offered an alternative to traditional virtue-ethical approaches that place heavy—and risky—bets on the power of individual practical rationality. While there is still an important role for the strategic application of individual powers of deliberation, self-monitoring, and self-control, it must be supplemented with systematic attention to the way "internal" cognitive processes interact with environmental factors such as interpersonal relationships, social and organizational settings, and institutional structures. Empirical research faces a similar challenge. The classic experimental paradigms in social psychology, such as those we have considered here, were designed precisely to disentangle observed occasions for action from the normative cues typically provided by subjects' long-standing personal relationships, routine social role expectations, and the like, as embedded in the familiar settings in which people usually go about their lives. This work has been extraordinarily illuminating, but there is more to be done. As Merritt (2009; cf. Bargh & Williams, 2006) argues, psychological research that situates observed cognition and behavior within interpersonal relationships can help us to understand in detail how environmental influences raise or lower the risk of individual ethical failure in real-world settings.

In placing this sort of emphasis on the social environment, we do not mean to suggest that the debate over character and situation has been resolved. On the contrary, we mean to suggest the opposite. The "character wars" represent only a beginning, an entrée into a more empirically informed way of doing moral psychology. As researchers with different theoretical predilections move together past these beginnings, they are finding that the issues at stake have a much broader resonance than discussions of character and virtue ethics, for the problem becomes the problem of determining in what circumstances human cognition deserves the philosophical honorific "practical rationality" (Doris, 2009).

References

Adams, Robert Merrihew. 2006. *A Theory of Virtue: Excellence in Being for the Good.* Oxford: Oxford University Press.

Adelmann, P. K., & R. B. Zajonc. 1989. "Facial Efference and the Experience of Emotion." *Annual Review of Psychology* 40: 249–280.

Allport, G. W. 1966. "Traits Revisited." *American Psychologist* 21: 1–10.

Annas, Julia. 2005. "Comments on John Doris's Lack of Character." *Philosophy and Phenomenological Research* 71: 636–642.

Anscombe, G. E. M. 1958. "Modern Moral Philosophy." *Philosophy* 33: 1–19.

Appiah, Kwame Anthony. 2008. *Experiments in Ethics*. Cambridge, MA: Harvard University Press.

Arpaly, Nomy. 2005. "Comments on Lack of Character by John Doris." *Philosophy and Phenomenological Research* 71: 643–647.

Asch, S. E. 1955. "Opinions and Social Pressure." *Scientific American* 193: 31–35.

Banaji, M. R., & D. A. Prentice. 1994. "The Self in Social Contexts." *Annual Review of Psychology* 45: 297–332.

Bargh, J. A. 1989. "Conditional Automaticity: Varieties of Automatic Influence in Social Perception and Cognition." In *Unintended Thought*, J. A. Bargh & J. S. Uleman (eds.). New York: Guilford Press, 3–51.

—— 1994. "The Four Horsemen of Automaticity: Awareness, Intention, Efficiency, and Control in Social Cognition." In *Handbook of Social Cognition*, vol. 1, J. R. S. Wyer & T.K. Srull (eds.). Hillsdale, NJ: Erlbaum, 3–42.

—— 1996. "Automaticity in Social Psychology." In *Social Psychology: Handbook of Basic Principles*, E. T. Higgins & A. W. Kruglanski (eds.). New York: Guilford Press, 169–183.

Bargh, J. A., & T. L. Chartrand. 1999. "The Unbearable Automaticity of Being." *American Psychologist* 54: 462–479.

Bargh, J. A., M. Chen, & L. Burrows. 1996. "Automaticity of Social Behavior: Direct Effects of Trait Construct and Stereotype Activation on Action." *Journal of Personality and Social Psychology* 71: 230–244.

Bargh, J. A., & E. L. Williams. 2006. "The Automaticity of Social Life." *Current Directions in Psychological Science* 15: 1–4.

Baron, J. 1994. "Nonconsequentialist Decisions." *Behavioral and Brain Sciences* 17: 142.

—— 2001. *Thinking and Deciding*. 3rd edition, Cambridge: Cambridge University Press.

Batson, C. Daniel. 2002. "Addressing the Altruism Question Experimentally." In *Altruism and Altruistic Love: Science, Philosophy and Religion in Dialogue*, S. G. Post et al. (eds.). New York: Oxford University Press, 89–105.

Batson, C. Daniel, B. Duncan, P. Ackerman, T. Buckley, & K. Birch. 1981. "Is empathic emotion a source of altruistic motivation?" *Journal of Personality and Social Psychology* 40: 290–302.

Batson, C. Daniel, K. O'Quin, J. Fultz, M. Vanderplas, & A. M. Isen. 1983. "Influence of self-reported distress and empathy on egoistic versus altruistic motivation to help." *Journal of Personality and Social Psychology* 45: 706–718.

Bazerman, H. M., & M. R. Banaji. 2004. "The Social Psychology of Ordinary Ethical Failures." *Social Justice Research* 17: 111–115.

Beecher, H. K. 1966. "Ethics and Clinical Research." *New England Journal of Medicine* 274: 1354–1360.

Blair, I. V. 2002. "The Malleability of Automatic Stereotypes and Prejudice." *Personality and Social Psychology Review* 6: 242–261.

Blass, T. 2000. *Obedience to Authority: Current Perspectives on the Milgram Paradigm*. Mahwah, NJ: Lawrence Erlbaum.

——2004. *The Man Who Shocked the World: The Life and Legacy of Stanley Milgram*. New York: Basic Books.

Bok, H. 1996. "Acting Without Choosing." *Nous* 30: 174–196.

Brandt, A. M. 1978. "Racism and Research: The Case of the Tuskegee Syphilis Study." *Hastings Center Report* 8: 21–29.

Brewer, M. B., & W. L. Gardner. 1996. "Who Is This 'We'? Levels of Collective Identity and Self Representations." *Journal of Personality and Social Psychology* 71: 83–93.

Broadie, A. 1968. "The Practical Syllogism." *Analysis* 29: 26–28.

Broadie, S. 1991. *Ethics with Aristotle*. New York: Oxford University Press.

Bush, L. K., C. L. Barr, G. J. McHugo, & J. T. Lanzetta. 1989. "The Effects of Facial Control and Facial Mimicry on Subjective Reactions to Comedy Routines." *Motivation and Emotion* 13: 31–52.

Ceci, S. J. 1996. *On Intelligence: A Bioecological Treatise on Intellectual Development*, expanded ed. Cambridge, MA and London: Harvard University Press.

Chartrand, T. L., & J. A. Bargh. 1999. "The chameleon effect: the perception–behavior link and social interaction." *Journal of Personality and Social Psychology* 76: 893–910.

Chen, M., & J. A. Bargh. 1997. "Nonconscious Behavioral Confirmation Processes: The Self-Fulfilling Consequences of Automatic Stereotype Activation." *Journal of Experimental Social Psychology* 33: 541–560.

Chen, S., H. C. Boucher, & M. P. Tapias. 2006. "The Relational Self Revealed: Integrative Conceptualization and Implications for Interpersonal Life." *Psychological Bulletin* 132: 151–179.

Clark, R. D., & Word, L. E. 1972. "Why Don't Bystanders Help? Because of Ambiguity?" *Journal of Personality and Social Psychology* 24: 392–400.

——1974. "Where Is the Apathetic Bystander?: Situational Characteristics of the Emergency." *Journal of Personality and Social Psychology* 29: 279–287.

Council for International Organizations of Medical Sciences (CIOMS). 2002. *International Ethical Guidelines for Biomedical Research Involving Human Subjects*. Geneva: World Health Organization.

Dana, J., & G. Loewenstein. 2003. "A Social Science Perspective on Gifts to Physicians from Industry." *Journal of the American Medical Association* 290: 252–255.

Darley, John M. 2005. "The Cognitive and Social Psychology of Contagious Organizational Corruption." *Brooklyn Law Review* 70: 1177–1194.

Darley, John M., & C. Daniel Batson. 1973. "From Jerusalem to Jericho: A Study of Situational and Dispositional Variables in Helping Behavior." *Journal of Personality and Social Psychology* 27: 100–108.

Dasgupta, N. 2004. "Implicit Ingroup Favoritism, Outgroup Favoritism, and Their Behavioral Manifestations." *Social Justice Research* 17: 143–169.

Dasgupta, N., & L. M. Rivera. 2006. "From Automatic Antigay Prejudice to Behavior: The Moderating Role of Conscious Beliefs About Gender and Behavioral Control." *Journal of Personality and Social Psychology* 91: 268–280.

DeJong, W., S. Marber, & R. Shaver. 1980. "Crime Intervention: The Role of a Victim's Behavior in Reducing Situational Ambiguity." *Personality and Social Psychology Bulletin* 6: 113–118.

DePaul, M. 1999. "Character Traits, Virtues, and Vices: Are There None?" In *Proceedings of the 20th World Congress of Philosophy*, vol. I. Bowling Green, OH: Philosophy Documentation Center, 141–157.

Detterman, D. K. 1993. "The Case for the Prosecution: Transfer as Epiphenomenon." In *Transfer on Trial: Intelligence, Cognition, and Instruction*, K. K. Detterman and R. J. Sternberg (eds.). Norwood, NJ: Ablex, 1–24.

Devine, P. G. 1989. "Stereotypes and Prejudice: Their Automatic and Controlled Components." *Journal of Personality and Psychology* 56: 5–18.

Dimberg, U. 1988. "Facial Electromyography and the Experience of Emotion." *Journal of Psychophysiology* 2: 277–282.

Doris, John M. 1998. "Persons, Situations, and Virtue Ethics." *Nous* 32: 504–530.

——2002. *Lack of Character: Personality and Moral Behavior*. Cambridge: Cambridge University Press.

——2005. "Précis" and "Replies: Evidence and Sensibility." *Philosophy and Phenomenological Research* 73: 632–635, 656–677.

——2009. "Skepticism about Persons." *Philosophical Issues* 19: 57–91.

Doris, John M., & Dominic Murphy. 2007. "From My Lai to Abu Ghraib: The Moral Psychology of Atrocity." *Midwest Studies in Philosophy* 31: 25–55.

Dovidio, J. F., K. Kawakami, & S. L. Gaertner. 2000. "Reducing Contemporary Prejudice: Combating Explicit and Implicit Bias at the Individual and Intergroup Level." In *Reducing Prejudice and Discrimination*, S. Oskamp (ed.). Mahwah, NJ: Lawrence Erlbaum, 137–163.

Drigotas, S. M., S. W. Whitton, C. E. Rusbult, & J. Wieselquist. 1999. "Close Partner as Sculptor of the Ideal Self: Behavioural Affirmation and the Michelangelo Phenomenon." *Journal of Personality and Social Psychology* 77: 293–323.

Eisenberg, N., R. A. Fabes, P. A. Miller, J. Fultz, R. Shell, R. M. Mathy, & R. R. Reno. 1989. "Relation of Sympathy and Personal Distress to Prosocial Behavior: A Multimethod Study." *Journal of Personality and Social Psychology* 57: 55–66.

Fazio, R. H., J. R. Jackson, B. C. Dunton, & C. J. Williams. 1995. "Variability in Automatic Activation as an Unobtrusive Measure of Racial Attitudes: A Bona Fide Pipeline?" *Journal of Personality and Social Psychology* 69: 1013–1027.

Fiske, Susan T. 1992. "Thinking Is for Doing: Portraits of Social Cognition from Daguerrotype to Laserphoto." *Journal of Personality and Social Psychology* 63: 877–889.

——1993. "Social Cognition and Social Perception." In *Annual Review of Psychology*, L. W. Porter and M. R. Rosenzweig (eds.). Palo Alto, CA: Annual Reviews, 44: 155–194.

Fiske, Susan T. 2003. *Social Beings: A Core Motives Approach to Social Psychology*. Hoboken, NJ: John Wiley & Sons, Inc.

Fitzsimmons, G. M., & J. A. Bargh. 2003. "Thinking of You: Nonconscious Pursuit of Interpersonal Goals Associated with Relationship Partners." *Journal of Personality and Social Psychology* 84: 148–164.

Flanagan, Owen. 1991. *Varieties of Moral Personality: Ethics and Psychological Realism*. Cambridge, MA: Harvard University Press.

Florack, A., M. Scarabis, & H. Bless. 2001. "When Do Associations Matter? The Use of Automatic Associations toward Ethnic Groups in Person Judgments." *Journal of Experimental Social Psychology* 37: 518–524.

Funder, D. C. 1991. "Global Traits: A Neo-Allportian Approach to Personality." *Psychological Science* 2: 31–39.

Gardner, W. L., S. Gabriel, & L. Hochschild. 2002. "When You and I Are 'We,' You Are No Longer Threatening: The Role of Self-expansion in Social Comparison Processes." *Journal of Personality and Social Psychology* 83: 239–251.

Gardner, W. L., S. Gabriel, & A. Y. Lee. 1999. " 'I' Value Freedom But 'We' Value Relationships: Self-construal Priming Mirrors Cultural Differences in Judgment." *Psychological Science* 10: 321–326.

Gilbert, D. T., & P. S. Malone. 1995. "The Correspondence Bias." *Psychological Bulletin* 117: 21–38.

Goldberg, L. R. 1993. "The Structure of Phenotypic Personality Traits." *American Psychologist* 48: 26–34.

——1995. "So What Do You Propose We Use Instead? A Reply to Block," *Psychological Bulletin* 117: 221–225.

Gourevitch, Philip. 1998. *We Wish to Inform You That Tomorrow We Will Be Killed with Our Families: Stories From Rwanda*. New York: Farrar, Straus & Giroux.

Haidt, Jonathan. 2006. *The Happiness Hypothesis: Finding Modern Truth in Ancient Wisdom*. New York: Basic Books.

Haidt, Jonathan, & J. Graham. 2007. "When Morality Opposes Justice: Conservatives Have Moral Intuitions that Liberals May not Recognize." *Social Justice Research* 20: 98–116.

Haney, C., W. Banks, & P. Zimbardo. 1973. "Interpersonal Dynamics of a Simulated Prison." *International Journal of Criminology and Penology* 1: 69–97.

Hansen, C. H., & Hansen, R. D. 1994. "Automatic Emotion: Attention and Facial Efference." *Advances in Experimental Social Psychology* 24: 319–359.

Harman, Gilbert. 1999. "Moral Philosophy Meets Social Psychology: Virtue Ethics and the Fundamental Attribution Error." *Proceedings of the Aristotelean Society* 99: 315–331.

——2000. "The Nonexistence of Character Traits." *Proceedings of the Aristotelian Society* 100: 223–226.

Hassin, R. R., J. S. Uleman, & J. A. Bargh. 2005. *The New Unconscious*. New York: Oxford University Press.

Hersh, Seymour M. 2004. *Chain of Command*. New York: HarperCollins.

Hodges, S. D., & D. M. Wegner. 1997. "Automatic and Controlled Empathy." In *Empathic Accuracy*, William Ickes (ed.). New York: Guilford Press, 311–339.

Hursthouse, Rosalind. 1999. *On Virtue Ethics*. Oxford and New York: Oxford University Press.

Isen, A. M., & P. F. Levin. 1972. "Effect of Feeling Good on Helping: Cookies and Kindness." *Journal of Personality and Social Psychology* 21: 384–388.

Johansson, P., L. Hall, S. Sikström, and A. Olsson. 2005. "Failure to Detect Mismatches Between Intention and Outcome in a Simple Decision Task." *Science* 310: 116-119.

Johansson, P., L. Hall, L., S. Sikström, B. Tärning, & A. Lind. 2006. "How Something Can Be Said About Telling More Than We Can Know." *Consciousness and Cognition* 15: 673–692.

Jones, E. E. 1990. *Interpersonal Perception*. New York: W. H. Freeman.

Jones, E. E., & J. W. Thibaut. 1958. "Interaction Goals as Bases of Inference in Interpersonal Perception." In *Person Perception and Interpersonal Behavior*, R. Tagiuri & L. Petrullo (eds.). Stanford: Stanford University Press, 151–178.

Jones, Renee M. 2006. "Law, Norms, and the Breakdown of the Board: Promoting Accountability in Corporate Governance." *Iowa Law Review*, 92: 105–158.

Kahneman, D., P. Slovic, & A. Tversky. 1982. *Judgment Under Uncertainty: Heuristics and Biases*. Cambridge: Cambridge University Press.

Kamtekar, Rachana. 2004. "Situationism and Virtue Ethics on the Content of Our Character." *Ethics* 114: 458–491.

Katz, I., & R. G. Hass. 1988. "Racial Ambivalence and American Value Conflict: Correlational and Priming Studies of Dual Cognitive Structures." *Journal of Personality and Social Psychology* 55: 893–905.

Kraut, Richard. 2008. "Aristotle's Ethics." In *The Stanford Encyclopedia of Philosophy (Fall 2008 Edition)*, Edward N. Zalta (ed.). URL = <http://plato.stanford.edu/archives/fall2008/entries/aristotle-ethics/>.

Kunda, Ziva. 1999. *Social Cognition: Making Sense of People*. Cambridge, MA: MIT Press.

Kupperman, Joel. 2001. "The Indispensability of Character." *Philosophy* 76: 239–250.

Latané, Bibb. 1981. "The Psychology of Social Impact." *American Psychologist* 36: 343–356.

Latané, Bibb, & John M. Darley. 1970. *The Unresponsive Bystander: Why Doesn't He Help?* Englewood Cliffs, NJ: Prentice-Hall.

Latané, Bibb, & S. Nida. 1981. "Ten Years of Research on Group Size and Helping." *Psychological Bulletin* 89: 308–324.

Leary, Mark R. 2001. "The Self We Know and the Self We Show: Self-esteem, Self-presentation, and the Maintenance of Interpersonal Relationships." In *Blackwell Handbook of Social Psychology: Interpersonal Processes*, G. J. O. Fletcher & M. S. Clark (eds.). Oxford: Blackwell, 457–477.

Lerner, J. S., & P. E. Tetlock. 1999. "Accounting for the Effects of Accountability." *Psychological Bulletin* 125: 255–275.

Levenson, R. W., & A. M. Ruef. 1992. "Empathy: A Physiological Substrate." *Journal of Personality and Social Psychology* 63: 234–246.

Markus, H., & S. Cross. 1990. "The Interpersonal Self." In *Handbook of Personality*, L. A. Pervin (eds.). New York: Guilford Press, 576–608.

Mathews, K. E., and L. K. Cannon. 1975. "Environmental Noise Level as a Determinant of Helping Behavior." *Journal of Personality and Social Psychology* 32: 571–577.

Mayer, Jane. 2006. "Annals of the Pentagon: The Memo." *The New Yorker*, February 27.

McConahay, J. G. 1986. "Modern Racism, Ambivalence, and the Modern Racism Scale." In *Prejudice, Discrimination, and Racism*, J. F. Dovidio & S. L. Gaertner (eds.). Orlando, FL: Academic Press, 91–125.

McDowell, John. 1997. "Virtue and Reason." In *Virtue Ethics*, R. Crisp & M. Slote (eds.). Oxford: Oxford University Press, 141–162.

McEvoy, S. P., M. Woodward, R. Cercarelli, C. Haworth, M. R. Stevenson, A. T. McCartt, & P. Palamara. 2005. "Role of Mobile Phones in Motor Vehicle Crashes Resulting in Hospital Attendance: a Case-Crossover Study." *British Medical Journal* 331: 428–432.

Meeus, Wim H. J., & Quinten A. W. Raaijmakers. 1995. "Obedience in Modern Society: The Utrecht Studies." *Journal of Social Issues* 51: 155–175.

Merritt, Maria. 2000. "Virtue Ethics and Situationist Personality Psychology." *Ethical Theory and Moral Practice* 3: 365–383.

——— 2009. "Aristotelean Virtue and the Interpersonal Aspect of Ethical Character." *Journal of Moral Philosophy* 6: 23–49.

Milgram, Stanley. 1974. *Obedience to Authority*. New York: Harper & Row.

Miller, Arthur G. 1986. *The Obedience Experiments: A Case Study of Controversy in Social Science*. New York: Praeger.

Miller, Arthur G., B. E. Collins, & D. E. Brief. 1995. "Perspectives on Obedience to Authority: The Legacy of the Milgram Experiments." *Journal of Social Issues* 51: 1–19.

Miller, Christian. 2003. "Social Psychology and Virtue Ethics." *The Journal of Ethics* 7: 365–392.

Millgram, Elijah. 2005. *Ethics Done Right: Practical Reasoning as a Foundation for Moral Theory*. Cambridge: Cambridge University Press.

Minow, Martha. 2007. "Living Up to Rules: Holding Soldiers Responsible for Abusive Conduct and the Dilemma of the Superior Orders Defense." *McGill Law Journal* 52: 1–54.

Mischel, Walter. 1968. *Personality and Assessment*. New York: John Wiley & Sons.

——— 1999. "Personality Coherence and Dispositions in a Cognitive-Affective Personality System (CAPS) Approach." In *The Coherence of Personality: Social-Cognitive Bases of Consistency, Variability, and Organization*, D. Cervone & Y. Shoda (eds.). New York and London: Guilford Press, 37–60.

Montmarquet, J. 2003. "Moral Character and Social Science Research." *Philosophy* 78: 355–368.

Moore, D. A., & G. Loewenstein. 2004. "Self-Interest, Automaticity, and the Psychology of Conflict of Interest." *Social Justice Research* 17: 189–202.

National Commission for the Protection of Human Subjects of Biomedical and Behavioral Research. 1979. *The Belmont Report.* United States Government Printing Office.

Neumann, R., & F. Strack. 2000. " 'Mood contagion': The Automatic Transfer of Mood Between Persons." *Journal of Personality and Social Psychology* 79: 211–223.

Niedenthal, Paula M. 2007. "Embodying Emotion." *Science* 316: 1002–1005.

Nisbett, Richard E. 2003. *The Geography of Thought: How Asians and Westerners Think Differently . . . and Why.* New York: Free Press.

Nisbett, Richard E., & Lee Ross. 1980. *Human Inference: Strategies and Shortcomings of Social Judgment.* Englewood Cliffs, NJ: Prentice-Hall.

Nisbett, Richard E., & Timothy D. Wilson. 1977. "Telling More Than We Can Know: Verbal Reports on Mental Processes." *Psychological Review* 84: 231–253.

Nosek, B. A., M. R. Banaji, & A. G. Greenwald. 2002. "Harvesting Implicit Group Attitudes and Beliefs from a Demonstration Web Site." *Group Dynamics: Theory, Research, and Practice* 6: 101–115.

Orlowski, J. P., & L. Wateska. 1992. "The Effects of Pharmaceutical Firm Enticements on Physician Prescribing Patterns: There's No Such Thing as a Free Lunch." *Chest* 102: 270–273.

Pennington, J. & B. R. Schlenker. 1990. "Accountability for Consequential Decisions: Justifying Ethical Judgments to Audiences." *Personality and Social Psychology Bulletin* 25: 1067–1081.

Pervin, L. A. 1994. "A Critical Analysis of Current Trait Theory." *Psychological Inquiry* 5: 103–113.

Peterson, Donald R. 1968. *The Clinical Study of Social Behavior.* New York: Appleton-Century-Crofts.

Power, Samantha. 2002. *"A Problem from Hell": America and the Age of Genocide.* New York: HarperCollins.

Ross, Lee, & Richard E. Nisbett. 1991. *The Person and the Situation.* Philadelphia, PA: Temple University Press.

Rudman, L. A., J. M. Feinberg, & K. Fairchild. 2002. "Minority Members' Implicit Attitudes: Ingroup Bias as Function of Group Status." *Social Cognition* 20: 294–320.

Sabini, John, & Maury Silver. 2004. "Situationalism and Character," *PsyCRITIQUES* 49: 607–609.

—— 2005. "Lack of Character? Situationism Critiqued." *Ethics* 115: 535–562.

Schlenker, B. R., & M. F. Weigold. 1992. "Interpersonal Processes Involving Impression Regulation and Management." *Annual Review of Psychology* 43: 133–168.

Sedikides, Constantine, & Jeffrey M. Jackson. 1990. "Social Impact Theory: A Field Test of Source Strength, Source Immediacy and Number of Targets." *Basic and Applied Social Psychology* 11: 273–281.

Shotland, R. L., & Stebbins, C. A. 1980. "Bystander Response to Rape: Can a Victim Attract Help?" *Journal of Applied Social Psychology* 10: 510–527.

Solomon, Robert C. 2003. "Victims of Circumstances? A Defense of Virtue Ethics in Business." *Business Ethics Quarterly* 13: 43–62.

—— 2005. "What's Character Got to do with it?" *Philosophy and Phenomenological Research* 71: 648–655.

Sreenivasan, Gopal. 2002. "Errors about Errors: Virtue Theory and Trait Attribution." *Mind* 111: 47–68.

Srull, T. K., & R. S. Wyer, Jr. 1979. "The Role of Category Accessibility in the Interpretation of Information about Persons: Some Determinants and Implications." *Journal of Personality and Social Psychology* 37: 1660–1672.

Stanovich, Keith. E. 2004. *The Robot's Rebellion: Finding Meaning in the Age of Darwin.* Chicago, IL and London: University of Chicago Press.

Swanton, Christine. 2003. *Virtue Ethics: A Pluralistic View.* Oxford: Oxford University Press

Taguba, A. M. 2004. "The 'Taguba Report' on Treatment of Abu Ghraib Prisoners in Iraq." (Article 15-6 Investigation of the 800th Military Police Brigade). Available at underline http://news.findlaw.com/hdocs/docs/iraq/tagubarpt.html (accessed June 8, 2007).

Teachman, B. A., K. D. Gapinski, K. D. Brownell, M. Rawlins, & S. Jeyaram. 2003. "Demonstrations of Implicit Anti-Fat Bias: The Impact of Providing Causal Information and Evoking Empathy." *Health Psychology* 22: 68–78.

Trope, Y. & A. Fishbach. 2005. "Going Beyond the Motivation Given: Self-Control and Situational Control Over Behavior." In *The New Unconscious*, R. R. Hassin, J. S. Uleman, & J.A. Bargh (eds.). New York: Oxford University Press, 537–565.

Tversky, A., & D. Kahneman. 1981. "The Framing of Decisions and the Psychology of Choice." *Science* 211: 453–463.

Upton, Candace (ed.). Forthcoming. *Virtue Ethics, Character and Moral Psychology.*

United States Code of Federal Regulations Title 45, part 46, Protection of Human Subjects.

Vernon, P. E. 1964. *Personality Assessment: A Critical Survey.* New York: Wiley.

Vranas, Peter B. M. 2005. "The Indeterminacy Paradox: Character Evaluations and Human Psychology." *Nous* 39: 1–42.

Wazana, A. 2000. "Physicians and the Pharmaceutical Industry: Is a Gift Ever Just a Gift?" *Journal of the American Medical Association* 283: 373–380.

Webber, Jonathan. 2006. "Virtue, Character and Situation." *Journal of Moral Philosophy* 3: 193–213.

—— 2007a. "Character, Common-Sense, and Expertise." *Ethical Theory and Moral Practice* 10: 89–104.

—— 2007b. "Character, Global and Local." *Utilitas* 19: 430–434.

Wegner, Daniel M. 2002. *The Illusion of Conscious Will.* Cambridge, MA: MIT Press.

Wegner, Daniel M., & J. A. Bargh. 1998. "Control and Automaticity in Social Life." In *The Handbook of Social Psychology*, 4th ed., vol. I, D. T. Gilbert, S. T. Fiske, and G. Lindzey (eds.). New York: McGraw-Hill, 446–496.

Wiggins, David. 1980. "Deliberation and Practical Reason." In *Essays on Aristotle's Ethics*, A. O. Rorty (ed.). Berkeley, Los Angeles, and London: University of California Press, 221–240.

Williams, Bernard. 1985. *Ethics and the Limits of Philosophy*. Cambridge, MA: Harvard University Press.

Wilson, Timothy D. 2002. *Strangers to Ourselves: Discovering the Adaptive Unconscious*. New York: Belknap.

12

Well-Being

VALERIE TIBERIUS AND ALEXANDRA PLAKIAS

1. Introduction

The question of what it is to achieve well-being is of obvious practical significance. Whatever well-being is exactly, the concept is meant to point to something we aim at for ourselves and ought to promote for others. Insofar as well-being is an action-guiding, or normative, notion that has a role in personal deliberation and public policy, accounts of well-being are subject to competing pressures. On the one hand, "well-being" aims to pick out an empirical phenomenon that can be measured, compared, and (one hopes) realized in people's lives: to achieve well-being is to enjoy a certain kind of life or set of experiences that we can investigate and influence. On the other hand, it has a kind of normative significance: it *makes sense* to promote well-being, procuring it is a *good* thing to do. In this chapter we aim to give an account of well-being that meets both of these demands.

Historically, philosophical conceptions of well-being (and related notions such as happiness and flourishing) have been responsive to the paired demands for normative and empirical adequacy.[1] Aristotle's conception of human flourishing (*eudaimonia*, in his Greek), for example, is clearly intended to be action guiding: for Aristotle (*NE:* I.8.1097b), *eudaimonia* is that at which everything aims, and his is an account of the *best* life for a human being. But Aristotle is also concerned with the empirical foundations of his conception of flourishing. In particular, since virtue is on his view necessary for happiness (NE I.8.1099b), he is pressed to give an account of the developmental psychology of virtue (*NE:* see II and III, esp. II.1–5). Utilitarians since Bentham (1789/1970) have been very concerned with the measurement of happiness, but they have also been at pains to argue for its value. Taking Aristotle and Bentham as our

[1] These notions are not coextensive, but it does make sense to compare accounts of each insofar as the account is put forward as describing the central goal of life; some of the complications this presents will emerge as we proceed.

examples, we can see, first, that questions about well-being are philosophical questions. Empirical psychological research may tell us how to measure pleasure, how to cultivate virtue, or what causes happiness, but it cannot tell us whether we ought to aim for pleasure, virtue, or happiness. Second, it makes a big difference what conception of well-being one adopts. Policies for promoting the development of virtue may be quite different from policies that produce more pleasure, and, for the individual deliberator, choosing one may be in conflict with choosing the other. Finally, we can see that though these questions are philosophical, the answers almost always make crucial empirical assumptions. For example, Aristotle (*NE,* esp. III.5) assumes that it is possible to inculcate robust and stable traits of character like the virtues, and Bentham (1789/1970, see esp. ch. 5 sec. 18–19) assumes that pleasures can be quantified and compared.

While it is true that philosophers interested in well-being have often been concerned about the empirical assumptions of their theories, few philosophers have made an effort to take account of the empirical research on this topic.[2] In large part, this is because this psychological research, particularly the burgeoning field of "positive psychology," is so new that philosophers have not had a chance to address it. We suspect, however, that another part of the explanation is uncertainty about the shape that a truly interdisciplinary study of well-being would take. In this chapter we employ a methodology that we hope will reduce this uncertainty. Our argument aims to characterize well-being in a way that is both empirically grounded and able to play the role in our ethical practice that it needs to play. *Normatively,* if our account of well-being ends up being something we have no reason to care about, then we have gone wrong somewhere. *Empirically,* if an account of well-being implies that it cannot be investigated, measured, and achieved, there is reason to look elsewhere. We might call this approach, following Haybron (2008a), a "reconstructive analysis."[3] In developing our own analysis, we hope to arrive at a conception that is both normatively and empirically adequate and also to provide the reader with some background and insight into the main concerns and issues in both empirical and philosophical approaches to well-being.

---

[2] Recent exceptions are Haybron (2008a) and Tiberius (2008). See also Haybron (2008b). L. W. Sumner (1996) briefly discusses the empirical research in his very influential book *Welfare, Happiness, and Ethics.* See also Peter Railton (unpublished ms).

[3] Haybron (2008a) distinguishes reconstructive analysis from conceptual analysis and a scientific naturalist approach that would treat the question of the definition of well-being as purely empirical. L. W. Sumner's (1996: 6–7) method for defining well-being is similar to reconstructive analysis, occupying a middle ground between the empirical and the conceptual.

With these goals in mind, our method for defending our preferred account of well-being will be to articulate the three main approaches to well-being in positive psychology—hedonism, eudaimonism, and life satisfaction—and to ask how well these theories meet the normative criterion. In Sections 2.1 and 2.2, we briefly argue that hedonism and eudaimonism, as represented in psychology, have difficulty explaining the normative status of well-being. Our intention is not to refute these theories (a feat that it would be foolish to attempt in a single contribution), but to motivate the turn to the life-satisfaction view, which we believe has an easier time accounting for the normative significance of well-being. Unfortunately, the life-satisfaction account of well-being has its own problems, which we consider in the remainder of Section 2. Given the instability of life-satisfaction reports, there is reason to wonder whether there is any stable phenomenon of "life satisfaction" that psychologists are investigating. If there isn't, then the life-satisfaction theory would not be empirically adequate. We argue, in Section 3, that solving this problem for the life-satisfaction theory leads to a modified life-satisfaction account, which is superior on both empirical and normative grounds. We call this account the Value-Based Life-Satisfaction Account. In the final sections of the chapter we refine this account and take up some objections to it.

2. Well-Being in Psychology

Positive psychology is a new field of psychological research that aims to correct a perceived imbalance in psychology as a whole. Since World War II, psychology has tended to focus on the negative—mental illnesses, weakness, stress, dysfunction—and how to remedy these problems when they occur; positive psychology, on the other hand, focuses on the positive aspects of human life and aims to help people live truly good lives rather than just avoid misery (Seligman, 2002). The fact that positive psychology is gaining in popularity among researchers is evident from the number of new academic anthologies and review articles that have appeared recently.[4] As one might

---

[4] Three very useful anthologies are *Flourishing: Positive Psychology and the Life Well-lived* (Keyes & Haidt, 2002), *The Positive Psychology Handbook* (Snyder & Lopez, 2002), and *Well-Being: The Foundations of Hedonic Psychology* (Kahneman, Diener, & Schwarz, 1999). *The American Psychologist* has devoted two issues to the topic that give a good overview of the state of research: Vol. 55 (1) (2000) and Vol. 56 (3) (2001). There is also a new journal devoted to positive psychology, *The Journal of Positive Psychology*, published by Routledge. The first issue of the journal begins with a report on the state of the field (Linley et al., 2006).

expect regarding such topics as happiness and the good life, positive psychology is also drawing attention outside the academy.[5]

According to Martin Seligman (2002), director of the Positive Psychology Center at the University of Pennsylvania, the new field of positive psychology has three pillars: positive subjective experience; positive individual character-istics (strengths and virtues); and positive institutions and communities. Given this broad account and the broad definition of "positive subjective experience," the research projects that fall under the rubric of positive psychology are very diverse.[6] Of the three areas, the first two have received the most attention, as seems reasonable; we need to understand what well functioning is before we can think about designing institutions to attain it. Since the topic of virtue gets much attention elsewhere in this volume, our chapter will focus on the first and most fundamental area of research in positive psychology: the nature of happiness, well-being, or flourishing. In this domain there are three distinct research paradigms distinguished by their views about which goal of human life we ought to measure: pleasure, life satisfaction, and eudaimonia.

2.1. Hedonism

Some of the most intriguing research in the hedonistic program has to do with people's ability to predict future pleasures and pains and to report on past pleasures and pains.[7] One of Kahneman's findings is that, in reflecting on their experiences, people's assessments of these experiences tend to observe what he calls the "peak-end" rule (Kahneman, 1999, 2000). This means that people put greater emphasis on the most pleasant (or most painful) point of a temporally extended experience and on the quality of the experience at the very end of it. People tend to remember less well the duration of the experience, even if they were in moderate pain for the duration.

---

[5] The *New York Times Magazine* and *Time* have both run cover stories, and popular books with yellow smiley faces on their covers abound; psychologist Dan Gilbert's recent book *Stumbling on Happiness* was, at least for a time, ubiquitous at airport booksellers.

[6] It should be noted that "positive psychology" is not the label that would be preferred by all psychologists. Some would prefer to describe their research as "well-being research" or "hedonic psychology." Since Martin Seligman has been very active in promoting this new field, his label seems to have the most currency at the moment. We shall use his definition of positive psychology as our working definition here.

[7] As an aside, one might think that this research does not, strictly speaking, fall into the category of positive psychology because it is focused on pain as well as pleasure. This has raised a criticism of positive psychology as a field, which is that it does not make sense to think about positive experiences in isolation from negative ones (see Lazarus, 2003). Many of the responses to this criticism point out that psychologists whose work is described as positive psychology do not ignore negative affect and emotions, and that the real point of the new field is to emphasize an aspect of psychology that has historically been ignored.

As Kahneman (2000: 697) describes the findings, "a simple average of the most extreme affect experienced during the episode (Peak) and the affect experienced near its end (End)" does an extremely good job of predicting the way the entire episode will be evaluated—in one study, researchers found a correlation of 0.67 between the Peak–End measure and patients' (retrospective) evaluations of the painfulness of a colonoscopy (Redelmeier & Kahneman, 1996).

Such discoveries have influenced the methods that hedonistic researchers use to measure pleasure and pain. New methods include real-time physiological measurements and online measures of experience ("Palm Pilot" studies), in which subjects are beeped at random intervals and asked to report their current hedonic state. This research should be of interest to philosophers inclined to accept hedonism insofar as they are interested in policy applications of their theories. The unreliability of retrospective self-reports complicates this application and may undermine some of the assumptions about what makes people happy that appear warranted from the armchair.

Another area of interest in hedonic research is adaptation. Studies have shown that at least in certain domains, a person's level of positive or negative affect will adapt to her circumstances. For example, several studies have observed hedonic adaptation to incarceration after a difficult initial adjustment period.[8] The oft-cited "Lottery Winners and Accident Victims" reports significant adaptation to paraplegia and quadriplegia caused by accidents (Brickman, Coates, & Janoff-Bulman, 1978). Recent research on adaptation is more cautious. It turns out that adaptation effects are limited to certain domains, that in some cases sensitization occurs instead of adaptation, and that there are other explanations for adaptation besides the existence of a hedonic set-point (Frederick & Loewenstein, 1999). Furthermore, according to Ed Diener, there is now good evidence that people can change their set-points and that they do not adapt to all conditions (Lucas et al., 2003, Lucas et al., 2004). That said, although some think claims about adaptation have been overblown, psychologists agree that hedonic adaptation is real and that it happens to a surprising extent.

Philosophical objections to hedonism as a normative account of the good for a person are numerous, and these objections seem likely to retain their force even with the advance of research in empirical psychology. In fact, psychological research on adaptation seems to make things worse for hedonism. Elijah Millgram (2000), for instance, has used this research on psychological adaptation as part of an argument against utilitarianism. The purpose of hedonic

---

[8] See Frederick & Loewenstein (1999: 311–313) for discussion.

states, he argues, is to indicate important changes in our circumstances and hence pleasant experiences are not the kind of thing that can be maximized.[9]

A second objection to hedonism as a normative account of well-being is its inability to distinguish between different kinds of pleasure. According to the psychologists' version of hedonism, the pleasure induced by taking soma is no less valuable than the pleasure caused by the birth of a child or the completion of an important project. Hedonism lacks the resources to draw distinctions between sources of pleasant affect, but many people share John Stuart Mill's (1871/1999, see esp. 56–59) intuition that some pleasures are better than others, independent of their quantity.[10] This criticism becomes especially pointed when we consider hedonism as a basis for policy: if the same amount of pleasure could be produced by piping mind-numbing muzak into the factory as by giving people more leisure time so that they could pursue projects they care about, hedonism cannot tell us where to invest our resources. Those who have the view that pleasures taken in activities that engage our capacities are better than drug-induced pleasures (and we suspect there are many in this camp) will find this position wrong-headed.

Finally, as has seemed obvious to many philosophers, there just seem to be things that are part of a good life (even a subjectively good life) that cannot be reduced to positive affect: for example, achievement, genuine friendship, and knowledge.[11] To see the point, consider the tortured artist who is living the life he wants to live despite a lack of pleasant affect. Or consider the famously tormented philosopher, Wittgenstein, whose alleged last words were: "Tell them I've had a wonderful life" (Monk, 1990: 579).

2.2. Eudaimonism

Worries about the normative significance of positive affect and other psychological notions are one reason to embrace eudaimonism. Eudaimonistic researchers develop accounts of well-being that focus on vital human needs and emphasize self-actualization or development rather than positive affect. Two such programs are Ryan and Deci's (2000, 2008) self-determination theory of well-being and Ryff and Singer's multidimensional account. Ryff and Singer's (1998) account "taps six distinct aspects of human actualization:

[9] Railton (unpublished ms) makes a similar argument.
[10] Mill distinguishes different *qualities* of pleasure. Hedonists in psychology have not followed Mill in attributing different worth to different kinds of pleasures. Philosophers have also been skeptical about this distinction; for a discussion of criticisms of Mill, see Feldman (1997), ch. 6.
[11] For the classic statement of the objection see Nozick (1974). See also Sumner's chapter on hedonism in his 1996 and Haybron (2008a). For defenses of hedonism, see Feldman (2004) and Crisp (2006).

autonomy, personal growth, self-acceptance, life purpose, mastery, and positive relatedness" (Ryan & Deci, 2001: 146). Ryan and Deci's account posits three basic human needs: autonomy, competence, and relatedness. The fulfillment of these needs, according to their theory (2000: 247), is essential for psychological growth, integrity, and well-being (by which they mean life satisfaction and psychological health).

Because of the emphasis on relatedness as a cause or constituent of well-being, the eudaimonistic paradigm has also fostered interesting work on the nature of good or positive relationships (Reis & Gable, 2003). One example with philosophical relevance is psychologist Shelly Gable's work on relationships, which shows that the quality of intimate relationships people have affects their well-being in ways that go beyond their direct contribution as a component of well-being. According to Gable, good, trusting relationships contribute to the construction of well-being by providing an outlet for capitalization on good fortune. By having subjects keep a diary of the "most important positive event of the day" and whether or not they shared this event with others, and then having subjects complete daily assessments of both life satisfaction and positive and negative affect, Gable et al. (2004: 241) found that "telling others about positive events [capitalization] was associated with higher positive affect and greater life satisfaction." In addition, receiving "active and constructive" responses to one's sharing increased these effects above and beyond the sharing itself. They offer several explanations for this phenomenon: sharing these events may allow one to relive the positive experience, and in doing so may increase the salience and accessibility of the event in one's memory. Furthermore, when others respond positively to such reports, this may enhance and strengthen the "social bond" one feels with others, while also reinforcing the impression that others are pleased on one's behalf, which, Gable et al. hypothesize, may increase self-esteem.

Consequentialism in moral philosophy is standardly understood as the view that the morally best action is the one that produces the best consequences overall, taking everyone into consideration (Sinnott-Armstrong, 2008). This view has been attacked on the grounds that it makes insufficient room for personal connections and the partiality we show toward our loved ones in virtue of our relationships with them (Williams, 1973; but see Railton, 1984). Lori Gruen (2003) has argued that Gable's work adds to the case for the importance of personal relationships in a consequentialist framework. Personal relationships, the thought is, have complex and pervasive causal influence on happiness that we miss if we focus only on the pleasures of friendship itself. In a survey of research on relationships and happiness, David Myers cites several studies that corroborate this hypothesis. For example, students who named five or more close friends with whom they had discussed important events during the last six months were 60% more likely to describe themselves as "very happy" than their peers who had fewer than five friends with whom they'd discussed such matters (Myers, 1999: 378).

The philosophical debate about whether the value of friendship can be accommodated within a consequentialist framework will not be settled by this empirical work. Even if Gruen is correct that Gable's research provides resources for the consequentialist, the charge that consequentialism misses the true value of friendship by putting it in the maximizing hopper still looms. However, this debate may be enriched by thinking about what exactly is important about friendship, and this is an area where empirical psychology has something to contribute.

The eudaimonistic program has also produced work on materialistic values (defined primarily in terms of money and status) and their relationship to well-being. Psychologists have found that, while income has relatively little effect on subjective well-being, caring a lot about income and possessions is a good predictor of low scores on many well-being indicators (Kasser, 2002). Kasser and Ryan (1996) found that subjects to whom financial success was important were more likely to suffer from depression and anxiety, and less likely to experience positive emotions. They were also less likely to report overall satisfaction with their lives. Interestingly, this result is found not only in adults, who are in the workplace, but also in teenagers who had not yet entered college (Kasser, 2002). Furthermore, Kasser reports that individuals who had attained their materialistic goals experienced no increase in subjective well-being, and that individuals who prioritized material achievements to the point of exclusion of non-materialistic achievements actually experienced lower subjective well-being overall than their counterparts who prioritized non-materialistic goals. Finally, attaining non-materialistic goals led subjects to experience an increase in subjective well-being, while attaining material goals caused no increase (Kasser, 2002).

Eudaimonism has in its favor that it can acknowledge differences between types of subjective experience. According to eudaimonism, pleasures that result from self-actualization or relating to other people would be more valuable than physical pleasures because the value of pleasure would be dependent on the satisfaction of a vital human need. It also makes sense of our well-documented inability to predict what will make us happy (Gilbert, 2006; Loewenstein & Schkade, 1999). To many of us, at times, it seems that if we just had a little bit more money, a bigger house, a better car, we would really be happier. This turns out to be much less often the case than one might have thought.

According to eudaimonism, this is because what matters is getting what we need, not getting what we want.

Eudaimonism makes sense of this phenomenon at a cost, however. The eudaimonistic paradigm builds quite specific norms into its account of well-being and thereby invites the charge that it creates too large a gap between well-being and subjective experience. This gap gives rise to concerns about the justification of eudaimonistic norms. If the justification of needs-based norms ultimately depends on the assumption that satisfying these needs brings us more pleasure, or makes us subjectively happier, then the theory on offer is not really a distinct alternative to hedonism or life satisfaction. Moreover, if this is *not* how needs-based norms are justified, it is difficult to see how eudaimonism can have a legitimate claim to be action-guiding in general (and not just for people who already identify with it). Since well-being is supposed to be a good *for* the subject (Sumner, 1996), norms that have authority in virtue of something external to the subject are suspect. In the context of policy application, these concerns take the form of the charge of paternalism.[12] Given that the eudaimonistic program relies on substantive normative assumptions about what constitutes a good life, the question might be posed: why should researchers' and academics' assumptions about what constitutes well-being serve as a guide to policy that will affect individuals who may not share those assumptions?

Unlike hedonism, eudaimonism gives advice and recommendations that are compelling from a normative standpoint. Our argument, though, is that eudaimonism must piggy-back on some other account of well-being for its normative force. Insofar as such theories furnish compelling advice about how to live, this is so because we want, prefer, or care about the things that eudaimonism tells us we need.

2.3. *The Life Satisfaction Program*

According to the life-satisfaction theory (LST), well-being consists in holding an overall positive appraisal or endorsement of your life. At first glance, LST seems well suited to answer our normative concerns. Unlike hedonism, LST can distinguish qualitative differences between pleasurable experiences and count them differentially as part of a person's well-being: if the subject does not find pushpin to be as important as poetry to how her life is going, then LST will place more value on poetry in its assessment. Unlike eudaimonism,

---

[12] Diener & Suh (2000: 4), for example, suggest that eudaimonism is paternalistic and that life satisfaction ought to be privileged because it is more democratic.

LST does not build in arbitrary external norms about what must be achieved for a life to go well: it is the subject's *own* norms that count.

Life-satisfaction researchers try to measure the degree to which people are satisfied with their lives overall. As Diener, Scollon, and Lucas (2003: 196) put it, "[p]resumably, individuals can examine the conditions in their lives, weigh the importance of these conditions, and then evaluate their lives on a scale ranging from dissatisfied to satisfied." Life satisfaction itself is "a positive cognitive/affective response on the part of a subject to (some or all of) the conditions or circumstances of her life" (Sumner, 1996: 156).[13] Subjective well-being (SWB), according to Diener and his colleagues, comprises life satisfaction, domain satisfaction, high positive affect, and low negative affect (Diener et al., 2003: 189).

Psychologists typically discover people's judgments of overall life satisfaction by using self-report measures. One of the most widely used scales for assessing life satisfaction is Ed Diener's *Satisfaction With Life Scale*, a five-item instrument designed to measure global assessments of life satisfaction.[14] Diener's scale asks subjects to indicate their level of agreement (on a 7-point Likert scale from "strongly agree" to "strongly disagree") with the following five items:

- In most ways my life is close to my ideal.
- The conditions of my life are excellent.
- I am satisfied with my life.
- So far I have gotten the important things I want in life.
- If I could live my life over, I would change almost nothing.

Self-reports, though important, are not the only method used. Peer-informant reports and online measures of experience (such as the Palm Pilot studies mentioned above in the context of hedonism) can also be used to measure life satisfaction and, according to Diener and Suh (2000: 6): "We will find ourselves standing on more firm ground if we find that our conclusions converge across measurement methods."

A major concern of life-satisfaction researchers has been to discover its causes and correlates. One reason for this might be an important study by Lykken

---

[13] We follow the philosopher Sumner here, since his definition of life satisfaction is consistent with most of what psychologists say and since psychologists' definitions are sometimes confused. For example, Diener, Scollon, & Lucas (2003: 196) *identify* life satisfaction with the judgment: "We refer to this global, cognitive judgment as life satisfaction." But this can't be what they really intend. After all, if we're not filling out a questionnaire, we're unlikely to be making such judgments explicitly; nevertheless there is a fact of the matter about our subjective well-being even when we are not filling out questionnaires or answering psychologists' questions.

[14] Other scales are sometimes used (e.g. Veenhoven, 1997; Andrews & Withey, 1976), but the differences between them are not significant for our purposes.

and Tellegen (1996), which showed that life satisfaction has a large genetic component. If well-being were entirely genetically determined, it would not be a helpful goal for social policy, short of technological advances in gene manipulation, or ethically suspect and politically untenable eugenics. Concerns about the practical applications of their work have therefore influenced psychologists to look into other causes. Fortunately for this research program, life satisfaction is not entirely a matter of one's genes; while there is evidence for a significant genetic contribution to subjective well-being, life-satisfaction researchers believe that there is enough evidence for an environmental contribution that it makes sense to think about well-being as something that might be influenced by personal effort or social intervention. (Of course, no one, save the most extreme Stoics,[15] doubts that many things that might affect our well-being are outside of our control, such as illness, bereavement, etc.; the point here is just that well-being is not genetically determined, and that, within certain limits, we can take actions and make decisions that will affect and change our well-being.)

In this light, life-satisfaction researchers have been particularly interested in correlations between life satisfaction and conditions of life over which people might have control. Their findings are that many things correlate well with life satisfaction: mental health, strong social ties, satisfying work, satisfying leisure time, goal achievement, self-esteem, and frequency of sex and exercise.[16] Recent work also shows that volunteer work and other altruistic actions are correlated with life satisfaction (Piliavin, 2002). One of the most robust correlations is with strong social ties. In one study, Diener and Seligman (2002) divided subjects into three groups (based on peer reports of affect, self-reports of life satisfaction, and self-reports of affect both global and daily): high-, average-, and low-happiness individuals. They found that all members of the high-happiness group reported having good social relationships (reports that were corroborated by informants), and therefore concluded that "social relationships form a necessary but not sufficient condition for high happiness."[17]

---

[15] See Annas (1993) and Nussbaum (1994) for discussion of the Stoic position.

[16] Correlations range from 0.48 for self-esteem to 0.68 for satisfying leisure time. For correlations with mental health, social ties, satisfaction with work and leisure, and frequency of sex and exercise are from Argyle (1999). Correlations with self-esteem are from Diener & Diener (1995). It is worth noting that the high correlations between life satisfaction and satisfying work and leisure time are based on surveys conducted in European nations. Argyle points out that the results have been found to be reversed in some Asian cultures, such as Japan. On the correlation of life satisfaction with goal attainment see Emmons (2003). Because of the flexibility of goals, some psychologists have come close to taking the satisfaction of goals to be the defining feature of well-being. See, for example, Oishi (2000); Schmuck & Sheldon (2001).

[17] Argyle (1999) also reports a large correlation between happiness and "strong social support" (0.50, although number of friends correlates much less strongly with happiness, at 0.15).

The discovery that people who are satisfied with their lives have close friendships and social ties will not come as a shock to anyone, of course: perhaps more surprising is what does *not* correlate with life satisfaction. Diener and Seligman, in the above study, found little or no difference between their groups when it came to activities such as eating, sleeping, religious participation, television watching, and factors such as income, grades, and physical attractiveness. Perhaps the most surprising result, at least to those not steeped in ancient philosophy, is that income is not a great predictor of life satisfaction or other well-being indicators. Diener and Biswas-Diener (2002) report that, across a wide range of individuals and societies the correlation between individual income and life satisfaction is only about 0.13. There is evidence that GDP per capita is not highly correlated with high life satisfaction (Diener & Oishi, 2000), and that a nation's economic growth does not correlate with an increase in life satisfaction (Diener & Biswas-Diener 2002).[18]

While it is well established that some expected strong correlations between wealth and happiness do not exist, it is important not to overstate the case. Getting one's basic needs met is surely an important factor in life satisfaction, and cross-cultural studies seem to confirm this idea. For example, mean national income correlates strongly with subjective well-being, with a correlation of 0.60 (Diener & Biswas-Diener, 2002).[19] Furthermore, at an individual level, correlations between income and SWB increase in strength as the wealth of the society decreases. Thus income is much more highly correlated with life satisfaction in the slums of Calcutta than in upper-class neighborhoods in the US. So, for example, Diener and Suh report correlations between income and life satisfaction in the US ranging from 0.10 to 0.15, whereas this correlation rises to 0.38 in South Africa, and Argyle reports a correlation of 0.68 in Tanzania. One explanation for these results is that, in very poor countries, greater income may mean the ability to meet basic human needs such as the needs for food, clothing, and shelter. Thus Argyle proposes, "money makes a greater difference to the quality of life when it is spent on food, housing, and other necessities than when it is spent on larger cars, works of art, antiques, and jewelry" (1999: 358). Finally, the research on income has generated some controversy over how to interpret small correlations between life satisfaction and income. Some psychologists are now arguing that these small correlations

---

[18] For a very recent challenge to this last claim (known as the Easterlin paradox—Easterlin, 1974), see Stevenson & Wolfers (2008).

[19] In this and other papers on the topic, Diener and his colleagues use life satisfaction as their primary indicator of subjective well-being; however, they do sometimes use additional measures, and emphasize that the addition of other measures—such as asking subjects about their financial satisfaction—does not significantly alter the results.

"result from the large variability in happiness between individuals but do not indicate trivial mean-level differences between rich and poor" (Diener, 2008: 499).

Cross-cultural studies have not been confined to questions about income. Life-satisfaction researchers have done significant work investigating cultural differences in causes of life satisfaction other than material resources.[20] An interesting finding is that life satisfaction is less highly correlated with self-esteem in so-called collectivist cultures (for example, Asian cultures) than it is in so-called individualistic cultures (for example, North American cultures) (Diener & Diener, 1995). This is not entirely surprising in light of the fact that individualist cultures characterize persons in terms of "personal attributes" rather than social context, whereas collectivist cultures employ a conception of the person that "understands persons in relation to group affiliations and social roles" (Doris & Plakias, 2008: 323; see Nisbett, 2003 for an in-depth discussion). Similarly, some psychologists argue that the correlation between life satisfaction and autonomy varies depending on whether one is in a collectivist or individualistic culture. These findings about autonomy have been disputed, however, on the grounds that the definition of autonomy used in the studies is incorrect. According to Richard Ryan and Edward Deci (2001: 160), "a major conceptual issue in research on autonomy and well-being concerns the constant confusion in the literature between independence (nonreliance) and autonomy (volition)." The authors argue that while the correlation between autonomy as freedom from other people and positive subjective states is culturally variable, there is good evidence for the claim that autonomy as "self-endorsement" correlates well with positive affect in all cultures.

Research on cultural differences may also be of interest to those interested in developing substantive accounts of human flourishing or well-being for the purpose of providing relevant standards for international justice and human rights. Diener and Seligman, two of the most prominent psychologists in this field, are keenly aware of the public policy implications of their research. Further, their recent work demonstrates an interest in promoting this use of the research. For example, they are involved in a project to develop national indicators of well-being, and have recently co-authored a paper in which they argue explicitly for including well-being measures in addition to standard economic measures in the assessment of policy. The conclusion of this jointly

---

[20] A number of studies have also been done to measure relative degrees of life satisfaction in different cultures. The data here show that Iceland, Denmark, and Switzerland are the happiest, closely followed by certain Latin American nations. Eastern European cultures (Bulgaria, Russia, and Belarus) are the least happy. Diener & Suh (1999).

authored paper gives a good indication of how this research might inform policy:

The existing findings suggest the following partial formula for high well-being:

- Live in a democratic and stable society that provides material resources to meet needs
- Have supportive friends and family
- Have rewarding and engaging work and an adequate income
- Be reasonably healthy and have treatment available in case of mental problems
- Have important goals related to one's values
- Have a philosophy or religion that provides guidance, purpose, and meaning to one's life. (Diener & Seligman, 2004: 25)

Diener and Seligman are not focused only on life-satisfaction research here, but they clearly think that satisfaction with life measures will play an important role in policy evaluation.[21]

2.4. *A Problem for the Life-Satisfaction Program*

The life-satisfaction program is well established and fruitful. It also seems not to be subject to the same worries about normative inadequacy that troubled psychologists' versions of hedonism and eudaimonism. Before we can conclude that LST is the way to go, however, we need to confront a serious problem that arises for it, namely, that the life-satisfaction program as it stands must treat all positive responses to the conditions of one's life as equally authoritative.

The life-satisfaction program presupposes that people make overall assessments of their lives that represent or express something important, something that answers to the concerns people have when thinking about well-being, and something that can be used to make meaningful comparisons between people or across the lifespan of a single person. We suggested above that these judgments are important in virtue of their expressing a relatively stable positive cognitive/affective attitude toward one's life.

According to some empirical studies, however, these assumptions are problematic. Such studies tell us that the judgments people make about how their lives are going as a whole are highly context-dependent. Judgments of overall life satisfaction (JOLS), it seems, are dependent on several variables: what information (memories, facts about oneself and one's options, and so forth)

---

[21] The use of happiness and life-satisfaction measures by governments to assess national progress is already under way in the UK and, to an even greater extent, in Bhutan (see www.number-10.gov.uk/su/ls/paper.pdf; also http://bhutanstudies.org.bt).

is accessible at the time of making the judgment, how the information is used (whether it is assimilated into the target of judgment or used as a point of comparison), one's perception of social norms, and one's mood.[22] These studies suggest either that JOLS are not reliable measures of people's stable feelings and life-satisfaction attitudes, or (worse) that life-satisfaction attitudes themselves are not stable responses to the relevant, objective conditions of life. We focus on the latter challenge to LST since the former challenge is not fundamental and could be solved by improving measurement tools, and since it seems to us that psychologists who press this criticism do indeed intend the latter, more serious challenge (Schwarz & Strack, 1999). On this view, JOLS and life-satisfaction attitudes are shaped by the information that is accessible to us at the time of making the judgment and by other factors such as mood. (In the discussion that follows we shall continue to talk about *judgments* of overall life satisfaction and to assume for the sake of argument that these judgments accurately represent underlying life satisfaction attitudes.) Which facts people happen to remember and think about while making a judgment about their lives shapes the way in which they construct the bits of their lives to be evaluated, and it helps to determine what we take the relevant standard of evaluation to be.

When psychologists manipulate the information that is accessible, they can change the kinds of judgments subjects tend to make. For example, priming subjects so that they are thinking about excitement makes these subjects more likely to evaluate their own lives in terms of how much excitement they have (Oishi et al., 2003). Similarly, some studies have shown that changing the item order on questionnaires influences the subjects' reports of life satisfaction. For example, Strack, Martin, and Schwarz (1988) asked students two questions: "how happy are you?" and "how many dates did you have last month?" When the general happiness question was presented first, there was no correlation between the two responses, but when the dating question was presented first, the correlation rose to 0.66.

Studies also show that memories of experiences and feelings can play different roles in the construction of life-satisfaction reports. Strongly valenced experiences, for example, can influence people's JOLS differently depending on how they are construed. Extreme negative experiences can cause people to evaluate their lives more positively if they are seen as the contrast class to how things are now, or they can cause people to evaluate their lives negatively if they are seen as part of the target of the judgment. How we attempt to answer

---

[22] For a review of this literature see Schwarz & Strack (1999). See also Kahneman (1999) and Oishi et al. (2003).

questions about how our lives are going also has effects on our answers. For example, the act of trying to explain a negative experience can cause people to become self-pitying and depressed, and so to evaluate their lives as going less well than otherwise (Martin & Tesser, 1989). JOLS are also influenced by the comparison class a person constructs for herself. What a person chooses as a point of comparison is again influenced by the information that is accessible at the time and also by the goals she is pursuing at that moment (Schwarz & Strack, 1999: 74). This phenomenon is illustrated by a study that demonstrated the effect that having a disabled person in the room has on people's reports about their well-being (Strack et al., 1990).[23] People tend to evaluate their lives as going better when there is a disabled person in the room than they do when the disabled person is not there, presumably because the disabled person changes the evaluative standard that the person uses in her judgment.

This study highlights the problem of intrapersonal comparisons given the practical nature of the notion of well-being. The average subject in this study makes two different assessments of the conditions of her life and the question is which (if any) is most relevant to her well-being. One could say that both assessments are relevant because well-being itself is variable from context to context. But this response abandons the plausible thought that well-being is a relatively stable state—as Aristotle famously remarked, "one swallow does not make a spring . . . nor does one day or a short time make us blessed and happy" (*NE:* I.7). Moreover, it would be seriously problematic for practical purposes. Insofar as our interest in well-being is driven by a concern to improve the conditions of people's lives, we need to have a stable basis of comparison. In other words, we need to know which of these assessments we should take as the basis for comparing subjects' well-being over time.

The problem with context sensitivity for psychological research in the life-satisfaction paradigm is that it introduces the suspicion that there isn't any stable disposition underlying the particular self-reports corresponding to a notion of life satisfaction that can be plausibly identified with well-being. An alternative explanation is that there is an underlying disposition but we do not have a good way of measuring it. Psychologists who have pushed this objection against the life-satisfaction program seem to think that in the absence of other evidence for a stable underlying disposition, the deeper skepticism is warranted (Schwarz & Strack, 1999).

---

[23] This experiment relies on the fact that people *assume* that disabled people are doing less well than non-disabled people. This may very well be an incorrect and prejudiced assumption, but it is the view many people seem to have.

2.5. *Stability After All?*

While some studies show life-satisfaction judgments to be variable and context-sensitive, there are other studies that indicate stability for a subset of life-satisfaction judgments. For example, the correlation between overall life satisfaction and domain satisfaction has been well established. A domain, in this context, is simply an aspect of an individual's life that the individual deems important to how her life is going in general. So, for example, Schimmack and Oishi (2005) asked their subjects to list the five most important aspects of their lives, and asked them how satisfied they were with these aspects. Examples of domains include "social relationships, achievements, conditions of your life, or the performance of your favorite sports team" (ibid.: 14). In their study, Schimmack and Oishi correlated subjects' satisfaction with these domains with life-satisfaction judgments and found high retest stability in judgments that correlated well with domain-specific satisfaction (this stability was also found when the domains were not self-generated but rather chosen from a list provided by the researchers). In other words, people who are satisfied in the domains they think are most important will report high overall life satisfaction consistently. Schimmack and Oishi report a general global-specific correlation of 0.70, meaning that subjects' ratings of satisfaction with "important domains" of their lives were highly correlated with overall ratings of global life satisfaction. Furthermore, item order did not appear to have a significant effect on correlations between satisfaction with specific (important) domains and global life satisfaction (ibid.: 15–17).

In addition, Schimmack and Oishi found high retest stability in life-satisfaction judgments and have argued that this stability is due to the fact that people rely on relevant and chronically accessible information in order to form the judgments.[24] These studies indicate that changes in *domain* satisfaction predict changes in *overall* life satisfaction.

Studies that demonstrate stability due to reliance on relevant sources also recognize that there are causes of variability in JOLS; for example, the studies are consistent with variation in JOLS that has to do with a person's mood.[25] Diener does not deny that there are sources of instability in life-satisfaction judgments, but he thinks that there is enough stability in them to support

[24] Retest correlation of global life-satisfaction judgments at the beginning and the end of a 3-month semester was 0.73 (Schimmack et al., 2002). See also Pavot & Diener (1993). Pavot & Diener's study shows a retest correlation of 0.82 over a 2-month period and 0.54 over a period of 4 years.

[25] In fact, Schimmack has shown that people can successfully eliminate the effects of mood when they are asked to do so. See Schimmack et al. (2002: 359).

the claim that they are meaningful.[26] These studies, therefore, do not entirely eliminate concerns about instability, but they do give us reason to think of them as measurement problems rather than as evidence that there is no stable underlying disposition to be measured.

Instability in JOLS causes a problem for the life-satisfaction program because it raises the suspicion that there is no object of measurement that corresponds to the original notion of overall life satisfaction. Given context effects, JOLS look like made-up pronouncements about how things are going overall that are really determined by temporary and situational factors. The research we have been discussing in this section tries to solve this problem by pointing to enduring factors that provide a basis for stable JOLS. The implication here is that only certain JOLS—those that report a stable condition of life—are closely related to well-being. JOLS are relevant to assessments of well-being, then, only if they abstract from mood and irrelevant distractions and focus on important domains.

It seems that overall life satisfaction that is based on satisfaction in important domains is stable enough for the purposes of psychological studies. Whether it meets the normative criterion central to philosophical accounts is the question we turn to next.

3. Life Satisfaction and Normativity

The problem of instability points to a different problem for life-satisfaction theories of well-being, one which is not necessarily solved by appeal to the conditions under which such judgments are stable. This problem is the *normative arbitrariness* of JOLS. The empirical studies highlight the problem of arbitrariness because they reveal that selective attention heavily influences a person's subjective point of view, and what people happen to attend to seems arbitrary in a way that other things do not.[27] The instability of life-satisfaction judgments in response to apparently arbitrary changes in circumstances (such as the weather) highlights the worry that such judgments

---

[26] According to Diener & Lucas (1999: 214), "Researchers know that the strong form of this hypothesis—that SWB judgments reflect only stable and meaningful conditions of people's lives—is untrue. Momentary factors such as current mood and even current weather conditions can affect judgments of life satisfaction . . . Yet in spite of these transitory influences, SWB is moderately stable across situations . . . and across the life span . . . suggesting that long-term SWB does exist."

[27] This is one of Haybron's (2007) main criticisms of life-satisfaction accounts. He thinks that life satisfaction varies with our perspective and that the choice of which perspective to take when judging how our lives are going is arbitrary.

are themselves arbitrary. Since well-being is supposed to be a normatively significant notion, the thought that it is made up of arbitrary assessments, or that the judgments that are relevant to it are arbitrarily chosen, is unsettling.

One obvious response to these problems is to give up on life satisfaction as the key to understanding well-being as a normative notion. One could do this by giving up on subjective well-being altogether or one could do it by substituting a different understanding of what precisely is relevant about subjective experience, for example, by returning to hedonism and the view that pleasurable subjective experiences are the key to well-being.

We want to resist both of these alternative directions. Instead, we seek to vindicate overall life satisfaction as crucial to well-being. The main reason for doing this is the need to ensure the *normative authority* of well-being so that we can justify the role it undoubtedly plays in discussions of practical reason and public policy. We can understand "normative authority" as the feature in virtue of which people have a reason to follow the imperatives of the normative theory. A theory of well-being that has normative authority, then, will be one that people have a reason to follow. For well-being in particular, these reasons must be motivating and justifying reasons. Therefore a good theory of well-being must make sure (1) that people (everyone to whom the theory is supposed to apply) will have some motivation to care about what the theory recommends and (2) that there are standards of justification (correctness or appropriateness) for these recommendations; there is no normativity without the possibility of error, nothing we *ought* to do unless we could fail to do it. We think a theory that takes life satisfaction to be central to well-being is best suited to meet these two criteria.

Life-satisfaction theories have a leg-up, we argue, because of the particular way in which they locate well-being in the subjective point of view. We will elaborate on this point in the next section. For now it will help to compare life-satisfaction theories with our two alternatives. Eudaimonist theories, insofar as they represent a distinct alternative, do not locate well-being in subjective experience at all, thus creating a gap between the theory's recommendations and people's motivations. Hedonism arbitrarily privileges a particular subjective experience (pleasure) without regard to how important this experience is from the subject's own point of view. Such arbitrary privileging will make the theory's recommendations seem unjustified to those who do not care most about pleasure. Of course, it remains to be seen how a life-satisfaction theory can solve this problem of arbitrariness; we turn to this problem in the next section.

3.1. *The Values-Based Life-Satisfaction Account*

The instability of life-satisfaction judgments gives rise to worries about the basis for these judgments and the underlying disposition they are meant to report. Once we acknowledge that people's judgments of life satisfaction can be influenced by all manner of variations in their circumstances, we begin to wonder why these judgments are normatively significant. If a person can make different assessments of how her life is going depending on whether she compares herself to someone worse off or better off than her, whether she factors in or ignores her current mood, or whether she thinks about her marriage, health, or career before thinking about her life overall, then it makes sense to ask which of these judgments matters and why. Insofar as they are concerned only with empirical adequacy, psychologists can solve the problem by insisting that the judgments that matter are whichever judgments lead to a stable object of measurement. But this does not answer our normative questions: the fact that something is stable does not guarantee that it is a good thing to promote. For example, a smoker may have a very stable desire for tobacco, but this does not necessarily make cigarettes good for him, even from his own point of view. In particular, restricting our attention to life-satisfaction assessments made on the basis of domains that are important to the subject will solve the problem only if subjectively important domains are themselves normatively significant.

Notice that the subjectively important domains that underlie stable life-satisfaction reports are very similar to a person's *values*. Insofar as values are a normative notion, introducing values into our life-satisfaction theory can help to answer the problem of normative arbitrariness. In short, the view we shall defend says that it is satisfaction with how one's life is going overall *with respect to one's values* that counts as well-being. In other words, life satisfaction constitutes well-being when it is a response to how life is going according to certain standards, and these standards are provided by a person's values.[28] Before elaborating the view, it will help to say more about the notion of a value.

We mean to be very inclusive about what counts as a value: values can include activities, relationships, goals, aims, ideals, principles, and so on. This is not the place to defend a fully developed conception of a value, but there are three features that we think are important if values are to play a role in an

---

[28] The view is similar to a subjective theory of happiness defended provisionally by Richard Kraut (1979), according to which the standards for happiness must be the agent's own standards. Kraut moved away from subjectivism in later work (1994).

account of well-being.[29] First, values must be normative from the point of view of the person who has them: that is, a person takes her values to provide good reasons for doing things. This must be the case if values are to answer the problem of normative arbitrariness. Second, values include an affective component: part of what it is to care about something in the way distinctive of valuing is to have some positive emotional response toward it. This must be the case if values are to provide the ground for the positive attitude of life satisfaction. Third, values are relatively stable, as they must be on our view since well-being itself is relatively stable.

This way of characterizing values introduces the possibility that values are subject to *standards* of justification. A value can be more or less reason-giving from a person's own point of view, more or less suited to produce positive emotions for a person, and more or less stable. This is convenient, because (as discussed above) if values are to solve the problem of normative arbitrariness, they must be subject to standards of correctness or appropriateness. We think that our rough characterization of values above suggests two such standards, which we might call the standard of affective appropriateness and the standard of information.[30] Information hasn't been mentioned yet, but its importance is clear: values that are sustained by false beliefs are unlikely to be stable because new information will put pressure on them to change. Moreover, values based on false beliefs about what one's emotional needs are, or what one will find satisfying, are unlikely to produce a positive emotional response over the long term. We shall call values that meet these standards of appropriateness *justified values*.

On our view, then, what a person in fact claims to value has *prima facie* authority that can be defeated when her holding these values does not adhere to the standards of affective appropriateness and information. For example, consider a young medical student who claims to value being a physician. The authority of her commitment as a goal for her life would be undermined if it were the case that the actual practice of medicine makes her miserable (in which

---

[29] See Tiberius (2000, 2008) for a more fully developed picture.

[30] If our theory is to retain the close relationship between well-being and subjective experience, it must be the case that the standards of affective appropriateness and information are standards that the person herself would count as making her values more justified. Whether or not people actually think their values ought to be informed and compatible with their emotional constitution is an empirical question that we cannot answer here. (Notice that this question opens the door for another interdisciplinary research project the aim of which would be to ascertain which norms of value improvement people accept.) We think it reasonable to assume that people want to be committed to things that fit their emotional natures, because negative affect has detrimental effects that are not confined to the subjective character of our experience. We also think it reasonable to assume that people want not to be misinformed, because false information has a way of frustrating long-term goals.

case the goal is not affectively appropriate) and her underlying motivation to be a doctor is a desire for her parents' approval (in which case the value is sustained by false beliefs about her real motivations). In this case the standards that make her values normative are not met. As long as we make room for the possibility of defeaters when the context requires, a psychologically realistic conception of a person's values can do the necessary work in a normative account of well-being.

Let us call the resulting account of well-being the *values-based life-satisfaction account* (VBLS). According to VBLS, life satisfaction is a positive cognitive/affective attitude toward one's life as a whole, and life satisfaction constitutes well-being when it is not defeated by considerations that undermine its normative authority. Defeaters can be of two types: first, life satisfaction does not count as well-being if it is not based on one's values at all (e.g. if the feeling of life satisfaction is primarily the result of an irrelevant change in circumstances, such as a change in the weather).[31] Second, life satisfaction does not count as well-being if the values that it is based on do not meet the standards for values, that is, if they are ill informed or ill suited to the person's affective nature. When life satisfaction is based on justified values, it is value-based life satisfaction and it constitutes well-being. The judgments of overall life satisfaction that a person makes when answering questions on a life-satisfaction scale are, on this view, *evidence* for value-based life satisfaction.

But now we have a problem. To what degree must life satisfaction be "undefeated" in order to count as well-being? Must it be entirely a response to how life is going according to one's values, without any influence at all from irrelevant circumstantial factors? Must the values in question be fully informed and perfectly emotionally appropriate? This sets the bar too high and has two undesirable implications—first, that well-being is quite significantly divorced from people's actual experiences,[32] and, consequently second, that well-being cannot be measured empirically. The problem is that life satisfaction and values must be somewhat idealized to solve the problem of arbitrariness, but too much idealization sacrifices both empirical accessibility and the close connection to the subject that well-being demands. Our question, then, is: how ideal is ideal enough?

[31] Our answer to the "experience machine objection" (Nozick, 1974) comes from this requirement. For those who value having real experiences, life satisfaction would not be a response to how they are succeeding at meeting their standards if it is based on false beliefs about how they are actually doing. Thus, we agree with Sumner (1996) that real experiences are privileged only for those who value them.

[32] This is a problem for so called full-information theories (Brandt, 1979; Griffin, 1986; Railton, 1986) of the good that idealize subjective responses to a very high degree. For criticisms see Rosati (1995), Velleman (1988), and Tiberius (1997).

Our answer to this question is: it depends. Before we can make this answer plausible, we need to insist that the important question to answer is an epistemological one, not a metaphysical one. In other words, what matters is how certain we must be when we make judgments about well-being that a person's life satisfaction is not defeated by its failure to meet the various standards. There is, obviously, another question about the nature of well-being itself: how ideal must life satisfaction be to *constitute* the stuff of well-being? We think this question does not need to be answered. Insofar as concerns about well-being are practical concerns that have to do with promoting one's own or others' well-being, it is the epistemological question that matters.

To answer the question of how certain we must be that life satisfaction meets the relevant standards, it will help to think about why it is such a common move in philosophy to idealize subjective states in order to account for normative notions. Of course, correcting for errors is desirable—but why? The reason is that judgments about normative notions like well-being lead people to act in ways that have significant costs that are supposed to be offset by significant benefits. We want the benefits to be likely, long term, and real, and we want the costs to be worth bearing. The problem with unidealized subject states (such as desires or feelings of life satisfaction) is that they can go awry in ways that make acting to promote them useless or counterproductive. To take a simple example, Peter Railton's (1986) dehydrated Lonnie wants to drink milk, which is actually bad for him because he is dehydrated. His desire for milk is uninformed and if Lonnie knew he were dehydrated he would want to drink clear fluids, which would help ameliorate his condition. If we try to promote Lonnie's well-being by attending to his *actual* desires, we will fail to benefit him in an obvious way. Since the cost of failure (Lonnie's death!) is high, an account of well-being that does not prevent such failures is a practical disaster.

Lonnie's case is easy. There is an obvious fact that he doesn't know (the fact that he is dehydrated), which if he did know would change his preferences in a way that would make them more beneficial (he would desire clear fluids). But real life is not so easy and there are many cases where someone making judgments about well-being will want to know "how much information is enough?" Or, for VBLS in particular, "how emotionally appropriate do the values have to be?" However, once we see that the question of how much idealization is needed is an epistemological question that arises in the practical context, we can also see that the answer to the question will depend on what is at stake in the particular practical context in question. The right degree of idealization, that is, depends on context. In some contexts, we maintain, it makes sense to question a person's claims about her values and to investigate further whether these claims adhere to the relevant standards. The more that is at stake, the more it will make sense to ask whether the person's claims about values follow the relevant norms. To put this more concretely, consider a norm that recommends reflecting on the facts. When circumstances demand particular care to ensure that our judgments about well-being are well founded, we should be more careful to ensure that the claims about values we are considering are not misinformed.

We have suggested that the contextual factors that can make a difference to whether or not we should take people's values and life satisfaction at face value have to do with the costs and benefits at stake. To take another example, this time focused on the first-person perspective, if our misguided medical student is contemplating a $40,000 student loan to finance her dream, she would do well to consider seriously whether the value she places on a medical career is well placed, given her interests and desires. When the potential costs of acting on her judgment that medicine is a good career for her are high, she ought to make sure the judgment is correct. Expected costs and benefits will also vary with respect to the kind of action that is being considered (a large-scale, expensive government program would require more scrutiny of judgments of well-being than other kinds of actions) and the reasons that there are for skepticism (we should be more inclined to investigate when a person says she doesn't care about having friends than we are when she says she doesn't value fine wine).

One might worry that a theory of well-being that makes use of idealization in *any* way creates the possibility of an undesirable gap between well-being and subjective experience. On one interpretation, this is a concern about a worrisome gap between affect and cognition.[33] The problem here is that according to VBLS it seems that we may be justified in judging that a person has achieved well-being even though she is in a persistent bad mood or has a depressed affect, because her life is going well according to the things she values. How much of a problem this is depends in large part on how much distance there can really be on this account between affect and values. Critics of life-satisfaction views seem to think that a large gap is possible so that a person could be clinically depressed and yet be achieving well-being (Haybron, 2008b). This would indeed be an unattractive implication, but it is unfair to saddle VBLS with it. On our view, serious depression will only be compatible with well-being if

---

[33] A related worry is about paternalism. If it is possible, according to VBLS, to judge that someone is not achieving well-being even though she thinks she is, then it seems that VBLS would recommend actions that promote her well-being despite how she herself feels about it. But this is not so. Paternalistic recommendations do not follow directly from a theory of well-being; a good deal of moral argument would be needed to get from here to there.

having commitments to values does not require affective engagement and if the person's values do not include her own happiness, enjoyment, positive affect, or mental health. Since value commitments do involve emotional engagement, and since most people do find these things to be important, a life consumed by serious depression is very unlikely to be found satisfying when attention is on values.

The possibility of a gap between well-being and subjective experience created by idealization may make some readers concerned about the empirical tractability of VBLS. At this point, therefore, it will be instructive to return to the empirical issue of measurement. One might think that the way we have altered life-satisfaction accounts makes them, once again, insufficiently empirically grounded. We do not think this is so, although we can only gesture here at how psychologists might use this conception of well-being to inform their research. First of all, VBLS implies that life satisfaction as measured by the SWLS and value-based life satisfaction occupy different spots on one continuum and, therefore, the former may be a starting point for ascertaining the latter. Indeed, standard life-satisfaction research is still useful, and life-satisfaction scales are still an important measure for VBLS. After all, as Schimmack and his colleagues have argued, people do make JOLS on the basis of chronically accessible information that tends to include domains that subjects find important, and important domains are, in our view, just values with a low degree of idealization. Life-satisfaction questionnaires might be reworded to guide people to think more explicitly about how their lives are going according to their own values. Ulrich Schimmack has done something like this already. In the introduction to the SWLS on his website, he says:

The Satisfaction With Life Scale is a short and reliable measure of life-satisfaction. Life-satisfaction is the cognitive component of subjective well-being (happiness). It allows people to consider the aspects that are most important to them and to evaluate how satisfied they are with them. Please think of the aspects that are most central to your life while answering the questions.[34]

Second, VBLS provides a natural justification for using alternative, non-self-report measures. If self-reports are imperfect indicators of the degree to which people's lives are actually going well according to their own values and standards, at least under certain conditions, then we should use other methods to assess this. Such methods might include objective measures of values that are widespread and likely to meet standards of information and emotional appropriateness such as friendship, family relationships, health, and good work.

---

[34] http://www.erin.utoronto.ca/~w3psyuli/survey/swls/swls.htm, last accessed January 8, 2009.

To sum up, according to the VBLS theory of well-being, well-being is satisfaction with one's overall conditions of life evaluated on the basis of standards provided by one's values. A person's actual attitudes of life satisfaction count as well-being unless they are defeated because they are influenced by irrelevant factors that have nothing to do with what the person cares about, or because the person is misinformed about the objects of her care, or because what the person says she cares about fits poorly with her affective nature. For those of us making judgments about our own or other people's well-being, there is a legitimate question about how certain we must be that these standards are met, and the answer to this question depends on the practical context.

We think that the VBLS theory meets the demand of normative adequacy. First, people to whom the theory is supposed to apply will indeed have some motivation to care about what the theory recommends because they are motivated by their own values. Second, according to VBLS there are standards of justification for judgments about well-being and so it is possible to "get it wrong." The theory also meets the demands for empirical adequacy because it does not insist that judgments of well-being must always be about highly idealized states that we cannot investigate. Further, because VBLS recommends thinking of real and idealized psychological states as on a continuum of idealization, it makes room for the relevance of one to the other.

4. Conclusion

The hedonistic and eudaimonistic research programs in positive psychology offer much to interest moral philosophers. However, as far as the underlying philosophical conceptions of well-being are concerned, there is something particularly compelling about the life-satisfaction view because of the connection it affords between well-being and subjective experience. Hedonism, while an attractive view for scientists because it makes few evaluative assumptions, may not provide the best account of the significance of well-being to choices people make about public policy and about our own lives. Eudaimonism, on the other hand, assumes too much and loses the presumed connection between well-being and subjective experience. The life-satisfaction view as articulated by psychologists excels at accommodating this connection, but risks having no explanation of the normative significance of well-being. The VBLS theory is to be preferred because it provides an explanation of the normative importance of well-being without sacrificing the relationship to subjective experience.

Our theory makes some empirical assumptions. It assumes that value-based judgments of life satisfaction are relatively stable over time and not too distant from the experience of real people. It also assumes that people have standards of justification to which they hold their values and that they are concerned to have better values rather than worse. These are empirical matters that matter philosophically. There are certainly many questions to be answered before we can fully evaluate the viability of the VBLS account. Positive psychology is a relatively young field and the work we have drawn on is still in its early stages. For now, we hope at least to have shown one way in which philosophical inquiry about the nature of the human good can benefit from attention to the empirical literature and conversation with positive psychologists. Given the problems raised for research programs in positive psychology, and given the inevitability of making normative assumptions in this area, we hope to have shown that psychologists will also benefit from the exchange.[35]

References

Andrews, F. M. & S. B. Withey (1976). *Social Indicators of Well-Being*. New York: Plenum Press.

Annas, J. (1993). *The Morality of Happiness*. Oxford: Oxford University Press.

Argyle, M. (1999). "Causes and Correlates of Happiness." In Kahneman, Diener, & Schwarz (eds.), 353–373.

Aristotle (1999). *Nicomachean Ethics*. Translated by Terence Irwin. Indianapolis, IN: Hackett.

Bentham, J. (1789/1970). *An Introduction to the Principles of Morals and Legislation*. J. Burns and H. Hart (eds.). New York: Oxford University Press.

Brandt, R. (1979). *A Theory of the Good and the Right*. Oxford: Clarendon Press.

Brickman, P., Coates, D., & Janoff-Bulman, R. (1978). "Lottery Winners and Accident Victims: Is Happiness Relative?" *Journal of Personality and Social Psychology*. 36 (8): 917–927.

Crisp, R. (2006). *Reasons and the Good*. Oxford: Clarendon Press.

Diener, E. (2008). "Myths in the Science of Happiness, and Directions for Future Research." In M. Eid and R. Larsen (eds.), *The Science of Subjective Well-Being*. New York: Guilford Press, 493–514.

Diener, E. & Biswas-Diener, R. (2002). "Will Money Increase Subjective Well-Being?" *Social Indicators Research*. 57: 119–169.

Diener, E. & Diener, M. (1995). "Cross-cultural correlates of life satisfaction and self-esteem." *Journal of Personality and Social Psychology*. 68: 653–663.

---

[35] The authors would like to thank the members of MPRG for helpful feedback on previous versions of this chapter. Special thanks for detailed comments are due to John Doris and Tim Schroeder.

Diener, E. & Lucas, R. (1999). "Personality and Subjective Well-Being." In Kahneman, Diener, & Schwarz (eds.), 213–229.

Diener, E., & Oishi, S. (2000). "Money and happiness: Income and subjective well-being across nations". In Diener and Suh (eds.),185–218.

Diener, E., & Seligman, M. (2002). "Very Happy People." *Psychological Science.* 13: 81–84.

——(2004). "Beyond Money Toward an Economy of Well-Being." *Psychological Science in the Public Interest.* 5 (1): 1–31.

Diener, E., & Suh, E. M. (1999). "National Differences in Subjective Well-Being." In Kahneman, Diener, & Schwarz (eds.), 434–449.

——(2000). *Culture and Subjective Well-Being.* Cambridge, MA and London: MIT Press.

Diener, E., Scollon, C., & Lucas, R. (2003). "The evolving concept of subjective well-being: the multifaceted nature of happiness." *Advances in Cell Aging and Gerontology.* 15: 187–219.

Doris, J. & Plakias, A. (2008). "How to Argue About Disagreement." In W. Sinnott-Armstrong (ed.), *Moral Psychology vol. 2: The Cognitive Science of Morality.* Cambridge, MA: MIT Press, 303–331.

Easterlin, Richard A. (1974). "Does Economic Growth Improve the Human Lot?" In Paul A. David & Melvin W. Reder (eds.), *Nations and Households in Economic Growth: Essays in Honor of Moses Abramovitz.* New York: Academic Press, Inc., 89–125.

Emmons, B. (2003). "Personal Goals, Life Meaning, and Virtue: Wellsprings of Positive Life." In Keyes & Haidt (eds.), 105–128.

Feldman, F. (1997). *Utilitarianism, Hedonism and Desert.* Cambridge: Cambridge University Press.

——(2004) *Pleasure and the Good Life: Concerning the Nature, Varieties, and Plausibility of Hedonism.* Oxford: Clarendon Press.

Frederick, S. & Loewenstein, G. (1999) "Hedonic Adaptation." In Kahneman, Diener, & Schwarz (eds.), 302–329.

Gable, S. L., Reis, H. T., Impett, E., & Asher, E. R. (2004). "What do you do when things go right? The Intrapersonal and Interpersonal Benefits of Sharing Positive Events." *Journal of Personality and Social Psychology.* 87: 228–245.

Gilbert, D. (2006). *Stumbling on Happiness.* New York: Knopf.

Griffin, J. (1986). *Well-Being: Its Meaning, Measurement and Moral Importance.* Oxford: Clarendon Press.

Gruen, L. (2003). Comments on Shelly Gable, "What do you do when things go right? The intrapersonal and interpersonal benefits of sharing positive events," Minnesota Workshop on Well-Being, October.

Haybron, D. (2007). "Life Satisfaction, Ethical Reflection, and the Science of Happiness." *The Journal of Happiness Studies.* 8 (1): 99–138.

——(2008a). *The Pursuit of Unhappiness.* Oxford: Oxford University Press.

Haybron, D. (2008b). "Philosophy and the Science of Subjective Well-Being." In *The Science of Subjective Well-Being*. Michael Eid & Randy Larsen (eds.). New York: Guilford, 17–43.

Kahneman, D. (1999). "Objective Happiness." In Kahneman, Diener, & Schwarz (eds.), 3–25.

—— (2000). "Experienced Utility and Objective Happiness: A Moment-Based Approach." In *Choices, Values, and Frames*. Kahneman & Tversky (eds.). Cambridge: Cambridge University Press, 673–692.

Kahneman, D., Diener, E., & Schwarz, N. (eds.) (1999). *Well-Being: The Foundations of Hedonic Psychology*. New York: The Russell Sage Foundation.

Kasser, T. (2002). *The High Price of Materialism*. Cambridge, MA and London: MIT Press.

Kasser, T. & Ryan, R. M. (1996) "Further examining the American dream: differential correlates of intrinsic and extrinsic goals." *Personality and Social Psychology Bulletin*. 22: 280–287.

Keyes, C. & Haidt, J. (eds.) (2002). *Flourishing: Positive Psychology and the Life Well-lived*. Washington, DC: American Psychological Association.

Kraut, R. (1979). "Two Conceptions of Happiness." *The Philosophical Review*. 88 (2): 167–197.

—— (1994). "Desire and the Human Good." *Proceedings and Addresses of the American Philosophical Association*. 68 (2): 39–54.

Lazarus, R. (2003). "Does the Positive Psychology Movement Have Legs?" *Psychological Inquiry*. 14 (2): 93–109.

Linley, P., Joseph, S., Harrington, S., & Wood, A. (2006). "Positive Psychology: Past, present, and (possible) future." *The Journal of Positive Psychology*. 1 (1): 3–16.

Loewenstein, G. & Schkade, D. (1999). "Wouldn't It Be Nice? Predicting Future Feelings." In Kahneman, Diener, & Schwarz (eds.), 85–105.

Lucas, R., Clark, A., Georgellis, Y., & Diener, E. (2003). "Re-examining adaptation and the setpoint model of happiness: Reactions to changes in marital status." *Journal of Personality and Social Psychology*. 84: 527–539.

Lucas, R. E., Clark, A. E., Georgellis, Y., & Diener, E. (2004). "Unemployment alters the set-point for life satisfaction." *Psychological Science*. 15: 8–13.

Lykken, D. & Tellegen, A. (1996). "Happiness is a stochastic phenomenon" *Psychological Science*. 7 (3): 186–189.

Martin, L. L. & Tesser, A. (1989). "Toward a motivational and structural theory of ruminative thought." In J. S. Uleman & J. A. Bargh (eds.), *Unintended thoughts*. New York: Guilford, 306–326.

Mill, J. S. (1871/1999). *Utilitarianism*. Roger Crisp, (ed.). Oxford: Oxford University Press.

Millgram, E. (2000). "What's the Use of Utility?" *Philosophy and Public Affairs*. 29 (2): 113–136.

Monk, R. (1990). *Ludwig Wittgenstein: The Duty of Genius*. New York: Penguin.

Myers, D. (1999). "Close Relationships and Quality of Life." In Kahneman, Diener, & Schwarz (eds.), 374–391.

Nozick, R. (1974). *Anarchy, State, and Utopia*. New York: Basic Books.

Nussbaum, M. (1994). *The Therapy of Desire: Theory and Practice in Hellenistic Ethics*. Princeton, NJ: Princeton University Press.

Oishi, S. (2000). "Goals as Cornerstones of Subjective Well-being: Linking Individuals and Cultures." In Diener and Suh (eds.), 87–112.

Oishi, S., Schimmack, U., & Colcombe, S. (2003). "The contextual and systematic nature of life satisfaction judgments." *Journal of Experimental Social Psychology*. 39 (3): 232–247.

Pavot, W. G., & Diener, E. (1993). "Review of the Satisfaction with Life Scale." *Psychological Assessment*. 5: 164–172.

Piliavin, J. A. (2002). "Doing Well by Doing Good: Benefits for the Benefactor." In Keyes & Haidt (eds.), 227–248.

Railton, P. (1984), "Alienation, Consequentialism and the Demands of Morality." *Philosophy and Public Affairs*. 13: 134–171.

——(1986). "Moral Realism." *The Philosophical Review*. 95 (2): 163–207.

——(unpublished ms). "The Problem of Well-Being: Respect, Equality, and the Self."

Redelmeier, D. & Kahneman, D. (1996). "Patients' Memories of Painful Medical Treatments: Real-time and Retrospective Evaluations of Two Minimally Invasive Procedures." *Pain*. 66 (1): 3–8.

Reis, H. & Gable, S. (2003). "Toward a Positive Psychology of Relationships." In Keyes & Haidt (eds.), 129–159.

Rosati, C. S. (1995), "Persons, Perspectives, and Full Information Accounts of the Good." *Ethics*. 105: 296–325.

Ryan, R. & Deci, E. (2000). "The 'What' and 'Why' of Goal Pursuits: Human needs and the self-determination of behavior. *Psychological Inquiry*. 11: 227–268.

——(2001). "On Happiness and Human Potential: A Review of Research on Hedonic and Eudaimonic Well-Being." *Annual Review of Psychology*. 52: 141–166.

——(2008). "Facilitating Optimal Motivation and Psychological Well-Being Across Life's Domains." *Canadian Psychology*. 49: 14–23.

Ryff, C. & Singer, B. (1998). "The Contours of Positive Human Health." *Psychological Inquiry*. 9: 1–28.

Schimmack, U., Diener, E., & Oishi, S. (2002). "Life-Satisfaction Is a Momentary Judgment and a Stable Personality Characteristic: The Use of Chronically Accessible and Stable Sources." *Journal of Personality*. 70 (3): 345–384.

Schimmack U. & Oishi, S. (2005). "Chronically accessible versus temporarily accessible sources of life satisfaction judgments." *Journal of Personality and Social Psychology*. 89, 395–406.

Schmuck, P. & Sheldon, K. (2001). *Life Goals and Well-Being: Towards a Positive Psychology of Human Striving*. Toronto: Hogrefe & Huber Publishing.

Schwartz, S. & Bilsky, W. (1987). "Toward a Universal Psychological Structure of Human Values." *Journal of Personality and Social Psychology*. 53 (3): 550–562.

Schwarz, N. & Strack, F. (1999). "Reports of Subjective Well-Being: Judgmental Processes and Their Methodological Implications." In Kahneman, Diener, & Schwarz (eds.), 61–84.

Seligman, M. E. P. (2002). "Foreword: The Past and Future of Positive Psychology." In Keyes & Haidt (eds.), xi–xx.

Sinnott-Armstrong, Walter (2008). "Consequentialism." *The Stanford Encyclopedia of Philosophy* (Fall 2008 Edition), Edward N. Zalta (ed.), URL = <http://plato.stanford.edu/archives/fall2008/entries/consequentialism/>.

Snyder, C. & Lopez, S. (eds.) (2002). *Handbook of Positive Psychology*. New York: Oxford University Press.

Stevenson, B. & Wolfers, J. (2008). "Economic Growth and Subjective Well-Being: Reassessing the Easterlin Paradox." CESifo Working Paper Series No. 2394. Available at SSRN: http://ssrn.com/abstract=1273524.

Strack, F., Martin L. L., & Schwarz, N. (1988). "Priming and communication: Social determinants of information use in judgments of life satisfaction." *European Journal of Social Psychology*. 18: 429–442.

Strack, F., Schwarz, N., Kern, C., & Wagner, D. (1990). "The salience of comparison standards and the activation of social norms: Consequences for judgments of happiness and their communication." *British Journal of Social Psychology*. 29: 303–314.

Sumner, L. W. (1996). *Welfare, Happiness and Ethics*. New York: Oxford University Press.

Tiberius, V. (1997). "Full Information and Ideal Deliberation." *Journal of Value Inquiry*. 31 (3): 329–338.

—— (2000). "Humean Heroism." *Pacific Philosophical Quarterly*. 81 (4): 426–446.

—— (2008). *The Reflective Life: Living Wisely With Our Limits*. Oxford: Oxford University Press.

Veenhoven, R. (1997). "Advances in Understanding Happiness." *Revue Québécoise de Psychologie*. 18: 29–79.

Velleman, J. D. (1988). "Brandt's Definition of Good." *The Philosophical Review*. 97 (3): 353–371.

Williams, B. A. O. (1973). "A Critique of Utilitarianism." In J. J. C. Smart & B. A. O. Williams, *Utilitarianism: For and Against*. Cambridge: Cambridge University Press, 77–151.

13

Race and Racial Cognition

DANIEL KELLY, EDOUARD MACHERY, AND RON
MALLON[1]

A core question of contemporary social morality concerns how we ought
to handle racial categorization. By this we mean, for instance, classifying or
thinking of a person as *black*, *Korean*, *Latino*, *white*, etc. While it is widely
agreed that racial categorization played a crucial role in past racial oppression,
there remains disagreement among philosophers and social theorists about the
ideal role for racial categorization in future endeavors. At one extreme of this
disagreement are short-term eliminativists who want to do away with racial
categorization relatively quickly (e.g. Appiah, 1995; D'Souza, 1996; Muir, 1993;
Wasserstrom, 2001/1980; Webster, 1992; Zack, 1993, 2002), typically because
they view it as mistaken and oppressive. At the opposite end of the spectrum,
long-term conservationists hold that racial identities and communities are
beneficial, and that racial categorization—suitably reformed—is essential to
fostering them (e.g. Outlaw, 1990, 1995, 1996). While extreme forms of
conservationism have fewer proponents in academia than the most radical
eliminativist positions, many theorists advocate more moderate positions. In
between the two poles, there are many who believe that racial categorization
is valuable (and perhaps necessary) given the continued existence of racial
inequality and the lingering effects of past racism (e.g. Haslanger, 2000; Mills,
1998; Root, 2000; Shelby, 2002, 2005; Sundstrom, 2002; Taylor, 2004; Young,
1989). Such authors agree on the short-term need for racial categorization
in at least some domains, but they often differ with regard to its long-term
value.

[1] We are grateful to the Moral Psychology Research Group for several useful discussions of this
material, and are particularly thankful to John Doris, Tim Schroeder, and Erica Roedder for their
many insightful comments on earlier drafts of this chapter. We would also like to thank Luc Faucher
for his feedback on a previous version. Remaining mistakes are ours. Finally, we would like to thank
Project Implicit (http://www.projectimplicit.net/) for permission to use their stimulus materials in this
chapter.

Our purpose here is not to delve into the nuances of this debate, nor is it to weigh in on one side or the other. Rather, we want to explore the intersection of these normative proposals with recent empirical work on the psychology of racial cognition. Race theorists often trade in normative arguments for conservationist or eliminativist agendas, and these normative arguments typically involve evaluations of the costs and benefits attached to those agendas (e.g. Boxill, 1984; Appiah, 1995; Muir, 1993; D'Souza, 1996; Outlaw, 1990, 1995, 1996). For instance, these types of evaluations are present in Outlaw's discussions of the benefits of racial communities (1995), Appiah's (1996) weighing of the costs and benefits of racial identification, Sundstrom's (2002) insistence on the value of racial categorization in social science, and Taylor's (2004) exploration of the social and ethical dimensions of racial classification, which weighs the value of employing racial categories in different ways against the costs. Such evaluations invariably involve background assumptions regarding the feasibility of the proposals, and the ease with which racial categorization and racism can be eliminated or reformed.

Given how pervasive these appeals to feasibility are, one might expect discussions regarding the role of human psychology in constraining or facilitating various reform proposals. Instead, contemporary race theory is nearly devoid of effort to engage the burgeoning literature from social psychology and cognitive science on racial categorization and racial prejudice. This is unfortunate, for, as we show, the surprising psychological forces at work in racial cognition and related behavior often bear directly on the revisionist goals of conservationists and eliminativists. Our aim, then, is to demonstrate the need for normative racial philosophy to more closely engage the contemporary psychology of racial categorization and racial prejudice.

We begin Section 1 by examining several positions within the philosophy of race in more detail, in the process pointing out where hitherto unappreciated facts about the psychology of race could have an impact upon the feasibility of reform proposals offered by philosophers. In Sections 2 and 3, we review two relatively separate sets of psychological literature: one from evolutionary cognitive psychology and the other from social psychology. Section 2 focuses on recent research on racial categorization, and argues that a large body of evidence shows that the content of racial thought is not a simple product of one's social environment, but is also shaped by the operation of certain evolved psychological mechanisms. Moreover, we show that this research has substantial implications for assessing the feasibility of eliminativist and conservationist proposals.

In Section 3, we turn to the question of racial evaluation, and consider recent studies of divergences between implicit and explicit racial cognition.

This research program suggests that implicit racist biases can persist even in persons sincerely professing tolerant or even anti-racist views, and that implicit racial evaluations can be insulated in important ways from more explicitly held beliefs. We then argue, once again, that these findings bear on the feasibility of proposals made in the philosophical literature on race, and may be used to help shape novel suggestions proposed in the conservationist spirit. We conclude that, although it has not received much discussion in the philosophy of race, the recent empirical work on racial cognition can have a direct impact upon the normative projects of race theory.

1. Race, Philosophy, and Psychological Research

1.1. *Thick Racialism and the Ontological Consensus*

The late nineteenth and early twentieth centuries were marked by the widespread endorsement of biologically rooted *racialist* doctrines—doctrines that divided human beings into putatively natural categories.[2] Such doctrines held that "natural" races exist, and that sorting people into racial groups on the basis of phenotypic features like skin color, hair type, and body morphology also served to sort them according to a range of other underlying properties that expressed themselves in a variety of physical, cultural, moral, and emotional differences among the various races. We shall call this view *thick racialism*. With the advent of modern genetics in the early twentieth century, it seemed obvious that the appropriate interpretation of such thick racialist claims was in terms of this emerging science of human heredity. In particular, it seemed that beliefs about the putative cultural, moral, and emotional differences between races would be vindicated by the discovery of specific and systematic genetic differences between races. However, subsequent research in biology, anthropology, social theory, as well as cognitive, social, and evolutionary psychology has brought about a consensus that thick racialism is false. The reasons for this *ontological consensus* that thick racialism is false are many, but an increased understanding of human genetic variation played an important role in undermining the supposition that there are genetic characteristics shared by all and only members of a race.[3]

---

[2] This is not to repeat the common claim that racialism was invented in the late nineteenth century (or at any other time, for that matter). See Section 2.1.

[3] Arguments referring to human genetic variation can be found in, e.g., Andreasen (1998: 206); Appiah (1996: 68); D'Souza (1996); Kitcher (2000: 87–88); Zack (1993: 13–15). They are rooted in pioneering work done in human genetics in the 1970s by Nei & Roychoudhury (1972, 1974), Lewontin (1972), and others. For a recent review of human genetic variation, see Brown & Armelagos (2001).

At the same time, there remains substantial debate about what could be called *thin racialism*, i.e. the idea that racial categorization might be useful in identifying *some* important genetic differences or other biological properties—for example, properties that might be useful for epidemiology, medicine, and forensic science.[4] Nevertheless, the important point for present purposes is that this ontological consensus against thick racialism is a point of agreement for all the authors we discuss below, and we shall take it for granted what follows.

1.2. *Eliminativism, Conservationism, and Psychology*

We shall call the normative philosophic position that recommends we do away with racial categories *eliminativism*. Eliminativists envisage a society in which there are no racial categorizations at all, typically because they believe that such categorizations are arbitrary and oppressive. For example, K. Anthony Appiah writes:

> The truth is that there are no races: there is nothing in the world that can do all we ask "race" to do for us. The evil that is done is done by the concept and by easy—yet impossible—assumptions as to its application.   (1995: 75)

Here Appiah articulates both of the ideas central to many contemporary eliminativist positions: the first being that thick racialism is false; the second that continued use of racial classification is oppressive.

In contrast, *conservationism* is the position that recommends we conserve racial categories, but do as much as we can to jettison their pernicious features. Conservationists are best understood as offering proposals for (at least short-term) rehabilitation of racial thinking, for conservationists typically advocate both the rejection of thick racialism and the eradication of racism, but hold that racial categories themselves should not be completely eliminated.[5] Outlaw, for example, agrees that "the invidious, socially unnecessary, divisive forms and consequences of thought and practice associated with race ought to be eliminated to whatever extent possible" (1995: 86), but thinks that "the continued existence of discernible racial/ethnic communities of meaning is highly desirable *even if, in the very next instant, racism and invidious ethnocentrism in every form and manifestation were to disappear forever*" (ibid.: 98; italics in original). Conservationists like Outlaw appear to recommend a system composed of discernible racial groups, but one wherein those groups share equal social worth, as opposed to being hierarchically ranked.

---

[4] See, e.g., the papers in *Nature Genetics* (Nov. 2004 Supplement); Gannett (2005); Root (2005).

[5] We follow the practice of using "racism" to involve both an endorsement of thick racialism *and* the evaluative ranking of races on the basis of the alleged natural distinctions between races.

Eliminativists and conservationists are best understood as revisionist: both suggest we reform current practices of racial categorization, but differ in whether it would be best to eliminate or rehabilitate them. Commitment to either type of reform, however, appears to entail commitment to substantive, if often tacit, psychological assumptions as well.

Consider first eliminativism. What exactly would eliminativists like to eliminate? Politically conservative eliminativists (e.g. D'Souza, 1996) are committed to the elimination of racial categorization *in public policy*. But many eliminativists (including a variety of liberal thinkers) have something much more sweeping in mind, and suggest reform extending from large-scale features of social organization all the way to *individual habits of thought and action*. In such normative proposals the psychological assumptions of eliminativism are fairly close to the surface. Consider, for example, a classic paper in which Richard Wasserstrom writes:

A nonracist society would be one in which the race of an individual would be the functional equivalent of the eye color of individuals in our society today. In our society no basic political rights and obligations are determined on the basis of eye color. No important institutional benefits and burdens are connected with eye color. Indeed, except for the mildest sort of aesthetic preferences, a person would be thought odd who even made private, social decisions by taking eye color into account.   (2001, [1980]: 323)[6]

Clearly, Wasserstrom's ideal involves a substantial reordering not only of contemporary social policies, but also of the patterns of categorization underwriting even personal behaviors and thoughts. Given this goal and the assumptions involved, work on the psychology of racial categorization and racism is obviously relevant to assessing the ease with which (or the extent to which) such ideals can be realized. Moreover, if it turns out that certain ideals cannot be realized, that same psychological work will be useful in determining what sort of less-than-ideal goals are more attainable.

With conservationism, the connections with psychology are more complicated, but it seems clear that conservationists, like Outlaw above, are typically committed to retaining racial categorization while eliminating racism and thick racialism.[7] Indeed, to the extent that individuals or groups can reap the (supposed) benefits of racial identification and categorization while avoiding harmful and distorting implications of racism, conservationism enjoys considerable appeal. But is this division of racial categorization from racial evaluation

---

[6] Note that Appiah's worry about the evil done by the *concept* of race suggests a similarly sweeping ideal.

[7] See Mallon (2004: sec. 2) for a similar interpretation of Mills (1998).

really, or even practically, possible? Here, too, there is strong reason to think information about human psychology is relevant to assessing conservationists' proposals.

In sum, both eliminativist and conservationist agendas include, often tacitly, goals of psychological reformation. In particular:

Eliminativists' Goal: Reducing the use of racial categories in thought and behavior.

Conservationists' Goal: The retention of racial categorization together with a rejection of thick racialism and pernicious racial discrimination.

As we shall go on to show, the extent to which these psychological aims can be achieved depends on the particular facts of racial cognition.

1.3. *Normative Proposals, Feasibility, and the Disregard of Psychology*

Costs of normative proposals can be evaluated along various dimensions, including economic, legal, and social ones. Naomi Zack (1998: 16), for example, considers whether completing the project of racial eliminativism is politically feasible given the protection the First Amendment provides to even mistaken thoughts and speech. We'll continue talking about the costs in terms of a proposal's "feasibility": the feasibility of a proposal is a function of the ease with which its goal can be reached. Neither "feasibility" nor "ease" is terribly precise, but we take the basic idea behind each to be clear enough to get our discussion going. Indeed, since we need some way to talk about different types of conditions that are relevant to assessing a proposal (economic, legal, social, psychological, etc.), insisting on greater precision would hinder the terms' usefulness.

One dimension that is rarely considered in these assessments is their *psychological* feasibility, the ease with which eliminativist and conservationist goals can be reached given the psychological facts about human racial cognition. This is puzzling. As we have seen, both eliminativist and conservationist proposals depend in substantial ways on our ability to reform our practices of racial categorization, and these in turn depend in part on the character of the psychology that underwrites these practices. Why, then, is there almost no engagement with the psychology of racial categorization by philosophers of race? The question is not one that can be simply answered by reference to disciplinary boundaries, for philosophical racial theorists typically engage research from a variety of sources, including history, sociology, and anthropology. Yet these same theorists make almost no effort to engage with psychological research, despite its obvious *prima facie* relevance.[8]

Rather than speculate on what motivates this *disregard of psychology*, we instead devote our efforts to showing how recent findings about racial cognition are indeed relevant to assessing the feasibility of both eliminativism and conservationism. Realistically evaluating eliminativist and conservationist goals can be accomplished only if one takes into account some of the more robust and surprising results in current psychology. Below, we shall describe two such areas of research and illustrate how they make the disregard of psychology in the normative racial literature untenable. Along the way, we also draw out some more detailed conclusions about how specific psychological results affect the feasibility of competing normative proposals.

2. Racial Categorization and Evolutionary Psychology

Both eliminativists and conservationists want to modify our practices of racial categorization: eliminativists by eliminating them, conservationists by doing away with thick racialism and mitigating the more unsavory evaluations that may accompany the use of racial categories. In this section, we shall review recent work in evolutionary cognitive psychology on racial categorization, and show how this work bears on the normative debates.

2.1. *Racial Categorization and Specialized Cognitive Mechanisms*

Racial categorization presents a puzzle for evolutionary-minded psychologists and anthropologists (Hirschfeld, 1996; Gil-White, 1999, 2001; Kurzban et al., 2001; for a critical review, see Machery and Faucher, 2005a). People classify themselves and others on the basis of physical, putatively racial properties, and seem to assume that these classifications group together people who share

---

[8] Paul Taylor (2004) is one of the few philosophers to offer an argument for the disregard of psychology. Taylor defends his decision not to consider psychological causes of racism on the grounds that he has "little sympathy for the idea that racism derives from the operation of innate, race-specific mechanisms . . . it's not clear to me why we need to appeal to some hard-wired mechanism that routinely cranks out organisms that indulge in racist exclusions. We'd still have to explain the peculiar forms of exclusion that the mechanism produces under specific cultural conditions, which seems to me to leave all of the interesting questions unanswered" (37–38). Taylor's case for the importance of culture in forming particular racialist and racist practices and racism is compelling, but it is the burden of this chapter to show that his exclusion of psychological factors is less so.

important biological properties (and perhaps also important psychological and moral properties). However, it is hard to account for this phenomenon with the explanatory resources favored by evolutionary psychologists, namely by appeal to something like a "race module"—an evolved cognitive system devoted to race and racial membership. First, it is difficult to identify a selection pressure that would have driven early humans to pay attention to physical properties now associated with race and putative racial differences, like skin color, body shape, etc. Long-distance contacts were probably rare during most of the evolution of human cognition, and our ancestors would have had little direct contact with groups whose members had substantially different physical phenotypes from their own. Moreover, as pointed out in the first section, there is an ontological consensus among researchers from a variety of disciplines that whatever else they might be, racial categories do not systematically map onto any biological categories that support robust physical, social, psychological, and behavioral generalizations.[9] Thus, even if contacts with people with substantially different phenotypical properties had been common during the evolution of humans, the adaptive benefit of classifying others on the basis of these properties would still be unclear.

Thus, rather than postulating a race module on the standard grounds, evolutionary psychologists instead propose that racial categorization is indeed subserved by a module, but that the module in question was initially selected for some function, one not related to race. Evolutionary psychologists theorize that this cognitive system contributes to our social cognition more broadly construed, and is a component of the collection of loosely affiliated cognitive systems that allow humans to navigate the social world. As we shall see below, much of the disagreement among evolutionary psychologists is over the nature and proper function of the cognitive system that now underlies racial thinking.

Some background will be useful in understanding these debates between proponents of the evolutionary-cognitive approach itself, for that approach stands in contrast to previous explanations of racial categorization that have been offered in psychology and the social sciences. These include social-ization explanations, perceptual salience explanations, and group prejudice explanations. Psychologists favoring explanations in terms of socialization have assumed that children are either explicitly taught to draw the distinctions used in racial categorization, or that they easily pick them up from the general social environment, even without anyone (e.g. parents, teachers, peers) explicitly

---

[9] It is doubtful that racial categories can even be used to express true generalizations about morphological characteristics of members of the same putative race, as there is a tremendous amount of morphological variation within a given recognized race (consider for example Ethiopians and Africans from West Africa). For discussion, see Diamond (1994).

instructing them in the use of racial categories (e.g. Allport, 1954). In contrast, evolutionary psychologists, while not denying that socialization plays some role, insist that it is not the whole story. Instead, they propose that our tendency to classify people racially is underwritten by an evolved cognitive system, whose development in children is to a large extent independent of teaching and socialization.

Another view at odds with the evolutionary approach holds that racial categorization results from the simple fact that people classify a wide variety of objects (animals, objects, etc.) into categories based on their *perceptually salient* features. The view just sees racial classification as a special case of this much more general tendency: since color is a salient visual property, skin colors trigger this domain-general categorization system, and as a result, people form and rely on racial categories (e.g. Taylor et al., 1978). In contrast, evolutionary psychologists reject the idea that racial categorization can be explained *merely* by the perceptual salience of skin color, and they argue that racial categorization results from a cognitive system that has evolved to deal with a specific domain in the social world, rather than with categories or perceptual salience in general.

Finally, some social psychologists maintain that racial categorization and racism are to be accounted for by a general tendency to form *group prejudices* about social groups, be they women, races, or social classes (e.g. Crandall & Eshleman, 2003). Evolutionary psychologists reject this idea on the grounds that not all social classifications and prejudices behave the same. They hold that not all classifications and prejudices are produced by the same cognitive system, and conclude that racial cognition should be distinguished from other forms of group-related cognition.

Evolutionary psychologists offer a variety of considerations in support of their distinctive approach to racial categorization. Although they differ on the details, each of the evolutionarily informed positions we shall consider sees racial categorization as a by-product of a fairly specialized cognitive system that evolved to deal with some specific aspect of the social environment. Before getting to the differences between the three positions within the evolutionary-cognitive camp, however, we shall review five lines of argument that undermine the socialization, perceptual salience, and group prejudice explanations just described.

First, and most controversially, evolutionary psychologists hold that people in *many* cultures and historical epochs have relied on skin color and other bodily features to classify their fellows, and have further believed that such classifications also group together people who share underlying biological commonalities. This is controversial because many social constructionist social scientists argue instead that racial categorization is the result of specific historical, political, or social circumstances in the recent history of Europe (see, e.g., Omi & Winant, 1994; Fredrickson, 2002). *Pace* social constructionists, however, there is evidence that across cultures and historical epochs—e.g. in Classical Greece and in the Roman Empire (Isaac, 2004)—people have relied on classifications that are similar to modern racial categories in two central respects. First, these classifications are supposed to be based on phenotypic properties: members are supposed to belong to the same racial category because they share some phenotypic, i.e. morphological or behavioral, properties. Second, people assume or act as if racial categories map onto biological categories: members who share the relevant phenotypic properties are assumed to share some important and distinctive set of underlying biological properties as well. This is not to deny that racial categorization varies across cultures and times in many respects, but rather to stress that these core elements of racial categorization are not a merely parochial cultural phenomenon.[10]

The presence of these common themes across different cultures is just what an evolutionary psychologist would expect, since evolutionary psychologists view racial cognition as a by-product of a cognitive system shared by all normally developing humans. In contrast, because socialization accounts cannot explain why these core elements should recur across times and cultures, they are at best incomplete.

Additionally, despite having such beliefs about racial properties at an early age (see below), children do not acquire the tendency to classify racially from their familial environments. If children were explicitly taught by their parents, or if they merely picked up the classifications their parents used even without being explicitly instructed in their use, one would expect children's beliefs about races to be similar to their parents' beliefs. However, this is not the case (Branch & Newcombe, 1986; Aboud & Doyle, 1996). This dissociation between parents and their children constitutes a second type of evidence against socialization explanations of the disposition to categorize racially.[11]

Third, explanations of racial cognition that rely on perceptual salience take for granted one of the very things they are supposed to be explaining, namely

---

[10] Further undermining the social constructionist view is that its proponents fail to agree on where, when, and why racial categorization appeared. Some locate it at the end of the Middle Ages (Fredrickson, 2002), others with the development of scientific biological classifications by Linnaeus and Blumenbach in the eighteenth century (Banton, 1978), while still others hold European social ideology from the end of the nineteenth century ultimately responsible (Guillaumin, 1980).

[11] Admittedly, the evidence discussed in this paragraph does not undermine every variant of the view that children are socialized into classifying racially. For instance, if children were taught to classify racially by their peers, rather than by their parents, the dissociation between their own beliefs and their parents' beliefs would not be problematic. Children may also just pick up the tendency to classify racially from their peers or from the broader social environment (without being instructed to do so).

why people classify each other on the basis of phenotypic properties like skin color. Color is not always intrinsically salient, or an important feature for categorization purposes. For example, we often do not pay attention to the color of artifacts, and, when we do happen to take their color into account, we rarely treat it as a property that is important for classificatory purposes (see, e.g., Brown, 1991; Keil et al., 1998). When children are trained to use a new tool of a particular color, afterward they show a tendency to use tools that have a similar shape, rather a preference for similar tools of the same color. Thus, in contrast to features such as their shape or rigidity, children do not treat color as an important property of tools or tool identity (Brown, 1991). Examples like these undermine the tacit assumption that colors are salient and important for classification in general. Hence, in the case of perceptual salience explanations of racial classification, the salience and importance of *skin* color needs to be explained, not assumed.

Fourth, social psychologists' emphasis on group prejudice is unable to account for the differences between different types of social classification and the different types of prejudices associated with each. Stereotypes about social groups vary substantially from one type of group to the next. To take only one example, stereotypes about political groups, such as Democrats and Republicans, do not seem to include the idea that these groups are biological kinds (Haslam et al., 2000). Races, on the other hand, *are* thought of as biological kinds (for some cross-cultural empirical evidence, see Machery and Faucher, ms). If all prejudicial stereotypes were produced by a unique cognitive system, or were driven by a single, general tendency to form stereotypes about social groups, we should not find such differences.

Fifth and finally, Lawrence Hirschfeld has provided an important body of experimental evidence that is *prima facie* inconsistent with the non-evolutionary explanations of racial categorization considered above, but that is congenial to the evolutionary approach (Hirschfeld, 1996). Hirschfeld amasses some striking evidence that 3- to 7-year-old preschoolers treat skin color differently from other properties. Unlike properties like body shape, for instance, preschoolers expect skin color to be constant over a lifetime and to be transmitted across generations. By contrast, they believe that body shape can change across a lifetime and is not necessarily transmitted across generations (ibid.: 97–101). These beliefs about racial properties reflect a kind of intuitive *essentialism*: racial properties are viewed as stable (racial properties do not change during one's lifetime), intrinsic (racial properties are thought to be caused by one's inner nature), innate (the development of racial properties does not depend much on one's rearing environment), and inherited (parents transmit their racial properties to their children). This sort of essentialism is also characteristic of children's and adults' folk biological reasoning (Gelman & Wellman, 1991). Because it is plausible that not all prejudices involve this form of essentialism, this makes up another form of evidence against the group prejudice explanation of racial categorization.[12]

Hirschfeld also provides some evidence that 3- and 4-year-old preschoolers pay attention to people's race when this information is presented verbally, but not when it is presented visually. On the one hand, when they are told a story involving various protagonists, children remember the race of these protagonists, even when they are not prompted to pay attention to it. However, when the story is presented by means of drawings, instead of verbally, children do not remember the race of the protagonists (Hirschfeld, 1996: ch. 6). This raises obvious problems for the view that intuitive racial categorization can be completely accounted for by appeal to the perceptual salience of skin color alone. Indeed, while Hirschfeld's experiments are not the final word on racial categorization, it is striking that his results would not be predicted by *any* of the three alternative approaches considered above.

In brief, evidence suggests the following. Racial categorization develops early and reliably across cultures; it does not depend entirely on social learning; it is, in some respects, similar to commonsense biological classification. Thus racial categorization seems to be neither the product of socialization alone nor of the perceptual salience of skin color alone. It does not appear to result from a general tendency toward group prejudice, either. Rather, this body of evidence is best explained by the hypothesis that racial categorization results from a specialized, species-typical cognitive system that, even if it did not initially evolve to deal with racial categorization, has been recruited for this purpose.

Evolutionary psychologists also infer a few more specific properties of the system underlying racial thought. Since the operation of the cognitive system is constant across cultures and certain aspects of it shielded from the influence of teaching, it is thought to be *canalized*: roughly speaking, a trait is environmentally canalized to the extent that its development is the same across different environments and environmental variables.[13] Given the specific properties of this capacity, namely the tendency to classify into races and the typical beliefs that accompany racial categorization, it appears to be driven by a cognitive system that is distinct from whatever cognitive system underlies

---

[12] *Some* other kinds of stereotypes, such as sexist stereotypes, also involve some form of essentialism (e.g. Haslam et al., 2000). However, what matters for the present argument is the fact that not *all* stereotypes involve some form of essentialism.

[13] For a more nuanced discussion of the notion of canalization, see Griffiths & Machery (2008).

stereotypes about other social categories. Finally, because it is species-typical, environmentally canalized, and functionally complex, this cognitive system is plausibly thought to be the product of evolution by natural selection.[14]

It is important to point out up front that, without further argument, such an evolutionary account of racial categorization in no way implies that racial categorization cannot be eliminated or modified. Consider the human taste for sweetness, which is also arguably the product of evolution by natural selection. It too develops early, reliably, and cross-culturally. However, during development, several factors determine whether or not and how much people will be attracted to sweet foods (Rozin, 1982). Thus, although it is a canalized product of natural selection, a person's taste for sweetness is not inevitable or completely impervious to modification. Analogously, racial categorization may thus result from an evolved cognitive system without being inevitable or unalterable. Understanding the possibilities for eliminating or modifying racial categorization, however, and discovering the most effective means of doing either, will depend on the specific empirical details of its development and operation.

2.2. *Controversies within Evolutionary Psychology*

Against this backdrop of broad theoretic agreement, disputes have emerged about the specific character of our capacity to make racial classifications. Hirschfeld (1996, 2001), Kurzban and colleagues (2001), and Gil-White (1999, 2001) have proposed three different accounts of the cognitive system that is assumed to underlie racial categorization. The dust has not settled yet, but the resolution of their disagreements may have an impact upon the debate between eliminativism and conservationism. In what follows, we briefly review each of these three accounts.

First, according to Hirschfeld (1996, 2001), racial categorization results from the interaction of an innate, evolved capacity for *folk sociological* thinking, on the one hand, and the specific social structure in which it is operating, on the other. The evolved function of the posited folk sociological mechanism is to identify the social groups in the social environment. Given the importance of social life during the evolution of human beings (e.g. Dunbar, 2003), the ability to map the social world was most likely selected for. According to

---

[14] It is worth emphasizing that the evolutionary psychological approach does not imply that the evolved cognitive system is the *unique* cause of racial categorization. For instance, Machery & Faucher (2005b) have proposed that people's disposition to classify racially results from the interaction of an evolved cognitive system and some form of social learning, which involves a disposition to imitate one's prestigious peers and a disposition to imitate the majority of one's peers.

Hirschfeld, an important aspect of this hypothesized cognitive system is that it essentializes whatever groups are salient in a given social environment: membership in these groups is associated with a set of immutable properties thought to be caused by some essence common to all group members. When societies are divided along racial lines, the folk sociological mechanism guides us in the identification and essentialization of these groups. In societies with a different social structure, of course, different social groups will be picked out and essentialized. In India, for instance, castes rather than races are the salient social groups, and Hirschfeld's view predicts that in such a social environment, Indians' folk sociological system will essentialize castes (for consistent evidence, see Mahalingam, 2003).

Kurzban, Tooby, and Cosmides (2001) offer a second account. Instead of positing a folk sociological mechanism that picks out the salient social groups in a given social environment, as Hirschfeld (2001) does, they argue that racial categorization results from a cognitive system whose function is to track *coalitions* (i.e. groups of individuals who cooperate with each other) in a given social environment. Kurzban and colleagues assume that races are coalitions in many modern settings, including contemporary American society; since the posited cognitive system tracks coalitions in the social environment, it picks out races in those modern societies.

To support this claim, they provide some intriguing evidence that adults' encoding of skin color and racial membership is influenced by whether racial membership is a relevant cue to coalitional membership. In their experiment, participants were shown pictures of the members of two basketball teams, where each team is composed of some black and some white players. Participants were also given a fictional verbal exchange between members of the teams. In the next stage of the experiment, participants were presented with individual sentences from the exchange, and asked to remember who uttered them. The experimenters then looked at the mistakes made by participants, and checked whether, when they were in error about who uttered a sentence, they mistakenly ascribed it to a basketball player of the same *race*, or to one on the same *team*. The resulting patterns of mistaken ascriptions were taken to indicate how participants classified the basketball players. For instance, if participants had categorized the players involved in the verbal dispute according to race rather than team, then when they made mistakes, they should have been more likely to ascribe a statement made by a white player to another white player than to a black player.

The results of this experiment were along the lines that Kurzban and his colleagues expected. When coalitional membership (i.e. membership in each basketball team) was not emphasized, participants implicitly categorized the individuals involved in the verbal exchange according to race. However, when coalitional membership was emphasized—by giving a distinctively colored jersey to the members of each multi-race team—participants appeared to rely much less on race. Kurzban and colleagues concluded that in the absence of any obvious indicators of coalitional boundaries, racial membership is often taken to be a cue to coalitional membership. This hypothesis explains why, when other indications of coalitional membership are made particularly evident or social environments make coalitional boundaries more salient, people are less prone to classify into races. Based on this conclusion, Kurzban and colleagues further suggest that if skin color were not a reliable cue to coalition membership—if, for instance, the social environment were structured differently—people would tend to classify much less on the basis of skin color.

The third account is offered by Gil-White (1999, 2001), who argues that evolution has selected for *an ethnic cognitive system*, that is, a cognitive system whose evolved function is to identify ethnic groups. In brief, at some point during the evolution of our species (around 100,000 years ago), our ancestors lived in groups called "ethnies," which were made up of (at least) several hundred or thousand culturally homogeneous members. Those ancestors displayed their membership to the group by means of specific ethnic markers, e.g. clothes, body paintings, etc. Gil-White maintains that it was important for our ancestors to map this dimension of the social world and argues that folk biology—the set of commonsense beliefs about animals and biological kinds together with the cognitive systems responsible for classifying and reasoning about animals and biological kinds—was recruited or "exapted" for this purpose (for further detail, see Gil-White, 2001).[15] As a result, we have evolved to pay attention to possible ethnic markers and to classify social actors on their basis. Moreover, because the folk biological system essentializes the entities it classifies, we now tend to essentialize the groups we discern on the basis of these ethnic markers. Finally, according to Gil-White, racial categorization can be driven by this cognitive system, because skin color and other racial properties (such as body type) are often taken to be ethnic markers. Because of this, races can be *mistaken* for ethnies by the ethnic cognitive system, despite the fact that they are, in general, *not* ethnies.

To summarize, controversies remain even among those who agree on the basic evolutionary-cognitive approach. In particular, disagreements center around details of how the cognitive system believed to now underlie racial categorization is structured, and what it initially evolved to do—track salient

---

[15] A trait is said to be exapted when it is used for something different than for what it was originally selected.

social groups, track coalitions, or track ethnies. The three accounts also suggest different reasons why skin color triggers this cognitive system.

2.3. Consequences for the Debate between Eliminativists and Conservationists

While interesting in its own right, the research on racial categorization in evolutionary psychology shows that there are some specific obstacles to the feasibility of eliminativism and conservationism that have been ignored by race theorists. To begin, each of these three accounts of racial cognition leads to a similar conclusion about eliminativism: any eliminativist proposal is committed not just to a substantial amount of social reform, but, in light of the constraints imposed by the psychology of racial categorization, to social reform of a fairly specific sort. This should feature in any serious cost–benefit analysis for or against eliminativism. Consider Hirschfeld's account: during development, the cognitive system that underlies racialism is triggered by the use of race terms ("black," "white," "Hispanic," etc.) by parents, peers, etc., when parents, peers, etc. refer to social groups or characterize individuals. Children rely on such terms to identify the important social groups in their social environment, and they essentialize such groups. Race terms are mapped onto specific visual cues (skin color, body shape, etc.) later in development (Hirschfeld, 1996: 136). Obviously, this account leaves many aspects of the development of racial categorization unspecified. However, it suggests that the feasibility of eliminating racial categories in part turns on the importance of races in people's social environment, and perhaps the prominence of racial terms in their vocabulary. If races are socially important, people will refer to them, and children are likely to develop a tendency to classify racially.

Kurzban, Tooby, and Cosmides's hypothesis leads to a similar conclusion. They propose, remember, that the salience of skin color depends on the coalitional status of races. People pay attention to races because races act as coalitions in many modern societies. Thus, if races continue to act—or seem to act—as coalitions, achieving the ideal of race blindness will be hindered by the fact that putative racial properties like skin color shared by putative coalition members will continue to be salient to our evolved coalitional cognitive system. Remarkably, however, Kurzban and colleagues conclude their (2001) article remarking on "how easy it was to diminish the importance of race by manipulating coalition" and suggesting that "the prospects for reducing or even eliminating the widespread tendency to categorize persons by race may be very good indeed" (15391). We are skeptical of this conclusion. If they are right, the existence of racial categorization is linked to the existence of racially based coalitions. These coalitions are reinforced by the economic and social divisions of contemporary societies, which are not themselves easily alterable. The prospects for eliminating racial categorization, on this story, are tied to the prospects for extensive economic and social reform, and may require putting an end to the sorts of economic, social, and even geographic segregation that continues to separate racial groups.

Kurzban et al.'s hypothesis also places interesting constraints on the type of programs that ought to be used to promote eliminativism. For example, programs where blacks help other blacks (e.g. programs that assign junior racial minority professionals to a senior minority mentor of the same race), for example, could tend to reinforce racial categories, if Kurzban et al. are right. On the other hand, programs in which members of *other* races help blacks (e.g. a classic affirmative action program in a predominantly white company) might not trigger coalitional thinking.

Although leading to a slightly different conclusion, Gil-White's views also suggest that eliminativism is committed to specific social reforms. According to him, as we saw, skin color and other phenotypic properties are often taken to be ethnic markers, that is, physical cues that indicate membership in ethnies. Nowadays, in most societies, social groups differ in many respects from the paleoanthropological ethnies in response to which ethnic cognition is supposed to have evolved. Nonetheless, like paleoanthropological ethnies, some modern groups may have substantial cultural homogeneity, in the sense that members of these groups endorse similar behavioral norms, and identify each other by similar markers. If, for some historical reason, racial distinctions in a given society map onto such groups, the posited ethnic cognitive system will be triggered not only by skin color and other phenotypic properties, but also by other cues (names, accents, behaviors, etc.). Arguably, this is the case of blacks in contemporary America.[16] If Gil-White's account is correct, eliminativism might require modifying the cultural structure of society—weakening perceived cultural differences between racial groups (such as blacks and whites in the United States). Given that such cultural differences are sometimes claimed to be constitutive of individuals' identities, this is an important and potentially controversial cost for eliminativism.[17]

We also note that the reforms suggested by Gil-White's account are of a different sort than the changes that would be required if Kurzban and

---

[16] Although this was not the case when African slaves arrived in the US. They came from different cultures in Africa.

[17] Of course, this cost is already explicitly considered in discussions of the value of racial identity in social theory (e.g. Outlaw, 1995, 1996; Appiah, 1996). What empirical models bring to the discussion are theories and evidence that bear on the question of whether culture and racial identity are, in fact, closely linked in folk racial thinking.

colleagues were right. Kurzban and colleagues' account of the nature of racial categorization suggests that to eliminate the tendency to classify racially, one should prevent the development of preferential cooperative links between members of the same race, and one should undermine these links if they already exist—that is, one should discourage Hispanics from preferentially helping Hispanics, blacks from preferentially helping blacks, and so on. By contrast, Gil-White's account suggests that to eliminate the tendency to classify racially, one should prevent members of the same race from developing shared cultural norms, or one should undermine such norms if they exist—that is, one should discourage Hispanics (or Asians, or blacks, or whites) from having a shared and distinctive accent, shared and distinctive behavioral norms, and so on.

Note that the need for such specific social reforms may not be an inescapable difficulty for eliminativism. Eliminativists are well aware that the thrust of their position is ambitious and calls for significant social change. Examples of reform with regard to race are not a mere or even distant possibilities, either: they are evident in actual societies, for instance in the form of affirmative action, school integration, and voting reform in American society. And, as we noted in Section 1, eliminativism can come in different strengths, or be targeted on different social domains. Nevertheless, it remains the case that evaluations of social reforms should include an assessment of the psychological feasibility of eliminativist proposals.

Conservationism, on the other hand, may not seem as affected by these consequences, since conservationists want to preserve racial distinctions. They do not have to change the cues that trigger the cognitive system that underlies racial categorization, and, thus, do not have to reform the social or cultural structure of our societies. Additionally, conservationists do not appear committed to anything that may entail the weakening of cultural or racial identities. Conversely, the evolutionary psychology considered in this section suggests that eliminativists *are* committed to such projects.

Nevertheless, the feasibility of conservationist goals will also be directly affected by which psychological view turns out to be correct. Hirschfeld's and Gil-White's accounts tentatively suggest that racial categorization and essentialism—i.e. the belief that racial groups are biological groups, whose members share an underlying essence that explains their shared physical, behavioral, and moral properties—are the product of the same cognitive system. Details and evidence are scarce at this point: particularly relevant is the fact that Hirschfeld does not adduce explicit evidence that moral properties are essentialized. Still, Hirschfeld's and Gil-White's accounts suggest that whenever people categorize racially (because races are salient social groups or because children take skin color and other physical properties to be ethnic markers), they essentialize the groups that are delineated. Thus, according to their accounts, conserving racial categorization while reforming its normative connotations may be hindered by the nature of the evolved cognitive system that underlies racial categorization. For example, an attempt to encourage people to adopt a nonessentialized metaphysics for race (of the sort suggested by, e.g., Omi and Winant, 1994; Mills, 1998; or Taylor, 2004) may be defeated or at least complicated by the very structure of the system underlying racial cognition. Of course, none of this implies that a nonessentialist conservationism is impossible. For, as illustrated above with the example of our taste for sweetness, the effects of an evolved and canalized cognitive system are not inevitable. But understanding the prospects of achieving a nonessentialist conservationism in light of this psychological research is certainly an important factor in the cost–benefit analysis of any specific conservationist proposal.

The situation would be very different if Kurzban, Tooby, and Cosmides's account turned out to be correct. For they propose that essentialism, on the one hand, and the salience of racial physical properties, on the other, stem from two different cognitive systems (Cosmides et al., 2003). Again, on this view, racial categorization is the product of a human coalitional system. Essentialism comes from our folk biology. If this is right, the nature of human racial psychology does not prevent the dissociation between racial categorization and its essentialist implications.

To summarize, recent evidence supports the idea that among the causes of racial categorization, one finds an evolved, canalized, and species-typical cognitive system. If true, these evolutionary hypotheses would reveal that there are some definite and significant problems for eliminativists and for conservationists alike. The three views considered here reinforce the thought that eliminativism is committed to some form of social reform. Moreover, as we saw, each view suggests that a distinct sort of social reform is needed for eliminativism, and each raises specific and difficult normative questions about the way in which the cultural or coalitional unity of a group would have to be compromised in order to eliminate racial categorization. Additionally, Hirschfeld's and Gil-White's views suggest that dissociating racial categorization and essentialism, as is proposed by conservationists, may be hindered by the nature of the cognitive system that underlies racial categorization, while Kurzban and colleagues' view is congenial to such proposals. In either case, neglecting psychology amounts to neglecting specific obstacles that need to be addressed in order for eliminativist or conservationist proposals for reform to be viable.

3. Racial Evaluation and Implicit Social Cognition

Racial categorization looks to raise problems both for eliminativists and conservationists. One might be tempted, however, to think those results weigh especially heavily against eliminativism, and tilt the balance of considerations toward conservationism. In this section, we suggest that the conservationist goal of reducing negative racial evaluation has problems of its own—problems that the disregard of psychology has kept from being addressed.

In social psychology, recent advances in experimental measurement techniques have allowed psychologists to explore the contours of our capacities for racial evaluation with great precision, and a set of unsettling results has emerged. Most relevant of these is a particular phenomenon that has been confirmed repeatedly: people who genuinely profess themselves to be tolerant, unbiased, and free of racial prejudice nonetheless often display signs of implicit racial bias on indirect experimental measures. These methods were designed to bypass one's explicitly held views, i.e. those available via introspection and self-report, and instead systematically probe the less transparent workings of attitudes, associations, and processes linked to categorization and evaluation. After reviewing the relevant findings, we shall go on to assess their implications for the normative debate between eliminativism and conservationism.

3.1. Indirect Measures and Implicit Cognition

Consider how you could find out about someone else's mathematical prowess, or their ability to distinguish the subtleties of red wines. Perhaps the most obvious way would be to simply *ask* that person outright, "How good are you at math? Can you integrate a multi-variable equation?" or "How educated is your wine palate? Can you appreciate the difference between a California merlot and a Chilean cabernet sauvignon?" Alternatively, you might take a more circuitous route, and proceed by giving the person a set of math problems or a wine taste test, and infer their mathematical abilities or wine sophistication from their performance on the respective tests. The first type of strategy depends for its reliability on the sincerity of the person's self-report, the absence of self-deception in their self-assessment, and their ability to introspectively access the relevant information. The second type, though less direct in some ways, has the advantage of bypassing all three of these obstacles.

For similar reasons, indirect strategies have become trusted instruments for investigating many cognitive capacities, and research on implicit social cognition is no exception. We shall call meausures that rely on such strategies *indirect measures*.[18] According to Nosek et al. (2007), most indirect measures are:

[M]easurement methods that avoid requiring introspective access, decrease the mental control available to produce the response, reduce the role of conscious intention, and reduce the role of self-reflective, deliberative processes.   (2007: 267)[19]

This description isn't definitive, but it gets across the flavor of indirect measures, the most prominent of which will be described in more detail below.

First, though, some terminological stipulations will lend clarity to the discussion. The term "implicit" is a source of potential confusion in this literature, as it is often applied to both the cognitive processes as well as the experimental measures used to probe them, and is treated as loosely synonymous with "automatic," "unconscious," and various other terms (Greenwald and Banaji, 1995; Greenwald et al., 1998; Cunningham et al., 2001; Eberhardt, 2005; Nosek et al., 2007). In what follows, we shall use "indirect" to describe measurement techniques, namely those that do not rely on introspection or self report, and reserve "implicit" only for mental entities being measured. Moreover, we will follow Banaji et al. (2001) and use 'implicit' to describe those processes or mechanisms operating outside the subject's conscious awareness, and "automatic" to denote those that operate without the subject's conscious control.

The Implicit Association Test (IAT)   The IAT has been the most widely used indirect measure, and has been consequently subjected to the most scrutiny.[20] It was initially conceived of as "a method for indirectly measuring the strengths of associations," designed to help "reveal associative information that people were either unwilling or unable to report" (Nosek et al. 2007: 269). At its heart, the IAT is a sorting task. Most instances of the IAT involve four distinct categories, usually divided into two pairs of dichotomous categories. For instance, an IAT might involve the category pairs *black* and *white* (called "target concepts"), on the one hand, and *good* and *bad* (called "attribute dimensions") on the other. In one common case, the exemplars of the

---

[18] Phelps et al. (2000) and Phelps et al. (2003) use this term to distinguish indirect from "direct" measures that use techniques like interviews or questionnaires that rely on verbal and written self-report.

[19] Thus characterized, indirect testing is not a particularly recent development to psychology (see, e.g., Stroop, 1935).

[20] The first presentation of the test itelf, along with the initial results gathered using it, can be found in Greenwald et al. (1998). Greenwald & Nosek (2001) and Nosek et al. (2007) both present more recent reviews of research using IATs, as well as assessments of the methodological issues generated by use of the test and interpretation of results. It should also be noted that there are several variants of this basic paradigm (e.g. Cunningham et al., 2001).

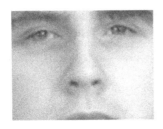

categories *black* and *white* are pictures of black and white faces, while exemplars of the other two categories are individual words, such as "wonderful," "glorious," and "joy," for *good*, "terrible," "horrible," and "nasty," for *bad*. During trials, exemplars are displayed one at a time, in random order, in the middle of a computer screen, and participants must sort them as fast as they can.

Crucial to the logic of the test is the fact that participants are required to sort the exemplars from the *four* categories using only *two* response options. For instance, they are told to press "e" when presented with any exemplar of *good* or any exemplar of *black*, and press "i" when presented with any exemplar of *bad* or any exemplar of *white*. Equally crucial to the logic of IATs is that they are *multi-stage* tests (often comprising five stages), and the response options (the "e" and "i" keys) are assigned to different categories in different stages. So one stage might require the participant to respond to exemplars of *good* or *black* with the "e" response option and exemplars of *bad* or *white* with the "i" response option, while the next stage assigns *bad* or *black* to the "e" response option and *good* or *white* to the "i" response option. Paired categories such as *good* and *bad*, or *black* and *white*, however, never get assigned to the same response options (each response option is assigned one "target concept" and one "attribute dimension"). When a participant makes a sorting error, it must be corrected as quickly as possible before he or she is allowed to move on to the next exemplar. Precise reaction times are measured by the computer on which the test is being taken, as is correction time and number of errors.[21]

Coarse-grained interpretation of performance is fairly straightforward. Generally speaking, the "logic of the IAT is that this sorting task should be easier when the two concepts that share a response are strongly associated than when they are weakly associated." More specifically, "ease of sorting can be indexed

---

[21] See the citations in previous footnote for a much more detailed and technically precise discussion of this technique. In order to get the feel of the test, however, one is much better off simply taking one; different versions of it are available at https://implicit.harvard.edu/implicit/demo/.

both by the speed of responding (faster indicating stronger associations) and the frequency of errors (fewer errors indicating stronger association)" (Nosek et al., 2007: 270). The idea can be illustrated with our example case. If a participant is able to sort exemplars faster and more accurately when *good* and *white* share a response option than when *good* and *black* share a response option, this fact is interpreted as an indirect measure of a stronger association between the two categories *good* and *white*, and hence an implicit preference for white, or, conversely, an implicit bias against black. This is called the IAT effect. The size of the relative preference or bias is indicated by the disparity between the speed and accuracy of responses to the same stimuli using different response option pairings. Finally, the associations thus revealed are taken to be indicative of processes that function implicitly and automatically, because the responses must be made quickly, and thus without benefit of introspection or the potentially moderating influence of deliberation and conscious intention. While the details of the method can seem Byzantine, the basic idea behind the test remains rather simple: stronger associations between items will allow them to be grouped together more quickly and accurately; the sophisticated set up and computerization just allow fine-grained measurement of that speed and accuracy.

Modern Racism Scale (MRS)   By way of contrast with indirect measures like the IAT, the MRS is a direct measure of racial attitudes, one that is often used in conjunction with the indirect measures. This is a standard self-report questionnaire that was designed to probe for racial biases and prejudices (McConahay, 1986). It poses statements explicitly about racial issues (e.g. "Over the past few years, Blacks have gotten more economically than they deserve"; "It is easy to understand the anger of Black people in America"; "Blacks are getting too demanding in their push for equal rights"), and allows participants to react to each statement by selecting, at their leisure, one of the responses, which range from Strongly Disagree to Strongly Agree.

The use of direct measures *together* with indirect measures is important because it is the conjunction of the two that supports the inference to not just automatic but *implicit* processes and biases in the sense discussed earlier. Recall that implicit processes operate outside the introspective access and awareness of participants, while automatic processes are those that operate beyond conscious control. There is much overlap, but these two terms are not completely coextensive; disgust responses, for example, may be automatic, but they are rarely implicit. That participants can exhibit biases on indirect measures, despite the fact that they report having no such biases when asked directly, lends support to the conclusion that what manifests in the indirect tests is indeed the result of processes that are unavailable to introspection and self-report.

3.2. *Evidence of Biases and their Effects*

3.2.1. *Implicit Racial Bias*   These types of indirect measures have been used to probe and reveal a wide variety of implicit biases, including age biases (e.g. Levy & Banaji, 2002), gender biases (e.g. Lemm & Banaji, 1999), sexuality biases (e.g. Banse et al., 2001), weight biases (e.g. Schwartz et al., 2006), as well as religious and disability biases (see Lane et al., 2007 for a review). Some of the first and most consistently confirmed findings yielded by these tests, however, center on racial biases.[22] Participants who profess tolerant or anti-racist views on direct tests often reveal racial biases on indirect tests. This result is quite robust; similar dissociations have been found using a wide variety of other indirect measures, including evaluative priming (Cunningham et al., 2001; Devine et al., 2002), the startle eyeblink test (Phelps et al., 2000; Amodio et al., 2003), and EMG measures (Vanman et al., 1997). In other words, it is psychologically possible to be, and many Americans actually are, *explicitly racially unbiased while being implicitly racially biased*.[23] Moreover, not only is it possible for two sets of opposing racial evaluations to coexist within a single agent, but, as we shall see, when it comes to altering and controlling them, the different types of biases may be responsive to quite different methods.

3.2.2. *Implicit Racial Bias and Behavior*   Perhaps a natural question to ask before going any farther is whether or not the biases revealed by indirect measurement techniques have any influence on judgments or ever lead to any actual prejudicial behavior, especially in real-world situations. Obviously, the question is important for a variety of reasons, not least of which is assessing

---

[22]   The first paper to showcase the IAT included the results from three separate experiments, one of which was a test for implicit racial biases in white American undergraduates (Greenwald et al., 1998). Results exhibited a now-familiar, but still disturbing, pattern: while most (19 of 26) of the participants explicitly endorsed an egalitarian, or even pro-black, position on the direct measures (including the MRS), all but one exhibited an IAT effect indicating implicit white preference. This was the first study using the IAT to investigate this phenomenon, but previous work using less sophisticated methods had revealed similar results (e.g. Devine, 1989; Greenwald & Banaji, 1995; Fazio et al., 1995). Since the initial 1998 paper, similar results from IATs have been reported so often and found so reliably that they have become a commonplace (Kim & Greenwald, 1998; Banaji, 2001; Ottaway et al., 2001).

[23]   While the fact that implicit and explicit racial biases can be dissociated is no longer a subject of much controversy, the relationship between the two is still very much in question. While early discussions stressed the complete independence of subjects' performances on direct and indirect tasks (Greenwald et al., 1998), follow-up work has shown that the two can be involved in complicated correlations (Greenwald et al., 2003; Nosek et al., 2007).

the feasibility of revisionist proposals offered by philosophers of race. Racial theorists (and others) skeptical of the relevance of this psychological literature might be inclined to simply dismiss it on the grounds that tests like the IAT measure mere linguistic associations or inert mental representations that people neither endorse nor act upon in real-world scenarios (see, e.g., Gehring et al., 2003). Others, who grant that the results of indirect tests (which usually turn on differences that are a matter of milliseconds) are of legitimate theoretic interest to psychologists,[24] might still remain skeptical that implicit biases, whatever they turn out to be, are powerful enough to make any practical difference in day-to-day human affairs.

We do not think that such skepticism is justified. First, we are impressed by mounting evidence that race and racial bias can still have measurable and important effects in real-world situations. In a field study by Bertrand and Mullainathan (2003), researchers responded to help-wanted ads in Boston and Chicago newspapers with a variety of fabricated résumés. Each résumé was constructed around either a very black-sounding name (e.g. "Lakisha Washington" or "Jamal Jones") or a very white-sounding name (e.g. "Emily Walsh" or "Greg Baker"). When the résumés were sent out to potential employers, those bearing white names received an astonishing 50% more callbacks for interviews. Moreover, those résumés with both white names and more qualified credential received 30% more callbacks, whereas those highly qualified black résumés received a much smaller increase. The numbers involved are impressive, and the amount of discrimination was fairly consistent across occupations and industries; in Bertrand and Mullainathan's own words:

In total, we respond to over 1300 employment ads in the sales, administrative support, clerical and customer services job categories and send nearly 5000 resumes. The ads we respond to cover a large spectrum of job quality, from cashier work at retail establishments and clerical work in a mailroom to office and sales management positions.   (3)

Interestingly, employers who explicitly listed "Equal Opportunity Employer" in their ad were found to discriminate as much as other employers.

Similar evidence of race and racial bias influencing real-world situations comes from a recent statistical analysis of officiating in NBA (National Basketball Association) games, which claims to find evidence of an "opposite race bias" (Price & Wolfers, ms). The study, which took into account data from the 12 seasons from 1991–2003, found evidence that white referees called slightly

---

[24] For instance, some psychologists see problems with the quick inference from IAT results to the attribution of implicit prejudice (Blanton & Jaccard, 2008; Arkes & Tetlock, 2004).

but significantly more fouls on black players than white players, as well as evidence of the converse: black referees called slightly but significantly more fouls on white players than on black players.

The racial composition of teams and refereeing crews was revealed to have slight but systematic influence on other statistics as well, including players' scoring, assists, steals, and turnovers. The study found that players experience a decrease in scoring, assists and steals, and an increase in turnovers when playing before officiating crews primarily composed of members of the opposite race. (For example, a black player's performance will fall off slightly when at least two of the three referees are white. For the purposes of the study all referees and players were classified as either black or not black.) These findings are especially surprising considering the fact that referees are subject to constant and intense scrutiny by the NBA itself, so much so that they have repeatedly been called "the most ranked, rated, reviewed, statistically analyzed and mentored group of employees of any company in any place in the world" by commissioner David Stern (Schwartz & Rashbaum, 2007).

While neither the IAT, nor any other indirect, controlled experimental technique was given to participants in either the NBA or the résumé studies, explanations that invoke implicit biases look increasingly plausible in both cases. Indeed, the sorts of real-world findings coming from these sorts of statistical analyses and field studies, on the one hand, and the types of automatic and implicit mental processes revealed by the likes of the IAT, on the other, appear to complement each other quite nicely. Explicit racism on the part of NBA referees or the employees responsible for surveying resumes and deciding whom to contact for job interviews may account for some fraction of the results, but given the conditions in which the respective groups perform their jobs, we are skeptical that appeal to explicit racism alone can explain all of the results. Especially in the heat of an NBA game, referees must make split-second judgments in high-pressure situations. These are exactly the type of situations where people's behaviors are likely to be influenced by automatic processes.

Moreover, researchers have begun to push beyond such plausible speculation and explicitly link indirect measures with behavior in controlled settings. These studies further confirm that when participants have to make instantaneous decisions and take quick action, racial biases affect what they do. Payne (2006) reviews a large body of evidence concerning participants who are asked to make snap discriminations between guns and a variety of harmless objects. Participants, both white and black, are more apt to misidentify a harmless object as a gun if they are first shown a picture of a black, rather than a picture of a white. This effect has become known as the "weapon bias." Similar results are found with participants who explicitly try to avoid racial biases.

Moreover, presence of a weapon bias correlates with performance on the racial IAT (Payne, 2005). This suggests that implicit racial biases may indeed lie behind the weapon bias. (For more discussion and a wider range of cases that link implicit biases of all sorts to behavior, see Greenwald et al., 2009.)

The real-world relevance of such findings is increasingly difficult to deny. It could help explain familiar anecdotes of sincerely egalitarian people who are surprised when they are called out for racist behavior or biased decision-making, especially when such accusations turn out to be legitimate. Another, more concrete example is provided by the highly publicized death of Amadou Diallo in 1999. He was shot and killed by New York police officers who thought he was drawing a gun, when in actuality he was just reaching for his wallet.

3.2.3. *Mitigating the Effects of Implicit Racial Bias*   In addition to its direct real-world relevance, this body of psychological research has implications relevant to normative racial theorists. Before discussing those implications, however, we wish to call attention to a relevant offshoot of this literature that investigates whether and how implicit biases can be brought under control, and whether their expression in behavior and judgment can be mitigated.[25] Preliminary evidence suggests that implicit biases and the downstream effects they typically give rise to can indeed be manipulated. Research is beginning to shed some light on the effectiveness, and lack thereof, of different methods for bringing them under control. We consider three different methods of mitigating the effects of implicit biases: manipulating the immediate environment, self-control, and blocking the development or acquisition of implicit bias.

First, some of these studies suggest that while implicit biases operate beyond the direct conscious control of the participants themselves, they can be rather dramatically influenced by manipulating aspects of a person's immediate *environment*, often their social environment. Dasgupta and Greenwald (2001) showed participants pictures of admired and disliked black and white celebrities (Denzel Washington, Tom Hanks, Mike Tyson, Jeffrey Dahmer) and found that exposure to admired blacks and disliked whites weakened the pro-white IAT effect. They also found that the weakening of the implicit bias measured immediately after exposure to the pictures was still present 24 hours later, while the subjects' explicit attitudes remained unaffected. Lowery et al. (2001) found that the implicit biases of white Americans (as measured by the IAT) could be lessened merely by having the participants interact with a black

---

[25] See the special issue of *Journal of Personality and Social Psychology* (vol. 81, issue 5, 2001), for an introductory overview and collection of articles devoted to this topic.

experimenter rather than a white experimenter. Richeson and Ambady (2003) showed situational differences can affect implicit biases: when white female participants were told they were going to engage in a role-playing scenario, either as a superior or a subordinate, immediately after they completed an IAT, those anticipating playing a subordinate role to a black in a superior role showed fewer traces of implicit racial bias than those anticipating play a superior role to a black in a subordinate role.

Other studies investigated the extent to which a participant can obliquely influence their own implicit biases by some form of *self-control*, either by actively suppressing their expression or indirectly affecting the implicit processes themselves. For instance, Blair et al. (2001) found that participants who generate and focus on counter-stereotypic mental imagery of the relevant exemplars can weaken their IAT effects. Richeson et al. (2003) present further brain-imaging and behavioral data suggesting that while so-called "executive" functions (in the right dorsolateral prefrontal cortex) can serve to partially inhibit the expression of racial biases on indirect tests, the act of suppressing them requires effort and (or perhaps in the form of) attention.

A different way to eliminate the pernicious effects of implicit biases might be to nip the problem in the bud, so to speak, and to keep people (young children, for instance) from acquiring or developing them in the first place. Research raises difficulties for this possibility, however. Preliminary evidence suggests that implicit biases are easier to acquire than their explicit counterparts. The same evidence suggests implicit biases are harder to alter once acquired, and are difficult to eliminate. This is given a rather striking experimental demonstration by Gregg et al. (2006). Participants in this study were told about two imaginary groups of people, the second of which was cast in a negative light in order to induce biases against its members. After they had been given this initial information, however, participants were told that the damning description of the second group was incorrect, the mistaken result of a computer error. Gregg and his colleagues then gave participants both direct and indirect tests, and found that while their explicit biases had disappeared, their implicit biases, as measured by an IAT, remained. Work on acquisition and the development of the capacity for implicit social cognition in general is still in its infancy, but initial forays into the area suggest that the development of the capacity for implicit bias is rapid, independent of explicit teaching, and distinct from the development of explicit biases (see Dunham et al., 2008).

These findings make up the beginning of a promising research program centered not only on implicit racial cognition itself, but on how the unwanted influence of implicit biases on judgment and behavior can be mitigated or brought under control. On the currently available evidence, it is not yet clear whether the most effective strategies act on the implicit biases themselves, or on ancillary processes that underlie their expression in behavior or judgments. The bulk of this work does suggest that, at the very least, the expression of implicit biases is not impossible to alter. Indeed, while they are inaccessible via direct introspection and appear not to require—indeed, can even *defy*—deliberation or conscious intention, these studies suggest that implicit biases can be affected by changes in the social environment and less direct forms of self-control. While blocking their development or acquisition may be an uphill battle, their expression can be restrained via strategic alterations of the social environment and specific forms of self-control.

3.3. *Consequences for the Debate between Eliminativism and Conservationism*

While it is fascinating in its own right, this body of work in social psychology is clearly relevant to a variety of philosophical issues concerning race.[26] To be forthright, the psychological story is still far from complete, and in a number of ways:

(a) the extent to which many of the results reported can be generalized from one culture to the next remains uncertain, as does the manner in which those results might be generalized;

(b) whether and which results can be generalized to racial groups beyond blacks and whites within a single culture (to include other putative racial groups such as Hispanics, Indians, Asians, etc.) is also uncertain (but see Devos et al., 2007);

(c) there is little systematic data concerning the ontogenesis of implicit racial biases (but see Baron & Banaji, 2006, Dunham et al., 2008);

(d) a more detailed account of the cognitive architecture underlying these implicit biases is needed, preferably one that can shed light on the admittedly live issue of how and how often the evaluations measured by the indirect tests are also involved in causal processes that lead to actual judgment and action;

(e) it is currently far from clear whether implicit biases of different types, for instance implicit racial biases, gender biases, age biases, disability biases, etc., all reflect the workings of the same set of cognitive mechanisms;

(f) more fine-grained and theoretically motivated distinctions are needed, since the term "group" used to interpret much of the data is probably too ambiguous to be of much serious use—as alluded to in Section 2,

---

[26] For an initial attempt to wrestle with the ethical implications of implicit racial biases, see Kelly & Roedder (2008), Faucher & Machery (forthcoming).

different sorts of groups, for instance coalitions, ethnies, families, political parties, or even professions may be cognized differently by distinct systems in the human mind.

We list these points not as an indictment or criticism, but by way of emphasizing the richness of the research project, and the breadth of the issues it might eventually be able to shed light on. Moreover, the contours of the emerging picture are already discernible, and they have implications of their own. Since many of those implications crucially involve not just racial categorization but *evaluation*, we shall here consider the impact they have on the conservationist position.

We noted at the outset that a typical conservationist position advocates retaining racial categorization while reducing or eliminating the belief that racial groups are biologically distinct, as well as racist evaluations that favor one group over another. In this way, the conservationist position is continuous with familiar social programs in the United States that attempt to diminish or redress racism and its effects while retaining racial categories. (For example, affirmative action is a program for which racial categories are indispensable.) At first, proposals along these lines seem both sensible and realistically achievable. Indeed, as has been noted in a number of places (Biernat & Crandall, 1999; Schuman et al., 1997; Phelps et al., 2000), the last couple of decades have shown a significant decrease in the expression of explicit racist attitudes, as measured by self-report. While this is surely a sign of progress, the results reported in the previous section suggest that the actual state of affairs is more complicated, and that achieving conservationist goals involves more than the reduction of explicit bias. That it is psychologically possible to be, and that many Americans indeed *are*, explicitly unbiased, but implicitly biased, suggests that maintaining racial categorization while at the same time purging racial categories of all of their derogatory evaluative baggage is committed to addressing two different families of evaluative states instead of just one. While no one is under the illusion that racism will be easy to eradicate,[27] the work in social psychology can help shed light on the exact nature of the difficulties involved. In turn, by disregarding that work, and the fact that implicit biases appear to exist in many explicitly unbiased people, conservationists are at risk of ignoring some of the obstacles that stand in the way of their own proposals.

We take the empirical research to have established a number of claims. A large body of evidence clearly indicates that implicit racial biases exist, and are fairly prevalent in the population. They are different from, and

---

[27] E.g. Outlaw (1995); Taylor (2004).

can coexist with, their explicit counterparts. Statistical analyses like those provided in Price and Wolfers's paper on the NBA, and field studies like those described in Bertrand and Mullainathan's résumé paper complement work done in controlled experimental settings, strongly suggesting that implicit biases indeed effect judgment and behavior, even in real-world situations. For conservationists, the broadest conclusion to draw from this is that to the extent that implicit biases have not been systematically taken into account, the feasibility of achieving their professed ideals remains largely unknown.

Additionally, explicit prejudices have declined steadily over the last several decades while implicit biases remain prevalent (although we lack similar data tracking the level of implicit bias through the same span of years). Whatever has been successful in bringing about the drop-off of explicit racial bias does not appear to have eliminated implicit bias. This suggests that not all racial evaluations can be revised and altered by the same methods. Hence, assessing the feasibility of specific conservationist proposals for dealing with negative racial evaluations should take into account not just implicit biases themselves, but the costs and benefits of implementing the sorts of techniques most likely to effectively deal with them.

Conservationists may take different stances in light of the existence and character of implicit racial biases. On the one hand, they may maintain that the proper ideal to strive for remains the complete eradication of negative racial evaluations, both explicit and implicit alike. If future research vindicates the preliminary results, then once implicit biases are taken into account, achieving such an ideal may be even more difficult that previously thought. Two ways that immediately come to mind of achieving the conservationist ideal are by blocking the acquisition or development of biases in younger generations, and by eradicating biases in those persons who are already harboring them. Recall, however, that initial findings indicate that implicit biases (a) develop quite early, often without benefit of explicit teaching (Dunham et al., 2008), (b) are easier to acquire than their explicit counterparts, and (c), especially relative to their explicit counterparts, appear difficult to eradicate (or reverse, i.e. flip from a negative to a positive valence) once acquired. As mentioned above, this is given a striking demonstration in Gregg et al. (2006), where participants had biases induced about a fictional group, only to be later told that the damning information used to induce the biases was incorrect; the participants' explicit biases against the group disappeared, but their implicit counterparts did not. Taking implicit biases into account raises serious challenges for both of the most obvious general strategies for doing away with implicit evaluations, and these challenges should be reflected in assessing the feasibility and cost associated with specific proposals based on them.

Psychological research might point the way to other less explored options, too. Future research may still help conservationists who remain committed to the ideal of complete eradication of racist evaluation by discovering more effective ways to deal with them at early stages of ontogeny, before they are fully developed or entrenched. Current research may also be mined for inspiration as well. For example, some studies have linked IAT effects with emotions, suggesting that implicit biases are often affect-laden (e.g. Phelps et al., 2000; Phelps & Thomas, 2003). If this turns out to be the case, emotion-based techniques may provide more effective means by which conservationists can achieve their goals. One interesting possibility emerges from work by Rozin (1997), who describes how *moralization*, which crucially involves emotional elements, has had effects both in the promulgation of vegetarianism and in the decrease of the acceptability of smoking. As such, moralization might be successful in the mitigation and elimination of implicit racial biases as well. Previously developed methods of social influence that appeal to emotions (and which may therefore fall under Rozin's concept of moralization) might also be successfully applied to implicit racial biases.[28] These might include, for instance, casting racist biases, judgments, and behaviors as not just wrong but shameful and viscerally disgusting. More speculatively, other sorts of emotion-based methods of persuasion may be recruited from advertising and marketing or political campaigning. Such methods may more effectively speak to implicit racial biases than straightforward education, rational discussion, or careful argumentation.

On the other hand, conservationists impressed by the psychological findings might abandon the idea of complete eradication of both implicit and explicit bias, and instead embrace a more pragmatic goal of eradication of explicit bias, together with some agenda of controlling or mitigating the expression of implicit biases (e.g. see Lengbeyer, 2004, who argues for a similar approach). Proposals for achieving this goal may center on the promulgation of techniques that are most effective in suppressing or bringing implicit biases under control. Such proposals, of course, need to be formulated in detail before they could be properly assessed, but they might be guided by the sort of research discussed in Section 3.2.3, which showed how implicit biases are not immune to certain forms of influence. For example, if future research bears out the preliminary findings that altering the social environment in targeted ways can reduce the expression of implicit biases, then the most effective conservationist proposals

---

[28] Although such proposals are certainly attractive, there are reasons to be cautious. For instance, Dan Fessler and his colleagues (Fessler et al., 2003) have argued that "moral" vegetarianism may have little to do with disgust-based moralization.

to mitigate the expression of racial bias might include suggestions for structuring the social environment in ways that the psychological research indicates is most helpful.

Other proposals may be inspired by the research on self-control. Here the conservationist gets a mixed bag. Preliminary research suggests that, on the one hand, individuals are able to suppress the expression of implicit racial biases in judgment and behavior. On the other hand, as indicated by the work of Richeson et al. (2003), Richeson and Shelton (2003), and Govorun and Payne (2006), effort and attention are required to exert this kind of self-control; indeed, Bartholow et al. (2006) have shown that alcohol consumption interferes with the capacity to intentionally control the expression of these biases. This may be construed as a cost that attaches itself to proposals that center on self-control. Implementing the widespread and consistent suppression of implicit biases may also require ensuring the vigilance and effort (and perhaps sobriety!) of those individuals who harbor them. Alternatively, future psychological research may help uncover additional techniques that can help enhance the effectiveness of self-control, as Blair and colleagues (2001) found of generating and focusing on counter-stereotypic mental imagery.

The main conclusion of this section is that the psychological work on implicit racial bias is directly relevant to the normative debate over race, and is especially important for conservationists. Individual proposals can be properly assessed only in light of the psychological research, and until implicit biases are systematically taken into account, the feasibility and costs associated with such proposals remain unclear. In addition to facilitating a more realistic assessment of extant proposals, the psychological work can also be a source of inspiration for novel positions and proposals in the conservationist spirit, and can also point the way towards more effective methods for achieving conservationist goals.

4. Conclusion

Our aim was not to weigh in on one side of the controversy between eliminativism and conservativism, but to point out an assumption apparently made by both sides of the debate, and show it to be untenable. That debate takes place against the backdrop of an acknowledged ontological consensus. United by the shared rejection of a biological basis of race, eliminativists and conservationists have proceeded to take the fields of biology and genetics to be by and large irrelevant to the normative racial debate. We have asserted that the normative debate takes place against the backdrop of a somewhat analogous, though generally *unacknowledged*, consensus that gives rise to the widespread disregard of psychology in that literature. In contrast to the attention paid to anthropological and historical factors, the philosophical literature on race fails to consider whether and how psychological factors could affect the feasibility of the various normative proposals that have been offered. We have argued that this disregard of psychology is unjustified, and have shown how empirical research on racial cognition is directly relevant to the goals held by normative racial theorists, and to the feasibility of the proposals made for achieving them.

References

Aboud, F. E., & Doyle, A. B. 1996. "Parental and Peer Influences on Children's Racial Attitudes." *International Journal of Intercultural Relations*, 20: 371–383.

Allport, G. W. 1954. *The Nature of Prejudice*. Cambridge, MA: Addison-Wesley.

Amodio, D. M., Harmon-Jones, E., & Devine, P. G. 2003. "Individual differences in the activation and control of affective race bias as assessed by startle eyeblink response and self-report." *Journal of Personality and Social Psychology*, 84: 738–753.

Andreasen, R. 1998. "A New Perspective on the Race Debate." *British Journal for the Philosophy of Science*, 49 (2): 199–225.

Appiah, K. A. 1995. "The Uncompleted Argument: Du Bois and the Illusion of Race." In L. A. Bell & D. Blumenfeld (1995), 59–78.

——1996. "Race, Culture, Identity: Misunderstood Connections." In K. A. Appiah & A. Guttmann (eds.), *Color Conscious: The Political Morality of Race*. Princeton, NJ: Princeton University Press, 30–106.

Arkes, H. & Tetlock, P. E. 2004. "Attributions of implicit prejudice, or Would Jesse Jackson 'fail' the Implicit Association Test?" *Psychological Inquiry*, 15 (4): 257–278.

Banaji, M. R. 2001. "Implicit Attitudes Can Be Measured." In H. L. Roediger, III, J. S. Nairne, I. Neath, & A. Surprenant (eds.), *The Nature of Remembering: Essays in Honor of Robert G. Crowder*. Washington, DC: American Psychological Association, 117–150.

Banaji, M. R., Lemm, K. M., & Carpenter, S. J. 2001. "Automatic and implicit processes in social cognition." In A. Tesser & N. Schwartz (eds.), *Blackwell Handbook of Social Psychology: Intraindividual Processes*. Oxford: Blackwell, 134–158.

Banse, R., Seise, J., & Zerbes, N. 2001. "Implicit Attitudes Toward Homosexuality: Reliability, Validity, and Controllability of the IAT." *Zeitschrift für Experimentelle Psychologie*, 48: 145–160.

Banton, M. 1978. *The Idea of Race*. Boulder, CO: Westview.

Baron, A. S., & Banaji, M. R. 2006. "The Development of Implicit Attitudes: Evidence of Race Evaluations from Ages 6 to 10 and Adulthood." *Psychological Science*, 17: 53–58.

Bartholow, B. D., Dickter, C. L., & Sestir, M. A. 2006. "Stereotype Activation and Control of Race Bias: Cognitive Control of Inhibition and Its Impairment by Alcohol." *Journal of Personality and Social Psychology*, 90: 272–287.

Bertrand, M., & Mullainathan, S. 2003. "Are Emily and Greg More Employable Than Lakisha and Jamal?: A Field Experiment on Labor Market and Discrimination." Poverty Action Lab Paper No. 3. http://povertyactionlab.org/papers/bertrand_mullainathan.pdf

Biernat, M., & Crandall, C. 1999. "Racial Attitudes." In P. Robinson, D. Shaver, & L. Wrightsman (eds.), *Measures of Political Attitudes*. San Diego, CA: Academic Press, 297–441.

Blair, I., Ma, J., & Lenton, A. 2001. "Imagining Stereotypes Away: The Moderation of Implicit Stereotypes Through Mental Imagery." *Journal of Personality and Social Psychology*, 81 (5): 828–841.

Blanton, H., & Jaccard, J. 2008. "Unconscious racism: A concept in pursuit of a measure." *Annual Review of Sociology*, 34: 277–297.

Boxill, B. 1984. *Blacks and Social Justice*. Totowa, NJ: Rowman & Allenheld.

Branch, C. W., & Newcombe, N. 1986. "Racial Attitude Development Among Young Black Children as a Function of Parental Attitudes: A Longitudinal and Cross-Sectional Study." *Child Development*, 57: 712–721.

Brown, D. 1991. *Human Universals*. New York: McGraw-Hill.

Brown, R. A., & Armelagos, G. J. 2001. "Apportionment of Racial Diversity: A Review." *Evolutionary Anthropology*, 10: 34–40.

Cosmides, L., Tooby, J., & Kurzban, R. 2003. "Perceptions of Race." *Trends in Cognitive Sciences*, 7 (4): 173–179.

Crandall, C. S., & Eshleman, A. 2003. "A Justification-Suppression Model of the Expression and Experience of Prejudice." *Psychological Bulletin*, 129 (3): 414–446.

Cunningham, W., Preacher, K., & Banaji, M. 2001. "Implicit Attitude Measures: Consistency, Stability, and Convergent Validity." *Psychological Science*, 12 (2): 163–170.

Dasgupta, N., & Greenwald, A. 2001. "On the Malleability of Automatic Attitudes: Combating Automatic Prejudice With Images of Admired and Disliked Individuals." *Journal of Personality and Social Psychology*, 81 (5): 800–814.

Devine, P. 1989. "Stereotypes and Prejudice: Their Automatic and Controlled Components." *Journal of Personality and Social Psychology*, 56: 5–18.

Devine, P., Plant, E., Amodio, D., Harmon-Jones, E., & Vance, S. 2002. "The Regulation of Explicit and Implicit Race Bias: The Role of Motivations to Respond Without Prejudice." *Journal of Personality and Social Psychology*, 82 (5): 835–848.

Devos, T., Nosek, B. A., & Banaji, M. R. 2007. "Aliens in their Own Land? Implicit and Explicit Ascriptions of National Identity to Native Americans and White Americans." Unpublished manuscript. Accessed @ http://projectimplicit.net/articles.php (06/08/2007).

Diamond, J. 1994. "Race without color." *Discover Magazine*, 15 (11): 83–89.

D'Souza, D. 1996. "The One-Drop-of-Blood Rule." *Forbes*, 158 (13): 48.

Dunbar, R. I. M. 2003. "The Social Brain: Mind, Language, and Society in Evolutionary Perspective." *Annual Review of Anthropology*, 32: 163–181.

Dunham, Y., Baron, A., & Banaji, M. 2008. "The development of implicit intergroup cognition." *Trends in Cognitive Sciences*, 12 (7): 248–253.

Eberhardt, J. L. 2005. "Imaging race." *American Psychologist*, 60: 181–190.

Faucher, L., & Machery, E. 2009. "Racism: Against Jorge Garcia's Moral and Psychological Monism." *Philosophy of the Social Sciences*, 39, 41–62.

Fazio, R., Jackson, J., Dunton, B., & Williams, C. 1995. "Variability in Automatic Activation as an Unobtrusive Measure of Racial Attitudes: A Bona Fide Pipeline?" *Journal of Personality and Social Psychology*, 69: 1013–1027.

Fessler, D. M. T., Arguello A. P., Mekdara, J. M., & Macias R. 2003. "Disgust Sensitivity and Meat Consumption: A Test of an Emotivist Account of Moral Vegetarianism." *Appetite*, 41 (1): 31–41.

Fredrickson, G. M. 2002. *Racism: A Short History*. Princeton, NJ: Princeton University Press.

Gannett, L. 2005. "Group Categories in Pharmacogenetics Research." *Philosophy of Science*, 72: 1232–1247.

Gehring, W. J., Karpinski, A., & Hilton, J. L. 2003. "Thinking about interracial interactions." *Nature Neuroscience*, 6 (12): 1241–1243.

Gelman, S. A., & Wellman, H. M. 1991. "Insides and Essences: Early Understandings of the Non-Obvious." *Cognition*, 38: 213–244.

Gil-White, F. 1999. "How Thick is Blood? The Plot Thickens . . . : If Ethnic Actors are Primordialists, What Remains of the Circumstantialists/Primordialists Controversy?" *Ethnic and Racial Studies*, 22 (5): 789–820.

—— 2001. "Are Ethnic Groups Biological 'Species' to the Human Brain?" *Current Anthropology*, 42 (4): 515–554.

Govorun, O., & Payne, B. K. 2006. "Ego Depletion and Prejudice: Strong Effects of Simple Plans." *Social Cognition*, 24: 111–136.

Greenwald, A., & Banaji, M. 1995. "Implicit Social Cognition: Attitudes, Self-Esteem, and Stereotypes." *Psychological Review*, 102 (1): 4–27.

Greenwald, A., McGhee, D., & Schwartz, J. 1998. "Measuring Individual Differences in Implicit Cognition: The Implicit Association Test." *Journal of Personality and Social Psychology*, 74 (6): 1464–1480.

Greenwald, A. G., & Nosek, B. A. 2001. "Health of the Implicit Association Test at Age 3." *Zeitschrift für Experimentelle Psychologie*, 48: 85–93.

Greenwald, A., Nosek, B., & Banaji, R. 2003. "Understanding and Using the Implicit Association Test: I. An Improved Scoring Algorithm." *Journal of Personality and Social Psychology*, 85: 197–216.

Greenwald, A. G., Poehlman, T. A., Uhlmann, E., & Banaji, M. R. 2009. "Understanding and Using the Implicit Association Test: III. Meta-analysis of Predictive Validity." *Journal of Personality and Social Psychology*, 97, 17–41.

Gregg, A. P., Seibt, B., & Banaji, M. R. 2006. "Easier Done than Undone: Asymmetry in the Malleability of Implicit Preferences." *Journal of Personality and Social Psychology*, 90: 1–20.

Griffiths, P. E., & Machery, E. 2008. "Innateness, Canalization, and Biologising the Mind." *Philosophical Psychology*, 21: 397–414.

Guillaumin, C. 1980. "The idea of race and its elevation to autonomous scientific and legal status." In UNESCO (eds.) *Sociological Theories: Race and Colonialism*. Paris: UNESCO.

Haslam, N., Rothschild, L., & Ernst, D. 2000. "Essentialist beliefs about social categories." *British Journal of Social Psychology*, 39: 113–127.

Haslanger, S. 2000. "Gender and Race: (What) Are They? (What) Do We Want Them To Be?" *Noûs*, 34 (1): 31–55.

Hirschfeld, L. W. 1996. *Race in Making: Cognition, Culture, and the Child's Construction of Human Kinds*. Cambridge, MA: MIT Press.

——2001. "On a Folk Theory of Society: Children, Evolution, and Mental Representations of Social Groups." *Personality and Social Psychology Review*, 5 (2): 107–117.

Isaac, B. H. 2004. *The Invention of Racism in Classical Antiquity*. Princeton, NJ: Princeton University Press.

Keil, F., Smith, W., Simons, D., & Levin, D. 1998. "Two dogmas of conceptual empiricism: implications for hybrid models of the structure of knowledge." *Cognition*, 65: 103–135.

Kelly, D., & Roedder, E. 2008. "Racial Cognition and the Ethics of Implicit Bias." *Philosophy Compass*, 3 (3): 522–540.

Kim, D.-Y., & Greenwald, A. G. 1998. "Voluntary controllability of implicit cognition: can implicit attitudes be faked?" Paper presented at meetings of the Midwestern Psychological Association, Chicago.

Kitcher, P. 2000. "Utopian Eugenics and Social Inequality." In Phillip Sloan (ed.), *Impllications of the Human Genome Project*. Notre Dame, IN: University of Notre Dame Press, 229–262.

Kurzban, R., Tooby, J., & Cosmides, L. 2001. "Can Race Be Erased? Coalitional Computation and Social Categorization." *Proceedings of the National Academy of Science*, 98 (26): 15387–15392.

Lane, K. A., Banaji, M. R., Nosek, B. A., & Greenwald, A. G. (2007). "Understanding and Using the Implicit Association Test: IV: Procedures and Validity." In B. Wittenbrink & N. Schwarz (eds.), *Implicit Measures of Attitudes: Procedures and Controversie*. New York: Guilford Press, 59–102.

Lemm, K., & Banaji, M. R. 1999. "Unconscious attitudes and beliefs about women and men." In U. Pasero & F. Braun (eds.), *Wahrnehmung und Herstellung von Geschlecht (Perceiving and performing gender)*. Opladen: Westdeutscher Verlag, 215–233.

Lengbeyer, L. 2004. "Racism and Impure Hearts." In Michael Levine & Tamas Pataki (eds.), *Racism in Mind: Philosophical Explanations of Racism and Its Implications*. Ithaca, NY: Cornell University Press, 158–178.

Levy, B., & Banaji, M. R. 2002. "Implicit ageism." In T. Nelson (ed.), *Ageism: Stereotyping and prejudice against older persons*. Cambridge, MA: MIT Press, 49–75.

Lewontin, R. C. 1972. "The Apportionment of Human Diversity." *Evolutionary Biology*, 6: 381–398.

Lowery, B., Hardin, C., & Sinclair, S. 2001. "Social Influence Effects on Automatic Racial Prejudice." *Journal of Personality and Social Psychology*, 81 (5): 842–855.

Machery, E., & Faucher, L. 2005a. "Why do we Think Racially?" In H. Cohen & C. Lefebvre (eds.), *Handbook of Categorization in Cognitive Science*. Orlando, FL: Elsevier, 1009–1033.

—— 2005b. "Social Construction and the Concept of Race." *Philosophy of Science*, 72: 1208–1219.

—— Ms. "The Folk Concept of Race: Experimental Studies."

Mahalingam, R. 2003. "Essentialism, Culture and Power: Representations of Social Class." *Journal of Social Issues*, 59: 733–749.

Mallon, R. 2004. "Passing, Traveling, and Reality: Social Construction and the Metaphysics of Race." *Noûs*, 38 (4): 644–673.

McConahay, J. 1986. "Modern Racism, Ambivalence, and the Modern Racism Scale." In J. F. Dovidio and S. L. Gaertner (eds.), *Prejudice, Discrimination, and Racism*, Orlando, FL: Academic Press, 91–125.

Mills, C. 1998. *Blackness Visible: Essays on Philosophy and Race*. Ithaca, NY: Cornell University Press.

Muir, D. 1993. "Race: The Mythic Root of Racism." *Sociological Inquiry*, 63: 339–350.

Nei, M., & Roychoudhury, A. K. 1972. "Gene Differences Between Caucasian, Negro, and Japanese Populations." *Science*, 177: 434–436.

—— 1974. "Genetic Variation Within and Between the Three Major Races of Man, Caucasoids, Negroids, and Mongoloids." *American Journal of Human Genetics*, 26: 421–443.

Nosek, B. A., Greenwald, A. G., & Banaji, M. R. 2007. "The Implicit Association Test at Age 7: A Methodological and Conceptual Review." In J. A. Bargh (ed.), *Automatic Processes in Social Thinking and Behavior*. Philadelphia, PA: Psychology Press, 265–292.

Omi, M., & Winant, H. 1994. *Racial Formation in the United States*. New York: Routledge.

Ottaway, S. A., Hayden, D., & Oakes, M. 2001. "Implicit Attitudes and Racism: The Role of Word Familiarity and Frequency in the Implicit Association Test." *Social Cognition*, 18 (2): 97–144.

Outlaw, L. 1990. "Toward a Critical Theory of 'Race'." In D. T. Goldberg (ed.), *The Anatomy of Race*. Minneapolis, MN: The University of Minnesota Press, 58–82.

—— 1995. "On W.E.B. Du Bois's 'The Conservation of Races'." In L. A. Bell & D. Blumenfeld (eds.), *Overcoming Racism and Sexism*. Lanham, MD: University Press of America, 79–102.

—— 1996. *On Race and Philosophy*. New York: Routledge.

Payne, B. K. 2005. "Conceptualizing Control in Social Cognition: The Role of Automatic and Controlled Processes in Misperceiving a Weapon." *Journal of Personality Social Psychology*, 81: 181–192.

—— 2006. "Weapon Bias: Split-second Decisions and Unintended Stereotyping." *Current Directions in Psychological Science*, 15: 287–291.

Phelps, E., & Thomas, L. 2003. "Race, Behavior, and the Brain: The Role of Neuroimaging in Understanding Complex Social Behaviors." *Political Psychology*, 24 (4): 747–758.

Phelps, E., Cannistraci, C., & Cunningham, W. 2003. "Intact Performance on An Indirect Measure of Race Bias Following Amygdala Damage." *Neuropsychologia*, 41: 203–208.

Phelps, E., O'Connor, K., Cunningham, W., Funyama, S., Gatenby, C., Core, J., & Banaji, M. 2000. "Performance on Indirect Measures of Race Evaluation Predicts Amygdala Activation." *Journal of Cognitive Neuroscience*, 12 (5): 729–738.

Price, J., & Wolfers, J. Manuscript. "Racial Discrimination Among NBA Referees." Accessed @ http://bpp.wharton.upenn.edu/jwolfers/research.shtml (06/08/2008).

Richeson, J., & Ambady, N. 2003. "Effects of Situational Power on Automatic Racial Prejudice." *Journal of Experimental Social Psychology*, 39: 177–183.

Richeson, J. A., & Shelton, J. N. 2003. "When Prejudice Does Not Pay: Effects of Interracial Contact on Executive Function." *Psychological Science*, 14: 287–290.

Richeson, J., Baird, A., Gordon, H., Heatherton, T., Wyland, C., Trawalter, S., & Shelton, N. 2003. "An fMRI Investigation of the Impact of Interracial Contact of Executive Function." *Nature Neuroscience*, 6 (12): 1323–1328.

Root, M. 2000. "How We Divide the World." *Philosophy of Science*, 67(Proceedings): 628–639.

—— 2005. "The Number of Black Widows in the National Academy of Sciences." *Philosophy of Science*, 72: 1197–1207.

Rozin, P. 1982. "Human food selection: The interaction of biology, culture and individual experience." In L. M. Barker (ed.), *The Psychobiology of Human Food Selection*. Amsterdam: Ellis Horwood, 225–254.

—— 1997. "Moralization." In A. Brandt and P. Rozin (eds.), *Morality + Health*. New York: Routledge, 379–402.

Schuman, H., Steeh, C., Bobo, L., & Kryson, M. 1997. *Racial Attitudes in America: Trends and Interpretations*. Cambridge, MA: Harvard University Press.

Schwartz, A., & Rashbaum, W. 2007. "N.B.A. Referee is the Focus of a Federal Inquiry." *The New York Times*, July 21. http://www.nytimes.com/2007/07/21/sports/basketball/21referee.html

Schwartz, M. B., Vartanian, L. R., Nosek, B. A., & Brownell, K. D. (2006). "The influence of one's own body weight on implicit and explicit anti-fat bias." *Obesity*, 14 (3): 440–447.

Shelby, T. 2002. "Foundations of Black Solidarity: Collective Identity or Common Oppression." *Ethics*, 112: 231–266.

—— (2005). *We Who Are Dark: The Philosophical Foundations of Black Solidarity*. Cambridge, MA: Belknap Press of Harvard University Press.

Stroop, J. 1935. "Studies of Inteference in Serial Verbal Reactions." *Journal of Experimental Psychology*, 18: 643–662.

Sundstrom, R. 2002. "Racial Nominalism." *Journal of Social Philosophy*, 33 (2): 193–210.

Taylor, P. 2004. *Race: A Philosophical Introduction*. Cambridge, UK: Polity Press.

Taylor, S., Fiske, S., Etcoff, N., & Ruderman, A. 1978. "The Categorical and Contextual Bases of Person Memory and Stereotyping." *Journal of Personality and Social Psychology*, 36: 778–793.

Vanman, E. J., Paul, B. Y., Ito, T. A., & Miller, N. 1997. "The modern face of prejudice and structural features that moderate the effect of cooperation on affect." *Journal of Personality and Social Psychology*, 73: 941–959.

Wasserstrom, R. 2001 1980. "Racism and Sexism." *Philosophy and Social Issues: Five Studies*. Notre Dame, IN: Univ of Notre Dame Press. Reprinted in *Race and Racism*, ed. B. Boxill. New York: Oxford University Press, 307–343.

Webster, Y. 1992. *The Racialization of America*. New York: St. Martin's Press.

Young, I. M. 1989. "Polity and Group Difference: A Critique of the Idea of Universal Citizenship." *Ethics*, 99: 250–274.

Zack, N. 1993. *Race and Mixed Race*. Philadelphia, PA: Temple University Press.

—— 1998. *Thinking About Race*. Belmont, CA: Wadsworth Publishing.

—— 2002. *Philosophy of Science and Race*. New York: Routledge.

Acknowledgments

Work on this volume was facilitated by semiannual gatherings of the Moral Psychology Research Group. We are very pleased to acknowledge the following institutions for their support of our meetings: the Philosophy Department and the Leslie Center for the Humanities, Dartmouth College; the College of Liberal Arts and the Center for Philosophy of Science, University of Minnesota; the Center for Philosophy of Science and Arts and the Science Faculty Research and Scholarship Program, University of Pittsburgh; the Rutgers University Research Group on Evolution and Higher Cognition; the Philosophy Department and Philosophy–Neuroscience–Psychology Program, Washington University in St. Louis. Here, as elsewhere, the Washington University Philosophy Department relied on the generous support of Ned and Jane Sadaka.

Final editing was completed while John Doris was an Autonomy–Singularity–Creativity fellow at the National Humanities Center; he wishes to thank Director Geoffrey Harpham, Deputy Director Kent Mullikan, and the extraordinary staff of the Center (especially Karen Carroll, for her excellent editorial services). Doris is also grateful for funding from the American Council of Learned Societies, the National Endowment for the Humanities, and the Research Triangle Park Foundation of North Carolina.

We are very much indebted to Peter Momtchiloff of Oxford University Press for his erudition and patience.

The Moral Psychology Research Group

Index of Names

General Index

Lightning Source UK Ltd.
Milton Keynes UK
UKHW020304060120
356364UK00001B/3/P